THE OTHER SIDE OF
CALVINISM

Books by Laurence M. Vance

The Other Side of Calvinism
A Brief History of English Bible Translations
The Angel of the Lord
Archaic Words and the Authorized Version
A Practical Grammar of Basic Biblical Hebrew
Double Jeopardy: The NASB Update
Christianity and War and Other Essays Against the Warfare State
King James, His Bible, and Its Translators
Greek Verbs in the New Testament and Their Principal Parts
War, Foreign Policy, and the Church
Guide to Prepositions in the Greek New Testament
The Myth of the Just Price and the Biblical Case for Laissez Faire
Guide to Nouns in the Greek New Testament
Guide to Adjectives in the Greek New Testament
Guide to Pronouns in the Greek New Testament
The Revolution that Wasn't
Rethinking the Good War
Galatians 1 & 2: Exposition, Commentary, Application
The Quatercentenary of the King James Bible
The War on Drugs Is a War on Freedom
War, Christianity, and the State: Essays on the Follies of Christian Militarism
Social Insecurity
War, Empire, and the Military: Essays on the Follies of War and U.S. Foreign Policy
The Making of the King James Bible-New Testament
Gun Control and the Second Amendment
Free Trade or Protectionism?
The Free Society
Erasmus on Christianity, War, and Soldiers
Abortion, Republicans, and Libertarians
Education in a Free Society
School Choice for Whom?
Foreign Aid Folly
Health Care Freedom
The Origin of the Chapters and Verses in the Bible
The Text of the King James Bible

THE OTHER SIDE OF
CALVINISM

by

Laurence M. Vance

Vance Publications
www.vancepublications.com

The Other Side of Calvinism
Copyright © 1991, 1999 by Laurence M. Vance
All Rights Reserved

Revised Edition
Sixth Printing 2021

ISBN 978-0-9628898-7-5

Library of Congress Catalog Card Number: 99-71074

Cover print of the Synod of Dordrecht courtesy of:
Prentenkabinet van de Universiteit Leiden

Published and Distributed by: Vance Publications
P.O. Box 780671, Orlando, FL 32878
E-mail: vancepub@vancepublications.com
Website: www.vancepublications.com

Printed in the United States of America

TABLE OF CONTENTS

PREFACE ix

1 Introduction to Calvinism 1
    Calvinism 2
    Calvinism and Arminianism 5
    Calvinism in History 10
    Calvinism and the Baptists 15
    Hyper-Calvinism 28
    Calvinism and Calvinists 33

2 The Origin of Calvinism 37
    Calvin and Augustine 37
    The Influence of Augustine 39
    Catholicism and Augustine 40
    The Church Fathers and Augustine 41
    The Age of Augustine 43
    The Life of Augustine 47
    Pelagianism and Augustine 50
    The Theology of Augustine 52
    From Augustine to the Reformation 59
    The Reformation 61
    The Reformers 65

3 John Calvin 69
    The Age of Calvin 72
    The Life of Calvin 76
    Calvin and Geneva 82
    Calvin and Servetus 89
    Calvin's Institutes 100
    The Theology of Calvin 105

4 James Arminius 115
    The Age of Arminius 117
    The Life of Arminius 122
    The Theology of Arminius 126

	Calvin and Arminius	131
	Calvinism and Arminius	133
	Arminianism	138
5	**The Five Points of Calvinism**	**143**
	The Five Points of Calvinism	145
	Four-Point Calvinism	147
	The Synod of Dort	148
	The Canons of Dort	156
	The Westminster Assembly	159
	The Westminster Standards	175
	Baptist Confessions of Faith	178
6	**Total Depravity**	**185**
	Definitions	186
	Total Inability	187
	The Importance of Total Depravity	189
	The Depravity of Man	191
	Depravity and the Will	201
	Salvation and the Will	214
	Analogies	219
	Proof Texts	223
	The Other Side of Total Depravity	232
7	**Unconditional Election**	**241**
	Definitions	242
	The Essence of Calvinism	245
	God's Decree	250
	Lapsarian Systems	281
	Reprobation	302
	Proof Texts	333
	God's People	335
	Given to Salvation	341
	Ordained to Salvation	344
	Chosen to Salvation	348
	Elected to Salvation	364
	Predestinated to Salvation	380
	Elect Infants	397
	The Other Side of Unconditional Election	401
8	**Limited Atonement**	**405**
	Definitions	405
	Accusations	409
	Four-Point Calvinism	412

The Atonement	414
Arguments	422
Proof Texts	342
Calvin's Calvinism	459
The Other Side of Limited Atonement	470

9 Irresistible Grace 475

Definitions	477
God's Will	479
Effectual Calling	490
Proof Texts	500
Repentance and Faith	513
New Testament Salvation	521
Infant Salvation	530
Evangelism	536
The Other Side of Irresistible Grace	550

10 Perseverance of the Saints 555

Definitions	556
Conclusions	559
Eternal Security	562
Arminianism	564
Proof Texts	569
Perseverance	573
Lordship Salvation	577
Preservation	586
Arminius	590
The Other Side of Perseverance of the Saints	593

Appendixes

1	The Remonstrance	597
2	The Counter-Remonstrance	599
3	The Opinions of the Remonstrants	601
4	The Canons of Dort	607
5	The Lambeth Articles	627
6	The Westminster Confession of Faith	629
7	The Second London Confession of Faith	641

NOTES	653
BIBLIOGRAPHY	741

Indexes

1 Subject 761
2 Name 767
3 Scripture 773

PREFACE

The philosophical speculations of Calvinism, although they have been debated for hundreds of years, have masqueraded as sound Bible doctrine for much too long. The resultant theological implications, under pretense of orthodoxy, have been the dominant influence in all facets of theology. They have been accepted as authoritative, but only to the detriment of the Scriptures. The subject of Calvinism has also been fiercely debated since the time of the Reformation more than any other topic. Unlike baptism, which was the main bone of contention between the Baptists and other groups, the bitter controversy about Calvinism has infected all the various denominations at one time or another. This leavening is part of the other side of Calvinism.

So why another work on Calvinism? Although there exists an abundance of material on the subject, the overwhelming majority is from the Reformed viewpoint, which is inherently Calvinistic. The Baptist contribution to the debate comes chiefly from the Calvinistic groups. This leaves a definite void as far as a balanced treatment of the issue is concerned. The result is a disproportionate, intimidating presentation of one side which is then equated with orthodoxy. So mainly because of the sheer volume of the supporting apparatus alone, Calvinism has established a foothold on theology. This is another facet of the other side of Calvinism.

The stream of books currently available in defense of Calvinism is seemingly without end. And although it was stated a century ago by a Calvinistic theologian that "much more has been published" in opposition to than in defense of Calvinism,[1] such is certainly not the case now. Regarding the material published opposing the Calvinistic system, whether in whole or in part, three types can be distinguished. Most of the available literature consists of small pamphlets that are inherently limited in their effectiveness.[2] There are also some small books available from a variety of viewpoints that provide some helpful information.[3] Concerning what could be termed the major books against Calvinism, there are at present but a few.[4] There still exists the need for a definitive work which addresses and sufficiently answers all of the philosophical speculations and theological implications of the other side of Calvinism.

A shortage of works against Calvinism is not an adequate reason to begin an undertaking of this magnitude unless there be an important underlying cause. The salient determinant is the tremendously damaging nature of the Calvinistic system. The doctrines of Calvinism, *if really believed and consistently practiced*, are detrimental to evangelism, personal soul winning, prayer, preaching, and practical Christianity in general. This is even unintentionally admitted by a Calvinistic Baptist: "The doctrines taught in the Bible relating to the sovereignty of God, referred to in religious circles as 'Calvinism,' also as 'the doctrines of grace,' are doctrines of the Book that are the occasion for many people 'choking' on the Word. The misuse and abuse of these doctrines will deaden and kill."[5] Calvinism is therefore the greatest "Christian" heresy that has ever plagued the Church. This being the case, the thesis of this book is that Calvinism is not only Reformed doctrine, and therefore something that Baptists should not be connected with, but that it is *wrong* doctrine. But because of its controversial nature, there exists a tremendous ignorance of the true nature of Calvinism. Some schools deem the subject so controversial that they even forbid discussion of the subject.[6] The long and manifold influence of Calvinism on all areas of theology necessitates this examination of the other side of Calvinism.

Because of its underlying thesis, this book is not written from a neutral perspective. But then again, neither is any book written by a Calvinist. One of the most popular Calvinistic authors, Loraine Boettner, in his book on Calvinism, starts out thus: "The purpose of this book is to show that Calvinism is beyond all doubt the teaching of the Bible and of reason."[7] Let me unequivocally assert that the purpose of *this* book is to show that Calvinism is beyond all doubt *not* the teaching of the Bible *nor* of reason. One Calvinist boldly proclaims: "The perspective from which I have written is decidedly Calvinistic. That is not an apology. It is a warning. I want the reader to know from the beginning what I hope to accomplish. I have written with an agenda."[8] But if Calvinists can write with the express purpose of defending their views, then it stands to reason that their critics should be afforded this same privilege as well. Another Calvinist says: "It is our hope that the material contained in this survey will help to promote the spread of Calvinism and that many will thus be led to understand, to believe, and to propagate this Biblical system of doctrine."[9] But contrariwise, it is my hope that the material contained in this survey will help to *prevent* the spread of Calvinism and that many will thus be led to understand, to *not* believe, and to *cease* to propagate this *anti*-biblical system of doctrine. Still another Calvinist claims that his book was "written in the hope that much of the abuse that is hurled at the Calvinistic system of theology will be withdrawn."[10] But once again, this book was written in the hope that much of the abuse that is hurled at the Calvinistic system of theology will be *sustained*. And finally, another Calvinist states: "The purpose of this monograph is not to attack men personally. Rather, it is to protect the church from the heretical doctrines of anti-Calvinistic teachings."[11] Likewise, the purpose of this monograph is not to attack men personally. Rather, it is to protect the church from the heretical doctrines of *Calvinistic* teachings. So, although one Calvinist maintains that "the denial of Calvinism is a very grave mistake,"[12] it will be maintained throughout this work that the *acceptance* of Calvinism is a very grave mistake. This perspective is necessary in order to present the other side of Calvinism.

The first and only recourse, as well as the final authority for everything said herein, is of course the Holy Bible. Not only will the Bible be used to answer the philosophical speculations and theological implications of Calvinism, but it will be believed as written. And because they form such an intrinsic part of the book, most Scripture citations will be given in full. Since this is a biblical defense, the emphasis will be on what the Bible actually says, not what it has commonly been interpreted to teach. **"The word of God is not bound"** (2 Tim. 2:9) by the opinions of the Church Fathers, commentators, scholars, creeds, confessions, or any man's opinions or system of interpretation. Since only the Scripture is infallible, it is quite able to correct both the writer and reader, as well as the philosophical speculations and theological implications of the other side of Calvinism.

The structure of the book is rather straightforward and is naturally divided into two parts: a historical examination and a biblical analysis. The origin, development, and claims of Calvinism, as well as its namesake and chief antagonist, will be investigated in the light of history. Once this essential foundation is laid, the actual doctrines of Calvinism will be examined, both doctrinally and theologically, and analyzed in the light of Scripture by comparing Scripture with Scripture. Because of this logical format, a disparity in content will exist between the two parts as well as the individual chapters. But this is a necessary evil in order to preserve the unity of each subject and bring to light the even greater evil contained in the other side of Calvinism.

The format of the book is exactly as the Calvinists have desired. One Calvinist says: "It is high time that we open our hearts and minds to an honest appraisal of Calvin and Calvinism."[13] Exactly. And the only way to make an honest appraisal of Calvin and Calvinism is to, in the words of another Calvinist, "let Calvinism speak for itself."[14] Therefore, the amassing of statements by non-Calvinists against Calvinism as proof that Calvinism is false will not be found in this work. In order to let Calvinism speak for itself, the procedure to be followed will be a simple one, and one employed by the Calvinists themselves. Just as one Calvinist says he has quoted his opponents "at length that there might be no mistake about what they believe,"[15] so the Calvinists themselves will be extensively and eclectically cited that there might be no mistake about what they believe. This is both to prevent the cry of misrepresentation and to demonstrate the numerous contradictions that exist among the Calvinists themselves. Anything that could possibly be damaging to Calvinism will be documented from Calvinist or neutral sources. All quotations, including the use of bold, italics, and capitals, as well as spelling, grammar, and punctuation, appear exactly as in the original source. The bibliography is limited to works cited or mentioned and does not include all works consulted in this examination of the other side of Calvinism.

Readers of the first edition of this work (originally published in 1991) will notice that the same basic format and structure have been followed. Nevertheless, this is where the similarity between the two books ends. Although their basic thesis is the same, this edition is an entirely new work. Not only have the deficiencies of the first edition been corrected and some material omitted, but much new material has been added. Besides the original work being completely rewritten, the historical section has been greatly expanded with a much greater emphasis on primary sources. The reception of the first edition by the Calvinists was just as expected and predicated in the epilogue of that work. And since the literature espousing Calvinism did not suddenly cease with the publication of the first edition of this work, it was deemed necessary to significantly enhance this biblical defense against the philosophical speculations and theological implications of Calvinism: the other side of Calvinism.

Chapter 1
INTRODUCTION TO CALVINISM

The doctrines known as Calvinism owe their name to the French Reformer John Calvin (1509-1564), although called by other names until he showed up. Broadly speaking, and as acknowledged by Calvinists themselves, there are two ways in which the term *Calvinism* has been used: in a theological and a non-theological sense. The term itself began to be used in a quasi-theological sense during Calvin's lifetime—as he himself acknowledged.[1] In its present and historical theological sense, Calvinism is of course associated with the doctrine of predestination. As Boettner says: "In the minds of most people the doctrine of Predestination and Calvinism are practically synonymous terms."[2] Other uses of the term, which include historical, denominational, philosophical, and political designations, will be explored later.[3] Unless otherwise stated, any references to Calvinism are to be taken in its strict theological sense. But despite the fact that the term *Calvinism* has been used for hundreds of years, some Calvinists would rather dispense with it. The theologian Robert Dabney (1820-1898) asserted that "Presbyterians care very little about the name Calvinism."[4] More recently, David Engelsma insists that "the term, 'Calvinism,' is not the name by which we Calvinists prefer to have our faith called; nor do we prefer to call ourselves 'Calvinists.'"[5] There are several reasons why some Calvinists shy away from the term. The first, and most obvious, is because it "leaves the impression that we follow a man."[6] Secondly, as W. J. Seaton maintains: "There is scarcely another word that arouses such suspicion, mistrust, and even animosity among professing Christians as the word Calvinism."[7] And finally, Boettner informs us that "perhaps no other system of thought has been so grossly and grievously and at times so deliberately misrepresented as has Calvinism."[8] Nevertheless, because the term *Calvinism* is so widely accepted, and because Calvinists themselves acknowledge that

Calvinism and *Calvinist* are "useful terms,"[9] the designation will be used throughout this work. When a Calvinist aspires to draw attention away from the name of Calvin he normally uses the phrase "Doctrines of Grace" to describe his system.[10] But if Calvinism is the doctrine of grace found in the Bible then this implies that if you disagree with Calvinism then you are denying salvation by grace. This theological implication can be found in the writings of all who hold to the Calvinistic system. And this is just the beginning of the other side of Calvinism.

Calvinism

What exactly is Calvinism? How do the Calvinists define Calvinism? To begin with, Calvinism is glowingly described in vague terms:

> Calvinism is Religion at the height of its conception. Calvinism is evangelicalism in its purest and only stable expression.[11]

> The central thought of Calvinism is, therefore, the great thought of God.[12]

> Calvinistic Theology is the greatest subject that has ever exercised the mind of man.[13]

> Calvinism thus emerges to our sight as nothing more or less than the hope of the world.[14]

These glimmering characterizations of Calvinism are to be expected since they come from the mouth of the Calvinists themselves. However, others could not disagree more, and have described Calvinism in other terms:

> Calvinism, or the belief in election, is not simply blasphemy, but the superfetation of blasphemy.[15]

> The doctrine that an infinite God made millions of people, knowing that they would be damned.[16]

> Calvinism is, in many of its facets, a human philosophical system. It is a constantly divisive element in the church.[17]

> Calvinism is not accidentally but essentially immoral, since it makes the distinction between right and wrong a matter of positive enactment, and thereby makes it possible to assert that what is immoral of man is moral for God, because He is above morality.[18]

Naturally, in response to this the Calvinist would reply that "no theological system was ever more grossly misrepresented, or more foully or unjustly vilified than that which is commonly called Calvinism."[19]

Undaunted, the Calvinist next equates Calvinism with biblical Christianity:

> Calvinism is a system of pure Biblical belief which stands firmly on the Word of God.[20]

> It has been correctly said that Calvinism is pure biblical Christianity in its clearest and purest expression.[21]

> Calvinism is an attempt to express all the Bible and only the Bible.[22]

The popular Presbyterian preacher and author D. James Kennedy tells us why he is a Calvinist: "I am a Calvinist precisely because I love the Bible and the God of the Bible. The doctrines of the Calvinist theological system are the doctrines of the Bible. When you get to know what we actually believe you may find you too are a Calvinist, *especially* if you love the Lord Jesus Christ and desire with all your heart to serve Him."[23]

But if biblical Christianity is Calvinism, then any other system is necessarily false. And this is precisely just what the Calvinist would have everyone believe. According to the Calvinist, Calvinism is not just *a* scriptural system—it is the *only* scriptural system:

> We believe the Calvinistic system to be the only one set forth in the Scriptures and vindicated by reason.[24]

> Calvinism is the only system which is true to the Word of God.[25]

> It is questionable whether a dogmatic theology which is not Calvinistic is truly Christian.[26]

The Calvinist goes so far as to insinuate that anything short of his position leads to heresy and worse. Kenneth Talbot and W. Gary Crampton caution us that "any compromise of Calvinism is a step towards humanism."[27] Boettner doesn't stop with humanism: "There is no consistent stopping place between Calvinism and atheism."[28] Therefore, he insists that "the future of Christianity is bound up with that system of theology historically called 'Calvinism.'"[29] But the fact that Calvinists equate their doctrine with that contained in the Scriptures in itself means nothing, for every sect and cult that names the name of Christ makes the same profession.

What we need is for the Calvinists to be more specific. What *exactly* is Calvinism? Again, we hear from the Calvinists themselves:

> Calvinism is just a full exposition of and development of the sum and substance of what is represented in Scripture as done for the salvation of sinners by the three persons of the Godhead.[30]

> What Calvinism particularly asserts is the supernaturalism of salvation, as the immediate work of God the Holy Spirit in the soul, by virtue of which we are made new creatures in Christ our Redeemer, and framed into the sons of God the Father.[31]

> Calvinism, in this soteriological aspect of it, is just the perception and expression and defence of the utter dependence of the soul on the free grace of God for salvation.[32]

All of these men are basically saying the same thing: Calvinism is to be equated with the system and doctrine of salvation found in the Bible.

Some Calvinists, however, narrow these soteriological explanations down even further and identify Calvinism with the Gospel itself:

> Calvinism is the Gospel and to teach Calvinism is in fact to preach the Gospel.[33]

> Calvinism is the Gospel. Its outstanding doctrines are simply the truths that make up the Gospel.[34]

Even the Baptist Charles Spurgeon (1834-1892) declared: "It is a nickname to call it Calvinism; Calvinism is the gospel, and nothing else."[35] If Calvinism is the Gospel then it should line up with the Gospel as presented in the Bible. Therefore, it would be pertinent to compare the Gospel of Paul the Apostle to the gospel of John Calvin:

> **Moreover, brethren, I declare unto you the gospel which I preached unto you, which also ye have received, and wherein ye stand;**
> **By which also ye are saved, if ye keep in memory what I preached unto you, unless ye have believed in vain.**
> **For I delivered unto you first of all that which I also received, how that Christ died for our sins according to the scriptures;**
> **And that he was buried, and that he rose again the third day according to the scriptures (1 Cor. 15:1-4).**

> We call predestination God's eternal decree, by which he compacted with himself what he willed to become of each man. For all are not created in equal condition; rather, eternal life is foreordained for some, eternal damnation for others. Therefore, as any man has been created to one or the other of these ends, we speak of him as predestinated to life or death.[36]

The biblical Gospel is the good news about what Jesus Christ has done on the cross respecting our sins. The gospel of Calvinism is likewise good news—but only if you are one of the "elect." This is confirmed by Engelsma: "Calvinism is good news! It is Gospel, glad tidings! As the message of grace, it comforts us and all those who, by the grace of the Spirit, believe in Christ."[37] To the non-elect Calvinism is not good news at all—it is an eternal death sentence.

Calvinism and Arminianism

To further bolster their position, and because many Christians might be skeptical about wholeheartedly embracing the claim that Calvinism is the only real form of biblical Christianity, Calvinists insist that there are really only two tenable schemes among real Christians: Calvinism and Arminianism. The term *Arminianism* is derived from the name of the Dutch theologian James Arminius

(1560-1609), who will be studied in detail in chapter 4. Not only did Arminius not invent the term, he would certainly cringe at the thought of how his name has been used since his death. What we shall see throughout this work is that Arminianism is not limited to the supposed doctrines of Arminius, for according to Calvinists, Arminianism is anything contrary to Calvinism. And it cannot be emphasized enough that this arbitrary division of men into either Calvinist or Arminian is the strength of the Calvinistic system. Since most people know very little about Arminius, and much of the information they do know they got from a Calvinist, they hesitate to be identified with him. Therefore, if there are only two viewpoints: if you are not a Calvinist then you have to be an Arminian. Boettner informs us: "It must be evident that there are just two theories which can be maintained by evangelical Christians upon this important subject; that all men who have made any study of it, and who have reached any settled conclusions regarding it, **must be either Calvinists or Arminians.** There is no other position which a 'Christian' can take."[38] The Presbyterian theologian William Shedd (1820-1894) insists that "only these two general schemes of Christian doctrine are logically possible" and that "in the future, as the past, all evangelical believers will belong either to one dogmatic division or the other."[39]

Still not able to convince the ardent skeptic that Calvinism is biblical Christianity, the Calvinist begins by making a disdainful contrast between Calvinism and Arminianism:

> Calvinism is the eternal truth. Arminianism has always been an inveterate lie.[40]

> It is clear that Arminianism is anti-Scriptural, but that Calvinism is completely true to the Bible.[41]

> The Biblical truths of Calvinism are never so clear as against the erroneous ideas of the Arminian.[42]

And what are the "erroneous ideas of the Arminian"? George Curtiss (1835-1898), a professed Arminian from the last century, defines his doctrine as:

> Arminianism teaches that God in Jesus Christ made provision fully for the salvation of all those who, by repentance towards

> God and faith in our Lord Jesus Christ, accept the terms, and all who do thus accept are eternally saved. All who rebel against God, and refuse to accept of Jesus on the terms of proffered mercy, sink under Divine wrath, and are eternally lost.[43]

But this is not good enough for a Calvinist, for now "every man's salvation depends on the choice of his own free will."[44]

The Calvinist next attempts to silence the cynic by a series of subtle implications and innuendos coupled with outright falsehood. Once again we emphasize that *Arminian* is the designation given by the Calvinist to any doctrine that is not Calvinistic. Most of those so-labeled are not really Arminians at all. But what makes them renounce the name for Calvinism are shocking statements about Arminianism like these:

> Arminianism thought is best understood historically, as a compromise of the Reformation gospel with the humanistic motif of the autonomy of the human consciousness flowing out of the ancient pagan learning that had just been rediscovered in the Renaissance.[45]

> The last and greatest monster of the man of sin; the elixir of Anti-Christianism.[46]

> These doctrines are a perversion of the Truth of God and the way of salvation. They have no scriptural foundation.[47]

> Arminianism is the very essence of Popery.[48]

> Arminianism is the plague of the church and the scourge of sound doctrine.[49]

> ARMINIANISM is that rejected error which has become the most insidiously devised heresy ever to lay claim to Biblical support.[50]

Then to further assail Arminianism, it is described as ritualistic, ephemeral, aristocratic, unfavorable to civil liberty, caste fostering, and auspicious to the rich.[51] Who would dare claim to be an Arminian after statements like these? Thus, if there are *only* two systems then it is apparent that most men who desire to appear orthodox would claim to be a Calvinist.

Besides these contrasts with Calvinism and general attacks against Arminianism, the Calvinists further misrepresent their opponents by another form of deception: guilt by association. This argument goes much deeper than simply designating their opponents as Arminians, for once this connection is made, Arminians are classified with everything under the sun which is unorthodox or heretical. N. S. McFetridge (1842-1886) associates Arminianism with the heresies of Arianism, Socinianism, and Unitarianism.[52] Gordon Clark (1902-1986) lumps Arminians and Roman Catholics together like they were cognate systems.[53] George Whitefield (1714-1770) classifies Arminians with Arians, Deists, Infidels, and Socinians.[54] The most injurious association is to that of the ancient heresy of Pelagianism. Duane Spencer (1920-1981) informs us that "Arminianism is but a refinement of Pelagianism,"[55] while others moderately only employ the term "Semi-Pelagianism" in the onslaught against Arminianism.[56] The significance of Pelagianism to a study of Calvinism and Arminianism remains to be examined in the next chapter.

The fourth building block in the attempt of the Calvinists to denigrate Arminianism is the implication that Arminians believe in salvation by works. This is established by utilizing the full range of heretical associations. Since there are supposedly only two groups of Christians: if you are not a Calvinist then you are an Arminian. If you are an Arminian, then you hold to an amalgamation of Socinianism, Romanism, and Unitarianism, which in turn are based on Pelagianism; therefore: you believe in salvation by works. So not subscribing to Calvinism means that you are the subject of the following opinions:

> Arminianism teaches salvation mostly of grace but not all of grace.[57]

> Arminianism is by necessity *synergistic,* in that it conceives of salvation as the joint or mutual effort of both God and man.[58]

Thus, the very salvation of "Arminians" is called into question:

> Salvation as the Arminians describe it is uncertain, precarious, and doubtful.[59]

> I believe that some Arminians may be born-again Christians.[60]

Nowhere is the Calvinist/Arminian dichotomy more pronounced than in reference to salvation:

> One makes salvation depend on the work of God, the other on a work of man; one regards faith as part of God's gift of salvation, the other as man's own contribution to salvation; one gives all the glory of saving believers to God, the other divides the praise between God, Who, so to speak, built the machinery of salvation, and man, who by believing operated it.[61]

> There are in reality only two types of religious thought. There is the religion of faith, and there is the religion of works. We believe that what has been known in Church history as Calvinism is the purest and most consistent embodiment of the religion of Faith, while that which has been known as Arminianism has been diluted to a dangerous degree by the religion of works."[62]

The Calvinist maintains that only in Calvinism can we find the teaching of salvation by grace:

> Calvinism is the casting of the soul wholly on the free grace of God alone, to whom alone belongs salvation.[63]

> The doctrine that men are saved only through the unmerited love and grace of God finds its full and honest expression only in the doctrines of Calvinism.[64]

Therefore, it is not Calvinism but Arminianism that "appears as the gospel of Christ, but in reality is 'another gospel.'"[65] This is a serious allegation, for as Paul wrote to the Galatians: **"But though we, or an angel from heaven, preach any other gospel unto you than that which we have preached unto you, let him be accursed"** (Gal. 1:8). To maintain that only in Calvinism can the teaching of salvation by grace be found is to charge anyone who is not a Calvinist with believing in salvation by works. This accusation by itself is often enough to make Calvinists out of men who otherwise would not claim any title.

Once again it cannot be emphasized enough that this arbitrary division of men into either Calvinists or Arminians is the strength of the Calvinistic system. In this regard the weapons of Calvinism are ignorance and intimidation. When everything contrary to

Calvinism is labeled Arminianism, and Arminianism is presented in the worst possible light, it is no wonder that so many men have claimed to be Calvinists. Many think they are Calvinists because they hold the doctrine of eternal security. Others who accept the term do so because they believe in salvation by grace and the complete ruin of man in the Fall. Most just know they are not an Arminian and take the name of Calvin by default. Although Calvinists despise Arminius and identify him with every evil possible, the name of their dreaded adversary must be unremittingly invoked. John Goodwin (1593-1665) has well said about the Calvinists:

> The necessity and power of those tenets or doctrines, nick-named *Arminian,* is so great for the accommodating and promoting of the affairs of Christianity, that even those persons themselves who get a good part of their subsistence in the world by decrying them, and declaiming against them, yet cannot make earnings of their profession, are not able to carry on their work of preaching, with any tolerable satisfaction to those that hear them, without employing and asserting them very frequently.[66]

It is clearly evident that without the name of Arminius to use as an epithet of condemnation, the Calvinists would have a much harder time getting men to join their side.

Calvinism in History

After shocking his opponents with the dreaded errors of Arminianism; after making them feel guilty about not being a Calvinist; after associating his detractors with heretical groups and doctrines: the Calvinist turns to the historical argument. The tactics of deception are still the same, only moving to the scene of history. Here the Calvinist can simply omit reporting whatever is inimical to Calvinism and insist that "Calvinism has had a greater influence on human history and institutions than any other theology ever formulated by the church."[67] By deliberately blending the aforementioned theological and non-theological uses of the term *Calvinism,* and by equating Calvinism alone with Bible-believing Protestantism, Calvinists can put forth incredible claims for their system:

> Only Calvinism furnishes the necessary guarantees for any genuine intellectual and scientific activity.[68]

> Just ask yourselves what would have become of Europe and America, if in the 16th century the star of Calvinism had not suddenly arisen on the horizon of Western Europe.[69]

But because the two most abused senses of the term *Calvinism* are in relation to economics and politics, a further study of these two subjects is in order.

If the statements of the Calvinists regarding their system are taken at face value, it is John Calvin and not Adam Smith (1723-1790) who should be the father of modern economics.[70] In the sphere of economics, it has been asserted about Calvinism:

> The Calvinistic countries became the countries where the capitalistic system developed.[71]

> The Protestant 'work ethic' was developed from Calvin's teaching.[72]

> Calvinism is the most formidable enemy which socialism and communism face today.[73]

Because Calvin valued private property, capital, thrift, hard work, and rejected medieval usury laws, some connection is generally made between Calvinism and capitalism, usually centered around a discussion of the "thesis" of Max Weber (1864-1920) in his *The Protestant Ethic and the Spirit of Capitalism*.[74] But underlying all that is by said Calvinists about the role of Calvinism in economics there is the subtle implication that a rejection of Calvinism *in its theological aspect* opens the door to a rejection of capitalism and the free enterprise system. But as any student of even basic economic history knows, Calvin was no "laissez faire capitalist," many free market advocates are atheists, and many Calvinists today are downright socialists. A case in point is Calvin College. A textbook written by the faculty and published by the college for use in its introductory economics courses has recently been labeled by a Calvinist as "a totalitarian and socialist tract, written with religious fervor by admirers of serfdom and the Dark Ages."[75] So much for the Calvinist\capitalist dichotomy.

The political use of the term *Calvinism* is even more stretched. Civil and religious liberty are here made to depend on Calvinism:

> There is one thing all history testifies to, namely, that what the world calls Calvinism is the only doctrine that produces civil and religious liberty, pure and undefiled religion, national independence and prosperity whilst all other systems produce superstition, worldliness and national decay, only to end in lawlessness, Bolshevism and destruction.[76]

The Dutch Reformed theologian and Prime Minister of the Netherlands, Abraham Kuyper (1837-1920), insisted that "Calvinism has captured and guaranteed to us our constitutional civil rights."[77] Boettner claims that "in England and America the great struggles for civil and religious liberty were nursed in Calvinism, inspired by Calvinism, and carried out largely by men who were Calvinists."[78] And if that wasn't enough, regarding the United States in particular, it is maintained that Calvinism is responsible for the Revolutionary War and the Constitution.[79] The religious foundations of this country are well known and need not detain us here. What needs to be pointed out, however, is that by confounding Calvinism in its theological and non-theological senses, and equating Calvinism *in its theological aspect* with Protestantism in general, Calvinism can be made responsible for anything and everything good in history. And although the Calvinists are quick to point out that one of the things imported to this country from England was Calvinism, they often fail to mention that the plague of a united Church and State, a Calvinist theocracy, was also exported to this country. Honest Calvinists, however, admit that New England Puritan Calvinists persecuted dissenters, Quakers, heretics, and Baptists.[80] So once again it is evident that any claim made on behalf of Calvinism should be rejected unless it is limited to the strict theological usage of the term.

In confining the term *Calvinism* to its strict theological sense we can now examine the relevant historical arguments used in its defense. Naturally, we are informed that throughout history "Arminianism among Protestantism was in the minority," and conversely, that "historically, the Christian church has been predominantly Calvinistic."[81] As is to be expected, the Calvinist begins with the Bible: "Calvinism is merely a nickname by which

Reformed theologians refer to the dogma taught throughout Holy Scripture."[82] Then, it is a simple matter of progressing through time. The Apostle Paul was Calvinistic,[83] and so was "apostolic doctrine."[84] Leaving the New Testament period, we are then informed that "the writings of the Patristic period reveal strong leanings toward Calvinism."[85] Advancing further through history, it is declared that "a number of Calvinists" during the Middle Ages "graced the theological scene."[86] Boettner is quick to add that "the great majority of the creeds of historic Christendom" have taught the doctrines of Calvinism.[87] And bringing things up-to-date, Boettner declares: "From the time of the Reformation up until about one-hundred years ago these doctrines were boldly set forth by the great majority of the ministers and teachers in the Protestant churches."[88]

Regarding this "great majority" of Calvinistic men, the Calvinists wax eloquent:

> Among the past and present advocates of this doctrine are to be found some of the world's greatest and wisest men.[89]

> There can be little question, in fact, that Calvinism, or some modification of its essential principles, is the form of religious faith that has been professed in the modern world by the most intelligent, moral, industrious, and freest of mankind.[90]

Spencer notifies us that "throughout history many of the great evangelists, missionaries, and stalwart theologians held to the precious doctrines of grace known as Calvinism."[91] From Calvinism comes "the great theologians and scholars."[92] R. C. Sproul maintains that "the titans of classical Christian scholarship" are Calvinists.[93] McFetridge adds that "there is no other system of religion in the world which has such a glorious array of martyrs to the faith."[94] Without fail, most Calvinists will provide a long list of distinguished men who were Calvinists (so they claim) to prove that Calvinism must be true.[95] By far the man most cited as a Calvinist is the famed Baptist preacher Charles Spurgeon.[96] All of the Calvinistic writers treasure Spurgeon's Calvinism: the Baptists, naturally, to convince the Baptists; and the Pedobaptists, knowing that they can't attract the Baptists to their position, to do the next best thing—make a Reformed Baptist. The Reformed scholar referred to most often, excepting Calvin of course, is Loraine

Boettner, the author of *The Reformed Doctrine of Predestination.* Boettner, like Spurgeon, is held in high esteem by both Baptists and Pedobaptists alike.[97]

The affinity that Calvinists have for American history has already been seen. So besides the general statements made above, it remains now to present the claims of Calvinists regarding men in American history who were Calvinists. Boettner begins by insisting that: "Calvinism came to America in the Mayflower."[98] The Calvinism of the English Puritans and Pilgrims, Dutch and German Reformed, French Huguenots, and Scotch-Irish is heartily recounted by Calvinists as proof that all American Christians should be Calvinists.[99] Boettner relates the debt that American education owes to Calvinists: "Our three American universities of greatest historical importance, Harvard, Yale, and Princeton, were originally founded by Calvinists, as strong Calvinistic schools."[100] The Calvinism of Jonathan Edwards (1703-1758) and George Whitefield and their role in the First Great Awakening does not go unmentioned, and especially the latter's disputes with John Wesley (1703-1791) over Calvinism.[101] And in contrast, the "Arminianism" of Charles G. Finney (1792-1875), D. L. Moody (1837-1899), and Billy Sunday (1862-1935) is often disparaged.[102]

The Presbyterian theologian Charles Hodge (1797-1878) admirably sums up the historical argument:

> Such is the great scheme of doctrine known in history as the Pauline, Augustinian, or Calvinistic, taught, as we believe, in the Scriptures, developed by Augustine, formally sanctioned by the Latin Church, adhered to by the witnesses of the truth during the Middle Ages, repudiated by the Church of Rome in the Council of Trent, revived in that Church by the Jansenists, adopted by all the Reformers, incorporated in the creeds of the Protestant Churches of Switzerland, of the Palatinate, of France, Holland, England, and Scotland, and unfolded in the Standards framed by the Westminster Assembly, the common representative of Presbyterians in Europe and America.[103]

The reasoning of the Calvinists is simple: since the majority of great preachers and theologians, creeds and confessions, and Church Fathers and Protestant Reformers were Calvinistic—Calvinism must be true. Now, supposing for a moment that all of this is true—that the majority of great preachers and theologians were

Calvinistic, that the majority of creeds and confessions were Calvinistic, and that the majority of the Church Fathers and Protestant Reformers were Calvinistic—and even going beyond the Calvinist and allowing that the overwhelming majority of these men and documents were Calvinistic: does this prove the truth of Calvinism? Sproul, although using the historical argument himself, acknowledges it is possible that it doesn't: "To be sure, it is possible that Augustine, Aquinas, Luther, Calvin, and Edwards could all be wrong on this matter. . . . Again, that these agreed does not prove the case for predestination. They could have been wrong. But it gets attention."[104] Well, could the majority be wrong? Certainly they could all be wrong! As every Calvinistic Baptist would concede: all of the aforementioned men were wrong on baptism—they sprinkled babies. Does it not then stand to reason that they could correspondingly be wrong on predestination as well? And as every premillennial Calvinist would confess: all of the aforementioned men were wrong on the millennium—they were amillennial or postmillennial. Does it not further stand to reason that they could be just as wrong on the doctrines of Calvinism?

Calvinism and the Baptists

The controversy over Calvinism among the Baptists calls for special attention. Not only has this debate raged among the Baptists for hundreds of years, the greatest exponents of Calvinism today are not the Presbyterian or Reformed but the Baptists. The fact that a Baptist says he is not a Calvinist means nothing, for the Baptists, more than any other Calvinists, when seeking to draw attention away from the name of Calvin, use the phrase "Doctrines of Grace" as a metaphor for Calvinism.[105] Another term used by Baptists is "Sovereign Grace."[106] The term "grace" by itself is also used to stand for the doctrines of Calvinism.[107] One Calvinistic Baptist even wrote a book called *Grace Not Calvinism* in order to prove that he was not a Calvinist.[108] But just as was pointed out previously, if Calvinism is the doctrine of grace found in the Bible then this implies that if you disagree with Calvinism then you are denying salvation by grace. Some Calvinistic Baptists get downright offended when they are accused by non-Calvinists of being Calvinists. Joseph Wilson, the former editor of a Calvinistic Baptist newspaper, went on record as saying:

> We are Sovereign Grace Landmark Missionary Baptists. That's what we are. That's how we advertise ourselves. That's what we desire to be known as, and to be called by others. Call us this, and you will get no argument. We are not ashamed of this. We are glad to wear this label. Call us "Calvinists" and you offend us.[109]

The attempt of these "Sovereign Grace Baptists" to distance themselves from John Calvin by claiming to maintain the "Doctrines of Grace" and denying that they are Calvinists is not only insulting to all adherents and recipients of the doctrine of God's free grace in salvation, but has further obscured their true identity and therefore made necessary more diligent study of Calvinism and the Baptists.

All of the arguments thus far encountered that are used to prove the truth of Calvinism are continued by the Baptists who espouse this doctrine. The glowing statements about Calvinism that present it as the only true form of biblical Christianity are repeated with a vengeance:

> The doctrines of Calvinism, if believed, are a sovereign remedy against the two great heresies in the so-called Christian world, viz: ritualism, or sacramental salvation, on the one hand, and rationalism, on the other; the one the offspring of superstition, the other, the product of infidelity.[110]

> There is no such thing as preaching Christ and him crucified, unless you preach what now-a-days is called Calvinism.[111]

Milburn Cockrell, the editor of another Calvinistic Baptist newspaper, maintains that nothing proves the state of apostasy that most Baptist Churches are in more than "their departure from the doctrine of free and sovereign grace."[112] Indeed, he does not even recognize as a true Baptist church a church which is against Calvinism:

> We do not recognize as true churches those who denounce the doctrines of grace as the doctrines of the Devil. We will not grant a letter to nor receive a letter from any such so-called Baptist church. We grant that a church may be weak on sovereign grace and yet retain its church status, but we do not believe that a church which violently and openly opposes

sovereign grace can be a true New Testament Baptist Church.[113]

Cockrell never does explain the difference between "violently and openly" opposing sovereign grace and being "weak on sovereign grace." How "weak on sovereign grace" does a Baptist church have to be to forfeit its "church status"? And furthermore, who decides when the line has been crossed?

But in spite of their aversion to the name of Calvin, the Baptists have always made use of the Calvinist/Arminian dichotomy to fortify their position just like their Presbyterian and Reformed "cousins." Once again two things about Arminianism need to be emphasized. The first is that when a Calvinist uses the term, he never limits it to the supposed doctrines of James Arminius, for according to Calvinists, Arminianism is anything contrary to Calvinism. And secondly, the arbitrary division of men into either Calvinist or Arminian is the strength of the Calvinistic system, for if there are only two tenable viewpoints then if you are not a Calvinist you have to be an Arminian. Roy Mason (1894-1978) claims "the two terms are fixed and established" so that "whether a person wants to be labeled Calvinistic or Arminian or not, there is no way in which they can avoid it."[114] Once this two-tiered system is set up, the usual shocking statements about Arminianism are made:

> Arminianism is a modern form of the way of Cain, for it makes man's words, worth, and works to do more than Christ did. In truth Arminianism is paganism and popery under the banner of Christianity. It will culminate in the worship of a man in the person of the final Antichrist.[115]

> Adam and his wife were the first to demonstrate the philosophy which came eventually to be known theologically as "Arminianism." They devised a system of soteriology which, while it included some elements of divine revelation, rested squarely upon their own wisdom rather than upon God's.[116]

Once the Calvinist labels all his opponents as Arminians, the guilt by association argument is likewise used. Kenneth Good (1916-1991) reminds us that Pentecostals, Holiness, and Charismatics "are all definitely Arminian."[117] He also makes the doleful connection between Arminianism and Semi-Pelagianism.[118] Nevertheless, some

Calvinistic Baptists consider it a "cheap tactic," and despair of this division of all men into these two camps: "I wrote an article some years ago in which I pled with preachers, not to call other preachers Arminians or Calvinists. If they are Baptists, they are not Calvinists, and they are not Arminians."[119] But as we shall soon see, the Calvinists will not recognize any mediating position between Calvinism and Arminianism.

Because of their insistence that Calvinism is the Gospel, the Calvinistic Baptists have made some rash statements about "Arminianism" that some of their number have been forced to mitigate. Cockrell insists that "the Christ of Arminianism is not the Christ of the New Testament."[120] Wilson claims that "no one has ever been or ever will be saved in the way taught by Arminianism."[121] These are serious charges, for they insinuate that no one but a Calvinist can be saved. But some Sovereign Gracers tread lightly on this matter, for they admit that they were "saved under the preaching of an Arminian preacher and church."[122] Even Wilson himself acknowledges that "many of us were saved in Arminian churches under Arminian preaching."[123] So how does he get around his earlier statements? He explains: "Understand that I do verily believe that some (even many) Arminians are saved, but I adamantly insist that they were saved in the way taught by Sovereign Grace."[124] The fact that these saved Arminians may live their life in contempt of Calvinism is no problem, for these Arminians "will be Sovereign Gracers when they do get to heaven, and will shout on the banks of sweet and everlasting deliverance, rejoicing because their doctrine was false."[125]

Although the Calvinistic Baptists insist they have the right to reject the terms *Calvinist* and *Calvinism*, they will not accord this privilege to their opponents. Forrest Keener says Calvinism should be called "anti-Arminianism."[126] The aforementioned Wilson, who so adamantly rejects the label *Calvinist*, laments that those Baptists who are opposed to Calvinism "are ashamed of the word 'Arminian.'"[127] He says to his antagonists: "Call yourselves what you will; Arminian is what you are."[128] But suppose a detractor of Calvinism refuses the label? Wilson further contends that "you don't have to call yourself either; but not calling yourself either does not change the fact of what you are. Refusing to call yourself an Arminian does not change the fact that, that is what you are."[129] Good insists that "there are some Arminians who do not know that they are Arminians."[130] Because of this duplicity of the Calvinists, the terms *Calvinist* and *Calvinism* will be used throughout this book to apply to any man or doctrine that is Calvinistic—whether the designations are accepted or not. And in spite of the obsession that Calvinists have with the terms *Arminian* and *Arminianism,* they claim that "a sort of 'Calviphobia' develops in the Arminian mind" when the subject of Calvinism is broached.[131] But in view of the astounding and exaggerated things that have been said thus far about Arminianism, it is evident that it is the Calvinist who has a phobia due to his obsession with Arminianism. This is no more evident than when a Baptist simply chooses to identify himself as a Bible believer.

To those Baptists who accept the Bible as the final authority instead of the philosophical speculations and theological implications of Calvinism or Arminianism, the Calvinist reserves the most scorn. To call oneself a "Biblicist," instead of either a Calvinist or an Arminian, although it is particularly offensive to the adherents of both systems because it correctly implies that they are both unbiblical, is especially troubling to a Calvinist because of his adamant insistence that one must be either a Calvinist or an Arminian. In answer to those who say "the truth lies between Calvinism and Arminianism," Spurgeon replied: "It does not; there is nothing between them but a barren wilderness."[132] Good insists that those who claim the title of *Biblicist* seek "for a simplistic slogan in order to evade the issues or avoid the studies."[133] And while he commends the desire to be identified as a Biblicist, Good regards "the foundation of the reasoning" as "rather shaky. It actually does not have an adequate Scripture-basis."[134] The problem that Good has with Biblicists is that "they are not actually Biblicists at all."[135] They are actually "following the doctrinal system invented by Arminius."[136] In other words, they are Arminians—just like everyone else who is not a Calvinist. Curtis Pugh maintains that Biblicist pastors "ask church members to allow them to 'talk out of both sides of their mouths.'"[137] But believing that Calvinism is biblical, he simply regards himself "also as a Biblicist"[138] to stop the debate. Any attempt to be just a Bible-believing Baptist and you are labeled with the moniker of "Calminian,"[139] obviously a derivative from the *only* two accepted systems.

A corollary to the Calvinist/Arminian dichotomy, and one that is peculiar to the Baptists, is the former division of Baptists into two groups (where have we heard this before?) termed "General" and "Particular" Baptists—General Baptists holding that Christ died for all men in general, and Particular Baptists viewing the Atonement as only for the particular group of God's so-called elect.[140] In America these were called "Separate" and "Regular" Baptists.[141] After resurrecting these titles, Calvinists make statements extolling the virtues of the Calvinistic Baptists:

> Baptist orthodoxy was preserved among the Particular or Calvinistic Baptists."[142]

> Only the English Particular Baptists remained unscathed by the theological apostasy."[143]

Naturally, this implies that the General or Separate Baptists were somewhat less than orthodox. Good implies that we should identify with the Particular Baptists because they were the "largest body of Baptist churches,"[144] while Jack Warren, the editor of another Calvinistic Baptist newspaper, bids us to "return to the old paths and to our Particular Baptist roots."[145]

Some Baptists, however, refused to be wed to these arbitrary distinctions. In this country, as related by the Baptist historian David Benedict (1779-1874), an unusual association of churches was once formed in Western Pennsylvania called the "Covenanted Independent Baptists." Of these churches he relates: "These churches are, as they say, called by some Semi-Calvinists, by others, Semi-Arminians."[146] After discussing the types of Baptists in England, the English Baptist historian Thomas Crosby (c. 1685-1752) pertinently observed in his *The History of the English Baptists*:

> And I know that there are several churches, ministers, and many particular persons, among the *English Baptists,* who desire not to go under the name either of *Generals* or *Particulars,* nor indeed can justly *be ranked under either of these heads; because they* receive what they think to be truth, without regarding with what human schemes it agrees or disagrees with.[147]

And of this same time period, a more recent Baptist historian relates of a fund established in 1717 to assist needy ministers that it was "argued against restricting it to the Particular Baptists" since "many

Baptists did not go under either name."[148] So not all Baptists accepted these man-made designations, contrary to the ardent efforts of the Calvinists to force all their opponents into the Arminian camp.

Like their fellow Calvinists, the Sovereign Grace Baptists also use the historical argument when attempting to prove the truth of their doctrine. Naturally, they start with the Bible and simply progress through time. Mason begins by contending that "the Bible is a predestinarian book."[149] "Christ and His apostles" were Calvinistic, according to Milburn Cockrell.[150] The Apostle Paul was even a Sovereign Grace preacher.[151] Not wanting to limit it just to the apostles, Mason insists that "Christians of the New Testament times were strong believers in the greatness and sovereignty of God and consequently in the doctrines of election and predestination."[152] And besides appealing to the Calvinism of the Puritans, Covenanters, and Huguenots, he also relates that "the great theologians of history" and "most of the creeds of historic Christendom" have been Calvinistic.[153] Other Baptists likewise appeal to these Calvinistic creeds as proof of the truth of Calvinism.[154] Regarding the Baptists in particular, Mason maintains: "Baptists have been Predestinarians down through the centuries, from the days of Christ."[155] Garner Smith reiterates that "the doctrines of grace were believed and taught by Baptists before Calvin ever came on the scene."[156] Another adds that "the majority of Baptists have historically been Calvinistic."[157] Warren reminds us that "our heritage is one of Calvinism"[158] Wilson insists that Calvin got his Calvinism from the "Baptist preservation" of his doctrines.[159] Therefore Spurgeon could say: "The longer I live the clearer does it appear that John Calvin's system is the nearest to perfection."[160] Sometimes an appeal is made by Baptists to the Calvinism of the old Philadelphia Baptist Association (established 1707).[161] Other times the entreaty is to the Calvinism of the Baptist confessions of faith.[162] Even the non-Baptist Boettner appeals to the Calvinism of the Baptist confessions when seeking to prove the truth of Calvinism with the historical argument.[163] The Presbyterian McFetridge merely says: "The Baptists, who are Calvinists,"[164] and then goes on expecting the reader to just accept his statement.

Because the Presbyterian and Reformed groups are inherently Calvinistic, they have never appealed to individual men in history who were Calvinists as have the Baptists. From the Baptist authors we can find not only sections,[165] but whole chapters in books devoted to Calvinistic Baptists in history.[166] There are also books on the subject as well.[167] The stated thesis of one writer is that "Calvinism, popularly called the Doctrines of Grace, prevailed in the most influential and enduring arenas of Baptist denominational life until the end of the second decade of the twentieth century."[168] But even supposing without any reservation that this statement is true, how does that prove that Calvinism is true and that as a consequence all Baptists should be Calvinists? What is implied in the above thesis (and what the author spends the rest of his book attempting to prove) is that because the majority of great Baptist preachers, theologians, and missionaries were Calvinistic—Calvinism must be true. Besides the aforementioned Spurgeon, the roll call of Calvinistic Baptists reads as follows:

Isaac Backus (1724-1806)	W. B. Johnson (1782-1862)
Abraham Booth (1734-1806)	Adoniram Judson (1788-1850)
James P. Boyce (1827-1888)	Benjamin Keach (1640-1704)
John Brine (1703-1765)	William Kiffin (1616-1701)
John A. Broadus (1827-1895)	Hanserd Knollys (1599-1691)
John Bunyan (1628-1688)	John Leland (1754-1841)
William Carey (1761-1834)	Basil Manly Sr. (1798-1868)
B. H. Carroll (1843-1914)	Basil Manly Jr. (1825-1892)
Alexander Carson (1776-1884)	Patrick Hues Mell (1814-1888)
John Clarke (1609-1676)	Jesse Mercer (1769-1841)
John L. Dagg (1794-1884)	J. M. Pendleton (1811-1891)
Edwin C. Dargan (1852-1930)	J. C. Philpot (1802-1869)
Andrew Fuller (1754-1815)	Arthur W. Pink (1886-1952)
Richard Furman (1755-1825)	Luther Rice (1783-1836)
J. B. Gambrell (1841-1921)	John Rippon (1751-1836)
John Gano (1727-1804)	John C. Ryland (1723-1792)
John Gill (1697-1771)	John Skepp (c. 1670-1721)
J. R. Graves (1820-1893)	A. H. Strong (1836-1921)
Robert Hall (1728-1791)	John Spilsbery (1593-1668)
Alva Hovey (1820-1903)	H. Boyce Taylor (1870-1932)
R. B. C. Howell (1801-1868)	J. B. Tidwell (1870-1946)
Henry Jessey (1601-1663)	Francis Wayland (1796-1865)

The impressive list of names of prominent Baptists who supposedly were Calvinistic that is regularly compiled by the Sovereign Grace Baptists is supposed to so overwhelm the reader as to convince him that he ought to be a Calvinist if he is to be a historic Baptist. But if the Calvinism of the abovementioned men is actually checked, it will be found that it ranges from radical to mild and everything in between. Indeed, some of these Calvinists disputed with each other over the subject. So what exactly is the historic Baptist position?

Of these men there are three that stand out as having had the greatest influence: John Gill, Charles Spurgeon, and Arthur W. Pink—all Englishmen.

Called "Dr. Voluminous" because of his vast writings,[169] Gill is arguably the greatest scholar the Baptists have ever had, his Calvinism notwithstanding. At the age of twenty-one, he was called to pastor an already notable church at Goat's Yard Passage, Fair Street, Horselydown, in the London borough of Southwark.[170] Here he remained for over fifty years. Besides his commentary on the whole Bible, he is noted for his Body of Divinity and his numerous polemical writings on baptism and Calvinism. Most of Gill's works have been reprinted by The Baptist Standard Bearer.[171]

As was mentioned previously, Spurgeon is the one whom both Baptists and Pedobaptists appeal to as an example of a Calvinist who had a fruitful ministry. What is not generally known, however, is that Spurgeon was the successor of John Gill, albeit a few years later. Like his predecessor, Spurgeon assumed the pastorate at a young age and remained until his death. He is chiefly remembered for his sermons, which continued to be published for years after his death. The extent of Spurgeon's Calvinism is continually debated, with both sides using extracts from his sermons to prove their respective points. But although many non-Calvinists have sought to downplay his Calvinism, Spurgeon is the quintessential Calvinist. Good claims that "what David was to the forces of Israel in the days of Goliath, Spurgeon has been to the Calvinistic Baptists in our own times."[172] Naturally, his Calvinistic sermons have been extracted from the thousands he preached and published seperately.[173] Most of Spurgeon's works have been reprinted by Pilgrim Publications.[174]

Although an Englishman, Pink began his ministry in the United States after a short stint at Moody Bible Institute in 1910.[175] Beginning as a premillennial dispensationalist, Pink later rejected both teachings but remained a radical Calvinist throughout his life. He is best known for his books that grew out of the articles in his magazine *Studies in the Scriptures,* the most infamous one being *The Sovereignty of God,* first published in 1918.[176] Pink's

Calvinism upset some Calvinists so bad that an attempt was made to tone it down by The Banner of Truth Trust, by issuing, in 1961, a "British Revised Edition" of *The Sovereignty of God* in which three chapters and the four appendixes were expunged.[177] For this they have been severely criticized (and rightly so) by other Calvinists.[178] Most of Pink's works are in print today from a variety of different publishers.[179]

Among the roll call of Calvinistic Baptists can also be found four great leaders of the modern Baptist missionary movement: Adoniram Judson, Luther Rice, William Carey, and Andrew Fuller. Their professed Calvinism is especially valuable to Calvinists because it is used to prove that Calvinism is not incompatible with missionary work. Judson and Rice were American Congregationalists who later became Baptists: the former going to Burma and the latter raising funds in the United States. But whatever their *profession*, they proved by their actions on behalf of foreign missions the *pretense* of their "Calvinism." Carey, called the "father of modern missions,"[180] was an Englishman who went to India. He authored *Inquiry into the Obligation of Christians to Use Means for the Conversion of the Heathen,* and because of his proficiency in acquiring languages, was responsible for numerous versions of the Scriptures in other languages. And while it is true that Carey's missionary society was officially entitled the "Particular Baptist Society for the Propagation of the Gospel Among the Heathen," to maintain that Carey was a *consistent* Calvinist is another story. It is because of this disparity that John Ryland supposedly retorted to Carey at his appeal for the use of means in mission work: "Young man, sit down. When God pleases to convert the heathen, he will do it without your aid or mine."[181] While pastoring at Kettering, England, Fuller issued *The Gospel Worthy of All Acceptation* in 1785 and was instrumental in the formation of the Baptist missionary society that sent Carey to India. Thus their actions prove that it is only in spite of their Calvinism that these men undertook their missionary efforts.

Because the designations *Regular* and *Separate*, as well as *Particular* and *General*, are no longer used to denominate Baptists, most Calvinistic Baptists have some sort of name identifying themselves as Calvinists. Since the Baptist aversion to the name of Calvin precludes them from using his name, one can find prefixes like "Sovereign Grace," "Hardshell," "Primitive," "Old," "Old

School," "Strict," "Orthodox," or "Reformed." The "Gospel Standard Baptists" are a Calvinistic group and so are the "Continental Baptist Churches." The name of "Missionary Baptists" that some Calvinistic Baptists take upon themselves is a misnomer. All Baptists should be missionary Baptists. The reason that the Sovereign Grace Baptists use the aforementioned term is to distinguish themselves from the stricter Primitive Baptists—the ones who practice their Calvinism. These Baptists are all quick to emphasize their Calvinism, so it isn't hard to recognize most of them. However, some Baptists are hard to pin down. One will find Baptists with Calvinistic leanings in the various Baptist associations and fellowships, as well as among those who are strictly independent. There has of late even been a resurgence of Calvinism in the Southern Baptist Convention.[182] Upon inquiry, most of these men will affirm their Calvinism; however, this is not to say that all of them publicly preach and teach these opinions nor put them into practice. Some of these men are what might be called "closet-Calvinists," since they keep their Calvinism, like the proverbial skeleton, in the closet, lest their church members take to heart what their pastor believes and stop visitation and giving to missions. This is not to imply that these men disdain visitation and missions—quite the contrary—they might be ardent about visiting and support many missionaries. They are woefully inconsistent; they never resolutely employ their theology. One Calvinist has rather accurately termed these men "shelf-Calvinists," since their Calvinism is mainly to be found on their library shelves.[183] Several newspapers are published by the Calvinistic Baptists (*The Christian Baptist,* Atwood, Tennessee; *The Berea Baptist Banner,* Mantachie, Mississippi; *The Baptist Examiner,* Ashland, Kentucky; the *Baptist Evangel,* Saginaw, Texas), and they maintain some small colleges (Baptist Voice Bible College, Wilmington, Ohio; Landmark Baptist Theological Seminary, Fort Worth, Texas; Lexington Baptist College, Lexington, Kentucky), but one would never know these publications and schools were Calvinistic without further inquiry. So, as was mentioned at the beginning of this section, the fact that a Baptist says he is not a Calvinist means nothing. It often takes diligent study in order to identify whether or not a Baptist church, school, or preacher is Calvinistic. Occasionally, however, a group of Sovereign Grace Baptists do put out a directory of their churches.

The concerted attempt of the Calvinistic Baptists to equate Calvinism with Baptist orthodoxy is not shared by their Presbyterian and Reformed "cousins." These two groups are basically the same in doctrine: the term *Reformed* emphasising the doctrines of the Reformation and the term *Presbyterian* emphasising their form of church government. The history of how each group developed will be found in the next four chapters. But in relation to the Baptists, it should first be pointed out that the Presbyterian and Reformed denominations consider their theology to be that of biblical Christianity:

> It is my firm conviction that the only theology contained in the Bible is the Reformed theology.[184]

> Christianity comes to its fullest expression in the Reformed Faith.[185]

> The apostolic doctrine was that of Reformed Theology.[186]

To appeal to a broader spectrum of Christianity, however, sometimes the term *Reformed* is de-emphasized. The title of the widely-adopted theology textbook by the Reformed theologian Louis Berkhof (1873-1957) was changed from *Reformed Dogmatics* to *Systematic Theology,* and similar changes were made to some of his other books as well.[187]

There are two doctrines that are central to the Reformed Faith: Covenant theology and Calvinism. The first is abhorrent to all Baptists and the second is treasured by the Sovereign Grace Baptists. This antinomy of the Baptists is one reason for this work, for as will be maintained throughout this book, Calvinism is not only *wrong* doctrine, it is *Reformed* doctrine. That Reformed theology is to be identified with Covenant theology there is no doubt.[188] The relationship is so strong that Sproul even avows that "Reformed theology has been nicknamed 'Covenant theology.'"[189] But the adherents of Reformed theology likewise identify it with Calvinism:

> This term is often used synonomously with the term *Calvinistic* when describing a theological position.[190]

> The great advantage of the Reformed Faith is that in the

framework of the Five Points of Calvinism it sets forth clearly what the Bible teaches concerning the way of salvation."[191]

Predestination can be taken as a special mark of Reformed theology.[192]

So Calvinism is to be equated with Reformed theology—not just by mere acquiescence, but being a fully cognate term. The aforementioned D. James Kennedy relates why he is a Presbyterian: "I am a Presbyterian because I believe that Presbyterianism is the purest form of Calvinism."[193] Moreover, Kuyper maintains that "Calvinism means the completed evolution of Protestantism."[194] Talbot and Crampton further insist that "if the church does not return to her Reformational shorings, she will reap the worldwind of a truncated gospel and man centered faith."[195] But if Calvinism is the quintessence of Protestantism; the culmination of the Reformation, then it is built on a spurious foundation, for as even the Calvinistic Baptists would agree, the Reformation was just that: a *reformation,* not a complete *return* to biblical Christianity. When Loraine Boettner wrote his book *The Reformed Doctrine of Predestination,* he inadvertently told the plain truth: predestination in the Calvinistic system is a Reformed doctrine just like the Catholic Mass is a Catholic doctrine. Calvinism is therefore distinctly a Reformed doctrine, the Baptists notwithstanding.

Although Kenneth Good maintains that Baptists can be Calvinists (his book *Are Baptists Calvinists?*) without being Reformed (his book *Are Baptists Reformed?*), those of the Reformed persuasion disagree:

> It is our contention that a Reformed Baptist is really an impossibility. The Baptist who defends free will, man's initiative in the work of salvation, resistible grace, the altar call, the free and well-meaning offer of the gospel, etc., is the Baptist who is consistent. The Baptist who defends dispensationalism, in whatever form it takes, is the Baptist who consistently maintains his position. The Baptist, on the other hand, who maintains the doctrines of grace and repudiates dispensationalism is inconsistent in his theology. I do not deny that he may, in his theology, be a Calvinist. I do not deny that he may truly repudiate dispensationalism. But he is guilty of a happy inconsistency for all that.[196]

Those who hold to the truth of infant baptism have generally maintained that the ideas of believers' baptism and sovereign grace are mutually exclusive, and that those who hold to these two positions hold a contradictory view of salvation.[197]

One cannot be a Presbyterian or Reformed without being a Calvinist, but one can certainly be a Baptist. A Calvinistic Baptist should be a misnomer, because, in the words of the Dutch Reformed Herman Hanko: "A Baptist is only inconsistently a Calvinist."[198]

Hyper-Calvinism

When the true position of a Calvinist is finally exposed, he will usually claim that he is being misrepresented. Therefore, another type of Calvinism has been invented, and it is to it that every objection against the Calvinistic system is consigned. The adherents of this fictitious scheme are referred to by various terms: "ultra-Calvinists," "extreme Calvinists," "high-Calvinists," "Hard-shells." The favorite designation for this group is "hyper-Calvinists."[199] The trouble is, *hyper-Calvinism* is an ambiguous term. To an "Arminian," all Calvinists might be considered hyper-Calvinists. To an admirer of Spurgeon, any Calvinist to the right of him could be a candidate for a hyper-Calvinist. To one group of Calvinistic Baptists, another Calvinistic group they don't like might be dismissed as hyper-Calvinists. Many consider a hyper-Calvinist to be a Calvinist who goes beyond the teachings of John Calvin.[200] But to say that a person could go beyond the teachings of Calvin is not accurate, for when we examine Calvin's views in chapter 7, we will see that Calvin was (as is to be expected) true to his name. And finally, because the soteriological aspect of Calvinism has *theological speaking* become identified with the depravity of man, salvation by grace, and eternal security, conventional Calvinists are often referred to as hyper-Calvinists.

So just what is a hyper-Calvinist? Since it is the Calvinists themselves who regularly make this judgment, we must of necessity hear from them:

> The present writer would define hyper-Calvinism as a view of predestination that would deny or minimize human responsibility to repent and believe the gospel because of an inability to do

> so in light of the doctrine of total depravity. Furthermore, hyper-Calvinism would deny the necessity of a universal offer of the gospel.[201]
>
> Hyper-Calvinism in its attempt to square all gospel truth with God's purpose to save the elect, denies there is a universal command to repent and believe, and asserts that we have only warrant to invite to Christ those who are *conscious* of a sense of sin and need.[202]
>
> Hyper-Calvinism is the denial that God, in the preaching of the gospel, calls everyone who hears the preaching to repent and believe. It is the denial that the church should call everyone in the preaching. It is the denial that the unregenerated have a duty to repent and believe.[203]

But as one of the above writers also related of hyper-Calvinism: "It would be impossible to define it in a manner that would be acceptable to all."[204] One Sovereign Grace Baptist insists "you would find a thousand different definitions of a hyper-Calvinist among the religions of the world."[205]

The only proper use of the term *hyper-Calvinist* is in *practice* not *profession*. As one writer has said: "When we talk about 'hyper-Calvinism' we are not talking about the extending of Calvin's doctrines to a place beyond which he taught, but we are merely talking about an overemphasis on what he taught."[206] The Calvinists and the so-called hyper-Calvinists believe, teach, and preach the same things about Calvinism—the "hyper-Calvinist" just puts them into practice more consistently than the Calvinist. Spurgeon, who was criticized by "hyper-Calvinists" contemporary with him,[207] just as he is today,[208] said about the doctrine of his critics:

> I do not think I differ from any of my Hyper-Calvinistic brethren in what I do believe, but I differ from them in what they do not believe. I do not hold any less than they do, but I hold a little more, and, I think, a little more of the truth revealed in the Scriptures.[209]

Because they believe that they are the true Calvinists, those who are denominated as hyper-Calvinists do not accept the label. In fact, no one has ever countenanced the label. Those accused of hyper-

Calvinism have even retaliated with a neologism of their own to brand what they consider as "a teaching that falls below the level of true Calvinism."[210] Apparently coined by David Engelsma,[211] "hypo-Calvinism" has since been used as a term of condemnation by other critics of what they consider to be something less than true Calvinism.[212]

But even though Calvinists refuse to accept the label, and often cannot agree on just what exactly a hyper-Calvinist is, they are adamant in their insistence that Calvinism and hyper-Calvinism are poles apart:

> A Hyper-Calvinist and a Calvinist are two entirely different people.[213]

> Hyper-Calvinism is an aberration from true Calvinism.[214]

And although Calvinists incessantly lament that Calvinism is not distinguished from hyper-Calvinism,[215] they relish attacks on hyper-Calvinism. They use the term to make themselves look orthodox much the same as they use the label *Arminian*. They are great at articulating what they *don't* believe, so as to draw attention away from what they *do* believe. By crusading against the errors of both hyper-Calvinism and Arminianism, the Calvinist can take the middle road and appear to be orthodox. This is exactly what Spurgeon did in his day:

> Now I, who am neither an Arminian nor a hyper-Calvinist, but a Calvinist of Calvin's own stamp, think I can stand between the two parties. Believing all that the hyper-Calvinist believes, and preaching as high doctrine as ever he can preach, but believing more than he believes; not believing all the Arminian believes, but still at the same time believing that he is often sounder than the hyper-Calvinist upon some points of doctrine.[216]

Once again it is apparent that the true difference between a Calvinist and a hyper-Calvinist is one of practice not profession. A Calvinist of "Calvin's own stamp" is too much of a Calvinist.

So just who are these hyper-Calvinists, what did they teach, and when did the teaching of hyper-Calvinism originate? The roots of hyper-Calvinism are usually traced to the "doctrinal antinomianism" of John Saltmarsh (c. 1612-1647), John Eaton (1575-1641), and

Tobias Crisp (1600-1643).[217] The birth of hyper-Calvinism is said to be the publication in 1707 of *God's Operations of Grace but No Offers of His Grace* by Joseph Hussey (1660-1726).[218] Lewis Wayman (d. 1764), who wrote *A Further Enquiry after Truth* in 1739, and Richard Davis (1658-1714), who wrote *Truth and Innocency Vindicated Against Falsehood* in 1692, are also cited as contributors.[219] The Baptist John Skepp, author of the posthumously published 1722 work with the formidable title of *The Divine Energy: or the Efficacious Operations of the Spirit of God in the Soul of Man, in His Effectual Calling and Conversion: Stated, Proved, and Vindicated. Wherein the Real Weakness and Insufficiency of Moral Persuasion, Without the Super-addition of the Exceeding Greatness of God's Power for Faith and Conversion to God, Are Fully Evinced. Being an Antidote Against the Pelagian Plague,* is usually blamed for the introduction of hyper-Calvinism among the Baptists.[220] There are two distinguishing characteristics of this hyper-Calvinism: the denial of the free offer of the Gospel to all men, and the denial that it is the duty of all men who hear the Gospel to repent and believe.[221] This latter point resulted in a theological controversy known as the Modern Question: whether saving faith in Christ is a duty required of all sinners.[222] Those answering in the negative made a distinction between "legal and evangelical repentance" and "common and saving faith."[223] According to Engelsma, hyper-Calvinism "manifests itself in the practice of the preacher's addressing the call of the gospel, 'repent and believe on Christ crucified,' only to those in his audience who show signs of regeneration, and thereby of election, namely, some conviction of sin and some interest in salvation."[224]

The most infamous man usually charged with hyper-Calvinism is the Particular Baptist John Gill.[225] Besides his own doctrines, Gill is usually regarded as a hyper-Calvinist because he wrote a preface to the hymns of Richard Davis in 1748, edited John Skepp's *Divine Energy* in 1751, published the works of Crisp in 1755, and was close to John Brine, who had written *Defense of the Doctrine of Eternal Justification* in 1732.[226] Spurgeon even said of his predecessor: "The system of theology with which many identify his name has chilled many churches to their very soul, for it has led them to omit the free invitations of the gospel, and to deny that it is the duty of sinners to believe in Jesus."[227] The problem that Calvinists (including Spurgeon) have with Dr. Gill is that he consistently practiced his Calvinism. For this he will not be faulted here. The man who is viewed as rescuing the Particular Baptists from the hyper-Calvinism of Gill is the pastor of his old church at Kettering, Andrew Fuller.[228] Thus, Baptists were divided into Gillites and Fullerites.[229] Spurgeon was even called a "Fullerite" early in his ministry.[230] Attacked by both Calvinists and Arminians,[231] Fuller declared about the Calvinistic Baptists: "Had matters gone on but a few years the Baptists would have become a perfect dunghill in society."[232] The complete title to his aforementioned 1785 work is *The Gospel Worthy of All Acceptation: or the Obligation of Men Fully to Credit and Cordially to Approve Whatever God Makes Known. Wherein Is Considered, the Nature of Faith in Christ, and the Duty of Those Where the Gospel Comes in That Matter.*[233] Here he elaborated on what he had previously written in his confession of faith:

> I believe it is the duty of every minister of Christ plainly and faithfully to preach the Gospel to all who will hear it; and as I believe the inability of men to spiritual things to be wholly of the *moral,* and therefore of the criminal kind, and that it is their duty to love the Lord Jesus Christ and trust him for salvation though they do not; I therefore believe free and solemn addresses, invitations, calls, and warnings to them to be not only *consistent,* but directly *adapted,* as means, in the hand of the Spirit of God, to bring them to Christ. I consider it as a part of my duty which I could not omit without being guilty of the blood of souls.[234]

It should not be supposed, however, that Fuller was anything less than a strict Calvinist. He said himself: "I do not believe every thing that Calvin taught, nor any thing because he taught it; but I reckon strict Calvinism to be my own system."[235] So as has been maintained throughout this section, hyper-Calvinism is merely the consistent practice of one's Calvinism.

In more recent times, there are others who have been labeled, for one reason or another, as hyper-Calvinists. Among the Baptists in England the Gospel Standard Baptists have been so disparaged.[236] In this country the Primitive Baptists are considered hyper-Calvinists by the Sovereign Grace Baptists, although the usual term for their doctrine is "hardshellism."[237] If there is one man who is pictured as the consummate hyper-Calvinist it is certainly Arthur W. Pink. Outside of the Baptists there is the Protestant Reformed Church, which has been called hyper-Calvinistic by the Christian Reformed Church.[238] The differences between these two Reformed bodies will be examined later.

Calvinism and Calvinists

There remains yet the question of just what exactly it is that determines whether a man is a Calvinist. The rejection of the term means nothing, because as we have seen, for a man to refuse the label does not mean that he is not a Calvinist. So who are the Calvinists? As mentioned on several occasions, the Presbyterian and Reformed groups are inherently Calvinistic. The differences in doctrine between Presbyterian and Reformed individuals and churches are rather insignificant, especially in relation to the doctrines of Calvinism. Therefore, their theologians are without exception all Calvinistic. This would include:

Herman Bavinck (1854-1921)	Herman Hoeksema (1886-1965)
G. C. Berkouwer (1903-1996)	Abraham Kuyper (1837-1920)
Louis Berkhof (1873-1957)	J. Gresham Machen (1881-1937)
J. Oliver Buswell (1895-1977)	John Murray (1898-1975)
Gordon H. Clark (1902-1985)	William G. T. Shedd (1820-1894)
William Cunningham (1805-1861)	Henry B. Smith (1815-1877)
Robert L. Dabney (1820-1898)	James H. Thornwell (1812-1862)
John Dick (1764-1833)	Francis Turretin (1623-1687)
Jonathan Edwards (1703-1758)	Cornelius Van Til (1895-1987)
Archibald A. Hodge (1823-1886)	Geerhardus Vos (1862-1947)
Charles Hodge (1797-1878)	Benjamin B. Warfield (1851-1921)

Because these men are for the most part conservative and orthodox, Calvinism has been equated with orthodoxy and therefore established a foothold on theology. And because they have written the majority of the theology books, it is very difficult to find a work on systematic theology that is not Calvinistic.

The identification of the Baptists who are Calvinists is, as we have seen, a different matter. Not only do most of them disdain the name of Calvin, but they have tremendous differences among themselves. Some are amillennial; some are premillennial. Some are KJV-only; others use modern versions. Some are local church-only; others allow for a universal church. Some use only fermented communion wine; others use only grape juice. Some send out missionaries; others send no missionaries. Some believe in mandatory women's head coverings; others think it is optional. Some allow instrumental church music; others permit no music. Some give Gospel invitations; others don't give any. Some are closed communion; others are open communion. Some allow divorced preachers; others permit none. Some are strongly dispensational; others are only moderately dispensational. Thus, the Calvinistic Baptists differ among themselves to a substantial degree. Nevertheless, their Calvinism is the one common bond which unites them.

So what is Calvinism? What is it that makes a man a Calvinist? Although Bible believers who reject Calvinism do not agree with the Calvinist/Arminian dichotomy, in one respect the Calvinists do have a point:

> The Arminian will say that man is elect because he believes. The Calvinist asserts that man believes because he is elect.[239]

> Thus according to the Arminian, the reason one accepts and another rejects the gospel is that *man* decides; but according to the Calvinist, *God* decides.[240]

> What is the real question at issue? I think I can tell you very plainly. It is the question whether a man is predestinated—if for the moment we concede to our adversaries in the debate their loose use of that term—it is the question whether a man is predestinated by God to salvation because he believes in Christ or is enabled to believe in Christ because he is predestinated.[241]

So what it all comes down to is this: Are men elected to salvation or are they not? That is the issue among Christians. The issue is not as Warfield says, that "there are fundamentally only two doctrines of salvation: that salvation is from God, and that salvation is from ourselves."[242] No Christian disagrees with that, although that is how a Calvinist will shift the issue to make his system look like it alone teaches salvation by grace. Wilson is even more subtle: "What is the decisive factor as to whether or not one is a sovereign gracer or an Arminian as to salvation. It is this: The sovereign gracer teaches that the final decisive factor as to whether or not one is saved is the will and work of God, while the Arminian teaches that the final decisive factor as to whether or not one is saved is the will and/or work of man."[243] Now, no true Christian believes that works have any part in his salvation; however, the role of the will of man is a separate issue. By combining the two, the Calvinist once again implies that only his system teaches salvation by grace. The issue is: election to salvation. All Calvinists, whether they be Presbyterian or Reformed, Primitive Baptist or Sovereign Grace Baptist; all Calvinists, whether they be premillennial or amillennial, dispensational or covenant theologist; all Calvinists, whether they go by the name or not; all Calvinists have one thing in common: God, by a sovereign, eternal decree, has determined before the foundation of the world who shall be saved and who shall be lost. To obscure the real issue, a vocabulary has been invented to confuse and confound the Christian. The arguments about supralapsarianism and infralapsarianism, total depravity and total inability, reprobation and preterition, synergism and monergism, free will and free agency, common grace and special grace, general calling and effectual calling, perseverance and preservation, and the sovereignty of God are all immaterial. The stumbling block for the Calvinist is the simplicity of salvation, so upon rejecting this, a system has to be constructed whereby salvation is made a mysterious, arcane, incomprehensible, decree of God. Thus, the basic error of Calvinism is confounding election and predestination with salvation, which they never are in the Bible, but only in the philosophical speculations and theological implications of Calvinism: the other side of Calvinism.

Chapter 2
THE ORIGIN OF CALVINISM

John Calvin did not originate the doctrines that bear his name. This is stated emphatically by Calvinists: "The system of doctrine which bears the name of John Calvin was in no way originated by him."[1] Dabney insists that "John Calvin no more invented these doctrines than he invented this world which God had created six thousand years before."[2] But if this is true then why are Calvin's teachings about predestination called Calvinism? Boettner replies that "it was Calvin who wrought out this system of theological thought with such logical clearness and emphasis that it has ever since borne his name."[3] Edwin Palmer (1922-1980) asserts that Calvin "was the most eloquent and systematic expositor of these truths."[4] Boettner credits Calvin with a "deep knowledge of Scripture," a "keen intellect," and "systematizing genius" as the reasons that he was able to set forth and defend these doctrines as never had been done before.[5] Calvin just "set forth what appeared to him to shine forth so clearly from the pages of Holy Scripture."[6] So once again we are told that Calvinism, whether so designated or not, is just the system of doctrine contained in the Scriptures. This in itself, of course, means nothing, for every sect and cult that names the name of Christ, including the Roman Catholic Church, makes the same profession.

Calvin and Augustine

If the doctrines of Calvinism are not from "the pages of Holy Scripture," then where did Calvin get his system? Let us hear from some well known and respected Reformed Calvinists themselves:

> John Calvin was part of a long line of thinkers who based their doctrine of predestination on the Augustinian interpretation of St. Paul.[7]

> There is hardly a doctrine of Calvin that does not bear the marks of Augustine's influence.[8]
>
> The main features of Calvin's theology are found in the writings of St. Augustine to such an extent that many theologians regard Calvinism as a more fully developed form of Augustinianism.[9]
>
> The system of doctrine taught by Calvin is just the Augustinianism common to the whole body of the Reformers.[10]

Secular historians like Will Durant (1885-1981) speak likewise: "Calvin based his ruthless creed upon Augustine's theories of the elect and the damned."[11] The Baptist Good grants that "Augustine may be regarded as the father of the soteriological system which now goes by the name of 'Calvinism.'"[12] Spurgeon acquiesces that "perhaps Calvin himself derived it mainly from the writings of Augustine," but then is quick to add that "Augustine obtained his views, without doubt, through the Spirit of God, from the diligent study of the writings of Paul, and Paul received them of the Holy Ghost, from Jesus Christ."[13] Calvin himself also stated: "Augustine is so wholly with me, that if I wished to write a confession of my faith, I could do so with all fulness and satisfaction to myself out of his writings."[14] Some Calvinists have even preferred the term *Augustinianism* over *Calvinism*.[15]

Augustine and Calvin are, in the eyes of the Calvinist, the premier theologians:

> These two extraordinarily gifted men tower like pyramids over the scene of history.[16]
>
> Calvin and Augustine easily rank as the two outstanding systematic expounders of the Christian system since Saint Paul.[17]
>
> The two most scientific theologians of Christendom.[18]

Even Baptists seeking support for their Calvinism cite Augustine and Calvin as "great theologians."[19]

The only problem with the men who correctly trace Calvinism back to Augustine is that once doing so they say: "Augustinianism is but the thetical expression of religion in its purity."[20] Good even maintains that "the Biblical faith, which had been commonly accepted but never formally organized, finally found theological expression in Augustine."[21] So we are right back to where we started from: Calvinism, whether called "Augustinianism" or some other term, is biblical Christianity. Therefore, an examination of Augustine and his system are necessary before moving on to John Calvin himself.

The Influence of Augustine

The influence of Augustine upon history in general and Christianity in particular is incalculable—but not surprising—since, like Calvin, he was an extensively prolific writer. Although most of Augustine's works are extant, his two most famous works, the *Confessions* and the *City of God,* are printed by numerous publishers and are still excerpted in most secular history books. And not only are his own works voluminous, the tremendous assortment of literature that his life and writings have inspired is equally undeterminable. Students at Calvin Theological Seminary have the option of taking a three semester hour course on "The Life and Thought of St. Augustine."[22] When a modern Calvinist endeavors to substantiate Calvinism by an appeal to men, the first name mentioned is always that of Augustine.[23] Even Arminius appealed to him when Augustine agreed with him on a particular interpretation.[24] And while it is certainly no surprise that Augustine made it on to the cover of *Christian History* magazine,[25] the fact that he was featured in *Time* magazine as "the second founder of the faith" shows the continued influence of Augustine.[26] Yet whether or not this influence has been good or bad remains to be seen.

The man Augustine has been glowingly lauded by Calvinists:

> One of the greatest theological and philosophical minds that God has ever so seen fit to give to His church.[27]

> Saint Augustine was one of the greatest Christian thinkers of all time.[28]

> The greatest Christian since New Testament times.[29]

> Assuredly greatest man that ever wrote Latin.[30]

The greatest psychologist and political thinker since Aristotle.[31]

Some would even place him in a trinity: "After Jesus and Paul, Augustine of Hippo is the most influential figure in the history of Christianity."[32]

Although the influence of Augustine is indeed great, the Calvinists have been quite generous in what they ascribe to him. The Presbyterian N. L. Rice (1807-1877) claims that Augustine's "labors and writings, more than those of any other man in the age in which he lived, contributed to the promotion of sound doctrine and the revival of true religion."[33] That is quite a statement, and it remains to be seen just what Augustine's "sound doctrine" and "true religion" really were, but consider what Warfield credits to Augustine:

> Augustine determined for all time the doctrine of grace.[34]
>
> The whole development of Western life, in all its phases, was powerfully affected by his teaching.[35]
>
> The entire political development of the Middle Ages was dominated by him.[36]
>
> He was in a true sense the creator of the Holy Roman Empire.[37]

The most remarkable statement by Warfield, however, is that "it is Augustine who gave us the Reformation."[38] Arthur Custance informs us that "the Reformation was essentially a revival of Augustinianism, as Augustinianism was a recovery of Pauline theology."[39] Although the Reformation was the culmination of many ideas and events, most of them directed against the corruption of the Catholic Church, to assign Augustine a major part in it is to twist the facts of history, for as we shall presently see, not only did he differ from Martin Luther (1483-1546) and the celebrated Pauline principle of the Reformation, the Roman Catholic Church itself has a better claim on Augustine than do the Calvinists.

Catholicism and Augustine

It is certainly not customary that those whom Protestants extol are at the same time embraced by the Roman Catholic Church as well. But such is the case with Augustine. He, along with Jerome (331-420), Ambrose (340-397), and Gregory the Great (c. 540-604), was one of Catholicism's original four "Doctors of the Church"[40] He has a feast day in the Catholic Church on August 28 (the day of his death).[41] The Catholic encyclopedia denominates him the founder of Western Christianity and applauds the "greatness of his achievement as thinker and theologian."[42] On the 1,600th anniversary of Augustine's conversion, Pope John Paul II termed him the "common father of our Christian civilization."[43] One Vatican official says that through Augustine: "I learned to believe, to know faith and to love the church."[44] Like any Roman Catholic relic, the bones of Augustine were transported all over Europe.[45] So the Calvinists are not the only ones who appeal to Augustine for their system of theology, for as one historian said: "There is scarcely a single Roman Catholic dogma which is historically intelligible without reference to his teaching."[46]

Augustine was first and foremost a Roman Catholic. All Calvinists, if they are honest, admit this. Warfield concedes that Augustine was "in a true sense the founder of Roman Catholicism."[47] Philip Schaff (1819-1893) calls him the "principal theological creator of the Latin-Catholic system as distinct from the Greek Catholicism on the one hand, and from evangelical Protestantism on the other."[48] Which means, as another writer so candidly asserted: "The first real 'Roman Catholic.'"[49] It is only because Augustine was so hypocritical that Warfield counts him as "both the founder of Roman Catholicism and the author of that doctrine of grace which it has been the constantly pursued effort of Roman Catholicism to neutralize."[50] Yet, the Baptist Tom Ross, after admitting that Augustine was "no friend to Baptists,"[51] cites him as "the renowned Catholic theologian" when he seeks a pre-Reformation ally who "believed the doctrines of grace."[52] But even though Calvinists delight in claiming Augustine as one of their own, not all Catholics are willing to give him up so easy.[53]

The Church Fathers and Augustine

During the time between the apostles of the New Testament and Augustine, numerous sects and heresies arose. But this was predicated by the Apostle Paul: **"For I know this, that after my departing shall grievous wolves enter in among you, not sparing** the flock. **Also of your own selves shall men arise, speaking perverse things, to draw away disciples after them"** (Acts 20:30). There is some debate, however, even among the Calvinists themselves, as to whether the doctrine of predestination, as it is understood by Calvinists, was taught before Augustine. We are usually told, with no documentation whatsoever, general statements like: "The writings of the Patristic period reveal strong leanings toward Calvinism."[54] Occasionally an effort is made to cite patristic authors,[55] but no Calvinist has ever improved upon the attempt of John Gill in his *The Cause of God and Truth*.[56] Yet, against the quotations from the Church Fathers presented as proof that they were Calvinistic, there stand three glaring objections. To begin with, most of the quotations adduced are highly ambiguous and must have Calvinism read into them in order to teach it. Secondly, the quotations cited do not address the real issue. Just because a church father mentions the depravity of man and the free grace of God in salvation does not mean he is teaching Calvinism, but that is what Calvinists want you to believe. And finally, for every Patristic quotation advanced in favor of Calvinism, two others may be proffered against it.

In spite of the attempts of some Calvinists to remove the stigma from Augustine being classified as what one Calvinist calls, the "first true Predestinarian,"[57] the majority of Calvinists make him just that. C. Norman Sellers acknowledges that "Augustine differed from the Fathers who preceded him in that he taught the absolute sovereignty of God."[58] And not only did he differ from the previous Fathers, Boettner declares that "he went far beyond the earlier theologians."[59] He then further says regarding the Calvinistic idea of salvation by an irresistible, eternal decree: "This cardinal truth of Christianity was first clearly seen by Augustine."[60] Warfield insists that Augustine "recovered for the Church" this cardinal truth.[61] Custance goes so far as to say that Augustine "was perhaps the first after Paul to realize the Total Depravity of man."[62] It should be remembered that it is the Calvinists themselves who are presenting Augustine "as a major link between Paul and Calvin."[63] Most of them so readily admit that "the doctrine of Predestination received such little attention" before Augustine,[64] that even Calvinistic Baptists concede that "Augustine may be regarded as the father of the soteriological system which now goes by the name of 'Calvinism.'"[65] This is even confirmed by secular historians: "These questions were seldom agitated from the time of St. Paul to that of St. Augustin."[66]

But whether or not any of the early Church Fathers taught what today is considered "Calvinism" is really very immaterial for two reasons given by the Calvinists themselves. The first is the fact that the real issue was *never* whether salvation was received by the free will of man or by an irresistible decree. Because of the age in which they lived, Gill informs us that "the pens of the first Christian writers were chiefly employed against Jews and Pagans, and such heretics who opposed the doctrine of the Trinity; and who either denied the proper deity or real humanity of Christ; and therefore it is not to be expected that they should treat of the doctrines now in debate among us."[67] And secondly, as Gill the Baptist knew so well: "The writings of the best of men, of the most early antiquity, and of the greatest learning and piety, cannot be admitted by us as the rule and standard of our faith. These, with us, are only the Scriptures of the Old and New Testament: to these we appeal, and by these only can we be determined."[68] With so much resting on Augustine, and being placed there by the Calvinists themselves, an examination of the theology of Augustine, together with a comparison of his theology with the Scriptures, is imperative.

The Age of Augustine

In order to better understand Augustine and his theology, a brief survey of the age in which he lived is pertinent, for Augustine lived during a very unique period in the history of the Christianity. Beginning with the persecution of the apostles after the ascension of Christ (Acts 4:1-3, 5:17-18) and the subsequent martyrdoms of Stephen (Acts 7:58-59) and James (Acts 12:1-2), the early Christians suffered almost continuous persecution. But as the church father Tertullian (c. 150-c. 220) articulated, persecution only increased the number of Christians: "Nor does your cruelty, however exquisite, avail you; it is rather a temptation to us. The oftener we are mown down by you, the more in number we grow; *the blood of Christians is seed.*"[69] But after almost three hundred years of bitter persecution, Christianity was thrust into a dubious position of ascendancy.

Constantine (c. 272-337) became the sole ruler of the Western branch of the Roman empire after defeating Maxentius (c. 283-312) at the famous Battle of the Mulvian Bridge, near Rome, in 312. It was here that Constantine claimed to have seen a vision of a shining cross that led to his victory. The historian Eusebius (c. 265-339), Constantine's greatest admirer, recorded from the mouth of Constantine:

> He said that about noon, when the day was already beginning to decline, he saw with his own eyes the trophy of a cross of light in the heavens, above the sun, and bearing the inscription, CONQUER BY THIS. At this sight he himself was struck with amazement, and his whole army also, which followed him on this expedition, and witnessed the miracle.[70]

Later that night in his sleep, Constantine claims to have been visited by Christ himself and commanded to make a standard in the likeness of the cross he had seen.[71] After supposedly attributing his victory to the "Christian God," Constantine joined with Licinius (c. 265-325), one of the emperors of the East, in issuing in 313, at Milan, a decree of toleration toward Christianity. Licinius soon defeated a rival in the east and Constantine in turn vanquished Licinius in 324, thus becoming the last sole ruler of the Roman empire.

The *Edict of Milan,* as the decree of toleration has come to be called, not only proscribed the persecution of Christians, it allowed for the restoration of confiscated property, recognized Christianity, and declared the absolute liberty of conscience in religious matters. Constantine and Licinius said in part:

> We have, therefore, determined, with sound and upright purpose, that liberty is to be denied to no one, to choose and to follow the religious observances of the Christians, but that to each one freedom is to be given to devote his mind to that religion which he may think adapted to himself, . . . every one who has the same desire to observe the religion of the Christians may do so without molestation. . . . we have granted to these same Christians freedom and full liberty to observe their own religion.[72]

Although at first glance this proclamation appears to be admirable, it was actually the beginning of the unholy alliance of the Church and State that was to plague true churches until well after the Reformation. Just as Balaam could not curse the children of Israel (Num. 23:7-8), and therefore caused them, through his counsel (Num. 31:16), to commit fornication (Rev. 2:14) and to join themselves to Baal (Num. 25:5), with the result that God ordered them to be killed (Num. 25:5), so the Church, beginning in the time of Constantine, since it could not be compromised by persecution, was seduced, as the children of Israel were, to join with the world.

If Constantine had merely followed the bare letter of the Edict of Milan and left the Christians alone he would have gone down in history with a much better reputation than he has enjoyed. But such was not the case, for Constantine soon afterward extended special privileges to what he considered to be the Church while withdrawing all privileges from not only the pagan Romans, but what he considered "heretics" as well. He exempted the Christian clergy from certain municipal duties and taxes, abolished pagan customs that Christians deemed offensive, and contributed liberally to the support of the clergy and the building of churches.[73] To one group of Christians, however, Constantine refused support. The Donatists of North Africa, who had separated themselves from the established Church, were deprived of their churches and persecuted by an edict of Constantine.[74] Then in 325, the first general church council, the Council of Nicaea, was summoned by Constantine to deal with the Arian controversy. Nothing confirms the lamentable state of the Church more than the calling of this church council by the State, for not only did Constantine side against Arius (256-336), he advocated the suppression of his writings in the harshest terms:

> If any treatise composed by Arius should be discovered, let it be consigned to the flames, in order that not only his depraved doctrine may be suppressed, but also that no memorial of him may be by any means left. This therefore I decree, that if any one shall be detected in concealing a book compiled by Arius, and shall not instantly bring it forward and burn it, the penalty for this offense shall be death.[75]

Constantine was relentless in his pursuit of "heretics." He forbid those outside of the catholic church to assemble, either publically or privately, and confiscated their property.[76] Thus, the very things Christians had endured themselves were now being practiced in the name of Christianity.

As he was approaching death, Constantine finally requested that he be baptized. He referred to baptism as "the salvation of God," "that seal which confers immortality," and "the seal of salvation."[77] Believing in baptismal regeneration, he had deferred baptism until he was near death so as to obtain forgiveness of his past sins and not have the chance to sin much more. He died soon afterward and was placed in a gold coffin and taken to the city of his namesake: Constantinople. In spite of the praise heaped upon him by Eusebius, Constantine was responsible for laying the foundation of one of the greatest errors to plague the Church: the union of Church and State. Even though Constantine was instrumental in the deaths of his wife, nephew, and son,[78] F. F. Bruce (1910-1990) still contends that "there is no reason to doubt the genuineness of Constantine's acceptance of Christianity, in spite of his barbaric outbursts which deface the record of his reign from time to time."[79] The historian Andrew Miller (1810-1883), however, is probably more accurate in his assessment: "A crucified Saviour, true conversion, justification by faith alone, separation from the world, were subjects never known by Constantine."[80]

What Constantine started, the emperor Theodosius (reigned 379-395) finished. After the death of Constantine, and the subsequent division of the empire among his sons, laws were passed against heathen sacrifices and heathen temples were pillaged.[81] This had the effect of bringing many unregenerate pagans into the Church. The first order of business for Theodosius was to issue an edict which declared to all subjects that they "steadfastly adhere to the religion which was taught by St. Peter to the Romans, which has been faithfully preserved by tradition."[82] He further ordered that "the adherents of this faith be called *Catholic Christians*," and forbid, under heavy penalty, "heretics" to meet in their churches.[83] Theodosius, like Constantine, also summoned an ecumenical church council. The First Council of Constantinople, which Theodosius called in 381, reaffirmed the Nicene creed as the only orthodox faith and condemned all "heresies."[84] In 391 Christianity was virtually made the official religion as all forms of pagan worship were forbidden.[85] But only what the emperor deemed to be orthodox Christianity was accepted. Christian "heretics" were forbidden to assemble, give instruction in their faith, and practice ordination.[86] Many were threatened with fines, confiscation of their property, banishment, and death.[87] Consequently, even though Christianity was the "official" religion, true Christians, like they did when paganism was in the ascendancy, were forced to go underground.

The results of imperial edicts and decrees and the unholy alliance of Church and State have been admirably summarized by the historian William Jones (1762-1846):

> The Scriptures were now no longer the standard of the Christian faith. What was orthodox, and what heterodox, was, from henceforward, to be determined by the decisions of fathers and councils; and religion propagated not by the apostolic methods of persuasion, accompanied with the meekness and gentleness of Christ, but by imperial edicts and decrees; nor were gainsayers to be brought to conviction by the simple weapons of reason and scripture, but persecuted and destroyed.[88]

Thus was the sad condition of the official Church at the time that Augustine began to exert his influence near the end of the fourth century.

The Life of Augustine

Aurelius Augustinus was born on November 13, 354, at Tagaste in Roman North Africa (modern-day Algeria) and died in nearby Hippo on August 28, 430. He was the son of a pagan father, Patricius, supposedly converted just before his death, and a Christian mother named Monica.[89] At the age of twelve, Augustine was sent to school at nearby Madaura, where he struggled with Greek.[90] During a year at home when he was sixteen, Augustine says "the thorns of lust grew rank over my head."[91] Although his mother warned him "not to commit fornication," he dismissed her advice as "womanish counsels" and indulged himself, even embellishing his exploits so as to surpass his friends.[92] At seventeen, Augustine went off to Carthage for further studies. At Carthage, he fell deeper into sin, claiming to have "befouled, therefore, the spring of friendship with the filth of concupiscence" and "dimmed its lustre with the hell of lustfulness."[93] It was here that he took a mistress and had a bastard child, Adeodatus.[94] And it was also here that Augustine experienced a conversion, but not to Christianity.

While reading the Roman orator Cicero (106-43), Augustine

became enamored with philosophy and turned to the Manichaean religion.[95] Founded by Mani (216-276), who was executed by the Persian government,[96] Manichaeism was a Gnostic religion drawing on Zoroastrianism, Buddhism, and Christianity.[97] Surprisingly, some elements of Manichaeism were to surface later in Augustine's Christian theology. In the dualism of the Manichaean system, the world was a struggle between Light and Darkness.[98] The Manichees were to assist in the separation of Light from the world by asceticism, celibacy, poverty, and vegetarianism—all practiced later by Augustine.[99] It is also interesting that the Manichees were divided into two groups: a minority, termed the Elect, and the majority, known as Auditors or Hearers.[100] For the next nine years Augustine was an ardent Manichaean, and made numerous converts.[101] After returning to his hometown to teach grammar, he left again for Carthage to teach rhetoric.[102] After eight years at Carthage, Augustine became disillusioned with Manichaeism and left for Rome.[103] When he discovered that the students in Rome did not like to pay their school bills, he took another position in Milan.[104] It was here that he sent away his mistress, took another, and then experienced another conversion, this time to Christianity.

While at Milan, three elements led to the conversion of Augustine. He first came under the influence of Neoplatonic philosophy, a revival of Platonism by the pagan philosophers Plotinus (c. 205-270) and Porphyry (c. 232-302).[105] Surprisingly, however, this philosophy did contribute to Augustine's spiritual quest, but only because of his Manichaean background and the fact that he read into Neoplatonism elements of Christianity that did not exist in it.[106] He also began attending the preaching of Ambrose, from whom he learned the allegorical method of interpreting the Scriptures.[107] But perhaps the greatest factor, and one that is often overlooked, is his reading of the Pauline epistles.[108] While under a period of great conviction, Augustine supposedly threw himself down under a fig tree and wept, but then heard a child's voice repeating "take up and read."[109] This he interpreted as "a command to me from Heaven to open the book, and to read the first chapter I should light upon."[110] The text he opened to was in the book of Romans:[111]

> **Let us walk honestly, as in the day; not in rioting and drunkenness, not in chambering and wantonness, not in**

strife and envying. But put ye on the Lord Jesus Christ, and make not provision for the flesh, to *fulfil* the lusts *thereof* (Rom. 13:14).

Soon afterward, Augustine resigned his teaching post, began writing, and prepared for baptism the following Easter.[112] His baptism was by immersion,[113] which continued to be the usual form of baptism.[114] After the death of his mother, Augustine went to Rome for a year and then returned to his hometown for three years of monastic study.[115] During a visit to the town of Hippo in 391, Augustine was ordained a presbyter and founded a monastery.[116] In 396 he became the bishop of Hippo, where he was to remain until the end of his life.[117] He died at the age of seventy-five as Hippo was being besieged by the Vandals.

One reason for Augustine's lasting influence is his tremendous literary output. His *Confessions,* written soon after he became a bishop, recount the story of his life until his return to North Africa after his conversion. Indeed, there is more in his *Confessions* on his conversion than there is in any of Calvin's works. His *Retractions,* written near the end of his life, are a systematic review and correction of his works. One of the most enduring of Augustine's works, the *City of God,* was begun on occasion of the sack of Rome by Alaric the Goth (c. 370-410) in 410.[118]

The theological works of Augustine were likewise written in response to what he perceived to be heresy. Three "heresies" in particular were the object of his literary campaigns. The first was the Manichaean heresy. Beginning soon after his conversion, Augustine took up his pen against his former religion.[119] He also publically debated Manichaean leaders.[120] Soon afterward, he turned his attention to the Donatists. While Augustine and the Catholics emphasized the unity of the Church, the Donatists insisted upon the purity of the Church and rebaptized all those who came to them from the Catholics—considering the Catholics corrupt.[121] The third great controversy that occupied Augustine was his dispute with the Pelagians. This is his most significant theological conflict, and one which bears directly on the subject of Calvinism, for as the Calvinists David Steele and Curtis Thomas maintain: "The basic doctrines of the Calvinistic position had been vigorously defended by Augustine against Pelagius during the fifth century."[122] And it is because of the modern comparison of the opposing systems of Augustinianism and Pelagianism to Calvinism and Arminianism that Pelagius and his system demand further study.

Pelagianism and Augustine

Just as a study of Arminius and Arminianism is requisite to a study of Calvinism, so a look at Pelagius and Pelagianism is in order if we are to fully understand Augustinianism. This is necessary because of the continuous stream of rhetoric from the Calvinists about all men being divided into two classes: one teaching what they believe and the other opposed to everything they believe. McFetridge claims that "Augustine and Pelagius stood in much the same attitude to each other as Calvin and Arminius in the sixteenth century. Hence Calvinism is frequently and correctly called Augustinianism; and Arminianism, Semi-Pelagianism. These are the two systems which are now most extensively held, and with the one or the other of them all other Christian theological systems have organic sympathies."[123] Therefore, since these arbitrary distinctions are adduced in support of their cause, the Calvinistic approach will have to be followed. As mentioned in the Introduction, Arminianism is frequently associated with Pelagianism so as to add insult to injury. The label *Pelagian* is dubiously invoked to damn any doctrine felt to threaten the primacy of grace. Boettner indomitably tells us: "The ancestry of Arminianism can be traced back to Pelagianism as definitely as can that of Calvinism be traced back to Augustinianism. Arminianism in its radical and more fully developed forms is essentially a recrudescence of Pelagianism."[124] Charles Hodge asserts that Arminianism was once known as Semi-Pelagianism.[125] Like the modern attacks made on Arminianism, in its day Pelagianism was also associated with every heresy in existence at the time. Jerome lumps Pelagius with the Gnostics and Manichaeans.[126] Although it is true that in their original form, "the two views were developed independently before the authors became acquainted with each other,"[127] Augustine's doctrines of sovereign grace were mainly a reaction to Pelagius.[128] This is even admitted by Calvinists.[129] The problem with Pelagius is that nearly all of the information on him comes from Augustine and the writings of modern-day Calvinists, and as one historian has commented, his name "has become indelibly associated with the heresy which minimizes the need for Grace."[130]

Although it is certain that Pelagius was born in Britain, the date of his birth is generally placed between the years 350-380.[131] It is also indisputable that he moved to Rome and lived there for some time before the controversy with Augustine.[132] He was shocked upon his arrival due to the low morals of the city,[133] and not only do Calvinists acknowledge that he was of blameless character,[134] Augustine himself does likewise.[135] Like Augustine, Pelagius disputed against the Manichaeans and wrote extensively against numerous heresies.[136] It was while he was in Rome in 405 that Pelagius had his first encounter with Augustine. The occasion was a certain bishop quoting to him a passage from Augustine's *Confessions:* "Give what Thou commandest, and command what Thou wilt."[137] Pelagius was incensed because he felt that this made man a mere puppet in the hand of God.[138] After the fall of Rome, Pelagius and Caelestius, one of his converts, made their way to North Africa.[139] They landed at Hippo but Augustine was out of town in Carthage, still disputing with the Donatists.[140] They did however, exchange letters.[141] Pelagius and Caelestius then removed to Carthage, and Pelagius went on to Palestine, while Augustine returned to Hippo disappointed that he had missed him.[142] Thus, unlike Calvin and Arminius, who did not live during the same time period, Augustine and Pelagius never met each other personally, even though they could have.

At Carthage it was Caelestius who promoted the views of Pelagius. After he sought ordination, Caelestius was accused of heresy for his views.[143] The principal charges were that he taught that "Adam's fall injured himself alone, not the human race" and that "children come into the world in the same condition in which Adam was before the fall.[144] Caelestius was excommunicated and withdrew to Ephesus.[145] It was after this that Augustine produced the first of his anti-Pelagian writings: *On the Guilt and the Remission of Sins, and Infant Baptism.* Although the debate between Augustine and Pelagius centered on the questions of free will and original sin, the initial opposition to Pelagius was over the purpose of infant baptism.[146] Pelagius taught that children are born in a neutral condition with the capacity for good or evil.[147] They are like Adam except for the fact that they were not yet conferred with the use of reason.[148] Pelagius taught that when Adam fell it had no effect on his posterity: the only relation of Adam's sin to the human race is that of a bad example.[149] Although Pelagius did not deny the need for infant baptism, he did deny that it was required to wash away original sin since he believed children were born innocent. Baptism, according to Pelagius, is the mark of sanctification.[150] In opposition to Pelagius on baptism, Augustine, the great champion of predestination, held that baptism was necessary for the remission of sins. And if baptism was essential, then the sooner the better, hence the baptism of infants. So it is not just Pelagius who holds unorthodox theological views, for as we shall shortly see, Augustine is just as culpable. Because of his deficient view of the fall of Adam, Pelagius also entertained heretical opinions on the atonement of Christ. The crucifixion of Christ was not an atonement for sin, it merely gave men an example of human perfection to follow.[151] On the subject of free will, Pelagius asserted that man had a free will to not only follow Christ's example, but to live without sin.[152] Pelagianism was condemned at the Council of Milevis in 416 and the Council of Carthage in 418.[153] But just because Pelagianism is unorthodox does not necessarily mean that Augustinianism is to be equated with authentic New Testament Christianity. Therefore, the doctrines of Augustine himself must yet be tried by the word of God.

The Theology of Augustine

The most important thing about Augustine that we are concerned with is his theology. Converting to Christianity and writing volumes of material does not necessarily guarantee that one will always be correct in his doctrine. This is especially true in the case of Augustine since he has been called "the father of orthodox theology."[154] The theology of Augustine, even though he lived hundreds of years ago, is exceptionally relevant to the study of Calvinism because of the emphasis put on Augustine by the Calvinists themselves, for no man who accepted the Bible as his final authority would be concerned with anything Augustine said if it didn't agree with the Scriptures.

Since the Scriptures are the final authority for the Christian, it is especially pertinent to examine Augustine's view of the Bible itself. Augustine's view of the inspiration and authority of the Scripture on the surface appears to be satisfactory until one questions what he included as the Scripture. Regarding the New Testament, Augustine accepted all twenty-seven books as canonical.[155] But when it came to the Old Testament canon, which was already settled long before the time of Christ, he accepted the Apocrypha, which he admitted the Jews rejected,[156] as part of the Old Testament:

> There are other books which seem to follow no regular order, and are connected neither with the order of the preceding books nor with one another, such as Job, and Tobias, and Esther, and Judith, and the two books of Maccabees, and the two of Ezra, which last look more like a sequel to the continuous regular history which terminates with the books of Kings and Chronicles. Next are the Prophets, in which there is one book of the Psalms of David; and three books of Solomon, viz., Proverbs, Song of Songs, and Ecclesiastes. For two books, one called Wisdom and the other Ecclesiasticus, are ascribed to Solomon from a certain resemblance of style, but the most likely opinion is that they were written by Jesus the son of Sirach. Still they are to be reckoned among the prophetical books, since they have attained recognition as being authoritative.[157]

Augustine also quoted the apocryphal books of Baruch,[158] Bel and the Dragon,[159] Susanna,[160] and the Song of the Three Children.[161] He believed the Septuagint was divinely inspired,[162] and wrote to Jerome requesting him to translate the Old Testament from it instead of the Hebrew.[163]

Although he claimed to believe the words of the Bible, Augustine's interpretation of the Bible was based on the allegorical method of Origen (c. 185-254) and the Alexandrian school.[164] This was founded upon a "gross misinterpretation"[165] of a passage in 2 Corinthians: **"Who also hath made us able ministers of the new testament; not of the letter, but of the spirit: for the letter killeth, but the spirit giveth life"** (2 Cor. 3:6), in which Augustine made the *spiritual* the real meaning of the Bible.[166] Thus, the six days of creation may not have been literal.[167] And although he claims to have once adhered to premillennialism,[168] and recognizes its adherents as "Chiliasts,"[169] Augustine was properly an amillennialist, not accepting a literal thousand-year reign of Christ, but, as admitted by Calvinists, teaching that the Millennium was the age between the First and Second Advents.[170] However, he also taught postmillennialism in holding that the present age was a conflict between the city of God and the city of Satan consummating in the Second Advent of Christ.[171] Not only did his allegorizing lead him to mistake the **"first resurrection"** of Revelation 20 as the spiritual resurrection of the believer,[172] he considered the devil to be presently bound: "Now the devil was thus bound not only when the Church began to be more and more widely extended among the nations beyond Judea, but is now and shall be bound till the end of the world, when he is to be loosed."[173] He also equated the Church with the kingdom and had the Church reigning now: "Therefore the Church even now is the kingdom of Christ, and the kingdom of heaven. Accordingly, even now His saints reign with Him."[174] Berkhof also acknowledges that Augustine was one of the first to assert "the authority of tradition and of the Church in the interpretation of the Bible."[175] Another contributing factor to Augustine's fallacious system of interpretation was his latent Neoplatonism. Ignoring the warning against philosophy in Colossians 2:8, Augustine made every attempt to synthesize Christianity and philosophy. It is admitted by Calvinists that "Augustinianism as a philosophy frequently used Platonic terms to set forth Christian concepts."[176] Even Warfield consents that Augustine's Christian philosophy was built "largely out of Platonic materials."[177] Schaff comments that "he could never cease to philosophize, and even his later works, especially De Trinitate [On the Trinity] and De Civitate Dei [City of God], are full of profound speculations."[178] Augustine confessed that he knew no Hebrew[179] and of Greek it has been said: "On the testimony of Augustine's works he had a limited working knowledge of biblical Greek, a very slight working knowledge of patristic Greek and apparently no working knowledge of classical Greek."[180] So although he professed orthodoxy on the inspiration of Scripture, his subsequent acceptance of the Apocrypha as authoritative coupled with his faulty hermeneutics render his profession somewhat tarnished.

On baptism Augustine not only departed from the Bible, he was an innovator when it came to infant baptism. By misinterpreting John 3:5, Titus 3:5, and 1 Peter 3:21 he taught baptismal regeneration.[181] He held to the damnation of infants who were not baptized. This is not only conceded by Calvinists,[182] it is stated by Augustine himself:

> So that infants, unless they pass into the number of believers through the sacrament which was divinely instituted for this purpose, will undoubtedly remain in this darkness.[183]

Let there be then no eternal salvation promised to infants out of our own opinion, without Christ's baptism.[184]

As nothing else is effected when infants are baptized except that they are incorporated into the church, in other words, that they are united with the body and members of Christ, unless this benefit has been bestowed upon them, they are manifestly in danger of damnation.[185]

Infants dying without baptism are consigned to *limbus infantum*.[186] Here, on the outskirts of hell, Augustine believed they received lighter punishment: "In may therefore be correctly affirmed, that such infants as quit the body without being baptized will be involved in the mildest condemnation of all."[187] The only thing that can take the place of baptism is martyrdom.[188]

Since Augustine is regarded by Calvinists as "in a true sense the founder of Roman Catholicism,"[189] it is no surprise that he maintained a number of Roman Catholic heresies besides baptismal regeneration. He taught that Mary was sinless and promoted her worship.[190] He allowed for the intercession of saints[191] and the adoration of relics together with miracles attributed to them.[192] He was the first who defined the so-called sacraments as a visible sign of invisible grace,[193] and adds confirmation, marriage, and ordination to the Lord's Supper and baptism.[194] The memorial of the Lord's Supper became that of the spiritual presence of Christ's body and blood.[195] To Augustine the only true church was the Catholic Church. Writing against the Donatists, he asserted:

The Catholic Church alone is the body of Christ, of which He is the head and Saviour of His body. Outside this body the Holy Spirit giveth life to no one, seeing that, as the apostle says himself, "The love of God is shed abroad in our hearts by the Holy Ghost which is given unto us;" but he is not a partaker of the divine love who is the enemy of unity. Therefore they have not the Holy Ghost who are outside the Church.[196]

He believed in an apostolic succession of bishops from Peter as one of the marks of the true church.[197] The "impenitent Augustinian and Calvinist,"[198] Bruce, even concedes that "it is quite true that much of Augustine's doctrine of the Church leads on to the mediaeval identification of the kingdom of God with the visible ecclesiastical organization (with the corollary of papal supremacy over secular governors, in view of the supremacy of the city of God over the earthly city)."[199] Boettner also admits that Augustine was the one who gave the doctrine of purgatory its first definite form.[200] Augustine dressed in black and lived a celibate, ascetic life of voluntary poverty and communism.[201] He is even acknowledged as "one of the creators of the Western monastic tradition. For it was he more than anyone else who was responsible for that combination of the monastic life with the priesthood which ultimately became one of the distinctive features of Western monasticism."[202] Not only did Augustine believe in celibacy, he also had some rather peculiar ideas about sex. To Augustine, the great sin behind human misery was sexual intercourse.[203] Neglecting the biblical admonitions on marriage (1 Cor. 7:2; Heb. 13:4), he thought sex was always shameful[204] and was sinful if not for the purpose of procreation.[205] Augustine also accepted polygamy over monogamy if it was solely for propagation.[206] Further ignoring Paul's instructions (1 Tim. 4:3), Augustine was also a vegetarian.[207]

The most relevant aspect of Augustine's theology is his Calvinism—his belief in the predestination of the elect and the related doctrines that accompany it. Just like a modern-day Calvinist, Augustine believed in the two-fold predestination of the elect and the reprobate:

> That owing to one man all pass into condemnation who are born of Adam unless they are born again in Christ, even as He has appointed them to be regenerated, before they die in the body, whom He predestinated to everlasting life, as the most merciful bestower of grace; whilst to those whom He has predestinated to eternal death, He is also the most righteous awarder of punishment.[208]

Augustine asserted that the number of the elect is fixed: "I speak thus of those who are predestinated to the kingdom of God, whose number is so certain that one can neither be added to them nor taken from them."[209] He insisted that none of the elect could perish,[210] and also that predestination was synonymous with foreknowledge: "Consequently sometimes the same predestination is signified also under the name of foreknowledge."[211] But in spite of his teaching on the certainty of predestination, Augustine claimed that no one could be sure of his predestination and salvation: "For who of the multitude of believers can presume, so long as he is living in this mortal state, that he is in the number of the predestinated?"[212] Yet, when it came to preaching his doctrine of predestination, Augustine advised some caution. Instead of saying: "And if there are any of you who obey, and are predestinated to be rejected, the power of obedience shall be withdrawn from you, that you may cease to obey," Augustine recommends a switch to the third person so as not to be "excessively harsh" to the congregation: "But if any obey, and are not predestinated to His kingdom and glory, they are only for a season, and shall not continue in that obedience unto the end."[213]

Regarding the free will of man to accept or reject God's gift of eternal life through Jesus Christ, Augustine at first held to free will:

> For the soul cannot receive and possess these gifts, which are here referred to, except by yielding its consent. And thus whatever it possess, and whatever it receives, is from God; and yet the act of receiving and having belongs, of course, to the receiver and possessor.[214]

> God no doubt wishes all men to be saved and to come into the knowledge of the truth; but yet not so as to take away from them free will, for the good or the evil use of which they may be most righteously judged.[215]

He then acknowledges that he changed his view and made faith an irresistible gift of God given to the elect.[216] The will of God became the cause of all things.[217] Consequently, the **"all men"** in First Timothy 2:4 whom God wills to be saved means either "the human race in all its varieties of rank and circumstances" or "that no man is saved unless God wills it."[218]

When it came to the perseverance of the elect, Augustine contradicted himself, as even Berkhof recognized: "But while Augustine is a strict predestinarian, there is also here an element in his teachings that is foreign to his main thought, namely, the idea that the grace of regeneration can again be lost. He holds that only those who are regenerated *and persevere,* or in whom, after loss, the grace of regeneration is restored, are finally saved."[219] Augustine himself gives his conflicting views on perseverance:

> We, then, call men elected, and Christ's disciples, and God's

children, because they are to be so called whom, being regenerated, we see to live piously; but they are then truly what they are called if they shall abide in that on account of which they are so called.[220]

It is, indeed, to be wondered at, and greatly to be wondered at, that to some of His own children—whom He has regenerated in Christ—to whom He has given faith, hope, and love, God does not give perseverance also.[221]

But they who fall and perish have never been in the number of the predestinated.[222]

Berkhof even goes on to distinguish "some elements" in the teachings of Augustine that "were in conflict with the idea of man's absolute dependence on the grace of God, and pointed in the direction of ceremonialism and work-righteousness."[223]

Even if Augustine was completely orthodox on all of the above doctrines and his antagonists were entirely unorthodox, there is nothing in Scripture to warrant the persecution of those whom he disagreed with doctrinally. But this is exactly what Augustine did. Although he first held that "heretics" should be won by "instruction and conviction," he later abandoned this view and advocated force against so-called heretics.[224] None were persecuted by Augustine as were the Donatists. He first attempted to bring them under the laws against heretics enacted by Emperor Theodosius.[225] To this the Donatist bishop Gaudentius said: "The Lord Christ, the Saviour of souls, sent fishermen, not soldiers, for the propagation of his gospel; he who alone can judge the quick and the dead has never sought the aid of a military force."[226] After the Council of Carthage, which was called due to the influence of Augustine,[227] much persecution took place. The historian Edward Gibbon (1737-1794) describes the odious results:

300 bishops, with many thousands of the inferior clergy, were torn from their churches, stripped of their ecclesiastical possessions, banished to the islands, and proscribed by the laws, if they presumed to conceal themselves in any of the provinces of Africa. Their numerous congregations were deprived of the rights of citizens and of the exercise of religious worship. By these severities, which obtained the warmest approbation of Saint Augustine, great numbers of Donatists were reconciled to

the Catholic Church.[228]

After the enactment of more stringent civil laws against them, the Donatists were then threatened with death if they continued to assemble.[229] Augustine's proof text that he used to justify religious persecution was taken from the Lord's parable of the great supper: **"And the lord said unto the servant, Go out into the highways and hedges, and compel *them* to come in, that my house may be filled"** (Luke 14:23). Using the phrase **"compel them to come in,"** Augustine advocated violence against the Donatists.[230] He said on one occasion:

> It is indeed better (as no one ever could deny) that men should be led to worship God by teaching, than that they should be driven to it by fear of punishment or pain; but it does not follow that because the former course produces the better men, therefore those who do not yield to it should be neglected. For many have found advantage (as we have proved, and are daily proving by actual experiment), in being first compelled by fear or pain, so that they might afterwards be influenced by teaching.[231]

The historian J. A. Neander (1789-1850) accurately perceived that Augustine's theory "contains the germ of the whole system of spiritual despotism, intolerance, and persecution, even to the court of the Inquisition."[232]

The fact that Augustine was not only doctrinally incorrect on so many things but also persecuted those whom he disagreed with should be cause for alarm, for if Augustine was wrong on so much why would anyone think he was correct when it came to the doctrine of predestination?

From Augustine to the Reformation

Although Calvinists are quick to jump back from the doctrines of predestination held by Calvin to Augustine, they are short on its adherents between the two of them. Boettner himself says: "From the time of Augustine until the time of the Reformation very little emphasis was placed on the doctrine of Predestination."[233] Custance explains that "gradually Augustinian theology was emasculated by Roman Catholic theologians as a whole, who retained only his emphasis upon the Church of Rome as the sole vehicle of God's dealings with man and the sole channel of salvation."[234] After the death of Augustine, Pelagianism was again condemned at the Council of Ephesus in 431.[235] However, various schemes that attempted to mediate between Pelagianism and Augustinianism continued to be propagated. These have been labeled both Semi-Pelagianism and Semi-Augustinianism.[236] A "moderate Augustinianism" is supposed to have been officially adopted at the Second Council of Orange in 529.[237] But to a few men during the time between Augustine and the Reformation, the word "moderate" can not be applied.

There are several notable adherents to Augustine's doctrine of predestination between the time of Augustine and the Reformation. The most referred to, however, by Calvinists, is Gottschalk, the German monk.[238] Gottschalk (c. 803-869) was placed by his parents in a monastery at an early age, but when he came of age and sought to leave, he was denied and transferred to another.[239] Here Berkhof says that Gottschalk "found rest and peace for his soul only in the Augustinian doctrine of election, and contended earnestly for a double predestination."[240] For this he was summoned before the Synod of Mainz (848) and "boldly professed his belief in a two-fold predestination, to life and to death."[241] Gottschalk was condemned and then summoned before yet another synod. This time he was not only condemned, but deposed from the priesthood, scourged, and imprisoned for life in another monastery.[242]

Another adherent to Calvin and Augustine's doctrine of predestination was Thomas Bradwardine, one time Archbishop of Canterbury. Bradwardine (c. 1290-1349) was acclaimed for his learning in theology, math, and physics as "Doctor Profundus."[243] He was appointed as the chaplain to the King Edward III (1312-1377) of England and accompanied him on his campaigns to the continent.[244] Bradwardine was not only a strong believer in predestination, he believed that God "immutably ordained all that comes about, with His will as the instrument in attaining His decrees."[245] He was heavily influenced by Augustine.[246] Still another predestinarian was Gregory of Rimini, so-named because he was born in Rimini, Italy. Gregory (c. 1300-1358) was called the "torturer of infants" for his views on the fate of unbaptized infants.[247] He too was influenced by Augustine.[248] There is no doubt that despite the reverence of the Roman Catholic Church for Augustine during the Middle Ages, its official position was closer to Pelagianism. Thus, Calvinists attribute a departure from Augustine's views on predestination and free will as a move toward Rome. And as we shall see, the same thing is done with the Reformation.

The Reformation

The Reformation has been acclaimed by Calvinists as the greatest event in history since the time of Christ.[249] Whatever social, economic, and political factors one considers that led up to it, and whatever ancillary results that came from it, the Reformation was primarily a "revival of religion."[250] The central issue of the Reformation, as recognized by Calvinists, was justification. Cunningham observes that justification "was the great fundamental distinguishing doctrine of the Reformation, and was regarded by all the Reformers as of primary and paramount importance."[251] Sproul maintains that "the Reformation focused on the question, *How* is a person justified?"[252] After correctly stating that "the justified person must possess righteousness," Sproul asks the question that he calls "the heart of the Reformation controversy," namely, "How does the sinner acquire the necessary righteousness?"[253] The Calvinists are correct about the main tenant of the Reformation but where they go wrong is in connecting it with Augustine.

Understanding the crux of the Reformation is very important because of what the Calvinists have thus far said about Augustine. It is to be remembered that Warfield considers Augustine as both "the founder of Roman Catholicism,"[254] and the one "who gave us the Reformation."[255] This paradox he explains as "the ultimate triumph of Augustine's doctrine of grace over Augustine's doctrine of the Church."[256] Thus, Warfield equates Augustine's "doctrine of grace" with the celebrated Pauline principle of the Reformation: justification by faith. But was the Reformation really a "revival of Augustinianism"?[257] The answer is to be found in an Augustinian monk who once reflected: "I hoped I might find peace of conscience with fasts, prayer, vigils, with which I miserably afflicted my body; but the more I sweated it out like this, the less peace and tranquility I knew."[258]

The catalyst of the Reformation is universally acknowledged by all as the day that Martin Luther nailed his ninety-five theses against indulgences on the Wittenberg church door in October of 1517. Luther is significant because of the relentless insistence by Calvinists that Luther was an Augustinian monk,[259] as if that was the reason Luther came to see the truth of justification by faith. For as McFetridge admonishes us: "Be it remembered that Luther was an Augustinian or Calvinistic monk, and that it was from this rigorous theology that he learned the great truth, the pivot of the Reformation and the kindling flame of civilization—salvation, not by works, but *by faith alone.*"[260] But as an Augustinian monk, it is apparent from Luther himself that salvation by faith was the last thing on his mind:

> I was a good monk, and I kept the rule of my order so strictly that I may say that if ever a monk got to heaven by his monkery it was I. All my brothers in the monastery who knew me will bear me out. If I had kept on any longer, I should have killed myself with vigils, prayers, reading, and other work.[261]

Yet the question still remains: Was the Reformation doctrine of justification by faith a *recovery* of Augustine or a *repudiation* of him? We must go back to Luther to find out.

After being ordained as a Roman Catholic priest, Luther received his doctorate in 1512.[262] His first Bible lectures were on the Psalms (1513-1515), followed by Romans (1515-1516) and Galatians (1516-1517).[263] It was during his study of the book of Romans that he began to see the truth of justification by faith. Luther recounts:

> Then I began to comprehend the "righteousness of God" through which the righteous are saved by God's grace, namely, through faith; that the "righteousness of God" which is revealed through the Gospel was to be understood in a passive sense in which God through mercy justifies man by faith, as it is written, "The just shall live by faith." Now I felt exactly as though I had been born again, and I believed that I had entered Paradise through widely opened doors.[264]

In Luther's new view of justification the sinner is declared righteous because of the imputation of Christ's righteousness. Justification is by faith alone *(sola fide)* and by grace alone *(sola gratia)*.

The Reformation view of justification was in direct contrast to the Roman Catholic view of justification prevalent at that time. And as Sproul correctly says: "To grasp the full significance of the issue of justification, we must turn our attention to the meaning of the Reformation doctrine of justification by faith alone."[265] The Reformers conceived of justification as a *judicial act* and not a *gradual process*. Thus, justification was seen in the biblical sense as the opposite of condemnation:

> **If there be a controversy between men, and they come unto judgment, that *the judges* may judge them; then they shall justify the righteous, and condemn the wicked (Deu. 25:1).**

> **He that justifieth the wicked, and he that condemneth the just, even they both *are* abomination to the LORD (Pro. 17:15).**

Instead of becoming justified by God's grace and human merit, and instead of becoming justified through faith and works, the Reformers grounded justification in the free gift of Christ's righteousness imputed to the sinner by grace alone and through faith alone:

> **But to him that worketh not, but believeth on him that justifieth the ungodly, his faith is counted for righteousness. Even as David also describeth the blessedness of the man, unto whom God imputeth righteousness without works (Rom. 4:5-6).**

The Reformation view of justification was repudiated by the Roman Catholic Church at the Council of Trent (1545-1563). The longest decree fashioned at the Council of Trent was that on the doctrine of justification. After sixteen chapters establishing the Catholic doctrine, there were attached thirty-three canons against the Protestant view, all of which end in "let him be anathema." Canon nine is representative:

> If anyone saith that by faith alone the impious is justified; in such wise as to mean that nothing else is required to cooperate in order to the obtaining the grace of justification, and that it is

no in any way necessary that he be prepared and disposed by the movement of his own will; let him be anathema.[266]

These canons of the Council of Trent have never been repudiated by the Roman Catholic Church.

The Reformation view of justification not only constituted a drastic break with Rome, but Augustine as well, for Augustine did *not* hold the same view of justification as the Reformers. This is acknowledged by the Reformed Calvinists themselves. Cunningham concedes that "it is true that even Augustine, notwithstanding all his profound knowledge of divine truth, and the invaluable services which he was made the instrument of rendering to the cause of sound doctrine and of pure Christian theology, does not seem to have ever attained to distinct apprehensions of the forensic meaning of justification."[267] He even calls Augustine's views about justification "defective and erroneous."[268] Schaff asserts that "the Pauline doctrine of justification as set forth in the Epistles to the Romans and Galatians, had never before been clearly and fully understood, not even by Augustin."[269] The Reformed theologian Berkhof admits that Augustine "does not conceive of justification in a purely forensic sense. While it includes the forgiveness of sins, this is not its main element. In justification God not merely *declares* but *makes* the sinner righteous by transforming his inner nature. He fails to distinguish clearly between justification and sanctification and really subsumes the latter under the former."[270] According to Berkhof: "The doctrine of justification by faith, so vital to a true conception of the way of salvation, is represented in a way that can hardly be reconciled with the doctrine of free grace."[271] And not only was Augustine wrong on justification, Schaff reveals that the antagonist of Augustine, who supposedly represents the antithesis of salvation by grace, was right on the matter: "Pelagius understands in the Protestant sense of *declaring* righteousness, and not (like Augustine) in the Catholic sense of *making* righteous."[272]

But it is not only the Reformed Calvinists who see a distinction between Augustine's doctrine of justification and their own, the Calvinistic Baptists and even Luther himself do likewise. The Baptist historian Timothy George, who believes that "Reformed and Baptist are not mutually exclusive terms,"[273] maintains that Luther redefined justification "in a non-Augustinian framework."[274] According to George, Augustine's "whole theology of justification" was influenced by Greek philosophy.[275] He then further contrasts the views of Luther and Augustine: "Luther believed that he had recovered the original meaning of the Greek verb used by Paul in Romans. Augustine and the scholastic tradition had interpreted it as 'to make righteous,' whereas Luther insisted on its legal connotation, 'to declare righteous.'"[276] That Augustine's doctrine of justification was defective there is not doubt, for as George points out: "For Augustine, too, the infusion of grace through the sacramental-penitential system of the church continued the process of justification begun in baptism."[277] But the strongest evidence that Luther, the Augustinian monk, *rejected* Augustine rather than *received* him is from his own mouth: "Augustine got nearer to the meaning of Paul than all the Schoolmen, but he did not reach Paul. In the beginning I devoured Augustine, but when the door into Paul swung open and I knew what justification by faith really was, then it was out with him."[278] So by the words of the Calvinists themselves, to say that it was Augustine "who gave us the Reformation"[279] is an impossibility if one looks to him for sound doctrine on justification.

The Reformers

To bolster their claims for the truth of Calvinism, Calvinists frequently appeal to the supposed Calvinistic doctrine of the other leading Reformers. Sometimes it is just general statements like Calvinism is "the theology of the Reformation,"[280] or Calvinism was "adopted by all the Reformers."[281] But on other occasions it is more specific: "Luther, Calvin, Zwingli and all the other outstanding reformers of that period were thorough-going predestinarians."[282] We have already evaluated the doctrine of Augustine and have seen that although he did teach the doctrines of what is now called Calvinism, that is the only thing he has in common with modern-day Calvinists, for they would repudiate almost everything else he taught. But what of the other Reformers? Did they teach the predestination usually associated with John Calvin? As we shall presently see, when a Calvinist invokes the name of a Reformer as an ally of Calvin on predestination he is usually correct. But this raises questions concerning the extent of, the emphasis of, the relevance of, and the reasons for the "Calvinism" of the other

Reformers.

Since Sproul claims that "virtually nothing in John Calvin's view of predestination, however, was not first in Martin Luther, and before Luther in Augustine,"[283] we shall examine Luther first. There is no disputing that Luther held what would be considered Calvinistic doctrines, regardless of the opinions of his Lutheran descendants.[284] What is disputed, however, is how much of a "Calvinist" he was. Luther, like many of the Reformers, held to the double predestination of the elect and reprobate.[285] But as Cunningham comments on Luther's Calvinistic doctrines, he "was never led to explain and apply, to illustrate and defend some of them, so fully as Calvin did."[286] Yet, Sproul still maintains that Luther wrote more about predestination than did Calvin,[287] while Augustus Toplady (1740-1778) insisted that Luther "went as heartily into that doctrine as Calvin himself. He even asserted it with much more warmth, and proceeded to much harsher lengths in defending it than Calvin ever did, or any other writer I have met with of that age."[288] But anyone who reads the works of Luther and compares them with the works of Calvin would see immediately that such is not the case. Luther's "Calvinism" must be extracted from his vastly eclectic writings, for he never wrote a systematic defense or exposition of predestination like Calvin did. The fact that Luther embraced the doctrine of predestination, however, is apparent in his book *De Servo Arbitrio* (The Bondage of the Will), penned in 1525 against a 1524 work of Desiderius Erasmus (1467-1536) entitled *Diatribe Seu Collatio De Libero Arbitrio* (Discussion or Collation Concerning Free-Will).[289] In *The Bondage of the Will,* which he counted as his best book, [290] Luther appeals to Augustine as he ardently denies that man has a free will.[291]

Although it is Luther whom is appealed to first, the other Reformers are likewise invoked as comrades in the search for Calvinistic Reformers. Huldreich Zwingli (1484-1531), the German Reformer in Zurich, Switzerland, likewise held to predestination.[292] Often referred to as the "third man" of the Reformation,[293] Zwingli claimed: "I did not learn my doctrine from Luther, but from God's Word itself."[294] Indeed, Zwingli is noted for his dispute with Luther over the significance of the Lord's Supper.[295] George argues that Zwingli's "doctrines of providence and predestination were, if anything, even more clearly delineated" than those of Luther.[296] Heinrich Bullinger (1504-1575), the successor to Zwingli in Zurich and author of the Second Helvetic Confession (1566), is often summoned as a witness for predestination,[297] although it is admitted that he was more moderate on the subject than both Luther and Zwingli.[298] Martin Bucer (1491-1551), the leading German Reformer at Strasbourg, is another Reformer cited as teaching predestination.[299] Bucer had a tremendous influence on Calvin, and Calvin testified of Bucer that "nobody within my memory has been gifted with more exacting diligence in the interpretation of the Scriptures."[300] But as one of Bucer's biographers stated: "Perhaps Calvin also chose many of his theological beliefs from Bucer's collection, as some worthy historians have claimed. Unfortunately they have not been able to find sufficient external evidence on the subject to lift it out of the realms of controversy."[301] Theodore Beza (1519-1605), Calvin's successor at Geneva and the editor of the Greek New Testament, is often said, even by Calvinists, to be more "Calvinistic" than Calvin.[302] Philip Melanchthon (1497-1560), an intimate associate of Luther and author of the Augsburg Confession (1530), is one Reformer that Calvinists shy away from. Although he at first held to a strict doctrine of predestination, Melanchthon moderated his views considerably.[303] He carried on a correspondence with Calvin but was not persuaded of his views on predestination.[304] Cunningham laments Melanchthon's "influence he seems to have exerted in leading the Lutheran churches to abandon the Calvinism of their master, and even contributing eventually to the spread of Arminianism among the Reformed churches."[305]

The Calvinistic views of the Reformers on predestination and free will were a direct reaction to the false views of salvation propagated by the Roman Catholic Church at the time. Just as Augustine's doctrine of predestination was a reaction to Pelagius, so the predestination of the Reformers was a reaction to Rome. No one can deny that the greatest antithesis to salvation by works is salvation by an absolute, irresistible decree of predestination. This explains why the Reformers might be inclined to embrace "Calvinism." But the cardinal issue of the Reformation was salvation by grace through faith alone versus salvation by faith plus merit or works or the Church. Whether or not salvation was by an eternal decree of predestination that resulted in an irresistible gift of faith to the elect was not the original concern. It is because Calvinists frequently confuse the issue that many who disdain the teaching of salvation by works are led to accept the doctrines of Calvinism because they see no other alternative. One thing is for certain, whatever "Calvinism" that Augustine and the Reformers had: "It was Calvin who wrought out this system of theological thought with such logical clearness and emphasis that it has ever since borne his name."[306] And it is to John Calvin that we now turn.

Chapter 3
JOHN CALVIN

As we have seen in the previous chapter, John Calvin was not the originator of that theological system known as Calvinism. We are told that he merely "uncovered truths that had been in the Bible all the time,"[1] or that "Augustine had taught the essentials of the system a thousand years before Calvin was born."[2] But although John Calvin was not the originator of that theological system known as Calvinism, he obviously had such a strong connection with it that his name is inseparably linked to it. As Custance says: "Mention of the words Election or Predestination today, in any but a theological environment, almost inevitably brings to people's minds the name of Calvin."[3] George rightly says of Calvin: "Most Christians, including most Protestants, know only two things about him: He believed in predestination, and he sent Servetus to the stake."[4] But it is not just a question of *knowing* these two things about him, for as Otto Scott remarks: "No Christian leader has ever been so often condemned by so many. And the usual grounds for condemnation are the execution of Servetus and the doctrine of predestination."[5] Nevertheless, the prodigious impact of Calvin upon Christianity has yet to be fathomed. Besides the additions to the English language of the noun *Calviniana,* the adjectives *Calvinistic* and *Calvinian,* and the epithets *Calvinist* and *Calvinism,* we are blessed with such institutions and organizations as Calvin College, Calvin Seminary, the *Calvin Theological Journal,* the International Congress on Calvin Research, the Calvin Translation Society, the Calvin Foundation, and the H. Henry Meeter Center for Calvin Studies, which contains over 3,000 books and 12,000 articles concerning John Calvin.[6] The majority of Calvin's writings are still available today, which is quite an exploit considering that he lived over 400 years ago. There are extant over 2000 of Calvin's sermons,[7] while Calvin's complete works occupy fifty-nine volumes in the *Corpus Reformatorum.*[8] College and seminary students at both Presbyterian and Reformed schools have the option of taking a whole course on John Calvin.[9] Moreover, Calvin has the eminence of being mentioned in every dictionary, encyclopedia, and history book: both secular and sacred. However, he also has the ominous distinction of being denominated, on the one hand, commendable, and on the other hand, contemptible. As one of Calvin's biographers has so aptly recounted: "No man in the history of the Church has been more admired and ridiculed, loved and hated, blessed and cursed."[10]

Those who admire Calvin commendably have expressed themselves on various aspects of his life:

> John Calvin stands out in the history of the church as one who was more vividly aware than almost any other of the mighty working of God in human history and of God's call to his people for service in the world.[11]

> No servant of Christ, probably since the days of the apostles and of the Gospel witnesses of their century, has been more grossly misrepresented or more maliciously maligned than the faithful, fearless and beloved Calvin.[12]

> Calvin's labors were so highly useful to the Church of Christ, that there is hardly any department of the Christian world to be found that is not full of them.[13]

> He was the most Christian man of his generation.[14]

> Calvin made such a mark upon his age and, even beyond it, exercised an influence which does not yet seem likely to decline.[15]

Theodore Beza, the successor to Calvin at Geneva, and one who knew him intimately, testified: "I have been a witness of Calvin's life for sixteen years, and I think I am fully entitled to say that in this man there was exhibited to all a most beautiful example of the life and death of the Christian."[16]

Like Augustine, Calvin has been equated by many Calvinists with the Apostle Paul:

> Calvin brought to light forgotten doctrines of the Apostle Paul.[17]

> Calvin easily ranks as one of the outstanding systematic expounders of the Christian system since Saint Paul.[18]

> Next to Paul, John Calvin has done most for the world.[19]

Calvin himself compared attacks on his person to those made against the Apostle Paul.[20] The most ineffable distinction, however, to be heaped upon Calvin is that he was "virtually the founder of America."[21]

But just as there are two sides to every story; indeed, just as light follows darkness, so there is another side to the reputation of John Calvin. Those who abhor Calvin contemptibly have likewise expressed themselves on Calvin's life:

> If Calvin ever wrote anything in favor of religious liberty, it was a typographical error.[22]

> Calvin has, I believe, caused untold millions of souls to be damned.[23]

> It was the fact that Calvin's own character was compulsive-neurotic which transformed the God of Love as experienced and taught by Jesus, into a compulsive character, bearing absolutely diabolical traits in his reprobatory practice.[24]

> And with respect to Calvin, it is manifest, that the leading, and to me at least, the most hateful feature in all the multiform character of popery adhered to him through life—I mean the *spirit of persecution.*[25]

> We shall always find it hard to love the man who darkened the human soul with the most absurd and blasphemous conception of God in all the long and honored history of nonsense.[26]

Perhaps the most infamous lasting characterization of Calvin was uttered by Voltaire (1694-1778): "The famous Calvin, whom we regard as the Apostle of Geneva, raised himself up to the rank of Pope of the Protestants."[27] This title was first used against Calvin by Servetus,[28] and has been confirmed as just by Calvinists.[29]

Since Schaff maintains of Calvin that "the better he is known, the more he is admired and esteemed,"[30] a look at the life of Calvin is in order before his theology is examined. But as Calvin is often labeled by Calvinists as a man of his age, especially when seeking to justify him in the Servetus affair, the time in which he lived is likewise relevant. The lack of a historical consciousness in studies of Calvin has of late been bemoaned by some of his modern biographers. William Bouwsma laments that Calvin's thought has been treated "ahistorically,"[31] while David Steinmetz mourns the attempt to reconstruct Calvin's theology "with little or no reference to his contemporaries."[32] Therefore, and rightly so, any attempt to understand Calvin's theology must take into account not only Calvin the man, but the age in which he lived as well.

The Age of Calvin

Calvin lived, like Augustine, during a very unique period of church history. The Reformation, which officially began with Martin Luther in Germany, was beginning to infect the rest of Europe. This is especially true because of the unity between Church and State that was still in existence at this time. In Calvin's native France, the German Reformer's writings were declared heretical in 1521.[33] During the reigns of Francis I (1515-47) and his son Henry II (1547-49), those charged with "Lutheranism" were severely persecuted, some to the point of death.[34] The first Protestant churches were not officially organized until 1555,[35] and it was not until the Edict of Nantes in 1598 that toleration was extended.[36] And as we shall presently see, Calvin would himself have to leave his native land to avoid persecution.

The Roman Catholic authorities in Germany did not take too highly to the spread of Lutheranism in Luther's native land. After the Diet of Worms in 1521, an edict was signed by the Holy Roman Emperor, Charles V (1500-1558), that not only denounced Luther and his followers, but authorized the burning of Lutheran books as well.[37] But because the German empire was at this time a loose confederation of seven electorates, small principalities, and free cities, it was difficult to enforce the Edict of Worms, for the question of religion was in a great measure dependent upon the civil authorities in each area.[38] This difficulty, coupled with a tremendous increase in the publication of literature, including Luther's German New Testament in 1522, led to the division of Germany into two separate camps—Catholic and Protestant.

The conflict in Germany was temporarily abated at the Diet of

Speyer in 1526. There the Protestant princes were able to obtain a temporary forbearance of the Edict of Worms. The Committee of Princes appointed by the Diet proposed that a general council should be convened to settle the religion question, but until such time, "every State shall so live, rule, and believe as it may hope and trust to answer before God and his imperial Majesty."[39] The Protestants interpreted this decision as giving them the legal right to practice their religion unmolested. Lutheranism flourished, and almost all of North Germany became Protestant within three years.[40] It is to be remembered, however, that the Church-State idea was still ingrained upon the minds of the people. Religious toleration is not religious liberty. The civil authorities decided the religion of their territories, and Protestants were at times just as intolerant as Catholics.[41]

At the Second Diet of Speyer, convened in 1529, the religious toleration that emanated from the Diet of 1526 was rescinded. The Lutherans in turn put forth an official protest on April 25, and it is from this document that the name *Protestant* was applied, first to Lutherans, and then to all who opposed the Catholic Church.[42] In 1530 another Diet assembled at Augsburg[43] to plan for war against the Turks. But fearing that a divided empire could not successfully repel them, it was proposed to first settle the religious differences that divided Germany. The Lutherans, on June 25, presented a "statement of their grievances and opinions relating to the faith."[44] Written by Melanchthon, the Augsburg Confession, as the statement came to be called, is still accepted by Lutherans today. After the Augsburg Diet, in which the emperor gave the Protestants until April 15, 1531, to submit, the Protestants formed the Schmalkald League (at Schmalkalden) to defend themselves.[45] War was averted, however, at the Diet of Nuremberg in 1532, when the Protestants were granted a "recess."[46] But after the death of Luther in 1547, the emperor invaded Germany with his Spanish Catholic troops with disastrous consequences for the Protestants. The emperor then issued what is known as the Augsburg Interim, an ambiguous document designed to placate the Protestants, but one that the people could not be coerced to accept.[47] Religious peace was not finally concluded until the Peace of Augsburg in 1555.

Although Huldreich Zwingli is known as the first Swiss Reformer, the Reformation in Switzerland was not directly dependent on him like the German Reformation was on Luther.

This is evident by the names the respective believers in Germany and Switzerland were called. The Lutherans, obviously, were so called after Luther, but the Christians in Switzerland, since they were more "reformed" than the Lutherans, came to be referred to as *Reformed*.[48] And though both branches of the Reformation were agreed in their stand against the doctrines and tyranny of Rome, it was the Swiss attempt to reform the worship and morals of the Church that grew out of the humanism of the Renaissance.[49] Yet, before the Reformation of the sixteenth century, Switzerland played little role in the history of Europe compared to what was to transpire after Zwingli began his ministry in Zurich in 1519.

At the time of the Reformation, Switzerland was a confederation of thirteen cantons and a number of free cities like Geneva. The Swiss had successfully maintained their independency since the uniting of the original three German-speaking cantons in 1291. Like the rest of Europe, however, Switzerland was subject to the Pope, and only Roman Catholicism was tolerated. And like the rest of Europe, the clergy were corrupt, with immorality rampant among the priests.[50] But signs of reform were evident in the German-speaking cantons, most notably in the city of Basel, where the university became a center of learning and the printing press the means for its dissemination.[51] The Reformation, however, was not inaugurated in Basel, it was to proceed from Zurich, the home of Huldreich Zwingli.

Zwingli was born in Wildhaus, high in the Swiss Alps, on January 1, 1484. Like most children at that time, he was a member of a large Catholic family. After excelling in his early Latin studies, young Zwingli entered the University of Vienna in 1498. In 1502 he enrolled in the University of Basel, earning two degrees while teaching Latin at another school.[52] He was ordained a priest in 1506 and assumed his first charge at Glarus, southeast of Zurich.[53] Zwingli remained in Glarus for ten years, during which time he also served as a chaplain with a contingent of Swiss mercenaries.[54] He was by this time an accomplished musician, a classical scholar, a Swiss patriot, and a Roman priest.[55] He then undertook to learn Greek that he might study the New Testament.[56] He also corresponded with Erasmus and later visited him in Basel.[57]

In 1516 Zwingli removed from Glarus to nearby Einsiedeln. Here he read extensively the works of Erasmus and began to preach against the abuses of the Catholic Church.[58] He later wrote of this period:

> I began to preach the gospel before anyone in my locality had so much as heard the name of Luther: for I never left the pulpit without taking the words of the gospel as used in the mass service of the day and expounding them by means of the Scriptures; although at first I relied much upon the Fathers as expositors and explainers.[59]

After two years in Einsiedeln, news of Zwingli's abilities spread and he was called to Zurich. Here he shocked his parishioners by preaching straight through the books of the New Testament.[60] And although not officially breaking with Rome, Zwingli preached against indulgences and Lenten fasts.[61] On October 10, 1522, he resigned as a priest and became a preacher employed by the city.[62] A series of public disputations were then held in which Zwingli insisted on the primacy of Scripture and attacked the Mass as "a blasphemous undertaking."[63] The Mass was soon abolished and the Lord's Supper was celebrated in its place.

It is Zwingli's interpretation of the Lord's Supper that sets him apart from Luther. Zwingli held, and rightly so, that the Lord's Supper was a memorial, and that the elements merely represented the body and blood of Christ. Luther, on the other hand, held to the presence of Christ in the elements, although he rejected the Catholic doctrine of transubstantiation. The controversy between Luther and Zwingli culminated in the Marburg Colloquy in 1529. Here the two Reformers met for the first and only time. And although they agreed on fourteen out of fifteen articles that were drawn up, they did not reach a consensus on the Communion issue.[64]

The Reformation in Switzerland spread rapidly throughout the other cantons, most notably in Basel under John Oecolampadius (1482-1531).[65] By 1530 it was firmly established in the leading cities of Switzerland.[66] Meanwhile, war broke out between the Protestant and Catholic cantons. Then, after a brief period of peace, they commenced fighting again. This time, however, Zwingli was tragically killed in battle on October 11, 1531. His successor in Zurich was Heinrich Bullinger, who preached there until his death in 1575. Bullinger was an able replacement, not only maintaining a correspondence with Calvin, Melanchthon, Bucer, and Beza, but having a part in the First Helvetic Confession (1536) and authoring the Second Helvetic Confession (1566).[67]

Although the reform movements in Germany and the German cantons of Switzerland differed as to their cause, leaders, and practices, there is one thing that they both agreed on: those who dissented from them were not to be tolerated. This included not only the Catholics, but that noble group of "heretics" who thought the Reformers did not go far enough. Zwingli called them *Wiedertäufer* (Anabaptists). In Zwingli's Zurich they were ordered to have their infants baptized.[68] Rebaptism was made a crime punishable by death.[69] On January 5, 1527, Felix Manz was bound and thrown in the river by the Zurich authorities because he "had become involved in Anabaptism."[70] Executions and banishments followed in other Swiss cantons as well.[71] In Germany they fared no different. They were persecuted by both Catholics and Protestants. The aforementioned Second Diet of Speyer in 1529 decreed that "all Anabaptists, male or female, of mature age, shall be put to death, by fire, or sword, or otherwise, according to the person, without preceding trial."[72] The problem Luther had with Baptists was not that they immersed (Luther himself at one time acknowledged immersion as scriptural and even immersed his own son[73]), but that they rebaptized. The Lutherans and the Reformed likewise practiced intolerance toward each other. It was an age of change and controversy, and Calvin was to be right in the middle of both.

The Life of Calvin

Although secular historians have downplayed the significance of Calvin to the sixteenth century, there is no doubt that Calvin remains "a seminal figure in European history."[74] But as a recent biographer of his laments, even scholarly treatments of Calvin "remain quasi-hagiographical."[75] This is to be expected from zealous Calvinists, just as the opposite is to be predicted from his detractors. Therefore, to avoid the charge of bigotry, everything said hereafter that could be construed as damaging to Calvin follows in the main only those writers in sympathy with him.

John Calvin was a Frenchman, born Jean Cauvin, on July 10, 1509, in Picardy at Noyon, France: sixty miles northeast of Paris. It is from his Latinized name, Joannes Calvinus, that we derive his name in English. Luther was already twenty-five when Calvin was born, but Calvin hardly outlived the other Reformers, dying on May

27, 1564, at only fifty-four years of age. His father was Gerald Calvin, a notary, who worked for the local Roman Catholic bishop managing the business affairs of the cathedral.[76] John was one of five sons, two dying in infancy. Calvin's mother died when he was about three and his father remarried a widow and subsequently fathered two daughters. It is interesting to note that Calvin likewise married a widow and had his only son die in infancy. The family was Roman Catholic. Due to a financial embarrassment, his father was excommunicated and died in 1531, the year in which his older brother Charles was also excommunicated as a priest for heresy.[77] His younger brother, Antoine, and one sister, Marie, left Romanism with him, but one sister remained a Papist.[78]

At the age of twelve, Calvin received part of the revenue of a chaplaincy in the Cathedral of Noyon:

> 19 May 1521. M. Jaques Regnard, secretary to the Reverend Father in God, Monseigneur Charles de Hangest, Bishop of Noyon, reported to the chapter that the Vicars General of the said Monseigneur had given to Jean Cauvin, son of Gerald, aged twelve years, a portion of the Chapel of La Gesine, vacant by the absolute resignation of Master Michel Courtin.[79]

This was a common custom at the time: appointing a boy to a church office, thereby putting him on the payroll, while a priest did the work.[80] The income from this benefice was used to fund Calvin's education.[81]

About this time, Calvin was sent to Paris, where he studied Latin, as all higher education at this time was in Latin.[82] Beza relates that in the preliminary grammar course, Calvin "left behind his fellow-students."[83] Calvin was quiet and never shared in the amusements of his peers, reprimanding their disorders.[84] He then enrolled in the University of Paris at the College de Montague, where Ignatius Loyola (1491-1556) was to study a few years later.[85] After completing his masters degree, Calvin transferred to the University of Orleans to study law.[86] This was due to his father, who realized that his son could make more money in law than in the priesthood. Calvin wrote: "My father had intended me for theology from my childhood. But when he reflected that the career of the law proved everywhere very lucrative for its practitioners, the prospect suddenly made him change his mind."[87] At Orleans, Calvin was considered a teacher rather than a pupil, conducting classes when the professor was absent.[88] His next quest for higher education led him to the University of Bourges to study under the famed jurist, Andrea Alciati (1492-1550).[89] It was also here that he began his study of Greek under the famed German scholar Melchior Wolmar (1496-1561).[90] Upon the death of his father, Calvin returned to Paris to study literature and the Greek and Roman classics.[91] He also further pursued his study of Greek and took up Hebrew as well.[92] It was also here that Calvin came under the influence of humanism and wrote his first book, a commentary on Seneca's *De Clementia,* but it was never a popular seller.[93] It was "the first production of a man famous for other things."[94]

It is to be remembered that the whole of Calvin's education and early life was spent as a Roman Catholic. Not much is known about the circumstances of Calvin's conversion since, in spite of his voluminous writings, he made only one reference to it.[95] A number of factors have been adduced as helping to bring about Calvin's conversion. His Latin teacher, Mathurin Cordier (1478-1564), is supposed to have spoken to Calvin about his misgivings about the Catholic Church.[96] His first Greek teacher, Wolmar, is also credited as an influence.[97] Calvin is said to have witnessed the burning of a Protestant martyr.[98] Pierre Robert (c. 1506-1538), known in history as Olivetan, was a cousin of Calvin who translated the Bible into French. A significant role in Calvin's conversion has been attributed to him.[99] Various friends of Calvin who, although Catholics, leaned toward the Reformation, have also been suggested.[100] A Lutheran merchant whom Calvin stayed with has also been named.[101] Beside the Scriptures,[102] and some writings of Luther,[103] Calvin had read some of the Church Fathers, Erasmus, and Augustine's *City of God.*[104] Yet Calvin himself never mentions any of these, except for Luther, whom he read when he "was beginning to emerge from the darkness of the papacy."[105] This fact is substantiated by Calvinists.[106]

As to the time and place of his conversion, Calvin has tossed to historians, in the words of Karl Barth (1886-1968), "a bone of fierce contention."[107] Various dates have been postulated from 1527 to 1534[108] for what Calvin called his "sudden conversion."[109] The only reference Calvin directly made to his conversion is found in the preface to his commentary on the Psalms, which was written in 1557:

And, in the first place, because I was so obstinately addicted to the superstitions of the papacy that it was very hard to draw me from that deep slough, by a sudden conversion He subdued and reduced my heart to docility, which, for my age, was over-much hardened in such matters. Having consequently received some taste and knowledge of true piety, I was forthwith inflamed with so great a desire to reap benefit from it that, although I did not at all abandon other studies, I yet devoted myself to them more indifferently. Now I was greatly astonished that, before a year passed, all those who had some desire for pure doctrine betook themselves to me in order to learn, although I myself had done little more than begin.[110]

Although he may have been converted as early as while he was studying law,[111] Calvin did not officially break from the Roman Church until he traveled to Noyon and gave up his benefice in the cathedral on May 4, 1534.[112] Calvin does quote the Bible in his commentary on Seneca, but only three times and in an incidental manner.[113] And as late as June of 1533, Calvin assisted a girl in gaining entrance to a nunnery.[114]

After finishing his law studies, Calvin traveled to Orleans and then back to Paris.[115] While in Paris, his intimate friend Nicholas Cop (c. 1501-1540) was named rector of the university and gave his inaugural address on November 1, 1533.[116] To the surprise of the authorities, Cop preached a mildly evangelistic address filled with the ideas of Erasmus and Luther.[117] Many Calvinists credit Calvin with the writing of Cop's discourse.[118] Nevertheless, both men were charged with heresy.[119] Cop fled to the Protestant city of Basel, while Calvin traveled about Europe as in exile, often using assumed names.[120] Between the time he left Paris and finally joined his friend Nicholas Cop in Basel there is great uncertainty as to exactly where Calvin was and what he did.[121] He supposedly journeyed back to Paris to meet with the Spanish physician Michael Servetus (whom he would later have burned at the stake), but for some reason the meeting never took place.[122] We do know that from Orleans in 1534 Calvin wrote his first theological work, *Psychopannychia,* in which he refuted the heresy that the soul merely sleeps between death and the resurrection, but that it was not published until 1542.[123] This heresy was supposedly held by some Anabaptists, although Barth acknowledges that "it is not certain whether Anabaptists advocated it."[124]

In October of 1534, some radical Protestants posted placards throughout Paris denouncing the Catholic Mass as blasphemous.[125] As a result of this, the Protestants suffered intense persecution and many were burned alive.[126] Calvin soon fled to Basel, by way of Strasbourg, where he was aided by the reformer Martin Bucer.[127] He arrived in Basel in early 1535 and was not only reunited with his friend Nicholas Cop, but became acquainted with the reformer Heinreich Bullinger as well.[128] While Calvin was in Basel two literary works were published which were to profoundly influence the Reformation. Olivetan published his French translation of the Bible in 1535 with two prefaces by Calvin, one in Latin and one in French, and Calvin completed and published the first edition of his *Institutes* in 1536.[129] Calvin then traveled to Italy and France before heading on to Strasbourg by way of Geneva.[130] And although he did not intend to stay in Geneva, from that day forward: "To speak of Calvin is to speak of Geneva."[131]

Calvin arrived in Geneva in July of 1536 with his brother Antoine and sister Marie. He intended to stay the night before going on to Strasbourg when the Genevan reformer Guillaume Farel (1489-1565), who had been in the city for two years already, heard that Calvin was in Geneva and pressed him to stay and help with the Reformation then in progress in the city against the Church of Rome.[132] Calvin relates that Farel "proceeded to warn me that God would curse my retirement and tranquility which I sought for my studies if I withdrew and refused to help when it was so urgently needed."[133]

After beginning as a "Reader in Holy Scripture," in which he lectured on the Pauline Epistles, Calvin soon assumed the office of pastor.[134] A catechism and a confession of faith were then presented to the city council along with a document entitled *Articles Concerning the Organization of the Church and of Worship at Geneva*.[135] After these were adopted by the Council, numerous laws were passed against vice and for the regulation of church worship and discipline.[136] Assent to the confession of faith was made mandatory for all citizens of Geneva and banishment was decreed for those who would not acquiesce.[137] Thus, as Schaff relates: "It was a glaring inconsistency that those who had just shaken off the yoke of popery as an intolerable burden, should subject their conscience and intellect to a human creed; in other words, substitute for the old Roman popery a modern Protestant popery."[138]

It was time for new elections in Geneva in early 1538 and a change in government subsequently took place. Calvin and Farel fell out of favor and were banished from the city in April of 1538.[139] Boettner, although trying to defend Calvin, nevertheless explains the reason why: "Due to an attempt of Calvin and Farel to enforce a too severe system of discipline in Geneva, it became necessary for them to leave the city temporarily."[140] After taking up residence in Basel, Calvin accepted the call from Bucer to come to Strasbourg and pastor the French refugee church.[141] Calvin again relates that he "resolved to live a private life, free from the burdens and cares of any public office until that most excellent servant of Christ, Martin Bucer, employing a similar kind of remonstration to me as that to which Farel had had recourse before, drew me to a new office."[142]

Strasbourg was at that time a free city in Germany where even Anabaptists were tolerated.[143] There Calvin labored for three years—preaching, teaching, and writing. He soon established a "vigorous ecclesiastical discipline" and "not only forbade the communion to the unworthy, but he required all who would partake of the Supper to present themselves to him for a previous spiritual interrogation."[144] While in Strasbourg, Calvin was married by Farel to one of his church members, Idelette de Bure, a widow with two children.[145] When asked what kind of girl he would prefer, Calvin replied: "I am not one of those insane lovers, who once smitten with the fine figure of a woman, embrace also her faults. This only is the beauty that allures me, if she be chaste, obliging, not fastidious, economical, and patient of my health."[146] Calvin and his wife had a son, Jacques, but he died in infancy, and Idelette herself died after nine years of marriage.[147] The death of his wife was "bitterly painful" for Calvin, and although he never remarried, he promised to take care of her children.[148]

During his stay in Strasbourg, Calvin was to write what has been called "the best apology for the Reformed faith written in the sixteenth century."[149] Jacopo Sadoleto (1477-1547), a Roman Catholic cardinal, wrote to the "dearly beloved Brethren, the Magistrates, Senate, and Citizens of Geneva" in which he sought to persuade the city to return to the Roman Catholic Church rather than follow the "innovations introduced within these twenty-five years by crafty men."[150] The letter of Sadoleto eventually made it to Calvin in Strasbourg and he answered masterfully in what has come to be called the *Reply to Sadoleto*. Soon afterward, when the government in Geneva was embroiled in turmoil, it was decided by the Genevan Council on September 21, 1540, that Calvin should be invited back.[151] An official invitation was extended to Calvin on October 22, but it was not until May of 1541 that Calvin's sentence of banishment was rescinded.[152] And although Calvin had earlier written about Geneva that "it would be better to perish at once than to be tormented to death in that chamber of torture,"[153] he acquiesced after repeated pleas by Farel.[154] Calvin returned to Geneva on September 13, 1541, in the words of one Calvinist, as "the stone which the builders had rejected."[155]

When Calvin arrived in Geneva, he entered the pulpit he had previously vacated and began to expound the Scriptures from the same place where he had left off in 1538.[156] He was to spend the rest of his life in Geneva—preaching, teaching, and writing—until his death twenty-three years later on May 27, 1564. He had suffered from numerous aliments during his life and his health deteriorated as he got older. His last words supposedly were: "The sufferings of this present time are not worthy to be compared with the glory that shall be revealed."[157] Calvin was buried in an unmarked grave, as he had wished.[158] Beza conducted the funeral and afterward wrote the first of many biographies of Calvin.[159] As the bulk of Calvin's writing and ministry occurred in Geneva, a further look at his second sojourn there is in order before an examination of his theology.

Calvin and Geneva

Although the French-speaking cantons of Switzerland embraced Protestantism later than the German ones, they soon eclipsed them in significance. The efforts of Guillaume Farel and Peter Viret (1511-1571) paved the way for the work of Calvin in Geneva, the city which was to become "the Protestant Rome."[160] When Calvin first arrived in Geneva in July of 1536, the city had only recently thrown off the yoke of Rome. Geneva was, until this time, a typical Roman Catholic city—divided into parishes, equipped with monasteries, nunneries, and ornate churches, and augmented by three hundred clerics.[161] Being on a trade route, Geneva had all the vices of a commercial city, vices from which the clergy were not exempted.[162] After years of political instability, the city of Geneva formed an alliance in 1526 with the neighboring cities of Freiburg and Bern.[163] In 1528, the city of Bern embraced the Reformation, due in a great measure to the efforts of Farel, who endured much persecution as he led a group of men in their efforts to evangelize French-speaking Switzerland.[164] Turning his sights on Geneva, Farel entered the city in October of 1532 only to be forced out soon afterward—with bruises to show for it.[165] Nevertheless, when a public disputation was called for between the Catholics and the advocates of reform, Farel returned to Geneva.[166] Finally, after much political and religious turmoil, the Mass was abolished and Geneva became an independent republic.[167] On May 21, 1536, the citizens of Geneva officially voted to "live in future according to his holy, evangelical laws and by the Word of God, and that we should abandon all masses and other ceremonies and papal abuses and everything which is attached to them."[168] The government of Geneva consisted at this time of a general assembly and three councils, the smallest of which, the Little Council (twenty-five members), being the most influencial.[169]

The rejection of popery by the city of Geneva did not necessarily mean that all of its citizens were now model Christians. Many simply went along with the Reformation for political reasons. The evils of a united Church and State—Catholic or Protestant—were not yet recognized. Consequently, "a set of severe regulations" were introduced, even before Calvin arrived in the city.[170] There were laws governing dress, music, games, church attendance, dancing, blasphemy, and oaths.[171] Education became free but compulsory.[172] One citizen who refused to attend sermons was imprisoned, forced to go hear sermons, and finally banished from the city.[173] Naturally, there were many residents of Geneva who rebelled against the strict system of discipline. It was into this unstable environment that Calvin entered in 1536. But rather than separating the Church from the State, Calvin used the power of the State to enforce his system of discipline.[174] A hair-dresser was imprisoned for two days for arranging a bride's hair in an unseemly manner.[175] Two Anabaptists were banished from the city on account of their theological views.[176] Penalties were assessed for making a noise or laughing during church.[177] A gambler was publicly punished.[178] Many of the leaders of the opposition to Calvin were among those who at first supported the reform efforts.[179] Thus, Calvin's "reign" in Geneva was doomed to failure.

Calvin's banishment and recall to Geneva has already been mentioned. Schaff maintains the inevitability of Calvin's return trip: "Calvin was foreordained for Geneva, and Geneva for Calvin. Both have made 'their calling and election sure.'"[180] We are told by Calvinists that "Calvin envisioned a model Christian community based on the Bible and patterned after the early church."[181] This has been variously termed a theocracy, a bibliocracy, a clerocracy, and a christocracy.[182] Calvin's first order of business was to submit to the city council his *Ecclesiastical Ordinances*. These ordinances, which were adopted on November 20, 1541, regulated the observance of baptism and communion and established the four church offices of pastors, doctors, elders, and deacons—corresponding to doctrine, education, discipline, and social welfare.[183] The elders were chosen by the magistracy and, together with the ministers, formed a consistory to regulate discipline.[184] After establishing ecclesiastical law, Calvin was called upon to codify the civil legislation.[185] His salary for preaching, however, was not paid out of the church collection but from the city treasury.[186] Thus, from the very beginning of his "ministry" in Geneva, Calvin was intimately involved with both Church and State. He counted among the duties of civil government "to cherish and protect the outward worship of God, to defend sound doctrine of piety, and the position of the church, to adjust our life to the society of men, to form our social behavior to civil righteousness, to reconcile us with one another, and to promote general peace and tranquillity."[187] The civil government also "prevents idolatry, sacrilege against God's name, blasphemies against his truth, and other public offenses against religion."[188] Yet Boettner still insists that "the Reformed soon came to demand complete separation between Church and State."[189] And of Calvin he incredibly adds: "Calvin was the first of the Reformers to demand complete separation between Church and State."[190]

The rules and regulations introduced in Geneva during Calvin's ministry left no area of life untouched. This is why Calvin has frequently been labeled "the Genevese dictator" who "would tolerate in Geneva the opinions of only one person, his own."[191] Besides the usual laws against dancing, profanity, gambling, and immodesty, the number of dishes eaten at a meal was regulated.[192] Attendance at public worship was made mandatory and watchmen were directed to see that people went to church.[193] Press censorship was instituted and books judged to be heretical or immoral were banned.[194] Interest on loans was capped at 5 percent.[195] The naming of children was regulated.[196] Naming a child after a Catholic saint was a penal offense.[197] During an outbreak of the plague in 1545, over twenty persons were burnt alive for witchcraft, and Calvin himself was involved in the prosecutions.[198] From 1542 to 1546, fifty-eight people were executed and seventy-six exiled from Geneva.[199] Torture was freely used to extract confessions.[200] The Calvinist John McNeil admits that "in Calvin's later years, and under his influence, the laws of Geneva became more detailed and more stringent."[201] Calvin was involved in every conceivable aspect of city life: safety regulations to protect children, laws against recruiting mercenaries, new inventions, the introduction of cloth manufacturing, and even dentistry.[202] He was consulted not only on all important state affairs,[203] but on the supervision of the markets and assistance for the poor.[204] Calvin was especially severe with incorrigible adulterers—he favored the death penalty.[205] Those guilty of fornication or adultery were fined and imprisoned.[206] Nevertheless, these laws did not stamp out adultery, for Calvin's own sister-in-law and stepdaughter were found guilty.[207] Calvin's theory of a theocracy is professed to be based on the Holy Scriptures, but as Schaff astutely observes: "It is impossible to deny that this kind of legislation savors more of the austerity of old heathen Rome and the Levitical code than of the gospel of Christ, and that the actual exercise of discipline was often petty, pedantic, and unnecessarily severe."[208]

It is not surprising that there was much opposition to Calvin among the residents of Geneva. Many who opposed Calvin during his first stay in the city were as equally antagonistic toward him when he returned. In 1547 a threatening letter was found on Calvin's pulpit:

> Gross hypocrite, thou and they companions will gain little by your pains. If you do not save yourselves by flight, nobody shall prevent your overthrow, and you will curse the hour when you left your monkery.[209]

Jacques Gruet, a known opponent of Calvin, was arrested for the deed. A search of his house uncovered some writings critical of the Scriptures and of Calvin.[210] Among the writings was a plea addressed to the magistrates of Geneva:

Everyone who maliciously and voluntarily hurts another deserves to be punished. But suppose I am a man who wants to eat his meals as he pleases, what affair is that of others? Or if I want to dance, or have a good time, what is that to do with the law? Nothing.[211]

After a month of torture, Gruet confessed and was sentenced to death: "You have outrageously offended and blasphemed against God and his holy Word; you have conspired against the government; you have threatened God's servants and, guilty of treason, merit capital punishment."[212] He was beheaded on July 26, 1547, with Calvin consenting to his death.[213] Several years later a heretical book of Gruet's was discovered and publicly burnt on Calvin's advice in front of Gruet's house.[214]

There was also some opposition in Geneva to Calvin's doctrine of predestination. In 1551 a medical doctor named Jerome Bolsec (c. 1520-1584) questioned Calvin's doctrine of predestination. After merely being reprimanded in May, Bolsec was arrested in October for affirming that "those who posit an eternal decree in God by which he has ordained some to life and the rest to death make of Him a tyrant, and in fact an idol, as the pagans made of Jupiter."[215] For this he was banished from the city in December and threatened with the whip if he returned.[216] The next year, Jean Trolliet, a city notary whom Calvin had previously rejected as a minister, attacked Calvin's view of predestination for making God the author of sin.[217] Calvin appealed to the city council and they ruled in his favor, declaring that "Calvin's book of the Institutes was a good and godly composition, that its doctrine was godly doctrine, that he was esteemed as a good and true minister of this city, and that thenceforward no one should dare to speak against this book and its doctrine."[218]

The doctrines of Calvin were not the only things that were spoken against in Geneva. Calvin himself was increasingly harassed and made the object of ridicule. Dogs were named after him and songs were written to mock him.[219] Guns were fired outside his window late at night.[220] In 1554 Calvin wrote "Dogs bark at me on all sides. Everywhere I am saluted with the name of 'heretic,' and all the calumnies that can possibly be invented are heaped upon me; in a word, the enemies among my own flock attack me with greater bitterness than my declared enemies among the papists."[221] Calvin also faced opposition from the city council for some of his ideas.[222]

Not everyone, of course, was opposed to Calvin. He certainly had his admirers, and was well respected by many who attended his preaching. The Scottish Reformer John Knox (1505-1572) spent several years in Geneva and termed it "the most perfect school of Christ that ever was in the earth since the days of the Apostles."[223] Numerous tributes have been recorded about how great it was to live in Geneva, but they are chiefly from refugees to Geneva who agreed with the faith of Calvin.[224] Ironically, Geneva became a haven for those who fled their native land due to religious persecution.[225] As a pastor, Calvin performed weddings, baptisms, and is reported to have preached 4,000 sermons after his return to Geneva.[226] He also introduced the practice of extempore prayer and congregational singing, although he was opposed to musical instruments.[227] In 1559 Calvin established the Academy of Geneva, with Beza as the first president, and attracted Protestant students from all over Europe.[228] By Calvin's death there were 1,600 students.[229] Two of the most famous students to study there were John Knox and James Arminius. Geneva was also home to exiles from England during the reign of Bloody Mary (1553-1558). It was also here that William Whittingham (1524-1579) translated the New Testament into English in what was to be called the Geneva Bible.

The harsh nature of Calvin's theocracy in Geneva has been dismissed by modern-day Calvinists because "we must not blame a man for the environment he is born into."[230] The idea is that Calvin was a product of his age—an age that knew nothing else but repressive laws and the mingling of the Church and State. Scott, seeking to defend Calvin, informs us:

> Neither Calvin nor Farel nor any other Reformer introduced the idea of monitoring morals in Geneva. The Vatican had done that, uncounted centuries before, and maintained that system for generations. But the Bishops grew lax in the late Middle Ages and indifferent during the Renaissance. In the early years of the Reformation, censorship of manners and morals remained a settled, accepted part of existing, ancient police regulations not only in Geneva, but in all Europe.[231]

It is also certainly true, as former Calvin College professor John Bratt (b. 1909) points out, that "many of the prohibitive rules and laws had been on the statute books long before Calvin's coming."[232] But instead of being ignored or removed, these laws were revived under Calvin. It is also repeatedly declared by Calvinists that Calvin held no civil or political office, could not vote, and was not even a citizen until 1559.[233] But this only mitigates against him, for if Calvin accomplished as much as he did without those benefits, how much more could he have achieved with them?

All the excuses given in defense of Calvin are immaterial if we take at face value what the Calvinists say about his knowledge of and reliance on the Scriptures. Another former Calvin College professor, Charles Miller (1919-1997), insists that "first and certainly basic in all of Calvin's thought is a dependence on Scripture."[234] We are also told that Calvin "was willing to break sharply with tradition where it was contrary to the Word of God."[235] So whatever the customs, traditions, and prejudices of his age, Calvin, because of his profound reverence for the authority of the Scriptures, should have been an iconoclast when it came to the Rome-like regulation of Genevan religion and society. But such is not the case, for Calvin, recognizing the errors of papal rulers, admonished Protestant rulers to emulate them: "Seeing that the defenders of the Papacy are so bitter and bold in behalf of their superstitions, that in their atrocious fury they shed the blood of the innocent, it should shame Christian magistrates that in the protection of certain truth, they are entirely destitute of spirit."[236] It is statements from Calvin like this that prompted the Baptist historian A. H. Newman (1852-1933) to remark: "Calvin virtually made every sin a crime, and so did not hesitate to make use of the civil power for the execution of church discipline. Calvin's view of the subordination of the civil power to the ecclesiastical does not appear to be radically different from the papal."[237] And although Calvin's actions are repeatedly dismissed because of the spirit of his age, it is not true that all Christians maintained a persecuting spirit. The Anabaptists, against whom Calvin wrote *Against the Anabaptists* in 1544, certainly did not believe in persecuting their opponents.[238] The historian George Fisher (1827-1909) correctly sums up the matter: "No historical student needs to be told what an incalculable amount of evil has been wrought by Catholics and by Protestants, from a mistaken belief in the perpetual validity of the Mosaic civil legislation, and from a confounding of the spirit of the old dispensation with that of the new."[239] It is even acknowledged by Calvinists that "the greater fruitage of Calvin's ideas elsewhere than in Geneva is due to the fact that in other areas they were not subjected to implementation by the civil state to the same degree as was true in Geneva."[240]

Calvin and Servetus

The subject of a church-state theocracy in Geneva and the intolerance that went with it brings us to what has been designated "the dark chapter in the history of Calvin which has cast a gloom over his fair name, and exposed him, not unjustly, to the charge of intolerance and persecution."[241] This blemish on Calvin's record has been distorted and explained away by Calvinists zealous to protect his reputation. Warfield insists that "Calvin possessed little influence in the tribunal which condemned and executed Servetus."[242] Henry Cole, the translator of two of Calvin's theological treatises, maintains that "Calvin is *falsely reported* to have been the prominent adviser" to the death of Servetus.[243] Kuyper charges that "history has been guilty of the great and far-reaching unfairness of ever casting in their teeth this one execution of fire of Servetus."[244] Philip Hughes argues that "Servetus was not burnt by Calvin, who had no authority to pronounce, or even to vote for, any such sentence."[245] Alister McGrath laments that Calvin has been singled out while the "greater claims to infamy of other individuals and institutions" have been overlooked.[246] Needless to say, the veracity of these statements remains to be proved.

Michaelem Serveto, known to us as Michael Servetus, was born in 1509 or 1511,[247] at Villanueva, in Aragon, Spain. Thus, he was about the same age as Calvin and, like him, was raised a Roman Catholic. He was educated at the University of Saragossa, and later studied law at the University of Toulouse.[248] Although Servetus was for several years employed by Juan Quintana, the confessor of the Holy Roman Emperor Charles V,[249] he showed up in Protestant Basel in 1530 where he met the reformer John Oecolampadius.[250] Here he published two attacks on the Trinity, *Seven Books on Errors about the Trinity*, in 1531, and *Two Books of Dialogues on the Trinity*, in 1532.[251] After his books were judged to be heretical, Servetus assumed the name of Michel de Villeneuve and went to Paris to study mathematics, geography, and medicine.[252] From Paris he removed to Lyons and edited an edition of Ptolemy's *Geography* and wrote some tracts on medicine and astrology.[253] Servetus returned to Paris in 1536, took degrees in medicine, and lectured in the university on geography and astrology.[254] Here he published two more works: a treatise on the use of syrups in medicine, in 1537, and a work on astrology, *Apologetic Dissertation on Astrology,* in 1538.[255] It was here that he also discovered the pulmonary circulation of the blood, years before William Harvey (1578-1658).[256] After conflicts in Paris over his teachings on astrology, Servetus left Paris to practice medicine and sometime after 1540 ended up in Vienne, a suburb of Lyons.[257] Here he both practiced medicine and edited books. A second edition of Ptolemy's *Geography* appeared in 1541, an edition of Pagnini's Latin Bible in 1542, and a seven-volume edition of the Bible.[258] Obviously, Servetus was very well-read and quite intelligent. Schaff credits him with knowing six languages.[259]

Servetus was to spend thirteen years at Vienne. On account of his increasingly unorthodox religious views he lived the life of a Roman Catholic, attending mass and editing an edition of Thomas Aquinas in Spanish.[260] Through a bookseller in Lyons, Servetus began a correspondence with Calvin. He sent Calvin a manuscript of a book he was working on and bombarded him with questions.[261] Calvin, replying that he did not have time to write whole books in answer to him, sent Servetus a copy of his *Institutes.*[262] He in turn returned the *Institutes* to Calvin with critical annotations in the margins, of which Calvin commented that there was hardly a page "that is not defiled by his vomit."[263] In 1553 Servetus published his answer to Calvin's *Institutes.* It was called *Christianismi Restitutio* (The Restoration of Christianity), and included thirty letters from Servetus to Calvin.[264] After a copy of the book reached Geneva, a friend of Calvin, Guillaume de Trie, wrote to his Catholic cousin in Lyons about Servetus:

> The man of whom I speak has been condemned by all the churches which you reprove, yet you suffer him and even let him print his books which are so full of blasphemies that I need say no more. He is a Portuguese Spaniard, named Michael Servetus. That is his real name, but he goes at present under the name of Villeneufve and practices medicine. He has resided for some time at Lyons. Now he is at Vienne where his book has been printed by a certain Balthazar Arnoullet, and lest you think that I am talking without warrant I send you the first folio.[265]

This got Servetus in trouble with the Roman Catholic authorities and he was arrested on April 4th. However, on April 7th he escaped and the Catholics had to settle for burning him in effigy.[266] The sentence on Servetus was: "To be burned alive in a slow fire until his body becomes ashes. For the present the sentence is to be carried out in effigy and his books are to be burnt."[267] After his escape from Vienne, Servetus foolishly went to Geneva and showed up in church on August 13—a Sunday when Calvin was preaching—and was promptly arrested.[268] After a trial in which Calvin played a part, Servetus was executed on October 27, 1553. The sentence this time was:

> We condemn thee, Michael Servetus, to be bound, and led to the place of Champel, there to be fastened to a stake and burnt alive, together with thy book, as well the one written by thy hand as the printed one, even till thy body be reduced to ashes; and thus shalt thou finish thy days to furnish an example to others who might wish to commit the like.[269]

His last words were: "O Jesus, Son of the Eternal God, have pity on me!"[270] It is truly ironic that Servetus was burned in effigy by the Catholics and in actuality by the Protestants.

Since Servetus was not burned at the stake for immorality, sedition, or any other crime against the state, but rather for holding theological opinions that were deemed heretical, a brief look at his theological views is in order. Although he regarded the Bible as the word of God, in each of his religious tenets he has a mixture of truth and error.[271] The principle charges against him were holding heretical opinions on the Trinity and infant baptism.[272] The Catholics, however, had something else against him, for he termed the Pope: "O vilest of all beasts, most brazen of harlots!"[273] To him the mass was a Satanic monstrosity and an invention of demons.[274] He further equated the Pope with the Antichrist and the seven-headed dragon in Revelation.[275] Regarding the Trinity, Servetus was not a Unitarian but had a strange view of the Trinity in a great measure peculiar to himself. He refers to Trinitarians as "tri-theists" and "atheists,"[276] and equated the Trinity with Cerberus, the three-headed dog of Greek mythology who guarded the entrance to the underworld.[277] He claimed to believe in the true Trinity.[278] But although his view of the Trinity comes closest to Sabellianism,[279] Williston Walker (1860-1922) suggests that the whole doctrinal controversy is epitomized in the distinction between the phrases "eternal Son of God" and "Son of the eternal God."[280] On baptism, Servetus regarded infant baptism as a "diabolical invention and infernal falsehood destructive of Christianity."[281] Yet, he still held to baptismal regeneration, only he believed it should be preceded by repentance and undertaken when one reached thirty years of age.[282] He even wrote two letters to Calvin on adult baptism and exhorted him to follow his example.[283] Regarding some other doctrines, Servetus likewise held a mixture of truth and error. He espoused the premillennial reign of Christ but interpreted the Book of Revelation historically.[284] He denied Calvin's doctrine of predestination but placed emphasis on the necessity of good works.[285] Now, although Servetus' theological views were not orthodox, they were by no means criminal, but that is why he was burned: for mental opinions not physical actions. But the irony of ironies is that although he was never tried like Servetus, Calvin himself was also several times accused of heresy. During his first sojourn in Geneva, he was accused of being an Arian, especially when he refused to subscribe to the Athanasian Creed.[286] And later, in 1543 and 1544, Calvin was again accused of holding unorthodox views of the Trinity and the deity of Christ.[287]

The fact that Calvin himself did not physically burn Servetus does not mean that he was not responsible. Seven years previously, Calvin wrote to Farel a letter in which he stated:

> Servetus lately wrote to me, and coupled with his letter a long volume of his delirious fancies, with the Thrasonic boast, that I should see something astonishing and unheard of. He takes it upon him to come hither, if it be agreeable to me. But I am unwilling to pledge my word for his safety, for if he shall come, I shall never permit him to depart alive, provided my authority be of any avail.[288]

And although Servetus vehemently affirmed, and Calvin equally denied, the charge that the original letter from Calvin's friend in Geneva to his Catholic cousin in Lyons was the work of Calvin himself, the historians are divided as to Calvin's complicity.[289] There is no doubt, however, that Calvin turned over letters written to him by Servetus, as well as pages from his *Institutes* upon which Servetus had inscribed marginal notes against infant baptism, to prove the identity of Servetus to the authorities in Vienne.[290] These were supplied through Calvin's friend, who wrote again to his cousin:

> All the rest is here right enough, the big book and the other writings of the same author, but I can tell you I had no little trouble to get from Calvin what I am sending. Not that he does not wish to repress such execrable blasphemies, but he thinks his duty is rather to convince heretics with doctrine than with other means, because he does not exercise the sword of justice. But I remonstrated with him and pointed out the embarrassing position in which I should be placed if he did not help me, so that in the end he gave me what you see. For the rest I hope by and by, when the case is further advanced, to get from him a whole ream of paper, which the scamp has had printed, but I think that for the present you have enough.[291]

All of this was done before Servetus even came to Geneva.

The account of the arrest of Servetus has already been mentioned. What needs to be added, however, is that Calvin himself was responsible for the arrest of Servetus. Beza admits that it was on Calvin's information to the magistracy that Servetus was put in prison,[292] which fact Calvin does not deny, as can be seen by letters he wrote during the trial. To Farel he wrote: "We have now new business in hand with Servetus. He intended perhaps passing through this city; for it is not yet known with what design he came. But after he had been recognized, I thought that he should be detained."[293] A couple of weeks later, Calvin wrote to a friend in Basel: "At length, in an evil hour, he came to this place, when, at my instigation, one of the Syndics ordered him to be conducted to prison; for I do not disguise it that I considered it my duty to put a check, so far as I could, upon this most obstinate and ungovernable man, that his contagion might not spread further.[294] As to why McGrath calls Calvin "an indirect first preferrer of charges,"[295] Francois Wendel (1905-1972) points out: "The Genevan law prescribed that every accuser must yield himself prisoner for the duration of the proceedings he was initiating, so that he himself should suffer an appropriate penalty if the accused were judged innocent."[296] Thus, Calvin's friend Nicolas de la Fontaine was detained instead of Calvin.[297] The trial lasted over two months and Calvin himself drew up a document of thirty-eight accusations against Servetus.[298] Five days into the trial, Calvin wrote to Farel:

"I hope that sentence of death will at least be passed upon him."[299] McGrath informs us that "the trial, condemnation, and execution (including the selection of the particular mode of execution) of Servetus were entirely the work of the city council, at a period in its history when it was particularly hostile to Calvin."[300] And although he further admits that Calvin served as "an expert theological witness," McGrath insists that such a witness "could have come from any orthodox theologian of the age, whether Protestant or Roman Catholic."[301] But this is immaterial, for Calvin, who should have known better, is the one who served as the "chief witness for the prosecution."[302] Calvin advocated the death penalty on the basis of a verse in the Mosaic law: **"And he that blasphemeth the name of the LORD, he shall surely be put to death,** *and* **all the congregation shall certainly stone him: as well the stranger, as he that is born in the land, when he blasphemeth the name** *of the LORD,* **shall be put to death"** (Lev. 24:16).[303]

We also know that Calvin was still bitter about Servetus missing an appointment with him in Paris years previously, for Calvin mentioned it when he recounted his last interview with Servetus: "I reminded him gently how I had risked my life more than 16 years ago to gain him for our Savior."[304] It is interesting to note that during the trial Servetus drew up a list of questions that Calvin should be asked. The sixth question was: "Whether he did not well know that it is not the office of a minister of the gospel to make a capital accusation and to pursue a man at law to the death?"[305]

It was not only before the trial and during the trial that Calvin expressed his hope for the death of Servetus, but after the trial as well. Within six months of the condemnation of Servetus, Calvin wrote a book defending his actions. In his *Defense of the Orthodox Trinity Against the Errors of Michael Servetus,* Calvin defended the use of the civil sword to execute religious "heretics" and maintained that "whoever shall now contend that it is unjust to put heretics and blasphemers to death will knowingly and willingly incur their very guilt."[306] Schaff correctly reflects that Calvin's arguments "are chiefly drawn from the Jewish laws against idolatry and blasphemy, and from the examples of the pious kings of Israel. But his arguments from the New Testament are failures."[307] After he wrote against the errors of Servetus, Calvin wrote to Bullinger and lamented: "Others speak with greater harshness, saying that I am, in fact, a master of cruelty and atrocity—that I now mangle with my pen the dead man who perished at my hands."[308] In a 1561 letter from Calvin to the marquis de Poet, high chamberlain to the King of Navarre, he says intolerantly: "Honour, glory, and riches shall be the reward of your pains: but above all, do not fail to rid the country of those zealous scoundrels who stir up the people to revolt against us. Such monsters should be exterminated, as I have exterminated Michael Servetus the Spaniard."[309] Nine years afterward, Calvin still justified his actions: "And what crime was it of mine if our Council at my exhortation, indeed, but in conformity with the opinion of several churches, took vengeance on his execrable blasphemies?"[310] All of Calvin's justifications for the death of Servetus were notably defensive.

It has correctly been pointed out by every Calvinist who has written on the subject that Calvin favored the sword rather than burning at the stake,[311] although Clark does go to extremes in trying to justify his mentor: "The story that he had Servetus burnt at the stake is an invention of Calvin's enemies. At least twice in his writings Calvin calls on Servetus' judges as witnesses that he urged them not to burn Servetus."[312] Again, this is certainly true. The passages in question can be found in two of Calvin's letters to Farel:

> I hope the sentence of death will at least be passed upon him; but I desire that the severity of the punishment may be mitigated.[313]

> He will be led forth to punishment to-morrow. We endeavored to alter the mode of his death, but in vain. Why we did not succeed, I defer for narration until I see you.[314]

However, the reason for this was that Calvin wanted Servetus executed as an offender against the State. Hughes, in seeking to exonerate Calvin, informs us that "the death penalty was imposed by the civil authorities."[315] However, the historian Leonard Verduin, writing for the Calvin Foundation, explains why: "Calvin wanted Servetus eliminated as an offender against the *civil* order. Death by fire was for offenders in the area of religion. Hence Calvin's concern in the matter."[316] Verduin further comments on Calvin's "plea of mercy":

> Some have tried to make something of the fact that, late in the trial of Servetus, Calvin put forth an effort to have the man destroyed in some other way than by fire. However, the fact is that Calvin was not opposed to *exterminatio* in the case of Servetus, merely against the proposed mode. Death by fire had been the punishment for heretics for more than a millennium, and Calvin, realizing that death for heresy was becoming questionable in the public mind, would have preferred execution by a means in which the sedition aspect rather than the heresy aspect of the man's deliction would stand out. In Calvin's mind, the one still implied the other—heresy implied sedition.[317]

If carried out, Calvin's plea would ensure escaping the blame for the deed, not proving that he was being merciful, as some of Calvin's defenders attempt to prove.

In spite of the documented facts of history, some Calvinists still seek to justify Calvin, as the Calvinist Cunningham asserts: "Some injudicious admirers of Calvin have attempted to exempt him from the responsibility of Servetus's death."[318] This is done in several ways. The first is by making general statements about Calvin and Servetus. McGrath informs us that "Servetus was the *only* individual put to death for his religious opinions in Geneva during Calvin's lifetime, at a time when executions of this nature were a commonplace elsewhere."[319] McNeil argues that although "many would be glad to damn and dismiss Calvin by a reference to Servetus," "no man ought to be judged solely by his worst acts."[320] W. Gary Crampton reminds us that Calvin "even sought to evangelize the blasphemer Servetus up to the day of his death."[321] Scott goes so far as to credit Servetus with destroying European Christianity if he was allowed to continue: "Left unchecked, Servetus would have unhinged both the Reformation and Catholicism, and left Europe bereft in the ashes of its faith centuries before that situation was actually realized."[322] As is evident by the above remarks, the subject of Servetus is a great embarassment to Calvinists.

The second way Calvin is justified is by making him a "child of his age."[323] Bratt maintains that "we must remember that Calvin simply reflected the ideas of his time."[324] McGrath insists that Calvin must be "contextualized," and reminds us that "every Christian body which traces its history back to the sixteenth century has blood liberally scattered over its credentials."[325] Wendel advocates "that it is contrary to a sound conception of history to try to apply our ways of judging and our moral criteria to the past."[326] McNeil tells us that Calvin's age was "an age of mass burnings and of mass butchery for religion."[327] Hughes excuses Calvin because it "was the custom of that age to burn heretics, and Calvin, in so far as he approved of what was done, was conforming to that custom."[328] He further explains that Servetus would have been executed "even if there had been no such person as Calvin in Geneva."[329] But making Calvin a "child of his age" is nothing but the same argument used by Calvinists in seeking to defend Calvin's regulation of Geneva.

The third means of justifying Calvin's burning of Servetus is by comparing him with the other Reformers. Boettner correctly says that "the other Reformers approved it and other death sentences against heretics."[330] Thus, Calvin was not alone in his views of killing heretics. During the trial, the city council of Geneva consulted with four other cities. Their reply was unanimously against Servetus.[331] After receiving the various replies, the sentence was passed by Geneva: "Their Lordships, having received the opinions of the Churches of Berne, Basel, Zurich and Schaffhausen upon the Servetus affair, condemned the said Servetus to be led to Champey and there to be burned alive."[332] Bullinger and Melanchthon also approved of the execution. During the trial of Servetus, Bullinger wrote to Calvin that "God had given the Council of Geneva a most favorable opportunity to vindicate the truth against the pollution of heresy, and the honor of God against blasphemy."[333] Melanchthon wrote to Bullinger in 1555: "I judge also that the Genevese Senate did perfectly right, to put an end to this obstinate man, who could never cease blaspheming. And I wonder at those who disapprove of this severity."[334] He also wrote to Calvin: "To you also the Church owes gratitude at the present moment, and will owe it to the latest posterity. I perfectly assent to your opinion. I affirm also that your magistrates did right in punishing, after a regular trial, this blasphemous man."[335] Martin Bucer insisted that "Servetus deserved to be disembowelled and torn to pieces."[336] Beza wrote a special word in defense of the execution: "Punishment was most deservedly inflicted on Servetus at Geneva, not because he was a sectory, but a monstrous compound of mere impiety and horrid blasphemy, with which he had for the whole period of thirty years, by word and writing, polluted both heaven and earth."337 But if the views of the other Reformers are not scriptural, then what difference does it make what they believed?

Surprisingly, the final manner in which Calvinists seek to justify Calvin is by comparing him with the papists. To exonerate Calvin, as some Calvinists have implied, by saying that Servetus would have been executed by the Catholics as well is to say that life in Geneva under the Gospel was same as life in a Catholic country under the Pope.338 In fact, it is worse, for as Schaff says: "Persecution deserves much severer condemnation in a Protestant than in a Roman Catholic, because it is inconsistent. Protestantism must stand or fall with freedom of conscience and freedom of worship."339 Ronald Wallace even admits that Catholics were not persecuted as long as they kept quiet.340 This further condemns Calvin. Hughes dismisses the execution of Servetus as "but a single drop in the ocean of savage tortures and persecutions and deaths that adherents of the Reformation were suffering in those days when it had become customary to hunt and destroy men like brutes."341 Scott bemoans the fact that "the rulers of Vienne have not been condemned, either by historians or theologians, for sentencing Servetus to death in absentia. Their names are not indissolubly linked to Servetus in arguments against Catholicism."342 But why should the Catholics be condemned any more than usual for doing what they already did for years? Roland Bainton reminds us of the historical roots of the laws which detained and condemned Servetus: "The law under which Servetus had first been imprisoned was that of the Holy Roman Empire; the law by which he was in the end condemned was that of the Codex of Justinian, which prescribes the penalty of death for two ecclesiastical offenses—the denial of the Trinity and the repetition of baptism."343 What difference then is there between Calvin and Torquemada (1420-1498) or the Reformers and the Inquisition?

Calvin is to be held culpable for the death of Servetus. To say that he was "no more guilty than his fellow-citizens,"344 is to abjure the facts of history. Verduin compactly summarizes the case against Calvin:

> The burning of Servetus—let it be said with utmost clarity—was a deed for which Calvin must be held largely responsible. It was not done in spite of Calvin, as some over-ardent admirers of his are wont to say. He planned it beforehand and maneuvered it

from start to finish. It occurred because of him and not in spite of him. After it had taken place Calvin defended it, with every possible and impossible argument.[345]

The verdict of the non-Calvinist historians is unanimous. The respected Lutheran historian, John Mosheim (1694-1755), judged in favor of Servetus.[346] The English historian Gibbon remarked: "I am more deeply scandalized at the single execution of Servetus than at the hecatombs which have blazed in the Auto da Fès of Spain and Portugal. The zeal of Calvin seems to have been envenomed by personal malice, and perhaps envy."[347] And the Baptist historian William Jones, although acknowledging "many doctrinal sentiments in common with Calvin," nevertheless said: "I strenuously deprecate every attempt to palliate the enormity of Calvin's conduct."[348] But it is not just non-Calvinists who have condemned Calvin, for even Calvinists themselves acknowledge his guilt:

> When all is understood, admirers of Calvin must still look upon it with shame.[349]

> In our judgment Calvin was guilty of sin.[350]

> There can be no doubt that Calvin beforehand, at the time, and after the event, explicitly approved and defended the putting him to death, and assumed the responsibility of the transaction.[351]

In 1903, some remorseful European Calvinists erected a monument to Servetus on which they engraved:

> On October 27, 1553, died at the stake at Champel, Michael Servetus, of Villeneuve d'Aragon, born September 29, 1511. Reverent and grateful sons of Calvin, our great Reformer, but condemning an error which was that of his age, and steadfastly adhering to liberty of conscience according to the true principles of the Reformation and of the gospel, we have erected this monument, on the 27th of October, 1903.[352]

This edifice no doubt helped placate the opponents of the Calvinists, but it was a few hundred years too late to help Servetus.

The reason why so much paper and ink has been given to the controversy between Calvin and Servetus is the same as that for

Calvin and Geneva: Calvin was supposed to be a Christian theologian who based all of his opinions on the Bible alone. This is the claim that the Calvinists adamantly make about him. As Gregg Singer says of him: "However much Calvin respected Augustine and the other early Fathers, he looked beyond them to the Scriptures which were, for him, the infallible rule of faith and practice."[353] Therefore, Calvin's conduct in the matter of Servetus is inexcusable if what the Calvinists say about him is true, for no Calvinist today would hardly advocate that the persecution of "heretics" was scriptural—whether by the State or the Church.

Calvin's Institutes

The greatest literary work to come from Calvin's pen is undoubtedly his *Christianae Religionis Institutio* (Institutes of the Christian Religion), commonly just referred to as his *Institutes*. It was begun during Calvin's exile from France and finished in 1535 while he was in Basel.[354] It was published at Basel in 1536 under the pretentious title of:

> *The Institute of the Christian Religion, Containing almost the Whole Sum of Piety and Whatever It is Necessary to Know in the Doctrine of Salvation. A Work Very Well Worth Reading by All Persons Zealous for Piety, and Lately Published. A Preface to the Most Christian King of France, in Which this Book is Presented to Him as a Confession of Faith. Author, John Calvin, of Noyon. Basel, MDXXXVI.*[355]

Calvin's *Institutes* underwent much revision and enlargement until the final edition in 1559.

Calvin prefaced his *Institutes* with a lengthy address to Francis I (1494-1547), the King of France. The preface alone has been called "one of the few masterpieces of apologetic literature."[356] Schaff reckons it "among the three immortal prefaces in literature."[357] In this preface Calvin tells the king:

> When I first set my hand to this work, nothing was farther from my mind, most glorious King, than to write something that might afterward be offered to Your Majesty. My purpose was solely to transmit certain rudiments by which those who are touched with any zeal for religion might be shaped to true

godliness.[358]

Yet Calvin had another purpose in mind, as he says: "It seemed to me that I should be doing something worth-while if I both gave instruction to them and made confession before you with the same work."[359] Calvin then made a plea on behalf of the French Protestants who had been mercilessly persecuted by the king since the Placards incident.[360] Calvin's appeal to the king was not based on liberty of conscience but on a desire to disassociate the French Protestants from the Anabaptists (who were deemed seditious and worthy of persecution) and to establish the French Protestants as the legitimate successors of apostolic Christianity and not the Catholic Church.[361] Calvin himself later said:

> This was why I published the *Institutes*—to defend against unjust slander my brothers whose death was precious in the Lord's sight. A second reason was my desire to rouse the sympathy and concern of people outside, since the same punishment threatened many other poor people. And this volume was not a thick and laborious work like the present edition; it appeared as a brief *Enchiridion*. It had no other purpose than to bear witness to the faith of those whom I saw criminally libeled by wicked and false courtiers.[362]

The first edition of Calvin's *Institutes* was written in Latin and contained six chapters. The first four, modeled after Luther's Catechism, consisted of expositions on the Ten Commandments, the Apostle's Creed, the Lord's Prayer, and the Sacraments, while the fifth and sixth chapters dealt with false sacraments and Christian Liberty.[363] The first edition sold out quickly and a second, also in Latin, was published in 1539.[364] This time, although the book was longer, the title was shorter, the words were interchanged to read *Institutio Christianae Religionis,* and the phrase "at length truly corresponding to its title" was included.[365] Calvin stated that his object in this edition was "to so prepare and train students of sacred theology for the study of the word of God that they might have an easy access into it, and be able to proceed in it without hindrance."[366] This second edition had seventeen chapters and was three times the size of the first.[367] The first French edition, *Institution de la religion chrestienne,* published in 1541, was translated by Calvin himself.[368] It has been called "one of the major influences in the evolution of the language from medieval to modern French."[369] After several more Latin and French editions, Calvin issued his final Latin edition in 1559:

> *Institute of the Christian Religion, now first arranged in four books and divided by definite headings in a very convenient way: also enlarged by so much added matter that it can almost be regarded as a new work.* [370]

This final edition contained eighty chapters and was viewed by Calvin as his definitive work.[371]

The importance of Calvin's *Institutes* to the development of the Reformed faith cannot be emphasized enough. The *Institutes* were soon translated into the other languages of the Europe and made the name *Calvin* a household word among Protestants.[372] The first English translation appeared in London in 1561.[373] Of the value of Calvin's *Institutes* it has been said:

> The masterpiece of Protestant theology.[374]

> One of the ten or twenty books in the world of which we may say without exaggeration that they have determined the course of history and have changed the face of Europe.[375]

> This book is the masterpiece of a precocious genius of commanding intellectual and spiritual depth and power. It is one of the few truly classical productions in the history of theology.[376]

Even the Roman Catholic historian, Wilhem Kampschulte (1831-1872), commented: "Without doubt the most outstanding and the most influential production in the sphere of dogmatics which the Reformation literature of the sixteenth century presents."[377] But in spite of this glowing report, most Roman Catholics did not appreciate Calvin's work, and it was suppressed by the Catholic Church and burned at Notre Dame in 1544.[378] Considering the time it appeared in history, Calvin's *Institutes* is certainly a remarkable work. But it is to be remembered that the *Institutes* is primarily a Reformed theology, and as one Calvinist terms it: "The authoritative expression of the Reformed theology."[379] Naturally, the Calvinistic Baptists who make recourse to Calvin's *Institutes* do so *only* when attempting to establish the truth of their doctrine of predestination.

Although Calvin was certainly an original thinker and professed to make the Bible his closest study, the sources of Calvin's thought in the *Institutes* is varied and wide ranging. As Walker remarks: "Calvin's mind was formulative rather than creative."[380] As one of the second generation of Reformers (Calvin was a generation younger than Luther, Zwingli, Melanchthon, and Bucer), Calvin was well versed in the writings of his forerunners. Luther and Bucer stand out in particular. Calvin read many of the works of Luther (translated into Latin), and Calvinists have long acknowledged his debt to the German reformer.[381] Warfield calls Bucer "Calvin's master in theology."[382] The influence of Bucer on Calvin has likewise been acknowledged by Calvinists, and especially regarding the doctrine of predestination.[383] Calvin himself even confessed: "I have particularly copied Bucer, that man of holy memory, outstanding doctor in the church of God."[384] Wendel also discloses that there are "striking analogies" between several passages in the *Institutes* and the works of Erasmus.[385] Calvin was familiar with the scholastic authors as well, especially Anselm (1033-1109), Lombard (1100-1160), Aquinas (1225-1274), and Bernard (1090-1153).[386] He also freely quoted ancient Greek and Latin authors.[387] And although Calvin knew the Church Fathers extremely well, "as no one else in the century,"[388] he regarded one in particular as "the best and most reliable witness of all antiquity."[389]

As we have seen in the previous chapter, this "best and most reliable witness" is none other than Augustine. There we saw that the name of Calvin is inseparably conjoined with that of Augustine. Talbot and Crampton insist that because "Augustine was so strongly Calvinistic, that John Calvin referred to himself as an Augustinian theologian."[390] Although it has been said by Calvinists that "Calvin uses Augustine's opinions only as corroboration of Scripture,"[391] it has also been admitted that at some points "he seems to rely on Augustine for the substance of an argument."[392] Once again it should be emphasized that it is the Calvinists themselves who connect Calvin with Augustine:

> Above all, Calvin regarded his thought as a faithful exposition of the leading ideas of Augustine of Hippo.[393]

> Throughout the Institutes Calvin's self-confessed debt to

> Augustine is constantly apparent.[394]
>
> He actually incorporates in his treatment of man and of salvation so many typical passages from Augustine that his doctrine seems here entirely continuous with that of his great African predecessor.[395]
>
> Upon points of doctrine he borrows from St Augustine with both hands.[396]
>
> He makes St Augustine his constant reading, and feels on an equal footing with him, quotes him at every opportunity, appropriates his expressions and regards him as one of the most valuable of allies in his controversies.[397]

Howbeit, to prove conclusively that Calvin was a disciple of Augustine, we need look no further than Calvin himself. One can't read five pages in Calvin's *Institutes* without seeing the name of Augustine. Calvin quotes Augustine over four hundred times in the *Institutes* alone.[398] He called Augustine by such titles as "holy man" and "holy father."[399] Calvin himself even stated: "Augustine is so wholly with me, that if I wished to write a confession of my faith, I could do so with all fulness and satisfaction to myself out of his writings."[400] Indeed, Calvin closes his introduction to the last edition of his *Institutes* with a quote from Augustine.[401]

In addition to his *Institutes,* Calvin wrote commentaries on the New Testament (except 2 John, 3 John, and Revelation—a book he acknowledged he could not fathom[402]) and most of the Old Testament (all but eleven books), as well as numerous treatises, sermons, and letters. As early as 1556 a complete set of Calvin's commentaries was published by Stephanus.[403] The bulk of Calvin's voluminous material is still in print today. And although his writings are over four hundred years old, they are still held in high esteem. Students at Calvin Theological Seminary can take courses on Calvin's *Institutes* and Calvin's commentaries.[404] But even though Calvin produced a wide variety of writings, the primary expression of Calvin's thought on any given subject is to be found in the *Institutes,* for Calvin himself regarded his commentaries as subordinate to his *Institutes.*[405] And it is to the *Institutes* that we must turn to see the theology of John Calvin.

The Theology of Calvin

Besides the failure of John Calvin to correctly interpret the New Testament in regards to the relationship between the Church and the State and the persecution of "heretics," there are other elements of his theology that are important to examine. Like Augustine, Calvin is not immune from criticism just because he was a great Reformer and wrote volumes of theological material. Moreover, a theological inquiry is especially pertinent in the case of Calvin because of the great theologian that Calvinists make him out to be. In his day, Melanchthon called Calvin "the theologian."[406] More recently we have been told:

> Possibly no theologian in history has so well combined the powers of Biblical exegesis, of clear and logical thought, of literary expression, and of pastoral concern in one powerfully integrated personality.[407]

> The first rank among interpreters of the age is deservedly assigned to John Calvin, who endeavored to expound nearly the whole of the sacred volume.[408]

> What John Calvin has to say can contribute significantly to contemporary Christian thinking.[409]

> It was he who gave the Evangelical movement a theology.[410]

Not all Calvinists, however, maintain such lofty opinions, for as Wendel concedes: "But sometimes, for the sake of logical coherence or out of attachment to pre-established dogmatic positions, he also did violence to the Biblical texts. His principle of Scriptural authority then led him to search the Scriptures for illusory support, by means of purely arbitrary interpretations."[411] Yet, George claims that Calvin "presented more clearly and more masterfully than anyone before him the essential elements of Protestant theology."[412] This being the accepted opinion, it is to Calvin's theology that we now turn.

In spite of their differences, the Reformers were united on one thing: an abhorrence of the papacy and the Roman Catholic system of relics, auricular confession, masses, and monasteries. Luther called the Pope "the Antichrist" and said that the Roman church was the "whore-church of the Devil."[413] He also burned the papal bull of his excommunication.[414] Calvin was just as incessant in his denunciation of the papal system, as Mosheim relates: "Few persons of his age will bear any comparison with Calvin for patient industry, resolution, and hatred of the Roman superstition,"[415] Calvin wrote several works against the Roman Church. His *Reply to Sadoleto* (1540) has already been mentioned. Calvin's *Treatise on Relics* appeared in 1543. This was followed in 1544 by another work entitled *On the Necessity of Reforming the Church*. And finally, *The Acts of the Council of Trent with the Antidote* in 1547, in which he says about the Council: "I will waste no further time exposing their impudence. But, as all can see, they are worse than useless; any one who is wise will, in future, take no notice of their decrees and be in no doubt about it."[416] Calvin likewise called the Pope "Antichrist."[417] Nevertheless, the error of Calvin and the other Reformers was to postulate a reformation instead of a complete rejection of the Roman Catholic Church. The determinant is inadvertently stated by Schaff: "All the Reformers were born, baptized, confirmed, and educated in the historic Catholic Church. They never doubted the validity of the Catholic ordinances, and rejected the idea of re-baptism."[418]

This failure of Calvin to completely reject the Roman Catholic Church and its ordinances has adversely affected his view of the New Testament Church and its ordinances. The error of Calvin's beliefs on the role of the State in the affairs of the Church and vice versa has already been mentioned. This is even confirmed by Calvinists: "He has no concept of a separation between religion and state, or of a non-Christian magistrate, or of toleration of plural churches."[419] And although Calvin distinguished between the visible and invisible church because he believed "that Holy Scripture speaks of the church in two ways,"[420] the way he explained both terms is contrary to the Bible teaching on ecclesiology. Calvin's invisible church was "that which is actually in God's presence, into which no persons are received but those who are children of God by grace of adoption and true members of Christ by sanctification of the Holy Spirit."[421] But in this "true" church Calvin included "not only the saints presently living on earth, but all the elect from the beginning of the world."[422] Thus, Calvin made no distinction between the Old and New Testaments as far as the Church as the body of Christ is concerned. He used the concept of eternal predestination to further the idea that the "true" church was known only to God.[423] Calvin's concept of the visible church was likewise flawed. He laid down as "distinguishing marks of the church" the "preaching of the Word and the observance of the sacraments"[424] rather than an assembly of born-again believers where these things take place. He said we should call the church our "mother" because "there is no other way to enter into life unless this mother conceive us in her womb, give us birth, nourish us at her breast, and lastly, unless she keep us under her care and guidance."[425] He also further adds that "away from her bosom one cannot hope for any forgiveness of sins or any salvation, as Isaiah and Joel testify."[426] So like his defense of his system of discipline in Geneva and the execution of Servetus, Calvin's arguments are continually drawn from the Old Testament instead of the New. And as Wendel acknowledges of Calvin: "Truth compels one to admit frankly that, despite all his fidelity to the Bible, he seems to have been searching the Scriptures more frequently for texts to support a doctrine accepted in advance, than to derive doctrine from the Scriptures."[427] Calvin's debt to Augustine for his teachings on ecclesiology has been acknowledged by Calvinists.[428] And not only did Calvin seek to refute the Anabaptists of his day on their concept of the church, like Augustine, he also reproached the Donatists of old.[429]

As mentioned in the preceding section, Calvin rejected the seven sacraments of the Catholics—reducing them to just two: baptism and the Lord's Supper. However, he still considered them to be sacraments. He agreed with Augustine's definition of a sacrament but sought to "give a fuller statement" to express it "more clearly."[430] He also claimed for the sacraments "the same office as the Word of God."[431] Calvin considered the sacraments to be "aids and means to our incorporation in Jesus Christ, or, if we are already of his body, to confirm us therein more and more until he unites us wholly with himself in the life of heaven."[432] But he agreed with Augustine that the benefits of the sacraments only accrue to the "elect."[433] Because of his concept of a sacrament, Calvin's teachings on the Lord's Supper and baptism require an individual examination.

At first Calvin's most controversial doctrine was not predestination but the idea that Christ's body is spiritually and really, though not physically, present in the elements at the Lord's Supper.[434] This doctrine was a great bone of contention between the Reformers. For although they were agreed in the matter of the predestination of the "elect," they strongly differed regarding the nature of the Lord's Supper. All the Reformers rejected the transubstantiation of the Roman Catholic Mass. But Luther was not far removed in his doctrine of consubstantiation, and Calvin in his idea of a spiritual presence. Zwingli alone held to the correct view of a memorial, which view Calvin termed "false and pernicious."[435] Although Calvin's theory of the Lord's Supper is first mentioned in the original edition of his *Institutes,* he was chiefly concerned with refuting the Roman Catholic doctrine of the Mass.[436] But in the final edition of his *Institutes* in 1559, Calvin devotes a whole chapter to both the errors of the Roman Mass and what he perceives to be the scriptural doctrine of the Lord's Supper. Besides in his *Institutes,* Calvin's view of the Lord's Supper was also set forth in his several theological treatises.[437]

There are, first of all, three commendable things about Calvin's doctrine of the Lord's Supper. First is his opinion of the Roman Catholic Mass. Of the Mass, Calvin said: "In it an unbearable blasphemy and dishonor is inflicted upon Christ."[438] Secondly, he strongly denounced the adoration of the host. He called it "idolatry," and declared that "those who have devised the adoration of the Sacrament" have "dreamed it by themselves apart from Scripture, where no mention of it can be shown."[439] And thirdly, Calvin opposed the withholding of the cup. He remarked that this Catholic practice was "so foreign to God's Word."[440] But in one respect he approached the view of the Catholics, for Calvin desired the frequent administration of the Lord's Supper "at least once a week."[441] However, he was willing to settle for communion once a month.[442] Nevertheless, the authorities in Geneva dictated that it should only be celebrated four times a year: Christmas, Easter, Pentecost, and the first Sunday in September.[443]

Calvin's actual view of the Lord's Supper was, according to the Presbyterian theologian Dabney: "Not only incomprehensible, but impossible."[444] Calvin himself said:

> The signs are bread and wine, which represent for us the invisible food that we receive from the flesh and blood of Christ.[445]

> That sacred partaking of his flesh and blood, by which Christ

pours his life into us, as if it penetrated into our bones and marrow, he also testifies and seals in the Supper.[446]

Our souls are fed by the flesh and blood of Christ in the same way that bread and wine keep and sustain physical life.[447]

Now, if anyone should ask me how this takes place, I shall not be ashamed to confess that it is a secret too lofty for either my mind to comprehend or my words to declare. And, to speak more plainly, I rather experience than understand it.[448]

Calvin's doctrine of the Lord's Supper is summarized by the Reformed theologian Berkhof as:

He believes that Christ, though not bodily and locally present in the Supper, is yet present and enjoyed in His entire person, both body and blood. He emphasizes the mystical communion of believers with the entire person of the Redeemer. His representation is not entirely clear, but he seems to mean that the body and blood of Christ, though absent and locally present only in heaven, communicate a life-giving influence to the believer when he is in the act of receiving the elements. That influence, though real, is not physical but spiritual and mystical, is mediated by the Holy Spirit, and is conditioned on the act of faith by which the communicant symbolically receives the body and blood of Christ.[449]

But Dabney and Berkhof are not the only Calvinists who believe Calvin to be obscure, for Wendel comments that "whatever may be the value of the arguments that Calvin adduces to justify his particular interpretation of the Eucharist, we must acknowledge that his doctrine leaves one with many obscurities, only imperfectly masked by an exegesis that is often peculiar, and by the appeal to mystery."[450] Calvin deplores those "who define the eating of Christ's flesh and the drinking of his blood as, in one word, nothing but to believe in Christ" because it seems to him "that Christ meant to teach something more definite, and more elevated, in that noble discourse in which he commends to us the eating of his flesh."[451] Thus, Berkhof admits again: "Sometimes he seems to place too much emphasis on the literal flesh and blood."[452] Calvinists even admit that Calvin relied heavily on Augustine for his view of the Lord's Supper.[453] So as alluded to previously, Calvin's doctrine of the Lord's Supper is intrinsically connected with his concept of a sacrament, as Wendel observes: "With regard to Augustine, his influence on this point is but one aspect of his more general influence throughout the Calvinist doctrine of the sacraments."[454] And it is this influence that also affects his teaching on baptism.

Although he maintained that baptism was not essential to salvation,[455] Calvin attached a great deal of significance to the rite and often made statements that would lead one to think he believed otherwise. He devoted two chapters of his *Institutes* to the subject. According to Calvin:

> Baptism is the sign of the initiation by which we are received into the society of the church, in order that, engrafted in Christ, we may be reckoned among God's children. Now baptism was given to us by God for these ends (which I have taught to be common to all sacraments): first, to serve our faith before him; secondly, to serve our confession before men. We shall treat in order the reasons for each aspect of is institution. Baptism brings three things to our faith which we must deal with individually. The first thing that the Lord sets out for us is that baptism should be a token and proof of our cleansing; or (the better to explain what I mean) it is like a sealed document to confirm to us that all our sins are so abolished, remitted, and effaced that they can never come to his sight, be recalled, or charged against us. For he will that all who believe be baptized for the remission of sins.[456]

Calvin disparaged those "who regarded baptism as nothing but a token and mark by which we confess our religion before men."[457] He connected baptism with salvation,[458] forgiveness of sins,[459] regeneration,[460] and assurance.[461] He also claimed that baptism was not only analogous to circumcision, but "has taken the place of circumcision."[462] However, he never mentions the subject of the baptism of females.

Because of his view of the meaning of baptism, Calvin advocated the baptism of infants—even claiming that infant baptism rests "on such firm approbation of Scripture."[463] In fact, those who opposed him on the subject were "frantic spirits" and "mad beasts."[464] God "will wreak vengeance upon any man who disdains to mark his child with the symbol of the covenant."[465] Although he rejected Augustine's thesis that unbaptized children go to limbo,[466]

Calvin did say that "infants are baptized into future repentance and faith, and even though these have not yet been formed in them, the seed of both lies hidden within them by the secret working of the Spirit."[467] Besides his appeal to circumcision, Calvin chiefly employed three texts to prove infant baptism:

> **For the unbelieving husband is sanctified by the wife, and the unbelieving wife is sanctified by the husband: else were your children unclean; but now are they holy (1 Cor. 7:14).**[468]
>
> **But Jesus said, Suffer little children, and forbid them not, to come unto me: for of such is the kingdom of heaven (Mat. 19:14).**[469]
>
> **For the promise is unto you, and to your children, and to all that are afar off,** *even* **as many as the Lord our God shall call (Acts 2:39).**[470]

Yet, as Wendel says of Calvin:

> Since it was not possible for him to adduce a single New Testament passage containing a clear allusion to infant baptism, he had to be content with indirect inferences and analogies drawn from circumcision and Christ's blessing of the children. Calvin has been much reproached for the weakness of this reasoning, in such contrast to the more rigorous exegetical methods he usually employed, at least in dealing with the text of the New Testament: and he himself seems to have been aware of the defects of his exegesis upon this point.[471]

On the mode of baptism, Calvin was equally wrong.

Like his fellow Reformers, Calvin not only baptized infants, he sprinkled them. And this in spite of the fact that in his *Institutes* he admits immersion as the proper mode: "But whether the person being baptized should be wholly immersed, and whether thrice or once, whether he should only be sprinkled with poured water—these details are of no importance, but ought to be optional to churches according to the diversity of countries. The word baptize means to immerse, and it is clear that the rite of immersion was observed in the ancient churches."[472] And not only was immersion observed in the ancient churches, it was the prevailing mode in

England at the time of Calvin and continued to be so until the reign of Queen Elizabeth I (1533-1603).[473]

Regarding the greatest event in the Bible as far as God is concerned—the Millennial reign of Jesus Christ—Calvin takes the amillennial position of the Roman Catholics. But because he made statements in his commentaries that could be considered postmillennial, he is sometimes claimed by advocates of both amillennialism and postmillennialism.[474] He was completely against any concept of a literal, earthly thousand-year reign of Christ:

> But a little later there followed the Chiliasts, who limited the reign of Christ to a thousand years. Now their fiction is too childish either to need or to be worth a refutation. And the Apocalypse, from which they undoubtedly drew a pretext for their error, does not support them. For the number "one thousand" does not apply to the eternal blessedness of the church but only to the various disturbances that awaited the church, while still toiling on the earth.[475]

Luther in like manner called the earthly kingdom of Christ "a dream."[476] Since Calvin believed that Christ's kingdom began at his first advent,[477] he felt that those who believe in a literal millennium "do not realize how much reproach they are casting upon Christ and his Kingdom."[478] And even though the teaching of amillennialism is built on an allegorical interpretation of Scripture, Boettner maintains that "Calvin led the way in discarding the custom of allegorizing the Scriptures."[479]

Calvin is of course best remembered for his doctrine of predestination. Yet Calvinists are insistent that predestination was not Calvin's main focus:

> This was not Calvin's main doctrine nor was it his starting point.[480]

> Although some scholars have suggested that predestination constitutes the centre of Calvin's thought, it is clear that this is not the case.[481]

> Contrary to the contention of most historians, Calvin did not lay unique stress on the doctrine of Predestination.[482]

McGrath insists that "others have read back into his writings the particular concern within later Reformed Orthodoxy for predestination."[483] H. Henry Meeter (1886-1963) claims that "it was only when the biblical doctrine of predestination was attacked" that Calvin "felt constrained to come to its defense."[484] Bratt mentions what he perceives as the limited coverage of predestination in the editions of Calvin's *Institutes:* "The doctrine is not mentioned in the first edition of the *Institutes*. He mentions it first in the edition of 1539 and then only in passing. It assumes prominence in later editions."[485]

Other Calvinists, however, disagree with this conclusion: "In the second edition of the *Institutes,* what Calvin added to his discussions of predestination was for the most part a defense, in which the doctrine of double predestination was strongly emphasized because it was on this point that the opposition was the greatest."[486] McGrath asserts that "from the edition of 1539 onwards, it is treated as a topic of importance in its own right."[487] A contemporary of Calvin, the Dutch Roman Catholic theologian Albert Pighius (c. 1490-1542) would disagree as well. After the publication in 1539 of the second edition of Calvin's *Institutes,* Pighius wrote a response to Calvin entitled *Ten Books on Human Free Choice and Divine Grace*.[488] He saw the book published in August of 1542 but died soon afterward.[489] Nevertheless, Calvin responded to Pighius's first six books in his 1543 work *A Defense of the Sound and Orthodox Doctrine of the Bondage and Liberation of the Human Choice Against the Misrepresentations of Albert Pighius of Kampen*.[490] In 1552 Calvin finished his answer to Pighius (whom he calls a "dead dog"[491]) in his *Concerning the Eternal Predestination of God*.[492]

The fact still remains: Calvin is intrinsically connected with the doctrine of predestination. The fact that early in his ministry he did not emphasize it is immaterial. The doctrine is firmly established as one of the foundations of Calvin's mature theological thought. And like most of his other teachings, Calvinists admit that Calvin was heavily influenced by Augustine in forming his doctrine of predestination.[493] The opposition to Calvin's doctrine of predestination by Bolsec and Trolliet has already been mentioned. Another who opposed Calvin with the same arguments was Sebastian Castellio (1515-1563). His attacks on Calvin's doctrine of predestination resulted in Calvin writing yet another defense of predestination in 1558 against "a certain worthless calumniator".[494] *A Defense of the Secret Providence of God.*[495] Castellio was one of the few outspoken advocates of religious toleration at this time in history. After the death of Servetus, whom he called a "murdered innocent,"[496] Castellio wrote a treatise condemning the execution and pleading for tolerance.[497] He also wrote a work against Calvin in 1554, but it was not published until both Calvin and Castellio were long dead.[498] During Calvin's lifetime, a collection of his sermons on the election of Jacob and the reprobation of Esau was also published.[499]

Calvin's emphasis on the doctrine of predestination was the cause for much controversy. It was causing so much trouble that the ministers of the neighboring city of Bern requested of Geneva on December 7, 1551, a "cessation of discussion" of the predestination issue for the sake of "the tranquility and peace of the church."[500] Calvin's fellow reformer Bullinger even wrote to him: "Believe me, many are displeased with what you say in your *Institutes* about predestination."[501] Paul Jewett maintains that Beza "found it necessary to spend more time defending Calvin's doctrine of predestination than anything else."[502] Since it is already apparent that Calvin was a "Calvinist," a complete treatment of his doctrine of predestination will be given in chapter 7 and elsewhere when related doctrines come up.

As mentioned previously in the sections on *Calvin and Geneva* and *Calvin and Servetus,* and even more so in regards to his theology, Calvin is without excuse when it comes to departing from the Scripture on *any* subject. It is not just that Calvinists make Calvin out to be a great theologian, he is regularly lauded as one of the greatest theologians. A typical example is Warfield: "He was distinctly a Biblical theologian, or, let us say it frankly, by way of eminence *the Biblical theologian of his age.* Whither the Bible took him, thither he went: where scriptural declarations failed him, there he stopped short."[503] So whatever the customs, traditions, and prejudices of his age; whatever knowledge he had of the writings of the Church Fathers or his fellow reformers that may have influenced him; whatever bad experiences he may have had before his conversion; however he was falsely slandered, ridiculed, and misunderstood by Christians: the other side of John Calvin is not only not without blemishes, it is fraught with notable departures from the Scriptures—as acknowledged by Calvinists themselves.[504] But what of his counterpart, James Arminius?

Chapter 4
JAMES ARMINIUS

Contrary to the anomalous abundance of material on John Calvin, there is scarcely to be found anything dealing with James Arminius the man, although the appellation derived from his name is maliciously thrown about by all manner of Calvinists. The life of James Arminius parallels in many respects the life of John Calvin. And like Calvin, he was not the originator of that system which bears his name. This is admitted by the most ardent of Calvinists:

> Paradoxical as it may sound, Arminius was not the first Arminian.[1]

> The opinions denominated Arminian had been substantially taught long before Arminius appeared.[2]

Not only do Calvinists admit that Arminius was not the author of Arminianism, they likewise acknowledge that he did not teach everything contained in that system which bears his name:

> Much of what is often classed under the general name of Arminianism contains a much larger amount of error, and a much smaller amount of truth, than the writings of Arminius.[3]

> The system of soteriology which is called "Arminianism" does not entirely represent the position of James Arminius.[4]

James Nichols (1785-1861), the translator of Arminius' works, had this to say about the relation of Arminius to Arminianism:

> The truly evangelical system of religious belief which is known in modern days under the name of ARMINIANISM, has acquired that appellation, not because ARMINIUS was the sole author of it, but, . . . because he collected those scattered and

often incidental observations of the Christian Fathers, and of the early Protestant Divines, which have a collateral relation to the doctrines of General Redemption, and because he condensed and applied them in such a manner as to make them combine in one grand and harmonious scheme, in which all the attributes and perfections of the Deity are secured to him in a clearer and more obvious manner than by Calvinism.[5]

Like Calvin, Arminius is either passionately esteemed or intensely despised. The admirers of Arminius have stated:

> James Arminius was the rightful restorer of the doctrine as it flowed from the lips of the impetuous Peter, the beloved John, the sweet-spirited James, the polished Paul, and all the apostles and early Fathers of the Church.[6]

> He appeared to me to be *a man who truly feared God,* of the DEEPEST ERUDITION, *uncommonly well versed in theological controversies,* and POWERFUL IN THE SCRIPTURES.[7]

> Arminius was a pious and godly man, prudent, candid, mild and placid, and most studious to preserve the peace of the Church.[8]

> Arminius was a faithful and energetic minister of the Gospel.[9]

Besides the disparaging remarks they have already made about Arminianism, it has further been asserted by Calvinists about Arminius himself:

> An adept practitioner of deceit and underhanded tactics, like many a heretic.[10]

> His character as to integrity, candour, and fidelity to his official pledges and professions, is covered with stains which can never by any ingenuity be effaced.[11]

> No matter how clearly his views represented a marked departure from the Reformed faith, he always hid himself under the cloak of orthodoxy.[12]

Unfortunately, this negative connotation of Arminius has been accepted without reservation by most Christians.

But in spite of the attacks made on him by Calvinists for his doctrine, some Calvinists have been honest enough to admit that, in regard to his character, Arminius was above reproach:

> A man of pleasing personality, refined in manners and appearance.[13]

> A most worthy man and undoubtedly a very earnest believer.[14]

> Arminius, in regard to talents, to learning, to eloquence, and to general exemplariness of moral deportment, is undoubtedly worthy of high praise.[15]

Even the Dutch Reformed theologian Homer Hoeksema (1923-1989) acknowledges Arminius as a "brilliant scholar."[16] Custance likewise applauds his "profound learning."[17] Yet, because the only references to Arminius are usually found in a book on Calvinism, ignorance of him is rampant. This ignorance of Arminius is so pervasive that even non-Calvinists regularly misrepresent him. But the widespread ignorance that exists about Arminius is perhaps greatest among those who have demeaned him the most: Calvinists. Most Calvinists have neither read his works nor studied the age in which he lived. They have been content to perpetrate ad nauseam the caricature of the man who remains an enigma to most Christians. In keeping with the nature of the book, this brief study aims to present the other side of Arminius—his life, his theology—but first, the age in which he lived.

The Age of Arminius

By the time Arminius was born, the Reformation was already firmly established in Germany and Switzerland. Such was not the case, however, in the Netherlands, the land of Arminius. The Reformation in the Netherlands coincided with its liberation from Spanish domination and the rise of the Catholic Counter-Reformation. The Netherlands, often referred to as the Low countries or simply Holland, consisted at this time in history of the modern Benelux countries of Belgium, the Netherlands, and Luxembourg. When the Hapsburg emperor of the Holy Roman Empire, Charles V, abdicated in 1555, control of the seventeen provinces of the Netherlands was given to his son, Philip II

(1527-1598), the king of Spain (1556-1598). During the reign of Charles V, the power of the Catholic Church was used to try to stamp out the ever increasing threat of "Protestantism." Edicts were issued against Lutherans and Anabaptists, as well as their writings, and many were burned alive.[18] An edict of 1550 commanded death by fire to the possessor of "any book or writing made by Luther, Oecolampadius, Zwingli, Bucer, or Calvin.[19] With renewed vigor, Philip pursued the same policies of his father until he left the Netherlands in 1559 for Spain, never to return.[20] Philip's half-sister, Margaret (1522-1586), was then appointed regent in his absence and instructed to continue his policies.

The next twenty years were marked by continual wars. Dissent was growing, however, against the tyranny of the Papists, and some toleration was extended.[21] Nevertheless, whatever possibilities of compromise that existed were shattered in 1576 when enraged rioters ransacked Catholic churches and destroyed all the images. After outbreaks of this iconoclasm spread, Philip sent the Duke of Alva (1507-1582), with thousands of Spanish Catholic troops, to subdue the Netherlands.[22] A council was then established to suppress heresy and sedition. This resulted in still more executions, and, as a contemporary historian described it:

> The gallows, the wheel, stakes, trees along the highways, were laden with carcasses or limbs of those who had been hanged, beheaded, or roasted; so that the air which God made for the respiration of the living, was now become the common grave or habitation of the dead.[23]

But under the leadership of William of Orange (1533-1584), the leaders of the Protestant and Catholic provinces signed an agreement (the Pacification of Ghent) to unite politically in order to repel the Spaniards.[24] This unstable union, however, was not to last long. In early January of 1579, the Catholic provinces formed a league at Arras to attempt a reconciliation with Spain.[25] The northern provinces, later the same month, formed a similar league at Utrecht, but to maintain their independence from Spain.[26] In July of 1581, the northern provinces declared their independence from Spain in the Act of Abjuration and went on to become a major European power. Meanwhile, the southern region remained under the yoke of Rome. This division precipitated the modern countries of the Netherlands in the north and Belgium in the south.

It goes without saying that the reform movements that were spreading across Europe did not delight the Roman Catholic Church. As a consequence, various measures were taken to combat the new "heresies" that were destroying the Church's grip on the people of Europe. And although there were attempts at reform in the Catholic Church that preceded the Reformation, these efforts became increasingly positive in the sixteenth century, culminating in what is known as the Counter-Reformation.

One of the most significant events in the history of Roman Catholicism in the sixteenth century is the founding of the Society of Jesus (the Jesuits) by Ignatius Loyola. After gathering a band of followers in 1534, Loyola was ordained to the priesthood in Venice in 1537, and then traveled to Rome where he met with Pope Paul III (1468-1549). In 1540 the Pope formally recognized Loyola's new society. The Jesuits were to be a holy militia, absolutely obedient to the Church and its hierarchy, and wholly dedicated to spreading the one, holy, apostolic, catholic Faith.[27] Education was the chief means used by the Jesuits for re-Catholicization.[28] Thus, in this country we presently have Georgetown, Loyola University, and other Jesuit schools.

Soon after the rise of the Jesuits, the most famous council in the history of Christianity was called for by Pope Paul III—the Council of Trent. The proceedings of this council, which formally convened on December 13, 1545, were held under three popes, during three periods of time, in twenty-five sessions, spread over eighteen years.[28] And although it convened at Trent, in Austria, the Council was dominated by the Italians.[30] At the Council of Trent, the traditional teachings of the Roman Catholic Church were reaffirmed and its opposition to Protestantism made manifest. The Apocrypha was accepted as canonical, tradition was made equal with Scripture, the Latin Vulgate was proclaimed the only authoritative Bible, and the authority of the Church to interpret the Scripture was maintained.[31] Of the decrees of the Council of Trent, the longest is that on Justification. Consisting of sixteen chapters and thirty-three canons, it expressly condemns the teaching of Luther and the Reformers. The decrees of the Council of Trent, which anathematize every non-Catholic in the world, have never been repudiated by the Catholic Church. The Council is even mentioned in the latest edition of the *Catechism of the Catholic Church* (1994).

Two other measures employed by the Roman Catholic Church

in the sixteenth century to combat "heresy" were the Index and the Inquisition. The prohibition and burning of writings deemed to be heretical was nothing new to the Church of Rome. After the invention of printing, however, this task was made much more difficult, especially with the flood of literature that appeared espousing Reformation doctrines and assailing Catholicism. The formidable task of suppressing heretical literature was taken up by Pope Paul IV (1476-1559) in 1559. His *Index of Prohibited Books* condemned all vernacular translations of the Bible as well as the works of Erasmus.[32] After the Council of Trent, Pope Pius IV (1499-1565) published a new index that absolutely prohibited the writings of the Reformers Zwingli, Luther, and Calvin.[33] The other tool employed by the Roman Church was the Inquisition. It likewise was nothing new, and most recently had been employed in Spain under the direction of the infamous Torquemada. The Papal Inquisition was reorganized by Pope Paul III in 1542 as The Congregation of the Holy Office.[34] With relentless zeal, the Papists sought to stamp out Protestant "heretics."

By the time Arminius began to minister in his native land, the established church was the Reformed Church. However, such was not always the case: Calvinism was actually the last reform movement to be established in the Netherlands. And furthermore, the reform movements in the Netherlands differ considerably from those in Germany and Switzerland. The Reformation in the Netherlands did not have an outstanding leader like Luther, Zwingli, or Calvin. It was not the result of one sect or faction, nor was it established by political means. But like the rest of Europe, and even more so in the case of the Netherlands, the Reformation was the result of a variety of factors.

Although the writings of Luther were soon circulating in the Low Countries, and many of its earliest preachers were followers of the German Reformer,[35] other factors predating the sixteenth century were also responsible for the Dutch Reformation. The Brethren of the Common Life, founded by Gerard Groot (1340-1384) in 1378, were not only known for their educational efforts, but for their emphasis on biblical studies and vernacular versions of the Scriptures.[36] There was not only a general knowledge of the Latin Vulgate among the people, but numerous translations of portions of the Bible into Dutch as well.[37] The emergence of Dutch humanism, which had a tremendous influence over education and culture, was also a factor in that it nurtured classical scholarship, and ultimately, New Testament studies.[38]

The early part of the sixteenth century in the Netherlands saw the rise to prominence of the Dutch humanist Erasmus of Rotterdam. Although maligned by Calvinists for opposing Luther on the question of free will, Erasmus not only published the first Greek New Testament in 1516, but criticized the Catholic Church as well in his celebrated work *The Praise of Folly*.[39] Numerous new translations of the Bible soon began to appear, and later, the writings of other Reformers besides Luther.[40] That the reform movements in the Netherlands did not follow the work of one man can be seen in the diverse groups that emerged during the sixteenth century. The Sacramentarians, who opposed both the Catholics and the Lutherans, denied the physical presence of Christ's body in the elements of communion.[41] The Anabaptists, and especially Menno Simons (1496-1561), from whom the Mennonites are named, were very prominent in the Netherlands. And just like in Switzerland, they were mercilessly persecuted for their views on baptism.[42] There are also the early Dutch Reformed leaders who were not necessarily Calvinistic. Before Arminius was even born, Anastasius Veluanus (1520-1570), in his book *The Layman's Guide,* which was circulated all over the Netherlands, explicitly rejected the predestination of the Calvinists.[43] Thus, from the very beginning of the Dutch Reformation, there were two types of "Reformed" Christians in the Netherlands.[44]

Although the introduction of Calvinism into the Netherlands can be traced back to the mid 1540s,[45] the first Calvinist congregations were actually formed in exile.[46] The writings of Calvin were widely circulated and his *Institutes* were translated into Dutch in 1560.[47] The strength of the Reformed Church in the Netherlands was its rapid organization. The earliest synod was held at Turcoing in 1563 followed by several more at Antwerp.[48] The development of a strong national church can be traced to the Synod of Emden in 1571. Here a plan of church government was approved, and rules were enacted to regulate funerals, marriage, clothing, adultery, drunkenness, and a host of other subjects.[49] It was also here that two important documents were officially adopted that were to play an important role in the subsequent history of the Reformed Church in the Netherlands: the Heidelberg Catechism and Belgic Confession of Faith.

The Heidelberg Catechism, named after the city of its birth in Germany, was drawn up by Zacharias Ursinus (1534-1583) and Caspar Olevianus (1536-1587), under commission from the elector Friedrich III of the Palatinate, and published in 1563.[50] Although originally written in German, it was soon afterward translated into Dutch and used by the Dutch Protestants. The Belgic Confession, written in what is now known as Belgium, was the work of Guido de Bres (1523-1567), the "Reformer of the Netherlands."[51] Written in French, it was intended, like Calvin's original *Institutes*, to be an apology for the persecuted French Protestants.[52] After its publication in 1561, it too was soon translated into Dutch for use by the Dutch Protestants. But as acknowledged by the Calvinists themselves, acceptance of these and any other creeds "was achieved by religious diplomacy rather than by the majority consent of the Calvinistic churches."[53]

The Dutch Calvinists, although in the minority, were leaders in the revolt against the Spanish. William of Orange even publically proclaimed himself a Calvinist in 1573.[54] Therefore, when the northern provinces attained independence in 1581, the Reformed Faith was made the official state religion.[55] Not only was all church property allotted to the Reformed, the funds to maintain it were provided by the state.[56] All ministers were subject to approval by the civil authorities.[57] The former Calvin College professor, Walter Lagerwey (b. 1918), admits that although "Calvinism was able to expand because of its close ties with the government," "this relationship was also detrimental and posed serious problems for the churches."[58] The most tenacious of Calvinists likewise acknowledge that the churches were financed and controlled by the government.[59] Thus, the twin evils of a denominational hierarchy and a Church-State setup were with the Dutch Reformed Church from the very beginning.

The tremendous changes that took place in the ecclesiastical history of the Netherlands during the sixteenth century were over by the time the ministry of Arminius began in 1587. However, new controversies would soon arise, but in the Reformed Church itself. And Arminius was right in the middle of them.

The Life of Arminius

James Arminius was a Dutchman who lived most of his life in his native Holland. He was born at Oudewater, on October 10,

1560, and died just forty-nine years later at Leiden on October 19, 1609.[60] As this would only make him four years old when Calvin died in 1564, it is clearly evident that Calvin and Arminius never debated the issue of Calvinism like it is commonly assumed. He was the third and youngest child of a smith whom he never knew, for Arminius' father died when he was an infant, which was just the opposite of Calvin, whose mother died. While a university student, Arminius Latinized his original Dutch name, usually given as Jacob Harmenszoon, in common imitation of other learned men.[61] He denominated himself Arminius, the name of the famous Germanic chieftain who resisted the Romans early in the first century.[62]

After the death of his father, Arminius was appointed a legal guardian, Theodorus Aemilius (d. 1574), a Protestant-leaning priest and cousin of his mother.[63] Aemilius took young James into his home at Utrecht and had him trained in Latin, Greek, and theology.[64] Upon the death of Aemilius when Arminius was fourteen, one more cousin of his mother, Rudolphus Snellias (1547-1613), resumed the role of guardian over Arminius.[65] Snellias, a linguist and mathematician from the University of Marburg in Germany, enrolled Arminius in the university in 1575.[66] It was the Reformer Philip Melanchthon who was instrumental in the founding of Marburg as the first Protestant university in 1527.[67]

Tragedy struck in 1575, interrupting the studies of the young Arminius. Spanish troops invaded Oudewater and massacred the town—killing his entire family, and capturing and hanging the Protestant minister. Oudewater had previously sided with the Protestant William of Orange resulting in a continual religious controversy that culminated in the said invasion. Upon hearing the news, Arminius, after two weeks of bitter lamentation, returned to his hometown to be confronted with death and destruction.[68] He swiftly journeyed back to Marburg, and after a short time there, returned by way of Rotterdam to his native land and enrolled in the new university at Leiden in 1576, where he was to spend the next five years. Oudewater, meanwhile, was not liberated from its Spanish occupation until December of 1576.

At the University of Leiden, a Protestant school founded in 1575 by William of Orange, Arminius distinguished himself above the rest of his classmates. His companion, Peter Bertius (c. 1564-1629), who would later deliver a funeral oration upon the death of Arminius, related that "if any of us had a particular theme or an essay to compose, or a speech to recite, the first step which we took in it, was, to ask for Arminius. If any friendly discussion arose among us, the decision of which required the sound judgement of a Palaemon [a Greek god of the sea], we went in search of Arminius, who was always consulted."[69] A professor at the university urged the students to imitate the example of Arminius and likewise complemented him for "the endowments of his genius, and his proficiency in learning and virtue."[70] After finishing his studies at Leiden, which included acquiring a competent knowledge of Hebrew,[71] Arminius accepted a grant from the Merchants' Gild of Amsterdam to further his theological studies at Geneva.[72] The grant came from a fund formerly used for "unnecessary superstition, drunkenness, and unbecoming carousing" when the guild members feasted after attending a special high mass, but, after the city became Protestant, now used for "godly and worthy purposes."[73] In return for the financial benefits, Arminius signed an agreement to exercise his ministry in the Reformed church at Amsterdam.[74]

Since its founding in 1559, the academy at Geneva had attracted a number of Dutch ministerial students. Arminius matriculated at Geneva on January 1, 1582, during the course of lectures on the Book of Romans by the Reformed patriarch, Theodore Beza.[75] Like his stay at the University of Marburg, Arminius' residence at Geneva was short lived. However, this time the *tragedy* was the offense taken by some to his private lectures which opposed their system of logic. Arminius followed the system of Peter Ramus (1515-1572), a noted critic of Aristotle (384-322).[76] Arminius then removed to the University of Basel in the summer of 1583.[77] The faculty at Basel esteemed him so highly that they offered to promote him to doctor of theology, but Arminius refused on the grounds of his youth.[78] The next year saw him return to Geneva to resume his studies. Arminius left Geneva in 1586 and visited the Italian cities of Padua and Rome. It was the occasion of this trip to Rome that the enemies of Arminius charged him with consorting with the Catholics.[79] Yet Arminius himself remarked of his trip that it was beneficial to him, for he saw at Rome *"'the mystery of iniquity'* in a more foul, ugly, and detestable form than his imagination could ever have conceived."[80] After returning briefly to Geneva, Arminius reported to Amsterdam in the fall of 1587, his training for the ministry now completed.

Amsterdam was the center of Dutch commercial life. Like most European cities, it was solidly Roman Catholic at the beginning of the sixteenth century. And although it had in it various dissenters, it was not until 1578 that the religious conflicts that had raged since the beginning of the century were settled—in favor of the Protestants. Arminius soon passed examinations to be admitted as a "preacher on trial," and was formally ordained on August 27, 1588.[81] He was the first native Hollander to minister in the Reformed church in Amsterdam.[82] The aforementioned Peter Bertius relates that "as soon as he was seen in the pulpit, it is impossible to describe the extraordinary grace and favour which he obtained from men of all ranks."[83] The other ministers of the city likewise paid homage to his erudition.[84] After serving as a pastor for two years, Arminius married the daughter of a prominent merchant and subsequently fathered twelve children—three dying in infancy. He remained in Amsterdam a total of fifteen years, until 1603, performing the usual pastoral duties and bearing many official responsibilities on behalf of the ministers of Amsterdam, serving as a secretary, treasurer, delegate, president, and representative.[85]

Meanwhile, back at the University of Leiden, the plague had taken the famed divinity professor, Franciscus Junius (1545-1602), and Arminius was chosen to succeed him.[86] He moved to Leiden in June of 1603, his large family necessitating two houses near the university. In conjunction with this appointment, Arminius received his doctor of theology degree, defending theses on the nature of God.[87] His disputation then became his first published work, for although he wrote extensively while in Amsterdam (chiefly theological treatises), nothing was published during that time.[88] And though Arminius likewise wrote extensively during his years at Leiden, most of his works were not published until after his death.[89] The currently available three-volume set containing most of the works of Arminius is a reprint of the nineteenth-century edition of James and William Nichols.[90] Sickness followed Arminius to Leiden and he became increasingly ill and was often confined to bed.[91] Controversy likewise daunted him, and his enemies were relentless.[92] He suffered numerous personal attacks and engaged in seemingly endless theological controversies over Calvinism—enduring them to the end—and died in his own home in the presence of his friends and family.

The Theology of Arminius

Although modern Calvinistic writers give the impression that Arminius was nothing less than a rank heretic, a cursory glance at his writings is all it takes to see that this is simply not the case, for Arminius was just as orthodox on the cardinal doctrines of the Christian Faith as any Calvinist, ancient or modern. And though the writings of Arminius are obtainable, they are seldom if ever read by anyone—especially Calvinists. But it is to his works that one must go to see his theology—not to any preacher, writer, or theologian, be they Calvinist or Arminian. One Calvinist even admits that "the theology of Jacob Arminius has been neglected both by his admirers and by his detractors."[93] The doctrinal sentiments of Arminius regarding Calvinism will be explored during the doctrinal analysis of the particular points of Calvinism, but regarding the fundamentals of the Christian Faith, Arminius' doctrinal beliefs are considered below.

Regarding the most important thing about what a man believes—the inspiration and authority of Scripture—Arminius was perfectly orthodox. He stated about the Bible:

> The authority of the word of God, which is comprised in the Scriptures of the Old and New Testament, lies both in the veracity of the whole narration, and of all the declarations, whether they be those about things past, about things present, or about those which are to come; and in the power of the commands and prohibitions, which are contained in the Divine word. Both of these kinds of authority can depend on no other than on God, who is the principal Author of this word; both because he is Truth without suspicion of falsehood, and because he is of Power invincible. On this account, the knowledge alone that this word is Divine, is obligatory on our belief and obedience; and so strongly is it binding, that this obligation can be augmented by no external authority.[94]

Arminius considered the Bible infallible,[95] and accepted as canonical all sixty-six books.[96] He always carried his New Testament with him,[97] and stated that of the perusal of the Holy Scriptures: "I earnestly inculcate more than any other person, as the whole university as well as the consciences of my colleagues will testify."[98] He regarded as "foolish and blasphemous" the Catholic claim that the Scriptures "are not authentic except by the authority of the Church."[99] And he likewise considered himself "as by no means bound to adopt all the private interpretations of the Reformed."[100] Therefore, it is not surprising that the writings of Arminius are saturated with references to Scripture.

Like Calvin and the other Reformers, Arminius was strongly anti-Catholic, classifying himself beside ones who said the Pope was "the adulterer and pimp of the Church, the false prophet, the destroyer and subverter of the Church, the enemy of God and the Antichrist."[101] He was called "a consummate and most successful assailant of the Papists."[102] Arminius never hesitated to describe in no uncertain terms his opinion of the Pope and those who follow him. He wrote in his theses *On Idolatry* that "the Roman Pontiff is himself an idol: And that they who esteem him as the personage that he and his followers boastingly depict him to be, and who present to him the honour which he demands, by those very acts shew themselves to be idolaters."[103] He also declared that "a reform must not be expected from any one who is elevated to the Roman Pontificates," and that "the Pope shall be destroyed at the glorious advent of Christ."[104] After some of his enemies accused him of "the defection of many persons to Popery,"[105] Arminius issued in writing his strongest denunciation of the Papacy:

> I openly declare, that I do not own the Roman Pontiff to be a member of Christ's body; but I account him an enemy, a traitor, a sacrilegious and blasphemous man, a tyrant, and a violent usurper of most unjust domination over the Church, the man of sin, the son of perdition, that most notorious outlaw.[106]

Regarding the Catholic Mass, Arminius affirmed that "it is impious, for any expiatory sacrifice now to be offered by men for the living and the dead."[107] He regarded the Mass as opposed to "the nature, truth and excellence of the sacrifice of Christ."[108] And finally, he advocated stern measures against Popery: "While all pious teachers ought most heartily to desire the destruction of Popery, as they would that of the kingdom of Antichrist, they ought with the greatest zeal to engage in the attempt, and, as far as it is within their power, to make the most efficient preparations for its overthrow."[109] The charge that Arminius had Catholic sympathies is obviously groundless.

On the nature and attributes of the members of the Godhead,

Arminius is again completely orthodox. He believed in the "Holy Trinity,"[110] taught that God created "all things out of nothing,"[111] and maintained that "God is capable of every thing which is possible."[112] Arminius expounded upon the infinity, immensity, impassibility, immutability, omnipresence, unity, essence, and eternity of God—just like any Calvinistic theologian.[113] The opinions of Arminius concerning the Lord Jesus Christ are likewise consonant with the Bible and Calvinistic authorities. He believed Christ was eternal,[114] and described him as "the Son of God and the Son of man; consisting of two natures, the divine and the human, inseparably united without mixture or confusion."[115] He identified him as the Jehovah of the Old Testament,[116] who became a man,[117] and was crucified for us.[118] Arminius believed in the literal death, burial, resurrection, and ascension of Christ.[119] He regarded the Atonement of Christ as "single, expiatory, perfect, and of infinite value."[120] On the Holy Spirit, Arminius maintained that the Spirit was "of the same Divinity with God the Father and the Son."[121] It is certainly apparent that Arminius was an orthodox Trinitarian.

On the fall and depravity of man, Arminius was just as orthodox as the most radical Calvinist. He believed in the complete ruin of man because of the sin of Adam. Because of this transgression: "Man fell under the displeasure and the wrath of God, rendered himself subject to a double death, and deserving to be deprived of the primeval righteousness and holiness in which a great part of the image of God consisted."[122] This condemnation is "common to the entire race and to all their posterity," for "whatever punishment was brought down upon our first parents, has likewise pervaded and yet pursues all their posterity: So that all men 'are by nature the children of wrath,' (Ephes. ii, 3,) obnoxious to condemnation, and to temporal as well as to eternal death."[123] Without being liberated by Jesus Christ, Arminius insisted that man "would remain oppressed for ever."[124] He further characterized man as hopelessly lost:

> In his *lapsed and sinful state,* man is not capable, of and by himself, either to think, to will, or to do that which is really good; but it is necessary for him to be regenerated and renewed in his intellect, affections or will, and in all his powers, by God in Christ through the Holy Spirit, that he may be qualified rightly to understand, esteem, consider, will, and perform whatever is truly good.[125]

Thus, Arminius described man's present condition in language that any Calvinist could agree with.

Because he concluded that man was in a lost, sinful condition, Arminius ascribed salvation entirely to God through Christ: "I believe that sinners are accounted righteous solely by the obedience of Christ; and that the righteousness of Christ is the only meritorious cause on account of which God pardons the sins of believers and reckons them as righteous as if they had perfectly fulfilled the law."[126] He described the Reformation doctrine of justification by faith with the vocabulary befitting Martin Luther:

> It is a Justification by which a man, who is a sinner, yet a believer, being placed before the throne of grace which is erected in Christ Jesus the Propitiation, is accounted and pronounced by God, the just and merciful Judge, righteous and worthy of the reward of righteousness, not in himself but in Christ, of grace, according to the gospel, to the praise of the righteousness and grace of God, and to the salvation of the justified person himself.[127]

Arminius even offered to subscribe to Calvin's statements on justification as found in his *Institutes*:

> My opinion is not so widely different from his as to prevent me from employing the signature of my own hand in subscribing to those things which he has delivered on this subject, in the Third Book of his *Institutes*; this I am prepared to do at any time, and to give them my full approval.[128]

He likewise characterized the doctrine of sanctification:

> It is a gracious act of God, by which He purifies man who is a sinner, and yet a believer, from the darkness of ignorance, from indwelling sin and from its lusts or desires, and imbues him with the Spirit of knowledge, righteousness and holiness; that, being separated from the life of the world and made conformable to God, man may live the life of God, to the praise of the righteousness and of the glorious grace of God, and to his won salvation.[129]

And regarding the security of the believer, the sentiments of Arminius were exactly like those of the Calvinists of his day. He even argued that "at no period have I asserted 'that believers do finally decline or fall away from faith or salvation.'"[130] Arminius also believed that one could have assurance of salvation: "With regard to the certainty of salvation, my opinion is, that it is possible for him who believes in Jesus Christ to be certain and persuaded, and, *if his heart condemn him not,* he is now in reality assured, *that he is a Son of God, and stands in the grace of Jesus Christ.*"[131] The doctrinal sentiments of Arminius regarding the salvation of a sinner are consonant with those of any Calvinist.

On some other matters, Arminius was like his fellow Reformed believers. He held to the baptism of infants by sprinkling—just like Calvin and the Reformed churches today.[132] He was also opposed to the Anabaptists, and disputed with some of them in their homes.[133] In 1600 Arminius was even asked to write "a short refutation of all the errors of the Anabaptists."[134] However, by 1605 the refutation was still not forthcoming, as Arminius was too busy.[135] But even though he advocated the Reformed Church-State setup, and contended with those outside of the Reformed Church, Arminius was known for his tolerance, and there is no record of any persecution practiced against "heretics."

Although Arminius believed he was at liberty to expound the word of God according to the dictates of his conscience, he was always very careful in what he taught and sought to avoid controversy and schism. During a debate with Petrus Plancius (1552-1622), Arminius declared that "he always exercised extreme caution in the doctrines which he taught, lest any of them might be perverted to root up the foundations of the Christian Faith."[136] He clearly stated the aim of his Christian life:

> With regard to Ambition, I possess it not, except that honourable kind which impels me to this service,—to inquire with all earnestness in the Holy Scriptures for Divine Truth, and mildly and without contradiction to declare it when found, without prescribing it to any one, or labouring to extort consent, much less through a desire to "have dominion over the faith of others," but rather for the purpose of my winning some souls for Christ, that I may be a sweet savour to Him, and may obtain an approved reputation in the church of the Saints.[137]

Even in his will Arminius maintained this position and exalted the Scripture, as this extract from his will shows:

Above all, I commend my soul, on its departure out of the body, into the hands of God, who is its Creator and faithful Saviour; before whom also I testify, that I have walked with simplicity and sincerity, and *"in all good conscience,"* in my office and vocation; and that I have guarded with the greatest solicitude and care, against advancing or teaching any thing, which, after a diligent search into the Scriptures, I had not found exactly to agree with those sacred records; and that all the doctrines advanced by me, have been such as might conduce to the propagation and increase of the truth of the Christian Religion, of the true worship of God, of general piety, and of a holy conversation among men,—and such as might contribute, according to the word of God, to a state of tranquility and peace well befitting the Christian name; and that from these benefits I have excluded the Papacy, with which no unity of faith, no bond of piety or of Christian peace can be preserved.[138]

Arminius deserves to be classified as an orthodox Dutch Reformed theologian.[139] He was a native, born at Oudewater, and was trained for the ministry at Leiden. He pastored at Amsterdam and then trained ministers at Leiden. He knew no other church but the Dutch Reformed Church, subscribing to its creeds, and defending it against all others. Even after this brief study of the theology of Arminius, the words of Bertius, uttered at the close of his funeral oration upon the death of Arminius, ring clear: "There lived in Holland a man whom they who did not know could not sufficiently esteem, whom they who did not esteem had never sufficiently known."[140] His theology was orthodox, but unlike Calvin, he exercised tolerance toward those whom he disagreed with. In the words of the famed lawyer Hugo Grotius (1583-1645): "Condemned by others, he condemned none."[141]

Calvin and Arminius

It would seem on the surface that no two men could be more dissimilar than Calvin and Arminius. But the two figureheads of opposing systems of theology not only parallel each other in many ways, there is a direct connection between them. Both were plagued by sickness and died in the prime of their ministry, Calvin at fifty-four and Arminius at forty-nine. Both were enveloped in controversy throughout their ministries. Both excelled in their educational attainments and had the benefit of attending several of the leading universities. Both exercised a tremendous influence over their followers. Nevertheless, there are some notable differences between the two. Arminius wrote no commentaries nor a formal systematic theology like Calvin's *Institutes*. His writings, and even his extant personal letters, are all theological in nature.[142] The greatest difference is perhaps their upbringing—not the fact that Arminius was Dutch and Calvin French—but that the influences on Arminius were decidedly Protestant.

Although they never knew each other, Arminius knew of Calvin and had a direct connection with him. It is to be remembered that the academy in Geneva where Arminius received his theological training was the very school founded by Calvin. Arminius studied under Beza, the successor of Calvin. Beza even wrote to Amsterdam an appeal for their continued financial support of Arminius:

> To sum up all, then, in a few words: let it be known to you that from the time Arminius returned to us from Basel, his life and learning both have so approved themselves to us, that we hope the best of him in every respect, if he steadily persist in the same course, which, by the blessing of God, we doubt not he will; for, among other endowments, God has gifted him with an apt intellect both as respects the apprehension and the discrimination of things. If this henceforward be regulated by piety, which he appears assiduously to cultivate, it cannot but happen that this power of intellect, when consolidated by mature age and experience, will be productive of the richest fruits. Such is our opinion of Arminius—a young man, unquestionably, so far as we are able to judge, most worthy of your kindness and liberality.[143]

And although the works of Arminius are never read by modern-day Calvinists, Arminius not only advocated that Calvin's *Institutes* be read,[144] he offered, as we have seen, to subscribe to Calvin's doctrinal sentiments as found in them.[145] And after the Scriptures themselves, Arminius highly recommended Calvin's commentaries: "I exhort them to read the commentaries of Calvin, on whom I bestow higher praise than Helmichius [a Dutch theologian (1551-1608)] ever did, as he confessed to me himself. For I tell them, that his commentaries ought to be held in greater estimation, than all that is delivered to us in the writings of the Ancient

Christian Fathers: So that, in a certain eminent Spirit of Prophecy, I give the preeminence to him beyond most others, indeed beyond them all."[146]

Calvinism and Arminius

The connection between Calvin and Arminius naturally leads to the question of what the opinions of Arminius were regarding Calvinism. Obviously, he was opposed to it, or any system of theology contrary to Calvinism would not be called Arminianism. It has been commonly maintained that Arminius was enamored with Beza while at Geneva and fully accepted his doctrine of predestination until, upon further study a few years later, he repudiated it.[147] But as this is an oversimplification at best, it deserves further examination before examining the disputes that Arminius had over the doctrines of Calvinism.

Soon after entering the ministry at Amsterdam, Arminius was embroiled in controversy over the predestination issue that would only later relent with his death. In 1578, two ministers from Delft, Arent Corneliszoon (1547-1605) and Reynier Donteklok (c. 1545-c. 1611), had debated Calvinism with the Dutch humanist and Secretary of State Dirck Coornhert (1522-1590).[148] Coornhert, who had earlier had a dispute with Calvin that resulted in Calvin writing *Response to a Certain Hollander* in 1562,[149] believed that Calvinism "represented God as the author of sin."[150] He then wrote *Responses to Arguments of Beza and Calvin*.[151] This was followed in 1589 by a work authored by Corneliszoon and Donteklok entitled *An Answer to Some of the Arguments Adduced by Beza and Calvin; From a Treatise Concerning Predestination, on the Ninth Chapter of the Epistle to the Romans*.[152] Arminius was asked by the ministers of Amsterdam to refute Coornhert, but he was instead persuaded by Martinus Lydius (c. 1539-1601), a former pastor in Amsterdam, to refute the book by the two Delft ministers.[153] It is supposedly during his preparation to refute Corneliszoon and Donteklok that Arminius underwent a theological transformation and "became a convert to the very opinions which he had been requested to combat and refute."[154] Although this is sometimes reported accurately,[155] the two requests of Arminius have often been conflated to Arminius rejecting Calvinism while seeking to answer Coornhert.[156] Nevertheless, the story of his transformation from Calvinism to "Arminianism" is also sometimes just mentioned as a consequence of his studies.[157] As to whether Arminius was ever in *complete* agreement with the Calvinism of Beza there is no way of knowing. He did write to a friend at Basel in 1591 that "there is a lot of controversy among us about predestination, original sin, and free will,"[158] but he never elaborated further. The only time Arminius is recorded as changing his views is in a letter written in 1608, but as to what these old or new opinions were remains a mystery: "Neither am I ashamed to have occasionally forsaken some sentiments which had been instilled by my own masters, since it appears to me that I can prove by the most forcible arguments that such a change has been made for the better."[159] So regardless of how it came about, the fact is that Arminius was now publically on record as being opposed to the established Calvinism of the Reformed Church.

Arminius had four significant disputes over Calvinism during his ministry—three while in Amsterdam and one in Leiden. It is from three of these that Arminius would write some of his major works. The first contention was with his fellow-minister Petrus Plancius. In addition to serving as a minister in Amsterdam, Plancius was skilled in cartography, astronomy, and navigation.[160] Because of his achievements in these areas, he played an important role in Dutch exploration and trade.[161] However, he was also a Calvinist: a zealous Calvinist, and one of the first to propagate Calvin's doctrines in the Dutch Reformed Church.[162] Plancius opposed Arminius throughout his pastorate in Amsterdam and his professorship in Leiden, and continued to assail him even after his death.[163] The next controversy over Calvinism was with the aforementioned Franciscus Junius, whom Arminius replaced as divinity professor at Leiden. Junius carried on a correspondence with him concerning predestination, and after the death of Arminius, the material was published as *Friendly Conference of James Arminius with Francis Junius about Predestination Carried on by Means of Letters*.[164] The last argument over Calvinism while he was still at Amsterdam was with the Cambridge professor William Perkins (1558-1602). Perkins, in reply to an earlier work against predestination, penned a work entitled *On the Mode and Order of Predestination, and on the Amplitude of Divine Grace*. After purchasing the book, Arminius wrote to Perkins: "I thought I perceived some passages of yours which deserved examination by the rule of truth. Wherefore I deemed that it would not be amiss if I should institute a calm conference with you respecting that little book of yours."[165] Although Perkins died before Arminius could complete his reply, it resulted in the publication of *Examination of Perkins' Pamphlet on the Order and Mode of Predestination,* but not until after the death of Arminius.[166] Upon his removal to Leiden, Arminius was immediately opposed by Franciscus Gomarus (1563-1641), one of the professors. Gomarus first tried to prevent Arminius from joining the faculty and then contended with him over predestination right up until his untimely death.[167] He was such a extreme Calvinist that the Calvinists in Holland were later called Gomarists.[168] The controversy between Arminius and Gomarus became so heated that there were disputes among both the theology students and the textile workers.[169] From this continual dispute came the work *Examination of The Theses of Dr. Francis Gomarus Respecting Predestination* and the *Declaration of Sentiments,* which was delivered by Arminius in 1608 before the States of Holland at The Hague.[170] While engaged in disputes with these men over the subject of predestination, Arminius also had to defend himself from some frivolous charges that call for further study.

Because he opposed their system of doctrine, the Calvinists impunged Arminius with charges of Roman Catholicism, Socinianism, and Pelagianism. The trite association with Catholicism was made because since the Catholics rejected the Reformed view of predestination, anyone else who did so must have Catholic sympathies.[171] Another heresy that Arminius was charged with is Socinianism.[172] Arising during the lifetime of Arminius, this movement was named after Laelius Socinus (1525-1562) and his nephew, Faustus Socinus (1539-1604). Their doctrine was that of Unitarianism: rejection of the Trinity and a denial of the true nature of the Atonement.[173] Needless to say, the Socinians rejected predestination, which is why Arminius is classified with them. But perhaps the most injurious association, and one that is still made today,[174] is to that of Pelagianism. This was a favorite charge of the enemies of Arminius,[175] but one which he vehemently repudiated.[176] Arminius clearly recognized in his day this incessant tactic still employed by Calvinists to impugn any detractors from Calvinism: "If any contradiction be offered to this doctrine, God is necessarily deprived of the glory of his grace, and then the merit of salvation is attributed to the free-will of man and to his own powers and strength,—which ascription savours of Pelagianism."[177] It is interesting to note, although Calvinists never mention it, that in 1549 Calvin was also forced to defend himself from charges of Pelagianism.[178]

Besides being unjustly associated with heretics who likewise rejected Calvinism, Arminius was accused of departing from the creeds accepted by the Reformed churches: the Heidelberg Catechism and the Belgic Confession.[179] To the charge that he taught contrary to the accepted creeds, Arminius responded with vigor. He stated on more than one occasion that he "taught and wished to teach nothing that was in any wise repugnant" to the official Confession and Catechism.[180] Yet, because of his high opinion of Scripture, Arminius never put the established creeds above the word of God: "I confidently declare, that I have never taught any thing, either in the Church or in the University, which contravenes *the Sacred Writings,* that ought to be with us the sole rule of thinking and of speaking, or which is opposed to *the Dutch Confession of Faith,* or to the *Heidelberg Catechism.*"[181] In advocating a national synod to examine the Confession and Catechism, Arminius again exalted the Scripture above what he called the works of men:

> That it may openly appear to all the world that we render to *the word of God alone* such due and suitable honour, as to determine it to be *beyond* (or rather *above*) *all disputes,* too great to be the subject of any exception, and worthy of all acceptation. Because these pamphlets are *writings that proceed from men,* and may on that account contain within them *some portion of error,* it is there proper to institute a lawful enquiry, that is, in a national Synod, whether or not there be any thing in those productions which requires amendment.[182]

Arminius proposed that the Confession be made as brief as possible, containing as few articles as possible, and that only scriptural expressions be used.[183] He wished to see the "explanations, proofs, digressions, redundancies, amplifications and exclamations" omitted and only the truths "necessary to salvation" retained.[184] As to what in these two creeds could be considered debatable or incorrect, the answer is very little, for each one contains only one ambiguous reference to election—one very ambiguous reference. Question fifty-four in the Heidelberg Catechism is a case in point:

> Q. What believest thou concerning the "holy catholic church" of Christ?
> A. That the Son of God from the beginning to the end of the world, gathers, defends, and preserves to himself by his Spirit and word, out of the whole human race, a church chosen to everlasting life, agreeing in true faith; and that I am and for ever shall remain, a living member thereof.[185]

The corresponding article in the Belgic Confession is article sixteen:

> We believe that all the posterity of Adam, being thus fallen into perdition and ruin by the sin of our first parents, God then did manifest himself such as he is; that is to say, merciful and just: Merciful, since he delivers and preserves from this perdition all whom he, in his eternal and unchangeable council of mere goodness, hath elected in Christ Jesus our Lord, without any respect to their works: Just, in leaving others in the fall and perdition wherein they have involved themselves.[186]

It was during some controversy over Arminius' preaching on Romans 9 in 1593 that he appeared before the consistory and affirmed his assent to the Confession, but reserved the right to interpret the second *all* in article sixteen to refer to believers.[187] What is truly ironic about these creeds is that the Calvinists themselves altered them. Franciscus Junius had abridged article sixteen and edited article thirty-six years before his controversy with Arminius.[188] Arminius even pointed out that other Reformed churches had revised their confessions and that the Belgic Confession had in fact been revised.[189]

It is Arminius' interpretation of predestination that is the crux of his argument with Calvin. Rather than applying predestination to unbelievers (as did Calvin), Arminius applied it only to believers. In his *Declaration of Sentiments,* Arminius even appealed to the Heidelberg Catechism in defense of his view. Question twenty of that erstwhile document reads:

> Q. Are all men then, as they perished in Adam, saved by Christ?
> A. No; only those who are ingrafted into him, and receive all his benefits.[190]

The comment of Arminius is noteworthy: "From this sentence I infer, *that God has not absolutely predestinated any men to salvation; but that he has in his decree considered [or looked upon] them as believers.*"[191] Arminius summarized his views of predestination as "an eternal and gracious decree of God in Christ, by which He determines to justify and adopt believers, and to endow them with life eternal, but to condemn unbelievers, and impenitent persons."[192] He called this predestination "the foundation of Christianity, of our salvation, and of the assurance of salvation."[193] Arminius reduces the controversy over Calvinism to the same two questions mentioned previously: "Do we believe, *because we have been elected?*" or "Are we elected, *because we believe?*"[194] This was the main issue in Arminius' day; it was the main issue in the subsequent Calvinism-Arminianism debates; it remains the main issue in these same debates today.

Arminianism

As we have seen throughout this chapter, Arminius was an orthodox Dutch Reformed theologian whose only real fault (if it be considered a fault) was to disagree with the established doctrines of Calvinism. But as we have seen in chapter 1 of this work, Arminianism has been charged with every heresy imaginable. So what has particularly given Arminius a bad name is not necessarily his theology but the theology of some of his so-called followers. The Reformed theologian Berkhof recognized this and concluded: "It is a well-known fact that Arminius himself did not depart as far from the Scripture truth and from the teachings of the Reformers as did his followers."[195] And as the Calvinist Cunningham rightly maintains: "Calvin and Arminius must not be held responsible for any opinions which they have not themselves expressed."[196] Mention the term *Arminianism* today and the first thing that comes to mind is the doctrine of conditional security; that is, the teaching that one can lose his salvation unless he does something. But as will be seen in the chapter on the Perseverance of the Saints, Arminius did not believe this teaching. This is even admitted by honest Calvinists.[197] And contrary to what Calvinists would have us believe, this is in many cases the only thing that would render an "Arminian" unorthodox.

Although the terms *Arminian* and *Arminianism* were invoked soon after the death of Arminius,[198] they eventually were broadened to impugn anyone who was opposed to Calvinism.[199] And as we have seen in chapter 1, this arbitrary division of Christians into two classes has been the strength of Calvinism. With only two opinions to consign men to, it was easy to associate Arminianism with every conceivable heresy and blame it for any cases of apostasy. But heresy can not just be limited to "Arminianism," for the Calvinists themselves have had their share of it. Many Presbyterian congregations in England during the eighteenth century became Unitarian.[200] In this country, in 1924, 1300 Presbyterian ministers signed the Auburn Affirmation, a document which basically repudiated the fundamentals of the faith.[201] The apostasy of the great Calvinist stronghold, Princeton Seminary, is well known.[202] Speaking of Calvinism in Switzerland, Germany, and France, the former Calvin College professor Charles Miller elaborates:

> In all three areas salvation came to be assumed as the natural right of birth. In Calvinist Switzerland and in Germany baptism was presumed to assure salvation and was not only a right but an obligation of citizenship. In France, regardless of life, confession, or intellectual convictions, birth into a Huguenot family presumed not only membership in the Reformed Church but ultimately salvation.[203]

These Calvinist shortcomings cannot all be blamed on Arminianism, for these "heretics" were all professing Calvinists.

The real followers of Arminius—those who voluntary claim the name—are of three types. His immediate (and true) descendants, because of the prominent place they had in the subsequent history of the Reformed Church in the Netherlands, are discussed in the next chapter. The second group begins with John Wesley, the founder and impetus of Methodism, who revived the name of Arminius and named his journal *The Arminian Magazine*.[204] The third body of Arminians are those among the Mennonites, Baptists, and "Evangelicals" who claim the name. But seeing as the Nazarenes, Wesleyans, Pentecostals, and other Holiness groups of today are the spiritual descendants of Wesley, it is pertinent to examine the man whom Spurgeon called "the modern prince of Arminians."[205]

John Wesley was born in 1703 at Epworth, England, a descendant of ministers on both sides of his line. Although his grandfathers were Nonconformists, his parents, Samuel (1662-1735) and Susanna (1669-1742), joined the established church of England before he was born. While at Oxford, John, his brother Charles (1708-1788), and George Whitefield were members of what was termed "The Holy Club."[206] For their holy and methodical living they were named "methodists," hence the Methodist Church. But in spite of his religion, Wesley was not converted until 1738. After his conversion he traveled throughout England the rest of his life preaching and organizing Methodist societies, but as it was never his intention to found a new denomination, he remained loyal to the Church of England all his life.[207] The first Methodist conference, in which standards for doctrine, liturgy, and discipline were adopted, was held in 1744.[208] In 1778 *The Arminian Magazine* was born, later becoming *The Methodist Magazine,* followed by *The Methodist Quarterly Review.*[209] In 1771 Wesley sent Francis Asbury (1745-1816) to America as a missionary. Known as the "Wesley of America"[210] and the "father of Methodism in the United States,"[211] Asbury preached throughout America and became a general superintendent of the newly organized Methodist Episcopal Church in 1784.[212] The Methodist movement in America soon eclipsed that in England. Besides Arminianism, Wesley and the Methodists were known for their doctrine of "perfectionism" or "entire sanctification." The Methodist Church today, however, is not known for anything but complete apostasy.

If John Wesley had never called himself an Arminian, the Calvinists certainly would have, for Wesley was one of the most ardent foes of Calvinism. And as Spurgeon says of Wesley: "To ultra-Calvinists his name is as abhorrent as the name of the Pope to a Protestant: you have only to speak of Wesley, and every imaginable evil is conjured up before their eyes, and no doom is thought to be sufficiently horrible for such an arch-heretic as he was."[213] So in the opinion of Calvinists, Wesley ranks right up there with Arminius. And like Arminius, Wesley engaged in several notable disputes with Calvinists. He split with Whitefield over the issue and clashed with Augustus Toplady and the Particular Baptist John Gill.[214] Wesley considered Calvinism to be "the very antidote of Methodism, the most deadly and successful enemy which it ever had."[215] In this he followed his mother, who wrote to him at Oxford: "The doctrine of predestination as maintained by rigid Calvinists, is very shocking, and ought utterly to be abhorred, because it charges the most holy God with being the author of sin."[216] Wesley's major works against Calvinism include *Serious Thoughts upon the Perseverance of the Saints* (1751) and *Predestination Calmly Considered* (1752). Wesley was not alone in his criticisms of Calvinism. His brother Charles the hymnwriter penned numerous verses against Calvinism. Wesley's associate John Fletcher (1729-1785) also wrote against Calvinism in his *Checks to Antinomianism*. He labored to show that Arminianism was not be to identified with Pelagianism.[217] The premier systematic theologian of Methodism was Richard Watson (1781-1833), who wrote his "Arminian" *Theological Institutes* in 1823. And further like Arminius, Wesley was deemed unorthodox, but like Arminius, he appealed to Calvin to prove his orthodoxy: "I think on justification, just as I have done any time these seven-and-twenty years; and just as Mr. Calvin does. In this respect, I do not differ from him an hair's breadth."[218] To this even Spurgeon concurs: "Wesley not only preached justification by faith very clearly, but so he did the total ruin of our race; and, whatever some of his followers may do, he himself did teach the inability of the creature."[219] With his denial of perseverance and his perfectionism, John Wesley departed further from Arminius than the Dutchman's immediate successors. But in spite of his faults, Wesley was not the heretic that Calvinists make him out to be.

The Methodist Church which Wesley founded, like all denominational churches, soon split into several factions. Some of these Arminian spiritual descendants of Wesley are still with us. The Wesleyan Church began in 1843 as the Wesleyan Methodist Church, but after a merger with the Pilgrim Holiness Church (founded in 1897) in 1968, it acquired its present name.[220] The Church of the Nazarene, as it has been called since 1919, is a result of the merger of three holiness groups in 1907 and 1908.[221] Further removed from Wesley are the various Holiness groups, all of which are "Arminian" in theology even though they may not claim the name. The Free Will Baptists in America are the true Arminian Baptists, contrary to the Calvinist-Arminian dichotomy that the Calvinistic Baptists espouse. They can be traced back to the work of Benjamin Randall (1749-1808) in 1780, who was converted under Whitefield.[222]

The followers of Arminius have forfeited the privilege of wearing the name *Arminian*. They have departed much further from him than he would ever condone. The old Edinburgh Encyclopedia judiciously expanded upon this theme:

> But the most eminent of those who became Arminians, or who ranked among the professed followers of Arminius, soon adopted views *of the corruption of man, of justification, of the righteousness of Christ, of the nature of faith, of the province of good works, and of the necessity and operations of grace,* that are quite contrary to those which he had entertained and published: Many of them, in process of time, differed more or less from one another, on some or all of these points. Even the Confession of Faith, which was drawn out for the Arminians by Episcopius, and is to be found in the second volume of his Works, cannot be referred to as a standard: It was composed merely to counteract the reproach of their being a society without any common principles. Every one was left entirely at liberty to interpret its language in the manner that was most agreeable to his own sentiments. Accordingly, so various and inconsistent are their opinions, that could Arminius peruse the unnumbered volumes which have been written as expositions and illustrations of Arminian doctrine, he would be at loss to discover his own simple system, amidst that heterogeneous mass of error with which it has been rudely mixed; and would be astonished to find, that the controversy which he had unfortunately, but conscientiously, introduced, had wandered far from the point to which he had confined it, and that with his name dogmas were associated, the unscriptural and dangerous nature of which he had pointed out and condemned.[223]

If the Calvinists would forever disconnect the name of Arminius from what is known as the Arminian system, then, and only then, would the label *Arminian* denote a most worthy profession.

Chapter 5
THE FIVE POINTS OF CALVINISM

The doctrines of Calvinism are usually defined and discussed as the Five Points of Calvinism. These five points are the sum and substance of the Calvinistic system: the distinguishing mark which separates Calvinists from all other Christians. This is stated in no uncertain terms by all Calvinists:

> The Calvinistic system especially emphasizes five distinct doctrines. These are technically known as the Five Points of Calvinism, and they are the main pillar on which the superstructure rests.[1]

> Calvinism, then, can rightly be viewed as certain basic doctrines, the so-called "five points of Calvinism."[2]

> The five points provide a classic framework which is quite well adapted for the expression of certain distinguishing emphases of Calvinism.[3]

In keeping with the Baptist practice of disassociation from the name of Calvin, Tom Ross terms these points "the five points of the doctrines of grace."[4] And although most Calvinists emphasize that Calvin did not formulate these points, they do claim that "it was Calvin who developed these truths, systematically and fully; and therefore, they came to be called by his name."[5] Spencer claims they were developed "in honor of the great French theologian, John Calvin."[6] Custance rejoins in more detail:

> So there they are: the Five Points, the five great asseverations of the Pauline-Augustinian-Calvinistic system of Reformed Faith which together constitute a satisfying, defensible, coherent, and thoroughly biblical confession that is realistic with respect to man's powers, position, and need, and honouring to God in its

unqualified adherence to the principle of sovereign grace.[7]

So even though Calvin himself did not formulate the Five Points, they are "truly representative of his theology."[8] But before exploring the claims of the Calvinists for the Five Points, it should be noted that there is some dissension among Calvinists regarding the Five Points.

To these five points, Mason adds an unnamed sixth.[9] Leonard Coppes thinks there should be ten, with infant baptism and covenant theology among the ones added,[10] which is not a bad idea considering the strictly Reformed history and nature of Calvinism. "To restrict it to five points," says Palmer, "is to misjudge and dishonor the man and movement that bears his name."[11] So he does them several times better, maintaining that "Calvinism is not restricted to five points: it has thousands of points."[12] But he doesn't stop there, for he later expands this to: "Calvinism has an unlimited number of points."[13] Another Calvinist claims that associating Calvinism with the Five Points "unduly limits the perspective of Calvinism."[14] But on the other hand, some Calvinists are ready to dispense with the points altogether. The famed Presbyterian theologian Dabney remarked that "historically, this title is of little accuracy or worth; I use it to denote certain points of doctrine, because custom has made it familiar."[15] The Baptist Good laments: "While this mnemonic system has been helpful in many ways, it sometimes has given wrong impressions. It has also been badly distorted to mean what its authors never intended it to say, and it has been caricatured to provide material for all sorts of ridicule. For these, and possibly other reasons, considerable doubt has been raised as to its current validity in correctly and adequately expressing what those who believe in the doctrines of grace really mean to say."[16] But regardless of how many points Calvinism has, the important thing is the claim made for them by the Calvinists.

Like Calvinism in general, the claim is made for the Five Points of Calvinism that they are nothing but biblical Christianity:

Firmly based as they are upon the Word of God.[17]

There is independent Scriptural support for each of the five points.[18]

The Bible contains an abundance of material for the development of each of these doctrines.[19]

As to the origin and propagation of the Five Points, Clyde Everman states: "It was God Himself that originated the five statements of grace."[20] Mark Duncan asserts that "Christ taught the doctrines which have come to be known as the five points of Calvinism."[21] It is further maintained that "this teaching was held to be truth by the apostles."[22] The Sovereign Grace Baptists insist that "Baptists have believed and taught these doctrines from the beginning of the first Baptist Church."[23] Indeed, one is not a "true Baptist"[24] and there can be no "true Baptist churches"[25] unless the Five Points of Calvinism are believed and taught. The Presbyterian Sproul, however, refers to the five points as the "Five Points of Reformed Theology,"[26] something the Baptists would object to. But not only should the Five Points of Calvinism be taught: they should be preached. Ben Rose insists that the "disputed points of Calvinism are preachable," and "a doctrine that is not preachable is not worth having."[27] The latest and most appalling use of the Five Points of Calvinism is in making them the first point of the Five Points of Christian Reconstruction.[28] This new and growing movement emphasizes the covenant theology and postmillennialism of Reformed theology but with an added twist: theonomic ethics; meaning: we are still under the Old Testament law. But as this is opposed even by those within the Reformed camp,[29] it is not relevant to our discussion of Calvinism.

The Five Points of Calvinism

The Five Points of Calvinism are commonly given under the acronym TULIP. To those in the medical profession, TULIP is a reference to a form of laser surgery for prostate problems (Transurethral Ultrasound-guided Laser-Induced Prostatectomy).[30] To the average man, however, a TULIP is just a flower. But the mention of the word in theological circles brings none of these things to mind, for any reference to a TULIP immediately connotes the Five Points of Calvinism. The Calvinist Coppes combines both the floral and the theological ideas: "The TULIP is but one of the flowers in the beautiful garden of truth."[31] The truth of the TULIP system remains to be seen. For now, however, it is necessary to survey the teachings behind the letters that make up this well-known acronym.

The TULIP acronym represents the following:

> Total Depravity
> Unconditional Election
> Limited Atonement
> Irresistible Grace
> Perseverance of the Saints

Total Depravity is the teaching that the unregenerate man is totally dead in sin to the extent that he has the inability to freely accept Jesus Christ. Unconditional Election is the teaching that God, by a sovereign, eternal decree, unconditionally elected a certain number of men to salvation. Limited Atonement is the teaching that Jesus Christ, by his death on the cross, only made an atonement for the group of men previously elected to salvation. Irresistible Grace is the teaching that God irresistibly overpowers the will of the elect sinner with his grace and regenerates him, granting him faith and repentance to believe on Jesus Christ. Perseverance of the Saints is the teaching that all of the elect who have been regenerated by God will persevere in the faith and ultimately die in a state of grace. The importance of these five points to Calvinism can be seen by what Calvinists equate them to.

Calvinists are adamant in their instance that the Five Points of Calvinism, the TULIP, are the Gospel:

> These five doctrines form the basic framework of God's plan for saving sinners.[32]

> God's plan of salvation revealed in the Scriptures consists of what is popularly known as the Five Points of Calvinism.[33]

The Sovereign Grace Baptist Fred Phelps claims that **"the preaching of the cross"** (1 Cor. 1:18) is "an ellipsis, standing for the Five Points of Calvinism."[34] He then not only implacably insists that "if you do not know the Five Points of Calvinism, you do not know the gospel, but some perversion of it,"[35] but: "If you do not have a thorough knowledge and understanding of the Five Points of Calvinism you are truly in darkness and ignorance of all divine truth. And, if you do not have an intelligent belief in and love for the Five Points of Calvinism, you have no rational religion, but are bound up in superstition and religious lies."[36] Just as the average preacher tries to mention the Gospel in every message, so the Calvinist does the same—but his Gospel is the Five Points of Calvinism. Spurgeon, even though he was a Calvinist, recognized this even in his day: "We have some ministers, excellent brethren, who never preach anything else. They have a kind of barrel-organ that only plays five tunes, and they are always repeating them. It is either Election, Predestination, Particular Redemption, Effectual Calling, Final Perseverance, or something of that kind; it is always the same note."[37] If the Five Points of Calvinism is the Gospel, can one be a Calvinist while at the same time rejecting one of the points? Some Calvinists think so.

Four-Point Calvinism

Some men, recognizing the repugnancy of Limited Atonement, yet still holding to the predestination of the Calvinistic system, claim to be only four-point Calvinists. The original four-point Calvinists were Moyse Amyraut (1596-1664), a French professor of theology at the Academy of Saumur (1624-1664), which had the largest enrollment of Reformed divinity students at that time,[38] and John Davenant (1576-1641), an Englishman who wrote *A Dissertation on the Death of Christ.* [39] In more recent times, the teaching of four-point Calvinism was held by the eminent dispensational theologian Lewis Sperry Chafer (1871-1952), founder of Dallas Theological Seminary,[40] and other Baptists whom he has influenced.[41] Many Baptists in the General Association of Regular Baptist Churches are four-point Calvinists.[42] There are also a great number of Baptists, many of whom are "closet Calvinists," who hold to this teaching.

The theological compromise known as four-point Calvinism is what is known as "blessed inconsistency," which will be proved in chapter 8 on the Atonement. The five-point Calvinists recognize this fact and don't hesitate to condemn those who only follow them 80 percent:

> In order for one to be consistent he must hold all five points of Calvinism.[43]

> The Five Points of Calvinism all tie together. He who accepts one of the points will accept the other points.[44]

> The five points are logically related such that any one of them implies the other four.[45]

But not only do five-point Calvinists condemn their four-point "cousins" for the "absurdity and folly" of their view,[46] they further insist that the whole Calvinistic system itself is in jeopardy if one of the points is denied:

> Prove any one of them false and the whole system must be abandoned.[47]

> Granted any one of these five points, the rest must follow inevitably; deny any one of them and the whole structure is endangered. One cannot satisfactorily defend some points but not others.[48]

> These five doctrines form a harmonious whole. Not one of them can be changed without giving disharmony to the whole and causing confusion as to how men are really saved.[49]

We will take the exact position as the five-point Calvinists, only we will reverse the argument: all five points will be rejected and none will be accepted.

The Synod of Dort

The Five Points of Calvinism, the TULIP, are taken from the Canons of Dordrecht (usually shortened to Dordt or Dort), formulated at the Synod of Dort in 1619. Although there had been other synods at Dort,[50] this one is referred to as "the great synod,"[51] and is acknowledged by Calvinists as having both historical and religious significance. As the first truly national synod,[52] Dort "marks the close of the first period in the history of the Reformed churches in the Netherlands"[53] and serves as "a symbol of the triumph of orthodox Calvinism in the Netherlands."[54] This "triumph" of Calvinism was over what was termed Arminianism. The conflict had raged since Arminius had first come to Leiden to teach. And while we have already seen that Arminius wished to teach nothing that was contrary to the Belgic Confession and Heidelberg Catechism, he did advocate a national synod to examine the accepted creeds of the Dutch churches. And although far removed from the simple New Testament church found in the Bible, because of the denominational hierarchy of the Dutch churches and the Church-State setup that existed in the Netherlands, the only way controversy could be officially settled was by a national synod. Arminius never lived to see his petition fulfilled, but fulfilled it was. But to understand the Canons properly, it is first necessary to review the conflict in the Reformed churches in the Netherlands preceding the National Synod of Dort, for too often, as Carl Bangs relates, the church history of the Netherlands is given simplistically as: "Calvinism came in, Arminius nearly ruined it, the Synod of Dort restored it."[55]

The controversy over predestination in the Dutch Reformed Church did not suddenly end with the premature death of Arminius in 1609. It actually increased, both in intensity and scope, until finally culminating in the Synod of Dort. There were three issues that led to this "great synod." First was the problem of the relationship between the Church and the State. The problem was not, however, whether they should be separate, but rather the extent of the control of the State over the Church. Secondly, the status of the creeds. The examination and possible revision of the Belgic Confession and Heidelberg Catechism was adamantly opposed by the Calvinists. And third, the controversy over predestination, without which a synod of this magnitude would never have taken place. It is also to be remembered that the Arminians were still in the Dutch Reformed Church: there was still no separate church to which they could freely worship according to the dictates of their conscience.

After the death of Arminius, four men assumed the leadership of the Arminian party: two preachers and two lawyers. John Uytenbogaert (1557-1644), who studied at Geneva under Beza, was an intimate friend of Arminius. It was he who sought the appointment of Arminius to the faculty of the University of Leiden.[56] Uytenbogaert preached at the Hague and served as a chaplain to Prince Maurice (1567-1625), the son and successor of William of Orange and the military leader of the Netherlands. He suffered greatly for his opinions, for he was not only exiled after the Synod of Dort, but had his goods confiscated as well.[57] Simon Episcopius (1583-1643) was schooled at Leiden under Arminius and later became professor of theology in place of Gomarus. He was the chief spokesman for the Arminians at the Synod of Dort, and like Uytenbogaert, was banished after the Dort synod.[58] John Van Oldenbarnevelt (1549-1619) gave support to the Arminians in his office as advocate-general of Holland. By refusing to call for a national synod, he prolonged the inevitable censoring of the Arminians. Although a national hero for helping William of Orange negotiate the Union of Utrecht, he was falsely charged with treason and suffered the ultimate price for his views: he was beheaded on May 13, 1619, as the Synod of Dort was concluding.[59] The aforementioned Hugo Grotius was the fourth leader of the Arminians. Educated at Leiden, he was a famed lawyer who gained world-wide recognition for his work on international law.[60] He advocated the right of the States-General to exert full authority over the churches. Although tried with Oldenbarnevelt, he was sentenced to life in prison, but managed to escape with the help of his wife, and eventually became the Swedish ambassador to Paris.[61] Grotius is father of the unorthodox Governmental view of the Atonement, but this view was not held by Arminius or the Arminians of that time.

Soon after the death of Arminius, his sympathizers presented to the States-General a notable document that has come to be known as the Remonstrance. On January 14, 1610, a private meeting of forty-six Arminian ministers was held at Gouda at the instigation of Uytenbogaert.[62] Here a remonstrance (a protest) against Calvinism was drawn up by Uytenbogaert and signed by those present.[63] The Remonstrance assailed Calvinistic doctrines because they were "not contained in the Word of God nor in the Heidelberg Catechism, and are unedifying—yea, dangerous—and should not be preached to Christian people."[64] The Remonstrance also proffered five positive points of Arminian belief. These five articles, the complete text of which can be found in appendix 1,[65] can be summarized as follows:

> 1. God has decreed to save those who shall believe on Jesus Christ and persevere in faith; leaving the unbelieving in sin to be condemned.
> 2. Jesus Christ died for all men, providing redemption if a man believe on him.
> 3. Man is in a state of sin, unable to of himself do anything truly good, but needs to be born again.
> 4. Man cannot without the grace of God accomplish any good deeds or movements, but this grace can be resisted.
> 5. Believers have power to persevere, but as to whether they can

fall away, that must be more particularly determined out of the Holy Scriptures.

Soon afterward, Uytenbogaert authored what has been termed "the sixth point of the Remonstrance,"[66] his tract *On the Office and Authority of a Higher Christian Government in Church Affairs,* in which he advocated the complete hegemony of the State over the Church.[67] The Remonstrance was given to Oldenbarnevelt and introduced to the States of Holland in July of 1610.[68] This was in direct response to the decision of the States of Holland on November 23, 1608, in which it was ordered that "any ministers who had objection to the Confession and Catechism were to address them to the States, not to a classis or local synod, and the States would forward them to a national synod."[69] To the dismay of the Calvinists, a resolution was passed on August 22nd declaring:

> That preachers of the opinions expressed in this Remonstrance being in the actual ministry should be free from the censure of other preachers, and that in the examination of new ministers, following the Church's custom, men should not proceed further than the five articles (especially on the subject of predestination).[70]

The Calvinists replied to the Remonstrance later that year with seven articles in what has become known as the Counter-Remonstrance.[71] This Calvinistic response, the complete text of which can be found in appendix 2,[72] can be summarized as follows:

> 1. Because the whole race has fallen in Adam and become corrupt and powerless to believe, God draws out of condemnation those whom he has chosen unto salvation, passing by the others.
> 2. The children of believers, as long as they do not manifest the contrary, are to be reckoned among God's elect.
> 3. God has decreed to bestow faith and perseverance and thus save those whom he has chosen to salvation.
> 4. God delivered up his Son Jesus Christ to die on the cross to save only the elect.
> 5. The Holy Spirit, externally through the preaching of the Gospel, works a special grace internally in the hearts of the elect, giving them power to believe.
> 6. Those whom God has decreed to save are supported and

preserved by the Holy Spirit so that they cannot finally lose their true faith.
7. True believers do not carelessly pursue the lusts of the flesh, but work out their own salvation in the fear of God.

The States of Holland, on December 23, 1610, ordered that a "friendly conference" should be held between the two parties at the Hague in March of the following year.[73] Accordingly, on March 11, 1611, six Remonstrants (as the Arminians were called), including Episcopius and Uytenbogaert, met with six Counter-Remonstrants (as the Calvinists were called), under the leadership of Petrus Plancius and Festus Hommius (1576-1642).[74] The Remonstrants sought for toleration of their views; the Counter-Remonstrants for a national synod to declare these views heretical. No agreement was reached, however, and the conference ended in failure nine days later.[75]

After the conference at the Hague, a bitter controversy ensued between the two parties which could have been avoided if the churches were independent of each other and the State. A similar conference between three Remonstrants and three Counter-Remonstrants was held at Delft in 1613 but proved to be as great a failure as the previous one.[76] In 1614 the States of Holland issued a peace resolution, drafted by Grotius, that outlawed discussion of the disputed five points in the pulpit.[77] A volatile pamphlet war then ensued.[78] The Calvinists sought to incite the public against the Arminians, denouncing them with the usual charges of heretics, Pelagians, and Socinians.[79] But just like today, there were men in the Reformed Church who did not identify themselves with either party.[80] The controversy turned into a political battle, with Oldenbarnevelt favoring the Arminians and Maurice the Calvinists. There had always been tension between Maurice and Oldenbarnevelt after the latter negotiated a truce with Spain in 1609, but after a controversy between Uytenbogaert and Maurice, the prince openly sided with the Counter-Remonstrants in 1617.[81] In 1618 the way was cleared for a national synod. Grotius and Oldenbarnevelt were arrested, and Remonstrant magistrates were replaced with supporters of the Counter-Remonstrants.[82]

It was decided to hold the national synod at Dort, a Calvinist stronghold in south Holland. No national synod had been held since 1586, and no more would take place for two hundred years.[83] On June 25, 1618, letters of invitation were sent to the following

THE FIVE POINTS OF CALVINISM

foreigners requesting that they send some of their learned theologians as delegates:[84]

> King James of England
> Deputies of the Reformed churches of France
> Elector of the Palatinate and Brandenburg
> Count of Hesse
> Reformed republics of Switzerland
> Dukes of Wetterau
> Republic of Geneva
> Republic of Bremen
> Republic of Emden

The delegates from France were not allowed to attend by order of the king so their place was marked by a symbolic empty bench.[85] Two delegates from Brandenburg were appointed but did not attend due to Lutheran opposition.[86] The Synod of Dort was the largest synod ever held of Reformed churches.[87] In addition to twenty-six foreign delegates, there were sixty Dutchman, including Gomarus and Hommius.[88] Cunningham insists that "they were themselves personally the most able and learned divines of the age, many of them having secured for themselves, by their writings, a permanent place in theological literature."[89] But he also admits that "the divines who composed the Synod of Dort generally held that the civil magistrate was entitled to inflict pains and penalties as a punishment for heresy" but that the Arminians advocated "toleration and forbearance in regard to differences of opinion upon religious subjects."[90] So although the Remonstrants and the Counter-Remonstrants both held to a Church-State alliance, the Remonstrants did not seek to use the State to punish their opponents.

The Synod of Dort convened on November 13, 1618, and closed in May of 1619.[91] Because of the various nationalities present, all of the proceedings were done in Latin.[92] Each member of the Synod took the following oath:

> I promise before God, in whom I believe, and whom I worship, as being present in this place, and as being the Searcher of all hearts, that during the course of the proceedings of this Synod, which will examine and decide, not only the five points, and all the differences resulting from them, but also any other doctrine,

I will use no human writing, but only the word of God, which is an infallible rule of faith. And during all these discussions, I will only aim at the glory of God, the peace of the Church, and especially the preservation of the purity of doctrine. So help me, my Savior, Jesus Christ! I beseech him to assist me by his Holy Spirit![93]

John Bogerman (1576-1637), who had translated Beza's tract on the punishment of heretics into Dutch, was elected president.[94] Bogerman had earlier participated in a conference with Gomarus, Uytenbogaert, and Arminius in which he went so far as to say that "the Scriptures must be interpreted according to the Catechism and the Confession."[95] To this Arminius replied: "How could one state more clearly that they were determined to canonize these two human writings, and to set them up as the two idolatrous calves at Dan and Beersheba?"[96] The first month of the synod was spent on matters other than the Arminian controversy.[97] The rest of the 180 sessions of the synod were taken up with the doctrines surrounding the five points.[98] One of the Swiss delegates to Dort insisted: "If ever the Holy Spirit were present in a Council, he was present at Dort."[99] An English delegate, Joseph Hall (1574-1656), who was replaced because of his ill health, declared that "there was no place upon earth so like heaven as the Synod of Dort."[100] There was some controversy, however, regarding the subject of Limited Atonement. Two of the English delegates, John Davenant and Samuel Ward (d. 1643), held, with the creed of the English church, that the Atonement was unlimited.[101] King James had even instructed that the English divines "should not oppose the Article of universal Redemption"[102] But the deck was stacked, as Schaff says: "The fate of the Arminians was decided beforehand."[103] John Wesley observed many years later that Dort was as impartial as the Council of Trent.[104] And Matthias Martinius (1572-1630), a delegate from Bremen who favored the Arminians, said that there were "some divine, some human, and some devilish" elements in the work of the synod.[105] It comes as no surprise that the synod condemned the Arminian tenets as unscriptural and issued the infamous Canons of Dort setting forth the Five Points of Calvinism.

There were three other groups represented at the Synod of Dort that are not often mentioned. First of all, there were present eighteen political commissioners assigned by the States-General.[106] And not only was the Dort synod called by the State and supervised by the State, all the expenses, including those of the foreign delegates, were borne by the State as well.[107] Secondly, in keeping with the civil nature of the synod, the sessions were public, and attended by crowds of spectators.[108] And third, there were thirteen Remonstrants cited to appear at the Synod, but they were summoned as defendants, not seated as delegates. On December sixth, at the twenty-second session, the Arminians were allowed to make their first appearance to defend their doctrines.[109] Simon Episcopius headed the small group of thirteen Arminians.[110] From December 13 to 17 the Remonstrants presented in writing their opinions concerning the five points of doctrine under dispute.[111] These "Opinions" of the Remonstrants, the complete text of which can be found in appendix 3,[112] are an expansion of the five points of the Remonstrance mentioned earlier. But after only a month the Remonstrants were dismissed, if you can call it that. President Bogerman burst forth with these words of dismissal:

> The foreign delegates are now of the opinion that you are unworthy to appear before the Synod. You have refused to acknowledge her as your lawful judge and have maintained that she is your counterparty; you have done everything according to your own whim; you have despised the decisions of the Synod and of the Political Commissioners; you have refused to answer; you have unjustly interpreted the indictments. The Synod has treated you mildly; but you have—as one of the foreign delegates expressed it—"begun and ended with lies." With that eulogy we shall let you go. God shall preserve His Word and shall bless the Synod. In order that she be no longer obstructed, you are sent away! You are dismissed, get out!"[113]

And thus, on January 14, the Remonstrants appeared before the synod for the last time. Upon removing from the premises, Episcopius proclaimed: "The Lord God shall judge between us concerning the tricks and lies you have laid to our charge."[114]

After the synod was over, the Arminians were prohibited from publishing anything related to the synod, but managed to issue anonymously a pamphlet entitled: *The Nullities, Mismanagement and unjust Proceedings of the National Synod held at Dort in the years 1618 and 1619*.[115] In early July, the thirteen Remonstrants were called before the States-General and asked to recant and agree to cease preaching their doctrines, or suffer banishment from the country.[116] Over two hundred Arminian ministers were then deposed from their pulpits and many of these were banished for refusing to keep silent.[117] A harsh Calvinistic theocracy was then established in which only Calvinism could be publically proclamated.[118] But fortunately, it was short-lived, for after the death of Prince Maurice in 1625, the Remonstrants were allowed to return under his brother and successor, Frederick Henry (1584-1647), and permitted to establish churches and schools throughout Holland, with certain restrictions.[119] They formed a denomination known as the Remonstrant Brotherhood and established their own theological college.[120] Thus, the true descendants of Arminius are the Dutch Remonstrants, not Wesley and those who call themselves Arminians.

The Canons of Dort

At the conclusion of the Synod of Dort, the Canons of Dort were issued:

> The judgment of the National Synod of the Reformed Belgic Churches. Held in Dort, in the years of our Lord, 1618 and 1619. At which very many theologians of the Reformed Churches of Great Britain, Germany, and France, were present; concerning the five heads of doctrine controverted in the Belgic Churches.[121]

Because the Five Points of Calvinism are taken from these canons, they are held in great esteem by Calvinists:

> No synod or council was ever held in the church, whose decisions, all things considered, are entitled to more deference and respect.[122]

> Five thoroughly Calvinistic Canons, in which the doctrines of the Reformation, and particularly of Calvin, on the disputed points are set forth with clearness and precision.[123]

> The Canons function as a bulwark, a defense, of the truth of God's Word concerning our salvation.[124]

But as one Calvinist accurately perceives: "Few creeds formulated by the Christian churches have received either such fulsome praise or bitter criticism as the *Canons of Dort.*"[125]

The Canons of Dort, the complete text of which can be found in appendix 4,[126] consist of four articles with a rejection of errors adjoined to each. There was also a preface, conclusion, and sentence against the Remonstrants, but these are usually omitted when the Canons are printed. Like the proceedings of the Synod, the Canons were issued in Latin, which was still the universal language in scholarly and scientific circles. The Canons actually contain five articles of doctrine: the Five Points of Calvinism, but appearing under four articles, the third and fourth being combined. Although it is sometimes thought that the five points presented by the Arminians were a reply to the Five Points of Calvinism as expressed by the Canons of Dort, such is not the case. The order of the Canons follows that of the Remonstrance and the Opinions of the Remonstrants. This is different from the regular TULIP designation, for Unconditional Election is treated first, followed by Limited Atonement, Total Depravity and Irresistible Grace, and then Perseverance of the Saints. The Canons of Dort are quite lengthy, but the TULIP acronym, although brief, is an accurate summation of them.

Even though there were foreign delegates at the Synod of Dort, the Canons were only officially adopted, with the exception of the Reformed Church of France (which sent no delegates), by the Dutch.[127] Calvinists admit, however, that the Canons of Dort are "the most controversial creedal statement of the Reformed churches."[128] In 1816 the Canons were dropped as a creedal statement by the Dutch Reformed Church.[129] This was followed in 1834 by the formation of a rival Reformed Church by the stricter Calvinists that "did not meet with the approval of the national church or government."[130] A second major secession from the official church took place in 1886 under Abraham Kuyper.[131] During this time of turmoil in the Dutch Reformed Church, many Calvinists left their native land for America, settling in Michigan. Consequently, Grand Rapids, Michigan, is a Calvinist stronghold today. It is in the United States that the Canons of Dort still live. Together with the Belgic Confession and the Heidelberg Catechism, the Canons of Dort make up the "Three Forms of Unity" accorded almost canonical status by the Reformed churches in America. At Reformed Bible College in Grand Rapids, Michigan, one can take a whole course on these three forms of unity.[132] And not only that, the college "bases its instruction on the infallible Word of God as interpreted" in these creedal documents.[133] At Calvin Theological Seminary, also in Grand Rapids, students can likewise take a course on the Reformed confessions.[134] In fact, the Three Forms of Unity are "basic to the seminary's life, thought, work, and spirituality."[135] The formula of subscription for ministers in the Reformed Church says in part:

> We the undersigned . . . do hereby, sincerely and in good conscience before the Lord, declare by this our subscription that we heartily believe and are persuaded that all the articles and points of doctrine contained in the Confession and Catechism of the Reformed Churches, together with the explanation of some points of the aforesaid doctrine made by the National Synod of Dordrecht, 1618–'19, do fully agree with the Word of God.[136]

The difference between the Canons of Dort and all other creeds and confessions is that the Dort document deals with one specific thing: the Five Points of Calvinism; whereas all other creeds are of a general nature, covering all manner of subjects and doctrines. It is the Five Points of Calvinism, as embodied in the Canons of Dort, that remain the sum and substance of Calvinism. So although the Reformed have their Three Forms of Unity, it is the Dort Canons that reign supreme. The Reformed theologian Homer Hoeksema acknowledges this fact: "The Heidelberg Catechism and the Belgic Confession must be maintained, *but always in the light of and in harmony with the further interpretation given at Dordrecht.*"[137] This adherence to Dort is to be expected from those of the Reformed persuasion, but not from the Baptists, for Baptists who follow the Five Points of Calvinism are in actuality following a Dutch Reformed, State-Church creed. Yet, the Baptist Kenneth Good insists that "Dort rendered a great service to Baptists."[138] He even maintains that "Baptists can nevertheless subscribe to the Canons of Dort without compromise."[139] To repudiate the Canons is to be an Arminian.[140] But Baptists who subscribe to these Canons are not only conforming to a Dutch Reformed, State-Church creed, they are following Augustine, for as the Reformed theologian Herman Hanko asserts: "Our fathers at Dordrecht knew well that these truths set forth in the Canons could not only be traced back to the Calvin Reformation; they could be traced back to the theology of Saint Augustine who lived almost a millennium before Calvin did his work in Geneva. For it was Augustine who had originally defined these truths."[141] Custance insists that the Five Points were "formulated implicitly by Augustine."[142]

Although the Canons of Dort are the main result of the Synod of Dort, they are not the only thing that transpired during the Synod. The first order of business was the question of a new Dutch translation of the Bible.[143] It was finally decided that six men were to work on the translation, three for each Testament.[144] Work was not begun until 1626, and the Bible was not finished until 1637.[145] Known as the Statenbijbel (the States Bible), it is still in use today. The ironic thing about the Synod of Dort is that the Calvinists did the very thing for which they anathematized the Arminians for wanting to do: they revised the Belgic Confession. The major change was in article thirty-six on the magistrate,[146] but because the French, Latin, and Dutch texts disagreed among themselves and each other, they were also subjected to a careful revision.[147]

The Westminster Assembly

After the Synod of Dort, the controversy over Calvinism shifted from the Continent to England. And although it is from the Canons of Dort that we get the Five Points of Calvinism, it is an English confession of faith that has come to be regarded as "the most systematically complete statement of Calvinism ever devised."[148] That the Westminster Confession of Faith, drawn up by the Westminster Assembly (1643-1649), has achieved this significance is a tribute to the temporary triumph of the Reformed Faith over Anglicanism. Due to the close relationship between Church and State that existed at the time, the acceptance of Calvinism in England, culminating in the Westminster Assembly, is deeply intertwined with the civil and religious history of England. And although the Westminster Assembly is far removed from the beginning of the English Reformation, the causes and intentions of the Assembly cannot be properly understood without recourse to the Reformation.

The Reformation in England proceeded unlike the Reformation anywhere on the Continent. It not only had more underlying causes, but progressed slower, lasted longer, and underwent more changes than any Continental reform movement. There is much more to the

Reformation in England than the familiar story of how King Henry VIII (1491-1547), because he wanted a divorce, separated the Church of England from Rome and declared himself the head of the Church. It is the story of how a solidly Roman Catholic country became the greatest Protestant nation on the face of the earth. But unlike on the Continent, where the names of Luther, Melanchthon, Calvin, and Zwingli were associated with the Reformation, the Reformation in England is intimately connected with the development of the English Bible.[149] As the Reformation in England parallels the Tudor-Stuart period of English history, it is necessary to start at the beginning of this period.

The year 1485 marks the beginning of the reign of the first Tudor, Henry VII (1457-1509). His reign began as his predecessors had begun with England thoroughly under the hegemony of the Roman Catholic Church. Just a few years previously, King Edward IV (1442-1483) addressed the pope as "blessed father," "most Holy Father," and "your Holiness."[150] The Church possessed tremendous wealth and lands while filling the government with its bishops. Opinions contrary to the established doctrine of the Roman Church were regarded as heretical and suppressed by the state. The propositions of John Wycliffe (c. 1320-1384), who regarded the Mass as "a veritable abomination of desolation in the holy place,"[151] were condemned by the Convocation of Canterbury in 1382.[152] Pope Innocent VIII (1432-1492), in a Papal Bull in 1486, recognized Henry VII as the new ruler of England with the words: "His Holiness confirmeth, establisheth, and approveth the right and title to the crown of England of the said our sovereign lord Henry VII."[153]

The official Bible at this time was the Latin Vulgate; the unofficial was the English translation of Wycliffe, completed in 1382. The attitude toward the Bible in English can be seen by the infamous Constitution adopted by the Provincial Council at Oxford in 1408: "We therefore enact and ordain that no one henceforth on his own authority translate any text of Holy Scripture into the English or other language, by way of a book, pamphlet, or tract, and that no book, pamphlet, or tract of this kind be read, either already recently composed in the time of the said John Wyclif, or since then."[154] But since printing was not introduced into England until 1476, the circulation of any Bible was very limited.

When Henry VIII assumed the throne of England in 1509, he

was a loyal son of the Catholic Church just like his father. Lollards and other "heretics" were still being burnt at the stake. Indeed, Andreas Ammonius (1477-1517), the secretary of Henry VIII, wrote from London in 1511 to Erasmus that "many heretics furnish a daily holocaust."[155] But although England was officially Catholic, all was not well with the people in matters of religion. There was controversy over investitures, praemunire, annates, and papal bulls, but this was not the result of doctrinal discord. Likewise, the state of the church was regarded as corrupt, not doctrinally, but morally. Anti-clericalism was widespread. The difference between the reign of Henry VIII and his predecessors was that the invention of printing and the revival of learning had now combined to engender books and tracts against the authority and corruption of Rome.

Three significant works had a part in the English Reformation before Henry's celebrated divorce. First was the Greek New Testament of Erasmus, issued in 1516. Erasmus had previously spent some time in England, so although his work was published on the Continent, it was well received in England by many at Oxford and Cambridge.[156] Secondly, the writings of Luther were soon transported in England and widely circulated.[157] However, the official response to Luther in England was the public burning of his books.[158] Luther's book against Rome, *The Babylonian Captivity of the Church,* was answered by Henry VIII himself in his *The Defence of the Seven Sacraments.* For this Henry received from Pope Leo X (1475-1521) the title "Defender of the Faith," but from Luther the epithet "a crowned ass."[159] It was also during this period that William Tyndale (1494-1536) gave to the world the first New Testament in English translated directly from the Greek. The response in England to Tyndale's Bible was the same as Tyndale himself would suffer later—burning. In two proclamations in 1530, Henry VIII attempted to suppress Tyndale's work. The first prohibited anyone "to preach, teach, or inform anything openly or privily, or compile and write any book, or hold, exercise, or keep any assemblies or schools in any manner of wise contrary to the Catholic faith."[160] It even contained an index of forbidden books including Tyndale's recent translation of parts of the Old Testament.[161] In his second proclamation, Henry insisted that "it is not necessary the said Scripture to be in the English tongue and in the hands of the common people."[162] It was then forbidden to "buy, receive, keep, or have the New Testament or the Old in the English tongue."[163] In 1535, Tyndale was imprisoned, tried as a heretic, and condemned to death. Before he was burned, however, he was heard to cry out: "Lord, open the King of England's eyes."[164]

Meanwhile, Henry VIII, being unable to secure a divorce to marry Anne Boleyn (1507-1536), had his marriage to Catherine of Aragon (1485-1536) declared null and void after secretly marrying Anne in January of 1533. The Act of Supremacy in 1534 established Henry as "the only supreme head in earth of the Church of England."[165] Thus, the break with Rome was political not doctrinal. And although it is certainly true that Pope Paul III condemned Henry and commanded, "on pain of excommunication," that his subjects "utterly and entirely withdraw themselves from obedience to the said King Henry,"[166] and that Henry dissolved the monasteries because they contained "manifest sin, vicious, carnal and abominable living,"[167] the Church of England was still Catholic in doctrine. In 1536 Henry devised what came to be called The Ten Articles. This confession of faith for the English Church retains the Romish practices of baptismal regeneration, invocation of saints, and transubstantiation.[168] In 1539, The Six Articles were issued by the king. The first of these articles strongly defended transubstantiation, the denial of which resulted in "pains of death by way of burning."[169] So although Henry lived and died a Catholic in doctrine, the officially sanctioned break with Rome paved the way for a real reformation of the Church of England.

After Tyndale's effort, several other English Bibles were produced. Encouraged by Thomas Cromwell (1485-1540), Myles Coverdale (1488-1569) produced the first complete translation of the Bible into English in 1535. In June of 1536, Cromwell wrote to his bishops with the injunction that they "cause the bible in English to be laid forth openly in your own houses and that the same be in like manner openly laid forth in every parish church."[170] Coverdale's associate, John Rogers (1500-1555), assembled Tyndale's completed works into a Bible with Coverdale's translation for the remainder of the Old Testament. The entire work was then slightly revised and issued in 1537 under the pseudonym of Thomas Matthew. Like the Coverdale Bible, the Matthew Bible was dedicated to King Henry VIII. The archbishop of Canterbury, Thomas Cranmer (1489-1556), requested of Cromwell that the Matthew Bible be given license by the king that it "may be sold and read of every person, without danger of any act, proclamation, or ordinance heretofore granted to the contrary, until such time that we the bishops shall set forth a better translation."[171] The license was approved, not only for the Matthew Bible, but also for a revised edition of Coverdale's Bible. Thus, by the end of 1537, there were two Bibles circulating in England "set forth with the King's most gracious license." William Tyndale's prayer was answered.

In 1538 the Second Royal Injunctions of Henry VIII were drawn up by Thomas Cromwell. The second of these injunctions called for "one book of the whole Bible of the largest volume, in English, and the same set up in some convenient place within the said church that you have cure of."[172] Coverdale was enlisted to revise both the text and the notes of Matthew's Bible to provide a Bible to fulfill Cromwell's injunction. On account of its large size, the new Bible, which appeared in 1539, was popularly termed the Great Bible. The title page, thought to be the work of the famous painter Hans Holbein (1497-1543), shows a corpulent Henry VIII handing out copies of the Bible to Cranmer and Cromwell, who in turn distribute the Bible to the people. The Great Bible was ordered by Henry in 1541 "to be fixed and set up openly in every of the said parish churches."[173] However, after 1541, no more English Bibles were printed during the reign of Henry VIII. The closing years of Henry's reign were marked by a return back toward Catholicism. In 1546, the year before he died, Henry proclaimed that "the New Testament of Tyndale's or Coverdale's translation" was forbidden.[174] But soon afterward, as if to halt the return toward Rome, Henry died. But although he repudiated the Pope, he nevertheless retained Catholic doctrine and persecuted "heretics." His lasting legacy, the results of which he never intended, was to approve the use of the English Bible in the churches and for the people.

The death of Henry brought his young son Edward VI (1537-1553) to the throne. Edward was decidedly for the Reformation and opposed Roman "idolatry and superstition."[175] Edward Seymour (1505-1552), his Protestant uncle, was proclaimed Lord Protector. During Edward's reign his father's Six Articles were repealed, the chantries were dissolved, and communion was permitted in both kinds.[176] The marriage of priests was also legalized.[177] Naturally, Bible printing flourished under the young king. In an injunction issued soon after his accession to the throne,

Edward instructed that "one book of the whole Bible, of the largest volume, in English" be "set up in some convenient place" in the church where the people may "resort unto the same and read."[178] In two Acts of Uniformity, the Book of Common Prayer was established.[179] Although the first Prayer Book represented somewhat of a compromise between Rome and the principles of the Reformation, the second edition of 1552 was the most Protestant document thus far in English history. Nevertheless, the Presbyterians later condemned the book as "an unperfecte booke, culled and picked out of that popishe dunghill, the Masse book, full of all abhominations."[180] During the brief reign of Edward, the Forty-two Articles of Religion were drawn up by Cranmer and published in the year of Edward's death.[181] This was the first Protestant confession of faith in England. The reform measures that were gradually taking place in England came to an end with Edward's premature death on July 6, 1553. He had the best of intentions, and "my Lord and God, save this realm from popery, and maintain it in true religion," was his dying prayer.[182] But beginning in the time of Edward, there arose a party in England who desired a more complete reformation, although it was not till later that they acquired the name of *Puritans.*

The death of Edward VI brought his sister Mary (1516-1558) to the throne. Being a Roman Catholic, her views on the Bible were diametrically opposed to those of her brother Edward. Mary's first proclamation on religion forbid "all and every her said subjects" to preach, read, interpret, or teach "any Scriptures or any manner points of doctrine concerning religion."[183] This was followed by acts repealing those statutes passed under the reigns of Edward and Henry that were against the Catholic Faith.[184] After her marriage to the ardent Catholic Philip II of Spain, Mary prohibited by proclamation the reading or possession of any books or writings by Luther, Calvin, Coverdale, Tyndale, and Cranmer, as well as the Book of Common Prayer "or any other like book" that contained "false doctrine contrary and against the Catholic faith and the doctrine of the Catholic Church."[185] The death penalty was ordered for violators.[186] After Mary revived various statutes against heresy,[187] several hundred became martyrs including Thomas Cranmer, John Rogers, and the Edwardian bishops Nicholas Ridley (c. 1500-1555) and Hugh Latimer (c. 1485-1555).[188] It was Latimer who remarked to Ridley at the stake: "We shall this day light such a candle by God's grace in England, as I trust never shall be put out."[189] For her cruelty, "Bloody" Mary was deemed "that horrible monster Jezebel of England" by John Knox.[190] The result of this persecution was that about eight hundred Protestants left England for the Continent.[191] Some of these "Marian Exiles" settled in Geneva, where, under the guidance of William Whittingham (1524-1579), the New Testament was yet again translated into English. This translation is most notable for its strongly anti-Catholic notes such as that in Revelation 9:11 where the pope is identified as the "anti-Christ, King of hypocrites, and Satan's ambassador." Upon the death of Mary in 1558, the Old Testament of what came to be called the Geneva Bible was translated and the completed Bible dedicated to the new queen, Elizabeth I.

The reign of Elizabeth brought a complete reversal of Mary's oppressive policies for Catholicism and against the Bible. By an Act of Supremacy, the authority of the pope was once again abolished, communion under both kinds was revived, and the heresy laws revitalized by Mary were repealed.[192] By an Act of Uniformity, the use of the Book of Common Prayer was re-established.[193] Various acts were also passed during the reign of Elizabeth against Roman Catholics, including the ordering of the Jesuits to "depart out of this realm of England."[194] In her Injunctions for Religion, the familiar command for "one book of the whole Bible of the largest volume in English" to be set up in the churches was resurrected.[195] All "ecclesiastical persons" were commanded to "discourage no man from the reading of any part of the Bible," because it is "the very lively word of God."[196] And instead of prohibiting opinions contrary to the "Catholic faith and the doctrine of the Catholic Church" as had her sister Mary, Elizabeth enjoined that "no man shall willfully and obstinately defend or maintain any heresies, errors, or false doctrine contrary to the faith of Christ and his holy Scripture."[197] During the reign of Elizabeth, Archbishop Matthew Parker (1504-1575) organized a group of bishops to revise the Great Bible. Called the Bishops Bible, the Convocation of Canterbury in 1571 decreed that "every archbishop and bishop should have at his house a copy of the holy Bible of the largest volume as lately printed at London."[198] To counter the flood of Protestant Bibles, English Papists who left England for the Continent issued their own English Bible. The New Testament was published in 1582 at Rheims, France, with a preface that stated this version "followeth the Greeke far more exactly then the Protestants translations."[199] The Old Testament was translated at Douay but not published until 1609-1610. Hence, this version came to be called the Douay-Rheims Bible. It was also during the reign of Elizabeth that the Thirty-Nine Articles of the Church of England were formulated. After appearing in Latin in 1563, they were revised and published in English in 1571.[200] By an act of parliament in 1571, it was made mandatory that all ecclesiastical persons subscribe to the Thirty-Nine Articles.[201] These articles have remained the doctrinal creed of the Church of England to this day. But just as during the reign of Edward VI, there was a party who desired a more complete reformation in the Church of England. The Puritans (as they were now called), led by Thomas Cartwright (1535-1603), a professor at Cambridge, objected to the popish practices in the prayerbook and preferred a Presbyterian to an Episcopal form of church government.[202] When Parliament met in 1572 the Puritans published *An Admonition to the Parliament* in which more reforms were sought.[203] This was countered by John Whitgift (1544-1600) in his *Answer to a Certain Libel Entitled An Admonition to the Parliament,* thus intensifying the conflict between the Puritans and the established church.[204] So, although the reign of Elizabeth ended the external conflict with Rome, it was followed by the internal conflict between Prelacy and Puritanism.

When Elizabeth died in 1604 the throne passed to the king of Scotland, James VI (1566-1625), who then became James I of England. Unlike that in England, the Reformation in Scotland proceeded swiftly. Through the efforts of John Knox, the Scottish parliament in 1560 rejected the jurisdiction of the Pope and adopted the twenty-five articles of the Scotch Confession of Faith.[205] In 1567, when the infant James VI was crowned king, the Scottish Parliament officially established the reformed church.[206] Under Knox's successor, Andrew Melville (1545-1622), the Presbyterian form of church government was firmly established.[207] Thus, just as in England, because of the faulty Church-State concept, needless controversy ensued between the advocates of Episcopacy and Presbyterianism. When James left his native land for England, he was presented by the Puritans with the Millenary Petition, so called because "they, to the number of more than a thousand ministers, groaned under the burden of human rites and ceremonies, and cast themselves at this majesty's feet for relief."[208] This gave rise to the famous Hampton Court Conference the next year where the Puritans, led by Dr. John Reynolds (1549-1607), were allowed to state their case. But as the king was averse to Presbyterianism, the Puritans were ordered to conform.[209] However, there is one lasting result of this conference that is still with us today. King James acquiesced to the suggestion by John Reynolds that "the Bible be new translated, such as are extant not answering the original."[210] And thus the King James Bible was born. England was now firmly Protestant, but the Puritan controversy persisted, and because of their influence in Parliament, there was continual conflict in both the government and the church.

Charles I (1600-1649), the son of King James, came to the throne upon the death of his father in 1625. It was during his reign that the Westminster Assembly was called, although he was engaged in a civil war with the Parliament at the time. The conflict with the Puritans that he inherited intensified as Charles attempted to rule without Parliament and, through the determined efforts of Archbishop William Laud (1573-1645), enforce Episcopacy.[211] And because the Parliament became increasingly identified with Puritanism, the Reformation in England that began as a contest between king and pope now became a contest between king and parliament.[212] In 1638, after Charles attempted to impose the Anglican liturgy on the Church of Scotland, the Scots rebelled and adopted the "National Covenant," pledging themselves against the actions of the king that "do sensibly tend to the re-establishment of the Popish religion and tyranny, and to the subversion and ruin of the true Reformed religion, and of our liberties, laws, and estates."[213] War followed, and in 1640 Charles was constrained to call a Parliament, the first in twelve years, to finance his army.[214] But as this "Short Parliament" (meeting less than a month) resisted the king, he was forced to call another. This "Long Parliament" (so called because it met until 1660) not only waged a civil war against the king, but abolished episcopacy, ejected two thousand royalist ministers, entered into the "Solemn League and Covenant" with the Scots against Prelacy, summoned the Westminster Assembly, executed Archbishop Laud, and eventually executed the king himself in 1649.[215]

There is one important factor in the rise of the Puritans that has not heretofore been mentioned: Calvinism. Although derivatives from Calvin's name first appeared in English in 1566,[216] the influence of Calvin can be traced back to the reign of Edward VI. Calvin had an interest in English affairs. He wrote letters to both the young king and Protector Somerset (c. 1506-1552), as well as to Archbishop Cranmer.[217] Cranmer even asked Calvin to come to England.[218] Calvin dedicated his commentary on First Timothy to Somerset and his commentary on Isaiah to Edward. John Knox was one of Edward's chaplains.[219] During the reign of Edward, Reformed theologians from the Continent were welcome in England. Martin Bucer taught at Cambridge and spent his last years in England.[220] When Mary became queen, the English exiles who settled in Geneva and translated the Geneva Bible certainly came under the influence of Calvin. And during the reign of Elizabeth, Calvin's *Institutes* were translated into English in 1561.[221] The *Institutes* were used as a textbook on theology at both Oxford and Cambridge.[222] Other works of Calvin were also translated into English.[223] Calvin was even requested to send a minister to the French congregation in London.[224] The Thirty-Nine Articles were mildly Calvinistic, rejecting Limited Atonement. In the late sixteenth century the University of Cambridge became a stronghold of Calvinism. The Cambridge professor William Perkins, who has been called "the greatest of the sixteenth-century Puritans theologians,"[225] was a very influential Calvinist, and produced voluminous writings.[226] His criticism by Arminius has already been mentioned. Not everyone at Cambridge, however, accepted Calvinism. The Frenchman Peter Baro (1534-1599), Margaret Professor of Divinity, opposed Perkins and advocated "free will and salvation possible to all men."[227] Calvinists claim he was "the first person who taught Arminianism in the Church of England."[228] In 1595 a controversy over Calvinism erupted at Cambridge and resulted in the adoption of nine Calvinistic articles that read like an English Canons of Dort. The Lambeth Articles (so called because they were approved by divines at Lambeth Palace, London), the complete text of which can be found in appendix 5,[229] were never approved by Elizabeth.[230] At the close of the Tudor period in English history, Calvinists were to be found among both Churchmen and Puritans. English Calvinism was not yet equivalent to Puritanism.[231]

Controversy over Calvinism likewise manifested itself during the reign of the first English Stuart king. At the Hampton Court Conference, Dr. John Reynolds requested of King James, but to no avail, that "the nine orthodoxal assertions concluded on at Lambeth might be inserted into the Book of Articles."[232] The name of Arminius became known in England after the king campaigned against Conrad Vorstius (1569-1622) as a replacement for Arminius at Leiden. Concerning Arminius, the king's declaration in the Vorstius affair mentioned that "it was our hard hap not to hear of this Arminius before he was dead."[233] It has already been mentioned that King James sent delegates to the Synod of Dort. He was of Scottish Calvinism stock but believed that his view of the monarchy depended on the preservation of Episcopacy.[234] And although James publically supported Calvinists,[235] the predestination issue was to him of secondary importance.[236] Thus, the translators of the King James Bible included both Calvinists and anti-Calvinists,[237] and James instructed the English delegates at Dort to "mitigate the heat on both sides," and to advise the Dutch "not to deliver in the pulpit to the people those things for ordinary doctrines which are the highest points of schools and not fit for vulgar capacity, but disputable on both sides."[238] The Canons of Dort were published in English in 1619,[239] but when the Calvinistic controversy heightened after the Synod of Dort, James began to favor the Arminians because of the Calvinists' insistence that no temporal ruler could be the head of the Church.[240] Preachers were instructed by order of the king not to preach the doctrines of Calvinism:

> No preacher, of what title soever under the degree of a bishop or dean at the least, do from henceforth presume to preach in any popular auditory deep points of Predestination, Election, Reprobation, or of the Universality, Efficacy, Resistibility or Irresistibility of God's Grace, but leave those themes rather to be handled by learned men, and that moderately and modestly by way of use and application, rather than by way of positive doctrines, being fitter for the schools than for single auditories.[241]

The label *Arminian* was now used by Puritans to impugn those who rejected Calvinism.[242] Arminianism (opposition to Calvinism) was termed Pelagianism.[243] But as usual, some did not go along with the contrived Calvinist-Arminian debate. The noted anti-Calvinist Richard Montagu (1577-1641) asserted that "he was neither an Arminian, nor a Calvinist, nor a Lutheran, but a Christian."[244] Although Calvinists could still be found among both Puritans and Episcopalians, a notable shift occurred during the reign of Charles I. Arminianism was redefined as not just being in opposition to Calvinism, but in opposition to "all that Puritans objected to in the Church."[245] Archbishop Laud promoted Churchmen who were anti-Calvinistic.[246] In the name of the "peace and quiet"[247] of the Church, Charles prohibited preaching on predestination. Thereafter, due in part to the works of Montagu, Calvinism became increasingly identified with Puritanism.[248] There were debates in Parliament over Calvinism throughout the 1620s.[249] It was the Calvinists, however, who eventually won out. Thus, the Long Parliament, in 1642, ordered the printing of a book by John Owen (1616-1683) entitled *A Display of Arminianism*, which assails Arminianism and upholds the doctrine of Limited Atonement.[250]

It is into this charged atmosphere that the Westminster Assembly was summoned. McNeil terms the Assembly "the last great effort to establish a Calvinist system in England."[251] On June 12, 1643, an ordinance calling for an assembly of divines was issued:

> An Ordinance of the Lords and Commons in Parliament, for the calling of an Assembly of learned and godly Divines, and others, to be consulted with by the Parliament, for the settling of the Government and Liturgy of the Church of England, and for vindicating and clearing of the Doctrine of the said Church from false aspersions and interpretations.[252]

Although even Calvinists admit that much of what has been written about the Assembly's members "has been more than a little hagiographical in nature,"[253] of the Assembly it has been said:

> One of the most learned bodies ever assembled on this earth for the formulation and promulgation of Christian truth.[254]

> A more zealous, intelligent, and learned body of divines seldom ever met in Christendom.[255]

> One is impressed with the unusual godliness and scholarship that were represented by those brought together by God for this Assembly.[256]

The members of the Westminster Assembly have also been compared with those of Synod of Dort: "The Christian world, since the days of the apostles, had never a Synod of more excellent divines (taking one thing with another), than this and the Synod of Dort."[257] There is no question that the delegates to the Assembly were both godly and scholarly. The majority of them held both bachelor's and master's degrees and served in a pastoral position.[258] Each member of the Assembly took the following oath:

> I, _____, do seriously promise and vow, in the presence of Almighty God, that in this Assembly, whereof I am a member, I will maintain nothing in point of doctrine but what I believe to be most agreeable to the Word of God; nor in point of discipline, but what I shall conceive to conduce most to the glory of God, and the good and peace of his Church.[259]

And although the Assembly was made up a diverse group of men, Calvinists are quick to inform us that "we should remember that all of the Westminster divines were Calvinists."[260]

The Westminster Assembly consisted of 151 members: 121 English divines, 10 members of the House of Lords, and 20 of the House of Commons. Among those summoned were Archbishop James Ussher (1581-1656) and the famed rabbinical scholar John Lightfoot (1602-1675). Ussher declined his invitation, and others, for various reasons, never appeared either.[261] The average daily attendance was about that of the first day: sixty-nine.[262] The moderator of the Assembly was William Twisse (c. 1578-1646), who had earlier written a reply to Arminius' critique of Perkins.[263] One of his assistants was John White (1575-1648), the great-grandfather of John Wesley.[264] The diverse group of men who made up the Assembly belonged to four parties, and can be distinguished by the form of church government they preferred. Although some Episcopalians were summoned, they all either refused the invitation or dropped out, except one who was expelled.[265] The Presbyterians were in the majority, as most of the Puritans favored that form of government.[266] The next party was the Independents, who favored a congregational church government and therefore were in conflict with the Presbyterians.[267] Finally, there were the Erastians. Named after Thomas Erastus (1524-1583), they maintained the authority of the State over the Church. Although very small in number, they had the support of Parliament,[268] which is substantiated by the fact that it was Parliament which called the Assembly in the first place. Absent was any divine who was not ordained in the Church of England, except for two French Reformed pastors serving in London.[269] After the Solemn League and Covenant was adopted in September by the Parliament and the members of the Assembly for "the reformation and defence of religion, the honour and happiness of the King, and the peace and safety of the three kingdoms of Scotland, England, and Ireland,"[270] a delegation from Scotland made up of two commissioners and four divines joined the Assembly.[271] But like the Synod of Dort, the presence of government officials at an ostensibly religious assembly raises some questions about its legitimacy.

The purpose of the Westminster Assembly, according to the ordinance that called it, was "to consult and advise of such matters and things, touching the premises, as shall be proposed unto them by both or either of the Houses of Parliament, and to give their advice and counsel therein to both or either of the said Houses, when, and as often as, they shall be thereunto required."[272] Specifically, the Parliament sought advice "for the settling of the Government and Liturgy of the Church of England."[273] Like the Synod of Dort, the expenses of the members of the Assembly were borne by the State.[274] Because the faulty Church-State concept is clearly manifested in the history of the Westminster Assembly, Calvinists are forced to admit the results of this union:

> The Assembly was the creature of Parliament and was never able to escape from Parliamentary supervision.[275]

> We must never, in any consideration of the work of the Assembly, forget that that body was clearly and completely subservient to the political authority of Parliament.[276]

> In earthly and political terms it was answerable, not to the King of Kings, but to the Lords and Commons of the English Parliament.[277]

Robert Baillie (1602-1662), one of the Scottish divines at the Assembly, stated during the time in question: "You know this is no proper Assembly, but a meeting called by the parliament to advise them in what things they are asked."[278] The Assembly was prohibited from divulging any of the results of their deliberations without the expressed permission of Parliament.[279] So as Schaff concludes: "The chief fault of the Assembly was that it clung to the idea of a national State Church, with a uniform system of doctrine, worship, and discipline, to which every man, woman, and child in three kingdoms should conform."[280]

Although the king prohibited the meeting of the Assembly, it was convened anyway on July 1, 1643, at Westminster Abbey (hence the name) and closed on February 22, 1649, after 1163 numbered sessions.[281] It is truly ironic that the Thirty Years' War began with the Synod of Dort and ended with the Westminster Assembly. The Assembly continued as a committee for the examination of ministers until 1652.[282] After the Westminster Divines were divided into committees, daily sessions were held from nine to two with committee meetings in the afternoons, although this schedule was later reduced to just weekly sessions.[283] The first task taken up by the Assembly was a modification of the Thirty-Nine Articles of the Church of England to make them more Calvinistic.[284] But after finishing the revision of the first fifteen articles, the Solemn League and Covenant was adopted and the focus of the Assembly changed to that of bringing "the Churches of God in the three kingdoms to the nearest conjunction and uniformity in religion, Confession of Faith, Form of Church Government, Directory for Worship and Catechizing."[285] So accordingly, the remainder of the Assembly was taken up with preparing the so-called "four parts of uniformity."[286]

From October of 1643 to April of 1645, by order of Parliament, the Assembly worked on documents concerning the government and worship of the church:

> Upon serious consideration of the present state and conjuncture of the affairs of this kingdom, the Lords and Commons assembled in Parliament do order, that the Assembly of Divines and others do forthwith confer and treat among themselves, of such a discipline and government as may be most agreeable to God's Holy Word, and most apt to procure and preserve the peace of the Church at home, and nearer agreement with the Church of Scotland, and other Reformed Churches abroad, to be settled in this Church in stead and place of the present Church government by archbishops, bishops, their chancellors, commissaries, deans, deans and chapters, archdeacons, and other ecclesiastical officers, depending upon the hierarchy, which is resolved to be taken away; and touching and concerning the

Directory of Worship, or Liturgy, hereafter to be in the Church: and to deliver their opinions and advices of and touching the same to both or either House of Parliament with all convenient speed they can.[287]

After this was done the Assembly proceeded with a confession of faith. Although preliminary work on a confession began in 1644, it was not until April of 1645 that Parliament enjoined the Assembly to prepare a confession of faith.[288] This occupied the Assembly until December of 1646. Work on a catechism was begun in September of 1646, but beginning in January of 1647, it was decided that "tuo formes of Catechisme may be prepared, one more exact and comprehensive, another more easie and short for new beginners."[289] Therefore, the remainder of the time was spent on the formulation of two catechisms, thus completing the "four parts of uniformity."

Before the Westminster Assembly was over, a Presbyterian system of church government was established in England. Thus, an attempt was made to enforce absolute uniformity in religion throughout England—just like the Anglicans had done—but it was short-lived. Because it was the creature of Parliament, any change in that body was liable to affect the Assembly. Thus, when the army, which was now controlled by the Independents, gained the ascendancy, the significance of the Assembly decreased along with the Parliament itself. The result of conflict between Parliament and the army was the purge of Parliament (called Pride's Purge, after Col. Thomas Pride [d. 1658]), in December of 1648, of the Presbyterians.[290] After this substantial reduction of Parliament (termed the Rump Parliament), the king was executed and England was declared a commonwealth, thus beginning the Interregnum (the period between reigns). In 1653 the Rump Parliament was itself dismissed and Oliver Cromwell (1599-1658) assumed power as Lord Protector. During the Protectorate of Cromwell religious toleration was extended to all Protestants (excepting Anglicans).[291] Many Baptists were even in his army.[292] After the death of Cromwell, and the overthrow of his son Richard (1626-1712), who succeeded him, the Protectorate gave way to the recalled Rump Parliament and finally the restored Long Parliament. In 1660 the monarchy was restored in the person of Charles II (1630-1685). However, with the monarchy came the restoration of Episcopacy and the repudiation of both Presbyterianism and Puritanism. But although Episcopacy remains to this day the established church in England, the Westminster Assembly still lives. Three hundred and fifty years after the convening of the Assembly, in 1993, Calvinists (mainly from America) met at Westminster Abbey to commemorate the Assembly and hold a conference highlighting its history and significance.[293] The literary products of the Assembly, however, have been continually used by Calvinists since their inception.

The Westminster Standards

Because of the decision of the Westminster Assembly to prepare two catechisms, the "four parts of uniformity" resulted in the production of five documents. Known as the Westminster Standards, only the confession of faith and the two catechisms are commonly used today. According to Presbyterian Calvinists: "The Confession and Catechisms represent the single best expression of the doctrine contained in the Scriptures."[294] The first two productions of the Assembly, *The Form of Presbyterial Church Government* and *The Directory for Public Worship,* were completed in 1644.[295] Although the former was not ratified by the English Parliament, the latter was established by ordinance in January of 1645 to replace the Book of Common Prayer.[296] However, both documents were adopted by the Scottish General Assembly in February of the same year.[297] The completed confession of faith was sent to Parliament in December of 1646 with the title: *The Humble Advice of the Assembly of Divines, Now by Authority of Parliament sitting at Westminster, concerning a Confession of Faith, presented by them lately to both Houses of Parliament.*[298] But as the House of Commons required Scripture proofs to be added, the confession was again submitted to Parliament in April of 1647 with the addition to the title of the phrase "with the Quotations and Texts of Scripture annexed."[299] It was not until June 20, 1648, that Parliament, after making some changes and omissions, ordered the publication of the confession under the title: *Articles of Christian Religion approved and passed by both Houses of Parliament, after Advice had with the Assembly of Divines by authority of Parliament.*[300] It is the original unexpunged text, however, that was adopted by the Scottish General Assembly in 1647.[301] And it is this same text, known as the Westminster Confession of Faith, that Presbyterians the world over have accepted ever since. The two catechisms, called (on account of their size) the Larger and the Shorter, were presented to Parliament without Scripture proofs in October and November, respectively, of 1647, while the proofs were provided on April 14, 1648.[302] But although both catechisms were adopted by the Scots in July of 1648, the English Parliament only approved the Shorter Catechism.[303]

The merits of the Westminster Confession of Faith have been acknowledged by Calvinists and non-Calvinists alike:

> The most complete, the most fully elaborated and carefully guarded, the most perfect, and the most vital expression that has ever been framed by the hand of man, of all that enters into what we call evangelical religion.[304]

> The ablest, clearest, and most comprehensive system of Christian doctrine ever framed.[305]

> It far more nearly approaches the full proportions of a theological treatise, and exhibits far more depth of theological insight, than any other.[306]

But Calvinists in particular regard the Westminster Confession as embodying their beliefs. Boettner calls it "the most perfect expression of the Reformed Faith."[307] McNeil terms it "a classic of Calvinism."[308] Warfield maintains that there is nothing in the Westminster Confession "which is not to be found expressly set forth in the writings" of John Calvin.[309] Some disagree, however, and claim that "Westminster theology, then, represents a substantial departure from the thought of John Calvin."[310] Nevertheless, Calvinists regard the Westminster Confession as an authority. Shedd refers to it as "the rule of faith."[311] Another terms it "the official creed of Presbyterianism."[312] Students at Westminster Theological Seminary in Philadelphia can take a course on the Westminster Assembly and examine its theology by "a study of the Westminster Confession of Faith."[313] And not only have numerous commentaries on the Confession appeared over the years, it has been translated into many languages since the first foreign translation into German in 1648.[314]

The Westminster Confession of Faith, relevant portions of which can be found in appendix 6,[315] contains thirty-three chapters, each divided into paragraphs. The longest is that on the Bible, containing ten paragraphs; the most infamous is that on predestination. The chief basis for the Confession was the strongly Calvinistic Irish Articles of Religion drawn up by Archbishop Ussher in 1615.[316] The Westminster Confession encompasses all the major doctrines of the Christian Faith. Thus, it differs from the Canons of Dort, which only relate to Calvinism. As mentioned previously, the form of the accepted Confession is that of the original produced by the Westminster Assembly and not the one approved by Parliament, which omitted chapters thirty and thirty-one, and several whole paragraphs.[317] The edition of the Confession currently in use in America is slightly different than the British edition. The differences chiefly consist in the omission of some phrases regarding the relationship between the church and the civil authorities.[318]

Although the Westminster Catechisms have likewise been lauded by Calvinists and their opponents, the Larger Catechism has, as related by Warfield, "taken a somewhat secondary place."[319] And whereas Calvinists consider the Larger Catechism "a full, balanced, edifying summary of the Christian faith,"[320] of the Shorter Catechism it has been said:

> A masterpiece of literary economy and clarity.[321]

> If the Westminster Assembly had done nothing more than produce the Shorter Catechism they would be entitled to the everlasting gratitude of the Christian church.[322]

> No product of the Divines has been more widely diffused or has exercised a deeper influence than their "Shorter Catechism."[323]

Like the Westminster Confession, the Shorter Catechism is considered "a classic of Calvinism."[324] It is also considered an authority. The Puritan theologian Richard Baxter (1615-1691) considered the Shorter Catechism, next to the Bible, "probably the best book in the world."[325] Schaff maintains that it "is one of the three typical Catechisms of Protestantism which are likely to last to the end of time."[326] Master of Divinity students at Reformed Theological Seminary are required to memorize the Shorter Catechism.[327] And also like the Westminster Confession, the Catechisms have been the subject of commentaries and have been translated into other languages.[328]

The Westminster Larger Catechism contains 196 questions and answers; the Shorter only 107. It is at the beginning of the Shorter Catechism that we find the most famous catechismal question and answer:

> Q. What is the chief end of man?
> A. Man's chief end is to glorify God, and to enjoy him forever.

Warfield credits Calvin as "the ultimate source of the opening question and answer of the Westminster Shorter Catechism."[329] Both Catechisms, however, have the distinction that each answer incorporates the corresponding question, thus forming a complete statement of faith in itself. And like the Westminster Confession of Faith, the Larger and Shorter Catechisms remain to this day the doctrinal standards of most Presbyterian churches.

With the restoration of the monarchy in England, these standards of the Westminster Assembly, which were intended to replace the Thirty-Nine Articles, came to naught as far as the English Church was concerned. But even though the work of the Westminster Assembly was repudiated in England, its Standards have remained "the fullest and ripest symbolical statement of the Calvinistic system of doctrine."[330] But again, some Calvinists disagree, claiming that "Westminster theology hardly deserves to be called Calvinistic—especially if that term is to imply the thought of Calvin himself."[331] Yet nevertheless, subscription to the Westminster Standards is still mandatory for ministers in conservative Presbyterian churches. But in spite of the admiration for these Standards, as the Presbyterian theologian William Shedd relates: "The doctrines of Calvinism formulated in the Westminster Standards are represented by many persons as destining the vast majority of the human race to an eternity of sin and misery."[332] Thus, beginning with the Cumberland Presbyterians in the early part of the nineteenth century, some Presbyterians have sought to revise the Standards in those places where the doctrines of Calvinism occur.[333]

Baptist Confessions of Faith

Baptists, because of their emphasis on the authority of

Scripture, have historically never been a creedal people. However, this does not mean that they have never produced confessions of faith or catechisms. Rather, the creedal documents that the Baptists have composed were often prepared for apologetic reasons because they were at times so misrepresented by their opponents. Out of the numerous Baptist confessions of faith that have been written there are three that are held in great esteem by the Calvinistic Baptists, with two of these being directly related to the Westminster Confession of Faith. It is therefore necessary to complete this chapter by examining these Baptist confessions of faith that are still invoked by Baptists when seeking to prove that Calvinism is the historic Baptist position.

The first confession to be considered is what has been termed the First London Confession. This confession was first issued in 1644 by seven Particular Baptist churches in London.[334] Naturally, it was both Baptistic and Calvinistic. Containing fifty-two articles, the title page read:

>   The CONFESSION OF FAITH
> Of those CHURCHES which are commonly (though falsly)
>   called ANABAPTISTS;
>   Presented to the view of all that feare God, to examine by the
>   touchstone of the Word of Truth: As likewise for the taking off
>   those aspersions which are frequently both in Pulpit and Print,
>   (although unjustly) cast upon them.

The Confession was vehemently opposed by the Episcopalian minister Daniel Featley (1582-1645). He had earlier participated in a disputation with the Baptists but was now in prison after being expelled from the Westminster Assembly.[335] In the last chapter of his book *The Dippers dipt. or, The Anabaptists duck't and plunged Over head and Eares, at a Disputation in Southwark,* Featley took issue with six articles of the new Baptist confession.[336] The Baptists, in 1646, then issued a new edition of their confession in which significant changes were made.[337] It also contained a dedication to Parliament, just as Featley's book:

> To the Right Honorable the Lords, Knights, Citizens and Burgesses in Parliament Assemblies. Right Honorable and Most Noble Patriots, In as much as there hath been a book (Featley's) lately presented unto you, in whose Dedicatory Epistle there are

many heinous accusations unjustly and falsely laid against us, we conceived it necessary to make some declaration of our innocency, and (to that end) humbly to present into your view this our Confession of Faith.[338]

But as has been proven, the revised edition of the First London Confession weakened the "distinctive Baptist character of some of the articles."[339] Shortly after this revised confession appeared, Benjamin Cox (b. 1595-c. 1661) issued what he called *An Appendix to a Confession of Faith* in which, in twenty-two articles, he expanded upon some points in the Confession.[340] This appendix, however, was not published with the Confession until 1981.[341] Other editions and reprints of the Confession also appeared later.[342]

After the restoration of the monarchy in England in 1660, there was a renewed persecution of dissenters from the Church of England. To maintain a united front, it was only natural that the groups of dissenters attempt to show the extent of agreement among themselves in regards to doctrine. The Congregationalists (Independents) had adopted the Westminster Confession of Faith in a slightly revised form in 1658. Termed the Savoy Declaration (because it was drawn up at Savoy Palace, London), it was mainly the work of the Independents who took part in the Westminster Assembly.[343] Thus, the Baptists, in order to show their agreement with the Presbyterians and Congregationalists, met in 1677 and, basing their work on the Westminster Confession, produced what has come to be called the Second London Confession.[344] Containing thirty-two articles, the title page read:

A CONFESSION OF FAITH
Put forth by the ELDERS and BRETHREN Of many
CONGREGATIONS OF
Christians (baptized upon Profession of their Faith) in *London*
and the Country.

After the Act of Toleration was issued in May of 1689, the Baptists got together again and in the course of their deliberations approved the 1677 confession and published it with the following prefix:

We the Ministers and Messengers of, and concerned for, upwards of one hundred baptized congregations in England and Wales (denying Arminianism) being met together in London, from the third of the seventh month to the eleventh of the same, 1689, to consider of some things that might be for the glory of God, and the good of these congregations; have thought meet (for the satisfaction of all other Christians that differ from us in the point of Baptism) to recommend to their perusal the confession of our faith, which confession we own, as containing the doctrine of our faith and practice, and do desire that the members of our churches respectively do furnish themselves therewith.[345]

It was signed by thirty-seven ministers, including Hanserd Knollys, William Kiffin, and Benjamin Keach.[346]

The Second London Confession of Faith, relevant portions of which can be found in appendix 7,[347] although based on the Westminster Confession, nevertheless contained enough changes to make it a Baptist confession of faith. Good terms it both "genuinely Baptistic and truly Calvinistic."[348] The principle changes were the omission of material in chapter VII on the covenants, the insertion of a new chapter XX entitled "Of the Gospel, and of the extent of the Grace thereof," the omission of chapters XXX and XXXI on "Of Church Censures" and "Of Synods and Councils," the expansion and rewriting of chapter XXV on the Church, the omission of material in chapter XXVII on the Sacraments, and the alteration of chapter XXVIII on baptism. The main section on Calvinism, however, is taken almost verbatim from the Westminster Confession. This is acknowledged by Calvinistic Baptists: "The London Confession of 1689 expressed its unreserved Calvinistic soteriology in language practically copied from the Westminster Confession."[349] Because of its reliance on the Westminster Confession, the Second London Confession has been criticized by some Calvinistic Baptists who advocate the superiority of the earlier London confession.[350] But as other Calvinistic Baptists have shown, the First London Confession was not only based on earlier non-Baptist sources, its revised edition toned down the Baptist emphasis of the first edition.[351] The Second London Confession is still held in reverence today among certain groups of Calvinistic Baptists. For example, the International Fellowship of Reformed Baptists (IFRB), formed in 1990, holds membership open to "individual ministers, Christian workers or local churches which subscribe to the doctrines of grace as set forth in the Baptist Confession of Faith of 1689."[352]

The Second London Confession made its way to the American colonies with the Particular Baptists who came to the new world. It was first adopted in an official sense by the Philadelphia Baptist Association on September 25, 1742.[353] Eventually termed the Philadelphia Confession of Faith, the first edition was printed by Benjamin Franklin (1706-1790).[354] The only difference between the London Confession and its American counterpart is the addition of two articles, bringing the total number to thirty-four. The two new articles, "Of Singing of Psalms in Public Worship" (XXIII) and "Of Laying on of Hands" (XXXI), are due to the influence of Elias Keach (1667-1701), the son of the famed signer of the Second London Confession.[355] Because of their symmetry, all subsequent references to the Second London Confession of Faith include the Philadelphia Confession as well, and vice versa.

Although the Canons of Dort only encompass the doctrines of Calvinism, the Five Points are embodied in the other Calvinistic creeds that have been mentioned. Modern-day Sovereign Grace Baptists make much ado over the consonance of election found in these Baptist confessions but paradoxically reject the confessions when it comes to other points. So the fact that the most well-known Baptist confessions of faith in history are Calvinistic means just that: a historical fact. The historical argument used by the Baptists to prove that all real Baptists should be Calvinistic is bogus. To begin with, the "historic position" of Philadelphia Confession enjoins the laying on of hands—a practice no Sovereign Grace Baptist Church employs today. And secondly, the Sovereign Grace Baptists today, the vast majority of whom are premillennial in their eschatology, disavow the amillennialism of not only the Philadelphia Confession of Faith, but both London Confessions and the Westminster Confession as well.

In closing this historical section of the book, a quote from the Calvinists Steele and Thomas is pertinent before moving on to the doctrinal section. In making the same transition in their book *The Five Points of Calvinism,* they state: "No attempt whatsoever has been made in this section to prove the truthfulness of the Calvinistic doctrines. Our sole purpose has been to give a brief history of the system and to explain its contents. We are now ready to consider its Biblical support."[356] The very opposite of this statement is here maintained, for heretofore no attempt whatsoever has been made in this section to prove the *untruthfulness* of the Calvinistic doctrines.

Our sole purpose has been to give a brief history of the system and to explain its contents. We are now ready to consider its *lack* of Biblical support.

Chapter 6
TOTAL DEPRAVITY

The first point of the TULIP system is Total Depravity. And this is as far as we can be in agreement with the Calvinists on this point. The problem we have is not with the doctrine of depravity itself, for it is a biblical doctrine. Our disagreement with the Calvinists is with what they mean when they say they believe in Total Depravity. Terms must be accurately defined before they can be profitably used. The first article of faith for a Mormon is: We believe in God, the Eternal Father, and in His Son Jesus Christ, and in the Holy Ghost. Sound orthodox? But a pretense of orthodoxy is just that: a *pretense*. Anyone who knew anything about Mormonism would recognize immediately that their *profession* was in direct contradiction to everything they really believe. Likewise, when a Jehovah's Witness claims to believe that Jesus Christ is the Son of God, he is not denoting the same belief of the Deity of Christ held by any Christian. Moreover, the use of words like "gay" and "liberal" must be qualified, lest an entirely different meaning be put on them than what was intended.

Now, concerning the term Total Depravity, it is not difficult to define. Depravity is simply "moral corruption"—see any dictionary. The word *deprave* is from the Latin *depravare*, which is made up of the intensive *de*, signifying "completely," and *pravus*, meaning "crooked." Thus, "completely crooked" or "totally depraved." Yet, the Calvinists insist on prefixing this with the designation *total*. Now, it is possible to say *total* and mean that man is all bad: speech, thoughts, actions, etc. Or, one could assert that all of mankind is bad: races, genders, ages, etc. But this will not do for the Calvinist. Total Depravity to a Calvinist has nothing to do with man's sinful nature or fallen condition, although he will emphasize these truths. When a Calvinist says that he believes in Total Depravity, he is giving you a smoke screen, however true it may be, to cover up the fact of what he really believes.

Definitions

What does the Calvinist mean when he professes to believe in Total Depravity? The Westminster Confession of Faith, in Chapter VI, entitled "Of the Fall of Man, of Sin and of the Punishment Thereof," states of the Fall of Adam and Eve:

> II. By this sin they fell from their original righteousness and communion with God, and so became dead in sin, and wholly defiled in all the parts and faculties of soul and body.
> III. They being the root of all mankind, the guilt of this sin was imputed; and the same death in sin, and corrupted nature, conveyed to all their posterity descending from them by ordinary generation.
> IV. From this original corruption, whereby we are utterly indisposed, disabled, and made opposite of all good, and wholly inclined to all evil, do proceed all actual transgressions.

This is certainly scriptural, and something that any Bible-believing Christian could agree with.

Modern-day Calvinists define Total Depravity in similar terms:

> Total Depravity means that the natural man is never able to do any good that is fundamentally pleasing to God, and, in fact, does evil all the time.[1]

> We mean by this doctrine, therefore, that man is *thoroughly crooked, wicked, and sinful by nature* in himself, and by *position* before God. This corrupt nature he received *in* Adam's fall into sin, and *from* Adam, and is evidenced in every man's *choice* and *practice* of sin, in which he is *like* Adam.[2]

> When Calvinists speak of man as being totally depraved, they mean that man's nature is corrupt, perverse, and sinful throughout.[3]

Once again, any Bible-believing Christian could agree with these definitions. So what is the problem? The problem is that this is not the whole story. When a Calvinist talks about Total Depravity, he means a great deal more than these descriptions of man's depravity. Because some Calvinists sense that "the term *total depravity* can be misleading and perhaps say more about man's sinful condition than

Scripture permits,"[4] other terms are sometimes used to describe the first point of the TULIP. Some prefer "radical" depravity.[5] C. Samuel Storms mentions "pervasive" or "extensive" depravity,[6] while Sproul prefers the new compound "radical corruption."[7] But calling Total Depravity by these other designations can never change the fact of what it really is.

Total Inability

When a Calvinist says Total Depravity, what he really means is Total Inability, which has nothing to do with Total Depravity at all, but is rather the supposed *result* of it. One Sovereign Grace Baptist simply says: "Total depravity is the cause of total inability and total inability is the result of total depravity."[8] Good explains that "inability is related to depravity as a portion of a circle is related to the whole."[9] But according to the Calvinists, man's inability is not just that "human nature has been and is utterly corrupted by sin so that man is totally incapable of doing anything to accomplish his salvation."[10] This is still not the whole story. The Calvinistic doctrine of depravity is unpretentiously stated by Calvinists as referring to man's inability to freely believe on Jesus Christ for salvation. Talbot and Crampton authenticate this proposition: "The Bible stresses the total inability of fallen man to respond to the things of God; he is not able to do so. This is what the Calvinist refers to as *'total depravity.'*"[11] Pink further expands upon the nature of man's inability: "As a *creature* the natural man is responsible to love, obey, and serve God; as a *sinner* he is responsible to repent and believe the Gospel. But at the outset we are confronted with the fact that the natural man is *unable* to love and serve God, and that the *sinner,* of himself, *cannot* repent and believe."[12] So the inability had nothing to do with man's depravity and need of a savior at all, but rather concerned man's inability to do what he is time after time commanded by God to do:

> **And saying, The time is fulfilled, and the kingdom of God is at hand: repent ye, and believe the gospel (Mark 1:15).**
>
> **And the times of this ignorance God winked at; but now commandeth all men everywhere to repent (Acts 17:30).**

This brings us to the real meaning of Total Depravity. Pink

acknowledges what he and all Calvinists really believe about Total Depravity when he says that it is the freedom of the will to resist or yield that "defines our conception of human depravity."[13] Total Depravity is therefore a *negative* doctrine. When one thinks of the depravity of man, thoughts of man's *positive* actions usually come to mind: sinful thoughts, sinful words, sinful deeds. But Total Depravity is not about anything the sinner does, it concerns what the sinner is not able to do.

So, when consulting the Westminster Confession to back up the first point of Calvinism, the proper place to look is not the aforementioned Chapter VI, but rather Chapter X, "Of Free Will," which says in part:

> III. Man, by his fall into a state of sin, hath wholly lost all ability of will to any spiritual good accompanying salvation: so as, a natural man, being altogether averse from that good, and dead in sin, is not able, by his own strength, to convert himself, or to prepare himself thereunto.
> IV. When God converts a sinner, and translates him into the state of grace, he freeth him from his natural bondage under sin; and, by his grace alone, enables him freely to will and to do that which is spiritually good; yet so, as that by reason of this remaining corruption, he doth not perfectly, nor only, will that which is good, but doth also will that which is evil.

The Canons of Dort echo this description of man's "inability":

> Therefore all men are conceived in sin, and by nature children of wrath, incapable of saving good, prone to evil, dead in sin, and in bondage thereto, and without the regenerating grace of the Holy Spirit, they are neither able nor willing to return to God, to reform the depravity of their nature, nor to dispose themselves to reformation.[14]

Although some Calvinists actually term their first point Total Inability,[15] most simply say "total depravity or inability" like they mean the same thing.[16] Others are more subtle and just stick with the term Total Depravity but define it as Total Inability.[17] As to why more Calvinists don't use the correct term, Palmer admits that the term Total Inability "suffers from being too negative."[18] But in spite of this confusing array of terminology, and no matter what a Calvinist calls the first point of the TULIP, the import is clear: man is unable to repent and believe the Gospel which God commands him to do. The fact that neither Total Depravity nor Total Inability are mentioned in the Bible does not deter a Calvinist, he just counters with "both wordings are revealed in the Word of God in other ways of expressing their modern connotation."[19]

To direct you away from the aspect of inability, the Calvinists imply that you are confusing inability with something they call "absolute depravity."[20] This is due in part to the ploy of the Calvinists when confronted with their true position. As we saw in chapter 1, the Calvinist has a peculiar habit of changing the subject or informing you what he *doesn't* believe when confronted with objections to his position. But once again we are bogged down in an abyss of terminology. Sproul prefers the term "utter depravity,"[21] while his mentor John Gerstner (1914-1996) contrasts *total* with "utter and extreme and ultimate depravity."[22] Absolute depravity has been defined as: "One expressing the evil of his sin nature as much as possible at all times."[23] The Calvinists correctly insist that this is not the case; therefore, the Christian is led to believe that Total Depravity is orthodox since he obviously agrees with the Calvinist in disdaining absolute depravity. Talbot and Crampton even call the teaching of absolute depravity "hyper-Calvinistic."[24] But just when the Calvinists' unique vocabulary was becoming understandable, the Protestant Reformed theologian Herman Hanko rejects the contrast between *total* and *absolute*, insisting that this distinction "is intended precisely to leave room for some good which man is able to perform."[25] He believes it was invented "to soften the truth of total depravity."[26] Another theologian of the Protestant Reformed Church, David Englesma, asserts that the debate about absolute depravity "is not even useful for understanding the real issue at stake in the controversy over the spiritual condition of fallen man."[27] So as we shall see throughout this work, Calvinists often have substantial differences among themselves—extending even to the doctrines of Calvinism.

The Importance of Total Depravity

The importance of Total Depravity to the Calvinistic system cannot be underestimated. Without it, the whole TULIP is destroyed, as Hanko says: "A denial of total depravity leads to a denial of sovereign grace. This in turn leads to a denial of limited atonement and unconditional election. And the preservation of the saints necessarily falls by the wayside."[28] Englesma is more direct: "Deny this doctrine, and the whole of Calvinism is demolished."[29] And not only the TULIP, for Hanko further insists that "if this truth is denied, softened, vitiated in any respect, it becomes impossible to preserve any of the truth of God's Word."[30] Total Depravity is one of the three essential points of Calvinism, the other two being Unconditional Election and Irresistible Grace. These three points are the essence of the Calvinistic system. The denial of the other two points, Limited Atonement and the Perseverance of the Saints, does not affect the basic premise of the Calvinism.

But additionally, Total Depravity is also the foundation of Calvinistic system. Gerstner asserts that "most of the problems which people have with the doctrine of predestination really are not problems concerning predestination but problems concerning total depravity."[31] He also informs us that "anyone who sees and believes that man is totally depraved and yet is saved would necessarily believe that he was elected to salvation."[32] Total Depravity necessitates the doctrines of Unconditional Election and Irresistible Grace. If all men are unable to repent and believe the Gospel, then it logically follows that if any of them are to be saved then God must first determine who they are (Unconditional Election) and then "irresistibly" overcome their "inability" (Irresistible Grace) so they can repent and believe the Gospel. So if Total Depravity is true, then there is nothing anyone can do except claim Lamentations 3:26 as his life verse:

> *It is* **good that** *a man* **should both hope and quietly wait for the salvation of the LORD (Lam. 3:26).**

If the Calvinistic doctrine of Total Depravity is true, all one can do is *hope* that he is the subject of Unconditional Election, and if he is, then quietly *wait* for God to save him by Irresistible Grace. It is as simple as that. But conversely, if Total Depravity is proven to be spurious, the rest of the TULIP withers. If man does *not* have inability, then he can be saved without the other points of Unconditional Election and Irresistible Grace. Because Total Inability is said to be the result of Total Depravity, a study of the depravity of man is in order before an analysis of the Calvinistic theological implication of it.

The Depravity of Man

The doctrine of man's depravity is very important to the Bible-believing Christian who refuses the label *Calvinist* or *Arminian*. From the standpoint of soteriology, the depravity of man is extremely significant. It is here that we see man's fallen sinful condition and hence the whole reason for salvation in all its aspects. The Calvinist Seaton accurately stated: "If we have deficient and light views about sin, then we are liable to have defective views regarding the means necessary for the salvation of the sinner."[33] Any denial or weakening of man's depravity will also cause one to have erroneous views on other Bible doctrines as well, as Pink recognizes: "A man's orthodoxy on this subject determines his viewpoint on many other doctrines of great importance."[34] And not only that, a man must be lost before he can be saved. Now, it is true that all men are lost, but unless a man really believes that as a result of his sin and depravity he is indeed lost, he has the "inability" to be saved. So, recognizing that most orthodox Christians believe in the depravity of man as it is taught in the Bible, the Calvinist uses the doctrine of man's depravity to make his doctrine of Total Depravity look orthodox. By focusing on man's depravity instead of its supposed result, the Calvinist subtly gains adherents to his position. The next step is to convince everyone that the Calvinists alone have a monopoly on the belief in the depravity of man. This is not hard to do given the state of apostate Christianity today. Calvinists further insist that if one denies *their* doctrine of Total Depravity, then sin and the Fall of man could not be taken very seriously, man must not be depraved, and that ultimately one would have to believe in some form of salvation by works. Hanko contends that "those who deny the truth of Total Depravity are also those who soften the harsh realities of sin."[35] Boettner claims that "only Calvinists seem to take the doctrine of the fall very seriously."[36] Rose implies that to deny Total Depravity is to "hold that mankind is basically good."[37] Custance argues that if a man has the ability to merely respond "favorably to the moving of the Holy Spirit in his heart" then "salvation a joint effort."[38] But in spite of the best efforts of the Calvinists, it will be maintained throughout this chapter that one does not have to be a Calvinist to believe in the depravity of man and all that the Bible says about it.

The study of history is the study of man's depravity: wars, starvation, rape, beatings, torture, murder, genocide, holocausts, enslavement, corruption, tyranny, theft, lies, deceit, pornography, adultery, abortion, infanticide. The list is endless. But in spite of the increases in all areas of technology, and the best efforts of governments and the United Nations, man is a failure, and is growing worse. The empirical evidence for the depravity of man parallels the testimony of the Scriptures. And it is in the Scriptures themselves that the true doctrine of the depravity of man must be found, not in a Reformed creed or a Calvinistic theology book. So if "inability" is the result of Total Depravity, then it behooves us to first examine man's depravity and then the claims for its conjectured result.

There is obviously a tremendous difference between the original creation and the world as it now exists:

And God saw every thing that he had made, and, behold, it was very good. And the evening and the morning were the sixth day (Gen. 1:31).

And **we know that we are of God, and the whole world lieth in wickedness (1 John 5:19).**

Contrary to the theories of Charles Darwin (1809-1882), man did not evolve—he fell. The fall of Adam in Genesis chapter three is of the utmost importance, for as Pink correctly maintains: "The Divine record of the Fall is the only possible explanation of the present condition of the human race. It alone accounts for the presence of evil in a world made by a beneficent and perfect Creator. It affords the only adequate explanation for the universality of sin."[39] Man was created **"upright"** (Ecc. 7:29), in the **"image of God"** (Gen. 1:26), **"a little lower than the angels"** (Psa. 8:5), and crowned with **"glory and honour"** (Psa. 8:5). He was created to **"replenish the earth," "subdue it,"** and **"have dominion"** over it (Gen. 1:28), all for God's pleasure (Rev. 4:11). But man fell, and it is the fall of Adam that explains how man went from **"upright"** to "depraved."

The fall of Adam is so important to the doctrine of salvation itself that, as Pink relates: "By denying the Fall, the imperative need of the new birth has been concealed."[40] The Bible explicitly states that it is because of Adam's willful sin (1 Tim. 2:14) that man is in the state he is in:

Wherefore, as by one man sin entered into the world, and death by sin; and so death passed upon all men, for that all have sinned (Rom. 5:12).

For as by one man's disobedience many were made sinners, so by the obedience of one shall many be made righteous (Rom. 5:19).

In fact, the unsaved man is not only said to be in Adam's image (1 Cor. 15:49), but in Adam (1 Cor. 15:22). Pink sums it up admirably:

> The relationship of our race to Adam or Christ divides men into two classes, each receiving nature and destiny from its respective head. All the individuals who comprise these two classes are so identified with their heads that it has justly been said: "There have been but two men in the world, and two facts of history." These two men are Adam and Christ; the two facts in history are the disobedience of the former, by which many were made sinners, and the obedience of the latter, by which many were made righteousness. By the former came *ruin,* by the latter came *redemption;* and neither ruin nor redemption can be Scripturally apprehended except as they are seen to be accomplished by those representatives, and except we understand the relationships expressed by being "in Adam" and "in Christ."[41]

The fall of Adam plunged man into sin and death: imputed sin (Rom. 5:12-19), natural sin (Eph. 2:3), personal sin (Rom. 3:23); physical death (1 Cor. 15:21), spiritual death (Eph. 2:1), eternal death (Rev. 20:14-15).

Because of his relationship to Adam, in the sight of God, the unsaved man is not just sick or corrupt, he is dead: **"And you *hath he quickened,* who were dead in trespasses and sins"** (Eph. 2:1). This spiritual death began before birth:

Who can bring a clean *thing* out of an unclean? not one (Job 14:4).

Behold, I was shapen in iniquity; and in sin did my mother conceive me (Psa. 51:5).

This spiritual death is present at birth:

> **Yet man is born unto trouble, as the sparks fly upward (Job 5:7).**

> **The wicked are estranged from the womb: they go astray as soon as they be born, speaking lies (Psa. 58:3).**

This spiritual death is manifest in youth:

> **The imagination of man's heart is evil from his youth (Gen. 8:21).**

> **His bones are full of the sin of his youth, which shall lie down with him in the dust (Job 20:11).**

It is because **"that which is born of the flesh is flesh"** (John 3:6), that man is born wrong and therefore **"must be born again"** (John 3:7).

Concerning the depravity of human nature, it has aptly been said: "In truth, no doctrine of the Scriptures is expressed in more numerous or more various forms, or in terms more direct or less capable of misapprehension."[42] In his fallen, depraved, spiritually dead condition, man is described a number of ways in the Bible: **"ungodly"** (Rom. 5:6), **"children of disobedience"** (Col. 3:6), **"children of wrath"** (Eph. 2:3), **"servants of sin"** (Rom. 6:20), **"abominable and filthy"** (Job 15:15), **"foolish, disobedient, deceived"** (Tit. 3:3). Man is like the grass that withereth (Isa. 40:6-7), a sheep gone astray (Isa. 53:6), and a troubled sea (Isa. 57:20). Man is also likened to **"dust"** (Psa. 103:14), **"a wild ass's colt"** (Job 11:12), and **"a worm"** (Job 25:6). Man is in darkness (1 Pet. 2:9), blinded by Satan (2 Cor. 4:4). Therefore, his thoughts are vanity (Psa. 94:11), he lives a vain life (Ecc. 6:12), and walks in a vain show (Psa. 39:6).

This depravity of man is universal:

> **For all have sinned, and come short of the glory of God (Rom. 3:23).**

> **For *there is* not a just man upon the earth, that doeth good, and sinneth not (Ecc. 7:20).**

Deep down inside, man is a dark abyss of sin and wickedness:

> **And he said, That which cometh out of the man, that defileth the man.**
> **For from within, out of the heart of men, proceed evil thoughts, adulteries, fornications, murders,**
> **Thefts, covetousness, wickedness, deceit, lasciviousness, an evil eye, blasphemy, pride, foolishness:**
> **All these evil things come from within, and defile the man (Mark 7:20-23).**

These things come out of the heart because the heart itself is corrupt:

> **The heart *is* deceitful above all *things*, and desperately wicked: who can know it? (Jer. 17:9).**

> **Because sentence against an evil work is not executed speedily, therefore the heart of the sons of men is fully set in them to do evil (Ecc. 8:11).**

Therefore, it is not man's wicked deeds that make him depraved, but his depravity is the cause of his wicked deeds. In his unregenerate state, the best efforts of man are not good enough:

> **Every man at his best state is altogether vanity (Psa. 39:5).**

> **But we are all as an unclean *thing*, and all our righteousnesses are as filthy rags; and we all do fade as a leaf; and our iniquities, like the wind, have taken us away (Isa. 64:6).**

Because of his depraved condition, everything man does is tainted with sin:

> **An high look, and a proud heart, *and* the plowing of the wicked, *is* sin (Pro. 21:4).**

> **The sacrifice of the wicked *is* abomination: how much more, *when* he bringeth it with a wicked mind? (Pro. 21:27).**

The Bible indictment of man is severe but justified. Jonathan Edwards accurately concluded over two hundred years ago: "The reality and greatness of the depravity of man's nature appears in this, that he has a prevailing propensity to be *continually* sinning against God."[43] He also correctly related that "not only a constant commission of sin, but a constant increase in the habits and practice of wickedness, is the true tendency of man's depraved nature, if unrestrained by divine grace."[44]

The depravity of man—not his environment, education, or class—is what explains the carnage of human history. It has correctly been said that "every period in history in the story of mankind ends in apostasy."[45] Using the biblical division of mankind into three groups: **"Give none offence, neither to the Jews, nor to the Gentiles, nor to the church of God"** (1 Cor. 10:32), we can see the truth of this principle. First the Gentiles. Adam and Eve lived in the most optimum conditions that have ever existed—but they fell. God wiped out the world and began again with Noah because of the condition the world was in:

> **And God saw that the wickedness of man was great in the earth, and *that* every imagination of the thoughts of his heart was only evil continually (Gen. 6:5).**
>
> **The earth also was corrupt before God, and the earth was filled with violence.**
> **And God looked upon the earth, and, behold, it was corrupt; for all flesh had corrupted his way upon the earth (Gen. 6:11-12).**

At the tower of Babel, God again had to intervene with man. This time he confounded their language and scattered them abroad (Gen. 11:7-8). From this until the time of Christ, God suffered all nations to walk in their own ways (Acts 14:16), "winking" at their ignorance, but he **"now commandeth all men every where to repent"** (Acts 17:30). This does not mean that Gentiles are not religious—to the contrary—they are very religious, but **"the things which the Gentiles sacrifice, they sacrifice to devils"** (1 Cor. 10:20). The Gentiles, **"which know not God"** (1 Thes. 4:5), walk **"in the vanity of their mind"** (Eph. 4:17) being **"carried away unto these dumb idols"** (1 Cor. 12:2).

The nation of Israel fared no better. God called out Abraham to make a great nation (Gen. 12:1-3). This in turn was passed on to Isaac (Gen. 17:19) and Jacob (Gen. 28:3-4). Jacob then went down into Egypt where his sons became a great nation (Exo. 1:7). After Israel became enslaved, God remembered his covenant with Abraham, Isaac, and Jacob (Exo. 2:24-25), declaring: **"Israel is my son, even my firstborn"** (Exo. 4:22). God chose Israel to be a peculiar people above the other nations (Deu. 14:2). It was a pure case of "sovereign election," as the Calvinist would say. But the nation of Israel did evil from their youth (Jer. 32:30). They rebelled against God (Deu. 9:7), provoked him to wrath (Deu. 9:8), murmured (Exo. 16:23), and became stiffnecked (Exo. 32:9); prompting God to kill some by fire (Num. 11:1), the plague (Num. 11:33), and finally almost consuming the whole nation (Exo. 32:10). Israel was commanded not to defile themselves with the ways of the other nations (Lev. 18:24), nor to make any covenant with them (Exo. 34:12), but to utterly destroy them (Deu. 7:2), showing no pity (Deu. 7:16). Instead, the children of Israel **"walked in the statutes of the heathen"** (2 Kgs. 17:8), and did **"worse than the heathen whom the LORD had destroyed"** (2 Chr. 33:9). God finally sent them into captivity in Babylon under Nebuchadnezzar (Dan 1:1-2). And although many Jews returned to their homeland under Ezra and Nehemiah, they never regained their prominence over the nations. When their Messiah showed up to deliver them, they crucified him and declared: **"His blood *be* on us, and on our children"** (Mat. 27:25); therefore: **"The wrath is come upon them to the uttermost"** (1 Thes. 2:16).

The history of the Church age is the same: apostasy. To compare the simple organization of the churches in the New Testament with the proliferation of denominations, sects, and cults all claiming to be the "true church" is to see quite a formidable contrast. The development of the Roman Catholic Church, with its history of corruption, persecution, politics, and false doctrine, is one of the greatest tragedies of history. But even in his day, the Apostle Paul warned of coming apostasy:

> **For I know this, that after my departing shall grievous wolves enter in among you, not sparing the flock.**
> **Also of your own selves shall men arise, speaking perverse things, to draw away disciples after them (Acts 20:29-30).**

The worldly, impotent, effeminate condition of the Church today needs no further elaboration. This too was prophesied by the Apostle Paul:

> Now the Spirit speaketh expressly, that in the latter times some shall depart from the faith, giving heed to seducing spirits, and doctrines of devils (1 Tim. 4:1).
>
> For the time will come when they will not endure sound doctrine; but after their own lusts shall they heap to themselves teachers, having itching ears;
> And they shall turn away *their* ears from the truth, and shall be turned unto fables (2 Tim. 4:3-4).

What does the Bible say about the depravity of man? **"The scripture hath concluded all under sin"** (Gal. 3:22).

Everything that the Calvinists say about the depravity of man is certainly in line with what the Scriptures say. Yet, as has been stated previously, and will be reiterated throughout this chapter, one does not have to be a Calvinist to believe in the truth of man's depravity. The two men whom Calvinists consider to be the basest of Arminians—Arminius and Wesley—do not differ from the Calvinists on this important subject at all. We saw in chapter 4 that, on the fall and depravity of man, Arminius was just as orthodox as the most radical Calvinist. Because of the sin of Adam: "Man fell under the displeasure and the wrath of God, rendered himself subject to a double death, and deserving to be deprived of the primeval righteousness and holiness in which a great part of the image of God consisted."[46] This condemnation is "common to the entire race and to all their posterity," for "whatever punishment was brought down upon our first parents, has likewise pervaded and yet pursues all their posterity: So that all men 'are by nature the children of wrath,' (Ephes. ii, 3,) obnoxious to condemnation, and to temporal as well as to eternal death."[47] He further characterized man as hopelessly lost:

> In his *lapsed and sinful state,* man is not capable, of and by himself, either to think, to will, or to do that which is really good; but it is necessary for him to be regenerated and renewed in his intellect, affections or will, and in all his powers, by God in Christ through the Holy Spirit, that he may be qualified rightly to understand, esteem, consider, will, and perform whatever it truly good.[48]

Because it cannot be disputed that Arminius described man's

present condition in language that any Calvinist could agree with, this fact has been acknowledged by honest Calvinists:

> The language of Augustine, Martin Luther, or John Calvin is scarcely stronger than that of Arminius.[49]

> The statements of Arminius himself, in regard to the natural depravity of man, so far as we have them upon record, are full and satisfactory.[50]

Wesley's statements on the fall and depravity of man are likewise consonant with Scripture:

> If we were not ruined by the first Adam, neither are we recovered by the second. If the sin of Adam was not imputed to us, neither is the righteousness of Christ.[51]

> Man in his natural state, is altogether corrupt, through all the faculties of his soul: corrupt in his understanding, his will, his affections, his conscience, and his memory.[52]

> By the grace of God, know thyself. Know and feel that thou wast shapen in wickedness, and in sin did thy mother conceive thee; and that thou thyself hast been heaping sin upon sin, ever since thou couldest discern good from evil. Own thyself guilty of eternal death; and renounce all hope of ever being able to save thyself.[53]

And like they were forced to admit about Arminius, honest Calvinists also acknowledge that Wesley's "descriptions of the fall were as dark as any of those found in Augustine, Luther, or Calvin."[54]

Because of man's spiritual condition, there is a **"great gulf fixed"** (Luke 16:26) between God and man: **"How then can man be justified with God? or how can he be clean *that is* born of a woman?"** (Job 25:4). Man has a serious problem. In relation to God, unregenerate men are said to be his **"enemies"** (Rom. 5:10), under the **"condemnation"** (John 3:18) and **"wrath of God"** (John 3:36). The natural man is **"alienated from the life of God"** (Eph. 4:18), **"guilty before God"** (Rom. 3:19), and **"cannot please God"** (Rom. 8:8). But if salvation is **"by grace"** (Eph. 2:8) and **"not of works"** (Eph. 2:9), then what could a man possibly do to escape this horrible predicament? The answer is: he can't *do* anything. Man has the "inability" to do anything to save himself, merit God's favor, or demand that God save him. So as the disciples once asked: **"Who then can be saved?"** (Mat. 19:25). If what the Bible says about man is true, how could anyone ever possibly be saved? There are two alternatives: the Bible and TULIP Calvinism. The Bible says:

> **And brought them out, and said, Sirs, what must I do to be saved?**
> **And they said, Believe on the Lord Jesus Christ, and thou shalt be saved, and thy house (Acts 16:30-31).**

But as we have seen, because of their connotation of Total Depravity, the Calvinist would have to say:

> *It is* **good that** *a man* **should both hope and quietly wait for the salvation of the LORD (Lam. 3:26).**

That is the difference between the Bible and Calvinism. In the Bible the sinner believes and he is saved; in Calvinism the sinner *hopes* he is one of the "elect" and then *waits* for God to save him if he is.

The issue then is whether a man can believe of his own free will. Pink asks the defining question: "Does it lie within the province of man's will to accept or reject the Lord Jesus Christ as Saviour?"[55] The question here does not concern whether a man has the *natural* ability in and of himself to repent and believe the Gospel without the word of God and the conviction of the Holy Spirit. That is not the issue, although that is what the Calvinist would like everyone to think the issue is. But no one who believes what the Bible says about the depravity of man would assent to such a proposition. Therefore, the heart of the matter is whether a man has the free will to respond to the word of God and the Holy Spirit *without* being the subject of Unconditional Election and Irresistible Grace. Again, Pink concludes: "Granted that the Gospel is preached to the sinner, that the Holy Spirit convicts him of his lost condition, does it, in the final analysis, lie within the power of his own will to resist or to yield himself up to God?"[56] The Calvinist would answer in the negative. But whether this is true remains to be seen.

Depravity and the Will

As we have seen, the problem with Calvinism is not what it teaches about the depravity of man but rather what it teaches about the result of this depravity. The Calvinistic result is recounted by Spencer: *"Total Depravity* insists that man does not have a 'free will' in the sense that he is *free* to trust Jesus Christ as his Lord and Saviour."[57] The denial that man has the free will to repent and believe the Gospel is part of the broader teaching that man, because of his depravity, has the inability to do anything good at all:

> Inasmuch as Adam's offspring are born with sinful natures, they do not have the ABILITY to choose spiritual good over evil. Consequently, man's will is no longer free (i.e., free from the dominion of sin) as Adam's will was free before the fall. Instead, man's will, as the result of inherited depravity, is in bondage to his sinful nature.[58]

So "even though man is born with the freedom to choose what he so desires, he no longer has the ability to choose good (righteousness). His every desire is to do evil in the sight of God."[59] Man "has only the power to choose between evils and since he sometimes chooses the lesser evil, he appears to be choosing the good."[60] The fallacy of this idea will be addressed later.

As a philosophical question that has been debated for centuries, and continues to be debated among philosophers to this day, the question of whether man has a free will is not just limited to Calvinism. There is one notable difference, however, between a deterministic philosopher and a Calvinist. No philosopher who denies to man a free will does so on the basis of man's depravity. And as we shall see in the next chapter, there is another aspect to the denial of free will by the Calvinists that is likewise espoused by no philosopher. In fact, the other facet of this denial actually renders the present debate about man's will completely irrelevant because of what the Calvinists believe about predestination. But since the doctrine of Total Depravity is ultimately built on the premise that a man **"dead in trespasses and sins"** (Eph. 2:1) cannot of his own free will accept the salvation offered in Jesus Christ, the very nature of the will itself must first be considered.

Regarding the essential nature of the will of man, there is no disagreement between Calvinists and their opponents. The classic definition is that of Jonathan Edwards:

> The faculty of the will is that faculty or power or principle of mind by which it is capable of choosing: an act of the will is the same as an act of choosing or choice.[61]

Pink simply says: "The will is the faculty of choice, the immediate cause of all action."[62] Other Calvinists have either copied verbatim this definition[63] or defined it in similar terms.[64] Therefore, whether one consults a dictionary or a Calvinist makes no difference: so far both are in agreement. But like the term Total Depravity, it is the first word in the expression "free will" that is the subject of controversy. The will of man is regulated by his nature and is influenced from without, as Pink again comments: "There is something which *influences* the choice; something which *determines* the decision."[65] But contrary to the Calvinists, this has never been disputed by any Christian who believed what the Bible said about man's depravity. Freedom is not the absence of influences. So to convince the skeptic that his doctrine of free will is correct, the Calvinist first invents a caricature of the "Arminian" position:

> In Arminian theology, for man to be free, nothing may determine his choices; they must be completely spontaneous. But this is logically and biblically impossible. There is no such thing as an uncaused action. Every choice man makes is caused by something (i.e., some inner disposition), otherwise, he couldn't choose. The concept of an uncaused choice is selfcontradictory. No choice can be completely spontaneous. If this Arminian concept of free will is taken to its logical conclusion, then it would be sinful to preach the gospel to fallen man. Why? Because it would be an attempt to *cause* him to turn to Christ, which would be a violation of his free will.[66]

The Calvinists then resurrect the old "guilt by association" argument and associate their opponents with Pelagians, Roman Catholics, and Finneyites in addition to Arminians.[67]

The debate over man's will hinges on the meaning attached to the word *free*. It is only by assigning to their opponents a broad and erroneous view of the word *free* that the Calvinists can make outrageous statements like:

Free will is nonsense.[68]

Free will is the invention of man, instigated by the devil.[69]

Free will makes man his own savior and his own god.[70]

The heresy of free will dethrones God and enthrones man.[71]

If the theory of free-will were true, it would give the possibility of repentance after death.[72]

Gerstner bids us to "pull down that banner of free will, which is a false symbol of a nonexisting entity."[73] Clark audaciously insists: "It is obvious that the Bible contradicts the notion of free will that its acceptance by professing Christians can be explained only by the continuing ravages of sin blinding the minds of men."[74]

But in spite of their attack on "freewillism,"[75] Calvinists do believe that man has a free will. The problem, however, is the significance of the word *free*. Tom Ross explains: "Man's will is free only within the boundaries of his nature. It is free in only one sense; it is free to act according to its sinful nature."[76] Nature is that which characterizes and impels; a principle of operation; a power impelling to action. But according to the Calvinists, the will is a servant—free to act *only* according to nature. Boettner claims that "only the Calvinistic principle that the will is determined by the nature of the person and the inducements presented, reaches a conclusion in harmony with that of Scripture."[77] Tom Wells maintains that "the natural man's will is bound to what he is."[78] This brings us back to the distinction between total and absolute depravity: whether man exercises the evil of his nature at all times. When Calvinists seek to prove Total Depravity, the difference between the two is insisted on, but when they attempt to support their concept of the will, it is ignored. Thus, even Calvinists have sharply criticized Calvin for his extreme views on the will of man in his fallen state: "His view of the fallen will not only manifests an inconsistency; it is defective as well."[79]

To prove that the natural man can only exercise his will in accordance with his depraved nature, Calvinists make some analogies. The first is to God himself. God is holy, and because of his nature he *cannot* sin. So God himself has inability.[80] The second is similar. For the saved man who has been regenerated,

God will one day **"change his vile body"** (Phil. 3:21) that he too may be holy with the inability to sin again.[81] Both of these statements are certainly true. Reference is then made to Adam: "In unfallen Adam the will was *free*, free in *both* directions, free toward good and free toward evil."[82] Once again, no one is disputing this assertion. The Lord Jesus Christ is then mentioned as being impeccable, that is, not able to sin because of his divine nature.[83] But since he was **"the second man"** (1 Cor. 15:47), **"the last Adam"** (1 Cor. 15:45), **"made in the likeness of men"** (Phil. 2:7), and **"in all points tempted like as *we are yet* without sin"** (Heb. 4:16), it is sometimes maintained that Christ was indeed like Adam, with his will free toward good or evil. Nevertheless, all would agree that now, in his risen, glorified state, the Lord Jesus Christ has the inability to sin. Last is the unregenerate man. Pink concludes:

> Now in contradistinction from the will of the Lord Jesus Christ which was biased toward good, and Adam's will which, before his fall, was in a condition of moral equipoise—capable of turning toward either good or evil—the *sinner's* will is *biased toward evil,* and therefore is free in one direction only, namely in the direction of evil. The sinner's will is *enslaved* because it is in bondage to and is the servant of a depraved heart.[84]

Naturally, the Calvinist offers scriptural "proof" for the truth of his doctrine:[85]

> **Even so every good tree bringeth forth good fruit; but a corrupt tree bringeth forth evil fruit.**
> **A good tree cannot bring forth evil fruit, neither *can* a corrupt tree bring forth good fruit (Mat. 7:17-18).**
>
> **O generation of vipers, how can ye, being evil, speak good things? for out of the abundance of the heart the mouth speaketh.**
> **A good man out of the good treasure of the heart bringeth forth good things: and an evil man out of the evil treasure bringeth forth evil things (Mat. 12:34-35).**

The idea here being that since man has a depraved nature he can only do according to that nature.

Now, it is certainly true that unregenerate men are **"the servants of sin"** (Rom. 6:20), **"dead in trespasses and sins"** (Eph.

2:1), and are **"by nature the children of wrath"** (Eph. 2:3). But does this mean that they can *only* act according to their nature? If it does then they not only have the inability to accept Jesus Christ, they have the inability to do anything good whatsoever, for the teaching that fallen man can exercise his will only in accordance with his depraved nature is why the Calvinist maintains that man has the inability to do anything good at all. These two ideas are sometimes referred to as "spiritual inability" and "moral inability."[86] There are basically four things wrong with the teaching that the natural man can act only according to his nature. Two of them concern a man forgotten in the previous analogies—the saved man, while the other two pertain to the unregenerate man—man's nature after the Fall and man's ability in the state of depravity.

First of all, concerning the saved man, one would think that if an unsaved man is like a **"corrupt tree"** (Mat. 7:17) that can only produce rotten fruit then a saved man must be like a **"good tree"** (Mat. 7:17) that can only produce good fruit. This is exactly how Boettner interprets it.[87] He says that "in this similitude the good and evil trees represent good and evil men."[88] Of these men he maintains that "one class of men is governed by one set of principles, while the other class is governed by another set of basic principles."[89] He insists that "it is impossible, then, for one and the same root to bring forth fruit of different kinds."[90] But is this interpretation true? Does a saved man *always* produce good fruit? Does a man stop sinning when he is saved? Don't some Christians bring forth bad fruit? And what about those who produce **"no fruit"** (Mark 4:7), where do they fit in? And what about the context of these passages in Matthew? The context is false prophets who come in sheep's clothing (Mat. 7:15). They looked and acted like sheep (Mat. 7:21). It was only by their fruit—their false teaching—that they could be discovered for what they really were (Mat. 7:16).

Secondly, one would think that man's "totally inability" would be rectified by salvation since all Calvinists claim that the natural man had "inability" and the saved man had "ability." But the Apostle Paul still acknowledged his "inability" *after* his salvation:

For that which I do I allow not: for what I would, that do I not; but what I hate, that do I.
If then I do that which I would not, I consent unto the law that *it is* **good.**

> Now then it is no more I that do it, but sin that dwelleth in me.
> For I know that in me (that is, in my flesh,) dwelleth no good thing: for to will is present with me; but *how* to perform that which is good I find not.
> For the good that I would I do not: but the evil which I would not, that I do.
> Now if I do that I would not, it is no more I that do it, but sin that dwelleth in me (Rom. 7:15-20).

And not just the Apostle Paul, but all Christians: **"For the flesh lusteth against the Spirit, and the Spirit against the flesh: and these are contrary the one to the other: so that ye cannot do the things that ye would"** (Gal. 5:17). So even the "elect" have "inability."

The nature of man after the Fall was correctly perceived by J. B. Heard (b. 1828) over one hundred years ago: "The mystery of human nature seems to lie in this, that men are born into the world with a living body and soul, but with a dead or dormant spirit."[91] Even though the Calvinists acknowledge that Adam died spiritually, only the trichotomist can properly explain the results of the Fall and therefore man's depravity. And not only the Fall, but as Heard relates, without the distinction between soul and spirit "the doctrine of the new birth is incomplete" and "the doctrine of the indwelling of the Holy Ghost would be utterly unmeaning."[92] This is not to say that all Calvinists reject the tripartite nature of man, nor that all non-Calvinists receive it. But as Pink the trichotomist recognizes about man's Fall: "That does not mean that either his soul or spirit, or any part thereof, ceased to be."[93] However, the debate over whether the constitution of man is a trichotomy or a dichotomy is really irrelevant since Calvinists can be found on both sides of the issue.[94] So as Boettner the dichotomist states of man: "While he is dead spiritually, that does not mean that his spirit is inactive or unconscious."[95]

Now, concerning the nature of unregenerate man after the Fall, the focus is usually on what man lost. But as Pink recognizes, there is also something that man *gained* by his fall into sin:

> Through sin man obtained that which he did not have before (at least in operation), namely, *a conscience*—a knowledge of both good and evil. This was something which unfallen man did not

possess, for man was created in a state of innocency, and innocence is ignorance of evil. But as soon as man partook of the forbidden fruit he became conscious of his wrongdoing, and his eyes were opened to see his fallen condition. And conscience, the moral instinct, is something which is now common to human nature. Man has that within him which witnesses to his fallen and sinful condition![96]

That man now had a conscience after he fell can be seen by comparing the attitude of Adam and Eve before and after the Fall:

And they were both naked, the man and his wife, and were not ashamed (Gen. 2:25).

And the eyes of them both were opened, and they knew that they *were* **naked; and they sewed fig leaves together, and made themselves aprons (Gen. 3:7).**

To the dismay of the Dutch Reformed theologian Homer Hoeksema,[97] the Canons of Dort echo the Scripture on this point:

There remain, however, in man since the fall, the glimmering of natural light, whereby he retains some knowledge of God, of natural things, and of the differences between good and evil, and discovers some regard for virtue, good order in society, and for maintaining an orderly external deportment. But so far is this light of nature from being sufficient to bring him to a saving knowledge of God, and to true conversion, that he is incapable of using it aright even in things natural and civil. Nay further, this light, such as it is, man in various ways renders wholly polluted, and holds it in unrighteousness, by doing which he becomes inexcusable before God.[98]

The remnant of man's fallen spirit is his conscience. Conscience does not behold God, but only his law, as Pink explains: "Conscience is the still small voice of God within the soul, testifying to the fact that man is not his own master but responsible to a moral law which either approves or reproves."[99] The knowledge of good and evil gives man a conscience. It is one thing that separates man from the animals. Just as there is a **"great gulf fixed"** (Luke 16:26) between God and man, so too between man and the animals. Without a conscience man is on the level of an animal when it comes to spiritual things and can no more believe on Jesus Christ than a dog or cat can. Conscience also explains the distinction between total and absolute depravity—why depraved man does not express the evil of his sin nature at all times. This is not to imply that man is not depraved or always follows his conscience, although this is what the Calvinist will accuse his opponents of believing. The relative state of depravity a man is in does affect his conscience. Men are said to have an evil conscience (Heb. 10:22), a defiled conscience (Tit. 1:15), a seared conscience (1 Tim. 4:2), and a weak conscience (1 Cor. 8:12). A defective view of the nature of man after his fall into sin is what leads to the false teaching of man's inability to act contrary to his nature. And once again, it is a Calvinist who points out Calvin's mistake on the matter: "Calvin retains in the fallen state so little of the will as it was created that he cannot explain adequately the moral character of human action in that state, when it still makes choices between good and evil."[100]

The final thing wrong with the teaching that the natural man can act only according to his nature concerns man's ability in the state of depravity. First of all, it is on the basis of the conscience that a depraved sinner who has never heard the Gospel has "ability":

> **For when the Gentiles, which have not the law, do by nature the things contained in the law, these, having not the law, are a law unto themselves:**
> **Which shew the work of the law written in their hearts, their conscience also bearing witness, and *their* thoughts the mean while accusing or else excusing one another (Rom. 2:14-15).**

This is confirmed by a Calvinist: "This accusing and excusing suggests further that the fallen conscience still faces the choice between doing good or evil."[101] But what about the existence of a "natural motivation to moral goodness in the fallen will" that has been corrupted by the Fall?[102] Again, an honest Calvinist: "The answer has to be yes; for it is the most reasonable interpretation of the Pauline language. The burden of proof is on Calvin to defend his view that the fall reduced the nature of the will as God created it to a spontaneous and exclusive pursuit of evil."[103] And secondly, after saying to the Jews that his doctrine was not his but God's (John 7:16), the Lord Jesus Christ laid down a principle that directly appeals to man's will: **"If any man will do his will, he shall know of the doctrine, whether it be of God, or *whether* I speak of myself"** (John 7:17). Pink even confirms the fact of man's "ability":

> In this declaration our Lord laid down a principle of supreme practical importance. He informs us how *certainty* may be arrived at in connection with the things of God. He tells us how spiritual discernment and assurance are to be obtained. The fundamental condition for obtaining spiritual *knowledge* is a genuine heart-desire to carry out the revealed will of God in our lives. Wherever the heart is right God gives the capacity to apprehend His truth.[104]

These comments by Pink show that the Calvinistic teaching that man's will is not free because it can only act according to his depraved nature is disproved by not only the Bible, but Calvinists as well.

A true view of man's fallen nature and depraved condition shows that man does have the "ability" to do "good." Sometimes it is generic statements that apply to anyone:

> **A good *man* leaveth an inheritance to his children's children: and the wealth of the sinner *is* laid up for the just (Pro. 13:22).**
>
> **A merry heart doeth good *like* a medicine: but a broken spirit drieth the bones (Pro. 17:22).**
>
> **But glory, honour, and peace, to every man that worketh good, to the Jew first, and also to the Gentile (Rom. 2:10).**
>
> **Servants, *be* subject to *your* masters with all fear; not only to the good and gentle, but also to the froward (1 Pet. 2:18).**

Other times it is the unregenerate in general that do "good":

> **And if ye do good to them which do good to you, what thank have ye? for sinners also do even the same (Luke 6:33).**
>
> **For they that are such serve not our Lord Jesus Christ, but their own belly; and by good words and fair speeches deceive**

the hearts of the simple (Rom. 16:18).

There are also occasions when specific individuals are mentioned as either doing good or having the capability of doing good. Abimelech and a couple of his companions, all of whom hated Isaac (Gen. 26:27), who was a type of Christ (Gen. 22:2), were unregenerate, yet it is recorded that they replied to Issac:

> **That thou wilt do us no hurt, as we have not touched thee, and as we have done unto thee nothing but good, and have sent thee away in peace: thou *art* now the blessed of the LORD (Gen. 26:29).**

God himself even recognized that the wicked could do "good":

> **And God came to Laban the Syrian in a dream by night, and said unto him, Take heed that thou speak not to Jacob either good or bad (Gen. 31:24).**

The principle of right action with a deceitful, wicked heart (Jer. 17:9) is confirmed by Jesus Christ: **"If ye then, being evil, know how to give good gifts unto your children, how much more shall your Father which is in heaven give good things to them that ask him?"** (Mat. 7:11). A deed can be good no matter what the motive is.

If in fact unregenerate men can be "good" and do "good," which the above Scriptures clearly show, then how does this correspond with the Scriptural declarations that no one does anything good?

> **For *there is* not a just man upon earth, that doeth good, and sinneth not (Ecc. 7:20).**

> **They are all gone out of the way, they are together become unprofitable; there is none that doeth good, no, not one (Rom. 3:12).**

In the ultimate sense, the Lord Jesus Christ is the only man who ever lived **"without sin"** (Heb. 4:16) and always **"went about doing good"** (Acts 10:38). He was good because he was God (Mark 10:18). And while the passage in Romans is literally true if contrasting the natural man with the Lord Jesus Christ, the hyperbolic language that is evident when the verse is examined in its context is employed for reasons to be presently discussed. The verse in Ecclesiastes is merely relaying the fact that everyone sins, much like Solomon said earlier (1 Kgs. 8:46). So if unregenerate men can be "good" and do "good," what are the implications of this to the subject at hand? First of all, it is certainly true, as Boettner articulates, that "fallen man is so morally blind that he uniformly prefers and chooses evil instead of good."[105] And, as Edwards stated: "There is a propensity in man's nature to that sin, which in heinousness and ill-desert immensely outweighs all the value and merit of any supposed good, that may be in him, or that he can do."[106] There is not a man who has studied history, read what the Bible says about the depravity of man, and confirmed his research by empirical evidence that would disagree with these statements by these two notable Calvinists. But the truth of these two observations does not demand the inability of man that we find in the Calvinistic system. There is an important distinction between *right* action and *righteousness* action. As the Calvinist Donald Grey Barnhouse (1895-1960) explains: "Total depravity does not mean that there is no good in man, but that there is no good in man which can satisfy God."[107]

To get around this clear teaching of Scripture, Calvinists have invented a difference between "relatively good works" and "truly good works."[108] But owing to their propensity to overwhelm the English language with theological terms, these are also referred to as "relative" and "absolute" good,[109] "natural" and "spiritual" good,[110] and "non-moral" and "moral" good.[111] To insist, however, that the unregenerate man can do "good," does not imply that anything he does is pleasing to God or contributes to his salvation in any way. So when Walter Chantry announces that "any sinner who supposes that his will has the strength to do any good accompanying salvation is greatly deluded and far from the kingdom,"[112] he is just blowing smoke, for no one who believes what the Bible says about salvation and man's depravity has ever taught such a thing. However, this was the error of Erasmus in his debate over free will with Luther. When Erasmus said that "by freedom of the will we understand in this connection the power of the human will whereby man can apply to or turn away from that which leads unto eternal salvation,"[113] he gave a very ambiguous and imprecise definition. Thus, he can also say that man can "by means of these and other ethically good works, apply in a way for obtaining the ultimate grace,"[114] and talk about "meritorious human acts."[115] Now, all of this does not mean that Luther was correct in his denial of free will, but it does mean that there is an alternative to Calvinism. Like the attempts of the Calvinists to describe all men as either Calvinists or Arminians, the Calvinists would like nothing better than to connect all of their opponents on the free will issue with Erasmus. But God is neither obligated nor aroused to save any man no matter what that man does. Grace is any move of God toward man. Whatever free will man has is irrelevant in this respect.

In contrast to Erasmus are the historical antagonists of the Calvinists: Arminius and Wesley. In response to the attacks of the Calvinists, Arminius had a public disputation on free will. In his "On the Free Will of Man and its Powers" Arminius made statements about the result of man's depravity that no "Arminian" would ever consent to:

> In this state the Free Will of man towards the True Good is not only wounded, maimed, infirm, bent, and weakened; but it is also imprisoned, destroyed, and lost: And its powers are not only debilitated and useless unless they be assisted by grace, but it has no powers whatever except such as are excited by Divine grace.[116]

In answer to the question: "Wherein may we come to the very edge of Calvinism?" Wesley replied: "In ascribing all good to the free grace of God. (2) In denying all natural free-will, and all power antecedent to grace. And (3) In excluding all merit from man; even for what he has or does by the grace of God."[117] To connect Arminius, Wesley, and any opponent of Calvinism with *all* the views of Erasmus is dishonest.

It should be apparent that owing to his depravity, man sins by his own volition and desire, not because his will can only follow his nature. The problem of the will is whether to yield to the flesh: **"Know ye not, that to whom ye yield yourselves servants to obey, his servants ye are to whom ye obey; whether of sin unto death, or of obedience unto righteousness"** (Rom. 6:16). There are several phases which occur when any man sins: presentation, illumination, debate, decision, action. It is not a sin to be presented with something; neither is it a sin to receive illumination as to whether something is right or wrong. However, once debate starts: sin enters—regardless of whether the decision is ever made to perform the act. This is illustrated a couple of different ways in the Bible:

> **And Achan answered Joshua, and said, Indeed I have sinned against the LORD God of Israel, and thus and thus have I done:**
> **When I saw among the spoils a goodly Babylonish garment, and two hundred shekels of silver, and a wedge of gold of fifty shekels weight, then I coveted them, and took them; and, behold, they** *are* **hid in the earth in the midst of my tent, and the silver under it (Jos. 7:20-21).**

> **But every man is tempted, when he is drawn away of his own lust, and enticed.**
> **Then when lust hath conceived, it bringeth forth sin: and sin, when it is finished, bringeth forth death (Jam. 1:14-15).**

Pink's two examples of "moral inability" are explained in the context, as even he himself records:

> **And when his brethren saw that their father loved him more than all his brethren, they hated him, and could not speak peaceably unto him (Gen. 37:4).**

> **Having eyes full of adultery, and that cannot cease from sin; beguiling unstable souls: an heart they have exercised with covetous practices; cursed children (2 Pet. 2:14).**

Pink explains that it was because **"they hated him"** that they **"could not speak peaceably unto him."**[118] And again, regarding the second passage, he says that the reason they **"cannot cease from sin"** is that their eyes are **"full of adultery."**[119] In both of these instances the inability was not the result of man's innate depravity but a specific sin. Although sin is described in the Bible in a number of ways: **"the transgression of the law"** (1 John 3:4), **"all unrighteousness"** (1 John 5:17), **"whatsoever** *is* **not of faith"** (Rom. 14:23), **"to him that knoweth to do good, and doeth** *it* **not"** (Jam. 4:17), the unregenerate man does not sin because he has the inability to do anything good, he sins because he yields to his depraved nature and willfully chooses to do so.

Salvation and the Will

When faced with such clear evidence for the free will of man, the Calvinist retreats and admits that man has a free will, but not pertaining to his acceptance of salvation. Luther claimed of man: "With regard to God, and in all that bears on salvation or damnation, he has no 'free-will.'"[120] If one dissents from this thesis, the old familiar accusations about denying salvation by grace pop up again:

> When the Arminian notion of free will is taken to its logical conclusion, it makes man his own saviour and denies the necessary and miraculous work of the Holy Spirit in regeneration.[121]

> The ideas of free grace and free will are diametrically opposed. All who are strict advocates for free will are strangers to the grace of the sovereign God.[122]

One way the Calvinists seek to get rid of the idea of free will as pertaining to salvation is by the use of the cognate although somewhat ambiguous term "free agency":

> Man is a free agent. But man has not a free will.[123]

> Free agency we may believe in, but free will is simply ridiculous.[124]

Other Calvinists likewise maintain this dichotomy.[125] Palmer explains the difference: "The term *free agency* has been used in theology to designate that a man is free to do what he wants to do; and *free will* has been used to indicate the kind of freedom that no man has—namely, the ability or freedom to choose either good or evil, either to believe on Christ or to reject Him."[126] However, as is the case with most of the finer points of the TULIP, there is much discord among the Calvinists. Some introduce another term: "free moral agent." The theologian Charles Hodge explains that "the doctrine of man's inability, therefore, does not assume that man has ceased to be a free moral agent."[127] But this is contradicted by the

Hardshell Baptist Eddie Garrett, who alleges: "Before the fall, Adam was a free agent. Man is a free agent now, and he will be a free agent in eternity. But man is a fallen creature, totally depraved, therefore he is not a free **moral** agent and does not have free will."[128] Pink likewise rejects both free will and free agency: "'Free moral agency' is an expression of human invention and, as we have said before, to talk of the freedom of the natural man is to flatly repudiate his spiritual ruin."[129] But Talbot and Crampton differ: "To maintain that man does not have free moral agency would be to allege that he could never make a choice about anything at all. That would be absurd."[130] Yet Pink insists of man that "to affirm that he is a *free* moral agent is *to deny that he is totally depraved*."[131]

This distinction between free agency and free will leads some Calvinists to make some curious statements about man and his free will:

He is free to turn to Christ, but not able.[132]

It is your decision to choose or reject Christ but it is not of your own free will.[133]

But whether it be free will, free agency, or free moral agency, the result is still the same: the unregenerate sinner has the inability to accept Christ of his own free will. If man cannot believe then how can he be held responsible for not doing so? Pink has the answer: "In and of himself the natural man has power to reject Christ; but in and of himself he has not the power to receive Christ."[134]

Not only does the Calvinist insist that man's will can only act according to nature, he further errs regarding the function of the will itself. Just like the "Arminian" position was misrepresented in regard to the influences on the will, so the Calvinist puts forth a false teaching that his opponents supposedly believe:

Men's hearts are so vile, it is utterly impossible that anything holy should issue from them. They can no more change their nature by an effort of will than a leper might heal himself by his own volition.[135]

Apart from God's sovereign grace, man is absolutely incapable of saving himself. He has neither the **will** nor the **power** to change his wicked heart.[136]

He cannot renew his own will, change his own heart, nor regenerate his bad nature.[137]

Change his nature? Regenerate himself? What non-Calvinist has ever insisted that any man by exercising his free will can change his nature or cause himself to be regenerated? All that is meant by the claim that man has a free will in the matter of salvation is that he has the ability to respond to the word of God and the conviction of the Holy Spirit. The fact that most men choose to reject Christ and remain in their sin shows the extent of man's depravity, but does not change the fact that man has a free will to do otherwise. A man is only free if he is able to have chosen to do otherwise. If a Calvinist wants to say that man can only choose the lesser of two evils then that is fine. In that case accepting Jesus Christ would be a lesser evil than going to hell. But, the Calvinist responds, fear is not the proper motive. Yet, to a guilty sinner facing the prospect of suffering an everlasting penalty, fear is a very healthy motive.

There are two pillars upon which the idea rests that man cannot accept Jesus Christ of his own free will:

Which were born, not of blood, nor of the will of the flesh, nor of the will of man, but of God (John 1:13).

So then *it is* not of him that willeth, nor of him that runneth, but of God that showeth mercy (Rom. 9:16).

These two phrases, **"nor of the will of man** (John 1:13), and **"it is not of him that willeth"** (Rom. 9:16), are applied without exception by Calvinists to the will of man to receive Jesus Christ. Manford Kober maintains that "if the two verses prove anything, it is that man does not have a free will when it comes to the matter of salvation."[138] The way this is done is standard operating procedure for the Calvinists. They do it by taking a word or phrase out of a verse and making it say whatever they want. A word or phrase can be used to prove anything if it is divorced from its context.

The verse from John cannot be examined without noticing the context:

He was in the world, and the world was made by him, and

> the world knew him not.
> He came unto his own, and his own received him not.
> But as many as received him, to them gave he power to become the sons of God, *even* to them that believe on his name:
> Which were born, not of blood, nor of the will of the flesh, nor of the will of man, but of God (John 1:10-13).

Calvinists often list verse thirteen as a reference after statements like that of Custance: "What could possibly be a plainer statement than this of the fact that salvation is conferred upon a select number who are conceived by the Holy Spirit and born again by the will of God alone."[139] Pink comments: "The will of the natural man is opposed to God, and he has *no will* Godward until he has been born again."[140] What the Calvinists are implying is that a man has the inability to receive Christ of his own free will. In essence what the Calvinists have done is taken the phrase **"received him"** out of verse twelve and substituted it for **"born"** in verse thirteen. This gives us: "Which received him, not of blood, nor of the will of the flesh, nor of the will of man, but of God." But verse thirteen is giving us the source of the new birth, not the reason why men receive Christ. The source of the new birth is given three times negatively before it is given once positively. Anyone who is born again is said to be born of God to the exclusion of three things. The new birth is **"not of blood."** The source of the new birth is not physical generation, inheritance, or natural descent. The new birth is not **"of the will of the flesh."** The source of the new birth is not reformation, self-development, or self-effort. The new birth is not **"of the will of man."** The source of the new birth is not relatives, preachers, or priests. The threefold negation emphasizes the fact that the source of the new birth is **"of God"** and not of man. And why does God give anyone the new birth? God gives the new birth to **"as many as received him."** The new birth is God's work, but the receiving of Christ is man's.

The next fragment of a verse is from Romans 9, but again the context must be examined:

> **For he saith to Moses, I will have mercy on whom I will have mercy, and I will have compassion on whom I will have compassion.**

> So then *it is* not of him that willeth, nor of him that runneth, but of God that showeth mercy (Rom. 9:15-16).

In commenting on verse sixteen, Calvinists uniformly apply the phrase **"it is not of him that willeth"** to the will of man to receive salvation:

> God does indeed rule over all so that salvation is completely dependent upon Him.[141]

> Nor is the sinner's salvation to be in any way attributed to either pliability of heart or diligence in the use of means.[142]

> The application of salvation is all of grace and is accomplished solely through the almighty power of God.[143]

This phrase even appeared on the title page of Jonathan Edwards' 1754 book *Freedom of the Will*.[144] But why did God speak verse fifteen to Moses? Was he telling him about his plans to only have mercy on the "elect" and to damn the rest? God spoke to Moses after he requested to see his glory (Exo. 33:18-19). Moses was then granted his desire while in the cleft of the rock (Exo. 33:22). The salvation of a "totally depraved sinner" was not even remotely connected with this event. So what then is **"not of him that willeth"**? Is it salvation? Is it predestination? The answer is found right in the verse: **"But of God that sheweth mercy."** This is reinforced by noting the **"so then"** at the beginning of the verse which refers us back to the previous one, the subject of which was God showing mercy. God's mercy is not merely a response to man's will or man's efforts to obtain it. It must be received under his terms and conditions. But doesn't God have to have mercy on a man before he can be saved? Yes, he certainly does: **"Not by works of righteousness which we have done, but according to his mercy he saved us, by the washing of regeneration, and renewing of the Holy Ghost"** (Tit. 3:5). But God's mercy is not limited to just the "elect":

> **For as ye in times past have not believed God, yet have now obtained mercy through their unbelief:**
> **Even so have these also now not believed, that through your mercy they also may obtain mercy.**

For God hath concluded them all in unbelief, that he might have mercy upon all (Rom. 11:30-32).

The mercy of God does not even have to be related to salvation. Jesus Christ showed mercy to numerous people that resulted in their physically healing, not their salvation (Mat. 9:27, 15:22, 17:15, 20:30).

The fact that a man has a free will to believe on Jesus Christ for salvation does not mean that he will choose to accept God's offer of grace. Having a free will is one thing; using it correctly is another. As Boettner observes: "Man's fallen nature gives rise to a most obdurate blindness, stupidity, and opposition concerning the things of God."[145] As a consequence of his depravity, man cannot do anything good that is fundamentally pleasing to God so as to merit his favor. He cannot demand that God save him. He cannot contribute to his salvation. He cannot change his nature. He cannot save himself. This is what his "inability" consists of. The Bible affirms man's ability to respond to the Gospel while in a state of depravity: **"But God be thanked, that ye were the servants of sin, but ye have obeyed from the heart that form of doctrine which was delivered you"** (Rom. 6:17). The reason men don't respond to the Gospel is not because they have the inability to do so: **"And ye will not come to me, that ye might have life"** (John 5:40).

Analogies

It is from their false concept of man's depraved nature that the Calvinists attempt to bolster their doctrine of Total Depravity. There are three analogies that are used to do this: dead men, babies, and creatures. These analogies are based on three verses of Scripture:

> And you *hath he quickened,* who were dead in trespasses and sins (Eph. 2:1).

> Jesus answered and said unto him, Verily, verily, I say unto thee, Except a man be born again, he cannot see the kingdom of God (John 3:3).

> Therefore if any man *be* in Christ, *he is* a new creature: old

things are passed away; behold, all things are become new (2 Cor. 5:17).

By comparing an unregenerate sinner to a dead man, a baby, and a creature, Calvinists attempt to prove that man has the inability to repent and believe the Gospel. But as we shall presently see, each one of these analogies is disparaged by no less a Calvinist than Arthur W. Pink.

The first is very important to the Calvinists since it actually mentions the fact of man's spiritual death: **"dead in trespasses and sins"** (Eph. 2:1). This is called by Sproul: "A predestination passage par excellence."[146] But while it is true that salvation is spoken of as being **"passed from death unto life"** (John 5:24), all Calvinists, without fail, make analogy between their doctrine of Total Depravity and *physically* dead men in general, or in an attempt to get scriptural, to Lazarus in particular (John 11:43-44).[147] The comparison runs as follows:

> A dead man cannot exercise faith in Jesus Christ.[148]
>
> A dead man is utterly incapable of willing anything.[149]
>
> A dead man cannot cooperate with an offer of healing.[150]
>
> The corpse does not restore life to itself; after life is restored it becomes a living agent.[151]

Custance uses the Jehovah's Witness proof text: **"The dead know not any thing"** (Ecc. 9:5), and reasons: "A corpse does not cry out for help."[152] Now, all of the above postulations are true—if one is referring to *physically* dead men. But as Sproul inadvertently stated: "Spiritually dead people are still biologically alive."[153] Spiritually dead men can walk, have a conversation, and fulfill desires (Eph. 2:2-3). Being dead in sin does not mean to be unconscious. Death never means a cessation of being. Thus, even the regenerated man is said to be dead, doctrinally speaking (Rom. 6:2; Col. 3:3). And regarding physically dead men, it should also be noted that a physically dead man can lift up his eyes, feel torment, see, speak, pray, and reason (Luke 16:23-28). Death is never non-existence, unless one is a Jehovah's Witness. The cadaver is not the real man; the rotting corpse is never the actual person. The unsaved dead who suffer **"the second death"** (Rev. 20:14) experience conscious torment (Mat. 13:42). A real analogy that illustrates the fact that a sinner is **"dead in trespasses and sins"** (Eph. 2:1) is the biblical story of the prodigal son who **"was dead, and is alive again; he was lost, and is found"** (Luke 15:24). And as was mentioned at the beginning of this section, Pink expressly discounted this analogy that his fellow Calvinists are so fond of: "Instead of attempting to draw analogies between spiritual and physical death and deriving inferences from them, we must stick very closely to the Scriptures and regulate all our thoughts by them."[154]

Some Calvinists, realizing that dead men still exist, go a step further, likening regeneration to the birth of a baby. But while it is true that salvation is spoken of as a birth: **"born again"** (1 Pet. 1:23), **"born of God"** (1 John 3:9), Calvinists once again seek an exact parallel in an attempt to prove the validity of Total Depravity:

> The infant does not procreate itself, but must be born of its parents in order to become a living agent.[155]

> A baby never desires or decides to be born. He never contributes an iota toward his own birth. In the whole process from conception through birth, he is completely passive and totally unable to control his birth.[156]

> We cannot have a birth of ourselves; a babe cannot be born of itself; nothing can have its original from itself, for it would then be before and after itself; it would be and would not be, at the same time.[157]

> The new birth is solely the work of God the Spirit and man has no part or lot in it. This from the very nature of the case. Birth altogether excludes the idea of any effort or work on the part of the one who is born. Personally we have no more to do with our spiritual birth than we had with our natural birth.[158]

But in a natural birth, conception and birth are separated by a period of nine months; in a spiritual birth, no such period exists. Pink, although the author of the last quote, repudiates himself, as well as all other Calvinists, when he appropriately says: "When treating of regeneration under the figure of the new birth, some writers have introduced analogies from natural birth which

Scripture by no means warrants, in fact disallows. Physical birth is the bringing forth into this world of a creature, a complete personality, which before conception had no existence whatsoever. But the one who is regenerated *had* a complete personality before he was born again."[159]

The third analogy used by the Calvinists to augment their doctrine of Total Depravity is that of a creature. But while it is true that after salvation a man is spoken of as a **"new creature"** (2 Cor. 5:17), the Calvinist, in his effort to substantiate the doctrine of Total Depravity, seeks an exact parallel between the creation of a creature and the salvation of a sinner:

> What creature has ever successfully resisted his own creation or made any active contribution to his own creation?[160]

> Non-being—nothingness—can never produce itself. The very concept of creation necessarily implies total passivity and inability on the part of the object that is to be created. What is true in the physical realm is also true in the spiritual realm: individuals are totally unable to make of themselves new creations in Christ.[161]

But once again, Pink aptly states the case against Calvinism: "Regeneration is not the creating of a person which hitherto had no existence, but the renewing and restoring of a person whom sin had unfitted for communion with God, and this by the communication of a nature of principle of life, which gives a new and different bias to all his old faculties."[162]

Another reason these analogies all break down when viewed as an exact parallel to the salvation of a sinner is the matter of responsibility. Is an uncreated creature responsible for anything? If the unregenerate man corresponds to an uncreated creature, he most certainly could never be responsible for any deed: he wouldn't even exist! We also hasten to add, is a baby responsible for any of its actions before it is born? If not, then neither would an unsaved man be responsible for any of his. And finally, if you make an exact parallel between a physically dead man and a spiritually dead man and say that neither one can believe on Jesus Christ, then you likewise have to say that neither one cannot *not* believe. If a dead man can't accept Christ because he is dead then he can't reject him either. A dead *man* cannot believe on Jesus Christ, but a dead *sinner* can.

Proof Texts

In addition to these analogies and the verses relating to salvation and the will, the Calvinist has some additional proof texts for the doctrine of Total Depravity. But although Rose claims that "the doctrine of total depravity does not rest on a few scattered texts,"[163] their numbers are actually quite scant. And in keeping with the true nature of how the Calvinists define Total Depravity, none of their proof texts mention man's depravity at all but rather his supposed inability. There are three types of Scripture texts used to prove the Calvinistic doctrine of Total Depravity. The first type are those that mention someone who "cannot" do something:

> **Jesus answered and said unto him, Verily, verily, I say unto thee, Except a man be born again, he cannot see the kingdom of God (John 3:3).**

> **Why do ye not understand my speech?** *even* **because ye cannot hear my word (John 8:43).**

> *Even* **the Spirit of truth; whom the world cannot receive, because it seeth him not, neither knoweth him: but ye know him; for he dwelleth with you, and shall be in you (John 14:17).**

> **Because the carnal mind** *is* **enmity against God: for it is not subject to the law of God, neither indeed can be.**
> **So then they that are in the flesh cannot please God (Rom. 8:7-8).**

Naturally, the Calvinist assumes that these "cannot" do something because of the result of Total Depravity: Total Inability.

Secondly, there are those passages which speak of someone's "inability" but with an explicit reason given for it:

> **No man can come to me, except the Father which hath sent me draw him: and I will raise him up at the last day (John 6:44).**

> **And he said, Therefore said I unto you, that no man can**

come unto me, except it were given unto him of my Father (John 6:65).

Therefore they could not believe, because that Esaias said again,
He hath blinded their eyes, and hardened their heart; that they should not see with *their* eyes, nor understand with *their* heart, and be converted, and I should heal them (John 12:39-40).

And finally, there are the two paramount verses used to prove the Calvinistic doctrine of Total Depravity:

There is none that understandeth, there is none that seeketh after God (Rom. 3:11).

But the natural man receiveth not the things of the Spirit of God: for they are foolishness unto him: neither can he know *them*, because they are spiritually discerned (1 Cor. 2:14).

The way all of these passages are usually employed is in a list of verse references after some statement delineating man's inability to repent and believe the Gospel. But in addition to this assumption, the Calvinist also infers that they refer to all individuals. But since it is obvious that these verses are of three different types, they will be handled accordingly.

Of the first type of verses used to prove the truth of Total Depravity—those that mention someone who "cannot" do something—the attempt by the Calvinists to prove man's inability to repent and believe the Gospel from the first one is calumnious indeed. The verse in question says that **"except a man be born again, he cannot see the kingdom of God"** (John 3:3). Although usually just listed by Calvinists in a string of proof texts,[164] sometimes extended comments are made on the verse. Coppes remarks: "The ungodly, apart from the rebirth effected by the Holy Spirit (John 3:3, 8), cannot repent."[165] Others go so far as to redefine the word **"see."** Keener corrects it to "perceive" in his attempt to prove Total Depravity.[166] Robert Morey postulates: "Christ places regeneration by the Spirit as a requirement before one can 'see,' i.e., believe or have faith in the Kingdom of God. He states quite emphatically that a sinner who is born of the flesh can not believe the good news of the Kingdom until he is born by the Spirit."[167] But it should be pointed out that seeing is not necessarily believing:

> **But I said unto you, That ye also have seen me, and believe not (John 6:36).**
>
> **Jesus saith unto him, Thomas, because thou hast seen me, thou hast believed: blessed** *are* **they that have not seen, and** *yet* **have believed (John 20:29).**

And not only does the Bible say **"see"** and not "believe," it is discussing **"the kingdom of God,"** not "salvation." The verse means just what it says. Without the new birth, a sinner can neither **"see"** (John 3:3) nor **"enter"** (John 3:5) **"the kingdom of God"** (John 3:3, 5).

The next "cannot" passage is similarly abused: **"Why do ye not understand my speech?** *even* **because ye cannot hear my word"** (John 8:43). Calvinists regularly list this passage in the midst of a string of verses said to prove Total Depravity.[168] But unlike the previous verse under discussion, the subject here is not universal. It is the unbelieving Jews, here addressed twice as **"ye,"** that are under consideration. They could not hear Christ's word, not just because they were, like all of the unregenerate (Acts 26:18; Eph. 2:2), of their **"father the devil"** (John 8:43) and **"not of God"** (John 8:47), but additionally, because they did the lusts of their father (John 8:44) and did not believe Christ when he told them **"the truth"** (John 8:45, 46). And not only was their "inability" conditional, it was also not permanent, for Jesus had said earlier that because they were **"from beneath"** (John 8:23), they would die in their sins and not be able to go where he was going (John 8:21). Yet, they would only die in their sins if they did not believe (John 8:24). What is even more interesting is that two Calvinists concur. Calvin by his implicit silence,[169] and D. A. Carson by his explanation:

> Jesus does not say they fail to grasp his message because they cannot follow his spoken word, his idiom, but that they fail to understand his idiom precisely because they cannot 'hear' his message. The Jews remain responsible for their own 'cannot,' which, far from resulting from divine fiat, is determined by their

own desire (theolusin) to perform the lusts (tas epithymias) of the devil (8.44). This 'cannot,' this slavery to sin (8.34), itself stems from personal sin.[170]

It should also be pointed out that not being able to hear Christ's word is not necessarily equivalent to not being able to repent and believe the Gospel.

Contrary to the last verse in question, the next reference does apply to a group other than certain Jews: **"*Even* the Spirit of truth; whom the world cannot receive, because it seeth him not, neither knoweth him: but ye know him; for he dwelleth with you, and shall be in you"** (John 14:17). Only a handful of Calvinists list this verse as a proof text for Total Depravity.[171] It is obvious why. The world cannot receive the Holy Spirit because the world neither sees nor knows him. In contrast, the disciples do know him because he dwells with them. What does this have to with the inability of the world to get the Holy Spirit? The verse does not say the world *cannot* see him or know him. It merely says that the world cannot receive him **"because it seeth him not, neither knoweth him."**

The next reference is the last of the "cannot" passages used to support the doctrine of Total Depravity: **"Because the carnal mind *is* enmity against God: for it is not subject to the law of God, neither indeed can be. So then they that are in the flesh cannot please God"** (Rom. 8:7-8). Although it is normally just listed in a string of proof texts for Total Depravity,[172] Calvinistic commentators have also commented on this passage:

> Paul's assessment of persons apart from Christ may justly be summed up in the theological categories of 'total depravity' and 'total inability.'[173]

> 'Enmity against God' is nothing other than total depravity and 'cannot please God' nothing less than total inability.[174]

Although a saved man can **"walk after the flesh"** (Rom. 8:4), the unregenerate man is **"in the flesh"** (Rom. 8:8). As a consequence, men cannot do anything good that is fundamentally pleasing to God so as to merit his favor. The flesh cannot be changed, reformed, trained, improved, or reconciled to God *unless* and *until* God changes it. But to say that because of this "inability" a man cannot believe the Gospel is another matter. The Bible speaks of God being **"pleased"** with Enoch (Heb. 11:5), with Solomon's request (1 Kgs. 3:10), with choices made by eunuchs (Isa. 56:4), with making Israel his people (1 Sam. 12:22), when Israel was blessed (Num. 24:1), for his righteousness' sake (Isa. 42:21), when he revealed Christ to Paul (Gal. 1:16), with spiritual sacrifices (Heb. 13:16), and especially with his Son (Isa. 53:10; Mat. 3:17, 17:5; Col. 1:19). But there are two other occasions when God is said to be pleased. The first concerns man in general: **"When a man's ways please the LORD, he maketh even his enemies to be at peace with him"** (Pro. 16:7). And more relevant to the subject at hand: **"For after that in the wisdom of God the world by wisdom knew not God, it pleased God by the foolishness of preaching to save them that believe"** (1 Cor. 1:21). So although man has the inability in his flesh to please God, God is pleased when sinners believe the Gospel.

The second category of Calvinistic proof texts for Total Depravity are those passages which speak of someone's "inability" but with an explicit reason given for it:

> **No man can come to me, except the Father which hath sent me draw him: and I will raise him up at the last day (John 6:44).**
>
> **And he said, Therefore said I unto you, that no man can come unto me, except it were given unto him of my Father (John 6:65).**
>
> **Therefore they could not believe, because that Esaias said again,**
> **He hath blinded their eyes, and hardened their heart; that they should not see with *their* eyes, nor understand with *their* heart, and be converted, and I should heal them (John 12:39-40).**

The first two verses are part of a Calvinist trilogy in John chapter six. The first is actually the main proof text for the fourth point of Calvinism: Irresistible Grace. Because of this, it will be examined in that chapter. The second is likewise used to prove the second point of Calvinism: Unconditional Election, and will be considered in the next chapter. The other passage in John relates that the reason why some **"could not believe"** was because God **"blinded their eyes."** In the maze of Calvinistic theological terms this is called "reprobation," and properly goes under the subject of Unconditional Election. Thus, it will be analyzed in that chapter.

The first principle verse used to prove the doctrine of Total Depravity is part of the great declaration of the universal depravity of man found in Romans chapter three. Paul **"searched the scriptures"** (Acts 17:11), and gleaned from Isaiah and the Psalms the odious description of man found in this section of the word of God. The Calvinist Gerstner correctly maintains that "there probably is no portion of the entire Bible which emphasizes the undone condition of mankind more than the first three chapters of the Book of Romans, and no part of Romans more than Romans 3:10-20."[175] Recourse, therefore, will have to be made to the context:

> **As it is written, There is none righteous, no, not one:**
> **There is none that understandeth, there is none that seeketh after God.**
> **They are all gone out of the way, they are together become unprofitable; there is none that doeth good, no, not one.**
> **Their throat** *is* **an open sepulchre; with their tongues they have used deceit; the poison of asps** *is* **under their lips:**
> **Whose mouth** *is* **full of cursing and bitterness:**
> **Their feet** *are* **swift to shed blood:**
> **Destruction and misery** *are* **in their ways:**
> **And the way of peace have they not known:**
> **There is no fear of God before their eyes (Rom. 3:10-18).**

There is one phrase extracted from one verse in this section that is continually cited by Calvinists as proving their doctrine of Total Depravity: **"There is none that seeketh after God"** (Rom. 3:11).[176]

Before examining the phrase in question, it should be pointed out that the Calvinists are correct in some respects. Sproul affirms that instead of seeking God, men "seek after the benefits that only God can give them."[177] He also perceptively relates a delusive inference that is often drawn, that "because people are seeking what God alone can supply, they must be seeking God himself."[178] The Calvinists are also accurate in granting the initiative in saving sinners to God himself:

> For God so loved the world, that he gave his only begotten Son, that whosoever believeth in him should not perish, but have everlasting life (John 3:16).
>
> But God commendeth his love toward us, in that, while we were yet sinners, Christ died for us (Rom. 5:8).
>
> We love him, because he first loved us (1 John 4:19).

But to maintain from all this that a sinner *cannot* believe the Gospel when confronted with it is a TULIP of another color. Therefore, there are three things wrong with the use of this phrase by the Calvinists to prove the truth of their doctrine of Total Depravity: the design of the passage is not to teach man's inability, nothing is said about anyone not being able to seek God, and the fact that seeking God is not the same thing as believing the Gospel.

First of all, what the Calvinists seem to forget is that Paul, in establishing the universal guilt of both Jews and Gentiles (Rom. 3:1, 9), quotes from the Old Testament to give *weight* to his arguments, not to charge each individual of the human race in particular with every indictment, nor to teach the inability of the unregenerate man to believe on Jesus Christ. There is a difference between establishing the universal depravity of man and charging *individual* men with sins. For instance, Cornelius, an unregenerate sinner (Acts 11:14), was a **"just man, and one that feareth God, and of good report"** (Acts 10:22). He was a **"devout man, and one that feared God with all his house"** (Acts 10:2). This is even recognized by Calvinists: "Now we must not think that this passage is accusing every member of the human race of having committed all of these individuals sins."[179]

Secondly, nothing is said in the phrase in question (or the verse or context) about anyone not being able to seek God, although that is how every Calvinist reads it. The Bible commands men to seek God:

> Seek ye the LORD while he may be found, call ye upon him while he is near (Isa. 55:6).
>
> For thus saith the LORD unto the house of Israel, Seek ye me, and ye shall live (Amos 5:4).

> Seek ye the LORD, all ye meek of the earth, which have wrought his judgment; seek righteousness, seek meekness: it may be ye shall be hid in the day of the LORD'S anger (Zep. 2:3).

God set the bounds of the nations so they would seek him (Acts 17:26-27). The Bible even enjoins men to **"seek the LORD and his strength, seek his face continually"** (1 Chr. 16:11). But not only are men commanded to seek him, God declares that those who do seek him would find him (Jer. 29:13-14), and that he would reward them **"which diligently seek him"** (Heb. 11:6). The Bible says that men are blessed who seek God **"with the whole heart"** (Psa. 119:2). In fact, it is said to be evil not to seek God (2 Chr. 12:14) and worthy of death (2 Chr. 15:13). These commands to seek God are not in vain: **"I have not spoken in secret, in a dark place of the earth: I said not unto the seed of Jacob, Seek ye me in vain: I the LORD speak righteousness, I declare things that are right"** (Isa. 45:19). This does not mean that a man who has rejected God will be able to find him whenever he desires: **"Then shall they call upon me, but I will not answer; they shall seek me early, but they shall not find me"** (Pro. 1:28).

And finally, seeking God is not the same thing as believing the Gospel. Seeking God is not enough. A Jew who desires to seek God under the commands of the Old Testament is just as lost as the Gentile who doesn't. Salvation is never obtained by seeking God:

> I said therefore unto you, that ye shall die in your sins: for if ye believe not that I am *he,* ye shall die in your sins (John 8:24).

> Jesus saith unto him, I am the way, the truth, and the life: no man cometh unto the Father, but by me (John 14:6).

If the reason that men don't seek God is not because they have Total Depravity, then what is it? The reason men don't seek God is simple: **"The wicked, through the pride of his countenance, will not seek *after God:* God is not in all his thoughts"** (Psa. 10:4).

The second principle text used to prove that a man has the inability to repent and believe the Gospel—Total Depravity—is clearly interpreted in the context. The verse in question reads: **"But the natural man receiveth not the things of the Spirit of God:**

for they are foolishness unto him: neither can he know *them,* **because they are spiritually discerned"** (1 Cor. 2:14). Like the other Calvinistic proof texts for Total Depravity, this verse can usually be found among a string of verses cited as proof for Total Depravity.[180] However, it has also been said in regards to the verse in question:

> We are at a loss to understand how any one can take a plain common sense view of this passage of Scripture and yet contend for the doctrine of human ability.[181]

> The doctrine of total depravity states that fallen human nature is morally incapable of responding to the gospel without being caused to do so by divine intervention.[182]

> Until the Spirit of God awakens the soul we *cannot* hear.[183]

Calvin concluded from this verse that "faith is not something that depends on our decision, but it is something given by God."[184] Garrett contends that this verse "puts the alien sinner in a rather poor position to perform conditions in order to [gain] eternal life."[185] A Calvinist reads the verse like this: "But the natural man receiveth not Jesus Christ: for he is foolishness unto him: neither can he receive him, because he is spiritually discerned." All Calvinists, whether they admit it or not, have to read the verse just like this if they are using it to teach their doctrine of Total Depravity. The use of this verse proves again the fact that Total Depravity has nothing to do with man's depravity at all. It concerns his supposed inability to repent and believe the Gospel.

The context is clearly *things,* not Jesus Christ. This is infallibly determined by simply reading the chapter. *Things* are what is being discussed in 1 Corinthians 2:9-15. The word *things* occurs at least once in every verse. Those who have received **"the spirit which is of God"** can know spiritual things (1 Cor. 2:12). And how does one receive this spirit? **"And because ye are sons, God hath sent forth the Spirit of his Son into your hearts, crying, Abba, Father"** (Gal. 4:6). God gives the Holy Spirit to his sons that they might have spiritual understanding; he doesn't give his Spirit to "alien sinners" that they might be able to repent and believe the Gospel. And how does one become a son of God? **"But as many as received him, to them gave he power to become the sons of**

God, *even* **to them that believe on his name"** (John 1:12). Any man who has received Jesus Christ has the Spirit of God: **"In whom ye also** *trusted,* **after that ye heard the word of truth, the gospel of your salvation: in whom also after that ye believed, ye were sealed with that holy Spirit of promise."** (Eph. 1:13). The Calvinists would have us believe that because the natural man cannot understand spiritual things, he cannot receive Jesus Christ. But as the Calvinists Gordon Clark and Charles Hodge commented on the passage:

> When the verse here says that they do not know the doctrine, it means they do not know it as true; and the reason is immediately given: for it is spiritually evaluated.[186]

> What, therefore, the apostle here affirms of the natural or unrenewed man is, that he cannot discern the truth, excellence, or beauty of divine things.[187]

Receiving spiritual things and receiving Jesus Christ are two different things.

The three types of Scriptures used by the Calvinists to prove the truth of Total Depravity have one thing in common: none of them mention man's depravity at all. Total Depravity is truly a negative doctrine. The positive sinful actions of men—sinful thoughts, sinful words, sinful deeds—are not under consideration in any of the above examined verses. The Calvinist who talks about man's depravity and then lists these verses as proof texts is dishonest. The true nature of Total Depravity is Total Inability.

The Other Side of Total Depravity

As we have seen throughout this chapter, there is one idea that continually surfaces when a Calvinist says Total Depravity: Total Inability, which has nothing to do with Total Depravity at all, but is rather the supposed *result* of it. This is part of the other side of Total Depravity. Although man's fall into sin and depravity have been examined from the Bible, the fact that man is fallen and depraved is not the whole story. It is the "inability" of man to freely believe on Jesus Christ for salvation that is the real issue. Total Depravity is a negative doctrine in that it concerns what the sinner is not able to do. The proofs put forth for this doctrine by the

Calvinists have also been examined and found wanting. But because Total Depravity is the foundation of Calvinism, and necessitates the other points of the TULIP, its importance to the Calvinistic system cannot be underestimated. If all men are unable to repent and believe the Gospel, then it logically follows that if any of them are to be saved then God must first determine who they are (Unconditional Election) and then "irresistibly" overcome their "inability" (Irresistible Grace) so they can repent and believe the Gospel. But if it is true that "the doctrine of total depravity states that fallen human nature is morally incapable of responding to the gospel without being caused to do so by divine intervention,"[188] then how can a sinner respond to the Gospel? The Calvinists retort: "Once the soul is sovereignly regenerated, it willingly responds in saving faith to God's command to repent and believe the gospel, but not before."[189] This is another part of the other side of Total Depravity: how God actually overcomes the "inability" of the sinner, and will be examined in more detail when we get to the chapter on Irresistible Grace. So if Total Depravity is true, then there really is nothing anyone can do except *hope* that he is the subject of Unconditional Election, and if he is, then quietly *wait* for God to save him by Irresistible Grace. But if Total Depravity is a fraudulent doctrine, then the rest of the TULIP withers.

But before presenting the principles and Scriptures that further overthrow the doctrine of Total Depravity, it would be pertinent to examine why the Calvinists are so persistent in affirming this doctrine. The theory behind Total Depravity is simply this: for God to get the glory for salvation, man must be *unable* to accept or reject. Tom Ross elaborates: "The teaching of the natural man's total inability concerning salvation is not only scriptural, but it is a doctrine that gives all the glory to God in the salvation of sinners."[190] Hanko insists that "the truth of total depravity is the only truth which preserves intact the glory of God."[191] Perhaps it is from a good motive, or perhaps it is just from blindly following Calvinistic tradition, but the Calvinist is obsessed with the idea that if a man has the ability to respond then this somehow robs God of his glory. Yet, to those who reject Calvinism and ascribe their salvation to the grace of God alone, the theory behind Total Depravity is insulting. It implies that unless one is a Calvinist, God does not receive the full glory for an individual's salvation.

In spite of their pronouncement of man's inability, the Calvinists unhesitatingly contend that man is fully responsible for what he *cannot* do. This is yet another part of the other side of Total Depravity. Custance simply says: "Man's total incapacity does not absolve him from full responsibility."[192] The idea that man could not be accountable unless he had "ability" is misrepresented by the Calvinists:

> If man's responsibility to obey is to be gauged by his ability to perform, then as his behaviour degenerates and his ability is progressively reduced, he has less and less duty. The wholly evil man thus ends up by having no responsibility whatever, and must be accounted blameless![193]

But more often than this exaggeration, the Calvinist says that we should not "confuse this idea, of responsibility and ability."[194] Tom Ross uses the example of a drunk who, even though he has the "inability" to drive safely, is responsible for his actions.[195] Pink reminds us that "in commercial life the loss of ability to pay does not release from obligation."[196] He also correctly points out that God does "require what is beyond our own power to render."[197] So obviously, a man can be held responsible for something which he is not able to do. But as usual, this is not the whole story. Consider a worker at a widget plant who agrees to make ten widgets per hour. Because he of his own free will agrees to the terms he is responsible to make ten widgets. But what if he only has the ability to make five widgets? Is he still responsible for ten widgets? If he agreed to make ten then he is responsible *in spite of* his inability; if his inability to make ten is because the plant burns down, then he is not accountable *because of* his inability. Now, if this illustration seems a little simplistic, then what about the Calvinists' example of the drunk and the debtor? Who would ever question whether they were responsible for their actions? So although a man's freedom at the time of an action is not necessarily the basis for his accountability, there must be a historical relationship between some prior free action and the state a man is presently in in order for him to be responsible for his actions. A man under the influence of drugs is accountable for his actions only if he knowingly and willfully put himself in such a state (he took drugs). But a man under the influence of drugs is not accountable for his actions if he did not knowingly and willfully put himself in such a state (he was drugged). So, is a man responsible for something which he is not able to do? Yes and no. It depends on why he has inability. For a Calvinist to make a blanket statement like "man's responsibility does not consist in his ability to do what God requires"[198] is dishonest because it is only part of the picture.

In their further attempts to convince their opponents that man is fully responsible for what he *cannot* do, the Calvinists once again overwhelm us with theological terms that only serve to confuse the issue. Jonathan Edwards, in his book *Freedom of the Will*, taxes the reader with discussions of things like: natural necessity, moral necessity, natural inability, moral inability, general and habitual moral inability, particular and occasional moral inability.[199] Pink admits that "the *basis* or ground of human responsibility is human *ability*."[200] But he grounds the responsibility of man on his distinction between "natural ability" and "moral and spiritual ability."[201] Pink maintains that although man has the moral and spiritual inability to believe the Gospel, he is still accountable to God because he has the natural ability to do so.[202] He even acknowledges that "the natural man *could* come to Christ if he wished to do so."[203] It is here that we see the essence of Total Depravity, for according to Pink, Total Depravity has to do, not with the inability to repent and believe the Gospel, but rather with the will to do so:

> The inability of the sinner consists of *the want* of moral power *to wish* and will so as to actually perform.[204]

> The sinner's inability or absence of power is itself *due* to *lack of willingness* to come to Christ.[205]

This is more of the other side of Total Depravity. Pink maintains that infants and idiots are not responsible to God because they lack natural ability.[206] But is this the whole truth? An unregenerate sinner in a coma who is not an infant or an idiot likewise lacks "natural ability." Would any Calvinist suggest that one in such a state is not responsible to God? What Pink really meant to say was that anyone who lacks "natural ability" from his birth and never leaves that state—a three-year-old infant or a thirty-year-old idiot—is not responsible to God. And conversely, if a maniac in an insane asylum has the natural ability to pick up a Bible and read it but has the inability to will that he lift it—can he be held responsible for not doing so just because he has "natural ability"? Obviously not. So the question at hand does not concern man's so-called natural ability at all. It has to do with whether a man has the will to choose *contrary* to his depraved nature. If he *can*, then he has the ability to respond to spiritual things and is therefore responsible to do so; if he *can't*, then he has the inability to respond to spiritual things and is therefore not responsible to do so. Pink has man being held accountable for the exercise of spiritual duties because he has natural ability.

To yet further convince his opponents that Total Depravity does not negate man's responsibility, the Calvinist brings up the matter of ignorance. Boettner remarks: "This total inability, however, arises not merely from a perverted moral nature, but also from ignorance."[207] Now, it is true that ignorance is no excuse for breaking the law: **"And if a soul sin, and commit any of these things which are forbidden to be done by the commandments of the LORD; though he wist *it* not, yet is he guilty, and shall bear his iniquity"** (Lev. 5:17). The Calvinist would like everyone to believe that just as ignorance does not nullify responsibility, so Total Depravity does not abrogate man's accountability.

Because God is not only a sovereign God but a just God, no man can be condemned for his inability to do what God expressly commands him to do. Whatever theological deficiencies that Wesley may have had, he recognized of God that:

> He will punish no man for doing anything he could not possibly avoid; neither for omitting anything which he could not possibly do. Every punishment supposes the offender might have avoided the offence for which he is punished. Otherwise, to punish him would be palpably unjust, and inconsistent with the character of God our governor."[208]

So although it is indeed true that no man can be condemned for his inability to do what God has expressly commanded him to do, it is also accurate to state that he can be condemned for his *ignorance* or his *unwillingness*. Therefore, the principle that overthrows Total Depravity is this: A man can be condemned for his *ignorance* or his *unwillingness,* but never for his *inability* to do what God has commanded him to do. Inability is the ground of the salvation of infants and idiots. The attempts of the Calvinists to explain the salvation of infants by other means is absurd, as will be explored in chapter 9.

There are two types of Scriptures that overthrow the false notion of Total Depravity. The first type are those verses where there is a command to believe; the second type concerns those passages that imply the possibility of doing so. If the multitude and variety of the commands, exhortations, admonishments, and warnings in the Bible are to be taken seriously, then man must have the ability to respond to them either to his good or to his detriment. This is especially true when it concerns his salvation:

> **Look unto me, and be ye saved, all the ends of the earth: for I *am* God, and *there is* none else (Isa. 45:22).**

> **And saying, The time is fulfilled, and the kingdom of God is at hand: repent ye, and believe the gospel (Mark 1:15).**

> **And the times of this ignorance God winked at; but now commandeth all men every where to repent (Acts 17:30).**

> **And this is his commandment, That we should believe on the name of his Son Jesus Christ, and love one another, as he gave us commandment (1 John 3:23).**

> **And the Spirit and the bride say, Come. And let him that heareth say, Come. And let him that is athirst come. And whosoever will, let him take the water of life freely (Rev. 22:17).**

There are also the invitations of Jesus Christ himself in the New Testament to be considered:

> **Come unto me, all *ye* that labour and are heavy laden, and I will give you rest (Mat. 11:28).**

> **In the last day, that great *day* of the feast, Jesus stood and cried, saying, If any man thirst, let him come unto me, and drink (John 7:37).**

If Total Depravity is true, then what are we to make of these verses? Is God just mocking his creation? Would God present salvation to a man knowing that the man could never even will to receive it? The God of the Bible is not the god of Calvinism. God himself even vouches for the genuineness of his intentions: **"I have not spoken in secret, in a dark place of the earth: I said not unto the seed of Jacob, Seek ye me in vain: I the LORD speak righteousness, I declare things that are right"** (Isa. 45:19). Erasmus recognized this and used it against Luther in their debate over free will: "If it is not in the power of every man to keep what is commanded, all the exhortations in the Scriptures, and all the promises, threats, expostulations, reproofs, adjurations, blessings, curses and hosts of precepts, are of necessity useless."[209]

The other type of Scripture that overthrows the doctrine of Total Depravity concerns those passages that imply the possibility that a man can believe. There are no possibilities in TULIP Calvinism. But in the Bible it is clear that the possibility exists that a man could believe under a given set of circumstances:

> **Those by the way side are they that hear; then cometh the devil, and taketh away the word out of their hearts, lest they should believe and be saved (Luke 8:12).**
>
> **And ye will not come to me, that ye might have life (John 5:40).**
>
> **Forbidding us to speak to the Gentiles that they might be saved, to fill up their sins alway: for the wrath is come upon them to the uttermost (1 Thes. 2:16).**

These verses do not mean that under a given set of circumstances a man will always believe. But they do show that there is that possibility. And if there exists even the slightest possibility that a man could believe, the doctrine of Total Depravity falls by the wayside.

As has been maintained throughout this chapter, if Total Depravity is true, then there is absolutely nothing a man can do but *hope* he is one of the "elect" and *wait* for God to save him. And if a man can't do anything himself, then another man certainly could not do anything for him either. Yet, when it comes to the subject of missions and evangelism, the Calvinist insists upon their necessity: "In spite of charges to the contrary, the missionary who believes in the Reformed truth of total depravity is *not* unable to do the work of missions. He is *not* stymied in his work. Nor is he doomed to failure before he begins."[210] The doctrine of Total Depravity is even said to "properly equip one for being a missionary."[211] So not only are unregenerate men responsible for their "inability," regenerate men are likewise responsible to preach the Gospel to them even though they have the inability to receive it. This is yet more of the other side of Total Depravity. Although the absurdity of claiming to believe in Calvinism and evangelism will be examined in more detail in chapter 9, it should be pointed out here that if a man *really* believed in the first point of Calvinism he would never even think of the subjects of evangelism and missionary work. Calvinists who do otherwise only manifest their inconsistency.

It should be reiterated at the close of this chapter that a denial of the Calvinistic doctrine of Total Depravity does not entail in any way a rejection or toning down of the biblical doctrine of man's fall into sin and subsequent depravity. One does not have to be a Calvinist to believe in the depravity of man. But recognizing that most orthodox Christians believe in the depravity of man as it is taught in the Bible, Calvinists use the doctrine of man's depravity to make their doctrine of Total Depravity look orthodox. By focusing on man's depravity instead of its supposed result, the Calvinist subtly gains adherents to his position. Calvinists would like nothing better than to convince everyone that they alone have a monopoly on the belief in the depravity of man. The Calvinist is to be commended, however, for his insistence on the complete ruin of man in the Fall and salvation by grace as the only hope for a depraved sinner. This we can agree with. What we reject is the other side of Calvinism: the philosophical speculations of Total Depravity and theological implications of Total Inability.

Chapter 7
UNCONDITIONAL ELECTION

The second petal of the TULIP is Unconditional Election. Like the first point of Calvinism, the term Unconditional Election suffers from the addition of a contrived prefix to an otherwise biblical doctrine. We saw in the previous chapter that, although the depravity of man is a biblical doctrine, the supposed result of man's depravity—the inability of the sinner to believe—shows that Total Depravity is really Total Inability, and not about the depravity of man at all. Thus, although the doctrine of election is scriptural, the Calvinistic doctrine of Unconditional Election will be proved to be a perversion of it. But since there is so much theological baggage that goes along with Unconditional Election, this will of necessity make this the longest chapter out of those which examine the Five Points of Calvinism.

Unconditional election is necessitated by the foundational point of Calvinism—Total Depravity. Because of this necessity, one cannot logically reject one and not the other, as Seaton explains: "Our acceptance or rejection of total depravity as a true Biblical statement of man's condition by nature will largely determine our attitude towards the next point that came under review at the Synod of Dort."[1] And because of this necessity: "The doctrine of unconditional election follows naturally from the doctrine of total depravity."[2] The connection of this second "point" with the previous one is further explained by Boettner:

> If the doctrine of Total Inability or Original Sin be admitted, the doctrine of Unconditional Election follows by the most inescapable logic. If, as the Scriptures and experience tell us, all men are by nature in a state of guilt and depravity from which they are wholly unable to deliver themselves and have no claim whatever on God for deliverance, it follows that if any are saved God must choose out those who shall be the objects of His grace.[3]

Seaton gives us the converse: "If man is unable to save himself on account of the Fall in Adam being a *total* fall, and if God alone can save, and if *all* are not saved, then the conclusion must be that God has not chosen to save all."[4] Now, what these Calvinists are saying is the absolute truth. Therefore, as Gerstner succinctly concludes: "If the person does not believe election is necessary he invariably believes it is not necessary because man apart from election is able to believe and be saved."[5] So if the doctrine of Total Depravity can be disproved then Unconditional Election is rendered completely unnecessary.

As we saw in the previous chapter, Total Depravity, as the foundation of the TULIP system, consigned all men to the following lot in life:

It is good that *a man* should both hope and quietly wait for the salvation of the LORD (Lam. 3:26).

Recognizing the truth of this statement, Spencer reasons that Total Depravity "declares that lost man's only hope is in an election based on the Purpose or plan of God."[6] If the Calvinistic doctrine of Total Depravity is true, all one can do is *hope* that he is the subject of Unconditional Election, and if he is, then quietly *wait* for God to save him by Irresistible Grace. It is as simple as that. But conversely, if Total Depravity is proven to be spurious, the rest of the TULIP withers. But the false foundation of Total Depravity has indeed been proved to be spurious. So the first problem with Unconditional Election is that it is built on the false premise of Total Depravity. Therefore, if man does not have inability, he can be saved without Unconditional Election. This in and of itself, however, does automatically render Unconditional Election a false doctrine. If Unconditional Election is true, God could still "unconditionally" elect a sinner in spite of his ability to be saved without it. Therefore, it is still necessary to examine the claims of the Calvinists on their second point.

Definitions

What do the Calvinists mean by Unconditional Election? It should be obvious that *election* and *predestination* are the Bible terms used to prove this doctrine. And biblical terms they are. It is the Calvinistic perversion of these terms that is being questioned. Before entering into a discussion of election and predestination, or for that matter, any discourse, it is first necessary to define exactly what is under discussion. The words *election* and *predestination* must first be defined according to their common, ordinary meanings before charging into the Bible and trying to ascertain their import according to preconceived ideas and opinions. A simple dictionary is sometimes the first tool needed to begin a study of the Bible. The word *elect* means to "select" or "choose." Every four years we have an *election* where we *choose* a candidate. There is nothing special about the meaning of the word. The other dreaded word is *predestination*. Of this word, the forms *predestinate* and *predestinated* each occur only twice in the Scripture. *Predestinate* is obviously a compound word made up of the prefix *pre,* meaning "before," and *destine,* meaning "determine," hence *predestinate,* signifying to "determine beforehand." The questions to be answered are plainly not what election and predestination denote but rather who or what is elected? Why were they elected? What are they elected to or for? So although he holds extreme views on election, Pink is nevertheless correct when he maintains: "In view of the fact that the terms 'predestinated,' 'elect,' and 'chosen,' occur so frequently in the Word, one would surely conclude that all who claim to accept the Scriptures as divinely inspired would receive with implicit faith this grand truth."[7] But as the Calvinist Storms correctly surmises: "Clearly the terms used in the New Testament do not of themselves tell us anything definitive about the basis of divine election. That issue must be determined by the way in which each term is used, as well as other relevant statements in each context."[8]

Although we will see later in this chapter that Calvinists have an exact theological meaning for the words *election* and *predestination,* they themselves use the terms interchangeably as applying to God's choosing of certain ones to be saved. So to find out exactly what the Calvinists mean by Unconditional Election, an appeal is now made to the Calvinists themselves. Although believing the doctrine, Sproul laments that "the term *unconditional election* can be misleading and grossly abused."[9] To this we couldn't agree more, and will go even further than that, disregarding not only the term, but the doctrine as well. Some Calvinists prefer the term "sovereign election,"[10] while "sovereign grace" is the preferred designation among the Calvinistic Baptists.[11] But whatever one calls it, the misuse and misapplication of predestination and election found in the doctrine of Unconditional Election is still the same.

In defining Unconditional Election, all Calvinists, whether Baptist, Reformed, or "other," say basically the same thing, emphasizing different aspects:

> All who will finally be saved, were chosen to salvation by God the Father, before the foundation of the world, and given to Jesus Christ in the covenant of grace.[12]

> Election is, therefore, that decree of God which He eternally makes, by which, with sovereign freedom, He chooses to Himself a people, upon whom He determines to set His love, whom He rescues from sin and death through Jesus Christ, unto Himself in everlasting glory.[13]

> We mean, therefore, by this doctrine, that God, in eternity, chose or picked out of mankind whom He would save (by means of Christ's death and the work of the Holy Spirit), for no other reason than His own wise, just, and gracious purpose.[14]

These Calvinistic speculations have so permeated the entire spectrum of theology that no matter which systematic theology or theological dictionary one consults, therein is presented these false views of election.[15]

It would also be pertinent to explore how the Westminster Confession of Faith and the Canons of Dort describe Unconditional Election:

> By the decree of God, for the manifestation of His own glory, some men and angels are predestinated unto everlasting life, and others foreordained to everlasting death.[16]

> Election is the unchangeable purpose of God, whereby, before the foundation of the world, he hath out of mere grace, according to the sovereign good pleasure of his own will, chosen, from the whole human race, which had fallen through their own fault, from their primitive state of rectitude, into sin and destruction, a certain number of persons to redemption in Christ, whom he from eternity appointed the Mediator and Head of the elect, and the foundation of Salvation.[17]

So according to the Calvinists, Unconditional Election is a sovereign, eternal decree where God chooses who is going to be saved and who is going to be lost. It is no wonder that Tom Nettles claims of Unconditional Election: "Perhaps one of the most feared and ignored doctrines in contemporary evangelicalism."[18]

The Essence of Calvinism

The second point of the TULIP is the main teaching of it and determines whether one is to be classed as a Calvinist. This was discussed back in chapter 1, but not within the framework of Unconditional Election, since the Five Points of Calvinism had not been introduced. But whatever it is called, the issue is still the same: Are men elected to salvation or are they not? We saw in chapter 1 that it is the belief that God, by a sovereign, eternal decree, has determined before the foundation of the world who shall be saved and who shall be lost that is the essence of Calvinism. So even though Bible believers who reject Calvinism do not agree with the Calvinist/Arminian dichotomy, in this one respect the Calvinists do have a point: man is either elect because he believes or he believes because he is elect. All Calvinists, whatever their denomination or theological views on any other subject, and whether they go by the name *Calvinist* or not, have this one thing in common. Thus, the basic error of Calvinism is confounding election and predestination with salvation.

Because Unconditional Election is the essence of Calvinism, one must be absolutely committed to this point above all others, as Calvinists rightly maintain: "If any one of the five points of Calvinism is denied, the Reformed heritage is completely lost. But it is certain that the truth of unconditional election stands at the foundation of them all. This truth is the touchstone of the Reformed faith. It is the very heart and core of the gospel."[19] But on the other hand, some Calvinists attempt to downplay the significance of this second point. Warfield insists that "the doctrine of predestination is not the formative principle of Calvinism, the root from which it springs. It is one of its logical consequences, one of the branches which it has inevitably thrown out."[20] This contradictory analysis of Unconditional Election is also evident in a more general sense. Grover Gunn claims that "the doctrine of election is difficult, and God has not answered all our questions."[21] But Robert Haldane

(1764-1842) maintains that election "is a truth essential to the plan of salvation, and a truth most explicitly revealed. No truth in the Scripture is more easily defended."[22] One would certainly think that Calvinists, of all people, would gladly accept their own doctrines, but as acknowledged by the Calvinists themselves, this is not always the case. Nettles contends that "the doctrine of election provides a foundation for every legitimate enterprise of Christian endeavor."[23] But Keith Mathison remarks: "Like the doctrine of total depravity, the doctrine of unconditional election is not popular, even among the elect."[24] So like the other points of the TULIP, the Calvinists are never in agreement among themselves as to the correct terminology, importance, and nature of their doctrines, which will become more readily apparent the further we descend into the TULIP. One thing is for sure: "No man can claim ever to be either Calvinistic or Reformed without a firm and abiding commitment to this precious truth."[25] This doctrine is considered so important that students at Reformed Theological Seminary can take a theology elective on "The Doctrine of Election."[26]

Not only is the doctrine of election of supreme importance, but the Calvinists declare that it is synonymous with the Gospel. Custance asserts that "it *is* the Gospel," and that "every departure from the doctrine of Election in any degree has been a departure from the Gospel."[27] This fraudulent supposition is the standard party line for all Calvinists. If one denies their doctrine of Unconditional Election, he becomes the subject of the following conclusions:

> The reason we are prone to disbelieve this doctrine is that we are not humble enough.[28]

> By making election conditional upon something that man does, even if what he does is simply to repent and believe the gospel, God's grace is seriously compromised.[29]

> The doubter's trouble is not with the doctrine of election but with the doctrine of sin.[30]

The Calvinist also charges the opponents of Unconditional Election with teaching salvation by works:

> The bottom line is if you deny election, you deny salvation by

grace. To reject election is to reject salvation by grace and promote salvation by works.[31]

Those who declare that salvation is entirely by the grace of God, and yet deny the doctrine of election, hold an inconsistent position.[32]

We reject the doctrine of election because we really believe that we can ultimately save ourselves by our own doings.[33]

The Sovereign Grace Baptist Roy Mason is really insolent:

If unconditional election, predestination, and predeterminism are not true, then PROPHECY IS A FAKE AND A FRAUD![34]

If predestination and election are not so, what else? The answer is, THEN WE DON'T KNOW HOW EVERYTHING IS GOING TO TURN OUT IN THE END! MAYBE SATAN WILL DEFEAT GOD AND FINALLY WIN OUT![35]

If all one ever listened to were Calvinists, he would think that the entire Bible revolved around the doctrine of Unconditional Election:

The Bible not only teaches the doctrine, but makes it prominent—so prominent that you can only get rid of Election by getting rid of the Bible.[36]

The doctrine of election is a cardinal teaching of the Scriptures.[37]

The story of the Bible is the story of unconditional election.[38]

Beloved, if the Bible teaches anything at all, it teaches that God predestinated us unto salvation before the foundation of the world. The Bible teaches election from Genesis to Revelation. Throughout the ages, God has always worked on the basis of election.[39]

But finding Unconditional Election throughout the Bible is like the leaven **"which a woman took, and hid in three measures of meal, till the whole was leavened"** (Mat. 13:33). The Calvinist thrusts his doctrines of election and predestination into every conceivable Scripture text. Clark claims that "Isaiah has some two dozen verses that bear rather directly on the doctrine of predestination."[40] What he means is that there are some two dozen verses violently wrested to prove predestination, for the word neither occurs in Isaiah nor anywhere else in the Old Testament. Custance is even bolder: "Turning more specifically to the matter of Election to salvation, consider the following."[41] Then follows a list of twelve passages from the Old Testament in which election is not mentioned and salvation is not even in view.[42] Turning now to the New Testament, we find the same thing. Boettner audaciously declares: "There is hardly a chapter in the Gospel of John which does not either mention or imply election or reprobation."[43] But even after a statement like that he didn't give any verses. In answering the question, "I would like for you to list the Scriptures which teach that God elected individuals to salvation before the world began," one Sovereign Grace Baptist lists six Scriptures where election is not even mentioned.[44]

Once Unconditional Election is set forth as the sum and substance of all theology, various historical arguments are used to further cement it in place. Mason reminds us that "CHRISTIANS OF THE NEW TESTAMENT TIMES were strong believers in the greatness and sovereignty of God, and consequently in the doctrines of election and predestination."[45] No quotes from the Church Fathers are given, however, to substantiate this claim. Jewett appeals to the "great theologians" in history:

> Every theologian of the first rank from Augustine to Barth has affirmed the doctrine of election as basic to the Christian faith. These master theologians have also agreed in a material way on the essential content of the doctrine. They all contend that God's election is a righteous and holy decision that he makes according to his own good pleasure to redeem the objects of his electing love.[46]

Mason adds that "if Unconditional Election is not true, then the GREATEST PREACHERS AND BIBLE SCHOLARS OF THE PAST WERE UTTERLY DECEIVED."[47]

As further proof for the doctrine of predestination, Boettner appeals to Islam and worse:

> When we stop to consider that among non-Christian religions Mohammedanism has so many millions who believe in some kind of Predestination, that the doctrine of Fatalism has been held in some form or other in several heathen countries, and that the mechanistic and deterministic philosophies have exerted such great influences in England, Germany, and America, we see that this doctrine is at least worthy of careful study.[48]

Another twist to this Islamic association is to divert attention from the Calvinistic doctrine of predestination by disdaining the supposed fatalism of Islam as contrasted with Calvinistic predestination.[49] Seaton appeals to Jesus Christ himself: "What was the doctrine that Jesus preached in the synagogue at Nazareth but the doctrine of unconditional election?"[50]

And whom do Calvinists present as the greatest proponent of Unconditional Election? Berkhof? Pink? Spurgeon? Surely it is John Calvin? Why no, it is the Apostle Paul!

> In the Epistles of Paul, the great doctrine of predestination is taught again and again. In fact, it would hardly be too much to say that it forms the basis of everything else that Paul taught.[51]

> The Apostle Paul was an avowed, ardent, predestinarian, holding double predestination, election, and reprobation.[52]

> Who ever stated the doctrine of election more plainly or in more forcible language than did the Apostle Paul?[53]

The extent to which the Calvinist goes to maintain his Unconditional Election is extreme indeed. Any statement setting forth the slightest condition on which a sinner may receive the forgiveness of sins through God's provision in Christ supposedly belies Unconditional Election and makes even the simplest request to place faith in Christ a condition and therefore a work. Believing this to be true, Coppes stumbles all over himself trying to maintain man's responsibility: "The Scripture declares that God alone chooses who is to be saved. He is the sovereign author of salvation. This is not to say that men are mere robots or blocks which are divinely manipulated as a child manipulates a toy. Men are responsible beings. They are called upon to believe in and to obey God. Ultimately, however, eternal life does not depend upon man's decision but on God's."[54] This double-talk is typical of the

Calvinist's attempts to make palatable his TULIP philosophy.

God's Decree

The consonance of every definition given for Unconditional Election is that it was by a sovereign, eternal decree. The philosophical concept of God's decree is the basis for the Five Points of Calvinism. Stripped of all of its theological verbiage, the decree of God that the Calvinists talk so much about can be described as singular, eternal, sovereign, and all-encompassing. It remains, therefore, to examine each of these elements individually in order to correctly ascertain the implications of God's decree.

The title of the third chapter in the Westminster Confession of Faith is "Of God's Eternal Decree." This tells us two things that Calvinists believe about God's decree: it is singular and it is eternal. Although it is often referred to in the plural, "for the benefit of man's finite mind,"[55] the Calvinists are united in making the so-called decrees of God as really one decree embracing one purpose with many events. It is referred to in the plural for the sake of convenience in enumerating these events. For confirmation of this fact, we cite Buswell and Hodge respectively:

> Since God's decrees are immutable from eternity past to eternity future, and since God is consistent and "cannot deny himself" (II Tim. 2:13), it follows that the decrees of God may be regarded as one complex decree, including all things.[56]

> The decrees of God, therefore, are not many, but one purpose. . . . It is one scheme, and therefore one purpose. As, however, this one purpose includes an indefinite number of events, and as those events are mutually related, we therefore speak of the decrees of God as many, and as having a certain order.[57]

This decree is also said to be eternal. Once again we let the Calvinists state exactly what they believe. This time Hoeksema and Berkhof speak for the Calvinists:

> The decree of God is as eternal as the eternal God Himself.[58]

> The divine decree is eternal in the sense that it lies entirely in eternity. . . . The decree, however, while it relates to things

outside of God, remains in itself an act within the Divine Being, and is therefore eternal in the strictest sense of the word.[59]

So according to the Calvinists, God's decree is singular, and God's decree is eternal.

The next philosophical concept of God's decree is the sovereignty of God. This Calvinistic buzzword has been popularized by the book *The Sovereignty of God* by Arthur W. Pink, and is the ever present diatribe that we hear from the Calvinists. In fact, the sovereignty of God is often given precedence over election itself: "The doctrine of election is a part of the larger teaching that God is in sovereign control of every detail of history."[60] And while sometimes Calvinists claim that "predestination must never be looked upon as the sum and substance of the Reformed Faith,"[61] the concept of the sovereignty of God is always exalted:

> The basic principle of Calvinism is the sovereignty of God.[62]

> The secret grandeur of Calvin's theology lies in his grasp of the Biblical teaching of the sovereignty of God.[63]

> One cannot emphasize the sovereignty of God strongly enough! The all-out emphasis on the almighty sovereignty of Jehovah God is the truth and beauty of Calvinism.[64]

> The sovereignty of God is foundational to Christianity. It is the most basic principle of Calvinism.[65]

Talbot and Crampton further insist that the sovereignty of God is "the foundation upon which all is built," and that by rejecting it "the whole of biblical Christianity will fall with it."[66] Coppes is quick to add that "only the Calvinist, however, recognizes God's absolute sovereignty,"[67] implying that if one is not a Calvinist then he has a false conception of God.

This singular, eternal, sovereign decree is also said to be all-encompassing; that is, God, by his decree, has foreordained everything that ever happens in time. Once again, we look to the Calvinists themselves for their true position, for this is the only way to avoid the cry of misrepresentation often voiced by the Calvinists when their true views are exposed. Does God really foreordain all things? The Calvinist claims that he does:

> As a builder draws his plans before he begins to build, so the great Architect predestinated everything before a single creature was called into existence.[68]
>
> The Sovereignty of God over all, and his independency, clearly shew, that whatever is done in time is according to his decrees in eternity.[69]
>
> All things whatever arise from, and depend on, the divine appointment.[70]

Often times the Calvinist will just quote the reply to question seven of the Westminster Shorter Catechism: "The decrees of God are his eternal purpose, according to the counsel of his will, whereby, for his own glory, he hath fore-ordained whatsoever comes to pass."

When a Calvinist claims that God ordains all things, does he mean "all without exception" or "all without distinction"? When faced with an unlimited Atonement, the Calvinist clamors for "all without distinction" in order to limit the Atonement to the "elect." But as pertaining to the all-encompassing extent of God's decree, when the Calvinist says *all* he means "all without exception":

> God predestinates all things whatsoever, both animate and inanimate. His decree includes all angels, both good and evil.[71]
>
> All things turn out according to divine predestination; not only the works we do outwardly, but even the thoughts we think inwardly.[72]
>
> God has appointed where each person shall reside: the particular country in which he should be born, and the very city, town, village, and house in which we shall dwell, and how long he shall remain there.[73]

John Gill summarizes the Calvinists' position:

> In short, every thing respecting all the individuals of the world, that have been, are, or shall be, all correspond with the decrees of God, and are according to them; men's coming into the world, the time of it, and all circumstances attending it; all events and occurrences they meet with, throughout the whole time of life; their places of habitation, their stations, calling, and

employment; their circumstances of riches and poverty, of health and sickness, adversity and prosperity; their time of going out of the world, with every thing attending that; all are according to the determinate counsel and will of God.[74]

Can there be any doubt whatsoever about what the Calvinists believe? There is nothing that has ever happened or will happen that God's all-encompassing decree is not responsible for. It is just as Doris Day sang: "*Que sera sera,* whatever will be will be." Although the redundancy of this material seems sensational and overdone, it is necessary to combat not only the cry of misrepresentation of the Calvinists when confronted with their true position, but also the skeptical reader who still is not convinced that the Calvinist really thinks God has decreed everything that ever has or will take place.

How far does the Calvinist go with his insistence that everything has been decreed? Consider the fall of Adam. If God has foreordained everything then the Fall must be included as well:

> Even the fall of Adam, and through him the fall of the race, was not by chance or accident, but was so ordained in the secret counsels of God.[75]

> Surely, if God had not willed the fall, He could, and no doubt would, have prevented it; but He did not prevent it: ergo, He willed it. And if He willed it, He certainly decreed it.[76]

> Plainly it was God's *will* that sin *should* enter this world, otherwise it *would not* have entered, for nothing happens save as God has eternally decreed. Moreover, there was more than a bare *permission,* for God only permits that which He has purposed.[77]

> Not only did His omniscient eye see Adam eating of the forbidden fruit, but He *decreed* beforehand that he *should* do so.[78]

But to merely say that the Fall was ordained is an understatement. Gill claims it is certain "that the fall of Adam was by the determinate counsel and foreknowledge of God" because "the sufferings and death of Christ, by which is the redemption of men from that sin, and all others, were ordained before the foundation of the world; and which must have been precarious and uncertain, if Adam's fall was not by a like decree."[79] The Reformed theologian and historian Richard Muller admits about Beza's concept of the Fall: "God's decree of election and reprobation rendered it necessary that he infold man in sin and disobedience for the sake of the justice and utter mercy of the decree."[80] This implies that the fall of Adam was a means to an end: the means of bestowing grace on the "elect" and the means of magnifying this grace by damning the "non-elect." The result is a divine chess game in which Adam was an unwitting pawn.

But let's go a step further. If everything that takes place in time has been decreed, including the fall of Adam, then what about every other sin? The Calvinists again have the answer:

> It is even Biblical to say that God has foreordained sin. If sin was outside the plan of God, then not a single important affair of life would be ruled by God.[81]

> Nothing comes to pass contrary to his decree. Nothing happens by chance. Even moral evil, which he abhors and forbids, occurs "by the determinate counsel and foreknowledge of God."[82]

> All things including even the wicked actions of wicked men and devils—are brought to pass in accordance with God's eternal purpose.[83]

> Sin is one of the 'whatsoevers' that have 'come to pass,' all of which are 'ordained.'[84]

The teaching that sin is also foreordained by God is not limited to just modern Calvinists. It has been with Calvinism since the very beginning. Gomarus, the chief antagonist of Arminius, taught that "God moves the tongues of men to blaspheme."[85] During a controversy with the aforementioned Vorstius, the Reformed theologian John Piscator (1546-1625), professor at Herborn in Germany, stated that "God justly wills that sins be committed by us, and indeed absolutely wills that they be committed; nay, procures in time these sins themselves."[86]

As if everything they have said was not enough, the Calvinist will even go so far as to insist that God could not have absolute knowledge of future events unless he actually decreed them to happen:

> The idea that God knows the future without having planned it and without controlling it is totally foreign to Scripture.[87]
>
> If God did not foreordain all things, then he could not know the future. God foreknows and knows all things because He decreed all things to be.[88]
>
> Foreknowledge of future events then is founded upon God's decrees, hence if God foreknows everything that is to be, it is because He has determined in Himself from all eternity everything which will be.[89]

The theological implication behind this teaching is that if one denies the all-encompassing nature of God's so-called decree, then one is denying the omniscience of God.

Before going deeper into the TULIP, it might be a good idea to examine what the Bible actually says about this singular, eternal, sovereign, all-encompassing decree. Certainly the Scripture has much to say about this decree of God? Think again. The term is used of men more than it is used of God. In the Old Testament, Cyrus made a decree (Ezra 5:13), Darius made a decree (Ezra 6:1), Artaxerxes made a decree (Ezra 7:21), Nebuchadnezzar made a decree (Dan. 3:10), and Esther made a decree (Est. 9:32). In the New Testament we find that the Caesars (Luke 2:1; Acts 17:7) and the apostles (Acts 16:4) made decrees. To ascertain the decrees of God involves a simple reading of the Bible, not a systematic theology by Berkhof, Dabney, or Hodge. The word *decree* occurs forty-nine times in forty-eight verses, the word *decreed* occurs five times in five verses, while the plural *decrees* is used twice in as many verses. Yet, out of the fifty-six occasions when a form of the word *decree* is used, only eight times is it connected with God.

The decrees of God are recorded in the Scripture as follows:

> Concerning the rain (Job 28:26)
> Concerning the sea (Job 38:10; Pro. 8:29)
> Concerning Jesus Christ (Psa. 2:7)
> Concerning the heavens (Psa. 148:6)
> Concerning a consumption (Isa. 10:22)

Concerning the sand (Jer. 5:22)
Concerning Nebuchadnezzar (Dan. 4:24)

The first thing to be noticed about God's decree is that it is not just one decree—there are seven of them. Secondly, none of these decrees are said to be eternal. And thirdly, none of these decrees involve election or predestination. Yet Christopher Ness (1621-1705) proclaims: "Predestination is also called a **Divine decree.**"[90] Scripture? He couldn't possibly give one. There is no such thing as God's eternal decree of predestination—except in the philosophical speculations and theological implications of Calvinism.

Since no decree of election or predestination is mentioned in the Bible, the Calvinist insists that they are part of God's secret decrees. Boettner reminds us that the Calvinist is "under no obligation to explain all the mysteries connected with these doctrines."[91] Palmer contends that "we ought not to probe into that secret counsel of God."[92] He even acknowledges that the Calvinist's motto is Deuteronomy 29:29: **"The secret *things belong* unto the LORD our God: but those *things which are* revealed *belong* unto us and to our children for ever, that *we* may do all the words of this law."**[93] Since God's ways are not our ways, nor his thoughts our thoughts (Isa. 55:8-9), Unconditional Election is pawned off as the secret counsel of God that can't be understood. Yet, untold volumes have been written by Calvinists on the subject. So if the decree of predestination is a secret decree, how do the Calvinists know so much about it? Strong tells of "the farmer who, after hearing a sermon on God's decrees, took the break-neck road instead of the safe one to his home and broke his wagon in consequence, concluded before the end of the journey that he at any rate had been predestinated to be a fool, and that he had made his calling and election sure."[94] In the Bible, however, the misappropriation of the decrees of God by the Calvinists is no laughing matter: **"Woe unto them that decree unrighteous decrees, and that write grievousness *which* they have prescribed"** (Isa. 10:1).

The next philosophical concept of God's decree is the sovereignty of God. Although at first glance the sovereignty of God appears to be a scriptural doctrine, when the Calvinistic interpretation of the sovereignty of God is examined, it will be manifest that their interpretation differs substantially from the one an unbiased reader would adopt. The Calvinist perception of God as being absolutely sovereign is very much accurate; however, that doesn't mean that it takes precedence over his other attributes.

In the Bible, God is the one and only supreme Being. This is called the supremacy of God, and is described in the Bible as follows:

> **Thine, O LORD, *is* the greatness, and the power, and the glory, and the victory, and the majesty: for all *that is* in the heaven and in the earth *is thine;* thine *is* the kingdom, O LORD, and thou art exalted as head above all.**
> **Both riches and honour *come* of thee, and thou reignest over all; and in thine hand *is* power and might; and in thine hand *it is* to make great, and to give strength unto all (1 Chr. 29:11-12).**
>
> **For the LORD most high *is* terrible; *he is* a great King over all the earth (Psa. 47:2).**

The sovereignty of God is the exercise of his supremacy:

> **But our God *is* in the heavens: he hath done whatsoever he hath pleased (Psa. 115:3).**
>
> **And all the inhabitants of the earth *are* reputed as nothing: and he doeth according to his will in the army of heaven, and *among* the inhabitants of the earth: and none can stay his hand, or say unto him, What doest thou? (Dan. 4:35).**

We definitely agree with those Calvinists who say that to declare God sovereign is to declare that he is God.[95] How could God not be sovereign? Sovereignty is inherent with Godhood. We also agree with Pink when he states that "when we say that God is sovereign we affirm His right to govern the universe, which He made for His own glory, just as He pleases."[96] Pink is also correct in saying that "because God is *God*, He does as He pleases, only as He pleases, always as He pleases; that His great concern is in the accomplishment of His own pleasure and the promotion of His own glory; that He is the Supreme Being, and therefore Sovereign of the universe."[97]

So what is the problem with God's sovereignty? The problem is that Fidel Castro is sovereign. Saddam Hussein is sovereign. The

Pope is sovereign. Hitler, Stalin, and Mao were sovereign. When a Calvinist speaks of God's sovereignty he means arbitrariness. The end result of this teaching is a God who could change, by-pass, or ignore his own laws because of his so-called sovereignty. This antinomian God is described by Pink:

> There is no conflict between the Divine will and the Divine nature, yet it needs to be insisted upon that God is a law unto himself. God does what He does, not simply because righteousness requires Him so to act, but what God does is righteousness simply because *He* does it. All the Divine works issue from mere sovereignty.[98]

> Yet, let it be pointed out, on the other hand, that God is sovereign, high above all law, and by no means tied by the restrictions which He has placed on His creatures.[99]

> But though His creatures are bound by the laws He has prescribed them, God Himself is not. God is under no law, but is absolute Sovereign. . . . God possesses supreme authority, and when He pleases sets aside His own laws, or issues new ones contrary to those given previously. . . . Learn then, that God is bound by no law, being above all law.[100]

So by this arbitrary capriciousness, God could damn to hell men yet uncreated for no other reason than his sovereign good pleasure. This concept of the sovereignty of God as applied to salvation is summed up concisely by Herman Hoeksema: "God determines sovereignly who shall be saved, and who shall not be saved."[101] So what Hoeksema and all Calvinists really mean is that God arbitrarily chose certain ones for salvation or damnation on a whim.

The Bible paints a rather contrary picture of God than the caricature of the Calvinist. First and foremost of God's attributes is his holiness. As we all know, the most vile, profane, bloody, wicked dictator could be sovereign—yet unholy. God is declared to be absolute holiness:

> **The LORD *is* righteous in all his ways, and holy in all his works (Psa. 145:17).**

> **And one cried unto another, and said, Holy, holy, holy, *is* the LORD of hosts: the whole earth *is* full of his glory (Isa. 6:3).**

God is **"glorious in holiness"** (Exo. 15:11). His name is holy (Psa. 33:21); his throne is holy (Psa. 47:8). Because God is holy, he exercises his sovereignty only in ways consistent with his holiness. What the Calvinists have done is to exalt the sovereignty of God above all his other attributes. But what kind of man, unless he had a theological axe to grind, would do such a thing?

The final thing about this singular, eternal, sovereign decree is that it is said to be all-encompassing; that is, God, by his decree, has foreordained everything that ever happens in time. The first problem with this teaching is that there is some truth in what the Calvinists say. In seeking to prove the all-encompassing nature of God's decree, Pink says things like:

> Not as much as a fly can settle upon you without the Creator's bidding, any more than the demons could enter the herd of swine until Christ gave them permission.[102]

> Christ rules and overrules for the good of His Church the deliberations of the senate, the conflict of armies, the history of the nations.[103]

In rejecting the Calvinistic nature of an all-encompassing decree, no denial is being made of God's ability and right to influence and direct man as he so chooses. This may take the form of withholding (Gen. 20:6), guiding (Psa. 73:24), directing (Pro. 3:6), restraining (Psa. 76:10), hardening (Exo. 14:17), leading (Psa. 139:24), inclining (Psa. 119:36), or many other forms. But God's influence is not the same as God foreordaining every thought and action of man. The problem we have with the Calvinists is this: God's influence, direction, control, and permission are not the same as God's election, predestination, foreordination, and decree.

To further add insult to injury, the Calvinists claim that God could not have absolute knowledge of future events unless he actually decreed them to happen. This is a direct attack on the omniscience of God. What kind of power does it take know something one has already decreed to take place? The proof that the Bible is inspired and God is exactly who he claims to be is the fact that God knows what men will do in the future *without* divine foreordination of anything:

Behold, the former things are come to pass, and new things

> do I declare: before they spring forth I tell you of them (Isa. 42:9).

> Declaring the end from the beginning, and from ancient times *the things* that are not *yet* done, saying, My counsel shall stand, and I will do all my pleasure (Isa. 46:10).

To take away God's absolute omniscience under the guise of an all-encompassing decree is not only a deliberate rejection of the word of God, but a subtle attack on the nature of God himself.

It is perfectly clear by examining God's decrees in the Bible that they are not eternal. It is also apparent that there is no such thing as one decree which contains many parts. The true nature of the Calvinistic concept of the sovereignty of God has also been examined. But as concerning the all-encompassing nature of God's so-called decree, the Calvinist does present some semblance of scriptural proof for God foreordaining all things. This is not to say that he is correct. All it means is that the Calvinist has amassed enough Scripture to make himself look authoritative. The issue is concisely stated by Boettner: "The question which faces us then is, has God from all eternity foreordained all things which come to pass?"[104]

The best place to begin is the "haven of divine foreordination" for all Calvinists—the Book of Proverbs:

> The preparations of the heart in man, and the answer of the tongue, *is* from the LORD (Pro. 16:1).

> A man's heart deviseth his way: but the LORD directeth his steps (Pro. 16:9).

> The lot is cast into the lap; but the whole disposing thereof *is* of the LORD (Pro. 16:33).

> *There are* many devices in a man's heart; nevertheless the counsel of the LORD, that shall stand (Pro. 19:21).

> Man's goings *are* of the LORD; how can a man then understand his own way? (Pro. 20:24).

> The king's heart *is* in the hand of the LORD, *as* the rivers of water: he turneth it whithersoever he will (Pro. 21:1).

> **Many seek the ruler's favour; but *every* man's judgment *cometh* from the LORD (Pro. 29:26).**

Any verse that mentions God's direction, the fact that something has come "from the Lord," or anything similar, is also a candidate for a divine foreordination proof text.

And what do the Calvinists get out of these verses?

> This verse, rather clearly, is not restricted to the facts of conversion alone. It quite generally covers all the thoughts of one's heart and all the answers one gives to any question.[105]

> If the Lord *directs* the steps of a man, is it not proof that he is being controlled or governed by God? . . . Can this mean anything less than, that no matter what man may desire and plan, it is the will of his Maker which is executed?[106]

> It is amazing that anyone who calls himself a Christian and has read even a little part of the Bible can deny that God controls the mental operations of his creatures. The heart of man is in the hand of the Lord and the Lord turns man's heart in any direction the Lord pleases. The idea that man's will is free, independent of God, able to turn itself in any one of a dozen incompatible directions, is totally unbiblical and unchristian. As a clear denial of omnipotence, it dethrones God and takes man out of God's control.[107]

Other Calvinists merely list some of these verses as proof texts after making general statements about election.[108] The Calvinist viewpoint is clear: God has foreordained every word, thought, deed, and motive of every man, woman, and child anytime and all the time. The issue in these verses is not whether God can or does control, guide, direct, and influence man. According to the Calvinists, these verses prove that God has foreordained every act of every man. Therefore, with this Calvinistic postulation in mind, we will see if the Bible confirms or denies the Calvinistic position.

The first class of verses are those which mention some characteristic of man that is supposedly ordained by God: preparations, answers, steps, goings, judgments. It should be remembered that the Calvinist insists that in these verses is found proof that God has foreordained *all* things. But what about other characteristics that are not mentioned? Specifically, man's thoughts, dreams, plans, and actions? Well, responds the Calvinist, the foreordination of these things is implied. Implied by whom? Calvinists or the Bible? And what about these features of man which are supposedly ordained? Let's assume for a moment that they are. What does that have to do with the foreordination of angels, devils, or animals? Is this implied as well? But let's continue to assume the divine foreordination of all man's actions. What kind of a god is the result of this teaching? What if a man prepared (Pro. 16:1) to commit murder or rape? Suppose the answer (Pro. 16:1) of a man was vile and profane? Was the answer of Ananias and Sapphira (Acts 5:2-5) from the Lord? How about the false testimony of the witnesses against Jesus Christ (Mat. 26:60)? Consider the steps (Pro. 16:9) of a man as he commits robbery or assault. What about a man's goings (Pro. 20:24) into a bar or pornographic bookstore? Suppose a man judged (Pro. 29:26) that sodomy or incest was okay? To say that God doesn't ordain any of *these* things is to contradict everything that the Calvinists have said thus far about the all-encompassing nature of God's singular, eternal sovereign decree.

Two other similar verses concern the cast lot (Pro. 16:33) and the devices in a man's heart (Pro. 19:21). Although men may devise and cast lots, the disposing and counsel of the Lord can not be overcome. Man proposes, God disposes. What do these verses have to do with God foreordaining anything? God can decide the outcome of any lot (Lev. 16:8-10; Acts 1:24-26), as well as prevent man's devises (Gen. 11:4-8; Rev. 20:7-9).

Lastly, there is the matter of the king: **"The king's heart *is* in the hand of the LORD, *as* the rivers of water: he turneth it whithersoever he will"** (Pro. 21:1). Calvinists read the foreordination of every man into this verse. The sovereign Grace Baptist David West reasons: "If God can and does control the king, the most powerful man on earth, He also controls every other man."[109] But assuming for a moment that God ordains all the actions of all kings, how does that prove that all men are included? All men are not kings. How can it be said that all men who aren't kings are included? Is this also implied? And what about the king's hands and feet? Are they in the hand of God? The verse doesn't say they are.

This verse is illustrated in the person of Cyrus:

Now in the first year of Cyrus king of Persia, that the word

> of the LORD by the mouth of Jeremiah might be fulfilled, the LORD stirred up the spirit of Cyrus king of Persia, that he made a proclamation throughout all his kingdom, and *put it* also in writing, saying,
> Thus saith Cyrus king of Persia, The LORD God of heaven hath given me all the kingdoms of the earth; and he hath charged me to build him an house at Jerusalem, which *is* in Judah (Ezra 1:1-2).

Likewise, God calls Nebuchadnezzar **"my servant"** when he uses him to bring judgment on Israel (Jer. 25:9). No one is denying God the right or ability to use men and nations as he sees fit. Pink is certainly correct in maintaining that "the worst tyrants, when inflicting the greatest outrages, are the instruments of God, accomplishing his will."[110] But the Calvinist forgets the words of the Apostle Paul: **"What shall we say then?** *Is there* **unrighteousness with God? God forbid"** (Rom. 9:14). Did God eternally decree Herod to slay all the children under two years old (Mat. 2:16)? Did God sovereignly decree that Ahab covet Naboth's vineyard and thereby have him killed (1 Kgs. 21:1-13)? Did God foreordain the wickedness of Manasseh, who did much worse in his abominations than the heathen (2 Chr. 33:9)? God will yet work in the heart of kings (Rev. 17:17) to fulfill his purpose (Zep. 3:8). Is every sin they commit part of God's "sovereign eternal decree"? The error of the Calvinists in these verses in Proverbs is in reading the word *foreordained* into "of the Lord," "from the Lord," "directeth," "turneth," and similar expressions that speak of God's control or influence.

Other passages used by Calvinists to prove that God has foreordained every act of every man include those which seem to speak of the time of man's death being determined by God:

> Seeing his days *are* determined, the number of his months *are* with thee, thou hast appointed his bounds that he cannot pass (Job 14:5).

> A time to be born, and a time to die; a time to plant, and a time to pluck up *that which is* planted (Ecc. 3:2).

Since all life comes from God (Acts 17:25), no one is denying his right or ability to determine the end of an individual man's life.

God is even recorded as doing so with Jacob (Israel) and Moses:

> **And the time drew nigh that Israel must die: and he called his son Joseph, and said unto him, If now I have found grace in thy sight, put, I pray thee, thy hand under my thigh, and deal kindly and truly with me; bury me not, I pray thee, in Egypt (Gen. 47:29).**

> **And the LORD said unto Moses, Behold, thy days approach that thou must die: call Joshua, and present yourselves in the tabernacle of the congregation, that I may give him a charge. And Moses and Joshua went, and presented themselves in the tabernacle of the congregation (Deu. 31:14).**

God was going to kill Hezekiah but added fifteen years to his life (Isa. 38:5).

The problem with the Calvinists is three-fold. First of all, the Calvinist reasons that because these verses speak of God determining the time of man's death, this also means that God has foreordained everything that ever takes place. Clark remarks: "This very obviously indicates that God controls the length of one's life. This much predestination does not worry our opponents. It is, however, one of the many details which together show that God governs all his creatures and all their actions."[111] But it is a long way from God determining the end of a man's life to God predestinating all things before the foundation of the world. Secondly, the Calvinist has taken general statements about mankind and made them into individual decrees for each man. Cockrell claims that "no man shall leave this world until He has finished his predestinated career."[112] The Bible declares of man: **"The days of our years *are* threescore years and ten; and if by reason of strength *they be* fourscore years, yet *is* their strength labour and sorrow; for it is soon cut off, and we fly away"** (Psa. 90:10). Yet, it is apparent that individual men do not always die at exactly seventy or eighty years of age. Some men **"shall not live out half their days"** (Psa. 55:23). A man can die before his appointed time (Ecc. 7:17). Third, even though Calvinists claim that they believe in the absolute predestination of all things, they make statements that contradict what they claim to believe: "The fact that God has determined the day, hour, and minute of our death does not hinder the use of means for the preservation of life."[113] But if God has really sovereignly, eternally determined the date of one's death, how could anything man does "for the preservation of life" affect this in any way?

The crucifixion of Christ is an event that Calvinists use to prove that God has foreordained every act of every man:

> **Him, being delivered by the determinate counsel and foreknowledge of God, ye have taken, and by wicked hands have crucified and slain (Acts 2:23).**
>
> **For of a truth against thy holy child Jesus, whom thou hast anointed, both Herod, and Pontius Pilate, with the Gentiles, and the people of Israel, were gathered together, For to do whatsoever thy hand and thy counsel determined before to be done (Acts 4:27-28).**
>
> **Who verily was foreordained before the foundation of the world, but was manifest in these last times for you (1 Pet. 1:20).**
>
> **And all that dwell upon the earth shall worship him, whose names are not written in the book of life of the Lamb slain from the foundation of the world (Rev. 13:8).**

Clark reasons: "As this event, the death of Christ, was foreordained, so too every event is foreordained because God is omniscient; and no detail, not even the number of hairs on one's head, escapes his foreknowledge and deliberate counsel. Everything is a part of his plan. Of everything God says, 'Thus it must be.'"[114] He then jeers: "Must not they who say that God does not foreordain evil acts now hang their heads in shame?"[115] There are four problems with Clark's exegesis. To begin with, what does God being omniscient have to do with him foreordaining sin? The Calvinist subtly leads us to believe that if one rejects the idea that God has ordained sin then he doesn't believe that God is really omniscient. Second, Clark deduces that because these verses speak of God determining Christ's crucifixion, this also means that God has foreordained every other event that ever takes place. But as we have seen, this is an unwarranted deduction. Third, the crucifixion of Christ was an exceptional, one-time, event—the focal point of history. To casually infer the doctrines of Calvinism from this event is sacrilegious to say the least. And fourth, Clark has ignored the word **"foreknowledge"** in the last part of the phrase **"the determinate counsel and foreknowledge of God."** If God determined the crucifixion of his Son by a sovereign, eternal decree, with no foreknowledge at all involved (it was unconditional), then we are left with the ghastly, draconian thought that God decreed the death of his Son and then created man so he could fall and God could bring about his decree of the crucifixion.

To abrogate the foreknowledge in Acts 2:23, Pink suggests we "note the order here: first God's 'determinate counsel' (His decree), and second His 'foreknowledge.'"[116] He then insists that God's foreknowledge is *based* on his decrees.[117] This is nothing but the aforementioned teaching that God cannot know anything unless he previously decreed it, as Pink says elsewhere: "God foreknows what will be because He has decreed what shall be."[118] But not only does Pink contradict the Scripture, but Calvin himself. First of all, when faced with other Scriptures in which foreknowledge does not come after predestination and election, Pink has a problem:

> **For whom he did foreknow, he also did predestinate *to be conformed to the image of his Son, that he might be the firstborn among many brethren (Rom. 8:29).***

> **Elect according to the foreknowledge of God the Father, through sanctification of the Spirit, unto obedience and sprinkling of the blood of Jesus Christ: Grace unto you, and peace, be multiplied (1 Pet. 1:2).**

But this isn't all, for sometimes calling (Irresistible Grace in the Calvinistic system) precedes election (2 Pet. 1:10), salvation comes before calling (2 Tim. 1:9), sanctification precedes calling (Jude 1), and calling comes before choosing (Mat. 22:14). Therefore, to build a doctrine of an all-encompassing decree on the order of two words in one verse is ludicrous.

The second problem faced by Pink is with the namesake of Calvinism. In discussing the verses in question, Calvin gives a decidedly different (and more scriptural) interpretation than Pink:

> Luke deals here with two doctrines, the foreknowledge and the decree of God. And although the foreknowledge is first in order, because God sees what he wills to determine before He

determines it, Luke makes it secondary to the counsel and decree of God, so that we may know that God wills or resolves nothing which He has not long before directed to its particular end.[119]

It may, however, be asked, as Adam did not fall before the creation of the world, how was Christ appointed to be the Redeemer? For a cure ought to come after the disease. My reply is, that this is to be referred to God's foreknowledge, for doubtless before He created man, God foresaw that he would not stand firm for long in his integrity. Hence, according to His wonderful wisdom and goodness, He ordained that Christ should be the Redeemer, who would deliver the lost race of man from ruin. In this there shines forth more clearly the unspeakable goodness of God, in that He anticipated our disease by the remedy of His grace, and provided a restoration to life before the first man had fallen into death.[120]

This demonstrates once again that the Calvinists are in hopeless disagreement among themselves.

The subject of the crucifixion brings up an interesting question: who killed Jesus Christ? Was it the man who made the cross? Was it the ones who held him down or the ones who drove the nails? There rests a five-fold responsibility for the crucifixion:

> Judicially: the Romans (1 Cor. 2:8)
> Nationally: the Jews (Mat. 27:25)
> Physically: Jesus Christ (John 10:18)
> Theologically: God the Father (Isa. 53:10)
> Practically: mankind (2 Cor. 5:21)

If the Jews addressed in the Book of Acts were simply carrying out God's decree then they wouldn't be declared responsible—they would be declared obedient. Yet, they were the ones on whom the responsibility rested. They were accused of crucifying Christ (Acts 2:36, 4:10), delivering up, denying, and killing him (Acts 3:13-15), slaying and hanging him (Acts 5:30, 10:39), as well as betraying and murdering him (Acts 7:52).

Concerning his own crucifixion, Jesus Christ made an interesting statement: **"And truly the Son of man goeth, as it was determined: but woe unto that man by whom he is betrayed!"** (Luke 22:22). Although Jesus Christ had to be crucified, no one man was foreordained to do it. Notice what Jesus Christ said about his betrayer: **"Good were it for that man if he had never been born"** (Mark 14:21). If Judas had not been born then someone else would have done it. Paul says the same thing about Pilate and Herod: **"Which none of the princes of this world knew: for had they known** *it,* **they would not have crucified the Lord of glory"** (1 Cor. 2:8). So Pilate and Herod were not sovereignly ordained before the foundation of the world to crucify the Son of God. Pilate, in his "determinate counsel," wanted to let Christ go: **"The God of Abraham, and of Isaac, and of Jacob, the God of our fathers, hath glorified his Son Jesus; whom ye delivered up, and denied him in the presence of Pilate, when he was determined to let** *him* **go"** (Acts 3:13). No one is ever foreordained to commit any sin.

There is also the question to be considered of God foreordaining sin, which, as we have seen, the Calvinists answer in the affirmative, as Shedd says: "Even moral evil, which he abhors and forbids, occurs by the determinate counsel and foreknowledge of God."[121] The question of God and evil has engaged philosophers for centuries. Many philosophers believe that the existence of evil renders belief in God unreasonable, inconsistent, or contradictory. The Scottish philosopher David Hume (1711-1776) inquired concerning God:

> Is he willing to prevent evil, but not able? Then he is impotent. Is he able, but not willing? Then he is malevolent. Is he both able and willing? Whence then is evil?[122]

The Christian theodicy to the fact that God is omniscient, omnipotent, and wholly good, yet, evil exists, is that the whole argument is based on faulty logic. God being omniscient, omnipotent, and wholly good, yet, evil exists, is not unreasonable or contradictory unless two other propositions are added, namely:[123]

> 1. A perfectly good being would always eliminate evil so far as it could
> 2. There are no limits to what an omnipotent being can do

The are a number of reasons why the first proposition is false: the occurrence of a greater evil, the elimination of a good state of affairs, discipline or punishment, the occurrence of an ultimate good. And as for the second, when the Christian insists on the omnipotence of God, he does not mean that God is without limits in an absolute sense, but in a logical sense; that is, God cannot make a square circle or an immoveable rock. For God to create men who are free, rational, moral agents entails a "Free Will Defense" of evil.[124] Although it is not acceptable, Calvinists claim to have a simple answer to the problem of evil: God decrees it.

Turning from philosophy to the Bible, the Calvinistic proof texts for this pernicious doctrine say nothing about God ordaining the individual sinful actions of men:

> **I form the light, and create darkness: I make peace, and create evil: I the LORD do all these** *things* **(Isa. 45:7).**

> **Out of the mouth of the most High proceedeth not evil and good? (Lam. 3:38).**

> **Shall a trumpet be blown in the city, and the people not be afraid? shall there be evil in a city, and the LORD hath not done** *it*? **(Amos 3:6).**

Clark sees Calvinism in the verse in Isaiah and concludes: "The two theses most unacceptable to the Arminians are that God is the cause of sin and that God is the cause of salvation. . . . Isaiah in this verse makes Arminianism biblically impossible."[125] What he means is that if you deny man the free will to sin without God ordaining it then you infringe upon God's sovereignty. That the verses in question aren't referring to God ordaining sin is clear. Custance, certainly as much a Calvinist as Clark, explains:

> There is a significant difference in meaning between the words *evil* and *sin*, . . . When we learn that God does evil, appoints evil, intends evil, purposes evil, and even creates evil, we seem to be left with no alternative but to explain such passages away. And this we must do, of course, if evil and sin mean the same thing, for we cannot suppose that God is the author of sin. . . . It is indeed difficult to distinguish evil and wickedness, and goodness and righteousness, *in the abstract*. One must consider these words in their context. When man does evil it is usually sinful; when God does evil it cannot possibly be. . . . The basic difference from a biblical point of view is that evil and goodness are ethical in character and temporal in effect whereas, by

> contrast, sin and righteousness are moral in character and eternal in consequence. . . . It is very clear that while God can never be accused of committing wickedness, He is often expressly declared to be the author of evil. . . . Evil may in fact be good, seen in the long view, whereas wickedness can never be righteousness no matter how long a view we take. . . . It is clear therefore that evil per se is not to be equated with sin, and that God has every right to ordain evil as well as good in the working out of his purpose.[126]

To make no distinction between evil as opposed to good and sin is to impugn the nature of God.

Because God is holy, he not only hates sin, he cannot sin:

> **Therefore hearken unto me ye men of understanding: far be it from God, *that he should do* wickedness; and *from* the Almighty, *that he should commit* iniquity (Job 34:10).**

> **For thou *art* not a God that hath pleasure in wickedness: neither shall evil dwell with thee (Psa. 5:4).**

> ***Thou art* of purer eyes than to behold evil, and canst not look on iniquity: wherefore lookest thou upon them that deal treacherously, *and* holdest thy tongue when the wicked devoureth *the man that is* more righteous than he? (Hab. 1:13).**

It is perfectly clear in the Bible, however, that God does many times bring evil upon both individuals (2 Sam. 17:14, 1 Kgs. 14:10, 21:21) and nations (Neh. 13:18; Eze. 14:22; Dan. 9:14). It should also be noted that the individuals and the nation in the verses referred to are all part of the nation of Israel: the elect nation. Why does God bring evil upon anything? The Calvinist would have us believe that God arbitrarily decrees good over here and evil over there according to his sovereign will. But what does the Bible say? Here is a typical example of why God brings evil:

> **And say, Hear ye the word of the LORD, O kings of Judah, and inhabitants of Jerusalem; Thus saith the LORD of hosts, the God of Israel; Behold, I will bring evil upon this place, the which whosoever heareth, his ears shall tingle.**
> **Because they have forsaken me, and have estranged this**

place, and have burned incense in it unto other gods, whom neither they nor their fathers have known, nor the kings of Judah, and have filled this place with the blood of innocents; They have built also the high places of Baal, to burn their sons with fire *for* burnt offerings unto Baal, which I commanded not, nor spake *it*, neither came *it* into my mind (Jer. 19:3-5).

The Book of Jeremiah alone contains many passages just like this one (Jer. 6:19, 11:10-11, 16:10-11, 36:3). Notice in the above passage that God brought the evil because of the people's sins. And regarding their sins, God expressly declared that he didn't decree them: **"Which I commanded not, nor spake *it*, neither came *it* into my mind"** (Jer. 19:5). How could God decree and foreordain their sin if it never came into his mind? Why does sin take place? It is because of the depravity of man, a doctrine that the Calvinists seem to forget except when they are trying to prove the inability of man to respond to the Gospel.

As a last resort, the Calvinists appeal to the last half of Ephesians 1:11 for proof that God has ordained every act—good or evil: **"In whom also we have obtained an inheritance, being predestinated according to the purpose of him who worketh all things after the counsel of his own will"** (Eph. 1:11). The expression **"worketh all things after the counsel of his own will"** is used by Pink to no end as he seeks to convince his readers of the "absolute sovereignty of God."[127] Alvin Baker claims that passages like this "will not allow the placing of unbelief and sin outside the eternal counsel of God. God works 'all things,' including sin, according to His eternal will."[128] John Feinberg maintains that this verse "is perhaps the clearest expression" of the notion of God's sovereignty."[129] Clark concludes from this verse: "God works all things after the counsel of his own will. He does just as he pleases, with everything. Nothing whatever escapes his predetermination."[130]

The problem here is two-fold. To begin with, the verse says that God **"worketh all things,"** not that he "foreordaineth all things." Someone has been spending too much time studying the decrees of God and not enough time studying English. Secondly, God's counsel is not God's decree (assuming for the sake of argument that there is such a thing in the first place). So the error of the Calvinists is in equating God's working and counsel with

God's foreordination and decree. As proof that God's counsel is not God's decree, it should be noted that in the Bible, a man can reject the counsel of God:

> **But ye have set at nought all my counsel, and would none of my reproof (Pro. 1:25).**
>
> **They would none of my counsel: they despised all my reproof (Pro. 1:30).**
>
> **But the Pharisees and lawyers rejected the counsel of God against themselves, being not baptized of him (Luke 7:30).**

Now, we grant that God must allow this to take place, but that doesn't lessen its authenticity.

To summarize and succinctly refute the concept that God has foreordained everything that takes place, and to prove that there is no such thing as the all-encompassing nature of God's decree, thirteen reasons will here be presented:

1. God said so
2. God's nature
3. God's permission
4. Man's responsibility
5. Man's free will
6. Prayer
7. Calvinists' admissions
8. Calvinists' rejections
9. Philosophy
10. Contingency
11. Semantics
12. Chance
13. Common Sense

As concerning God, the first thing that negates this teaching is that he plainly says he doesn't decree everything. We saw in reference to God ordaining man's sin that God **"commanded not, nor spake *it*, neither came *it* into my mind"** (Jer. 19:5). How could God decree and foreordain sin if it never came into his mind?

Secondly, God's holy nature would not allow him to do such a thing. The second problem with this teaching is that it plainly makes God the author of sin. But when the Calvinist is faced with this charge, he retreats and begins to talk out of both sides of his mouth. Like Beza, who claims that while nothing "happens accidentally or apart from the just decree of God," "God himself is neither the author of sin nor a participant in the act of sinning."[131] But which is it? Does God ordain all things or does he not? This double-talk of the Calvinist is typical when he is confronted head-on with the implications of his doctrine. But God further declares: **"I have not spoken in secret, in a dark place of the earth: I said not unto the seed of Jacob, Seek ye me in vain: I the LORD speak righteousness, I declare things that are right"** (Isa. 45:19). God would never command a man to repent and then fix it so he couldn't in order to damn him. But this is exactly what the TULIP system does.

There is also the matter of God's permission. Often times God is said to do something when in fact he only permitted it to be done. Satan provoked David to number Israel (1 Chr. 21:1), but God was said to do it (2 Sam. 24:1). The best example is Job. Satan was the cause of Job's trouble (Job 1:12, 2:7), but Job (Job 1:21), the writer of Job (Job 42:11), and Satan himself (Job 1:11, 2:5) attributed it to God. This is further confirmed by Charles Hodge: "From these and similar passages, it is evident that it is a familiar scriptural usage, to ascribe to God effects which he allows in his wisdom to come to pass."[132] As pertaining to man, the doctrine that God has predestinated all things destroys man's responsibility. The Calvinist Jay Adams sees the problem: "The doctrines of divine sovereignty—embracing predestination, election, etc.—are frequently dismissed as foolish and dangerous teachings that, if accepted and believed, would destroy evangelism, human initiative and responsibility."[133] Exactly. But naturally, the Calvinists insist that it doesn't negate man's responsibility at all:

> The sovereignty of God also teaches that God is not the responsible author of evil, that man is a free moral agent who is not forced to sin and who is responsible for what he does.[134]

> God is neither the author of sin, nor sanctions it (approves of it). He is not responsible for sin, though He decreed it. Those guilty of sinning are responsible.[135]

This double-talk is also found in the Westminster Confession of Faith:

> God, from eternity, did, by the most wise and holy counsel of his own will, freely, and unchangeably ordain whatsoever comes to pass: yet so, as thereby neither is God the author of sin, nor is violence offered to the will of the creatures; nor is the liberty or

contingency of second causes taken away, but rather established.[136]

The Calvinist offers several explanations for dealing with "the apparent paradox of the sovereignty of God and the responsibility of man."[137] Gunn informs us that "the teachings of human responsibility and divine sovereignty are like two parallel lines that meet only in infinity."[138] Palmer insists: "This secret matter belongs to the Lord our God, and we should leave it there. We ought not to probe into that secret counsel of God."[139] J. I. Packer tells us to "refuse to regard the apparent inconsistency as real."[140] But even Calvinists themselves don't buy these explanations. Sproul correctly points out: "To say that parallel lines meet in eternity is a non-sense statement; it is a blatant contradiction."[141] Palmer and Packer have both been criticized for their views by other Calvinists.[142] But if God has foreordained every thought, word, and deed of man, then how could it be otherwise, if God is holy and just, that man's responsibility is negated?

As further pertaining to man, the doctrine that God has predestinated all things also destroys man's free will. To this proposition the Calvinists agree. Although he believes that sovereignty and responsibility are not antinomies, Clark maintains that sovereignty and free will "would be an antinomy and contradiction; for sovereignty means that God controls all things, including our wills, and free will means that our wills are not controlled by God. This is a clear contradiction. Only an insane person could believe both of these."[143] But as we saw in the previous chapter, the solution of the Calvinists is to deny free will altogether. It was there pointed out that the question of free will was a philosophical question that has been debated for centuries, and continues to be debated among philosophers to this day. The difference, however, between a deterministic philosopher and a Calvinist is that no philosopher denies to man a free will because of a sovereign, eternal, all-encompassing decree. So the idea that man has no free will is directly related, not just to the supposed Total Depravity of the sinner, but to the erroneous premise that all his actions were foreordained from eternity.

The result of believing that everything has been foreordained, with the subsequent denial of free will, reads like something written by a mad man. Typical is Gerstner in his booklet on free will:

> Dear reader, you have in your hands a booklet entitled *A Primer on Free Will*. I don't know you, but I know a good deal about you. One thing I know is that you did not pick up this book of your own free will. You picked it up and have started to read it, and now continue to read it, because you must do so. There is absolutely no possibility, you being the kind of person you are, that you would not be reading this book at this time. Still, you have not already put down the little book in indignation. If you had, you would not have read that sentence. A few of you may smilingly know how right I am. But some of you are angry because you think what I have said about you is foolish and absolutely false.[144]

But after saying that his book had to be picked up and read, he pleads: "Now, I say to those who are doubtful, and especially those who are angry, please do not put down the book."[145] But then he says again: "Am I not justified in saying that you *had to* pick up this book, and you now *have to* continue reading exactly where you are at this time?"[146]

The question at hand is stated by Boettner: "The problem which we face here is, How can a person be a free and responsible agent if his actions have been foreordained from eternity?"[147] Clark, after first insisting that "the Bible never actually mentions free will,"[148] then says: "The only reference to free will in the Bible is the 'free-will' offerings. These have nothing to do with the problem under consideration. Free-will offerings are merely offerings above those required by law. After a person had made all the offerings prescribed by law, he might out of gratitude for God's grace give something additional. This was called a free-will offering."[149] Clark is wrong on two counts. First of all, these freewill offerings, which are mentioned sixteen times in the Bible, have *everything* to do with the problem under consideration. As Clark explains: "After a person had made all the offerings prescribed by law, he might out of gratitude for God's grace give something additional." Note the phrase "he might." This implies that he had the free will to do it or not do it. And second, notice what else the Bible says about freewill: **"I make a decree, that all they of the people of Israel, and *of* his priests and Levites, in my realm, which are minded of their own freewill to go up to Jerusalem, go with thee"** (Ezra 7:13). Adam and Eve had free will (Gen. 2:16). During the time of the Judges the people **"willingly offered themselves"** (Jud. 5:2).

David encouraged Solomon to serve God **"with a willing mind"** (1 Chr. 28:9). During the time of Nehemiah some people **"willing offered themselves to dwell at Jerusalem."** (Neh. 11:2). In the New Testament, we find that prayer promises are based on free will: **"If ye abide in me, and my words abide in you, ye shall ask what ye will, and it shall be done unto you"** (John 15:7). Paul preached willingly: **"For if I do this thing willingly, I have a reward: but if against my will, a dispensation** *of the gospel* **is committed unto me"** (1 Cor. 9:17). Free will is not only a Bible doctrine, the term is actually used in the Bible. On the other hand, the terms Unconditional Election, sovereign grace, the sovereignty of God, and God's eternal decree are neither Bible doctrines nor Bible terms.

The last thing in relation to man which proves that God has not predestinated all things is prayer. The Bible is filled with examples of prayer and injunctions for Christians to pray:

> **Be careful for nothing; but in every thing by prayer and supplication with thanksgiving let your requests be made known unto God (Phil. 4:6).**
>
> **Pray without ceasing (1 Thes. 5:17).**
>
> **I exhort therefore, that, first of all, supplications, prayers, intercessions,** *and* **giving of thanks, be made for all men (1 Tim. 2:1).**

Does prayer change things? It did in the case of Moses (Deu. 9:18-20) and Hezekiah (2 Kgs. 20:1-6). Calvinists, however, insist that it doesn't. The Calvinists' attitude toward prayer can be seen in the answer given to a question about prayer to a panel of Calvinists. In response to the question: "Can prayer change things?" three Sovereign Grace Baptists replied:[150]

> *James O. Wilmoth:* We know that God has predestinated all things that happen. He worketh all things after the counsel of His own will. It is difficult to reconcile prayer and the unchanging will of God.
>
> *David S. West:* Prayer does not change things, nor does prayer change God or His mind.

Dan Phillips: What God has predestinated to be will always come to pass as He has purposed, and all the praying one can muster will not change that. No, prayer does not change things; however, it does change us.

The idea is: if God has already fixed everything, then who are we to infringe upon his sovereignty and request a change? The Calvinists' attitude toward prayer is summarized by the Sovereign Grace Baptist Joseph Wilson:

> No man can believe in the glorious, Biblical doctrine of absolute predestination, and believe that prayer changes things. The two are incompatible. They do not go together. If one is true, the other is false. Since predestination is true, it follows, as night follows day, that prayer does not change things.[151]

So when Robert Selph maintains that "everyone is a Calvinist when on his knees in prayer,"[152] he is lying, for the Calvinist position on prayer is not accepted by most Christians.

As pertaining to the Calvinists themselves, they also provide grounds for rejecting the concept that God has foreordained everything that takes place by an all-encompassing decree. To begin with, some Calvinists, even though they believe this doctrine, acknowledge the absurdity of it. N. L. Rice admits that divine foreordination seems "unscriptural, absurd and impious."[153] Palmer concedes that what he advocates is "illogical, ridiculous, nonsensical, and foolish."[154] Secondly, the idea of God ordaining sin has especially perplexed and disturbed some Calvinistic. To get around the obvious implications, some adopt a distinction between God's efficacious decrees and God's permissive decrees.[155] But changing the name doesn't alter a thing, it only adds to the confusing mass of TULIP terminology. For example, Talbot and Crampton hold that "the decree with reference to sin" is a permissive decree but not just "a **mere** permissive decree."[156] The Dutch Reformed theologian G. C. Berkouwer wonders how theologians can "at the same time speak, of God, as the all-causing one, and not say He is the cause of human sin."[157] Contrary to their Philadelphia Confession of Faith, some Sovereign Grace Baptists likewise balk at the idea that God has predestinated everything.[158] Although holding the doctrine of predestination to salvation, most Primitive Baptists reject predestination in an absolute sense.[159]

The final thing in relation to the Calvinists that calls their absolute predestination teaching into question is that this teaching is no different than other philosophical concepts which teach "what is to be will be." Although Calvinists go out of their way to distance themselves from fatalism,[160] they are in essence teaching the same thing. When a philosopher believes "what is to be will be" it is called determinism. When a Stoic believes "what is to be will be" it is called fate. When a Moslem believes "what is to be will be" it is called fatalism. But when a Calvinist believes "what is to be will be" it is called predestination. The only way the Calvinist gets away with it is by saying that predestination alone is a Bible doctrine.

The fact that there are verses in the Bible which show the contingency of an event is another proof that there is no such thing as God foreordaining everything by an all-encompassing decree. As we saw in the previous chapter, in the Bible it is clear that the possibility exists that a man could or could not believe depending on the circumstances:

> **Those by the way side are they that hear; then cometh the devil, and taketh away the word out of their hearts, lest they should believe and be saved (Luke 8:12).**

> **And ye will not come to me, that ye might have life (John 5:40).**

> **Forbidding us to speak to the Gentiles that they might be saved, to fill up their sins alway: for the wrath is come upon them to the uttermost (1 Thes. 2:16).**

These verses do not mean that under a given set of circumstances a man will always believe. But they do show that there is that possibility. And if there exists even the slightest possibility that a man could believe, the doctrine of God's sovereign, eternal decree falls by the wayside. There are no possibilities in TULIP Calvinism. There are many things in the Bible that aren't fixed. If the works that Christ did had been done in Tyre and Sidon they would have repented (Mat. 11:21), likewise Sodom (Mat. 11:23). God's dealings with his elect people the Jews were conditional (Deu. 5:33, 6:1-3, 11:16-17).

The next reason why God could not have foreordained everything that takes place by an all-encompassing decree is semantics. This has to do with the meaning, or an interpretation of the meaning, of words. If words have any meaning at all, then the Bible is clear in its denial that God has an all-encompassing decree:

> **For God so loved the world, that he gave his only begotten Son, that whosoever believeth in him should not perish, but have everlasting life (John 3:16).**
>
> **And the Spirit and the bride say, Come. And let him that heareth say, Come. And let him that is athirst come. And whosoever will, let him take the water of life freely (Rev. 22:17).**

This principle of "whosoever," which will be studied later in this chapter, expressly negates any all-encompassing decree.

Another reason that God could not have foreordained everything that takes place by an all-encompassing decree is chance. Does anything happen by chance? According to the Bible it does:

> **If a bird's nest chance to be before thee in the way in any tree, or on the ground, *whether they be* young ones, or eggs, and the dam sitting upon the young, or upon the eggs, thou shalt not take the dam with the young (Deu. 22:6).**
>
> **And by chance there came down a certain priest that way: and when he saw him, he passed by on the other side (Luke 10:31).**

This does not mean that God can't or doesn't know what is going to happen or that God has no control over his creation. What it does mean, however, is that there is no such thing as an all-encompassing decree of predestination.

The most natural answer to the idea of an all-encompassing decree is plain, ordinary common sense. If what is to be will be, then no one could possibly do anything but carry out the sovereign, eternal decree of God. In the Bible, a man cut his concubine up into twelve pieces and sent her into the coasts of Israel (Jud. 19:29). Was it by a sovereign, eternal decree? Some people burned their children in the fire to Molech and had sex with animals (Lev. 18:21-24). Was it according to the determinate counsel of God? I fully realize the extreme nature of the aforementioned arguments, but I am not the one who claims that God has foreordained every thought, word, and deed of man and beast. The documented evidence from the Calvinists themselves has been presented. To this abominable scheme of absolute predestination, Erasmus, whatever his faults, recognized hundreds of years ago:

> Let us assume the truth of what Wycliffe has taught and Luther has asserted, namely that everything we do happens not on account of our free will, but out of sheer necessity. What can be more useless than to publish this paradox to the world? Secondly, let us assume that it is true, as Augustine has written somewhere, that God causes both good and evil in us, and that he rewards us for his good works wrought in us and punishes us for the evil deeds done in us. What a loophole the publications of this opinion would open to godlessness among innumerable people? In particular: mankind is lazy, indolent, malicious, and, in addition, incorrigibly prone to every impious outrage. How many weak ones would continue in their perpetual and laborious battle against their own flesh? What wicked fellow would henceforth try to better his conduct? Who could love with all his heart a God who fires a hell with eternal pain, in order to punish there poor mankind for his own evil deeds, as if God enjoyed human distress?[161]

What shall we say to these things? If God doesn't decree all the sin and wickedness in the world then why does it take place? Obviously God permits it, but *permit* and *decree* are two different words. The mysterious, unexplained question is this: Why does God allow the things he does? God's thoughts are not our thoughts; his ways are not our ways (Isa. 55:8). He **"giveth not account of any of his matters"** (Job 33:13), and is not under any obligation to do so. The Apostle Paul expanded on these themes:

> **O the depth of the riches both of the wisdom and knowledge of God! how unsearchable** *are* **his judgments, and his ways past finding out!**
> **For who hath known the mind of the Lord? or who hath been his counsellor?**
> **Or who hath first given to him, and it shall be recompensed unto him again? (Rom. 11:33-35).**

The decrees of God are child's play alongside of the will of God.

But since the divine foreordination of all things is said to be an "*essential part* of a system of doctrines which has been called Calvinistic,"[162] one can not *consistently* hold to the Five Points of Calvinism without assenting to an all-encompassing decree which includes sin.

Lapsarian Systems

If God only has one decree, yet he has foreordained everything, then what about the decrees of election and predestination that we hear so much about? What is the difference, if any, between election and predestination? Because the technical nature of this discussion lends itself to the cry of misrepresentation being raised by the Calvinists, everything said about the different aspects of God's decree will be stated and defined by the Calvinists themselves.

As mentioned previously, in Calvinistic thought, God has one decree. This decree is eternal in nature and all-comprehensive in scope. W. E. Best summarizes the Calvinist position: "The decrees of God may be regarded in one complex decree including all things. The extent of God's decree covers everything before time, through time, and subsequent to time. It is unchangeable. There is no alteration in the Divine intention. No new act will ever enter the Divine mind. Furthermore, there will be no reversion of the Divine plan."[163] According to the Westminster Confession of Faith:

> By the decree of God, for the manifestation of His own glory, some men and angels are predestinated unto everlasting life, and others foreordained to everlasting death.[164]

So properly speaking, the part of this decree that concerns itself with the eternal destinies of men and angels is termed predestination; however, as Charles Hodge relates: "There is an ambiguity in the word predestination."[165] Sometimes predestination is used to describe the decree itself while other times it is applied to the actual election of men to salvation. In reality, however, it is just as Machen describes it: "The doctrine of predestination is just the doctrine of the divine decrees applied to the special sphere of salvation."[166] The fact that predestination in the Bible has nothing to do with God's decrees is irrelevant for the moment.

This predestination is further divided into two parts: election and reprobation. For confirmation of these distinctions, we cite Berkhof and the Southern Presbyterian theologian John Girardeau (1825-1898):

> Predestination includes two parts, namely, election and reprobation, the predetermination of both the good and the wicked to their final end, and to certain proximate ends which are instrumental in the realization of their final destiny.[167]

> Predestination is, by Calvinistic theologians, regarded as a generic decree including under it Election and Reprobation as specific decrees: the former predestinating some human beings, without regard to their merit, to salvation, in order to the glorification of God's sovereign grace; the latter foreordaining some human beings, for their sin, to destruction, in order to the glorification of God's retributive justice.[168]

The confusing nature of this terminology is explained by Sproul: "Often the term *election* is used as a synonym for *predestination*. Technically this is incorrect. The term *election* refers specifically to one aspect of divine predestination: God's choosing of certain individuals to be saved."[169] But it is also to be remembered, as Pink explains, that "predestination relates to *all* creatures, things, and events; but election is restricted to rational beings—angels and humans.'"[170]

The debate in Reformed theology concerns neither the extent nor the eternal nature of the decrees but rather the relation of the decrees of election and reprobation to the Fall. Within the scope of the divergent opinions maintained by the Calvinists, there surfaces three lapsarian systems of Calvinistic thought: supralapsarianism, infralapsarianism, and sublapsarianism. Best explains how these systems got their principal name: "The word lapsarian comes from the Latin word *lapsus* which means the 'doctrine of the fall.'"[171] Because God's decree is supposed to be a singular, eternal decree, the titles of these systems pertain not to the *actual* order of the decrees in relation to the Fall, but to their *logical* order, as Berkhof attests: "The eternity of the decree also implies that the order in which the different elements in it stand to each other may not be regarded as temporal, but only as logical."[172] This is important to keep in mind, because it means that all the following details about the order of God's supposed decrees is pure conjecture. But since it is necessary to a proper understanding of Calvinism, it is important to continue.

Among five-point Calvinists, the minority view, due to its foreboding overtones, is supralapsarianism, *supra,* from the Latin meaning "above," and the word for the Fall, *lapsus.* This scheme has God decreeing election while men are *creabilis et labilis* (certain to be created and to fall). The opposing view is infralapsarianism, from the Latin *infra,* meaning "below," and *lapsus.* Because of the charge that supralapsarianism makes God the author of sin and is the direct cause of the damnation of men, most Calvinists have digressed to the "infra" position in which men are considered *creatus et lapsus* (created and fallen). The initial difference between these systems is aptly stated by Berkouwer: "Originally it was a matter of different interpretations of the relationship between predestination and the fall. The question arose whether in the counsel of God the fall of man had been willed by Him."[173] This naturally led to a difference in the interpretation of the manner of the rejection of the "non-elect." The result of the former viewpoint was the damnation of the rejected according to the sovereign good pleasure of God, while the latter claimed to ground the underlying cause of condemnation on man's sin. From these disputes came the question concerning the succession of God's decrees as related to the Fall—one putting election and reprobation above (before) the Fall and the other below (after) the Fall.

The so-called decrees of God in the supralapsarianism system are as follows:

1. Election and reprobation
2. Creation
3. Fall
4. Atonement for elect
5. Salvation for elect

Thus, in this system, as Berkouwer again pertinently states, the Creation and the Fall "form, so to speak, the means by which that primary predestination decree becomes realized."[174] That is, God first decided to elect some men to heaven and reprobate other men to hell, so upon creating them, he made them fall, using Adam as a scapegoat, so it would look like God was gracious in sending the "elect" to heaven and just in sending the "reprobate" to hell. The distinctive feature of this scheme is its positive decree of reprobation. Reprobation is the deliberate, foreordained, predestinated damning of millions of souls to hell as a result of God's sovereign good pleasure and according to the **"counsel of his own will"** (Eph. 1:11). This teaching has historically been the most repulsive part of the TULIP system.

Since it is obviously so unscriptural and repugnant, supralapsarianism has come under much criticism. Because it was an important issue in his day, Arminius commented at length on this system. He believed that this doctrine of predestination was

> repugnant to the nature of God,
> repugnant to the justice of God,
> repugnant to the goodness of God,
> contrary to the nature of man,
> diametrically opposed to the act of creation,
> at open hostility with the nature of eternal life,
> opposed to the nature of eternal death,
> inconsistent with the nature and properties of sin,
> repugnant to the nature of divine grace,
> injurious to the glory of God,
> highly dishonourable to Jesus Christ our Saviour,
> hurtful to the salvation of men, and
> in open hostility to the ministry of the Gospel.[175]

He charged supralapsarianism with making God a sinner,[176] and concluded that this doctrine of predestination had been rejected, both now and formerly, by the vast majority of Christians.[177]

It is not just the dreaded Arminius who was opposed to supralapsarianism. The editor of the original *International Standard Bible Encyclopedia*, James Orr (1844-1913), had his own opinion:

> A doctrine of this kind, which bids us think of beings not yet conceived of as even created (therefore only *possibles*)—not to say as sinful—set apart for eternal blessedness or misery, and of the fall and redemption as simply means for effecting that purpose, is one which no plea of logical consistency will ever get the human mind to accept, and which is bound to provoke revolt against the whole system with which it is associated.[178]

King James of England, who sent delegates to the Synod of Dort, nevertheless went on record as against this system:

This doctrine is so horrible, that I am persuaded, if there were a council of unclean spirits assembled in hell, and their prince the devil were to put the question either to all of them in general, or to each in particular, to learn their opinion about the most likely means of stirring up the hatred of men against God their Maker; nothing could be invented by them that would be more efficacious for this purpose, or that could put a greater affront upon God's love for mankind, than that infamous decree of the late Synod, and the decision of that detestable formulary, by which the far greater part of the human race are condemned to hell for no other reason, *than the mere will of God, without any regard to sin;* the necessity of sinning, as well as that of being damned, being fastened on them by that great nail of the decree before-mentioned.[179]

But as we shall presently see, it is the Calvinists themselves who condemn this doctrine.

Since the adherents of supralapsarianism are in the minority, and the doctrine seems somewhat extreme, it is often referred to as hyper-Calvinism by those Calvinists who wish to divert attention from what they really believe and thereby make their form of Calvinism appear scriptural. Boettner is typical: "At the present day it is probably safe to say that not more than one Calvinist in a hundred holds the supralapsarianism view. We are Calvinists strongly enough, but not 'high Calvinist.' By a 'high Calvinist' we mean one who holds the supralapsarian view."[180] The easiest way to accomplish this diversion is to pit Arminianism against hyper-Calvinism and then take plain Calvinism as a mediating position. This makes Calvinism appear orthodox. So in 1990, Talbot and Crampton put out a book called *Calvinism, Hyper-Calvinism and Arminianism*, in which they attack what is termed extreme views so they can settle comfortably in the middle hoping no one will notice the difference. But as briefly mentioned in chapter one, the term *hyper-Calvinism* is highly ambiguous and concerns one's *practice* not *profession*. Most Calvinists not only don't mind attacks on hyper-Calvinism, they make them themselves. They use the term to make themselves look orthodox much the same as they use the label *Arminian*.

The system of supralapsarianism is not hyper-Calvinism and neither does it go beyond the teachings of John Calvin. In spite of the overwhelming evidence to the contrary, some have claimed that

Beza and others distorted "Calvin's Calvinism" in promoting the supralapsarian view.[181] Custance claims that Calvin started out "supra" but softened his position later years.[182] He calls Beza the "most ultra-Calvinist of the time."[183] Best insists that "Calvin could be classified as neither infralapsarian nor supralapsarian. He leaned more toward infralapsarianism."[184] Schaff contends that Calvin "carried the doctrine of the divine decrees beyond the Augustinian infralapsarianism" to "the very verge of supralapsarianism."[185] Some maintain that Calvin never held this belief at all,[186] while others that Calvin did not express himself clearly or consistently on this matter.[187] While consistency was not one of Calvin's greatest attributes, neither is it to be found in the majority of other Calvinists. Most Calvinists, including A. A. Hodge and Berkhof, who disagreed with Calvin on this point, as well as non-Calvinists, recognize that Calvin did hold to the "supra" position.[188] The only reason that there is some question is, like Limited Atonement, the issue had not reached such prominence in Calvin's day that it required its own vocabulary to understand it. A factor in the determination of Calvin's position is, as stated by the Dutch Reformed theologian, Klaas Dijk (1885-1968), that "the supra presentation is the one of the Reformation."[189] Luther, Zwingli, and Bucer being prime examples, with Bullinger and Melanchthon dissenting. Therefore, supralapsarianism is the *original* position of Calvinism.

The best and only honest way to see exactly what Calvin believed about predestination is to go to directly to his writings. "Calvin," we are told by former Calvin Theological Seminary professor Fred Klooster, "did not invent the doctrine of predestination, nor was he the first to teach it clearly. Calvin's name has become inseparably linked to this doctrine, however, probably because he, more than anyone else, was called upon to defend predestination against all sorts of opposition."[190] So as mentioned previously, although Calvin was not the originator of that theological system which emphasizes predestination, known commonly as Calvinism, he obviously had such a strong connection with it that his name is inseparably linked to it.

Although Klooster claims that Calvin "did not engage in speculative, frigid, theoretical reasoning in discussing predestination,"[191] Calvin's predestination has aptly been described as: absolute, particular, double.[192] This designation is true, and we shall presently see straight from Calvin's pen exactly what he believed about the predestination as it is recorded in his *Institutes*:

> We call predestination God's eternal decree, by which he compacted with himself what he willed to become of each man. For all are not created in equal condition; rather, eternal life is foreordained for some, eternal damnation for others. Therefore, as any man has been created to one or the other of these ends, we speak of him as predestinated to life or death.[193]

> As Scripture, then, clearly shows, we say that God once established by his eternal and unchangeable plan those whom he long before determined once for all to receive into salvation, and those whom, on the other hand, he would devote to destruction. We assert that, with respect to the elect, this plan was founded upon his freely given mercy, without regard to human worth; but by his just and irreprehensible but incomprehensible judgment he has barred the door of life to those whom he has given over to damnation.[194]

Klooster asserts that "almost everything that Calvin taught regarding predestination is included in these two summaries."[195] He maintains that "Calvin's doctrine of predestination is his attempt to faithfully echo what he heard the Scriptures say."[196]

Aside from these "two comprehensive definitions,"[197] perhaps the most infamous statement Calvin ever uttered was his *decretum horribile:*

> Again, I ask: whence does it happen that Adam's fall irremediably involved so many peoples, together with their infant offspring, in eternal death unless because it so pleased God? Here their tongues, otherwise so loquacious, must become mute. The decree is dreadful indeed, I confess. Yet no one can deny that God foreknew what end man was to have before he created him, and consequently foreknew because he so ordained by his decree.[198]

It is on this word *horrible* that the hymnwriter Charles Wesley based some of his verses against Calvinism:

> O Horrible Decree,
> Worthy of whence it came!

> Forgive their hellish blasphemy,
> Who charge it on the Lamb![199]
>
> God, ever merciful and just,
> With newborn babes did Tophet fill;
> Down into endless torments thrust;
> Merely to show His sovereign will.
> This is that *Horrible Decree!*
> This is that wisdom from beneath!
> God (O detest the Blasphemy!)
> Hath pleasure in the sinner's death.[200]

Now, it is true, as Clark explains, that "in Latin *horrible* does not mean horrible. It means awe-inspiring,"[201] but the thought is horrible none the less.

To realize the results of his system of predestination, Calvin necessarily believed that God directly ordained the fall of Adam:

> I freely acknowledge my doctrine to be this: that Adam fell, not only by the permission of God, but by His very secret counsel and decree; and that Adam drew all his posterity with himself, by his fall, into eternal destruction.[202]
>
> I, at the same time, witness as my solemn confession that whatever happened to, or befel, Adam was so ordained of God.[203]

It goes without saying that Calvin also believed that all things were foreordained by God's sovereign, eternal decree:

> God did certainly decree from the beginning everything which should befall the race of man.[204]
>
> My doctrine is that the will of God is the first and supreme cause of all things.[205]
>
> God foresees future events only by reason of the fact that he decreed that they take place.[206]
>
> But why shall we say "permission" unless it is because God so wills?[207]
>
> Nothing happens except what is knowingly and willingly

decreed by him.[208]

At the end of his treatise on predestination, Calvin even states: "No one will ever attempt to disprove the doctrine which I have set forth herein, but he who may imagine himself to be wiser than the Spirit of God."[209] Calvin full well deserves to have the TULIP system named in his honor.

After Calvin, Beza unhesitatingly maintained this rigid form of Calvinism:

> It is not satisfactory to identify the *massa* as the human race already fallen and corrupt, for Paul here seeks out prior causes and fastens on the mercy and justice of God and the manifestation of divine glory in a just decree.[210]

> The issue is that God decrees by his right and according to his will alone. How great an injury it would be to God if we were to conceive of his decree as resting on the result of human activity, or to hypothesize a second divine decree, a reactive decree, subsequent to the corruption of the creature.[211]

Next, we find two opponents of Arminius continuing the supralapsarian tradition: the Cambridge professor William Perkins and the Leiden professor Franciscus Gomarus.[212] The influence of Gomarus, however, was not enough to convince the Synod of Dort to rule in favor of the "supra" position.[213] William Twisse, the moderator of the Westminster Assembly, likewise failed to incorporate into the Westminster Confession his supralapsarian views.[214] He is even said by Berkhof to have developed predestination into "a rather extreme supralapsarian form."[215] The Particular Baptist John Gill also held to the "supra" view, but sought to incorporate elements of what is now known as infralapsarianism to prevent God from being the author of sin. On the two systems, Gill conceded:

> I think they both may be taken in; that in the decree of the end, the ultimate end, the glory of God, from which he does all things, men might be considered in the divine mind as creable, not yet created and fallen; and that in the decree of the means, which, among other things, takes in the mediation of Christ, redemption by him, and the sanctification of the Spirit; they might be considered as created, fallen, and sinful, which these

things imply.[216]

Although not many Baptists have been identified with this doctrine, there is one Baptist in history who brazenly proclaims his supralapsarianism:

> This writer unhesitatingly (after prolonged study) takes the Supralapsarian position, though he is well aware that few indeed will be ready to follow him.[217]

> I am a strong supra-lapsarian, and in my humble judgment, any one who is not firmly fixed there is bound to go astray in his subsequent thinking and postulates.[218]

The subject, of course, is Arthur W. Pink, of whom one of his biographers correctly said that he "was responsible for many pastors becoming Calvinists."[219] Published in 1918, the first edition of 2000 copies of his book *The Sovereignty of God* was understandably hard to sell.[220] Of this treatise, Arno Gaebelein (1861-1945) remarked:

> Mr. Pink used to be a contributor to our magazine. His articles on *Gleanings on Genesis* are good, and we had them printed in book form. But when he began to teach his frightful doctrines which make the God of Love a monster we broke fellowship with him. The book you have read is totally unscriptural. It is akin to blasphemy. It presents God as a Being of injustice and maligns His holy character. The book denies that our blessed Lord died for the ungodly. According to Pink's perversions He died for the elect only. You are not the only one who has been led into darkness by this book. Whoever the publisher is, and whoever stands behind the circulation of such a monstrous thing has a grave responsibility. It is just this kind of teaching which makes atheists.[221]

It has been thought that Pink started out as an infralapsarianism and then moved to the supralapsarianism position.[222] This could be inferred from one place in Pink's book *The Sovereignty of God*: "God's decree of Reprobation contemplated Adam's race as fallen, sinful, corrupt, guilty."[223] However, Pink, as all Calvinists, sometimes contradicted himself:

> God had a definite reason *why* He created men, a specific purpose why He created this and that individual, and in view of the eternal destination of His creatures, He purposed either that this one should spend eternity in Heaven or that this one should spend eternity in the Lake of Fire.[224]
>
> If there were some of Adam's descendants to whom He *purposed* not to give faith, it must be because He ordained that *they* should be damned.[225]
>
> If then God *has* foreordained *whatsoever* comes to pass then He must have decreed that vast numbers of human beings should pass out of this world unsaved to suffer eternally in the Lake of Fire. Admitting the general premise, is not the specific conclusion inevitable?[226]

As was mentioned in chapter 1, because Pink's views were deemed so radical, The Banner of Truth Trust 1961 edition of *The Sovereignty of God* removed the chapter on reprobation, claiming that their edition more accurately presented "Pink's mature thought."[227]

The purveyors of the supralapsarian form of Calvinism are the Dutch Reformed people. None of the Presbyterian theologians of note (Hodge, Dabney, Shedd) held to this position. However, among the Dutch there is not unanimous agreement. Kuyper, Vos, and Van Til held to supralapsarianism,[228] while Berkhof and Bavinck sought to synthesize the "supra" and "infra" ideals.[229] A conflict between the opposing sides of the debate culminated in the Synod of Utrecht in 1905, which concluded: "That our Confessions, certainly with respect to the doctrine of election, follow the infralapsarian presentation," but that "this does not at all imply an exclusion or condemnation of the supralapsarian presentation."[230] The "supralapsarian presentation" tradition survives today almost exclusively in the Protestant Reformed Church, a split from the Christian Reformed Church. Their premier theologian is Herman Hoeksema, who boldly stated: "We therefore place ourselves without reservation on the standpoint of supralapsarianism, and maintain that it is the scriptural and the only consistent presentation of the decree of God's predestination."[231] The curious thing about this doctrine is its insistence that God decreed the election and reprobation of men *before* their creation. For this reason the

Reformed theologian Otto Ritschl (1860-1944) more correctly termed it "supracreatianism."[232] But the debate concerned the Fall not man's creation. This makes supralapsarianism doubly liable to criticism. The fact that the reprobate are damned for their sins is just an afterthought, for according to this system, God decreed the damnation of men and created them explicitly for that purpose. Creation, the Fall, and sin were just the means for the realization of God's sovereign will.

To avoid making God the author of sin and other heinous implications of Calvin's "horrible decree," the original system has been modified in an attempt to make it palatable. This hybrid scheme is known as infralapsarianism. As mentioned previously, the decrees of election and reprobation in this system are below *(infra)* the Fall *(lapsus)*, meaning after it. This puts the order of the decrees as follows:

1. Creation
2. Fall
3. Election and reprobation
4. Atonement for elect
5. Salvation for elect

None of the decrees have changed, only the *supposed* order is different. This is like someone saying to Mrs. Lincoln: "Aside from *that*, how did you like the play?" But despite its placement, the decree of election is the same in both systems; it is the decree of reprobation that bothers the infralapsarians.

The way that the supralapsarians speak of the decree of reprobation is troubling to the infralapsarians. They (the "infras") prefer to speak of reprobation as a *negative* or *permissive* decree and object to it being spoken of in terms of a *positive* decree.[233] This is understandable, since the positive aspects of reprobation are quite foreboding. Although Gill preferred the term *rejection* "because the other word *reprobation*, through wrong and frightful ideas being affixed to it, carries in it, with many, a sound harsh and disagreeable,"[234] he grounded the damnation of those rejected on the good pleasure of God's will: "The moving, or impulsive cause of God's making such a decree, by which he has rejected some of the race of Adam from his favour, is not sin, but the good pleasure of his will."[235] Calvin likewise founded the damnation of the reprobate on God himself:

What of those, then, whom he created for dishonor in life and destruction in death, to become the instruments of his wrath and examples of his severity? That they may come to their end, he sometimes deprives them of the capacity to hear his word; at other times he, rather, blinds and stuns them by the preaching of it.[236]

It is utterly inconsistent to transfer the preparation for destruction to anything but God's secret plan.[237]

The Protestant Reformed theologian David Engelsma continues Calvin's legacy as seen by his positive, supralapsarian view of reprobation:

Scripture teaches that reprobation is God's sovereign, unconditional decree to damn some sinners. This is the inescapable implication of the Biblical doctrine that God has unconditional chosen some men, not all, unto eternal life.[238]

Reprobation asserts that God eternally hates some men; has immutably decreed their damnation; and has determined to withhold from them Christ, grace, faith, and salvation.[239]

It is no wonder that Boettner laments the propensity of Arminians to focus on reprobation "as though it was the sum and substance of Calvinism."[240] Thus, it is no surprise that John Wesley was very outspoken in opposing this system:

Sing, O hell, and rejoice ye that are under the earth. For God, even the mighty God, hath spoken and doomed to death thousands of souls, from the rising of the sun to the going down thereof. Here, O death, is thy sting. They shall not, cannot escape. For the mouth of the Lord hath spoken. Here, O grave, is thy victory. Nations yet unborn, or even they have done good or evil, are doomed never to see the light of life, but thou shalt gnaw upon them for ever and ever. Let all those morning stars sing together who fell with Lucifer, sun of the morning. Let all the sons of hell shout for joy. For the decree is past and who shall disannul it.[241]

In spite of their perceived differences, both groups are united in their avowal of reprobation, as seen by the words of Homer

Hoeksema the supralapsarian and Loraine Boettner the infralapsarian:

> The truth of election and reprobation stand or fall together. To deny election is to deny reprobation. To deny reprobation is to deny election. To believe election is to believe reprobation. To believe reprobation is to believe election.[242]

> Those who hold the doctrine of Election but deny that of Reprobation can lay but little claim to consistency. To affirm the former while denying the latter makes the decree of predestination an illogical and lop-sided decree.[243]

So even though both groups believe in "double predestination," they approach the subject differently. As Sproul observes: "The question then is not *if* predestination is double, but *how* it is double."[244] The view that election and reprobation are symmetrical is sometimes called "equal ultimacy." Sproul is quick to tell us that "though Calvinism certainly holds to a kind of double predestination, it does not embrace equal ultimacy."[245] He considers this doctrine "sub-Calvinism" or "anti-Calvinism."[246] But to confuse matters, Best maintains that infralapsarians "do not embrace double predestination," it is only supralapsarians who "believe in double predestination."[247] Now, what Best means by double predestination is the equal ultimacy doctrine. So, in distinguishing one Calvinist from another, it is important to understand how they define their terms.

To divert attention from the *positive* decree of reprobation, the adherents to the "infra" presentation join the Arminians in assailing the "supra" system. Boettner, copying Warfield,[248] maintains that "supralapsarianism goes to as great an extreme on the one side as does universalism on the other. Only the infralapsarian scheme is self-consistent with other facts."[249] Shedd remarks that "the supralapsarian order is liable to the charge that 'God creates some men in order to damn them,' because creation follows from reprobation. The infralapsarian order is not liable to this charge."[250] Spurgeon insists that it "is a doctrine which we as much detest as the Arminians themselves do."[251] Sproul tries to shock his readers with an emotional appeal: "Some argue that God first predestinated some people to salvation and others to damnation and then decreed the Fall to make sure that some folks would perish. Sometimes this dreadful view is even attributed to Calvinism. Such an idea was repugnant to Calvin."[252]

The way the infralapsarians make reprobation palatable is by splitting it into two parts. The first part is made unconditional like election, and is generally called "preterition," from the Latin *praeter,* "by," and *ire,* "to go," signifying "to pass by." The second part is then made conditional, and consists of God condemning men for their sin that they are still in because of being passed over. Girardeau and Cunningham explain it in detail from the Calvinist perspective:

> We have seen that the teaching of Scripture is, that out of his mere mercy, and according to the good pleasure of his sovereign will, he decreed to save some of the fallen and sinful mass who were thus contemplated as justly condemned . That is Election. The rest, consequently, were not elected to be saved, but were passed by and ordained to continue under just condemnation. That is Reprobation. There are two elements which it involves: first, a sovereign act of God, by which they were in his purpose passed by and left in the condition in which they were regarded as placing themselves. That is called Preterition. Secondly, there is a judicial act of God, by which they were in his purpose ordained to continue under the sentence of the broken law and to suffer punishment for their sin. That is called Condemnation.[253]

> In stating and discussing the question with respect to reprobation, Calvinists are careful to distinguish between the two different acts formerly referred to, decreed or resolved upon by God from eternity, and executed by him in time,—the one negative and the other positive,—the one sovereign and the other judicial. The first, which they call non-election, preterition, or passing by, is simply decreeing to leave—and, in consequence, leaving—men in their natural state of sin: to withhold from them, or to abstain from conferring upon them, those special, supernatural, gracious influences, which are necessary to enable them to repent and believe; so that the result is, that they continue in their sin, with the guilt of their transgression upon their head. The second—the positive judicial act,—is more properly that which is called, in our Confession, "fore-ordaining to everlasting death," and "ordaining those who have been passed by to dishonour and wrath *for their sin.*"[254]

The Canons of Dort likewise express this distinction:

> What peculiarly tends to illustrate and recommend to us the eternal and unmerited grace of election, is the express testimony of sacred Scripture, that not all, but some only are elected, while others are passed by in the eternal election of God; whom God, out of his sovereign, most just, irreprehensible and unchangeable good pleasure, hath decreed to leave in the common misery into which they have willfully plunged themselves, and not to bestow upon them saving faith and the grace of conversion; but leaving them in his just judgement to follow their own ways, at last for the declaration of his justice, to condemn and perish them forever, not only on account of their unbelief, but also for all their other sins. And this is the decree of reprobation which by no means makes God the author of sin (the very thought of which is blasphemy), but declares him to be an awful, irreprehensible, and righteous judge and avenger thereof.[255]

This split decree is also found in Chapter III of the Westminster Confession of Faith:

> III. By the decree of God, for the manifestation of his glory, some men and angels are predestinated unto everlasting life; and others foreordained to everlasting death.
>
> VII. The rest of mankind God was pleased, according to the unsearchable counsel of his own will, whereby he extendeth or withholdeth mercy, as he pleaseth, for the glory of his sovereign power over his creatures, to pass by; and to ordain them to dishonour and wrath for their sin, to the praise of his glorious justice.

One can see that without the latter article a supralapsarian interpretation would be required.

To add to the discord among the Calvinists and to confuse matters further, there is another school of thought to be examined, that of sublapsarianism. The prefix *sub* can be recognized immediately from its extensive use in English: submarine, submerge, subcontractor, etc. Therefore, both *infra* and *sub* imply the same thing: "below" or "after." Because of this, when Gill or Girardeau or Dabney mention sublapsarianism they are referring to what is more commonly known as infralapsarianism. Five-point Calvinists only recognize two tenable systems: supralapsarianism and infralapsarianism or sublapsarianism. But those Calvinists who reject Limited Atonement have added a third to accommodate their viewpoint. They propose the following order:

1. Creation
2. Fall
3. Atonement for all
4. Election and reprobation
5. Salvation for elect

So in this system, not only are the decrees of election and reprobation *after* the Fall, they are also *after* the Atonement. This scheme is also known as "hypothetical redemption," and was the position of Moyse Amyraut, the original four-point Calvinist.[256] What is now called sublapsarianism is the view of all four-point Calvinists. As will be pointed out in the next chapter, the debate about the Atonement is meaningless since only the elect will be saved anyway. So like their "infra" cousins, the sublapsarians seek to get around the bestial implications of a positive view of reprobation that parallels election.

Berkhof claims that "only Reformed theology does full justice to the doctrine of the decrees."[257] But once again the Scripture says of these decrees: **"Woe unto them that decree unrighteous decrees and that write grievousness *which* they have prescribed"** (Isa. 10:1). The contradictory and confusing nature of God's decrees as presented by the Reformed theologians rules out any possibility of God being the source of them. God **"cannot deny himself"** (2 Tim. 2:13), and neither is he **"the author of confusion"** (1 Cor. 14:33).

There are a number of problems with these Calvinistic theories as to the relation of sin and the Fall to election and reprobation. Obviously, supralapsarianism makes God the author of sin and directly responsible for the damnation of billions of souls. But the other two hypotheses are equally as contemptible. If God's decrees are really one decree, then as Dabney explains: "God's decree has no succession; and to Him no successive order of parts; because it is a contemporaneous unit, comprehended altogether, by one infinite intuition."[258] Therefore, there can be no separation of predestination into election and reprobation or any division of reprobation into preterition and condemnation. This one decree is also supposed to be eternal. Thus, there can be no difference between the lapsarian systems because, as Berkouwer affirms: "We cannot speak of before and after in God's eternal decrees as we do in time, hence the difference between supra and infra can be called imaginary because it implies the application of a temporal order to eternity."[259] It should also be remembered that this one, eternal decree is said to be all-encompassing in scope. Accordingly, as Chafer avows: "There is one comprehensive plan in which all things have their place and by which they proceed. With God there is one immutable decree embracing in itself every detail, even the falling of a sparrow."[260] Consequently, everything that happens, necessarily including sin, the Fall, and the ultimate damnation of certain men, is according to God's sovereign good will and purpose. Concerning the Fall in particular, if God decreed reprobation after the Fall which he likewise ordained, then as Berkouwer observes: "The fall must ultimately have been part of God's counsel and therefore it 'rests' in God's sovereign pleasure. But in that case the infra concept says the same as the supra."[261]

If there was a difference between the three lapsarian schools of thought when it came to reprobation one could never tell. Boettner the "infra" laments: "It is hard for us to realize that many of those right around us (in some cases our close friends and relatives) are probably foreordained to eternal punishment."[262] Chafer the four-point Calvinist comments on the origin of sin: "The Arminian approach to the solution of this problem assigns to God no relation to the advent of sin into the universe other than that He foreknew that it would eventuate. This view is wholly inadequate, since foreknowledge on the part of God carries with it, of necessity, all the force of a sovereign purpose. A thing cannot be foreknown that is not certain, and nothing is certain until God's sovereign decree makes it thus."[263] And as we shall presently see, all three of these groups even use the exact same Scriptures to substantiate reprobation! One can see now why so much time was spent on the all-encompassing nature of God's supposed eternal decree. If God has ordained *everything* for his glory then the reprobation of the wicked is his **"determinate counsel"** (Acts 2:23) and takes place **"according to the counsel of his own will"** (Eph. 1:11) no matter which lapsarian system one adheres to.

Regarding specifically the two-fold division of the decree of reprobation, to be consistent, the theologians should, as Dabney remarks: "Apply a similar analysis to the decree of election, and divide it into a selection and a prejustification. Thus we should have the doctrine of an eternal justification, which they properly reject as erroneous. Hence, the distinction should be consistently dropped in explaining God's negative predestination."[264] So Dabney is at least partially correct in making reprobation "a simple preterition."[265] However, there are two other problems. If God chose the "elect" he consequently didn't choose the "reprobate." Therefore, there is no such thing as a negative reprobation—a preterition. One cannot choose some without passing by others; the "elect" cannot be chosen out of the fallen mass of humanity without automatically passing by the "reprobate." To pass by someone who is not created is an impossibility. The only way reprobation can be a separate decree is with a yet to be created man who can either be created as "elect" or "reprobate." It is the Fall that is the real "decree of reprobation." But the fall of Adam effected the reprobation of all men, not just a certain class: **"For as in Adam all die, even so in Christ shall all be made alive"** (1 Cor. 15:22). So in a sense, all men are predestinated to everlasting death, but not unconditionally, for the Lord Jesus Christ provided a way out: **"Verily, verily, I say unto you, He that heareth my word, and believeth on him that sent me, hath everlasting life, and shall not come into condemnation; but is passed from death unto life"** (John 5:24).

When faced with the insurmountable difficulties in explaining the fatal contradictions inherent in his lapsarian systems, the Calvinist retreats into the mercy and sovereign grace of God. Berkouwer relates that "it is therefore not the most important question whether God in predestination has accepted man as already created and fallen or as not-yet-created and therefore before the fall, but the most important thing is that man's salvation is seen in the light of God's mercy."[266] Pink informs us that "the sufficient answer to all the wicked accusations that the doctrine of Predestination is cruel, horrible, and unjust, is that, *unless* God had chosen certain ones to salvation, *none* would have been saved."[267] The most often referred to dictum is that of Warfield: "The marvel of marvels is not that God, in his infinite love, has not elected all of this guilty race to be saved, but that he has elected any."[268]

These sentimental statements are negated, however, when it is remembered what the Calvinists really believe about God's decree. They are also built on a false premise, that of Total Depravity. It is no tribute to God's grace and mercy if he sovereignly elects a total depraved sinner out of a group he first rendered with Total Inability. The doctrine of Unconditional Election *demands* the doctrine of Total Depravity for its operation. Howbeit, supposing that God *didn't* foreordain everything and *really* permitted the Fall and *indeed* provided a universal atonement, would "sovereign election" magnify God's grace if no man could be saved without it? The real issue is whether God would be just in passing by (preterition) the rest. According to the Bible—he wouldn't. The God of the Calvinist is like the priest and the Levite who **"passed by"** the **"half dead"** man in the parable of the good Samaritan (Luke 10:31-32). And worse yet, God would also be like the thieves who **"stripped him of his raiment, and wounded *him*, and departed, leaving *him* half dead"** (Luke 10:30). To say that because God came back and **"had compassion *on him*, and went to *him*, and bound up his wounds"** (Luke 10:33-34) that he should be praised for his grace and mercy is absurd. Concerning the Samaritan who **"went to him"** (Luke 10:34), the Lord enjoined: **"Go, and do thou likewise"** (Luke 10:37). Certainly the Lord practices what he preaches.

The sovereign, eternal decree of election is supposed to breed humility. Baker reminds us that "no one should ever be so presumptuous as to assume his election."[269] Palmer piously states: "This, then, is the religious humility of the Calvinist. He confesses: I don't know. I can't understand everything, but since it is in the Bible that God is one hundred percent sovereign and yet that I am responsible, I believe."[270] So even though the Calvinist doesn't understand election and doesn't know for sure if he is elected since he can't presumptuously assume it, he still boldly claims that he, and the members of his family, are the part of the "elect." In reality, Unconditional Election leads to what is epitomized in this old Particular Baptist hymn:

> We are the Lord's elected few,
> Let all the rest be damned;
> There's room enough in hell for you,
> We won't have heaven crammed![271]

The attempt to delve into the mind of God *apart* from what he has revealed in the Bible is work of "dead orthodox" theologians who pass their philosophical speculations and theological implications from one generation to the next. Whether it be the Presbyterian route from Calvin to Hodge to Warfield, the Reformed route from Calvin to Kuyper to Berkhof, or the Baptist route from Calvin to Gill to Spurgeon, all the conjecture about the nature, order, and extent of God's decrees is just that. Although sharply disagreeing among themselves, the theologians never fail to laud and extol one another while minimizing each other's shortcomings. We have already seen the aggrandizement made over Augustine. Calvin likewise, although somewhat deservedly, was so eulogized. Clark is unreservedly said to have "stood in the tradition of Augustine and Calvin for many years."[272] But anyone who knew anything about the heresies of Augustine or the errors of Calvin would cringe from such a designation. The usual association is with just Calvin, as if that is supposed to signify one as being a great theologian. Berkouwer, it is claimed, "stands in the line of the great Reformer, John Calvin."[273] Van Til maintained that John Murray was "the greatest living Calvin scholar."[274] Boettner insisted that Warfield was "the outstanding theologian since John Calvin."[275] But the name of Calvin is not even necessary in some cases. So after the death of Warfield we are informed that "the mantle of Dr. Warfield, Calvinism's most distinguished expositor and defender of the last generation, seems to have fallen on Dr. Boettner's shoulders."[276] Caspar Hodge (1870-1937) labeled Machen at his death as "the greatest theologian in the English-speaking world."[277] He also accounted Warfield as excelling both the first professor at Princeton, Archibald Alexander (1772-1851), and its most famous professor, Charles Hodge, "in erudition."[278] Clark referred to the initial Princeton Hodge, Charles, as "America's greatest theologian."[279] Francis Patton (1843-1932), former president of Princeton, spoke of Warfield as "one of the three great masters of the Reformed theology of that day (the others being Abraham Kuyper and Herman Bavinck of the Netherlands)."[280] And A. A. Hodge joined Shedd in considering Dabney "the greatest teacher of theology in the United States."[281]

For all their learning and erudite scholarship, these giants of Presbyterian and Reformed orthodoxy were, however, not without their problems. Kuyper held to presumptive regeneration and eternal justification.[282] John Murray thought that Sunday was a Sabbath and consequently no public transportation could be used to get to church.[283] Boettner maintained that "it appears very plain that

Christianity is the future world religion. In the light of these facts we face the future confident that the best is yet to be."[284] But two of the greatest irregularities among some of the theologians were tobacco and the influence of evolution. Like its influence on the Baptist theologian A. H. Strong, evolutionary thought had made inroads into the theology of some Princeton theologians. Warfield did not at all insist on a literal six-day creation.[285] This in turn was passed on to his pupil, J. Gresham Machen,[286] who likewise influenced Boettner.[287] The supralapsarian Reformed theologian Herman Hoeksema both smoked and drank cocktails while he pondered God's decrees.[288] Machen delighted in "a Princeton room full of fellows smoking" and proclaimed: "What a wonderful aid tobacco is to friendship and Christian patience."[289] John Murray acknowledged: "There is plenty of tobacco around my habitat wherever it happens to be."[290] So although they speculated about God's decrees and all the subsequent theological nuances, many of the Reformed scholars and theologians didn't have enough faith in the Bible to reject the encroachment of Darwinism into Christianity or enough common sense to stay away from tobacco. And yet Calvinists expect us to believe Berkhof when he says that "only Reformed theology does full justice to the doctrine of the decrees."

Reprobation

Although the Calvinists can't agree among themselves about the decrees of God there is one thing they do agree on: God has elected certain ones to salvation and reprobated others. Since God's decrees with all the trimmings can't be found in the Bible, the Calvinist will emphasize his arbitrary distinctions of the "elect" and the "reprobate" since the actual words can be found in the Bible. We will examine reprobation first since Calvin claimed that "election itself could not stand except as set over against reprobation."[291] Reprobation, as concisely defined by one Calvinist, is "God's eternal decree that the destiny of certain men shall be everlasting death, whether one views it as God's passing those men by with the grace of election or as the determination to damn."[292] When it comes to actually proving this doctrine from the Bible, Gill professes that it "is spoken of but sparingly in scripture."[293] Yet Engelsma insists: "It must be very difficult to read the Bible without seeing reprobation."[294] He further boasts: "How can one remain ignorant of reprobation when he reads in the New Testament Matthew 11:25-27, John 10, Romans 9, 1 Peter 2:8, and Jude 4?"[295] To which we reply: The reason Engelsma can remain ignorant of the true Bible doctrine of reprobation is because, although forms of the word are actually mentioned in the Bible, none of the verses he lists contain any mention of it.

Although twisted in meaning by the Calvinists, reprobation, like election, is a biblical doctrine. In the Bible, a reprobate is someone unapproved and therefore rejected. To *probate* something is to prove it. *Probation* is a proving period. A *probe* is an examination. The prefix *re* means to do something again (retype, repossess), to go back (recede, return), or to intensify (research, regard): I *rewrote* the *report* so as to *refine* it. To *re-probate* something is to prove it again. So a *reprobate* is someone or something that is unapproved and stands rejected in a position to be proved or tried again. Even though he believes in eternal reprobation,[296] the Calvinist Alvin Baker nevertheless confirms the above definition.[297] So the point at issue is not what the word means, but rather:

    1. Does God make a man in a *reprobate* condition?
    2. Are men *reprobate* because of something they do?
    3. Is a *reprobate* in a permanent, irreversible condition?

So the first thing to be examined is the evidence for the Calvinist view of reprobation in the Bible instances where the term occurs.

Although the word *reprobation* does not occur in the Bible, the form *reprobate* occurs four times and the plural *reprobates* three times. The word *reprobate* occurs but one time in the Old Testament: **"Reprobate silver shall *men* call them, because the LORD hath rejected them"** (Jer. 6:30). In this case, the word **"reprobate"** is clearly defined in the verse with the reason for it given in the context. They were *reprobate* because they were *rejected.* Why were they rejected? Because of a sovereign, eternal decree? The Lord said: **"Stand ye in the ways, and see, and ask for the old paths, where *is* the good way, and walk therein, and ye shall find rest for your souls"** (Jer. 6:13). But they replied: **"We will not walk *therein*"** (Jer. 6:16). The Lord said again: **"Also I set watchmen over you, *saying,* Hearken to the sound of the trumpet"** (Jer. 6:17). But they replied again: **"We will not hearken"** (Jer. 6:17). Therefore, they were reprobate **"because they** have not hearkened unto my words, nor to my law, but rejected it" (Jer. 6:19). The **"determinate counsel and foreknowledge of God"** (Acts 2:23) **"according to the counsel of his own will"** (Eph. 1:11) had nothing to do with it.

Moving to the New Testament, we find that forms of the word *reprobate* are used six times in four contexts. The first occurrence is in Romans: **"And even as they did not like to retain God in *their* knowledge, God gave them over to a reprobate mind, to do those things which are not convenient"** (Rom. 1:28). Because they **"changed the glory of the uncorruptible God into an image made like to corruptible man"** (Rom. 1:23), God **"gave them up to uncleanness"** (Rom. 1:24). Because they **"changed the truth of God into a lie, and worshipped and served the creature more than the creator"** (Rom. 1:25), God **"gave them up unto vile affections"** (Rom. 1:26). And because they **"did not like to retain God in *their* knowledge"** (Rom. 1:28), God **"gave them over to a reprobate mind"** (Rom. 1:28). Just as God did not ordain their **"uncleanness"** or their **"vile affections,"** so God did not ordain their **"reprobate mind."** John Murray described a **"reprobate mind"** as "one abandoned or rejected of God and therefore not fit for any activity worthy of approbation or esteem."[298] And notice some of **"those things which are not convenient"** that those given over to a **"reprobate mind"** committed: unrighteousness, fornication, covetousness. After naming these sins (1 Cor. 6:9-10), Paul said about the Corinthians: **"And such were some of you"** (1 Cor. 6:11). The Gentiles whom God gave over **"to a reprobate mind"** were some of Paul's converts. This shows that although a reprobate mind was a mind that God could not approve, God did not make anyone a reprobate. A man is a reprobate because of something he does. And there is nothing that implies that a reprobate is in a permanent, irreversible condition.

The last two usages of the singular *reprobate* are found in the Pastoral Epistles:

> **Now as Jannes and Jambres withstood Moses, so do these also resist the truth: men of corrupt minds, reprobate concerning the faith (2 Tim. 3:8).**

> **They profess that they know God; but in works they deny *him,* being abominable, and disobedient, and unto every good work reprobate (Tit. 1:16).**

Why were some men "reprobate concerning the faith"? Because it was eternally decreed? Not at all. They were said to resist the truth because they were **"ever learning, and never able to come to the knowledge of the truth"** (2 Tim. 3:7). Clark says that these men "have flunked the test of faith."[299] This is in contrast to those who obey the words of Paul to **"study to shew thyself approved unto God"** (2 Tim. 2:15). Notice in the next verse that it is to **"every good work"** that these are reprobate; no one's salvation is even in view. When their profession is put to the test on a good work—they fail the test. In both cases, God did not make them reprobate. They were reprobate because of something they did. And there is nothing that implies that a reprobate is in a permanent, irreversible condition.

The plural *reprobates* occurs three times in as many verses:

> **Examine yourselves, whether ye be in the faith; prove your own selves. Know ye not your own selves, how that Jesus Christ is in you, except ye be reprobates?**
> **But I trust that ye shall know that we are not reprobates.**
> **Now I pray to God that ye do no evil; not that we should appear approved, but that ye should do that which is honest, though we be as reprobates (2 Cor. 13:5-7).**

The whole point of Paul's query was because the Corinthians sought **"a proof of Christ speaking in me"** (2 Cor. 13:3), not because Paul wondered whether the individual Corinthians were "elect" or "reprobate." As proof that Christ was speaking through him, Paul admonished the Corinthians to examine themselves. Their verdict concerning themselves will likewise be their verdict about him because they owe their salvation to him (Acts 18:1, 4, 8). To affirm that Christ was in them, the Corinthians had to affirm that Christ was indeed speaking through Paul. If they were not reprobates then Paul was not a reprobate. If Paul was a reprobate then so were they. Notice the contrast between **"prove"** and **"reprobates"** (2 Cor. 13:5) and **"approved"** and **"reprobates"** (2 Cor. 13:7). The reprobation had to do with failing a test and being disapproved. If Christ is not in a man then he is a reprobate. This does not mean that God made him a reprobate. It does mean, however, that a man is a reprobate because of something he does. And there is nothing that implies that a reprobate is in a permanent, irreversible condition. The Calvinist Charles Hodge even correctly says about **"reprobates"** that "the word is to be taken in its ordinary meaning, *disapproved, unworthy of approbation.*"[300]

On this passage in 2 Corinthians, Hodge makes an interesting deduction which proves the bogus nature of the Calvinist position on reprobation: "The word *reprobate*, in its theological sense, means one who is judicially abandoned to everlasting perdition. Such is obviously not its sense here, otherwise all those not now converted would perish forever."[301] John Murray likewise admits that the scriptural use of the term *reprobate* does not agree with Calvinistic use of the term.[302] Dabney also acknowledges the word *reprobate* is not "applied in the Scriptures to the subject of predestination."[303] So there we have it: Calvinists use the word *reprobate* in a theological sense, not a scriptural sense. And not only does the Bible usage of the word *reprobate* not confirm the Calvinists' position, it rather mitigates against it. Any reprobate in the Scripture got there not by creation, but by his own free will and depravity. Anyone who believed in Total Depravity should certainly understand how this could happen. Moreover, men are obviously reprobates because of something they do—not because "what is to be will be." And furthermore, no reprobate is in a permanent, irreversible condition, for as Hodge says: "Otherwise all those not now converted would perish forever." It is apparent then that the Calvinistic doctrine of reprobation cannot be proved from the Bible instances of the word. This is why Dabney laments that "the application of the word to the negative part of the decree of predestination has doubtless prejudiced our cause. It is calculated to misrepresent and mislead."[304]

If the theological implications of reprobation cannot be found in the word itself then how can the Calvinists teach it? Simple, they seize upon any verse dealing with judgment or condemnation and read reprobation into it. The key words or ideas that the Calvinists focus on are hardened, made, appointed, reserved, ordained, and blinded. Any verse which contains one of these words is a candidate for reprobation.

Because it combines the expression "of the Lord" with the mention of God hardening people, the account of the nations God commanded the Jews to exterminate is often cited as proof of reprobation:

There was not a city that made peace with the children of

> **Israel, save the Hivites the inhabitants of Gibeon: all** *other* **they took in battle.**
> **For it was of the LORD to harden their hearts, that they should come against Israel in battle, that he might destroy them utterly,** *and* **that they might have no favour, but that he might destroy them, as the LORD commanded Moses (Jos. 11:19-20).**

Seizing upon the phrase **"hardened their hearts,"** Pink endeavors to build a case for reprobation:

> What could be more plainer than this? Here was a large number of Canaanites whose hearts the Lord hardened, whom He had purposed to utterly destroy, to whom He showed *"no favour."* Granted that they were wicked, immoral, idolatrous; were they *any* worse than the immoral, idolatrous cannibals of the South Sea Islands (and many other places), to whom God gave the Gospel through John G. Paton! Assuredly not. Then why did not Jehovah command Israel to teach the Canaanites His laws and instruct them concerning sacrifices to the true God? Plainly, because He had marked *them* out for destruction, and if so, that from all eternity.[305]

Pink would have us believe that this hardening was completely arbitrary, not taking into account any circumstances whatsoever.

If these nations were already reprobated from all eternity then why did they need to be hardened in time? Was God making their reprobation and condemnation sure? So if it wasn't by a sovereign, eternal decree, then why did God harden their hearts so they would be destroyed by Israel? There is a reason for God wanting these nations destroyed, but it is not to be found in God's sovereignty or decrees. The sin and depravity of the nations was the only reason. What happened to the doctrine of Total Depravity? God plainly spelled out why the nations were to be destroyed:

> **Defile not ye yourselves in any of these things: for in all these the nations are defiled which I cast out before you:**
> **And the land is defiled: therefore I do visit the iniquity thereof upon it, and the land itself vomiteth out her inhabitants (Lev. 18:24-25).**

These things included incest (Lev. 18:6), adultery (Lev. 18:20), human sacrifice (Lev. 18:21), homosexuality (Lev. 18:22), and bestiality (Lev. 18:23). Because of these abominations, Israel was commanded to **"destroy them with a mighty destruction"** (Deu. 7:23). Yet, if Israel didn't obey God, they too would perish like the nations (Deu. 8:20). Nothing was decided in eternity past; all was conditional. As for why God didn't command Israel to teach the Canaanites like the cannibals on the South Sea Islands, the nation of Israel was never intended to inhabit the South Sea Islands; neither are we in the Church age commanded to kill Canaanites. Pink's argument about the South Sea heathen is completely irrelevant. It is not only irrelevant, it also contradicts his own teaching elsewhere, for just a few pages later, Pink correctly tells us why God purposed to destroy the Canaanites: "It was because of their awful wickedness and corruption."[306] In his commentary on Joshua, Pink also disdained any reference to an eternal decree of reprobation, declaring that the hardening was "because they had filled up the measure of their iniquities and were ripe for judgment."[307]

There are similar cases in Scripture of God hardening individuals, but not without reason and purpose. God hardened Sihon king of Heshbon that he might be delivered into hand of Israel (Deu. 2:30). Sihon was king of the Amorites at Heshbon (Num. 21:25). The Amorites worshipped false gods (Exo. 34:15). Israel was commanded to destroy their altars, break down their images (Exo. 34:13), and destroy the people (Deu. 7:2). The hardening had nothing to do with salvation at all. God later hardened the heart of the nation of Israel (Isa. 63:17)—his elect nation. Likewise, the disciples of Christ in the New Testament hardened their hearts (Mark 6:52, 8:17). Were they in danger of reprobation? The hardening of the heart is not an eternal decree. It is warned against time after time in the Bible:

> **He, that being often reproved hardeneth *his* neck, shall suddenly be destroyed, and that without remedy (Pro. 29:1).**

> **But exhort one another daily, while it is called To day; lest any of you be hardened through the deceitfulness of sin (Heb. 3:13).**

> **While it is said, To day if ye will hear his voice, harden not your hearts, as in the provocation (Heb. 3:15).**

The ultimate case of hardening, that of Pharaoh, king of Egypt during the Exodus, will be considered later, as it is one of the three proofs of reprobation in the "haven of reprobation" for all Calvinists—Romans 9.

The next "pillar of reprobation" for the Calvinist is found in the Book of Proverbs: **"The LORD hath made all *things* for himself: yea, even the wicked for the day of evil"** (Pro. 16:4). Clark inquires: "Is this not clear enough to force an Arminian to become a Calvinist?"[308] To which we reply: Is not "whosoever believeth" (John 12:46; Acts 10:43; Rom. 9:33; 1 John 5:1) clear enough to force a Calvinist to accept the Bible? For the standard Calvinist interpretation we cite Pink: "It expressly declares that the Lord made the wicked *for* the Day of Evil; *that was* His *design* in giving them being."[309] The first thing to be noticed is that the only way to accept the verse as a Calvinist is in the supralapsarian mold. To take it otherwise would necessarily destroy the Calvinistic implications. This leaves the majority of Calvinists who take the infralapsarian position as straddling a fence between making God the author of sin and missing one of the few opportunities to find his doctrine of reprobation in the Scripture. The import of the verse is two-fold: all creation has but one author (Gen. 1:1; John 1:3) and one end (Col. 1:16; Rev. 4:11). To accentuate this, God mentions a particular thing he created, **"the wicked,"** just like he does elsewhere (Col. 1:16; Gen. 1:16), and a certain event to bring about his purposes, **"the day of evil,"** just like he does elsewhere (Rom. 9:17; Phil. 2:9-11). The verse is discussing the use God makes of his creation, not the decisions he makes for them.

The Calvinist would lead us to believe that God made certain men wicked to fulfill the **"counsel of his own will"** (Eph. 1:11). To the contrary, man was made upright (Ecc. 7:29), and is corrupt because Adam fell. Even Satan was once perfect until he sinned (Eze. 28:15-17). Since God does all his pleasure (Isa. 46:10), and yet has no pleasure in the death of the wicked (Eze. 33:11), then he couldn't have created a man wicked to damn him in order to demonstrate his power. God has made all men the same in one sense:

> **The LORD looketh from heaven; he beholdeth all the sons of men.**
> **From the place of his habitation he looketh upon all the inhabitants of the earth.**

> He fashioneth their hearts alike; he considereth all their works (Psa. 33:13-15).

Although God doesn't make a man wicked, he makes the wicked subserve his own glory and purposes:

> The LORD bringeth the counsel of the heathen to nought: he maketh the devices of the people of none effect (Psa. 33:10).

> Surely the wrath of man shall praise thee: the remainder of wrath shalt thou restrain (Psa. 76:10).

The Calvinist would at least agree with this.

Turning now to the New Testament, we find two supposed examples of reprobation that use the word *appointed*. The first instance concerns the promise to Christians that **"God hath not appointed us to wrath, but to obtain salvation by our Lord Jesus Christ"** (1 Thes. 5:9). Pink states: "To say that God 'hath not appointed *us* to wrath,' clearly implies that there *are* some whom He *has* 'appointed *to* wrath,' and were it not that the minds of so many professing Christians are blinded by prejudice, they could not fail to clearly see this."[310] Wilson equates the word **"appointed"** in this text to God's decree and accordingly explains the nature of this wrath: "I believe that the 'wrath' of this text is the eternal wrath of God in eternal hell. I believe that the 'Salvation' of this text is the eternal salvation of all of God's elect from the hell they deserve."[311]

The error of the Calvinists is two-fold: making **"wrath"** the wrath of God in hell, and making **"salvation"** the salvation of God in heaven. Both errors are due to a failure to note the context. Is it not Pink who said: "Verses of Scripture must not be wrenched from their setting, but weighed, interpreted, and applied in accord with their context"?[312] The word *wrath* only occurs three times in 1 Thessalonians. Once it is a reference to the wrath of God being presently on someone: **"Forbidding us to speak to the Gentiles that they might be saved, to fill up their sins alway: for the wrath is come upon them to the uttermost"** (1 Thes. 2:16). The unregenerate man doesn't have to wait for the wrath of God: **"He that believeth on the Son hath everlasting life: and he that believeth not the Son shall not see life; but the wrath of God abideth on him"** (John 3:36). The other two times the word *wrath* appears, the context is the coming of Jesus Christ and his deliverance from **"the wrath to come"** (1 Thes. 1:10), not the salvation of the "elect" from hell. The **"great day of his wrath"** (Rev. 6:17) is not the wrath of God on a sinner in hell (Rev. 11:18, 15:1, 16:1). After saying that "a casual reading of Revelation chapters six through nineteen reveals that the time period known as the Tribulation period is going to be characterized by the wrath of God being outpoured from heaven upon the unconverted inhabitants of earth," the Sovereign Grace Baptist Tom Ross states that "the Bible makes it very clear that the saints are not destined to experience the wrath of God, but rather deliverance from the wrath to come."[313] And what are his two proof texts? The very two verses in 1 Thessalonians where the wrath of God is mentioned![314] Chafer likewise interpreted these passages.[315] So once again the words of some Calvinists overthrow the words of some others.

There is one other passage where the Calvinist uses the word *appointed* to prove reprobation: **"And a stone of stumbling, and a rock of offence, *even to them* which stumble at the word, being disobedient: whereunto also they were appointed"** (1 Pet. 2:8). For the Calvinist private interpretation (2 Pet. 1:20), we once again turn to Pink: "The 'whereunto' manifestly points back to the stumbling at the Word, and their disobedience. Here, then, God expressly affirms that there *are* some who have been 'appointed' (it is the same Greek word as in 1 Thes. 5:9) unto disobedience."[316] Warfield adds that the stumbling of the disobedient confirms the fact that they have been appointed to disbelief.[317] If this explanation be questioned then Pink makes an emotional appeal: "Our business is not to *reason* about it, but to *bow* to Holy Scripture. Our first duty is not to *understand*, but to *believe* what God has said."[318]

Pink, as Warfield, has conveniently forgotten to give the cross-references to the stone (Gen. 49:24; Psa. 118:22; Isa. 28:16) and the stumbling (Isa. 8:14; Mat. 21:44; Rom. 9:33). The disobedience is defined in the context as unbelief (1 Pet. 2:7), just as obedience is defined as belief in Romans 10:16. **"Whosoever believeth"** is found in the same passages as the stumbling stone (Isa. 28:16; Rom. 9:33; 1 Pet. 2:6). No man was appointed to stumble unless he did not believe (Rom. 9:32). The primary reference is to the rejection of Christ by the Jews (Rom. 9:31-32, 11:25). There is always a reason for anyone being **"appointed to** destruction" (Pro. 31:8). God will yet in the future send men **"strong delusion, that they should believe a lie: that they all might be damned"** (2 Thes. 2:11-12). But the reason is because they **"believed not the truth, but had pleasure in unrighteousness"** (2 Thes. 2:12). Even Pink recognizes this: "Just as the Jews of Christ's day despised His testimony, and in consequence, were 'blinded,' so a guilty Christendom which has rejected the Truth shall yet have sent them from God a 'strong delusion' that they may believe a lie."[319] No one was ever appointed to stumble, to destruction, or to damnation before the foundation of the world any more than Justus and Matthias were appointed to be the replacements for Judas by an eternal decree (Acts 1:23).

The next proof text for reprobation is like the aforementioned Proverbs 16:4 in that it contains the word *made:* **"But these, as natural brute beasts, made to be taken and destroyed, speak evil of the things that they understand not; and shall utterly perish in their own corruption"** (2 Pet. 2:12). Once again we hear from Pink: "Here, again, every effort is made to escape the plain teaching of this solemn passage. We are told that it is the 'brute beasts' who are 'made to be taken and destroyed,' and not the persons here likened to them."[320] But then all he says is that "'these' men *as* brute beasts, are the ones who, like animals, are 'made to be taken and destroyed.'"[321] Although he never does tell us *why* or *when* these men were **"made to be taken and destroyed,"** Pink is implying that these **"false prophets"** and **"false teachers"** (2 Pet. 2:1) have been foreordained **"to be taken and destroyed."**

But there are two problems with this interpretation. Are beasts foreordained **"to be taken and destroyed"** before the foundation of the world by a sovereign, eternal decree? And when a beast is **"taken and destroyed,"** does that mean that it goes to hell? The contrast of these men with the beasts **"made to be taken and destroyed"** is finished at the end of the verse: **"shall utterly perish in their own corruption."** There is a similar description of false teachers in Jude: **"But these speak evil of those things which they know not: but what they know naturally, as brute beasts, in those things they corrupt themselves"** (Jude 10). Notice in both cases that the **"corruption"** was their own doing: **"their own corruption," "they corrupt themselves."** God never makes a man in a reprobate condition; men are always reprobate because of something they do. No man deserves to be destroyed unless he earns it. The very next verse in the context in 2 Peter makes this perfectly clear. There we read that these men under consideration **"shall receive the reward of unrighteousness"** (2 Pet. 2:13). God has destroyed people, but we are told that was limited to **"them that believed not"** (Jude 5).

Although mentioned only scarcely by Calvinists,[322] there are two other passages that could be construed as proof texts for reprobation:

> **These are wells without water, clouds that are carried with a tempest; to whom the mist of darkness is reserved for ever (2 Pet. 2:17).**
>
> **Raging waves of the sea, foaming out their own shame; wandering stars, to whom is reserved the blackness of darkness for ever (Jude 13).**

The Calvinistic interpretation of these verses would be that the reprobate have been **"reserved"** for condemnation by a sovereign, eternal decree. And although it is surprising that more Calvinists have not appealed to these passages as proof texts for reprobation, the interpretation given above is exactly what they believe about reprobation no matter which words are used to describe it. But who is it that has eternal reservations for the **"mist of darkness"** and **"the blackness of darkness"**? The "non-elect"? The "reprobate"? According to the Bible it is false prophets and teachers who deny the Lord and **"bring upon themselves swift destruction"** (2 Pet. 2:1). It is ungodly men who deny the Lord and **"corrupt themselves"** (2 Pet. 2:12; Jude 10). The angels that sinned (2 Pet. 2:4; Jude 6), the unjust (2 Pet. 2:9), and the wicked (Job 21:30) are similarly "reserved." Even the earth is **"reserved unto fire against the day of judgment"** (2 Pet. 3:7).

Although the word *ordained* will be considered later in reference to salvation, because it occurs one time in reference to condemnation, it will be examined here in a verse that most Calvinists present as a proof text for reprobation: **"For there are certain men crept in unawares, who were before of old ordained to this condemnation, ungodly men, turning the grace of our God into lasciviousness, and denying the only Lord God, and our Lord Jesus Christ"** (Jude 4). Pink claims that "there can be no evading the fact that certain men are *'before of old'* marked out *by God* 'unto condemnation.'"[323] So Pink again restates the verse and says nothing we didn't already know. What he said by way of implication was that certain men were ordained to condemnation before the foundation of the world by a sovereign, eternal decree. What Pink actually said was correct, the question is *when* and *how* and *why* were they so ordained? The Puritan Thomas Manton (1620-1677) was more to the point: "From all eternity some were decreed by their sins to come unto judgment or condemnation." He then agreeingly notes that "this is one of the texts which divines bring to prove the general doctrine of reprobation."[324]

The root problem with their interpretation is that Calvinists are assuming that **"before of old"** means "before the foundation of the world." When God wants to say "before the foundation of the world," he does so (John 17:24; Eph. 1:4; 1 Pet. 1:20). Once the fallacy of this reasoning is recognized, the answer to all three of our pertinent questions can found in the context:

> **And Enoch also, the seventh from Adam, prophesied of these, saying, Behold, the Lord cometh with ten thousands of his saints,**
> **To execute judgment upon all, and to convince all that are ungodly among them of all their ungodly deeds which they have ungodly committed, and of all their hard** *speeches* **which ungodly sinners have spoken against him (Jude 14-15).**

The words of Enoch tell us *when* and *how* and *why* these were so ordained. But before getting to Enoch, Jude compares these false teachers with three events (Jude 5-7), three men (Jude 11), and three objects (Jude 12-13). In no case were the actions of anyone or anything the result of a sovereign, eternal decree. The day will come when God will **"execute upon them the judgment written"** (Psa. 149:9). But the greatest proof that Jude 4 doesn't refer to reprobation *as defined by the Calvinists* is not the Scripture. Alvin Baker, who strongly believes in reprobation *as defined by the Calvinists,* insists that "Jude 4 cannot be used to substantiate reprobation."[325] So in this case not only is the Scripture against the Calvinists—they are against themselves.

Before examining the "haven of reprobation" for all Calvinists—Romans 9, there is yet one more passage on reprobation to be considered. There are actually several related passages, all drawn from a very significant Old Testament prophecy of Isaiah:

> And he said, Go, and tell this people, Hear ye indeed, but understand not; and see ye indeed, but perceive not.
> Make the heart of this people fat, and make their ears heavy, and shut their eyes; lest they see with their eyes, and hear with their ears, and understand with their heart, and convert, and be healed (Isa. 6:9-10).

This prophecy is alluded to five times in the New Testament (Mat. 13:14-15; Mark 4:12; Luke 8:10; John 12:39-40; Acts 28:25-27). Before examining the Calvinist's arguments for reprobation, we should notice some important things about the passage in Isaiah. Twice we are told whom the passage is referring to: **"this people,"** which is obviously the nation of Israel. It is also apparent that the shutting of the eyes was not an eternal act, it takes place *after* the people are already born. They were not created with their eyes shut—they were God's elect people. The word *lest* signifies that the destiny of these people was not fixed by an unconditional decree. Some Jews did get saved later (Acts 14:1, 21:20). So all the elements necessary to prove the Calvinistic doctrine of reprobation are not only missing, the very opposite is present. No unconditional, eternal decree of reprobation could possibly be in view because not all of Israel were "reprobated," those that were doesn't include Gentiles, the shutting was in time, and nothing was fixed. Now, does this mean that the Calvinists don't use this text to teach reprobation? Not at all. But the typical way this passage is used to support the doctrine of reprobation is the same as that for most of the other Calvinistic proof texts—a list of verses is given or quoted after a statement of Calvinistic doctrine.

Of the five times this prophecy is alluded to in the New Testament, two are never used to teach reprobation because the subjects are said to close their own eyes instead of it being done to them:

> And in them is fulfilled the prophecy of Esaias, which saith, By hearing ye shall hear, and shall not understand; and seeing ye shall see, and shall not perceive:
> For this people's heart is waxed gross, and *their* ears are dull of hearing, and their eyes they have closed; lest at any time they should see with *their* eyes and hear with *their* ears, and

> should understand with *their* heart, and should be converted, and I should heal them (Mat. 13:14-15).

> And when they agreed not among themselves, they departed, after that Paul had spoken one word, Well spake the Holy Ghost by Esaias the prophet unto our fathers,
> Saying, Go unto this people, and say, Hearing ye shall hear, and shall not understand; and seeing ye shall see, and not perceive:
> For the heart of this people is waxed gross, and their ears are dull of hearing, and their eyes have they closed; lest they should see with *their* eyes, and hear with *their* ears, and understand with *their* heart, and should be converted, and I should heal them (Acts 28:25-27).

This variation is curiously never pointed out.

The passage in John which relates to Isaiah's prophesy is as follows:

> But though he had done so many miracles before them, yet they believed not on him:
> That the saying of Esaias the prophet might be fulfilled, which he spake, Lord, who hath believed our report? and to whom hath the arm of the Lord been revealed?
> Therefore they could not believe, because that Esaias said again,
> He hath blinded their eyes, and hardened their heart; that they should not see with *their* eyes, nor understand with *their* heart, and be converted, and I should heal them (John 12:37-40).

This passage was introduced in the previous chapter on Total Depravity because it mentions someone having the inability to believe. But as was mentioned there, there is a reason given for the inability besides the fact of Total Depravity. The reason why some **"could not believe"** is, according to the Calvinists, because God **"blinded their eyes"** by reprobation. This is why the study of these verses properly goes in the chapter on Unconditional Election.

Even though much could be made of the fact that God **"blinded their eyes,"** Calvinists seldom mention this passage except in passing or in a string of proof texts.[326] Pink, being a better Bible student than most Calvinists, remarks on why they were blinded: "Why? Because they had refused to believe on Christ? This is the popular belief, but mark the answer of Scripture—*that they should not* see with their eyes."[327] Pink is implying that this refers to "God's sovereign 'hardening' of sinners' hearts."[328] He maintains that for one to see reprobation in this passage requires not "prolonged searching or profound study, but a childlike spirit."[329] The trouble is, however, that Pink's interpretation is a pale horse, and death and hell follow it. Death and hell (Rev. 6:8) in this instance are personified as Pink's own arguments *against* the standard Calvinistic interpretation he just gave. And not only Pink, but other Calvinists contradict this interpretation as well.

In the same book in which he made the above comments, Pink, while attempting to prove that God hardens people, again refers to John 12:37-40, but this time he informs us that "it needs to be carefully noted here that these whose eyes God 'blinded' and whose heart He 'hardened,' were men who had deliberately scorned the Light and rejected the testimony of God's own Son."[330] And in his commentary on John, Pink stated:

> In consequence of their rejection of Christ, the nation as a whole was judicially blinded of God, that is, they were *left* to the darkness and hardness of their own evil hearts. But it is most important to mark the *order* of these two statements: in 12:37 they *did not* believe; here in 12:39, they *could not* believe. The most attractive appeals had been made: the most indubitable evidence had been presented: yet they despised and rejected the Redeemer. They *would not* believe; in consequence, God gave them up, and now they *could not* believe. . . . The fault was entirely theirs, and now they must suffer the just consequences of their wickedness. . . . This was God's response to the wicked treatment which Israel had meted out to His beloved Son. They had refused the light, now darkness shall be their dreadful portion. They had rejected the truth, now a heart which loved error should be the terrible harvest. Blinded eyes and a hardened heart have belonged to Israel ever since.[331]

Gill and Carson likewise reject Pink's earlier interpretation:

> I do not find that these words are cited by any of our writers to prove the decree of reprobation, or preterition, or any eternal purpose of God to blind the eyes, and harden the hearts of men, by any positive act of his, with a view to hinder their

> conversion, and that his decree of condemnation might take place.[332]
>
> It is clear in both Mark and John that those condemned are in any case *justly* condemned, i.e. they are rightly accountable for their unbelief (in John, cf. surrounding verses, especially 12.35-7, 44ff.) They are not forced into an unbelief they do not themselves want.[333]

This is yet another example of the Calvinists not only disagreeing among themselves, but contradicting themselves.

That these passages based on Isaiah's prophesy refer to the judicial hardening of a nation and not the sovereign hardening of individuals is perfectly clear. To further confirm it, it should be noted where in the Bible this prophecy from Isaiah appears. It was mentioned in the Gospels when the Jews rejected their Messiah and the mystery form of the kingdom was revealed. It was quoted in John when the Jews rejected Christ and he finished his public dealings with them. It was referred to by Paul in Acts when the Jews rejected the risen Christ and God turned to the Gentiles for the duration of the Church age. The original passage in Isaiah heralds the Tribulation where the Jews accept a false christ. So the passage in Isaiah didn't teach reprobation at all. Every place it occurred it was aimed at Israel as a nation. Individual Jews are still converted (Acts 14:1, 21:20) even during the period of official rejection (Rom. 11:25). But even though these passages concern Israel, this does not rule out any spiritual application. In this age of grace, the Devil has **"blinded the minds of them which believe not"** (2 Cor. 4:4) and takes away **"the word out of their hearts, lest they should believe and be saved"** (Luke 8:12). The lesson for individuals is clear: **"Seek ye the LORD while he may be found, call ye upon him while he is near"** (Isa. 55:6). Light rejected becomes lightning. God is under no obligation to reveal the truth to any man who doesn't desire it or has rejected it.

There is a related passage in Romans that also speaks of the judicial blindness of Israel:

> **What then? Israel hath not obtained that which he seeketh for; but the election hath obtained it, and the rest were blinded**
> (According as it is written, God hath given them the spirit of

> **slumber, eyes that they should not see, and ears that they should not hear;) unto this day (Rom. 11:7-8).**

Although these verses are occasionally referenced by Calvinists as proof texts for reprobation,[334] because it is so obvious from the context that this blindness was not only national in scope, but temporary in nature (Rom. 11:25), most Calvinists only use this passage in reference to election since the word actually occurs. Therefore, these verses will be examined under that topic along with the other two uses of the word *election* in Romans.

As mentioned previously, the "haven of reprobation" for all Calvinists is Romans 9. Of this chapter in the word of God, Calvinists have said:

> The most neglected chapter in the Bible.[335]

> It is safe to say that language cannot be chosen better adapted to teach Predestination at its height.[336]

> Romans 9 contains the *fullest* setting forth of the doctrine of Reprobation.[337]

> More than any other portion of the Word of God this chapter sets forth the doctrine of unconditional election and answers sufficiently the human objections.[338]

Out of all of their proof texts for their doctrines, Calvinists have here been the most prolific. Some Calvinist proof texts are used fairly often, and others are curiously avoided, but Calvinists of all stripes never fail to appeal to Romans 9 for proof of election and reprobation. But since Romans 9 is in the main referred to prove reprobation, and our subject at hand is reprobation, only the three "pillars of reprobation" in Romans 9 will be considered here.

Romans 9 is the first chapter in a larger parenthetic section of the Book of Romans. While Romans 1–8 deals with doctrinal issues, and Romans 12–16 deals with practical issues, Romans 9–11 is a parenthesis where is displayed God's present plan in dealing with the nation of Israel. Because of its importance, Romans 9–11, and even Romans 9 itself, have been the subject of many books from different perspectives.[339] Romans 9–11 is a parenthesis where the Jew is considered nationally, both alone (Rom. 9:1-5, 10:1-3,

11:1-10), and as contrasted with the Gentiles (Rom. 9:30-31, 10:12, 11:11-12). Since Romans 9–11 contains passages that specifically concern Israel, it is to be expected that Calvinists will generally misinterpret these passages more than any others. Proof of this will be found on numerous occasions throughout this book. But not only will the Bible be rejected, the Calvinists will also overthrow the interpretations of their fellow Calvinists the whole way through.

That Israel was an elect nation there is no doubt (Deu. 7:6-7; 1 Kgs. 3:8; Psa. 135:4; Isa. 45:4). Yet Israel was **"ignorant of God's righteousness"** (Rom. 10:3). They were **"a disobedient and gainsaying people"** (Rom. 10:21), with the result that **"the wrath is come upon them to the uttermost"** (1 Thes. 2:16). The problem then is this: How God could reject those whom he had elected (Rom. 11:1)? And as a consequence, what about the faithfulness of God and his word? This right away mitigates against Unconditional Election. And not only this, the burden throughout these chapters that Paul maintained for the salvation of the Jewish people as a whole (Rom. 9:1-3, 10:1-3, 11:12-14) also dampens the idea of the election and reprobation of all members of the human race. And as we shall presently see, the reprobation of individuals isn't even remotely connected with the three "pillars of reprobation" given to us by the Calvinists in Romans 9: **"Esau have I hated"** (Rom. 9:13), **"whom he will he hardeneth"** (Rom. 9:18), **"vessels of wrath fitted to destruction"** (Rom. 9:21).

The first passage concerns Jacob and Esau:

> **And not only** *this;* **but when Rebecca also had conceived by one,** *even* **by our father Isaac;**
> **(For** *the children* **being not yet born, neither having done any good or evil, that the purpose of God according to election might stand, not of works, but of him that calleth;)**
> **It was said unto her, The elder shall serve the younger.**
> **As it is written, Jacob have I loved, but Esau have I hated (Rom. 9:10-13).**

This familiar story was even the subject of a sixteenth-century play entitled *A mery and wittie Comedie or Enterlude, newely imprinted, treating upon the Histories of Iacob and Esau, taken out of the xxij. Chap. of the booke of Moses entituled Genesis.*[340] And what do the Calvinists have to say about Jacob and Esau?

> The unconditional election of Romans 9:11 is so patent that even a hurried reading forces it upon the mind.[341]

> We conclude, therefore, that the predestination of Jacob and Esau is a personal election and reprobation unto salvation and eternal desolation respectively.[342]

> How much instruction do these words 'The elder shall serve the younger,' contain, as standing in the connection in which they are quoted! They practically teach the great fundamental doctrines of the Prescience, the Providence, the Sovereignty of God; His predestination, Election, and reprobation.[343]

What the Calvinists have "practically" done is to insert the phrase **"Jacob have I loved, but Esau have I hated"** before **"for the children being not yet born"** to get an eternal, individual election or reprobation of the TULIP variety. John Piper simply says that Jacob and Esau "were appointed for their respected destinies before they were born."[344] According to Charles Cosgrove: "God loves Jacob and hates Esau before they are born."[345] To reinforce these private interpretations, Herman Hoeksema, under pretense of paraphrasing a simple nine-word phrase, adds to the word of God and comes out with: "Jacob have I eternally accepted in love; Esau have I eternally rejected as an object of My sovereign hatred."[346]

The **"and not only *this*"** of verse ten points us back to an earlier context:

> **Not as though the word of God hath taken none effect. For they *are* not all Israel, which are of Israel:**
> **Neither, because they are the seed of Abraham, *are they* all children: but, In Isaac shall thy seed be called.**
> **That is, They which are the children of the flesh, these *are* not the children of God: but the children of the promise are counted for the seed.**
> **For this *is* the word of promise, At this time will I come, and Sarah shall have a son (Rom. 9:6-9).**

Verses ten through thirteen are a continuation of verse nine, showing that Abraham's seed was to be called in Jacob as in Isaac. It could be argued from verse eight that Isaac was chosen because Ishmael was born of a bondmaid, so Paul anticipates what might be advanced by the Jews in opposition to the former type. His argument that there was an Israel within Israel (Rom. 9:6) is illustrated by the descendants of Isaac and Jacob being reckoned as the children of the covenant promise to the exclusion of all other descendants of Abraham. God made the same promises concerning "thy seed" and the land to Abraham (Gen. 17:7-8), Isaac (Gen. 26:3-4), and Jacob (Gen. 35:11-12). The **"purpose of God according to election"** (Rom. 9:11) had nothing to do with individual salvation or reprobation at all. It concerned the Messianic line of Abraham–Isaac–Jacob–Jesus Christ. As L. S. Ballard correctly ascertained: "To contend that this election was to salvation is preposterous, false, and as far from the truth as heaven is from hell, or as the east is from the west. It was an election to national preference or theocratic privileges and there is nothing akin to salvation in it."[347]

This truth is even more apparent upon examination of the Old Testament references to which Paul refers:

> **And the children struggled together within her; and she said, If *it be* so, why *am* I thus? And she went to inquire of the LORD.**
> **And the LORD said unto her, Two nations *are* in thy womb, and two manner of people shall be separated from thy bowels; and *the one* people shall be stronger than *the other* people; and the elder shall serve the younger (Gen. 25:22-23).**

So although the children were not born (Rom. 9:11), nothing took place before the foundation of the world—they were in the womb of Rebekah when it was said: **"The elder shall serve the younger"** (Gen. 25:23; Rom. 9:12). The Scripture also told us that individuals were not under discussion—nations were: **"two nations," "two manner of people"** (Gen. 25:23). And not only does the text not say "the elder shall be lost and the younger shall be saved," Esau as an individual never served Jacob; the very opposite happened. Jacob bowed down to Esau (Gen. 33:3), called him lord (Gen. 33:8), claimed to be his servant (Gen. 33:5), and urged him to accept gifts (Gen. 33:11).

The other passage under consideration was written hundreds of years later:

> **The burden of the word of the LORD to Israel by Malachi.**

> I have loved you, saith the LORD. Yet ye say, Wherein hast thou loved us? *Was* not Esau Jacob's brother? saith the LORD: yet I loved Jacob,
> And I hated Esau, and laid his mountains and his heritage waste for the dragons of the wilderness (Mal. 1:1-3).

Jacob and Esau had been dead for hundreds of years when the statement was made: **"Jacob have I loved, but Esau have I hated"** (Rom. 9:13). In Genesis we have a prophetic statement looking forward and in Malachi we have a historical statement looking backward. After the death of Jacob, the term *Jacob* always has reference to Israel as a nation, unless mentioned in connection with Abraham and Isaac or in recounting some event in the life of Jacob the individual. Even Calvin admits that it is the posterity of Jacob and Esau in view.[348] And as we made clear at the beginning of our study of Romans 9, the Calvinists cannot agree among themselves as to what is an example of reprobation and what is not. Berkouwer, joined by his fellow Dutchman, Herman Ridderbos (1910-1981), maintains that Romans 9 *does not* present the election and reprobation of Jacob and Esau as individuals, but sets forth the principle that God's election is not of works and that the destiny of Israel as a whole is in view.[349]

So how does the Calvinist make Romans 9:13 apply to individual election and reprobation? The first ploy is to admit that the references in Genesis and Malachi refer to Jacob and Esau *nationally* but that Romans 9 concerns Jacob and Esau *individually*. Then the Calvinist uses two arguments to prove election and reprobation. John Murray consents to the "national" proposition and then insists: "Yet we may not discount the relevance to Jacob and Esau themselves. Why was there this differentiation between Israel and Edom? It was because there was differentiation between Jacob and Esau. It would be as indefensible to dissociate the fortunes of the respective peoples from the differentiation of the individuals as it would be to dissociate the differentiation of the individuals from the destinies of the nations proceeding from them."[350] But by the reasoning of Murray, if the spiritual state of the descendants of Jacob and Esau paralleled them, then allowing for the election of Jacob and the reprobation of Esau, all their descendants would have to be either saved or lost respectively. A case could be made for Esau's posterity, but what about Jacob's? Were Dathan, Korah, and Abiram saved even though God opened the earth and cast them into the bottomless pit (Num. 16:31-33)? Were Nadab and Abihu saved in spite of God sending fire from heaven and burning them up (Lev. 10:1-2)? So to claim that God treated the progenies of Jacob and Esau like he did them would mean that salvation was automatic for the former's descendants and unobtainable for the latter's.

The second, and most popular alternative, is to claim that Jacob and Esau were not only types of their posterity, but of all men. Haldane explains: "In its obvious and literal meaning, what is said of Jacob and Esau must be true of all the individuals of the human race before they are born. Each one of them must either be loved or hated of God."[351] The fallacy of this argument is two-fold. First, assuming that Jacob and Esau were sovereignly elected and reprobated respectively, how does that prove that all men were likewise treated? To say that it is implied and logically fits the TULIP system is no way to teach Bible doctrine. And second, as has already been pointed out, God didn't hate Esau in eternity past. He was said to hate him *nationally* after observing his actions for hundreds of years.

The Calvinist also runs into another problem with his eternal love-hate interpretation, for Jesus Christ was said to love the rich young ruler who rejected him and **"went away grieved: for he had great possessions"** (Mark 10:22). The standard Calvinist teaching, as stated by Owen, is that God "hated the non-elect before their birth."[352] Now, as we have seen, there is an element of truth in every heresy of Calvinism. Pink is certainly correct in saying: "It has been customary to say God loves the sinner, though He hates his sin. But that is a meaningless distinction. What is there in a sinner but sin?"[353] This is corroborated by Scripture:

> **God judgeth the righteous, and God is angry *with the wicked* every day (Psa. 7:11).**

> **The sacrifice of the wicked *is* abomination: how much more, *when* he bringeth it with a wicked mind? (Pro. 21:27).**

But because this verse goes against Pink's idea that God eternally hated the non-elect, he claims that the rich young ruler "was one of God's elect, and was 'saved' sometime after his interview with our Lord."[354] Scripture? He didn't give any.

The greatest rebuke the Calvinists have ever received on these verses in Romans 9 which concern Isaac, Ishmael, Jacob, and Esau did not come from an Arminian or other non-Calvinist. It came from one of their own. The extended comments of the theologian J. Oliver Buswell, a five-point Calvinist, and the former president of Wheaton College (1926-1940), because they are not only true, but completely contrary to the vast majority of Calvinists, are here presented:

> There are several references to election in the early part of the ninth chapter of the epistle to the Romans which seem rather clearly to indicate election to the line of the ancestry of the Messiah, rather than to eternal salvation as such. When we read (v. 8), . . . Paul is referring to the fact that the Messianic line was to be perpetuated in Isaac, not in Ishmael. But we are certainly not to understand by this that Ishmael was necessarily among the reprobate, so far as eternal salvation is concerned. . . . The reference in Romans 9 to Jacob and Esau is similar. . . . In this case the comment with which Paul concludes the reference to Jacob and Esau coincides with the view that the "election" here referred to is an election to the Messianic line, and not an election of an individual to eternal life. . . . In the Malachi passage from which Paul quotes these words, the prophet is clearly referring not to the individual Esau, but to the people of Edom who had been a sinful and rebellious people, thought they were, according to the promises of God, eligible to be considered within God's covenant with Israel. There is nothing in the Genesis record to indicate that Esau, when Jacob returned to his home land, was other than a sincere worshiper.[355]

Our next concern is the reference to Pharaoh—of which Storms claims: "This episode in Scripture ranks second only to 'Jacob I loved, but Esau I hated' in terms of the disfavor in which it is held!"[356] The only disfavor, however, is in the eyes of the Bible-believing Christian who hates to see the Scripture misinterpreted by a Calvinist. The Bible says of Pharaoh:

> **For the scripture saith unto Pharaoh, Even for this same purpose have I raised thee up, that I might shew my power in thee, and that my name might be declared throughout all the earth.**
> **Therefore hath he mercy on whom he will *have mercy,* and whom he will he hardeneth (Rom. 9:17-18).**

Herman Hoeksema insists that "Pharaoh was sovereignly hated from eternity, even as was Esau."[357] But as we assented about Esau, suppose that Pharaoh was "sovereignly hated from eternity." How does that prove the damnation of billions of other "reprobates"? Pink assumes that it does: "The case of Pharaoh *establishes* the principle and illustrates the doctrine of Reprobation. If God actually reprobated Pharaoh, we may justly conclude that He reprobates all others whom He did not predestinate to be conformed to the image of His Son."[358] But contrariwise, if it can be proved that God did not reprobate Pharaoh, then we may justly conclude that God reprobates no man, at least according to the Calvinist view of reprobation, for God *does* "reprobate" all whom he *does not* predestinate to be conformed to the image of his Son. But no man is predestinated to be conformed to Christ's image until *after* he is saved. Consequently, all men are "reprobate" unless they accept Christ—by faith, not by Unconditional Election and Irresistible Grace.

That the purpose to which Pharaoh was raised up and the subsequent hardening had nothing to do with Pharaoh's eternal destiny is perfectly clear, both according to the Bible and the Calvinists. Pharaoh was said to be raised up to show God's power—not to be damned to hell by a sovereign, eternal decree. The purpose being that God might prove to Israel that he was the Lord who delivered them (Exo. 6:6-7, 10:1-2, 13:14-16), to show Pharaoh that he was the only God (Exo. 9:14), to show the Egyptians that he was the Lord (Exo. 7:5, 14:4, 18), and that his name might be declared throughout the whole earth (Exo. 9:16). These purposes were realized by Israel (Exo. 14:31), Pharaoh and the Egyptians (Exo. 14:17-18, 25), and throughout the earth (Jos. 2:10-11, 1 Sam. 4:7-8). For the word of a Calvinist, we again turn to Berkouwer: "It is clear that Paul does not want to direct our attention to the individual fate of Pharaoh, but that he speaks of him in order to show his place in the history of salvation, and it is certainly not permissible—as Calvin did—to draw conclusions here regarding the 'example' of stubbornness because of God's eternal decree, and regarding the rejection of the wicked."[359]

Then there is the question of God hardening Pharaoh. We have already seen similar cases in the Bible where God was said to harden individuals. None of them had to do with salvation or any eternal decree as seen by the fact that Israel—the elect nation—was hardened by God (Isa. 63:17). Therefore, it is fallacious of Herman Hoeksema to reason that as God hardens Pharaoh's heart to reprobate him so "God hardens the heart of all the wicked."[360] It should first be noted that before God ever touched Pharaoh, and before Moses ever went to see him, God in his foreknowledge said: **"And I am sure that the king of Egypt will not let you go, no, not by a mighty hand"** (Exo. 3:19). The reason God knew this is apparent from the first meeting that Moses had with Pharaoh:

> **And afterward Moses and Aaron went in, and told Pharaoh, Thus saith the LORD God of Israel, Let my people go, that they may hold a feast unto me in the wilderness.**
> **And Pharaoh said, Who *is* the LORD, that I should obey his voice to let Israel go? I know not the LORD, neither will I let Israel go (Exo. 5:1-2).**

A sovereign, eternal decree of reprobation had nothing to do with it.

Pharaoh uttered the most tragic words that a man could speak: **"I know not the LORD."** Knowing this is what caused God to determine to harden Pharaoh (Exo. 4:21, 7:3). Then God is said to harden him (Exo. 7:13, 9:12, 10:1, 20, 27, 14:8). But Pharaoh was also said to harden his own heart (Exo. 8:15, 32, 9:34). And twice, Pharaoh's heart was said to be hardened with no agent mentioned (Exo. 7:22, 9:35). In his zeal to send Pharaoh to hell, Storms alleges that when Pharaoh hardened his heart and no executor of the hardening is named, God really did it.[361] But there are several things to notice about this hardening. First, it was always in reference to letting Israel go, not believing or obeying what God said in reference to salvation (Exo. 4:21, 7:3-4, 10:1, 20, 27, 14:8). Secondly, if the decree of reprobation was eternal, what was God doing hardening Pharaoh's heart in time and on several occasions if he was already predestined to hell? Was he making his reprobation and condemnation sure? Perhaps the greatest error concerns the nature of hardening in general. When a brick, a piece of clay, an ice cube, or gasket sealer is hardened—it has already assumed its final shape. The hardening *hardens* it, not forms it. And note what the Calvinist John Murray tells us: "The hardening, it should be remembered, is of a judicial character. It presupposes ill-desert, and, in the case of Pharaoh, particularly the ill-desert of his self-hardening."[362]

There was some dissension in the Calvinistic camp regarding

Jacob and Esau. The subject of Pharaoh wrought even more division. But upon examination of the last stronghold of reprobation in Romans 9, most of the Calvinists have abandoned ship:

> **Nay but, O man, who art thou that repliest against God? Shall the thing formed say to him that formed *it*, Why hast thou made me thus?**
> **Hath not the potter power over the clay, of the same lump to make one vessel unto honour, and another unto dishonour?**
> ***What* if God, willing to shew *his* wrath, and to make his power known, endured with much longsuffering the vessels of wrath fitted to destruction:**
> **And that he might make known the riches of his glory on the vessels of mercy, which he had afore prepared unto glory,**
> **Even us, whom he hath called, not of the Jews only, but also of the Gentiles? (Rom. 9:20-24).**

Although there are many defectors, there still remains a remnant according to the election of Calvinism. According to Herman Hoeksema, because the potter has power over the clay, this proves "God's absolute sovereignty to determine the final destiny of men, either to honor or dishonor, to salvation and glory or to damnation and desolation."[363] However, while Hoeksema insists that the clay is not fallen mankind,[364] other Calvinists maintain that it is.[365] Calvinists continually refer to the **"vessels of wrath fitted to destruction"** as the reprobate.[366] Regarding these **"vessels of wrath,"** Pink simply says: "He fits the non-elect unto destruction by His fore-ordaining decrees."[367]

The potter and the clay was a common illustration in the Old Testament (Isa. 29:16, 45:9, 64:8; Jer. 18:1-6). Never is it a reference to anyone's salvation. Israel is said to be the clay (Isa. 64:8; Jer. 18:6). The clay is formed, not created. There was no clay before the foundation of the world, and neither is anyone said to be fitted or prepared before the foundation of the world. And although the **"vessels of mercy"** are said to be **"afore prepared unto glory"** by God, no agent is given in the case of those **"fitted to destruction."** Vessels are made empty, and bring honor or dishonor (2 Tim. 2:20) according to what is put in them. God doesn't *make* anyone honorable or dishonorable. So although Cosgrove claims that "in the course of explaining God's justice toward Israel, Paul affirms a doctrine of double predestination,"[368] it is only by segregating this passage from the rest of Romans 9–11 and reading into it election and reprobation that the Calvinist interpretation seems plausible.

The diverse interpretations of the commentators on this passage are irrelevant for two reasons. First, everything depends on how one interprets Romans 9 as a whole. This can be seen in the comments of Piper:

> It is clear therefore that in 9:21 Paul still has in mind the issue of unconditional election raised in 9:6-13. For those who remain unconvinced that Paul was concerned with the predestination of individuals to salvation and perdition in 9:6-13, this observation will not strengthen the case for seeing predestination of individuals in 9:21.[369]

Piper also appeals to "the clear and powerful statements of double predestination in Rom 9" as proof that God fit men for destruction before the foundation of the world in Romans 9:22.[370] John Murray does the same thing, but appeals to Romans 8: "Although in verses 22, 23 there is not direct reference to the decretive foreordination of God in the expressions 'fitted unto destruction' and 'afore prepared unto glory,' it is not possible to dissociate verse 24 from the earlier passage in which calling is given its locus in relation to predestination (8:28-30)."[371] So even though the passage in question does not in and of itself teach election and reprobation, Calvinists see these doctrines anyway because they read into it their idea of predestination that they perceive elsewhere. But could it not just as easily be said that because Unconditional Election is not found elsewhere that it is not an option here?

The second thing that renders the interpretations of these verses irrelevant is that it is the Calvinists themselves who overthrow the interpretations of some of their more radical "brethren." Is mankind a lump of clay that God molds for heaven or hell? The Calvinists John Murray and Charles Hodge reply:

> There is no warrant for the interpretation or objection that Paul represents God as esteeming mankind as clay and dealing with men accordingly. He is using an analogy and the meaning is simply that, in the realm of his government, God has the intrinsic right to deal with men as the potter, in the sphere of his occupation, deals with clay.[372]

> In the sovereignty here asserted, it is God as moral governor, and not God as creator, who is brought to view. It is not the right of God to create sinful beings in order to punish them, but his right to deal with sinful beings according to his good pleasure, that is here, and elsewhere asserted.[373]

Regarding the **"vessels of wrath,"** were they unconditionally **"fitted to destruction"** before the foundation of the world? Calvin thought so, but what about his followers?

> It must be said, however, that many no longer agree with Calvin's exegesis of this passage, not because they wish to minimize the sovereignty of God, but because they recognize that Paul's words cannot legitimately bear this interpretation.[374]

> The main thought is that the destruction meted out to the vessels of wrath is something for which their precedent condition suits them. There is an exact correspondence between what they were in this life and the perdition to which they are consigned.[375]

> This, however, is not to be understood in a supralapsarianism sense. God does not create men in order to destroy them.[376]

Are the **"vessels of wrath"** the individual "reprobate" members of the human race? Once more, the Calvinists will answer for us:

> In the preceding verse, Paul had declared that God exercised much long-suffering towards the *vessels of wrath*—that part of Israel which were not of Israel.[377]

> Furthermore, the apostle has in view the unbelief of Israel and the longsuffering with which God endures their unbelief.[378]

> It must be that Paul refers here to Israel. Just as God wanted to reveal His wrath against Pharaoh, so also against Israel but, simultaneously and through that, He shows His majesty and glory. Again, this is not an independent analysis of the destiny of individual man; it shows, rather, the acts of the electing God through the course of history.[379]

To take this passage in Romans 9 in anything but a supralapsarian sense destroys the whole TULIP system. This is why there are so many defectors from Calvin's position. Like everywhere else in Romans 9, the nation of Israel is in view. According to the Calvinists themselves, the **"vessels of wrath"** are the unbelieving Jews—not the "reprobate" so decreed from before the foundation of the world. What is said about Pharaoh and God showing his power is transferred to unbelieving Israel. The **"vessels of wrath"** were **"fitted to destruction"** because they **"stumbled at that stumblingstone"** (Rom. 9:32), were guilty of the blood of Christ (Mat. 27:25), and were enemies of the Gospel (Rom. 11:28). But just as Israel was showed mercy in the case of Pharaoh (Rom. 9:15-18), yet became **"vessels of wrath"** in the passage under consideration, so individual Jews who rejected Christ could become **"vessels of mercy"** if they accepted Christ (1 Tim. 1:13, 16), for they were forgiven by him (Luke 23:34). And even though Calvinists would all make Pharaoh a vessel **"unto dishonour,"** we are told in Exodus that the Lord said: **"I will get me honour upon Pharaoh"** (Exo. 14:17). Finally, by way of application, all men are **"vessels of wrath"** (Eph. 2:3), but God will have mercy on any man who receives Jesus Christ (Rom. 11:30-31; 1 Pet. 2:10). The fallacy behind all of the Calvinist interpretations in Romans 9 is in reading sovereign election and reprobation into Paul's arguments on the question of Israel.

For those Calvinists who firmly believe their doctrine of reprobation, it should be preached as part of **"all the counsel of God"** (Acts 20:27). Yet, Calvin agrees with Augustine in maintaining: "If any one should address the people and say, If ye believe not, it is because ye are predestinated of God to eternal destruction; such an one would not only foster his own indolence, but would indulge malice towards his hearers."[380] But Calvin and Augustine's hypothetical message is exactly the truth—if one is a real Calvinist. And the doctrine of reprobation is either false, or as Bunyan declares: "It is impossible that any should be reprobate, before God had both willed and decreed it should be."[381] Therefore, if reprobation is true, then there is nothing anyone can do about it. So whether "elect" or "reprobate," man's lot in life is still:

> *It is* **good that** *a man* **should both hope and quietly wait for the salvation of the LORD (Lam. 3:26).**

Reprobation should not be preached, but not for the reason given by Augustine and approved by Calvin. It should not be preached because not only is it patently false, it is truly a "horrible decree."

Once again, however, there is an element of truth in every heresy of Calvinism. Although God didn't make men in a reprobate condition, this in no way denies the judgment of God upon the wicked. Being omniscient and omnipresent, God is certainly aware of what is going on: **"The eyes of the LORD *are* in every place, beholding the evil and the good"** (Pro. 15:3). God remembers wickedness (Hos. 7:2), and will judge everything, including man's words (Mat. 12:36) and secrets (Rom. 2:16). The wicked will go to hell (Psa. 9:17), have fire and brimstone rained upon them (Psa. 11:6), and be consumed as the fat of lambs (Psa. 37:20). The Lord will mock and laugh at the wicked (Pro. 1:26) and vex them (Psa. 2:5). Yet, there is no unrighteousness in God (Psa. 92:15; Rom. 9:14). The problem with Calvinism is that none of this occurs because of a sovereign, eternal decree. So not only did God not make a man wicked, he will accept any man who turns from his wickedness (Eze. 33:19). Consequently, when a man is reserved, appointed, or ordained to condemnation, it is always because of something he did, not by an eternal decree of reprobation.

In concluding the subject of reprobation, the Calvinists are still divided. Baker insists that "there seems to be adequate scriptural support for the doctrine of reprobation."[382] But on the contrary, Bavinck remarks that "Scripture makes little mention of rejection as eternal decree" even while Dijk admits that "Scripture speaks of rejection solely as an act of God in time and history."[383] Commenting on the supralapsarian/infralapsarian debate among the Calvinists, the Calvinist Paul Jewett concludes that "when all is said and done, the problem of reprobation remains unresolved and, it would appear, unresolvable."[384] Palmer uses a proof for reprobation that no Sovereign Grace Baptist would ever dream of: "Just as surely as the church practices infant baptism, so also does it teach the truth of reprobation."[385] So although the Calvinists cannot agree among themselves as to the nature and order of God's decrees or the question of reprobation, there is one thing that unites them, yea, denominates them Calvinists: God has elected certain ones to be saved and they alone are the recipients of salvation. There are many arguments used by the Calvinists to prove that men are sovereignly elected by an eternal decree to salvation. But from supralapsarianism to sublapsarianism, and everything in between, the arguments are all the same. Therefore, we will provide a "balanced diet" of assorted Calvinists as we see how they use the Scripture to prove the counterpart of reprobation.

Proof Texts

As mentioned earlier, predestination and election are often used as cognate terms both applying to God's choosing of certain ones to be saved. And if all one ever listened to were Calvinists, he would think that the entire Bible revolved around these doctrines. But not only are election and predestination two completely different ideas, they are not even remotely given the emphasis in the Bible that they are by the Calvinists. There are two classes of proof texts given by the Calvinists in support of their "election to salvation" doctrine. The first is the argument that God has a special group of people—the "elect"—who were chosen to salvation before the foundation of the world. Calvinists see this in phrases which mention God's "people" or God's "sheep," as well as verses where the converse is implied. The other kind of proof text for Unconditional Election is a verse which contains a key word that the Calvinist reads as Unconditional Election. These verses are of five types, corresponding to the following ideas:

1. Given to salvation
2. Ordained to salvation
3. Chosen to salvation
4. Elected to salvation
5. Predestinated to salvation

Since these two classes of proof texts each contain several Scriptures to be examined, they will be considered individually, and, in the case of the latter, further divided into five sections.

But before examining the Calvinist proof texts for Unconditional Election, the fallacy that each one of them is based on should be noted. This fallacy is the whole idea that mankind is divided into two groups: the "elect" and the "reprobate." As we saw earlier in this chapter, God has made all men the same in one sense:

The LORD looketh from heaven; he beholdeth all the sons of men.
From the place of his habitation he looketh upon all the inhabitants of the earth.

> He fashioneth their hearts alike; he considereth all their works (Psa. 33:13-15).

Consequently, just as there is no such thing as God's one, eternal, sovereign, all-encompassing decree, so there is no such thing as the "elect" and the "reprobate."

The simple proof that salvation is not just limited to the "elect" is provided throughout the Scripture:

> In the last day, that great *day* of the feast, Jesus stood and cried, saying, If any man thirst, let him come unto me, and drink (John 7:37).

> To him give all the prophets witness, that through his name whosoever believeth in him shall receive remission of sins (Acts 10:43).

> As it is written, Behold, I lay in Sion a stumblingstone and rock of offence: and whosoever believeth on him shall not be ashamed (Rom. 9:33).

> Wherefore also it is contained in the scripture, Behold, I lay in Sion a chief corner stone, elect, precious: and he that believeth on him shall not be confounded (1 Pet. 2:6).

> Whosoever believeth that Jesus is the Christ is born of God: and every one that loveth him that begat loveth him also that is begotten of him (1 John 5:1).

> And the Spirit and the bride say, Come. And let him that heareth say, Come. And let him that is athirst come. And whosoever will, let him take the water of life freely (Rev. 22:17).

The first way to get rid of the promise that "whosoever will" may come is to ignore it and lie about its existence. Spencer simply claims that it "is not to be found in the Bible."[386] Realizing that it is not possible to get away with this, the other approach to achieve the same result is to advance that "the will to come is not prevenient to grace but subsequent to it as its fruit."[387] So behind every verse which admits of free will there exists a mysterious, philosophical, theological meaning *opposite* of what the verse says.

This enables a Calvinist to prate about believing in "whosoever will" while at the same time denying it. The most tragic example of this phenomenon is the book *Whosoever Will,* by the supralapsarian, Protestant Reformed theologian Herman Hoeksema. While stating that "it is absolutely sure that 'whosoever will may come.' And it is equally certain that whosoever comes will certainly be received,"[388] Hoeksema spends 164 pages postulating the following Calvinistic implications:

> In fact, the sinner is of himself neither capable nor willing to receive that salvation.[389]
>
> The saving grace of God, changing the heart of the sinner, precedes the will to come to Christ.[390]
>
> The will to come to Christ is rooted in, and is the outcome of God's unconditional, free and sovereign election of His own unto eternal life.[391]

Boettner likewise dismisses the idea that "whosoever will" may come: "The fact is that a spiritually dead person cannot will to come."[392] This brings us right back to the foundation of Calvinism: Total Depravity. But as the four-point Calvinist Lewis Sperry Chafer answered the scriptural gymnastics of his "brethren": "It is misleading to assert, as Dr. Warfield was wont to do, that 'whosoever God wills may come.'"[393] Yet this is what Calvinism reduces salvation to. God wrote the script billions of years ago and is now in the process of pulling the strings to bring about his desired carte blanche.

God's People

The first type of argument to be considered is whether God has a predetermined people waiting to be saved by Irresistible Grace. The premier text for this teaching mentions God's "people":

> **Then spake the Lord to Paul in the night by a vision, Be not afraid, but speak, and hold not thy peace:**
> **For I am with thee, and no man shall set on thee to hurt thee: for I have much people in this city (Acts 18:9-10).**

For the standard Calvinist interpretation, we cite another Protestant Reformed supralapsarian, David Engelsma, and a former GARBC Bible college president, David Nettleton:

> Before Paul and the gospel ever got to Corinth, the Lord had much people there by virtue of God's election of many in that city. The reason why Paul was sent there to preach and the reason why he had to remain there preaching, in the face of opposition, was the salvation of the elect in that city. Paul knew very well that God did not love all the Corinthians and that God did not desire to save all the inhabitants of that city.[394]

> It was predetermined that Paul would have success in Corinth. God assured him that He had much people there. Did this dull the edge of Paul's evangelism? Not at all. The opposite was true. Being assured that God had chosen many to salvation, Paul set out to reap the harvest.[395]

That the Lord had **"much people"** in Corinth there is no doubt—but who were they? The "elect"? The "predestinated"? If God already had **"much people"** in Corinth then what was Paul doing preaching there in the first place? If the **"much people"** who belonged to God from all eternity didn't hear the message of Paul and repent then what would have happened to them? Would they cease to be one of the "elect"? Are unsaved Gentiles ever spoken of as God's people? The Bible describes the unregenerate as **"children of disobedience"** (Eph. 2:2) and **"children of wrath"** (Eph. 2:3). The **"much people"** are defined in the chapter as Aquila and Priscilla (Acts 18:2), Silas and Timotheus (Acts 18:5), Justus (Acts 18:7), Crispus and his family (Acts 18:8), and **"many of the Corinthians"** (Acts 18:8). There is no such animal as an "elect unregenerate" child of God.

If God has his "people," then it follows that the rest of mankind are not his people due to the fact that they were not elected. This is precisely what the Calvinist sees in the Book of Revelation. God wrote in a book the names of the "elect," and those not written became the "non-elect":

> **And all that dwell upon the earth shall worship him, whose names are not written in the book of life of the Lamb slain from the foundation of the world (Rev. 13:8).**

> The beast that thou sawest was, and is not; and shall ascend out of the bottomless pit, and go into perdition: and they that dwell on the earth shall wonder, whose names were not written in the book of life from the foundation of the world, when they behold the beast that was, and is not, and yet is (Rev. 17:8).

Pink asserts that this is a "positive statement affirming that there *are* those whose names *were not* written in the Book of Life."[396] But this is exactly what the verse says. Custance is bolder: "And so also in Revelation 17:8 it seems that **'from the foundation of the world'** the names of the elect were entered in the 'account book' of God, which perhaps records the names of the participants in the covenant made by the Father with the Son."[397] But Custance "seems" that "perhaps" he is not too sure of his interpretation. Clark does not mince words: "The Lamb that was slain from the foundation of the world did not intend to save those whose names were not written in the book of life from the foundation of the world."[398] But in the verse he commented on, nothing is said about any names being written from the foundation of the world. Talbot and Crampton comment on the latter verse: "Several things should be noticed in this passage. First, some names have already been written down in the book of life before the foundation of the world and some have not. Will any be added? None! Will any be lost? None! The elect and the non-elect have been predetermined from all eternity. There is an absolute fixity to the number."[399] Thinking the Calvinists have the best of the argument, some correct the Scripture to avoid a conflict.[400]

The fallacy of the Calvinist suppositions is multi-faceted. The first problem is that the Calvinists continually read *before* whenever they see a verse that mentions the foundation of the world. But **"from the foundation"** means "from the foundation," and never signifies "before the foundation." The phrase in question occurs five times in the New Testament besides the two times it appears in the Book of Revelation. Notice that it couldn't possibly be a reference to before the foundation of the world: **"That the blood of all the prophets, which was shed from the foundation of the world, may be required of this generation"** (Luke 11:50). The second thing is that no mention is made about anyone's salvation. The Calvinist tries to make every verse in the Bible a reference to salvation. Third, there is no mention of the purpose for anyone's name being written or not written. Fourth, the book is called the **"book of life,"** not the "book of the elect." And finally, it should be noted that someone can have their name removed from the book of life.

> He that overcometh, the same shall be clothed in white raiment; and I will not blot out his name out of the book of life, but I will confess his name before my Father, and before his angels (Rev. 3:5).

> And if any man shall take away from the words of the book of this prophecy, God shall take away his part out of the book of life, and out of the holy city, and *from* the things which are written in this book (Rev. 22:19).

What is this but the "the reprobation of the elect"? The writing in the Lamb's book of life is not done with the pen of sovereign decrees nor the ink of arbitrary election.

The next Calvinistic proof text that God has a special group of people—the so-called elect—who were chosen to salvation before the foundation of the world concerns those verses which mention God's sheep:

> I am the good shepherd, and know my *sheep,* and am known of mine.
> As the Father knoweth me, even so know I the Father: and I lay down my life for the sheep.
> And other sheep I have, which are not of this fold: them also I must bring, and they shall hear my voice; and there shall be one fold, *and* one shepherd (John 10:14-16).

> But ye believe not, because ye are not of my sheep, as I said unto you (John 10:26).

These verses have suffered much misapplication due to the influence of the Calvinists. Pink informs us that "the name 'sheep' is synonymous with 'elect,' for such are 'sheep' before they believe, yea, before they are born."[401] Not only are the "elect" God's sheep, but "the elect have always been called sheep. Beloved, the saints of God have never been called goats, even before they were saved."[402] The reference to the **"other sheep"** of another fold is the Lord "here contemplating His elect among the

Gentiles."[403] Even though no forms of the word *election* appear in John's Gospel, Custance insists that "election is unequivocally maintained throughout the Old and New Testaments, and nowhere more clearly so than in the Gospel of John."[404] And where does he find election in John's Gospel? "As is clear from John 10:26 we must already be Christ's sheep to be believers. The Lord did not say, 'Ye are not my sheep because ye believe not,' but 'ye believe not because ye are not of my sheep'—which is a very different thing. Faith is not the cause of this life but the proof of it. We are not saved because we believe, but we believe because we are of his sheep."[405]

There are two major problems with this interpretation. First of all, if men are sheep before they believe then they already have eternal life: **"And I give unto them eternal life; and they shall never perish, neither shall any *man* pluck them out of my hand"** (John 10:28). If the sheep were never goats then how can they be born **"dead in trespasses and sins"** (Eph. 2:1)? No one among the unsaved Gentiles is ever called a sheep. Try pigs and dogs (Mat. 7:6, 15:26-27; 2 Pet. 2:1, 22). The Gentiles were **"without Christ, being aliens from the commonwealth of Israel, and strangers from the covenants of promise, having no hope, and without God in the world"** (Eph. 2:12). Can one of God's sheep go to hell? Why then must God's sheep believe on Christ?

The second problem concerns the identification of the sheep. Who are the sheep? According to Micaiah (1 Kgs. 22:17), Asaph (Psa. 74:1, 78:52, 79:13), the Psalmist (Psa. 44:11, 22, 95:7, 100:3), David (Psa. 119:176), Isaiah (Isa. 53:6), Jeremiah (Jer 23:1, 50:6, 17), Ezekiel (Eze. 34:6, 11, 12), and Jesus Christ (Mat. 10:6, 15:24): the sheep are Israel. Notice the condition of Israel in the Old Testament:

> **My people hath been lost sheep: their shepherds have caused them to go astray, they have turned them away *on* the mountains: they have gone from mountain to hill, they have forgotten their restingplace (Jer. 50:6).**

> **My sheep wandered through all the mountains, and upon every high hill: yea, my flock was scattered upon all the face of the earth, and none did search or seek *after them* (Eze. 34:6).**

Then notice a forgotten prophecy from the Lord:

> **For thus saith the Lord GOD; Behold, I, *even* I, will both search my sheep, and seek them out.**
> **As a shepherd seeketh out his flock in the day that he is among his sheep *that are* scattered; so will I seek out my sheep, and will deliver them out of all places where they have been scattered in the cloudy and dark day.**
> **And I will bring them out from the people, and gather them from the countries, and will bring them to their own land, and feed them upon the mountains of Israel by the rivers, and in all the inhabited places of the country.**
> **I will feed them in a good pasture, and upon the high mountains of Israel shall their fold be: there shall they lie in a good fold, and *in* a fat pasture shall they feed upon the mountains of Israel.**
> **I will feed my flock, and I will cause them to lie down, saith the Lord GOD.**
> **I will seek that which was lost, and bring again that which was driven away, and will bind up *that which was* broken, and will strengthen that which was sick: but I will destroy the fat and the strong; I will feed them with judgment (Eze. 34:11-16).**

Note also the New Testament counterparts:

> **But go rather to the lost sheep of the house of Israel (Mat. 10:6).**

> **But he answered and said, I am not sent but unto the lost sheep of the house of Israel (Mat. 15:24).**

When Christ came, his sheep—like Simeon (Luke 2:25), Anna (Luke 2:36-38), Zacharias and Elisabeth (Luke 1:5-6), the shepherds (Luke 2:8-20), and the disciples (John 1:40-49)—knew him (John 10:14), followed him (John 10:27), and received eternal life (John 10:28). We have here the separation of the Jewish sheep from the goats and the drawing of them to the Messiah. And as is clear to all but a Calvinist, sheep are never synonymous with the "elect"—ask any zoologist.

The next case of God's so-called unregenerate elect is also in the Gospel of John: **"He that is of God heareth God's words: ye** therefore hear *them* not, because ye are not of God" (John 8:47). Pink comments:

> First, it signifies, he that belongs to God by eternal election. A parallel to this is found in John 10:26, "Ye believe not, because ye are not of *my sheep.*" It is this which, in time, distinguished the elect from the non-elect. The former, in due time, hear or receive God's words; the latter do not. Second, "He that is of God" signifies, he that has been born of God, he that is in the family of God.[406]

Custance adds: "Such indeed is the implication also of John 8:47 addressed to those who the Lord well knew were not destined to become his sheep."[407] The trouble with John 8:47 is, in regards to Unconditional Election, it is a blank. Even Calvin himself didn't take this for eternal election.[408] The verse had to do with hearing, not anyone's salvation. Nothing was said about how one came to be **"of God."** No mention was made that those not **"of God"** were sovereignly decreed to be so. Every Calvinist who used this verse read the word *elect* into it when it never occurs anywhere in John's Gospel. The text is a general principle that those **"of God"** will be the ones that hear his word and those not **"of God"** will not. Could anything be plainer?

Given to Salvation

The other kind of proof text for Unconditional Election is a verse which contains a key word that Calvinists read as Unconditional Election. The first of these to be examined are those passages which contain the word *given.* Calvinists read the idea of the "elect" being "given to salvation" into two classes of verses. The first, and most extensive, class of verses are those which mention God the Father *giving* someone to God the Son:

> **All that the Father giveth me shall come to me; and him that cometh to me I will in no wise cast out (John 6:37).**

> **And this is the Father's will which hath sent me, that of all which he hath given me I should lose nothing, but should raise it up again at the last day (John 6:39).**

Custance and Palmer comment:

> The elect are the Father's gift to the Son. For these He died, and these will come as gifts to Him at the appropriate time.[409]

> It is clearly seen that those who will be raised up at the last day—all true believers—are given to Christ by the Father. And only those whom the Father gives to Christ can come to Him.[410]

That this will of the Father was not a sovereign, eternal decree is apparent from the fact that one of those given to Christ was a devil (John 6:70) who was lost (John 17:12), and some of those who came to him went back (John 6:66). And if the second half of John 6:37 is divorced from the first then the Calvinists have another problem: others besides the ones "elected" could come to Christ and be accepted as the first and not be cast out. This would mean that there were two wills of the Father corresponding to these two classes: that Christ should lose none of those given to him (John 6:39), and that **"every one which seeth the Son, and believeth on him, may have everlasting life"** (John 6:40).

Closely related to these two verses is the account of the real Lord's prayer found in John 17:

> **As thou hast given him power over all flesh, that he should give eternal life to as many as thou hast given him (John 17:2).**

> **I have manifested thy name unto the men which thou gavest me out of the world: thine they were, and thou gavest them me; and they have kept thy word (John 17:6).**

> **I pray for them: I pray not for the world, but for them which thou hast given me; for they are thine (John 17:9).**

> **And now I am no more in the world, but these are in the world, and I come to thee. Holy Father, keep through thine own name those whom thou hast given me, that they may be one, as we** *are* **(John 17:11).**

> **While I was with them in the world, I kept them in thy name: those that thou gavest me I have kept, and none of them is lost, but the son of perdition; that the scripture might be fulfilled (John 17:12).**

Father, I will that they also, whom thou hast given me, be with me where I am; that they may behold my glory, which thou hast given me: for thou lovedst me before the foundation of the world (John 17:24).

The Calvinists are united in joining these verses to John 6:37 and grasping at any form of the word *give* as proof that God the Father, by Unconditional Election, gave the "elect" to God the Son before the foundation of the world so he could make a Limited Atonement for them so God the Holy Spirit could overcome the Total Depravity of the "elect" with Irresistible Grace so they could partake of the Perseverance of the Saints.

Nothing is being overstated—the Calvinists read Unconditional Election into this chapter:

> I do not see how predestination could possibly be taught more clearly than it is in the whole of this high-priestly prayer of Jesus in the 17th chapter of John.[411]

> The fact that we are the gift of the Father to the Son, a circumstance that implies we are in some special way God's possession even before we come to the Son, is constantly reaffirmed by the Lord himself.[412]

> All believers, those presently such and those who will become such, constitute those given by the Father to Jesus.[413]

There is no doubt that some were given to Christ, but not only are they never called the "elect," they are defined as the disciples in the passage.

The ones given to Christ were men (John 17:6). Are all women lost? Jesus Christ manifested his name unto them (John 17:6). He hasn't manifested his name to anyone for almost two thousand years. The ones given to Christ kept God's word (John 17:6). Have all Christians kept God's word? Christ gave unto them the words of God (John 17:8). We have the Bible, but did Jesus Christ personally give it to us? Christ was with them in the world (John 17:12). He is now seated in heaven (Heb. 10:12). One of those given to Christ was lost (John 17:12). Can the "elect" become the "reprobate"? Jesus Christ prayed **"for them also which shall believe on me through their word"** (John 17:20). If the "elect" were given to

Christ then who are they **"which shall believe"**? Can the "non-elect" believe? Christ declared the Father's name unto them (John 17:26). He hasn't declared anything to anyone for almost two thousand years. Yes, a definite group is being given to Christ during his earthly ministry—not before the foundation of the world. The ones given are Jewish disciples. They are said to be his sheep (John 10:27). John baptized that Christ should be manifest to Israel (John 1:31). And although Israel as a whole received him not (John 1:11), he was known of his sheep (John 10:14).

Besides the class of verses which mentions God the Father *giving* someone to God the Son, there is another class to be considered. This next type contains two verses used by the Calvinists to teach Unconditional Election on the basis of something being *given* to the "elect":

And he said, Therefore said I unto you, that no man can come unto me, except it were given unto him of my Father (John 6:65).

For unto you it is given in the behalf of Christ, not only to believe on him, but also to suffer for his sake (Phil. 1:29).

Sometimes the verse in John is misread by the Calvinists and put into the same class as was previously looked at.[414] That this giving of the Father was not a sovereign, eternal decree is apparent from the fact that Jesus Christ said he would give **"everlasting life"** to the multitude (John 6:27). Was every member of this group one of the "elect"? It is evident that not everyone received everlasting life for some believed not (John 6:36). But since this verse is a companion to the main proof text for Irresistible Grace, John 6:44, it will be considered further in that chapter. The verse in Philippians is cited by Calvinists when seeking to prove that faith is God's gift to his "elect" so they can have their Total Depravity overcome by Irresistible Grace. But since not all Christians "suffer for his sake," an irresistible gift could not be in view. The idea that faith is God's gift to his "elect" will be considered in the chapter on Irresistible Grace.

Ordained to Salvation

The second word that Calvinists use to prove Unconditional

Election is *ordained*. And although there is really only one verse that they use, it is one of the main proof-texts employed by the Calvinists to substantiate Unconditional Election. It is also one of only two verses that seem to connect "election" with salvation: **"And when the Gentiles heard this, they were glad, and glorified the word of the Lord: and as many as were ordained to eternal life believed"** (Acts 13:48). Every Calvinist, no matter what else he believes, uses this verse to prove Unconditional Election. Every Calvinist claims that on the basis of this verse, every person who has ever been saved (Old or New Testament) or ever will be saved (Church age or Tribulation or Millennium) was **"ordained to eternal life"** before the foundation of the world by a sovereign, eternal decree. Nettleton claims that it is this verse that made him a Calvinist.[415] The verse alarms the non-Calvinists so much that some alter the text rather than face the Calvinistic implications.[416] On the other hand, Calvinists who would not hesitate to correct the Scripture in other places condemn those who would do so here.[417] There is no need to present any comments on this verse by Calvinists—there is no doubt what they will be. Palmer prates: "Here is another text with stunning clarity for whoever will read the Bible without preconceived notions about election."[418] Pink claims that "every article of human ingenuity has been employed to blunt the sharp edge of this scripture and to explain away the obvious meaning of these words, but it has been employed in vain, though nothing will ever be able to reconcile this and similar passages to the mind of the natural man."[419]

There are a number of problems with the Calvinists' interpretation of this verse. To begin with, the word *ordain* is used several different ways in the Bible, just as it is in any dictionary. Quite often it is used in connection with an office one is put into, both in the Old Testament (2 Kgs. 23:5; 1 Chr. 9:22; 2 Chr. 11:15; Jer 1:5; Heb. 5:1), and the New (Mark 3:14; John 15:16; Acts 14:23; 1 Tim. 2:7; Tit. 1:5). Sometimes it is used in the sense of choosing (2 Chr. 29:27; Dan. 2:24; Acts 1:22, 10:42, 17:31), establishing (Num. 28:6; 1 Kgs. 12:32, 33; Rom. 13:1; 1 Cor. 7:17; Heb. 9:6), preparing (Psa. 7:13; Isa. 30:33), making (1 Chr. 17:9; Isa. 26:12; Psa. 8:3), or deciding (2 Chr. 23:18; Acts 16:4; 1 Cor. 9:14; Eph. 2:10).

Not only does the word *ordain* mean several different things, it never is a reference to an unconditional, sovereign, eternal decree.

Take Judas for example: he was "ordained" with the other eleven disciples and sent forth the preach (Mark 3:14). Yet, he turned out to be a devil (John 6:70). Where are the priests who were ordained to offer sacrifices (Heb. 5:1)? God didn't accept their sacrifices after Calvary (Heb. 10:10-14). What about all the men who have been ordained to the ministry? Didn't some leave the ministry and go back into the world? Didn't God ordain the stars (Psa. 8:3)? Then why do we have falling stars? Do stars "fall from grace"? Does every pastor **"live of the gospel"** (1 Cor. 9:14)? Do all Christians practice good works? Even though **"God hath before ordained that we should walk in them"** (Eph. 2:10), Paul had to remind Christians about doing good works (Tit. 3:8, 14).

Although Calvinists maintain that Acts 13:48 is without a doubt in support of Calvinism, there are several things this verse does say that should be noted. It does say **"ordained"** instead of "foreordained." That is why the various connotations of the word were explained. It also says **"as many as"** instead of "all." **"As many as were ordained to eternal life"** does not mean that everyone who has ever believed fits that description:

> **Neither was there any among them that lacked: for as many as were possessors of lands or houses sold them, and brought the prices of the things that were sold (Acts 4:34).**

> **For before these days rose up Theudas, boasting himself to be somebody; to whom a number of men, about four hundred, joined themselves: who was slain; and all, as many as obeyed him, were scattered, and brought to nought (Acts 5:36).**

Another important thing to note is that this verse says **"Gentiles,"** not Jews or the Church. Acts 13:48 is in the middle of one of the turning points in the Book of Acts which show the gradual progression of the Gospel from **"the Jew first"** (Rom. 1:16) to the Gentiles. In Acts 7:54, the Jews at Jerusalem rejected Stephen. Then in Acts 13:46, the Jews in Asia Minor rejected Paul. In Acts 18:6, the Jews in Europe did likewise. In Acts 28:28, the rejection was final. God now calls from the Gentiles **"a people for his name"** (Acts 15:14) until **"the fulness of the Gentiles be come in"** (Rom. 11:25), for through the fall of the Jews **"salvation is come unto the Gentiles"** (Rom. 11:11). That this event with the Gentiles in Acts 13:48 was significant, and not just an isolated incident, can be seen by what was said about it afterward: **"And when they were come, and had gathered the church together, they rehearsed all that God had done with them, and how he had opened the door of faith unto the Gentiles"** (Acts 14:27). God didn't ordain any Gentile to eternal life until he sought for the truth (Acts 13:42). A similar case is that of the Gentile Cornelius (Acts 10:1). Cornelius was *"A* **devout** *man,* **and one that feared God with all his house, which gave much alms to the people, and prayed to God alway"** (Acts 10:2). Cornelius was accepted by God (Acts 10:4, 31, 35) because he sought for the truth—not because he was saved, although Luther adamantly insists that he was.[420] Cornelius still had to believe to be saved (Acts 11:17), and that is exactly what Peter preached (Acts 10:43).

That this event with Cornelius was also significant, can be seen by what was said about it afterward:

> **And the apostles and brethren that were in Judaea heard that the Gentiles had also received the word of God (Acts 11:1).**
>
> **When they heard these things, they held their peace, and glorified God, saying, Then hath God also to the Gentiles granted repentance unto life (Acts 11:18).**

This does not mean that all Gentiles are saved. Just like Peter saying that the Gentiles by his mouth **"should hear the word of the gospel, and believe"** (Acts 15:7) does not mean that all Gentiles are saved. But assuming that the Gentiles in Acts 13:48 were sovereignly elected according to the manner of Calvinism, no case could necessarily be made for any Jews. And assuming further the election of these Gentiles, how does that prove that all saved Gentiles who have ever existed were ordained to eternal life according to Acts 13:48?

There are also a number of things that Acts 13:48 does not say. It doesn't say one has to be ordained to believe. It doesn't say there are "reprobates" who can't be saved. It doesn't say that anyone was ordained unconditionally. It doesn't say that anyone was ordained before the foundation of the world. It doesn't say that anyone was ordained by a sovereign decree. It doesn't say that those who are ordained will believe. It doesn't say that everyone who was ever saved was ordained to believe. And the final thing this verse doesn't say is that every Calvinist has to use it as a proof text for Unconditional Election. The Calvinistic theologian Buswell, although believing in Unconditional Election, says about this verse: "Actually the words of Acts 13:48,49, do not necessarily have any reference whatever to the doctrine of God's eternal decree of election."[421] So as we have seen time and time again, it is the Calvinists themselves who often overthrow their own doctrines.

There is one more example of the word *ordained* being used to teach Unconditional Election: **"But we speak the wisdom of God in a mystery, *even* the hidden *wisdom,* which God ordained before the world unto our glory"** (1 Cor. 2:7). That this verse has nothing to do with Unconditional Election to salvation is explicitly clear. But that doesn't mean a Calvinist won't use it anyway. Clark comments: "This verse, unlike the previous passage, reflects only indirectly on God's predestination of particular persons. However, even the indirectness may perhaps have a point."[422] But to the contrary, this verse, unlike the previous passage, reflects *directly* on the Calvinists' propensity to read God's predestination of particular persons into every conceivable verse. Wisdom is being discussed in the verse, as it is in the whole chapter, as well as the previous one. Wisdom, not Unconditional Election.

Chosen to Salvation

Before examining the grossly misunderstood words *election* and *predestination,* there is one more term that is fastened upon, more than any other, to teach Unconditional Election. Since the basic meaning of *elect* is "choose," any form of the word *choose* occurring in Scripture is ripe for a TULIP interpretation. It doesn't matter whether salvation is even remotely connected with the passage, if someone is "chosen" then he is unconditionally, sovereignly, and eternally elected to salvation. The first passage to be considered is a pair of similar verses from Matthew:

> **So the last shall be first, and the first last: for many be called, but few are chosen (Mat. 20:16).**

> **For many be called, but few chosen (Mat. 22:14).**

Because they contain the word **"chosen,"** these two verses in

Matthew are referenced or quoted with others supposedly referring to Unconditional Election as if they too were proof texts.[423] Before commenting on each individual verse, several things should be noted about both verses as a whole. To make these verses refer to Unconditional Election, Calvinists have to add "to salvation" after each occurrence of the word *chosen*. The context of both passages, however, had nothing to do with **"the gospel of the grace of God"** (Acts 20:24). Both passages concern **"the kingdom of heaven"** (Mat. 20:1, 22:2), not heaven or salvation. And both passages are parables, not doctrinal statements on the plan of salvation. The first verse in question had to do with laborers (Mat. 20:1); salvation is a gift (Rom. 6:23; Eph. 2:8). In Matthew 22:14 the ones chosen are chosen because they accepted the invitation (Mat. 22:9) and had the prescribed wedding garment (Mat. 22:11). The ones chosen were **"bid to the marriage"** (Mat. 22:9), not foreordained to go. The ones chosen were **"good and bad"** (Mat. 22:10), not just the "elect." And finally, the ones chosen responded to a general invitation (Mat. 22:9), the invitation to a particular group was refused (Mat. 22:3).

There is also the question of the order of the words **"called"** and **"chosen"** in these two verses. As we saw in our study of Acts 2:23, Calvinists often base their doctrine of Unconditional Election on the order of the words in a verse. In Acts 2:23, since the word *counsel* preceded the word *foreknowledge,* Calvinists maintained that God's foreknowledge was based on his decrees. But note here that if the word **"chosen"** signifies election, then those **"called,"** which supposedly signifies Irresistible Grace, were called by Irresistible Grace before they were elected. And not only this, foreknowledge *precedes* predestination (Rom. 8:29), calling comes before election (2 Pet. 1:10), salvation comes before calling (2 Tim. 1:9), and sanctification precedes calling (Jude 1). When Calvinists can build a doctrine of an all-encompassing decree on the order of two words in a verse they will do so. But when the order of two words in another verse contradicts their system, they withhold comment.

The next verse containing a form of the word *choose* that is used as a proof text for Unconditional Election is in John:

Ye have not chosen me, but I have chosen you, and ordained you, that ye should go and bring forth fruit, and *that* your

> fruit should remain: that whatsoever ye shall ask of the Father in my name, he may give it you (John 15:16).

There are four ways to force eternal election into these verses. First, realizing that the text has to be stretched to the breaking point to prove an eternal predestination to salvation, the majority of Calvinists simply mention the verse with a group of other Scriptures as a proof text for Unconditional Election, hoping that no one will bother to look it up. The second type of argument is similar to the first, but with some explanation given—like when Clark comments: "That salvation rests on divine initiative and not on the will of man is indicated again in John 15:16, . . . This verse does not explicitly state that Christ's choice is irresistible, but the preceding verses have said so, and the following will say so again."[424] Third, you can quote the text like Boettner, pretend it refers to Unconditional Election, and then discuss salvation like that is what the verse was in reference to.[425] The final argument is to admit the verse has to do with service but simply ignore it and talk about salvation anyway. This is Nettleton's approach: "Since God chooses some individuals to serve Him, surely He chooses to save them first, since His saved ones serve Him. The entire plan is God's—the salvation, the means of salvation and the service which is the result."[426]

Before comparing Scripture with Scripture to arrive at the proper interpretation, another word from the Calvinists is in order. But this time from the Sovereign Grace Baptist, Clyde Everman, who correctly explained:

> I'm convinced that the above Scripture relates not to His choosing them to be children of God, but His workers through His church. God the Father has chosen us to be His children. This is not the work of the office of the Son. The Son, however, in His office, has chosen certain ones to make up His church and I'm convinced that John 15:16 relates to the same. Jesus, in fact, chose them for a specific purpose.[427]

So once again the Calvinists are their own downfall. But what saith the Scripture? In this verse, Jesus Christ was speaking to his disciples. He described them as not only **"chosen"** but **"ordained."** That Judas was included is apparent from other passages:

> **Jesus answered them, Have not I chosen you twelve, and one of you is a devil? (John 6:70).**
>
> **And he goeth up into a mountain, and calleth *unto him* whom he would: and they came unto him.
> And he ordained twelve, that they should be with him, and that he might send them forth to preach (Mark 3:13-14).**

Judas was chosen as one of the twelve, ordained, and called with the other eleven disciples. Was he one of the "elect" chosen and ordained to salvation by a sovereign, eternal decree and called by Irresistible Grace? The end result of reading Unconditional Election into these verses is a sovereignly elected, irresistibly called, ordained *devil* (John 6:70).

The next case of someone being "chosen to salvation" is that of the Apostle Paul:

> **But the Lord said unto him, Go thy way: for he is a chosen vessel unto me, to bear my name before the Gentiles, and kings, and the children of Israel (Acts 9:15).**
>
> **And he said, The God of our Fathers hath chosen thee, that thou shouldest know his will, and see that Just One, and shouldest hear the voice of his mouth (Acts 22:14).**

Custance says of Ananias and Paul: "Only once in Scripture did a man actually know that the unsaved man to whom he was called to minister the Gospel was numbered among God's elect."[428] That Paul was a chosen vessel there is no doubt, but Paul was already saved when he went to Ananias, and he wasn't chosen to salvation. Paul was chosen to bear the Lord's name (Acts 9:15), to know God's will (Acts 22:14), to see Christ and hear his voice (Acts 22:14), to be a minister and a witness (Acts 26:16), and to open the eyes of the Gentiles and turn them to God (Acts 26:18). Once again the Calvinists have failed to merely read the passages. However, there is one exception. Buswell, whom we have heard from before, says regarding the choosing of Paul: "There can be no doubt that in this context God used the word with reference to a specific function which the great Apostle was to perform."[429]

The reason a Calvinist envisions Paul as sovereignly elected before the foundation of the world is because he reads Unconditional Election and Irresistible Grace into Paul's testimony in Galatians:

> But it pleased God, who separated me from my mother's womb, and called me by his grace,
> To reveal his Son in me, that I might preach him among the heathen; immediately I conferred not with flesh and blood (Gal. 1:15-16).

Paul does not hesitate to regard himself like prophets in times past (Jud. 16:17; Jer. 1:5; Luke 1:15). The case of Jeremiah is also used to build a case for Unconditional Election, but as the Calvinist Storms explains, his election was not to "salvation and life" but to "office and service."[430] But rather than upholding Unconditional Election, this passage rather overthrows it, for election is supposed to be eternal. **"Separated me from my mother's womb"** could never have taken place before Genesis 1:1—ask Paul's mother. Paul was also separated on another occasion: **"As they ministered to the Lord, and fasted, the Holy Ghost said, Separate me Barnabas and Saul for the work whereunto I have called them"** (Acts 13:2). The Lord Jesus Christ was revealed in Paul *after* he was saved, not when God overcame his will with Irresistible Grace because of Unconditional Election. Paul classified himself as the chief of sinners (1 Tim. 1:15), not as an example of someone who had an eternal union with Christ. And besides, to compare the conversion of Paul with that of any Christian is rather ridiculous considering that the Lord appeared to him **"as one born out of due time"** (1 Cor. 15:8).

The next verse containing a form of the word *choose* that is used as a proof text for Unconditional Election is in 1 Peter:

> But ye are a chosen generation, a royal priesthood, an holy nation, a peculiar people; that ye should shew forth the praises of him who hath called you out of darkness into his marvellous light (1 Pet. 2:9).

Because it directly mentions Christians as being **"chosen,"** this verse is also listed with a group of other Scriptures as a proof text for Unconditional Election.[431] The connection of this verse with election will be dealt with under that subject. However, it should be noted that nothing was said about when the choosing took place, why it took place, or what it was for. It is also clear that individuals are not even the subject: **"chosen generation, a royal priesthood, an holy nation, a peculiar people."** A group of people is in view. This is even acknowledged by the Calvinist Storms, who correctly says that the church as a collective body is in view and not individuals.[432]

Before getting to the main proof texts for Unconditional Election that contain a form of the word *choose,* there is one occurrence of the word *choose* in each Testament which demonstrates conclusively the bogus nature of Unconditional Election as maintained by all Calvinists:

> **Blessed *is the man whom* thou choosest, and causest to approach *unto thee, that* he may dwell in thy courts: we shall be satisfied with the goodness of thy house, *even* of thy holy temple (Psa. 65:4).**

> **Hearken, my beloved brethren, Hath not God chosen the poor of this world rich in faith, and heirs of the kingdom which he hath promised to them that love him? (Jam. 2:5).**

The verse in the Psalms is also used to teach Irresistible Grace, and will be looked at again in that chapter. The last half of the verse is never quoted. Reference is simply made to the first half like it asserts Unconditional Election.[433] Berkouwer refers to the whole Psalm as one "on the election of God."[434] For an example of the incredible way this verse is often used to prove Unconditional Election, notice how a Sovereign Grace Baptist handles it: "'Blessed is the man whom thou choosest (election) and *causest* to approach unto thee' (irresistible grace), Psalm 65:4."[435] The verse, however, speaks of God's courts, God's house, and God's temple. The time of the choosing is not mentioned. New Testament salvation is not even remotely connected with the verse, the Psalm, nor the Psalm before or after it. The verse in the New Testament is likewise treated. It is described by Calvinists as "salvific" in nature,[436] adding further to the mass of TULIP terminology. It is incredulous that Calvinists would appeal to this verse as a proof text for Unconditional Election, but even some Baptists do so.[437] But consider the implications. Is every welfare recipient in Detroit, Chicago, and St. Louis one of the "elect"? Are all the food stamp recipients in Newark, Philadelphia, and New York "chosen to salvation"? Obviously not, but the use of these verses shows the lengths that Calvinists go to in order to prove that Unconditional Election is a Bible doctrine and not part of the philosophical speculations and theological implications of Calvinism.

The last two verses to be considered are used by Calvinists to prove Unconditional Election because they each contain the word *chosen:*

> **According as he hath chosen us in him before the foundation of the world, that we should be holy and without blame before him in love (Eph. 1:4).**
>
> **But we are bound to give thanks alway to God for you, brethren beloved of the Lord, because God hath from the beginning chosen you to salvation through sanctification of the Spirit and belief of the truth (2 Thes. 2:13).**

However, these two particular verses are not only the main proof texts for Unconditional Election that contain a form of the word *choose,* they are part of that small group of paramount Calvinistic proof texts for Calvinism. But since the verse in Ephesians is used more often, and has a lot of theological baggage connected with it, the verse in 2 Thessalonians will be considered first.

Regarding the phrase **"God hath from the beginning chosen you to salvation through sanctification of the Spirit and belief of the truth,"** Clark comments: "Salvation was the purpose of God's appointment and for this purpose he chose us. How could anyone resist and nullify what God did 'from the beginning'?"[438] Although the word does not occur in the verse, Pink sees predestination and reminds us that "instead of shrinking back in horror from the doctrine of predestination, the believer, when he sees this blessed truth as it is unfolded in the Word, discovers a ground for gratitude and thanksgiving such as nothing else affords."[439] But what of the "non-elect"? Such a doctrine is a "horrible decree" if one is numbered among the "reprobate." It then becomes a ground for **"cursing and bitterness"** (Rom. 3:14). Palmer connects the text with another Calvinistic proof text in Ephesians and says that "God chose them from the beginning; that is, from before the foundation of the world (Eph. 1:4)—from eternity."[440] Some non-Calvinists attempt to alter the text in hopes of silencing the Calvinists.[441]

That the Thessalonians were chosen **"from the beginning"**

there is no doubt. The question, however, as recognized by the Calvinists themselves, is: "from the beginning of what?"[442] Leon Morris, attempting to placate those who question that Paul uses this phrase in the sense of "from before the foundation of the world," says: "That this is an unusual expression in Pauline writings for 'from the beginning of time' is not significant."[443] But to the contrary, it is very significant, for the phrase "from the beginning" is never a reference to eternity past except when it refers to the Lord Jesus Christ (1 John 1:1, 2:13, 14). Sometimes the beginning of the created world is meant (Mark 13:19; Acts 15:18; Eph. 3:9; 2 Pet. 3:4). The majority of the time "from the beginning" is undefined yet easily determined from the context. The Devil **"was a murder from the beginning"** (John 8:44). He **"sinneth from the beginning"** (1 John 3:8). "From the beginning" can refer to Adam and Eve (Mat. 19:8). It often times has reference to the beginning of Jesus' public ministry (Luke 1:1-2; John 6:64, 8:25, 15:27). What did Peter mean when he **"rehearsed *the matter* from the beginning"** (Acts 11:4)? Paul said about the Jews: **"Which knew me from the beginning"** (Acts 26:5)? When did the disciples hear the commandment which they had **"from the beginning"** (1 John 2:7, 3:11; 2 John 5, 6)? What the Calvinists have done is to transport **"from the beginning"** back "before the foundation of the world" in order to line up this verse with their theology.

The Scriptures are self-interpreting, and, with the aid of a map, perfectly clear. Notice when **"from the beginning"** is defined as:

> **Now ye Philippians know also, that in the beginning of the gospel, when I departed from Macedonia, no church communicated with me as concerning giving and receiving, but ye only.**
> **For even in Thessalonica ye sent once and again unto my necessity (Phil. 4:15-16).**

While at Troas (located in the northwest corner of modern Turkey) Paul had a vision:

> **And a vision appeared to Paul in the night; There stood a man of Macedonia, and prayed him, saying, Come over into Macedonia, and help us.**
> **And after he had seen the vision, immediately we endeavoured to go into Macedonia, assuredly gathering that the**

Lord had called us for to preach the gospel unto them (Acts 16:9-10).

Paul left Troas and headed west to Samothracia and Neapolis (Acts 16:11). He then settled in Philippi (Acts 16:12). Here he had his first convert in Europe, Lydia (Acts 16:14). After the conversion of the Philippian jailer (Acts 16:30-34), Paul departed from Philippi and, going through Amphipolis and Apollonia, went to Thessalonica (Acts 17:1) and then to Berea (Acts 17:10). As any Calvinist could see by looking at the maps in the back of his Bible, these cities are all in Macedonia. Paul then travelled to Athens, which is in Greece (Acts 17:15). He defines the **"beginning of the gospel"** as when he **"departed from Macedonia"** (Phil. 4:15). Now, this does not mean when Paul left Macedonia for Greece, for we are told that **"even in Thessalonica ye sent once and again unto my necessity"** (Phil. 4:16). Thessalonica is still in Macedonia. Paul is saying that the **"beginning of the gospel"** was when he left Philippi to begin his departure from Macedonia. Philippi was **"the chief city of that part of Macedonia"** (Acts 16:12). The Philippians not only helped Paul when he was in Thessalonica (1 Thes. 2:9; 2 Thes. 3:8), but when he was in Corinth (2 Cor. 11:9), and when he was in Rome (Phil. 4:18). Macedonia is not a city, it is a province. Thus, Silas and Timotheus, who were in Berea (Acts 17:14), were said to **"come from Macedonia"** (Acts 18:5). The Thessalonians were chosen **"from the beginning"** (2 Thes. 2:13) to get the Gospel preached to them (Acts 16:10). Paul often referred to the Gospel coming to them (1 Thes. 1:5, 2:1-2; 2 Thes. 2:14).

It should also be noted that the **"salvation"** of the Thessalonians was **"through sanctification of the Spirit and belief of the truth,"** not by a sovereign, eternal decree. This is in direct contrast to those mentioned in the previous verse: **"That they all might be damned who believed not the truth, but had pleasure in unrighteousness"** (1 Thes. 2:12). The conditions for the salvation of the Thessalonians are stated in similar terms elsewhere: **"Elect according to the foreknowledge of God the Father, through sanctification of the Spirit, unto obedience and sprinkling of the blood of Jesus Christ: Grace unto you, and peace, be multiplied"** (1 Pet. 1:2). Paul rejoiced that the Thessalonians believed, not that they were predestinated by an eternal decree: **"For this cause also thank we God without ceasing, because** when ye received the word of God which ye heard of us, ye received *it* not as the word of men, but as it is in truth, the word of God, which effectually worketh also in you that believe" (1 Thes. 2:13).

The twin sister of 2 Thessalonians 2:13 is in Ephesians: **"According as he hath chosen us in him before the foundation of the world, that we should be holy and without blame before him in love"** (Eph. 1:4). The implications are obvious, but for the typical Calvinist viewpoint, we cite a Sovereign Grace Baptist:

> The Bible states in Ephesians 1:4 that we (Christians and those yet to be saved) were chosen in Him (elected in Christ) before the foundation of the world, that we should be holy (through Christ's imputed righteousness and of course in the rapture of the glorified body) and without blame (not one sin laid to our charge). We will stand before Him in love.[444]

This text is the epitome of all the "choose" verses used to teach Unconditional Election. Gill terms it "a strong proof of the doctrine of an eternal, personal, and unconditional election of men to grace and glory."[445] Storms holds that "next to Romans 9, Paul's comments in Ephesians 1 are generally regarded as the most important information we have about eternal election."[446] Cockrell believes that "perhaps no verse in the New Testament is shunned and hated more than my text. The carnal mind cannot bring itself to receive the plain teaching of this verse about the eternal, unconditional election of a people in Christ before the foundation of the world."[447]

There are a number of problems with using this verse to teach "an eternal, personal, and unconditional election of men." To begin with, the word *election* not only does not occur in the verse, it is not to be found in the entire Book of Ephesians. This is unconscionable since this is supposed to be one of the premier proof texts for Unconditional Election. Secondly, the choosing is said to be **"that we should be holy and without blame,"** not that we should be "in Christ" or saved. Perhaps this is why Calvinists continually quote only the first half of the verse. Third, when the second half of the verse is commented on, it is usually thrust into the future since Christians are not presently **"holy and without blame."** Calvinists are not united on the interpretation of this verse. In fact, judging from what they have written on the passage, it sometimes seems as though there is no *standard* Calvinist interpretation of this verse.

Regarding the expression **"in him,"** Storms acknowledges:

> It must be admitted that the clause *in Christ* is ambiguous. By itself, it says neither that we are elect because we are in Christ nor that we are elect in order that we shall be in Christ. Contrary to what some Calvinists would say, it is unlikely that Paul means we were chosen "to be" in Christ, insofar as the latter part of the verse declares that we were chosen "to be" holy and blameless.[448]

Calvinists can't seem to agree on just how to interpret this phrase:

> We are chosen 'in Christ' in the sense that this Son to whom the Father has given us is he through whom this election to life is made ours in experience.[449]

> It is, therefore, in Christ, *i.e.*, as united to him in the covenant of redemption, that the people of God are elected to eternal life and to all the blessings therewith connected.[450]

> When the text says 'he chose us in him' it probably means that God chose that the church would experience salvation 'through Jesus Christ.' He is the agent and person through whom the electing work of God would come to fruition.[451]

Regarding the phrase **"holy and without blame,"** Pink admits that "there has been much difference of opinion among the commentators as to whether this refers to that imperfect holiness of grace which we have in this world, or to that perfect holiness of glory which will be ours in the world to come."[452] And what is his preference? "Personally, we believe that both are included, but that the latter is chiefly intended."[453] After stating that "these two words have been the cause of considerable debate," Storms concludes: "All this persuades me that Paul is referring to that absolutely sinless, holy, and blameless condition in which we shall be presented to God at the second coming of our Savior."[454] But whatever else the verses teaches, and however they may disagree about the details, Calvinists are united in claiming this as a proof text for Unconditional Election.

The proper interpretation of the verse can be found by noting the **"according as"** at the beginning of the verse which connects it with the previous one:

> **Blessed *be* the God and Father of our Lord Jesus Christ, who hath blessed us with all spiritual blessings in heavenly *places* in Christ:**
> **According as he hath chosen us in him before the foundation of the world, that we should be holy and without blame before him in love (Eph. 1:3-4).**

The choosing had nothing to do with salvation but rather concerned our position in Christ. This is confirmed by reading one additional verse that wasn't on the TULIP circuit: **"And hath raised *us* up together, and made *us* sit together in heavenly *places* in Christ"** (Eph. 2:6). This is not future and neither can it be figurative, for the same thing is said of Jesus Christ: **"Which he wrought in Christ, when he raised him from the dead, and set *him* at his own right hand in the heavenly *places*"** (Eph. 1:20). As far as God is concerned, we are seated **"before him,"** holy, without blame, and blessed with all spiritual blessings. This is because we are part of Jesus Christ (1 Cor. 6:17; Eph. 5:30). Once a man gets "in Christ" he gets in on the choosing. God chose that whoever was in his Son would be **"blessed us with all spiritual blessings in heavenly *places*"** and **"holy and without blame before him in love."** The error of the Calvinists was in assuming the verse made mention of getting "in Christ."

The key to understanding the phrase **"in him"** is in another verse in the Pauline Epistles: **"Who hath saved us, and called *us* with an holy calling, not according to our works, but according to his own purpose and grace, which was given us in Christ Jesus before the world began"** (2 Tim. 1:9). This verse is usually listed with a group of others used as proof texts for Unconditional Election.[455] Some assorted Calvinists have commented:

> This giving of grace which he mentions is certainly meant to refer to the predestination by which we are adopted as God's children. I wanted to remind my readers of this, for often God is said to give us this grace only at the time when it begins to work effectively in us. But here Paul is dealing with what God determined with Himself from the beginning, so that then He gave it to people who were not yet born quite apart from any

consideration of merit.[456]

Paul declared clearly that the elect had been given grace before they ever existed.[457]

There was never a time that the regenerated person was not in a state of grace, because grace was given him in Christ eternally.[458]

Now, grace was not *physically* given to any man **"before the world began"** for the simple reason that there were no men around to give it to. But grace was **"given us in Christ Jesus."** God deposited grace in Christ before the world began, but it was only given to us when we got "in Christ." This grace **"is now made manifest by the appearing of our Saviour Jesus Christ"** (2 Tim. 1:10).

These two passages also bring to light an even greater error of the Calvinists. What some Calvinists have done is to take the phrases **"in him"** (Eph. 1:4) and **"in Christ Jesus"** (2 Tim. 1:9) and unite them with **"before the foundation of the world"** (Eph. 1:4) and **"before the world began"** (2 Tim. 1:9). The result of this union is the teaching that the "elect" were "in Christ" before the foundation of the world. Nothing is being overstated, this is exactly what some Calvinists believe. That this was not a *potential* but an *actual* union is made clear by Pink and Cockrell:

There was a mystical and eternal union subsisting between Christ and the Church, which formed the basis of that vital union which is effected by the Holy Spirit during a time state, the latter *making manifest* the former, the former being the ground upon which the latter is effected.[459]

The elect have a secret being in Christ and a union in Him from eternity (II Tim. 1:9). There is a federal union with Christ which is antecedent to all actual union and is the source of it because the elect are in Christ as their covenant Head.[460]

The one writer who, according to Pink, "appears to have been blest with a clearer insight into this great mystery," was the Particular Baptist John Gill.[461] Gill claimed that "there must be first a vital union to Christ, before there can be any believing in him."[462] His proof texts? Ephesians 1:3-4 and 2 Timothy 1:9.[463] The teaching of the "eternal union" of the "elect" with Christ is also based on a verse in Jeremiah: **"The LORD hath appeared of old unto me,** *saying,* **Yea, I have loved thee with an everlasting love: therefore with lovingkindness have I drawn thee"** (Jer. 31:3).[464] Since this verse is primarily used by the Calvinists to prove the validity of Irresistible Grace, it will be examined further in that chapter.

The consequence of this "eternal union" is that God eternally loved the "elect": "Beloved, there has never been a time that God has not loved those He gave to the Son."[465] But the end result of an "eternal union" and an "eternal love" is an "unregenerate, elect sheep" that is considered a child of God: "The elect were not aware that they were the elect until the Holy Spirit made the gospel real to them, for they were always the children of God."[466] But if the "elect" were always the children of God, could they have ever been children of the devil? This question was answered by a panel of Sovereign Grace Baptists:

> The unregenerate elect are lost sheep, not goats. The manifestation of their inherited fallen nature may be as bad as any of the non-elect, and they certainly are deserving of God's wrath; but they are not, were not, children of the devil.[467]

> I believe that a good understanding of God's eternal purpose concerning His elect will teach us that they have always been children of God and never been the children of the devil.[468]

> The elect of God have always been the children of God. . . . There is no way that the elect have ever been the children of Satan.[469]

But is this how the "elect" are described in the Bible?

> **And you *hath he quickened,* who were dead in trespasses and sins:**
> **Wherein in time past ye walked according to the course of this world, according to the prince of the power of the air, the spirit that now worketh in the children of disobedience:**
> **Among whom also we all had our conversation in times past in the lusts of our flesh, fulfilling the desires of the flesh and of the mind; and were by nature the children of wrath, even as others (Eph. 2:1-3).**

> That at that time ye were without Christ, being aliens from the commonwealth of Israel, and strangers from the covenants of promise, having no hope, and without God in the world (Eph. 2:12).

According to these passages, the "elect" were **"children of wrath"** (Eph. 2:3) **"without God"** (Eph. 2:12), not children of God.

But not only do Calvinists claim that the "elect" were "in Christ" before the foundation of the world, they also maintain that the "elect" were in Christ at the cross.[470] So what is the problem? The problem is a momentous event that took place between "before the foundation of the world" and the cross: the fall of Adam. This means that before the "elect" got **"in Adam"** (1 Cor. 15:22), they had a relationship with Christ:

> God's people had a super-creation and spiritual union with Christ before ever they had creature and natural union with Adam; that they were blessed with all spiritual blessings in the heavenlies in Christ (Eph. 1:3), before they fell in Adam and became subject to all the evils of the curse.[471]

> Every passage which makes mention of 'redemption' presupposes eternal election. Because 'redemption' implies a previous possession: it is Christ *buying back* and delivering those who were God's at the beginning.[472]

Consider the implications of this teaching: (1) The "elect" were "in Christ" before the foundation of the world. (2) The "elect" fell out of Christ and became lost "in Adam." (3) The "elect" got back "in Christ" at the cross. (4) The "elect" fell out of Christ again so they could be born "in sin." (5) The "elect" got back "in Christ" when God applied Irresistible Grace to them and they got saved. But if the "elect" fell out of Christ even once, what is to prevent them from falling again?

If this "oversimplification" be objected to, then the only other alternative is even more repugnant:

> Though, while all fell in Adam, yet all did not fall alike. The non-elect fell so as to be damned, they being left to perish in their sins, because they had no relation to Christ—He was not related to them as the Mediator of union with God. The non-elect had their all in Adam, their spiritual head. But the

> elect had all spiritual blessing bestowed upon them in Christ, their gracious and glorious Head (Eph. 1:3). They could not lose these.[473]

> The elect were "children" *from* all eternity and decreed to be so *unto* all eternity. They did not lose their sonship by the fall, neither by any corruption derived from that fall in their nature. "Children" they continued, though *sinful* children, and as such justly exposed to wrath. Nevertheless, this relationship could not be revoked by any after-acts in time: united to Christ from all eternity, they were always one with Him.[474]

So the Fall didn't affect the "elect." It was only the means of reprobating the "non-elect." Or if one is a supralapsarian, it is what God used to make it look like the "reprobate" deserved their fate. This scenario of a fall that really wasn't a fall enables Pink to claim that one can be dead "in sin" and yet be "in Christ" at the same time![475] Morey maintains that "while the elect sinner is 'in Christ' objectively from eternity, Christ is not 'in Him' subjectively until personal salvation. Thus the unregenerate elect sinner is both 'in' and 'out' of Christ at the same time."[476] So which is it? He loves me or he loves me not?

When mention is made of the pride and arrogance that Calvinists sometimes manifest because they consider themselves of the "elect," no overstatement is being made. This attitude is exemplified in the comments of the former editor of *The Baptist Examiner:*

> There was a time when, so far as I knew, I was not going to heaven; but was actually on my way to hell. In actuality, not one of the elect has ever for a moment been in real danger of going to hell. No man can truly believe in sovereign grace and question this statement. God's elect were, from eternity, predestinated to be conformed to the image of Jesus Christ. They were ordained to eternal life. They were chosen to be saved and predestinated unto the adoption of children. God looked on them as His dear children. He smiled upon them in electing love. In reality, they were as safe while living in sin and rebellion against God as they are now.[477]

Some Calvinists go so far as to teach that the "elect" were justified before the foundation of the world. A notable exponent of this teaching was John Brine:

> The elect were blest with all spiritual blessings in Christ before the foundation of the world: and therefore with Justification, for that is a spiritual blessing. "This grace by which we are justified, was given us in Christ from eternity, because from eternity God loved us in Christ, and made us accepted in him."[478]

In more recent times, Herman Hoeksema contended that "before God His people are justified from eternity; and He beholds them forever as perfectly righteous in Christ, and as such He blesses them."[479] But what is this but a complete overthrow of the Gospel? If the "elect" have from all eternity been justified children of God then why must they be regenerated and believe on Christ? Can an "eternally justified, elect" child of God go to hell? How could he even be said to be lost?

The result of the Fall is clear: it affected all men equally:

> **Wherefore, as by one man sin entered into the world, and death by sin; and so death passed upon all men, for that all have sinned (Rom. 5:12).**
>
> **For as in Adam all die, even so in Christ shall all be made alive (1 Cor. 15:22).**

The Bible also makes it perfectly clear that no one was ever "in Christ" until his salvation: **"Salute Andronicus and Junia, my kinsmen, and my fellowprisoners, who are of note among the apostles, who also were in Christ before me"** (Rom. 16:7). In Calvinism the "elect" are all put in Christ at the same time; in the Bible no one is put in Christ until he is saved.

Elected to Salvation

One would certainly think that if "there are a number of Scripture passages which support the Calvinist doctrine of divine election,"[480] then Bible verses which contain a form of the word *election* ought to be the strongest in support of this doctrine. We have examined a number of Calvinist proof texts for Unconditional Election, but none of them contained any form of this word. Yet, Calvinists insist that "it is hardly a matter of dispute that this is a very clear teaching of many passages in Scripture."[481] Engelsma claims that "election has a prominent place in the Gospel preached by the apostles."[482] Kober maintains that "no one was a stronger believe in election than the Apostle Paul."[483] But if what these Calvinists are saying is true, and if Unconditional Election is really the "sine qua non" of Calvinism,[484] then an appeal to those verses in the Scripture that contain a form of the word *election* should turn up some trace of the Calvinists' "election to salvation" doctrine if it is indeed scriptural.

As acknowledged by Calvinists, there are several things in the Bible that election refers to.[485] It is also a fundamental concept, with two main ideas, as H. H. Rowley (1890-1969) noted: "To the writers of the Old Testament Israel is the chosen people of God; to the writers of the New Testament the Church is the heir of the divine election."[486] But before examining each of these ideas, two other cases of election must be examined.

The first and foremost case of election is that of Jesus Christ. Obviously Jesus Christ did not need to be elected to salvation. No Calvinist would ever think of Jesus Christ being "elect" in the sense of God choosing to apply Irresistible Grace to him so he could be saved. When the word *elect* is applied to Christ its primary emphasis is not on selection but the valuation and worth of the subject described. This is confirmed by an infallible rule: comparing Scripture with Scripture. The first example is Matthew quoting a prophecy of Isaiah:

> **Behold my servant, whom I uphold; mine elect, *in whom* my soul delighteth; I have put my spirit upon him: he shall bring forth judgment to the Gentiles (Isa. 42:1).**

> **Behold my servant, whom I have chosen; my beloved, in whom my soul is well pleased: I will put my spirit upon him, and he shall shew judgment to the Gentiles (Mat. 12:18).**

The second is Peter, but this time doing just the opposite:

> **Therefore thus saith the Lord GOD, Behold, I lay in Zion for a foundation a stone, a tried stone, a precious corner *stone*, a sure foundation; he that believeth shall not make haste (Isa. 28:16).**

> **Wherefore also it is contained in the scripture, Behold, I lay in Sion a chief corner stone, elect, precious: and he that believeth on him shall not be confounded (1 Pet. 2:6).**

To this "Christological election"[487] Calvinists would agree.

The word *elect* is also once applied to the angels: **"I charge *thee* before God, and the Lord Jesus Christ, and the elect angels, that thou observe these things without preferring one before another, doing nothing by partiality"** (1 Tim. 5:21). Pink calls this a "most remarkable and little known example of divine election."[488] Like the election of Jesus Christ, this has nothing to do with salvation nor an eternal decree, for neither Christ nor the angels as a group fell. Yet here is the scenario Pink construes:

> If then, there are "elect angels" there must necessarily be non-elect, for there cannot be the one without the other. God, then, in the past made a selection among the hosts of heaven, choosing some to be vessels of honor and others to be vessels of dishonor. Those whom He chose unto His favor, stood steadfast, remained in subjection to His will. The rest fell when Satan revolted, for upon his apostasy he dragged down with himself one third of the angels (Rev. 12:4). Concerning them we read, "God spared not the angels that sinned, but cast them down to hell, and delivered them into chains of darkness" (II Peter 2:4). But those of them who belong to the election of grace are "the holy angels": holy as the consequence of their election, and not elected because they were holy, for election antedated their creation.[489]

It is to be remembered that, in the technical nuances of the Calvinistic system, the part of God's sovereign, eternal decree that concerns the eternal destinies of men and angels is termed predestination. This predestination is further divided into two parts: election and reprobation. Thus, what is true of the election and reprobation of men is also true of angels. This is the teaching of the Westminster Confession of Faith:

> By the decree of God, for the manifestation of his glory, some men and angels are predestinated unto everlasting life; and others foreordained to everlasting death.[490]

Therefore, Boettner adds: "Election extends not only to men but also and equally to the angels since they also are a part of God's creation and are under His government. Some of these are holy and happy, others are sinful and miserable. The same reasons which lead us to believe in a predestination of men also lead us to believe in a predestination of angels."[491] Gill even has these "non-elect" angels appearing before the judgment seat of Christ.[492]

There are several things wrong with the interpretation of Pink, Boettner, Gill, the Westminster Confession, and that of any Calvinists who go along with them. First of all, Revelation 12:4 takes place in the future, not before Genesis 1:1. Pink has been reading John Milton (1608-1674) instead of the Holy Bible. The second problem concerns the "reprobation" of the "non-elect" angels, and is recognized by Gill: "They could not be considered as fallen creatures, or in the corrupt mass, since the elect angels never did fall."[493] Therefore, since the angels never fell, no amount of theological hairsplitting about preterition and condemnation can explain away the positive reprobation of the "non-elect" angels. Since all the angels never fell, God had to have arbitrarily decreed the damnation of the "non-elect" angels (supralapsarianism) without considering their sin or fall (infralapsarianism). It had to be the **"counsel of his own will"** (Eph. 1:11) that some angels be created so they could be damned. And third, no angel was ever said to be elected before the foundation of the world by a sovereign, eternal decree. Some angels have already fallen (Gen. 6:2), and are captive in chains, in the darkness of hell, to be judged at a later day (2 Pet. 2:4; Jude 6) by their replacements (1 Cor. 6:3), the sons of God by faith (1 John 3:2). God "chose" the angels who didn't fall, hence they are denominated as **"elect angels."** The use of the term *elect* as applied to angels parallels that of Christ. The significance is not of selection but of appraisal or assessment. This is why they are also denominated as **"holy angels"** (Mat. 25:31).

The next thing that election refers to has been mentioned several times already—the election of the nation of Israel. Israel is said to be God's elect (Isa. 45:4, 65:9, 22). God chose Israel to be a peculiar people above the other nations (Deu. 14:2). It was a pure case of Unconditional Election. But individuals were only elect according to their relationship to the nation. God did not choose each individual Jew to be one of the elect. They were either born into it by being a descendant of Jacob or became a proselyte like Ruth, who chose of her own free will to be one of the "elect" (Ruth

1:16). The salvation and damnation of individuals was not the purpose of their election. We saw in Romans 9 that many members of the nation of Israel were "reprobate." Thus, there are five principles that can be established about the election of Israel:

1. Individuals are elect according to their relationship to the elect one
2. God did not choose each individual
3. The elect are elect because of their birth
4. Their election had nothing to do with salvation
5. Their election was not by a sovereign, eternal decree

This corporate election of Israel as a nation is also affirmed in the New Testament. Contrary to all amillennial and postmillennial Calvinists, God is not through with his elect nation (Rom. 11:25-27). It is the failure to recognize that Israel is still called the "elect" in the New Testament that is the cause for much misinterpretation of Scripture by Calvinists and non-Calvinists alike.

The greatest example of this misinterpretation is the Olivet discourse:

And except those days should be shortened, there should no flesh be saved: but for the elect's sake those days shall be shortened (Mat. 24:22).

For there shall arise false Christ's, and false prophets, and shall shew great signs and wonders; insomuch that, if *it were possible*, they shall deceive the very elect (Mat. 24:24).

And he shall send his angels with a great sound of a trumpet, and they shall gather together his elect from the four winds, from one end of heaven to the other (Mat. 24:31).

The context here obviously concerns a future tribulation period (Mat. 24:21, 29)—a future period of time called **"the time of Jacob's trouble"** (Jer. 30:7). Those addressed are not "elect sinners" waiting to be saved by Irresistible Grace, but Jewish saints. The context in Matthew 24:13 has nothing to do—directly or indirectly—with the salvation of anyone in the Church age under grace. And regarding Matthew 24, the premillennial Calvinist

Chafer correctly points out: "Here, as throughout this entire Olivet discourse, the 'elect' is Israel."[494]

Another tragic exegesis concerning Israel as an elect nation being mistaken for the Church is doubly twisted: **"Therefore I endure all things for the elect's sakes, that they may also obtain the salvation which is in Christ Jesus with eternal glory"** (2 Tim. 2:10). Pink comments: "That illustrates the principle: the apostle knew that in his evangelical labors he was being employed in executing God's purpose in carrying the message of salvation to His people. To that very end was the apostle sustained by divine providence and directed by the Spirit of the Lord."[495] And who are the "His people" that Pink refers to? Calvinists make the elect in this passage "God's people" who were elected before the foundation of the world. Pink, after including this verse with some others as proof texts for Unconditional Election, says that "many other passages might be quoted, but these are sufficient to clearly demonstrate that God has an elect people. God Himself says He has, who will dare say He has not!"[496] But if the "elect" were elected before the foundation of the world by an unconditional, efficacious, sovereign, eternal decree then they could never *not* obtain salvation whether Paul preached or not. To believe that Paul strove (Rom. 15:20) and labored in the Gospel (Phil. 4:3), enduring (2 Tim. 2:10) beatings, stonings, imprisonments, shipwreck, perils, pain, hunger and cold (2 Cor. 11:23-27) for the sake of the "elect" who would be saved anyway is the most preposterous excuse ever offered in support of Unconditional Election. Paul longed to see his fellow Jews saved (Rom. 9:1-3, 10:1-3, 11:12-14), but not by Unconditional Election. And besides the context speaking of a millennial reign (2 Tim. 2:12), the verse in question mentioned not just salvation, but salvation **"with eternal glory."**

There is also one ambiguous occurrence of Israel as God's elect: **"And shall not God avenge his own elect, which cry day and night unto him, though he bear long with them?"** (Luke 18:7). Who these elect are and how, why, and when they were "elected" is not specifically mentioned. Historically, God's **"own elect"** would be the Jews, likewise in the Gospels. Spiritually speaking, this text could apply to anyone that was saved in any period of time. Doctrinally however, there could be some reference to the Tribulation (Rev. 6:9-10). But regardless, the verse had to do with prayer (Luke 18:1), not a sovereign, eternal decree.

There are four more instances, all in Romans, of the election of Israel in the New Testament, but this time, since they for the most part concern only *part* of Israel, the Calvinist sees in them definite proof for Unconditional Election. The first verse in question has shown up before:

> (For *the children* being not yet born, neither having done any good or evil, that the purpose of God according to election might stand, not of works, but of him that calleth;) (Rom. 9:11).

We have already seen in our study of reprobation that Paul's argument about there being an Israel within Israel (Rom. 9:6) was illustrated by the descendants of Isaac and Jacob being reckoned as the children of the covenant promise to the exclusion of all other descendants of Abraham. The **"purpose of God according to election,"** as even admitted by Calvinists like Buswell, had nothing to do with individual salvation or reprobation at all. It concerned the Messianic line of Abraham–Isaac–Jacob–Jesus Christ. It was an election of national preference or theocratic privilege. The next verse, since it concerns the whole of Israel, is not much of a problem:

> As concerning the gospel, *they are* enemies for your sakes: but as touching the election, *they are* beloved for the fathers' sakes (Rom. 11:28).

That this refers to the whole of Israel and has nothing to do with salvation is acknowledged by Calvinists, including Calvin.[497]

The other two examples are also in Romans:

> Even so then at this present time also there is a remnant according to the election of grace (Rom. 11:5).

> What then? Israel hath not obtained that which he seeketh for; but the election hath obtained it, and the rest were blinded (Rom. 11:7).

Since both of these verses concern only a portion of Israel, the Calvinists read their doctrine of Unconditional Election into them more so than usual. Regarding the **"election"** in the above two verses, John Murray considers "it impossible to think of the election as anything other than the election unto salvation of which the apostle speaks elsewhere in his epistles."[498] So once again we are bogged down in Romans 9–11. We reiterate that the design of Romans 9–11 is God's present plan in dealing with the nation of Israel; a parenthesis where the Jew is considered nationally. The problem of how God could reject those whom he had elected is being considered. The personal election and reprobation of all the individual members of Adam's race is not even remotely under consideration. But supposing for a moment that the Unconditional Election of Jews *is* being discussed in these verses, how does that prove that all saved Gentiles who have ever existed were so elected?

Since Romans 11:5 begins with **"even so,"** we must turn to the preceding verses in the context:

> **I say then, Hath God cast away his people? God forbid. For I also am an Israelite, of the seed of Abraham, *of* the tribe of Benjamin.**
> **God hath not cast away his people which he foreknew. Wot ye not what the scripture saith of Elias? how he maketh intercession to God against Israel, saying,**
> **Lord, they have killed thy prophets, and digged down thine altars; and I am left alone, and they seek my life.**
> **But what saith the answer of God unto him? I have reserved to myself seven thousand men, who have not bowed the knee *to the image* of Baal (Rom. 11:1-4).**

The **"remnant according to the election of grace"** (Rom. 11:5) corresponds to the seven thousand men reserved to God. But once again the Calvinist focuses on the word **"reserved"** like he did in trying to prove reprobation. But why were these men reserved? Was it because of God's decree of Unconditional Election? They were reserved because they hadn't bowed to Baal. The Calvinist theologian Charles Hodge even states: "In Kings, God threatens the general destruction of the people, but promises to reserve seven thousand, who had not gone after false gods."[499] This idea of a remnant was also used by Paul in Romans 9:27, 29. But neither in Romans nor in the passages quoted by Paul from Isaiah (Isa. 1:9, 10:22) is individual salvation in view. As there was a remnant in the days of Elijah, so now there is a remnant. This proves that

"God hath not cast away his people."

Now we can pick up the rest of the context in Romans:

> Even so then at this present time also there is a remnant according to the election of grace.
> And if by grace, then *is it* no more of works: otherwise grace is no more grace. But if *it be* of works, then is it no more grace: otherwise work is no more work.
> What then? Israel hath not obtained that which he seeketh for; but the election hath obtained it, and the rest were blinded (Rom. 11:5-7).

The first thing to be determined is what it was that Israel sought after:

> But Israel, which followed after the law of righteousness, hath not attained to the law of righteousness (Rom. 9:31).

> For they being ignorant of God's righteousness, and going about to establish their own righteousness, have not submitted themselves unto the righteousness of God (Rom. 10:3).

So as John Murray says: "What Israel is represented as seeking for, though not stated in this verse, is the righteousness mentioned in 9:31; 10:3."[500] The next thing to ascertain is why the election obtained this righteousness and the others didn't:

> But to him that worketh not, but believeth on him that justifieth the ungodly, his faith is counted for righteousness (Rom. 4:5).

> Wherefore? Because *they sought it* not by faith, but as it were by the works of the law. For they stumbled at that stumblingstone;
> As it is written, Behold, I lay in Sion a stumblingstone and rock of offence: and whosoever believeth on him shall not be ashamed (Rom. 9:32-33).

> For Christ *is* the end of the law for righteousness to every one that believeth (Rom. 10:4).

Again, Murray concurs.[501]

Paul attributes the failure of Israel to obtain salvation to their rejection of the God appointed means of faith. To be in on the election of the nation is not enough, one must also be a partaker of the "election of grace." **"They which receive abundance of grace and of the gift of righteousness"** (Rom. 5:17) receive it by faith. Only the remnant who sought it by faith participate in the **"election of grace."** The reason being that **"it is of faith, that it might be by grace"** (Rom. 4:16). The remnant obtained salvation because they believed on Jesus Christ, not because they were unconditionally elected to be overcome by Irresistible Grace. The blinding of those who did not partake of the **"election of grace"** (Rom. 11:5) was because they sought it by works. That part of Israel which **"hath not obtained that which he seeketh for"** (Rom. 11:7) did not fail because they were hardened, they were hardened because they failed. Works nullify both faith (Rom. 4:5) and grace (Rom. 11:6). And yet, as pointed out previously, the blindness was national in scope and temporary in nature (Rom. 11:25). "Reprobate" Israel will one day become "elect" Israel.

We now take up the apex of this whole chapter on Unconditional Election. It is the election of the Church that all of the previous material has laid the groundwork for. This subject is of the utmost importance because the Calvinist postulates: "There is only one way that leads to salvation and that is the way of God's election."[502] One Calvinist advises us "not to be intimidated by the doctrine of divine election."[503] But upon examination of the New Testament references to the election of the Church, we are confronted with a rather dismal picture of any eternal decree. The verb *elected* occurs just once, the term *election* is used only twice, and the designation *elect* appears only six times. Although they appear in different contexts, these nine occurrences of a form of the word *elect* all have one thing in common: they are never connected with any decree of God—sovereign, eternal, or otherwise.

First is the verb *elected*: **"The *church that is* at Babylon, elected together with you saluteth you; and so doth Marcus my son"** (1 Pet. 5:13). Notice that no individual is under consideration and no mention is made of when, how, or why anyone was elected. So just because the word *elected* is found in the Bible does not mean anyone was elected according to the scheme of Unconditional Election.

Next is the term *election:*

Knowing, brethren beloved, your election of God (1 Thes. 1:4).

Wherefore the rather, brethren, give diligence to make your calling and election sure: for if ye do these things, ye shall never fall (2 Pet. 1:10).

Once again we emphasize that the fact of election is simply being maintained. No eternal decree, no reason given, and no means of election are even intimated at. The reference in 1 Thessalonians probably refers to the aforementioned manner in which the Thessalonians received the Gospel, which we covered in our comments on 2 Thessalonians 2:13. 2 Peter 1:10, although just stating the fact of election, overthrows the TULIP system so bad that it demands further study.

Pink attempts to scare away the opposition by saying it is "sheer blasphemy" if you disagree with his reading Unconditional Election into 2 Peter 1:10.[504] The TULIP destroying nature of the verse is apparent: calling comes before election, giving us TILUP. The reason Pink went into a frenzy is because all his life he taught that "effectual calling is the consequence of election, as it is also the manifestation thereof."[505] As we have seen, verses like 2 Thessalonians 2:13 are worded in such a way that the Calvinist can make a case for Unconditional Election based on the order of some of the key words. But here in 2 Peter 1:10, calling does not follow election, it precedes it. We saw just the opposite in 2 Timothy 1:9 (calling follows salvation) and Jude 1 (calling follows sanctification). Pink claims that the inverted order in 2 Peter 1:10 was because Christian experience was being dealt with and those addressed were believers, but when he runs into an unlimited atonement in 2 Peter 2:1, he contends that the book was written to Jews as he tries to explain away the verse.[506] Calvin takes a different approach: "He mentions *calling* first, though it comes later in sequence. The reason is that election is of greater importance and the proper order of a sentence is to put the most important words at the end."[507] Yet, when listing spiritual gifts in 1 Corinthians, Paul puts tongues last because it was the least important gift. In Acts 2:23, foreknowledge comes after the supposed predestination. And in 1 Thessalonians 2:13, **"belief of the truth"** is put last, after the alleged election. Would a Calvinist claim that man's believing is more important than God's election?

But regardless of "Christian experience" or "proper order," how could anyone **"give diligence"** to make sure a supposedly sovereign, eternal decree? If the decree of election was unconditional, sovereign, and eternal, and it was made by an omnipotent, sovereign God, then no one could possibly do anything to make it sure. That this calling has nothing to do with Irresistible Grace will be seen in the next chapter. Once again, however, it is the Calvinists who contradict the Calvinists. Realizing the anti-Calvinist overtones, Custance makes both the calling and the election relate to service, not salvation.[508]

Then there is the word *elect*. This word is applied to Christians but six times:

> **Who shall lay any thing to the charge of God's elect?** *It is* **God that justifieth (Rom. 8:33).**
>
> **Put on therefore, as the elect of God, holy and beloved, bowels of mercies, kindness, humbleness of mind, meekness, longsuffering (Col. 3:12).**
>
> **Paul, a servant of God, and an apostle of Jesus Christ, according to the faith of God's elect, and the acknowledging of the truth which is after godliness (Tit. 1:1).**
>
> **Elect according to the foreknowledge of God the Father, through sanctification of the Spirit, unto obedience and sprinkling of the blood of Jesus Christ: Grace unto you, and peace be multiplied (1 Pet. 1:2).**
>
> **The elder unto the elect lady and her children, whom I love in the truth; and not I only, but also all they that have known the truth (2 John 1).**
>
> **The children of thy elect sister greet thee. Amen (2 John 13).**

Not one of these verses says that election is a decree of God, that it is eternal, that it is unconditional, or that it results in salvation. The word **"elect"** in the above verses is simply a title for New Testament Christians signifying valuation or worth and appraisal or assessment. Thus, its use parallels the election of Jesus Christ and the angels. Like we saw in Luke 18:7, nothing is said in these verses about how, why, or when anyone came to be called **"elect."** The Calvinist has tried to make everyone think that because the word *elect* was found in various forms a number of times in the Bible that his doctrine of Unconditional Election must be biblical. But from looking at what is said about the **"elect"** in these verses, it is obvious that no one is elect until he is saved. The elect are said to be justified (Rom. 8:33), they are depicted as holy and beloved (Col 3:12), and they have faith (Tit. 1:1). No Calvinist would ever describe an unsaved man in such terms. But that is what they are doing if the "elect" in their system have been "elect" from all eternity.

To build a case for his doctrine using the forms of the word *elect*, the Calvinist must go elsewhere to get his doctrine and then read it back into every text where election is found. The starting place is 1 Peter 1:2, since salvation is mentioned in the same verse as election. But because foreknowledge is mentioned, the verse is then connected with Romans 8:29, 30. And whereas predestination is now introduced, the next "destination" is Ephesians 1:5, since it also contains the word. Seeing that the previous verse in Ephesians describes being chosen and mentions the phrase **"before the foundation of the world,"** 2 Thessalonians 2:13 is then picked up as another stop on the TULIP circuit. For added support, appeal is then made to Romans 9–11 and a few other assorted verses to teach the opposite of election—reprobation. But because it doesn't mention election as taking place before the foundation of the world, 1 Peter 1:2 is avoided by some Calvinists who see the hard time they would have proving Unconditional Election.[509] Buswell, who already contradicted his brethren on Acts 13:48, turns his pen to 1 Peter 1:2 and assails both Arminians who teach that "God's decree of election is based upon foreknown faith" and his fellow Calvinists who have reduced "Peter's phrase to a mere tautology."[510]

Due to the manifold influence of the Calvinists, election among Arminians and other non-Calvinists is also commonly thought to be "unto salvation." Then, to get rid of the Calvinistic implications, it is said to be based on foreknowledge. The Arminian position is found in article one of the Remonstrance where God elects those who "shall believe on this his Son Jesus, and shall persevere in this faith and obedience of faith, through this grace, even to the end." But as Gill recognizes: "I can see no need of their being elected at all; for when they have persevered unto the end, they are immediately in heaven, in the enjoyment of eternal life, and can have no need to be chose to it."[511] The Baptist theologian Henry Clarence Thiessen (1883-1947) states the classic non-Calvinist position: "By election we mean that sovereign act of God in grace whereby He chose in Christ Jesus for salvation all those whom He foreknew would accept him."[512] Unlike the Arminian viewpoint, this interpretation does not ground election on man's perseverance. But it still suffers from the same deficiency, for if God's knowledge is absolute, complete, and certain then anyone whom God knew would be saved needed no decree of election at all. So in reaction to the Calvinists, those who differ have equally blundered. Buswell astutely recognizes the problem:

> These words by Peter cannot be any proper syntactical exegesis be made to indicate that the basis or ground or reason of election is the foreknowledge of God. The preposition employed here, *kata* with the accusative, simply indicates the harmony of the items mentioned—election, and foreknowledge—and this text has nothing to say one way or the other as to the question whether election depends upon foreknowledge or whether foreknowledge depends upon election. The text simply says that the two are harmonious and parallel.[513]

This is easily confirmed by examining other scriptural uses of the term (cf. Mark 7:5; Eph. 2:2; Rom. 2:2). But even though he criticizes the non-Calvinist position, Buswell equally disdains the Calvinist position as well.

Calvinists who appeal to 1 Peter 1:2 as a proof text for Unconditional Election normally make foreknowledge into foreordination exactly like we will see the Calvinists do in Romans 8:29. Pink maintains that the foreknowledge here is not God's "prescience of all things, but signifies that the saints were all eternally present in Christ before the mind of God" because they were "chosen by Him as the special objects of His approbation and love."[514] Calvin comments that "God knew before the world was created those whom he had elected for salvation."[515] Warfield refers to this as "the elective foreknowledge of God."[516] This grammatical licentiousness will be covered in more detail when we get to Romans 8:29. For now, however, the word of a Calvinist will suffice. Once again Buswell aptly explains:

Aside from the point of syntax, that *kata* with the accusative does not connect identity, but implies two distinct parallel items, I must object to a subtle assumption which usually accompanies the cliche which I am describing. It is frequently held that God's knowledge is a subordinate attribute, dependent upon His will. . . . It is sometimes even argued that God is incapable of literal foreknowledge or prescience in the sense of cognitive apprehension of future events. Some so-called Calvinists have even taken the Thomistic position that for God to know and to do are identical. I wish to make it clear that in rejecting the Arminian interpretation of I Peter 1:1,2, I am by no means accepting the cliche which makes God's foreknowledge nothing but His decree of election. Divine election is one thing and divine foreknowledge is another thing. There is no disharmony between them, and no dependence of one upon the other is indicated in the Scripture.[517]

This is yet another example of a Calvinist directly contradicting his fellow Calvinists.

Although it has been pointed out several times before, it should be noted once again that in Acts 2:23, foreknowledge follows rather than precedes the **"determinate counsel"** of God. This forces the Calvinist to treat foreknowledge as foreknowledge, not foreordination, and major on the premise that God foreknows because he decrees. But here in 1 Peter 1:2, because election is said to be **"according to the foreknowledge of God,"** the Calvinist puts an entirely different spin on the word. But the passage in question said nothing about anyone being elected to anything. *Elect* is just a description with the means of receiving it given in the verse: **"through sanctification of the Spirit, unto obedience and sprinkling of the blood of Jesus Christ."** Pink makes much ado about the order of **"sanctification"** and **"obedience,"** and has God quicken the sinner before he believes.[518] Best dispenses with the whole idea of eternal election in 1 Peter 1:2, holding that the election in this verse "refers to God actually picking out the elect from among mankind and saving them by His grace."[519]

Believers are referred to in a number of ways in this epistle of Peter and it is here that we see the true connotation of election: **"But ye *are* a chosen generation, a royal priesthood, an holy nation, a peculiar people; that ye should shew forth the praises of him who hath called you out of darkness into his marvellous light"** (1 Pet. 2:9). There can be no doubt where these terms came from:

> **And ye shall be unto me a kingdom of priests, and a holy nation. These *are* the words which thou shalt speak unto the children of Israel (Exo. 19:6).**

> **For thou *art* an holy people unto the LORD thy God, and the LORD hath chosen thee to be a peculiar people unto himself, above all the nations that *are* upon the earth (Deu. 14:2).**

But rather than see the truth of election, the postmillennial and amillennial Calvinists have decided that God has permanently rejected Israel and therefore they get all of their blessings—but none of their curses. Calvinists have completely missed the significance of Christians being referred to by these designations.

Overlooked is the fact that as the nation of Israel was corporately elected so also was the Church as a body (Eph. 1:22-23; Col. 1:18). As recognized by Roger Forster and Paul Marston: "The prime point is that the election of the church is a corporate rather than an individual thing. It is not that individuals are in the church because they are elect, it is rather that they are elect because they are in the church, which is the body of the elect one."[520] William Klein came to similar conclusions: "In the old covenant a person entered the chosen nation of Israel through natural birth. In the new covenant a person enters the chosen body, the church, through the new birth. To exercise faith in Christ is to enter into his body and become one of the 'chosen ones.'"[521] But in reviewing Klein's work, Hanko at once condemns and presents the non-Calvinist position: "Klein's plea for a corporate view of election turns out to be a plea for a conditional view of election in which foreknowledge becomes prescience, and God's determination to save or to damn is based upon man's faith or unbelief."[522] But even Herman Hoeksema acknowledges that the "elect" are "one body, one legal corporation, represented by Christ Who is their head."[523] It is obvious that this body is comprised of individuals, but comprehending all men potentially and no man unconditionally. The election is of the body and comprehends individual men only in association and identification with the body; election has nothing to do with how any man gets into the body. The English nonconformist Calvinist Christopher Ness once said that "our election is typified by God's election of Israel."[524] This is true in a number of ways.

Just as the national election of Israel comprehended only those "in Jacob," so one must be "in Christ" to get in on election. Just as individuals in the Old Testament were only elect according to their relationship to the nation, so the election of anyone in the New Testament depends on their relationship to Jesus Christ. Just as God did not choose each individual Jew to be one of the elect, so he does not choose each individual Christian—they are born into it. The salvation and damnation of individuals was not the purpose of their election. Thus, the same five principles that were established about the election of Israel also apply to the Church:

1. Individuals are elect according to their relationship to the elect one
2. God did not choose each individual
3. The elect are elect because of their birth
4. Their election had nothing to do with salvation
5. Their election was not by a sovereign, eternal decree

No unsaved man was ever elected to anything. And just as the election of Israel did not require the reprobation of the Gentile world, so whosoever believeth (John 3:16; Rom. 9:33) is not condemned (John 3:18, 5:24) and has eternal life (John 3:36; 1 John 5:13). The basic error of Calvinism is confounding election with salvation. It is apparent, then, that the Calvinistic doctrine of election cannot be proved from any Bible instances of any form of the word. But what about predestination?

Predestinated to Salvation

The last type of proof text for Unconditional Election is a verse in which appears the dreaded word *predestination*. Unlike election, which is at least mentioned several times in the Bible, the subject of predestination occurs but sparingly. Yet, not only did Warfield assert that all the biblical writers were conscious of it,[525] Calvin claimed that Paul preached "the doctrine of predestination continually."[526] Realizing, however, that a form of the word *predestination* only occurs four times in the Scripture, another Calvinist simply says that it is "one of the most interesting doctrines in the Bible. It should be taught in kindergarten."[527] There is certainly nothing difficult in and of itself about the word *predestination* that would preclude such an endeavor, as the Calvinist theologian Buswell explains: "The word 'predestination' simply indicates the advance designation and arrangement of a horizon, or a situation, or an event. It is always the context which must determine who or what is predestinated and what is the condition to which the predestination is directed."[528] But one would think that if predestination is the prominent doctrine that Calvinists maintain it is, then those Bible verses which contain a form of the word ought to be the strongest in support of this doctrine. We have examined a number of Calvinist proof texts for Unconditional Election in which Calvinists see the idea of "predestination to salvation," but none of them contained any form of this word. But if what Calvinists say about predestination is true, then an appeal to those verses in the Scripture that contain a form of the word should turn up some trace of this doctrine if it is indeed scriptural. So, in taking up the subject of predestination, we will follow Calvin's advise to the letter: "Let this, therefore, first of all be before our eyes: to seek any other knowledge of predestination than what the Word of God discloses is not less insane than if one should purpose to walk in a pathless waste, or to see in darkness."[529]

The first thing to be determined is if the word *predestination*, as it is used in the Bible, matches the definitions given for predestination by the Calvinists. According to Calvinism:

> Predestination is the decree of God, whereby (according to the counsel of His own will) He fore-ordained some of mankind to eternal life, and refused or passed by others.[530]

> From the Bible we learn that predestination is the eternal counsel of God whereby He determines the eternal destiny of all men. It includes the sovereign election of some to eternal life through Jesus Christ, and the most righteous reprobation of others for their sins.[531]

It would also be pertinent once again to see how the Westminster Confession defines predestination:

> By the decree of God, for the manifestation of his own glory, some men and angels are predestinated unto everlasting life, and others foreordained to everlasting death.[532]

So properly speaking, as we saw back in the section on God's decree, the part of God's sovereign, eternal decree that concerns itself with the eternal destinies of men and angels is termed predestination.

With this in mind, we present the only four verses in the Bible in which predestination is mentioned:

> **Having predestinated us unto the adoption of children by Jesus Christ to himself, according to the good pleasure of his will (Eph. 1:5).**
>
> **In whom also we have obtained an inheritance, being predestinated according to the purpose of him who worketh all things after the counsel of his own will (Eph. 1:11).**
>
> **For whom he did foreknow, he also did predestinate *to be* conformed to the image of his Son, that he might be the firstborn among many brethren (Rom. 8:29).**
>
> **Moreover whom he did predestinate, them he also called: and whom he called, them he also justified: and whom he justified, them he also glorified (Rom. 8:30).**

There are several problems with the Calvinists' understanding of these verses that immediately come to mind. First, in none of these verses is predestination ever called a decree of God. Second, there is no mention in any of these verses of predestination taking place before the foundation of the world. Third, none of these verses mention any angels. Fourth, there is no mention in any of these verses of anyone being predestinated to salvation. Fifth, none of these verses contain any reference to judgment, condemnation, reprobation, or everlasting death. It is apparent that what the Bible says about predestination is irreconcilable with what the Calvinists say about predestination. This being the case, it remains to be seen just what the Calvinists say about predestination in these particular verses.

The first two occurrences of predestination are in Ephesians:

> **Having predestinated us unto the adoption of children by Jesus Christ to himself, according to the good pleasure of his will (Eph. 1:5).**
>
> **In whom also we have obtained an inheritance, being**

predestinated according to the purpose of him who worketh all things after the counsel of his own will (Eph. 1:11).

Because the context contains the word **"chosen"** and the phrase **"before the foundation of the world"** (Eph. 1:4), Calvinists connect these verses with those words and say that the "elect" were predestinated to salvation before the salvation of the world. However, the usual way this is done is to simply list one or more of these verses after making such a statement.[533] But not only is there no mention of when this predestination took place, it had nothing to do with who should or should not become a Christian. Predestination concerns only our destiny as Christians. This is why the term *predestination* is used. Like election, no unsaved man was ever predestinated to anything. But because the unregenerate sinner is born **"dead in trespasses and sins"** (Eph. 2:1), he is in a sense predestinated to hell, but not unconditionally, for his destination could be changed upon his acceptance of the Gospel.

To what then does this predestination refer to? According to the text, it has reference to **"the adoption of children by Jesus Christ to himself."** Besides our text here, adoption is only mentioned four other times in the Scripture (Rom. 8:15, 23, 9:4; Gal. 4:5), one of which being in reference to Israel (Rom. 9:4). Adoption concerns our legal status as sons. It has reference to privilege, not nature; position, not relationship. Regeneration concerns our nature, justification our standing, sanctification our character, and adoption our position. By regeneration we are *born* (1 Pet. 1:23) into God's family and are so designated sons of God (John 1:12; 1 John 3:2), but by adoption we *receive* (Gal. 4:5) the legal status of sons and the right to our inheritance (Eph. 1:11, 13). Adoption is not regeneration, as acknowledged by Berkhof: "The sonship by adoption should be carefully distinguished from the moral sonship of believers, their sonship by regeneration and sanctification."[534] Although adoption is spoken of in the present (Gal. 4:5), it awaits its ultimate realization until the future: **"And not only *they*, but ourselves also, which have the firstfruits of the Spirit, even we ourselves groan within ourselves, waiting for the adoption, *to wit*, the redemption of our body"** (Rom. 8:23). Thus, Pink comments on our text: "The 'adoption' to which we are predestinated (Eph. 1:5) we still await (Rom. 8:23)."[535] And if this be the case, predestination in Ephesians 1 could not possibly be a reference to "predestination to salvation." The predestination in Ephesians 1:5 is said to be **"to the praise of the glory of his grace"** (Eph. 1:6). This predestination entitles us to an inheritance (Eph. 1:11) **"that we should be to the praise of his glory"** (Eph. 1:12). This inheritance is said to be **"incorruptible, and undefiled, and that fadeth not away, reserved in heaven for you"** (1 Pet. 1:4). The **"earnest of our inheritance"** (Eph. 1:14) is the **"holy Spirit of promise"** (Eph. 1:13), also referred to as the **"firstfruits of the Spirit"** (Rom. 8:23), the **"Spirit of his Son"** (Gal. 4:6), and indicatively, the **"Spirit of adoption"** (Rom. 8:15). We are an **"heir of God"** (Gal. 4:7) and **"joint-heirs with Christ"** (Rom. 8:17) **"until the redemption of the purchased possession, unto the praise of his glory"** (Eph. 1:14). So until then we are **"waiting for the adoption, to wit, the redemption of our body"** (Rom. 8:23) when we are **"conformed to the image of his Son"** (Rom. 8:29).

The next two verses on predestination are part of a larger section in Romans 8 that Calvinists have described as a "golden chain" of grace or salvation:[536]

> **And we know that all things work together for good to them that love God, to them who are the called according to *his* purpose.**
> **For whom he did foreknow, he also did predestinate *to be* conformed to the image of his Son, that he might be the firstborn among many brethren.**
> **Moreover whom he did predestinate, them he also called: and whom he called, them he also justified: and whom he justified, them he also glorified (Rom. 8:28-30).**

Cockrell claims that "a good number of people believe that God should have left these verses of Scripture out of the Bible. Many do not understand them; others just simply do not believe them. Still others seek to explain away their plain sense in order to cling to their religious dogma."[537] That there be no misunderstanding of exactly what the Calvinists believe and teach, their standard interpretation is here given by one of their own:

> Paul is showing that there are five links in the chain of redemption: Foreknowledge, Predestination, Calling, Justification and Glorification. God foreknew those whom He wanted to

be His. He marked them off (predestinated) to be His and to be conformed to the image of His Son, Jesus Christ. Then in the proper time He called them and made them willing to come to Christ. When they came He justified them by imputing to them righteousness. And as the final and culminating action of His grace upon them He glorified them (note the past tense, for it is already accomplished in the divine mind).[538]

To question that this passage teaches that "God has from all eternity elected a certain number to everlasting life" is "to question the truth of this sacred text."[539] But although Romans 8 is often thought of as a citadel of Calvinism, it is actually one of their weakest links. Storms considers this passage as one of the two texts of which none "are more dear or necessary to the Arminian."[540] These verses have been maligned for so long by both Calvinists and Arminians that any departure from their respective "historic positions" is tantamount to heresy. Since this is neither a commentary on Romans nor a doctrinal treatise on salvation, an extended exegesis must necessarily give way to an analysis of the system erected by the Calvinists.

The first assumption made by the Calvinists (and many non-Calvinists) is that Romans 8 contains the elusive *ordo salutis* (order of salvation).[541] But even then the Calvinists can't come to an agreement. Herman Hoeksema admits that "there has always been a good deal of difference of opinion with regard to the order in which the benefits of salvation are bestowed upon the people of God."[542] So right away the *ordo* TULIP withers. Besides the incongruency of the Calvinists, there are two conclusive reasons why this is *not* the order of salvation. The first concerns the glaring omission of regeneration (Tit. 3:5) and sanctification (Jude 1). How can one even begin to have salvation without regeneration and sanctification? The second reason is that a contrary order is given, not once, but several times. This has been pointed out on many occasions but deserves more attention in light of our text. In Matthew 20:16 and 22:14, calling comes before "election," but in Romans 8:29 it is after predestination. In Acts 2:23 foreknowledge comes after the supposed predestination, but in 1 Peter 1:2 and Romans 8:29 it doesn't. In 2 Thessalonians 2:13 and 1 Peter 1:2, sanctification follows "election," but in Jude 1 it precedes calling. According to 2 Timothy 1:9 and 2 Peter 1:10, the order is salvation, calling, and then election. In Jude 1, however, one is sanctified, preserved, and then called. But in 1 Corinthians 6:11, the believer is washed, sanctified, and then justified.

The fallacy of trying to construct an *ordo salutis* without taking into account all of the scriptural evidence manifests itself in Pink's incredible explanation of the order in Jude 1:

> The *order* of the verbs here is most significant. The "sanctification" by the Father manifestly speaks of our eternal "election," when before the foundation of the world God, in His counsels, *separated* us from the mass of our fallen race, and appointed us to salvation. The "calling" evidently refers to that inward and invincible call which comes to each of God's elect at the hour of their regeneration (Rom. 8:30), when the dead hear the voice of the Son of God and live (John 5:25). But observe that in Jude 1 it is said they are "preserved" in Jesus Christ, and "called." Clearly the reference is to *temporal preservation prior to salvation*. As the writer looks back to his unregenerate days he recalls with a shudder a number of occasions when he was in imminent peril, brought face to face with death. But even then, even while in his sins, he was (because in Christ by eternal election) miraculously preserved.[543]

In Acts 2:23 Pink emphasized the secondary placement of foreknowledge. Then he changed his tune when the word occurred in 1 Peter 1:2. We have also seen the gymnastics he performed when faced with calling before election in 2 Peter 1:10. But here in Jude 1, when there was no way to make the order fit his system, Pink simply changed sanctification into election and then took a promise of eternal security (not perseverance) and made it into God preserving the "elect" so they could be "called" by Irresistible Grace. But what difference would it make whether God *temporally* preserved the "elect"? According to all Calvinists, the "elect" couldn't be lost if they tried. This is reminiscent of Paul enduring all things so the "elect" could be saved (2 Tim. 2:10) or God's longsuffering toward the "elect" so they could repent (2 Pet. 3:9). The "elect" will be preserved, saved, and brought to repentance no matter who does what. This is the underlying principle of Calvinism in general and Unconditional Election in particular. The *ordo* TULIP of Romans 8 is a artificial arrangement.

The next problem with attempting to build an *ordo salutis* on the basis of the order of the words in Romans 8 is justification.

There is no disagreement with the Calvinists on the doctrine of justification per se. The argument with the Calvinists concerns how the sinner obtains it, and will be considered in chapter 9 on Irresistible Grace. However, as we saw back in our discussion of Ephesians 1:4, some Calvinists—those who are consistent with their concept of the "elect" being "in Christ" from the foundation of the world—embrace the doctrine of eternal justification. John Brine, one of its notable adherents, not only made the statement: "Regeneration is the effect of justification,"[544] but further insisted that "because Paul was justified, reconciled, and adopted, even when in a state of unbelief, therefore he was converted in God's time."[545] Against the objection that men cannot be justified before they exist, he reasons: "If there is a personal election from eternity, there also may be a personal Justification from eternity, because the latter requires our existence no more than the former."[546] But if justification is eternal, then once again the *ordo* TULIP withers. It is to be remembered that the order in Romans 8:30 is: predestinate, called, justified. All Calvinists claim that predestination takes place in eternity. Likewise, all Calvinists insist that calling is Irresistible Grace and takes place in time. But if this is true, then how could justification be eternal if the strict order of the words is to be maintained? Not to mention that if the "elect" were justified from all eternity, then they would not need to be regenerated and believe on Christ. Could one of God's "eternally justified elect" go to hell?

The last weak link in this TULIP chain is glorification. Although the texts says **"and whom he justified, them he also glorified"** (Rom. 8:30), Calvinists are united in pushing this out into the future.[547] They claim that "the golden chain of grace reaches from eternity past to eternity future, or from everlasting predestination to everlasting beautification."[548] Nettles, however, makes the glory "all salvific blessings" to avoid the apparent paradox.[549] Although we will be glorified in the future as part of our predestinated end (Rom. 8:18; 1 Cor. 15:49; 1 John 3:2), until such manifestation (Rom. 8:19), we have been called to glory (1 Thes. 2:12; 1 Pet. 5:10; 2 Pet. 1:3), have the **"spirit of glory"** (1 Pet. 4:14), and are **"a partaker of the glory that shall be revealed"** (1 Pet. 5:1) **"to the obtaining of the glory of our Lord Jesus Christ"** (2 Thes. 2:14). God has already **"blessed us with all spiritual blessings"** (Eph. 1:3), made us **"holy and without blame before him"** (Eph. 1:4), and **"raised *us* up together, and made *us***

sit together in heavenly *places* in Christ" (Eph. 2:6).

The second fallacy of the Calvinists is that predestination is unto salvation. Some non-Calvinists have so succumbed to the *ordo* TULIP that their interpretation parallels that of the Calvinists. So, to get rid of the Calvinistic implications, it is said to be based on foreknowledge. But like 1 Peter 1:2, the non-Calvinist likewise errs in his interpretation. The genuine Arminian theologian, John Miley (1813-1895), states the standard Arminian explanation: "All who are foreknown of God as obedient to the divine call are predestinated to an ultimate blessedness."[550] It should be added, however, that this "obedience" entails slightly more than believing on Christ, for Miley espouses "the possibility of a final apostasy."[551] The Calvinists are certainly correct in assailing this "foresight of faith" theory: "The thing that strikes me about the Arminian interpretation of this passage is the utter absence of any reference to faith or free will as that which God allegedly foreknows or foresees in men."[552] The other non-Calvinist position is similar but takes a proper view of eternal security. It confounds predestination with election and makes both contingent upon God foreknowing who would accept Christ.[553] But the Calvinists also recognize the absurdity of this construal: "The predestinating of what one knows is going to happen is a meaningless exercise. . . . The concept of predestination, which connotes bringing events to pass, loses any integrity of meaning in this explanation."[554]

Calvinists who appeal to Romans 8:29 as a proof text for Unconditional Election because they see the word *predestination* generally take one of two approaches. The first alternative is based on the idea that "the divine foreknowledge is based upon the divine purpose—God foreknows what will be because He has decreed what shall be."[555] Boettner maintains that God's "foreknowledge is but a transcript of His will" and that it "rests upon His pre-arranged plan."[556] The way this is done is similar to how the Calvinists handled Acts 2:23. There we saw that, because **"foreknowledge"** was mentioned after **"the determinate counsel"** of God, Calvinists abrogated foreknowledge by grounding it on God's decree. But, it is asked, how can the Calvinists do this in Romans 8:29? Does it not mention foreknowledge first? Pink replies: "Note carefully the *order* in Acts 2:23 and Romans 8:28 (last clause) and 29."[557] Because Romans 8:29 begins with foreknowledge and not predestination, Pink goes back to the preceding verse so as to make foreknowledge appear second. The verses in question read:

And we know that all things work together for good to them that love God, to them who are the called according to *his* **purpose.**
For whom he did foreknow, he also did predestinate *to be* **conformed to the image of his Son, that he might be the firstborn among many brethren (Rom. 8:28-29).**

Pink elaborates: "The first word here, *'for,'* looks back to the preceding verse and the last clause of it reads, 'to them who are the called according to His purpose'—these are the ones whom He did 'foreknow and predestinate.'"[558]

There are two glaring problems with this interpretation. First, why stop at the last clause in verse twenty-eight? Why not go back to the phrase **"to them that love God"** and say that God's calling, foreknowledge, and predestination all depend on whether a man loves God? And second, the phrase in verse twenty-eight that Pink mentions, **"to them who are the called according to his purpose,"** is to the Calvinist, because it contains a form of the word *call,* the Irresistible Grace of his TULIP system. According to the order of the words, this would put calling (Irresistible Grace) before predestination (Unconditional Election). So once again the *ordo* TULIP withers. And as has been pointed out on several occasions, this contrary order is given many other times as well.

As mentioned briefly at the beginning of this chapter, the claim of the Calvinists that God could not have absolute knowledge of future events unless he actually decreed them to happen is a direct attack on the omniscience of God. What kind of power does it take know something one has already decreed to take place? To take away God's absolute omniscience under the guise of an all-encompassing decree is not only a deliberate rejection of the word of God, but a subtle attack on the nature of God himself. In their zeal to uphold their "divine determinism,"[559] Calvinists are actually denying not only God's "middle knowledge" (knowledge of what *will* or *could* or *would* happen), but his "simple foreknowledge" (knowledge of what *will* actually happen), and limiting God to possessing only "present knowledge" (knowledge of what *has* actually happened).[560] In this respect the Calvinists are no different than those philosophers and Arminians who deny to God absolute omniscience.[561] In fact, they have even gone beyond some of those who deny God's absolute omniscience, for at least some of them ascribe to God some knowledge of future events without any divine decree.[562]

The knowledge of God is presented in the Bible as infinite, as someone has aptly said: "Did it ever occur to you that nothing ever occurred to God?" God is a **"God of knowledge"** (1 Sam. 2:3). Job declared that God was **"perfect in knowledge"** (Job 37:16). Paul exclaimed: **"O the depth of the riches both of the wisdom and knowledge of God!"** (Rom. 11:33). David said: **"For *there is* not a word in my tongue, *but,* lo, O LORD, thou knowest it altogether"** (Psa. 139:4). The Lord knows the **"secrets of the heart"** (Psa. 44:21). And not only does he know **"the things that come into your mind, every one of them"** (Eze. 11:5), God knows **"all the imaginations of the thoughts"** (1 Chr. 28:9). The proof that the Bible is inspired and God is exactly who he claims to be is the fact that God knows what men will do in the future *without* divine foreordination of anything:

> **Behold, the former things are come to pass, and new things do I declare: before they spring forth I tell you of them (Isa. 42:9).**

> **Declaring the end from the beginning, and from ancient times *the things* that are not *yet* done, saying, My counsel shall stand, and I will do all my pleasure (Isa. 46:10).**

The Calvinist Jerom Zanchius (1516-1590) has stated it well: "God is, and always was so perfectly wise, that nothing ever did, or does, or can elude His knowledge. He knew, from all eternity, not only what He Himself intended to do, but also what He would incline and permit others to do. Consequently, God knows nothing now, nor will know anything hereafter, which He did not know and foresee from everlasting."[563] It is ironic that Calvinists would deny God's absolute omniscience yet perhaps the most exhaustive characterization of God's knowledge was written by their chief antagonist—Arminius:

> He knows all things possible, whether they be in the capability of God or of the creature; in active or passive capability; in the capability of operation, imagination, or enunciation: He knows all things that could have an existence, on laying down any

hypothesis: He knows other things than himself, those which are necessary and contingent, good and bad, universal and particular, future, present and past, excellent and vile: He knows things substantial and accidental of every kind; the actions and passions, the modes and circumstances of all things; external words and deeds, internal thoughts, deliberations, counsels, and determinations, and the entities of reason, whether complex or simple.[564]

He also stated that God likewise understands "all things and every thing which now have, will have, have had, can have, or might hypothetically have, any kind of being."[565]

Like the question of God and evil that has engaged philosophers for centuries, the problem of God's foreknowledge and man's freedom has likewise enamored both Christian and non-Christian philosophers.[566] Most philosophers who deny God's absolute omniscience do so because they believe that "God's omniscience is incompatible with human freedom."[567] Likewise, Arminians who reject God's absolute omniscience do so because they believe that "foreknowledge entails foreordination."[568] Calvinists, on the other hand, reject God's absolute omniscience because they wish to get rid of free will altogether for fear it will infringe upon their peculiar idea of divine sovereignty. Those who deny God's absolute omniscience often labor under the misconception that it is God's foreknowledge of a future event which renders it certain. William Lane Craig correctly explains God's foreknowledge:

> From God's foreknowledge of a free action, one may infer only that that action will occur, not that it must occur. The agent performing the action has the power to refrain, and were the agent to do so, God's foreknowledge would have been different. Agents cannot bring it about both that God foreknows their action and that they do not perform the action, but this is no limitation on their freedom. They are free either to act or to refrain, and whichever they choose, God will have foreknown. For God's knowledge, though chronologically prior to the action, is logically posterior to the action and determined by it. Therefore, divine foreknowledge and human freedom are not mutually exclusive.[569]

Therefore, it is fallacious to conclude, as Boettner does, that since "foreknowledge implies certainty," it of necessity follows that "certainty implies foreordination."[570] God's absolute omniscience provides the only key to the reconciliation of God's "sovereignty" and human freedom. If God knows with genuine certainty what any man could and would do in any situation, then he can bring about his purposes by ordering the appropriate situations without violating man's freedom.

The second hypothesis of the Calvinists on Romans 8:29 is that foreknowledge really means foreordination. Since predestination comes first in the Calvinistic system, but is listed second in Romans 8:29, the foreknowledge must be turned into foreordination since it "lies at the root of the whole process."[571] When foreknowledge follows what is considered predestination or election (Acts 2:23) it is taken as foreknowledge; when it doesn't (Rom. 8:28; 1 Pet. 1:2) it is regarded as foreordination. That the Calvinists really do exercise this grammatical licentiousness can be seen by how they define foreknowledge in what they consider to be "the classic passage in the issue of God's foreknowledge":[572]

> To "foreknow" on God's part means to "forelove." That God foreknew us is but another way of saying that he set his gracious and merciful regard upon us, that he knew us from eternity past with a sovereign and distinguishing delight.[573]
>
> Paul is using the Biblical idiom of "know" for "love," and he means, "whom God loved beforehand, he foreordained."[574]
>
> Defined Biblically, foreknowledge refers to a loving relationship which God sustains to certain individuals by choosing them.[575]
>
> It is never what God foreknew, but whom He foreknew, and it always has to do with foreordination, not foresight.[576]
>
> God's foreknowledge, then, is His eternal love for His chosen people.[577]
>
> God's foreknowledge, therefore, is not a reference to His omniscient foresight but to His foreordination.[578]
>
> What then does the word "foreknow" mean? It is practically synonymous with "forelove."[579]

Although he believed that foreknowledge was really foreknowledge in Acts 2:23,[580] Calvin insists that "the foreknowledge of God here mentioned by Paul is not mere prescience, as some inexperienced people foolishly imagine, but adoption, by which He has always distinguished His children from the reprobate."[581] So according to the Calvinists, foreknowledge is basically the same thing as election. This is further confirmed by a Sovereign Grace Baptist and former editor of *The Baptist Examiner*: "'Everlasting love' is a perfect Biblical definition of 'foreknowledge.' This everlasting love is almost a Biblical synonym for election. The meaning of 'foreknowledge' and 'election' are close akin in the Bible; so close that one can almost be used for the other."[582]

What the Calvinists have done is to turn an attribute of God, *foreknowledge,* into an act of God, *foreordination.* To disagree with their interpretation is to hold "the Arminian understanding of foreknowledge."[583] As is plainly apparent, the words *foreknow* and *foreknowledge* are compound words made up of the prefix *fore,* meaning "before," and the words *know* or *knowledge,* the basic meaning of which is obvious. Thus, *foreknow* means "to know beforehand" and *foreknowledge* means "knowledge of something beforehand." The addition of the prefix doesn't change the meaning of the word *know,* it only dates it. It is because the word *know* has several shades of meaning that Calvinists are able to attempt to turn it into foreordination in Romans 8:29. Thus, in commenting on this passage, John Murray says: "Many times in Scripture 'know' has a pregnant meaning which goes beyond that of mere cognition. It is used in a sense practically synonymous with 'love,' to set regard upon, to know with peculiar interest, delight, affection, and action."[584] Some scriptural examples would be:

> **And Adam knew Eve his wife; and she conceived, and bare Cain, and said, I have gotten a man from the LORD (Gen. 4:1).**
>
> **Who said unto his father and to his mother, I have not seen him; neither did he acknowledge his brethren, nor knew his own children: for they have observed thy word, and kept thy covenant (Deu. 33:9).**
>
> **And then will I profess unto them, I never knew you: depart from me, ye that work iniquity (Mat. 7:23).**

> Now learn a parable of the fig tree; When her branch is yet tender, and putteth forth leaves, ye know that summer is near (Mark 13:28).
>
> Wherefore I was grieved with that generation, and said, They do alway err in *their* heart; and they have not known my ways (Heb. 3:10).

That the word *know* has several shades of meaning is apparent from Scripture.

The concept of foreknowledge only surfaces six times. The passages in 1 Peter 1:2 and Acts 2:23 have already been examined. They merely state the fact of God's foreknowledge. Likewise, the bare fact that God foreknew someone appears in Romans 11:2. Our text in Romans 8:29 is also ambiguous, for as Sproul concludes: "All the text declares is that God predestines those whom He foreknows."[585] There remain two more examples of foreknowledge:

> My manner of life from my youth, which was at the first among mine own nation at Jerusalem, know all the Jews;
> Which knew me from the beginning, if they would testify, that after the most straitest sect of our religion I lived a Pharisee (Acts 26:4-5).
>
> Ye therefore, beloved, seeing ye know these things before, beware lest ye also, being led away with the error of the wicked, fall from your own stedfastness (2 Pet. 3:17).

The meaning here is obvious—prior knowledge. Out of the hundreds of times that a form of the word *know* appears in the Bible, it rarely signifies anything but to perceive, acknowledge, recognize, or understand. So as usual, there are several things wrong with the Calvinists' interpretation.

If the word *know* has the connotation of "that intimate relationship which exists between God and His elect, based solely on His electing grace,"[586] then the Calvinists are faced with several problems. The first thing that anyone with any common sense would immediately realize is that one can't have a loving relationship with someone who doesn't exist. Regardless of God's attributes of omniscience and omnipotence, the "elect" still did not exist before the foundation of the world. Second, the so-called elect were **"without God in the world"** (Eph. 2:12), not "foreloved" from all eternity. Third, if foreknowledge is really foreordination, then we are left with the tautology: "For whom he did foreordain, he also did predestinate." And not only this, the Sovereign Grace Baptist John Alber maintains that the phrase **"called according to his purpose"** in Romans 8:28 is "identical with predestination."[587] This would give us the nonsensical phrase: "Predestinated according to his purpose. For whom he did foreordain, he also did predestinate."

There are also three Scripture examples of a form of the word *know* which clearly overthrow the Calvinistic concept of foreknowledge: the idea that God had an eternal love for the "elect." Would any Calvinist claim that Jesus Christ had a relationship with any but the "elect"?

> **Now when he was in Jerusalem at the passover, in the feast** *day,* **many believed in his name, when they saw the miracles which he did.**
> **But Jesus did not commit himself unto them, because he knew all** *men* **(John 2:23-24).**

According to this passage, Christ **"knew all** *men,***"** not just the "elect." But not only did the Lord "know" all men, he did not "know" the "elect" until their conversion:

> **Howbeit then, when ye knew not God, ye did service unto them which by nature are no gods.**
> **But now, after that ye have known God, or rather are known of God, how turn ye again to the weak and beggarly elements, whereunto ye desire again to be in bondage? (Gal. 4:8-9).**

God could not have had an eternal, loving relationship with the "elect" if he never knew them.

The final passage concerns God foreknowing Israel. Would any Calvinist claim that all the Jews in the Old Testament were saved?

> **I say then, Hath God cast away his people? God forbid. For I also am an Israelite, of the seed of Abraham,** *of* **the tribe of Benjamin.**
> **God hath not cast away his people which he foreknew. Wot ye not what the scripture saith of Elias? how he maketh intercession to God against Israel, saying (Rom. 11:1-2).**

No Calvinist would dispute the fact that the **"his people"** in verse one is a reference to the entire nation of Israel. But according to verse two, God "foreknew" the whole nation of Israel. In this case foreknowledge couldn't possibly have anything to do with foreordination to salvation. The relationship God had with the nation of Israel didn't guarantee the salvation of everyone in the nation or else all Jews in the Old Testament would have been saved. But if **"foreknew"** means "foreordained," then all Jews would have been saved. Realizing this, some Calvinists try to make the phrase **"his people which he foreknew"** into "his elect which he predestinated."[588] But once again a Calvinist corrects his fellow Calvinists: "It is Israel as a whole that is in view in verse 1. The answers in the latter part of verse 1 apply to Israel as a whole. The first part of verse 2 is the direct reply unfolding what is implicit in the latter part of verse 1. It would be difficult to suppose that the denotation is abruptly changed at the point where this direct denial is introduced. It is more tenable, therefore, to regard 'his people' (vs. 1) and 'his people which he foreknew' (vs. 2) as identical in their reference and the qualifying clause in verse 2 as expressing what is really implied in the designation 'his people.'"[589]

If predestination is not unto salvation then to what does this predestination refer? According to the text, the believer is predestinated by God **"to be conformed to the image of his Son."** In addition to our text, we are given more information elsewhere:

> **And as we have borne the image of the earthy, we shall also bear the image of the heavenly (1 Cor. 15:49).**

> **Beloved, now are we the sons of God, and it doth not yet appear what we shall be: but we know that, when he shall appear, we shall be like him; for we shall see him as he is (1 John 3:2).**

Calvinists who properly identify predestination in Romans 8:29 only do so because they make foreknowledge into foreordination:

> "Foreknew" focuses attention upon the distinguishing love of God whereby the sons of God were elected. But it does not inform us of the destination to which those thus chosen are appointed. It is precisely that information that "he also foreordained" supplies, and it is by no means superfluous. . . .

"Conformed to the image of his Son" defines the destination to which the elect of God are appointed. The apostle has in view the conformity to Christ that will be realized when they will be glorified with Christ.[590]

So just as we saw regarding election, no unsaved man was ever predestinated to anything. The basic error of Calvinism is confounding election and predestination with salvation. It is only by constructing an *ordo salutis* to match his TULIP theology that the Calvinist is able to appeal to the predestination verses in Romans.

Elect Infants

If Unconditional Election is true; that is, if God unconditionally determined the eternal destiny of every member of the human race by a sovereign, eternal, all-encompassing decree, then certainly infants are included, for all men, whether "elect" or "reprobate," have to first be born as an infant before attaining adulthood. The problem, however, is what happens when an infant dies. The question of whether children who die in infancy are counted among the "elect" has plagued Calvinism since the very beginning. The mention of "elect infants, dying in infancy" in the Westminster Confession of Faith[591] has especially troubled the Calvinists.[592] In fact, the Cumberland Presbyterians were so troubled by this phrase that in 1813 they revised the wording of this article in the Westminster Confession.[593] Regarding the possibility that some infants who die are among the "reprobate," Spurgeon comments: "Among the gross falsehoods which have been uttered against the Calvinists proper, is the wicked calumny that we hold *the damnation of little infants*. A baser lie was never uttered. There may have existed somewhere, in some corner of the earth, a miscreant who would dare to say that there were infants in hell, but I have never met with him, nor have I met with a man who ever saw such a person."[594] So even though election is supposed to be sovereign and unconditional, Calvinists as a rule would insist that all children who die in infancy are part of the "elect."

Not all Calvinists, however, retreat from the obvious implications of Unconditional Election—that a dead infant is as equally liable to be "elect" or "reprobate." The most consistent Calvinist was Augustine, who held to the damnation of "non-elect" and non-baptized infants.[595] Among the Reformers, Zwingli was the only one who believed unconditionally in universal salvation for all infants by the Atonement of Christ.[596] As for Luther, George relates: "He believed in the salvation of unborn and unbaptized infants, although he was reluctant to preach this publicly lest the common folk grow lax in bringing their children to the baptismal font."[597] The case of Calvin is not quite as Boettner alleges: "It is sometimes charged that Calvin taught the actual damnation of some of those who die in infancy. A careful examination of his writings, however, does not bear out that charge."[598] But as Schaff remarks: "The attempts of Dr. Shields of Princeton to prove that Calvin believed in the salvation of all infants, is an entire failure."[599] Other Calvinists likewise admit that their namesake held to the damnation of some dead infants.[600]

Although most Calvinists deny that there are "reprobates" who die in infancy, when it comes to actually stating in unambiguous terms that all infants who die are saved, some Calvinists speak in hesitant tones:

> The question whether all infants, dying in infancy, are elect, and therefore saved, is one which the Confession did not undertake to decide. As it is not a matter concerning which the Scriptures speak definitely, it was wisely left where they put it.[601]

> Infants, it may be reasonably supposed, yea, in a judgment of charity it may rather be concluded, that they are all chosen, than that none are.[602]

> Our outstanding theologians, however, mindful of the fact that God's "tender mercies are over all His works," and depending on His mercy widened as broadly as possible, have entertained a charitable hope that since these infants have never committed any actual sin themselves, their inherited sin would be pardoned and they would be saved on wholly evangelical principles.[603]

Even the Calvinistic Baptists are ambivalent.

For an up-to-date look at how they feel about infant salvation, a panel of Sovereign Grace Baptists tackled the question: "Do you think all babies who die in infancy are the elect?"[604]

> *Harold Harvey:* Some adults are elect and some are non-elect, the same thing is true of infants. All of the non-elect infants will

live to maturity and become conscious of sin. Among the elect infants, some will be allowed to live to adulthood, while others will die as babies.

E. D. Strickland: Though I name no Scripture specifically, I think God saves them.

Jimmie B. Davis: David could indeed go to where the child was, and I'm sure that most would say that the child was with the Lord, but there is no scriptural way to prove that this is true of all babies who die in infancy.

James Green: Clearly these passages are not emphatic, but we tend to lean upon them for comfort and support of our belief that those who die in infancy are elect.

Only one out of four of the above panelists seems sure of the salvation of all infants.

This uncertain, wavering attitude of the Calvinists on the subject of the salvation of infants is a far cry from their dogmatic assertions about the reprobation of the adult "non-elect." Perhaps the words of Charles Wesley still linger in the ears of some Calvinists:

> God, ever merciful and just,
> With newborn babes did Tophet fill;
> Down into endless torments thrust;
> Merely to show His sovereign will.
> This is that "Horrible Decree"!
> This is that wisdom from beneath!
> God (O detest the Blasphemy)
> Hath pleasure in the sinner's death.[605]

Honest Calvinists acknowledge that some of their "brethren" held to the damnation of "reprobate" infants:

> Sad to say, not all of our Christian Reformed people dare to take the definite position that all believers' children who die in infancy are saved.[606]

That many of the elder Calvinists believed that there are some non-elect infants is undeniable.[607]

Best is one modern Calvinist who boldly asserts what is implied in Unconditional Election:

> Many religionists claim that children are safe until they reach the age of accountability (whatever that is), and then they are no longer safe. If that is true, what a shame that they're not either aborted or die before they reach that age. If they are safe until they reach the age of accountability, it is an act of mercy to abort one before it comes from the mother's womb or let it die before it reaches the age of accountability. Every person's sin took place in the past when he sinned in Adam. Conclusively, no one can prove from Scripture that all children who die in infancy go to heaven.[608]

The way the Calvinists get "elect" infants overthrows their whole system of Unconditional Election: covenant theology. Without giving any Scripture, Boettner claims: "The Scriptures seem to teach plainly enough that the children of believers are saved."[609] This is also taught in the Canons of Dort:

> Since we are to judge of the will of God from his Word, which testifies that the children of believers are holy, not by nature, but in virtue of the covenant of grace, in which they, together with the parents, are comprehended, godly parents have no reason to doubt of the election and salvation of their children, whom it pleaseth God to call out of this life in their infancy.[610]

To reinforce this teaching, Herman Hanko made the Jews of the dispersion in Acts 2:39 a reference to infant baptism in the Reformed Church.[611] He even insists that the salvation of infants must be denied if one holds to "the theory of adult baptism."[612] The subject of infant baptism confirms the *Reformed* nature of Calvinism. Herman Hoeksema despairingly refers to Gill and other like-minded Baptists as "so-called Calvinistic Baptists."[613] He maintains that "nothing could be more evident from the Scriptures" than that "baptism has come in the place of circumcision."[614] The Particular Baptist Spurgeon strongly disagreed, and stated about infant baptism: "A human and carnal invention, an addition to the word of God, and therefore wicked and injurious."[615] The covenant theology of Reformed Calvinism actually destroys Unconditional Election. What possible connection could "elect" parents have to do with a sovereign, eternal, unconditional, unchangeable, efficacious decree that affected their children? Calvinists adamantly insist that God unconditionally chose some to salvation and others to damnation. Why is it then that Charles Hodge and Herman Hoeksema, whose sons both succeeded them in some capacity, would insist that their sons were of the "elect"? If Unconditional Election is true, then any Calvinist who had six children could reasonably suppose that one or two were "reprobate." But as Spurgeon has pointed out: "There is no distinction between a child of godly or ungodly parents."[616] There couldn't possibly be, and any Calvinist who makes such a distinction demonstrates that he doesn't really believe his TULIP theology, at least where it concerns a member of his family. Reformed Calvinists who are always quoting Spurgeon in an attempt to convince Baptists to be Calvinists suddenly cease their appeals to him when the subject of baptism comes up.

The Other Side of Unconditional Election

The Calvinist Kenneth Johns laments that "the doctrine of unconditional election is not given its proper biblical emphasis in the pulpits of today."[617] But from what we have seen in this chapter, this is a good thing. And although Pink insists that "the only reason why any God-fearing soul believes in the doctrine of election is because he finds it clearly and prominently revealed in God's word,"[618] we have seen that the doctrine of election, which the Calvinist identifies with Unconditional Election, is only "prominently revealed in God's word" because the Calvinists have read it into every conceivable passage. This part of the other side of Unconditional Election is actually conceded by the Protestant Reformed theologian Herman Hanko: "It is the central truth of all the Scriptures. While it is literally taught in hundreds of places in God's Word, it is also the underlying truth upon which the whole of Scripture as the revelation of God in Christ is based. It is present in every passage, presupposed in every part, an integral truth of the whole of God's revelation."[619]

Although the notion of the "elect" being predestinated to salvation before the foundation of the world has been proven to be at complete variance with Scripture, the other side of this doctrine—that God predestinated the "reprobate" to damnation before the foundation of the world—has also been examined and found to be not only unscriptural but abhorrent. Therefore, Clark is correct when, in commenting on the section in chapter three of the Westminster Confession that "anti-Calvinists abominate,"[620] he says that what irritates "Arminians" without measure, although they "may not object too much to the idea that God predestinates some men to everlasting life," is "the idea that God has foreordained other men to everlasting death."[621] All attempts of the Calvinists to mitigate this concept of reprobation should be rejected. It should be remembered that Calvinists see election and reprobation as the twin branches of predestination, which they define as that part of the decree of God which concerns the eternal destinies of men and angels. But this is not all, for once the true nature of this sovereign, eternal, all-encompassing decree is realized, the fallacy of the Calvinists in equating election and predestination with salvation fades into the background. In commenting on the verses in John 17 which Calvinists use to teach Unconditional Election, Martyn Lloyd-Jones (1899-1981) unintentionally made a statement that brings out the other side of Unconditional Election like no other: "My friend, if you are a Christian, do you know that you were the object of God's interest and concern before the foundation of the world? All these things have been worked out in eternity, before time, so you must always remember that nothing can happen in time which will make the slightest difference."[622]

That the Calvinists really believe this fatalistic conclusion has been documented throughout this chapter. And if "nothing can happen in time which will make the slightest difference," then this confirms the state of all men as has been maintained throughout this work:

It is good that a man should both hope and quietly wait for the salvation of the LORD (Lam. 3:26).

The best one can do is *hope* he is one of the "elect." As Boettner expresses it: "No unconverted person in this life knows for certain that God will not yet convert and save him, even though he is aware that no such change has yet taken place."[623] Yet, Coppes still maintains that "predestination is the fount of assurance of salvation and God's answer to doubt."[624] This brings up another facet of the other side of Unconditional Election—seeking assurance of salvation in an arcane, mysterious, sovereign, eternal decree of predestination instead of in the clear statements of the Bible. Ronald VanOverloop comforts us with the thought that "those who wish a greater assurance of election must not be alarmed at the mention of reprobation, but must persist in the use of the means which God has appointed for the working of this assurance and wait prayerfully for a season of richer grace."[625]

We saw in the last chapter that when it comes to the subject of missions and evangelism, the Calvinist insists upon their necessity in spite of man's Total Inability to believe. The same is true on this point of the TULIP as well. VanOverloop again tells us that "the truth of election gives every preacher, whether pastor or missionary, the assurance that his efforts are not in vain."[626] Shedd and Warfield assure us that the number of the "elect" is far greater than the "reprobate."[627] But if, as Zanchius says: "We assert that the number of the elect, and also of the reprobate, is so fixed and determinate that neither can be augmented or diminished,"[628] and if, as Storms contends: "But eventually, if they are elect, in God's appointed time they will believe,"[629] what possible difference could it make whether one sent or withheld missionaries?

Another element of the other side of Unconditional Election is the confusing morass of terminology that Calvinists have introduced into theology, which is no more apparent than in this chapter. But John Wesley, even though he was an ardent Arminian, had enough sense to comprehend the real issue:

> Call it therefore by whatever name you please, Election, Preterition, Predestination, or Reprobation, it comes in the end to the same thing. The sense of all is plainly this: By virtue of an eternal, unchangeable, irresistible decree of God, one part of mankind are infallibly saved and the rest infallibly damned; it being impossible that any of the former should be damned, or that any of the latter should be saved. But if this be so, then is all preaching vain.[630]

Wesley also realized the practical result of Unconditional Election, charging it with "making all preaching vain, and tending to destroy holiness, the comfort of religion and zeal for good works, yea, the whole Christian revelation by involving it in fatal contradictions."[631] So in conclusion, the word of God is not bound by the other side of Unconditional Election: the philosophical speculations of election and the theological implications of predestination.

Chapter 8
LIMITED ATONEMENT

We come now to the middle point of the TULIP system, Limited Atonement. But while the Atonement of Christ is a biblical doctrine, the describing of it as *limited* changes things considerably. This is the same thing we encountered in our study of the first two points of Calvinism: the prefixing of a qualifying term to an otherwise scriptural one. The depravity of man is a biblical doctrine, but as we have seen, the Calvinistic doctrine of Total Depravity is not. Likewise, although the doctrine of election is also scriptural, the Calvinistic doctrine of Unconditional Election is certainly not. And although Calvinists have referred to Limited Atonement as "the heart of the matter in the Calvinist–Arminian debate,"[1] it is really not necessary to spend too much time on this point because it is not essential to the Calvinistic system. Limited Atonement is what one would call "deadwood" or "excess baggage" or "spare parts" or "slag." And aside from the supralapsarian doctrine of reprobation, Limited Atonement is the most objectionable part of the Calvinistic scheme. But in spite of the objectionable theological implications of Limited Atonement, it really is not much of a cause for alarm, due to the fact of its nonessentiality. Limited Atonement is simply "adding insult to injury," the injury being Unconditional Election. For if certain men are not of those elected to salvation, then what does it matter whether Christ died for them or not? It makes absolutely no difference whatsoever whether Christ died for the "non-elect," for in the system of TULIP Calvinism, the so-called non-elect couldn't possibly be saved whether Christ died for them or not. Due to its nonessential and objectionable nature, Limited Atonement is rejected by many modern Baptists and other non-Reformed who hold to Unconditional Election.

Although Limited Atonement is not requisite to the carrying out of the TULIP system, it is frequently federated with the previous point of Unconditional Election:

> These two doctrines must stand or fall together. We cannot logically accept one and reject the other. If God has elected some and not others to eternal life, then plainly the primary purpose of Christ's work was to redeem the elect.[2]

> It is in this truth of limited atonement that the doctrine of sovereign election (and, in fact, sovereign predestination with its two aspects of election and reprobation) comes into focus.[3]

Total Depravity *demands* that God must elect and irresistibly save any man who will ever be saved. But although the Atonement of Christ was necessary for the salvation of the "elect," it didn't have to be limited to them in order to maintain their election. This is what separates Limited Atonement from the rest of the TULIP. It is absolutely non-essential to the Calvinistic system. The fifth point of Calvinism, Perseverance of the Saints—as taught by Calvinists—is also dispensable, as will be seen in chapter 10.

Calvinists admit that their third point is the most controversial and therefore objectionable of the five. Spencer terms it "the most difficult" of the five.[4] Gunn considers it "the most misunderstood."[5] Talbot and Crampton maintain that Limited Atonement is "the hardest one of the *"Five Points Of Calvinism"* for Arminians to cope with."[6] John deWitt acknowledges that many consider Limited Atonement to be "the Achilles Heel of Calvinism."[7] But why is Limited Atonement so objectionable to non-Calvinists? Are not other doctrines of Calvinism equally as erroneous? The trouble with Limited Atonement is that it is so blatantly anti-Scriptural. Honest Calvinists even recognize that the Bible appears to support an unlimited Atonement in the majority of its texts.[8] Other Calvinists, however, are bold in their defense of Limited Atonement. Joseph Wilson, the former editor of *The Baptist Examiner,* argues that Limited Atonement is the strongest point of the TULIP system, "standing at the very fore of our onslaught against heretical views of salvation."[9] Therefore, he insists: "We cannot afford to give up this point. We cannot afford even to be weak or confused on this point. Give up this point, and we have lost the battle on the sovereignty of God in salvation."[10] A. A. Hodge likewise declares that Calvinism is overthrown if Limited Atonement is disproved:

> As far, then, as this question is involved in the Arminian controversy, we are ready to admit the reality of the great

importance which they attribute to it. If they could prove that the love which prompted God to give his Son to die, as a sin-offering, on the cross, had for its objects all men indiscriminately, and that Christ actually sacrificed his life with the purpose of saving all indifferently on the condition of faith, then it appears that their inference is irresistible that the central principle of Arminianism is true; that is, the principle which makes the destiny of the individual to depend upon his own use of divine grace, and not upon the sovereign good pleasure of God.[11]

Nevertheless, A. A. Hodge admits that the nature of the Atonement itself does *not* require that it be limited: "When thoroughly analyzed and accurately defined, the true doctrine that Christ satisfied the retributive justice of God by bearing the very penalty of the law, *does not* logically lead to any consequences which can be accurately expressed by the phrase *limited* Atonement."[12]

Definitions

Like Total Depravity and Unconditional Election, but even more so, Limited Atonement is called by other names to de-stigmatize the implications of the term. Mathison relates that although "the Calvinistic doctrine of the atonement has traditionally been called 'limited atonement,'" other words have been suggested "because of the misunderstanding surrounding the word 'limited.'"[13] Good alleges that the term Limited Atonement suffers from "being a somewhat *negative* designation."[14] Palmer claims that the term "may confuse people."[15] Rose maintains that Limited Atonement is "a misleading term."[16] Therefore, some Calvinists say "definite atonement."[17] Others prefer "particular atonement."[18] Still others embrace the description "specific."[19] One terms it "efficacious atonement."[20] Another "effective atonement."[21] It is also expanded to "definite and personal atonement."[22] Dabney rejects as ambiguous both the terms "limited" and "particular" when connected with the equally opaque term "atonement."[23] And if that wasn't enough to confuse the reader, the word *atonement* is often exchanged for *redemption,* giving us such designations as "particular redemption,"[24] "effective redemption,"[25] or "limited redemption."[26] But like the other "points," calling Limited Atonement by other names can never change the fact of what it really is.

So what is Limited Atonement? How do the Calvinists define it? To avoid the charge of misrepresentation in defining *exactly* what a Calvinist means by Limited Atonement, we will let the Calvinists define it for us:

> The doctrine of "limited atonement" which we maintain is the doctrine which limits the atonement to those who are heirs of eternal life, the elect.[27]

> Christ died *positively* and effectually to save a certain number of hell-deserving sinners on whom the Father had already set His free electing love.[28]

> The doctrine of limited atonement is simply that the cross of Christ provides a sure, secure and real salvation for everyone God intended it to save and for them alone.[29]

It would also be pertinent to see the doctrine of Limited Atonement as expressed by the Westminster Confession of Faith:

> The Lord Jesus, by his perfect obedience, and sacrifice of himself, which he, through the eternal Spirit, once offered up unto God, hath fully satisfied the justice of his Father; and purchased, not only reconciliation, but an everlasting inheritance in the kingdom of heaven, for all those whom the Father hath given unto him.[30]

One Calvinist who rejects Limited Atonement insists that it is not taught in the Canons of Dort,[31] but the Canons say otherwise:

> For this was the sovereign counsel, and most gracious will and purpose of God the Father, that the quickening and saving efficacy of the most precious death of his Son should extend to all the elect, for bestowing upon them alone the gift of justifying faith, thereby to bring them infallibly to salvation: that is, it was the will of God, that Christ by the blood of the cross, whereby he confirmed the new covenant, should effectually redeem out of every people, tribe, nation, and language, all those, and those only, who were from eternity chosen to salvation, and given to him by the Father; that he should confer upon them faith, which together with all the other saving gifts of the Holy Spirit, he purchased for them by his death; should purge them from all sin, both original and actual, whether committed before or after

believing; and having faithfully preserved them even to the end, should at last bring them free from every spot and blemish to the enjoyment of glory in his own presence forever.[32]

So Limited Atonement is just what it implies: Christ shed his blood and made an atonement only for the sins of the "elect."

Although most Calvinists do not deny that the Atonement of Christ on the cross has infinite saving potential, all of them maintain that Christ's blood was shed for the "elect" for the simple reason that God did not want any others to be saved. This is the theory behind Limited Atonement: Christ only made a limited Atonement for the "elect" because he did not want anyone else to be saved:

> The cross could save everyone if God had only intended it to do so.[33]

> As God doth not will that each individual of mankind should be saved, so neither did He will that Christ should properly and immediately die for each individual of mankind, whence it follows that, though the blood of Christ, from its own intrinsic dignity, was sufficient for the redemption of all men, yet, in consequence of His Father's appointment, He shed it intentionally, and therefore effectually and immediately, for the elect only.[34]

So we are right back to Unconditional Election again. According to the Calvinist, election saved no man, it only marked out certain ones who were to be saved by an atonement made just on their behalf. The reason the others were not elected? As we saw in the previous chapter: God wanted them to go to hell. Therefore, to make an issue out of Limited Atonement is a waste of time. If Christ died a thousand deaths for the "non-elect" they would still go to hell. Seaton sums up the debate on the extent of the Atonement: "The over-riding question must always be the Divine intention; did God *intend* to save all men, or did He not?"[35]

Accusations

The Calvinistic arguments in defense of Limited Atonement give evidence to the lengths that a Calvinist will go in order to keep his TULIP in full bloom. Much of the same intimidating accusations are leveled against those who reject Limited Atonement as are postulated for Calvinism in general or Unconditional Election in particular. Naturally, the Calvinist begins with the Bible: "Why does the **Calvinist** believe in *Limited Atonement?* For the simple reason that Christ and the holy apostles believed in it and taught it."[36] Like all the other "points," if you reject the third then you are an Arminian: "It is simply Arminian to teach that Christ died for all men."[37] Once the connection to Arminianism is made, the old "guilt by association" misrepresentation is resurrected:

> Though no one accuses the Arminians of being Roman Catholics, the two agree on one point at least, a fatal point, namely, that while Christ's sacrifice was necessary for salvation, it is not *sufficient*. Man must add some meritorious work of his own.[38]

> All Arians, Pelagians, semi-Pelagians, Socinians and Arminians, have in perfect consistency with their several systems, maintained the general and indefinite reference of the Atonement, while, on the other hand, as was to be expected, all true Augustinians and Calvinists have necessarily held that Christ died definitely and personally for the elect.[39]

> The Arminian theory that God is anxiously trying to convert sinners but not able to exert more than persuasive power without doing violence to their natures, is really much the same as the old Persian view that there were two eternal principles of good and evil at war with each other, neither of which was able to overcome the other.[40]

But is the Trinity to be rejected along with the Incarnation because Catholics believe both? These misrepresentations show that Calvinists will use any argument to impugn their opponents and bolster their position, no matter how inept, inane, or asinine it is.

As if the charge of Arminianism wasn't enough, the Calvinists make all sorts of derogatory accusations against their opponents. Those who deny Limited Atonement are said by Rose to "believe salvation is in part our own doing; they do not believe that we are fully and effectively delivered from sin by the grace of God alone."[41] He further maintains that "if some do not believe this doctrine, they must be ready to bear the weight of their own guilt, ready to atone for their sins the best way they can."[42] Boettner has his opponents disparaging God: "If Christ's death was intended to save all men, then we must say that God was either unable or unwilling to carry out His plans."[43] Calvinists maintain that if Christ did not make a Limited Atonement then somehow some of his blood was wasted:

> To them the atonement is like a universal grab-bag: there is a package for everyone, but only some will grab a package. Christ not only shed His blood, He also spilled it. He intended to save all, but only some will be saved. Therefore, some of His blood was wasted: it was spilled.[44]

> For if Christ died for all men and all men are not saved, the cross of Christ is of no effect. Calvary is a sham.[45]

But these accusations are groundless, if we are to believe the Presbyterian theologian Dabney: "Had every sinner of Adam's race been elected, the same one sacrifice would be sufficient for all. We must absolutely get rid of the mistake that expiation is an aggregate of gifts to be divided and distributed out, one piece to each receiver."[46] And as Boettner himself says: "Even if many fewer of the human race were to have been pardoned and saved, an atonement of infinite value would have been necessary in order to have secured for them these blessings."[47]

The Calvinists then further misrepresent their adversaries by insisting that "Arminians have long accused Calvinists of limiting the power of the atonement."[48] But no Arminian or other non-Calvinist has ever espoused such accusations. No orthodox Calvinist has ever limited the *power* of the Atonement: it is the *extent* that is limited. Calvinists then have the audacity to insist that it is their opponents who limit the Atonement:

> In actuality, it is the Arminian who depersonalizes the atonement and renders it powerless.[49]

> The Free-Willers even limit the atonement. They limit it to who-so-ever makes a commitment—that is, coming to the altar, mourner's bench, or being baptized.[50]

> It is not we who teach a limited atonement, but our opponents.

> That must be a limited redemption indeed which leaves the majority of those for whom it was designed in hell for ever.[51]

Calvinists actually insist that without the doctrine of Limited Atonement no salvation is even possible:

> A Christ for all is really a Christ for none![52]

> With a Christ that merited salvation for all men, but who cannot actually save the sinner unless the latter permits Him, salvation is utterly impossible.[53]

And like we have seen on the previous "points," Calvinists imply that anything less than Limited Atonement robs God of his glory:

> Only Calvinism with its effective atonement limits man's power and exalts God's power and glory.[54]

> Particular redemption ascribes all the glory of salvation to the Triune God.[55]

Not every Calvinist, however, would agree with all of the above accusations.

Four-Point Calvinism

As mentioned in chapter 5, some Calvinists who recognize the repugnancy of Limited Atonement, yet still hold to the predestination of the Calvinistic system, claim to be only four-point Calvinists. And although this teaching was held in the seventeenth century by the aforementioned Moyse Amyraut and John Davenant, English Deputy to the Synod of Dort, four-point Calvinism is generally of recent origin. But as acknowledged by Calvinists: "Considerable controversy has arisen among Calvinists themselves on the extent of the redemption accomplished at Calvary."[56] Therefore, the chief opponents of Limited Atonement are not Arminians, but rather, those denominated as four-point Calvinists. As Custance aptly states it: "The concept of Limited Atonement is perhaps the one point of the Five Points of Calvinism about which controversy among those who otherwise hold firmly to the Calvinist position has had the most serious consequences."[57] Good explains that because of the "difficulties attached to the third of the 'Five Points,' many who consider themselves to be Calvinists have deleted this particular tenet altogether from their system. They do not regard it as basic to essential Calvinism."[58] Tom Ross laments that "even those who profess to believe the doctrines of grace often shy away from this precious truth."[59] The reason a Calvinist would oppose the third point of the TULIP is to divert attention away from the fact that a four-point Calvinist still believes in the Unconditional Election of the Calvinistic system which consigns the reprobate to hell with no chance of being saved. This is similar to the arguments about hyper-Calvinism. By focusing his opponents' attention on what is labeled an extreme position that he doesn't believe, the Calvinist can take the middle road and appear to be orthodox. But Pink claims he would rather be a called a hyper-Calvinist than believe in an unlimited atonement.[60]

The four-point Calvinist Chafer, in enumerating the points of agreement between the two schools regarding the extent of the Atonement, inadvertently reveals the truth of the unimportance of Limited Atonement to the TULIP system: "The belief of one group is that God provides salvation for the elect to the end that the elect might be saved. The belief of the other group is that God provided salvation for all men to the end that the elect might be saved."[61] So what is the difference? If only the "elect" will be saved, does it really matter for whom Christ died? Recognizing this glaring inconsistency, the full-bloom TULIP Calvinists strongly condemn their "cousins":

> I have often thought that to be a four-point Calvinist one must misunderstand at least one of the five points. It is hard for me to imagine that anyone could understand the other four points of Calvinism and deny Limited Atonement. There always is the possibility, however, of the happy inconsistency by which people hold incompatible views at the same time.[62]

> Some have attempted to keep election and the sovereign working of the Holy Spirit, but at the same time deny limited atonement. Such a theory drives an unbiblical disjunction between the work of the Father, Son, and Holy Spirit.[63]

Gerstner insists that a rejection of Limited Atonement "is actually indicative of a thoroughgoing departure from Calvinism."[64] Thus, he attacks with a vengeance his fellow Calvinist Chafer for denying Limited Atonement.[65] But even the Arminian Robert Shank sees the inconsistency of the four-point position: "Why should Jesus bear the sins of men who have no prospect of forgiveness and whose inevitable destiny, by decree of God, is eternal perdition?"[66] The denial of Limited Atonement by some Calvinists conclusively proves that it is non-essential to the TULIP system.

The Atonement

Just as a denial of Unconditional Election is translated by Calvinists into a departure from salvation by grace, so the Calvinists imply that anyone who denies Limited Atonement rejects the true doctrine of the Atonement as found in the Bible. Therefore, an inquiry into the true nature of the biblical doctrine of the Atonement is in order to lay the groundwork for a rejection of Limited Atonement and a defense of an unlimited atonement. The death of Jesus Christ is universally acknowledged to be one of the most significant events in history. To the Christian, however, it is much more than just a historical event, it is the God-appointed atonement for sin. And as A. A. Hodge states: "The doctrine of the Atonement is evidently the central and principal element of the doctrine of Justification."[67] The Atonement is the distinguishing mark of Christianity. Buddha (c. 563-483) and Mohammed (570-632) never professed to die for anyone's sins. Although the Bible is clear in its description of the nature of the Atonement, the failure to believe it as written has resulted in a number of theories that are all notably deficient in one respect: Christ did not die *for* anyone's sins.

Before passing on to the scriptural design of the Atonement, we digress to first examine what the Atonement is *not*, by an examination of some of the divergent theories regarding it:

> 1. Ransom theory: first advocated by Origen (184-254), this theory maintains that the death of Christ constituted a ransom paid to Satan. Christ did not die *for* anyone's sins.[68]

> 2. Recapitulation theory: first advocated by Irenaeus (130-200), this theory maintains that Christ recapitulates in himself all the stages of human life, experiencing all that Adam did, and compensating for Adam's disobedience by his obedience. Christ

did not die *for* anyone's sins.[69]

3. Commercial theory: first advocated by Anselm (1033-1109), this theory maintains that the death of Christ restored the honor to God the Father that man's sin robbed God of. Christ did not die *for* anyone's sins.[70]

4. Moral Influence theory: first advocated by Abelard (1079-1142), this theory maintains that the death of Christ was a manifestation of the love of God toward the sinner to influence him. Christ did not die *for* anyone's sins.[71]

5. Example theory: first advocated by Socinians, this theory maintains that Christ died as a martyr as an example of obedience to inspire men to reform. Christ did not die *for* anyone's sins.[72]

6. Accident theory: popularized by Albert Schweitzer (1875-1965), this theory maintains that the death of Christ was merely an accident. Christ did not die *for* anyone's sins.[73]

7. Governmental theory: first advocated by Grotius, this theory maintains that the death of Christ was a demonstration that revealed God's hatred for sin in order to uphold respect for God's law. Christ did not die *for* anyone's sins.[74]

8. Mystical theory: advocated with some differences by various men, this theory is similar to the Moral Influence theory but maintains that a change is produced in man, not by a moral influence, but by a mystical union of God and man brought about by the Incarnation. Christ did not die *for* anyone's sins.[75]

As is evident, every one of these theories suffers from one major fault: Christ did not die *for* anyone's sins.

Turning now from man's postulations to the Bible's pronouncements, we can see the true nature of the Atonement: the idea of substitution. Christ died not just *on behalf of* others, but *in the place of* others. Specifically, the death of Christ was a penal substitution in which he became the sin-bearer and the curse-bearer:

For he hath made him *to be* sin for us, who knew no sin; that we might be made the righteousness of God in him (2

> Cor. 5:21).

> **Christ hath redeemed us from the curse of the law, being made a curse for us: for it is written, Cursed *is* every one that hangeth on a tree (Gal. 3:13).**

That the death of Christ was a penal substitution presupposes a number of things. The holiness and justice of God demand that the sinfulness of man be punished. The Lord Jesus Christ, because he alone was both God **"manifest in the flesh"** (1 Tim. 3:16) and a man **"holy, harmless, undefiled, separate from sinners, and made higher than the heavens"** (Heb. 7:26), was able to mediate between both parties: **"For *there is* one God, and one mediator between God and men, the man Christ Jesus"** (1 Tim. 2:5). God could not just forgive the sinner, for as Pink says: "The sinner is only forgiven on the ground of Another having borne his punishment."[76] It was for this reason that Jesus Christ came into the world:

> **This *is* a faithful saying, and worthy of all acceptation, that Christ Jesus came into the world to save sinners; of whom I am chief (1 Tim. 1:15).**

> **Wherefore when he cometh into the world, he saith, Sacrifice and offering thou wouldest not, but a body hast thou prepared me (Heb. 10:5).**

This he did voluntarily (John 10:17-18), completely (John 19:30), once for all (Heb. 10:10), by one offering (Heb. 10:14) that God **"might be just and the justifier of him which believeth in Jesus"** (Rom. 3:26). Yet, it should also be remembered that God was not obligated to make atonement for any man. He could save no one and still be holy and just. The grace of God is any move of God toward man.

Regarding the Atonement of Christ, the New Testament mentions the word *atonement* but one time: **"And not only *so*, but we also joy in God through our Lord Jesus Christ, by whom we have now received the atonement"** (Rom. 5:11). *The Atonement*, not like the many atonements of the Old Testament which just covered sin, but expressing the specific thing which Christ wrought in order to save men. Although the use of the term *atonement* is often disparaged,[77] Homer Hoeksema explains that "the term *atonement* covers such confessional terms as *redemption, redeem, purchase, satisfy, propitiatory sacrifice,* etc. And it covers such Scriptural terms as *reconciliation, propitiation, ransom, purchase,* etc. It simply looks at all these various Scriptural and confessional terms from a very basic point of view."[78]

The Atonement is set forth in the Scripture in a number of ways: Sacrifice, Ransom, Expiation, Propitiation, Reconciliation.

1. Sacrifice: The sacrifice was the divinely instituted provision whereby the sin might be covered and the liability to wrath and curse removed. It involved a substitutive endurance of the penalty or liability due to sin. Jesus Christ was to offer himself a sacrifice for our sins:

> Yet it pleased the LORD to bruise him; he hath put *him* to grief: when thou shalt make his soul an offering for sin, he shall see *his* seed, he shall prolong *his* days, and the pleasure of the LORD shall prosper in his hand (Isa. 53:10).

> Purge out therefore the old leaven, that ye may be a new lump, as ye are unleavened. For even Christ our passover is sacrificed for us (1 Cor. 5:7).

> And walk in love, as Christ also hath loved us, and hath given himself for us an offering and a sacrifice to God for a sweetsmelling savour (Eph. 5:2).

> Who needeth not daily, as those high priests, to offer up sacrifice, first for his own sins, and then for the people's: for this he did once, when he offered up himself (Heb. 7:27).

> By the which will we are sanctified through the offering of the body of Jesus Christ once *for all* (Heb. 10:10).

> But this man, after he had offered one sacrifice for sins for ever, sat down on the right hand of God (Heb. 10:12).

2. Ransom: The sacrifice of Christ was in the form of a ransom. A ransom is the securing of a release by the payment of a price. To be redeemed is to be delivered by the payment of a ransom. Redemption presupposes some kind of bondage or captivity. In his sacrificial death, Jesus Christ was our substitute, thereby redeeming

us:

> Even as the Son of man came not to be ministered unto, but to minister, and to give his life a ransom for many (Mat. 20:28).

> In whom we have redemption through his blood, *even* the forgiveness of sins (Col. 1:14).

> Who gave himself a ransom for all, to be testified in due time (1 Tim. 2:6).

> Who gave himself for us, that he might redeem us from all iniquity, and purify unto himself a peculiar people, zealous of good works (Tit. 2:14).

> Neither by the blood of goats and calves, but by his own blood he entered in once into the holy place, having obtained eternal redemption *for us* (Heb. 9:12).

> Forasmuch as ye know that ye were not redeemed with corruptible things, as silver and gold, from your vain conversation *received* by tradition from your fathers;
> But with the precious blood of Christ, as of a lamb without blemish and without spot (1 Pet. 1:18-19).

3. Expiation: The sacrificial ransom of Christ was a penal expiation in that it removed the guilt of sin by canceling and purging it out. Expiation respects the effect which satisfaction has upon sin or the sinner. This is accomplished by the vicarious suffering of our penalty by Jesus Christ:

> The next day John seeth Jesus coming unto him, and saith, Behold the Lamb of God, which taketh away the sin of the world (John 1:29).

> For he hath made him *to be* sin for us, who knew no sin; that we might be made the righteousness of God in him (2 Cor. 5:21).

> Who being the brightness of *his* glory, and the express image of his person, and upholding all things by the word of his

> power, when he had by himself purged our sins, sat down on the right hand of the Majesty on high (Heb. 1:3).

> How much more shall the blood of Christ, who through the eternal Spirit offered himself without spot to God, purge your conscience from dead works to serve the living God? (Heb. 9:14).

> For then must he often have suffered since the foundation of the world: but now once in the end of the world hath he appeared to put away sin by the sacrifice of himself (Heb. 9:26).

> For Christ also hath once suffered for sins, the just for the unjust, that he might bring us to God, being put to death in the flesh, but quickened by the Spirit (1 Pet. 3:18).

4. Propitiation: To propitiate means to placate, pacify, appease, conciliate—all of which presupposes the wrath and displeasure of God. For this cause the Liberals and Modernists are appalled at the idea of propitiation. To deny propitiation, however, is to deny the nature of the Atonement as a necessary satisfaction. God is holy and necessarily must **"be just and the justifier of him which believeth in Jesus"** (Rom. 3:26). Propitiation removes the judicial displeasure of God. It is the appeasing or turning away of the wrath of a righteous God against sin by the acceptance of Christ's death as a satisfactory substitute:

> Whom God hath set forth *to be* a propitiation through faith in his blood, to declare his righteousness for the remission of sins that are past, through the forbearance of God (Rom. 3:25).

> And he is the propitiation for our sins: and not for ours only, but also for *the sins of* the whole world (1 John 2:2).

> Herein is love, not that we loved God, but that he loved us, and sent his Son *to be* the propitiation for our sins (1 John 4:10).

5. Reconciliation: Reconciliation contemplates our alienation from God and the method of restoring us to his favor. The cause of

this alienation is our sin; the ground of it is the absolute holiness of God. On account of this holiness, enmity exists between God and man (Eph. 2:15-16) because our sin necessarily evokes this reaction of his holiness. The propitiatory sacrifice of Christ is the cause for reconciliation:

> **For if, when we were enemies, we were reconciled to God by the death of his Son, much more, being reconciled, we shall be saved by his life (Rom. 5:10).**
>
> **And all things *are* of God, who hath reconciled us to himself by Jesus Christ, and hath given to us the ministry of reconciliation;**
> **To wit, that God was in Christ, reconciling the world unto himself, not imputing their trespasses unto them; and hath committed unto us the word of reconciliation (2 Cor. 5:18-19).**
>
> **And that he might reconcile both unto God in one body by the cross, having slain the enmity thereby (Eph. 2:16).**
>
> **And having made peace through the blood of this cross, by him to reconcile all things unto himself; by him, *I say*, whether *they be* things in earth, or things in heaven.**
> **And you, that were sometime alienated and enemies in *your* mind by wicked works, yet now hath he reconciled (Col. 1:20-21).**
>
> **Wherefore in all things it behoved him to be made like unto *his* brethren, that he might be a merciful and faithful high priest in things *pertaining* to God, to make reconciliation for the sins of the people (Heb. 2:17).**

Calvinists would equally disparage all of the false theories of the Atonement as they would agree with the above biblical view of the Atonement. The problem is that they will not let their opponents do the same. A rejection of Limited Atonement does not mean that the doctrine of the Atonement as found in the Bible can not be believed. The Calvinists' argument with their opponents should be "limited" to the extent of the Atonement, not the nature of it. But to make their doctrine of Limited Atonement more palatable, Calvinists try to relate it in every way possible to those whom it was never intended: "the non-elect."

In an attempt to soften their doctrine of Limited Atonement, most Calvinists will advocate that the Atonement was *sufficient* for all men but *efficient* for only the "elect."[79] Although used inattentively by non-Calvinists, the adage was coined by Augustine,[80] and is called by Dabney: "The well known Calvinistic formula."[81] By quoting this formula, or talking about the Atonement having infinite saving potential,[82] Calvinists can make their opponents think that the Atonement had some relation to the "non-elect." There is, however, some dissension among the Calvinists. Sproul, although acknowledging that "the value of Christ's atonement is sufficient to cover the sins of the world," claims that it is the Arminians who use the formula that "Christ's atonement is *sufficient* for all, but *efficient* only for some."[83] Nettles maintains that the Atonement was not sufficient for all—it was sufficient only for the "elect"—and that the sufficient/efficient formula fails "to differentiate effectual and definite atonement from general atonement."[84] He calls on "Calvinistic Baptists (and Calvinists of all sorts) to reexamine the traditional formula of 'sufficient but efficient' and perhaps question its aptness as an accurate description of effectual or limited atonement."[85]

Another tactic used by Calvinists to relate their doctrine of Limited Atonement to the "non-elect" is to talk about the benefits of Christ's death to the world in general. According to Dabney, the death of Christ (1) "makes a display of God's general benevolence and pity towards all lost sinners," (2) "purchased for the whole human race a merciful postponement of the doom incurred by our sins, including all the temporal blessings of our earthly life, all the gospel restraints upon human depravity, and the sincere offer of heaven to all," and, although (3) "wilfully rejected by men, sets the stubbornness, wickedness and guilt of their nature in a much stronger light."[86] Boettner adds that the Atonement "forms a basis for the preaching of the Gospel and thus introduces many uplifting moral influences into the world and restrains many evil influences."[87] Others claim that the Atonement provides "common grace" to all men.[88] Cunningham insists that "the advocates of universal atonement, then, have no right to charge us with teaching that none derive any benefit from Christ's death except those who are pardoned and saved; we do not teach this, and we are not bound in consistency to teach it."[89] By denying that an atonement was made for them, but by extending the benefits of Christ's death to the "non-elect," some Calvinists have the audacity to say that they believe Christ died for all men:

> There is, then, a certain sense in which Christ died for all men, and we do not reply to the Arminian tenet with an unqualified negative.[90]

> Christ died for the whole created world (John 3:16), including Satan.[91]

But as the Dutch Reformed Calvinist Homer Hoeksema has aptly stated: "If Christ died for the elect only, then there are no possible benefits in that death of Christ for anyone else but those for whom he died."[92] This view alone is consistent Calvinism. And has been maintained throughout this chapter, even if Christ actually did make an atonement for all men, if certain men are not of those elected to salvation, then what does it matter whether Christ died for them or not? It makes absolutely no difference whatsoever whether Christ died for the "non-elect," for in the system of TULIP Calvinism, the so-called non-elect couldn't possibly be saved whether Christ died for them or not. It is only due to the objectionable nature of Limited Atonement that some Calvinists try to relate it in every way possible to those whom it was never intended.

Arguments

Before investigating the actual Scripture proof texts for or against Limited Atonement, it would be admissible to examine certain arguments presented by the Calvinists in behalf of Limited Atonement that have some semblance of credibility. These arguments are five in number: (1) A universal atonement demands a universal salvation. (2) Double jeopardy. (3) A universal atonement doesn't actually save anyone. (4) The relationship between Adam and Christ. (5) The sin of unbelief. Each one of them, however, suffers from the same fallacy, that of making the Atonement and its application the same thing.

The first reasonable postulation, and one that is the most common, is that a universal atonement demands a universal salvation. Calvinists believe that if the Atonement was unlimited in scope then it would result in the universal salvation of all mankind:

> It seems to follow from the idea of unlimited atonement that salvation is universal.[93]
>
> If Christ has paid the debt of sin, has saved, ransomed, given His life for *all* men, then *all* men will be saved.[94]
>
> If Christ's death secured salvation as Calvinism teaches, and it was also for every man as Arminianism teaches, then we would have to conclude that all people are saved.[95]

Sometimes this universalism argument is taken to ridiculous extremes:

> You cannot make good the assertion, "That Christ died for them that perish," without holding . . . "That all the damned souls would hereafter be brought out of hell."[96]
>
> If Christ died substitutionally for all mankind, bearing the divine penalty and guilt for the sins of all men without exception, it would appear that at the "great white throne" judgment there will remain no one to be punished, other than the fallen angels, and consequently all men would be saved.[97]

The truth of the doctrine of Limited Atonement will soon be made manifest. If belief in an unlimited atonement demands a universal salvation then the Atonement and its application are the same thing.

The next argument used by the Calvinists is that of "double jeopardy." The idea being that if Christ has paid for a man's sins then, legally speaking, it would be double jeopardy for him to be judged for those sins and sent to hell. Therefore, since all men are not saved, Christ could not have died for all men. Custance and Boettner explain their position:

> *No man can be held accountable for a debt that has already been paid for on his behalf to the satisfaction of the offended party.* But a double jeopardy, a duplication of indebtedness, is indeed involved if the non-elect are to be punished for sins for which the Lord Jesus Christ has already endured punishment. And this is what *un*-limited atonement means if interpreted in the universalistic sense that Christ died for the sins of all men. It follows therefore that if the unsaved are to be punished, the Lord cannot *also* have been punished substitutionally on their

account.[98]

> For God to have laid the sins of all men on Christ would mean that as regards the lost He would be punishing their sins twice, once in Christ, and then again in them. Certainly that would be unjust. If Christ paid their debt, they are free, and the Holy Spirit would invariably bring them to faith and repentance."[99]

To give weight to this supposition, a tear-jerking poem is often quoted in whole or in part:[100]

> If Thou hast my discharge procured,
> And freely in my place endured
> The whole of wrath Divine;
> Payment God will not twice demand,
> First at my bleeding Surety's hand,
> And then again at mine.

The theological implication behind this little dictum is that God would be unjust to condemn any man to hell for whom Christ died. In other words, the Atonement and its application are one and the same.

Some Calvinists argue that a universal atonement doesn't actually save anyone. They maintain that their opponents only believe in a potential atonement: "The Arminians also place a limitation on the atoning work of Christ, but one of a much different nature. They hold that Christ's saving work was designed to make possible the salvation of all men on the condition that they believe, but that Christ's death *in itself* did not actually secure or guarantee salvation for anyone."[101] Gerstner lamblasts the four-point Calvinist Chafer for teaching that Christ died to make all men "savable."[102] Owen explains the Calvinist position as: "Christ did not die for any upon condition, if they do believe; but he died for all God's elect, that they should believe, and believing have eternal life. Faith itself is among the principal effects and fruits of the death of Christ."[103] Therefore, as Dabney says: "Christ's work for the elect does not merely put them in a salvable state, but purchases for them a complete and assured salvation."[104] But if the Atonement itself purchased "a complete and assured salvation" for all the "elect," then the Atonement and its application are the same thing.

Another argument for Limited Atonement is the relationship sustained to the human race by Adam and Christ. Charles Hodge sums this up as:

> The sin of Adam did not make the condemnation of all men merely possible; it was the ground of their actual condemnation. So the righteousness of Christ did not make the salvation of men merely possible, it secured the actual salvation of those for whom He wrought.[105]

But if Christ's death "secured the actual salvation" of those for whom he died, then we repeat that the Atonement and its application are the same thing.

The last, and supposedly the strongest, rationalization for Limited Atonement is that which was first used by John Owen, the infamous antagonist of all unlimited redemptionists. In its original form, the brainstorm of Owen concerned the sin of unbelief as related to three supposed views of Christ's death. This has been corrupted in various ways by other Calvinists (to their misfortune) by changing the three views or divorcing them from the sin of unbelief.[106] The indomitable Owen speaks:

> God imposed his wrath due unto, and Christ underwent the pains of hell for, either all the sins of all men, or all the sins of some men, or some sins of all men. If the last, some sins of all men, then have all men some sins to answer for, and so shall no man be saved; . . . If the second, that is it which we affirm, that Christ in their stead and room suffered for all the sins of all the elect in the world. If the first, why, then, are not all freed from the punishment of all their sins? You will say, "Because of their unbelief; they will not believe." But this unbelief, is it a sin, or not? If not, why should they be punished for it? If it be, then Christ underwent the punishment due to it, or not. If so, then why must that hinder them more than their other sins for which he died from partaking of the fruit of his death? If he did not, then did he not die for all their sins? Let them choose which part they will.[107]

But again, if this philosophical speculation be accepted, then the Atonement and its application are the same thing.

If one's doctrine of the Atonement is built on a false premise then it naturally will lead to an erroneous conclusion. This false premise is making the Atonement and its application the same thing; that is, confounding the *provision* of a Savior with the *applying* of salvation. But before answering the polemics of the Calvinists, the views of several Calvinists are here presented so as to remove any doubt as to what they believe about the Atonement and its application:

> Not to open a door for them to come in if they will or can; not to make a way passable that they may be saved; not to purchase reconciliation and pardon of his Father, which perhaps they shall never enjoy; but actually to save them from all the guilt and power of sin, and from the wrath of God for sin.[108]

> What does redemption mean? It does not mean redeemability, that we are placed in a redeemable position. It means that Christ purchased and procured redemption.[109]

> To say that everything turns on the sinner's acceptance, is to affirm that Christ did nothing more for those who are saved than He did for those who are lost. It is not faith which gives Divine efficacy to the blood; it was the blood which efficaciously purchased faith.[110]

> If satisfaction of the debt of sin is made for any man, then that man's debt of sin and guilt is gone! it is no more! From the moment that satisfaction has been made, that debt is forever removed.[111]

> It was specifically designed for and limited to those whom the Father had given to the Son; and it effectively accomplished their salvation.[112]

> We enjoy an actual reconciliation unto God by his death.[113]

Best not only claims that "Christ's righteousness was imputed to all the elect when Jesus Christ died,"[114] but that "God justifies the elect" on the basis of this imputed righteousness.[115]

So what the Calvinists are saying is that the "elect" were actually saved, redeemed, reconciled, and justified by and at the instant of the Atonement. No Calvinist is being misrepresented; nothing is being taken out of context: the sins of the "elect" were *temporally* taken care of at Calvary. But if the nature of the

Atonement was such that it actually in and of itself provided salvation for those whom it was intended, then the "elect" could never have been born **"dead in trespasses and sins"** (Eph. 2:1). And consequently, how could men who were saved, redeemed, reconciled, and justified be **"by nature children of wrath"** (Eph. 2:3)? If this conclusion be objected to then the only other alternative is an unlimited atonement. If a Calvinist denies that the "elect" were *temporally* saved when Christ died on the cross, then he would have to admit that the *effects* of the Atonement were currently available for the "elect" to appropriate. Therefore, if the Atonement was of infinite value, which Calvinists would say is true, and would be the same whether more or fewer were saved by it, which Calvinists would also assent to, and the effects of the Atonement were currently available for the "elect," which Calvinists would have to affirm if they denied that the "elect" were actually saved at the cross, then the only thing that could prevent any man from being saved is his not being one of the "elect," not that the Atonement was not available for him. But just as we saw in the previous chapter, the so-called elect could not have possibly been saved at the cross for the simple reason that they did not exist.

An example from the Old Testament should settle the question of the application of the Atonement. The Passover, which Pink acknowledges as "one of the most striking and blessed foreshadowments of the cross-work of Christ to be found anywhere in the Old Testament,"[116] is a clear example of the principle that the Atonement and its application are to be distinguished. The blood of the slain passover lamb (Exo. 12:6, 21) became efficacious only after it was applied to the doorpost per instructions (Exo. 12:7, 22). When the Lord went through the land of Egypt he only passed over the houses where the blood was applied, not just where the lamb was slain. The death of the lamb saved no one: the blood had to be applied.

Surprisingly, this is even confirmed by Pink in his commentary on Exodus:

> In like manner to-day, it is not enough for me to know that the precious blood of the Lamb of God was shed for the remission of sins. A Saviour *provided* is not sufficient: he must be *received.* There must be *"faith* in His blood" (Rom. 3:25), and faith is a *personal* thing. *I* must exercise faith. I must by faith take the blood and shelter beneath it. I must place it between my

sins and the thrice Holy god. I must rely upon it as the sole ground of my acceptance with Him.[117]

Gerstner attacks the four-point Calvinist Robert Lightner for appealing to the analogy of the passover lamb to uphold his "contradictory pattern of thought," but never answers Lightner's argument.[118]

It should be obvious by now that the Bible differentiates between the *universal provision* and the *individual application* of the Atonement. The work of Christ is *complete* but *conditional;* the Atonement is *actual* but *potential*. If this is heresy then the only alternative is to say that the "elect" were saved before they were born. Boettner, when discussing a ransom, carelessly says: "The nature of a ransom is such that when paid and accepted it automatically frees the persons for whom it was intended."[119] So a ransom, according to Boettner, must not only be *paid*, it must be *accepted*. Likewise, the Atonement of Christ must not only be *made*, it must be *accepted*. The Bible distinction is apparent. There is a *universal provision* of Christ's death (Heb. 2:9), imputation of sin to Christ (Isa. 53:6), salvation (1 Tim. 4:10), redemption (2 Pet. 2:1), reconciliation (2 Cor. 5:19), propitiation (1 John 2:2), expiation (John 1:29), and sanctification (Heb. 10:29). There is also an *individual application* of Christ's death (Rom. 5:8), imputation of sin to Christ (2 Cor. 5:21), salvation (2 Tim. 1:9), redemption (Col. 1:14), reconciliation (2 Cor. 5:18), propitiation (1 John 4:10), expiation (1 John 3:5), and sanctification (Heb. 10:10).

The distinction between the universal provision and the individual application of the Atonement provides an answer to the arguments for Limited Atonement mentioned previously. The argument about a universal atonement demanding a universal salvation disappears when it is realized that since the so-called elect did not actually exist when Christ died on the cross, the effects of his Atonement would have to be available at the present time for any of them to be saved. The actual Atonement in and of itself not only did not result in a universal salvation, it did not result in the salvation of anyone until it was applied. Likewise, if it is "double jeopardy" for God to hold a man accountable for whom Christ died, then the only alternative is simple: all those for whom Christ died are automatically saved, having their sins expiated at the cross before they were born. Calvinists who maintain that a universal atonement doesn't actually save anyone are wrong on two counts. First of all, when a Calvinist denies that an unlimited atonement actually saves anyone, he leaves the impression that because it did not save anyone at the time it was made that it is powerless to save anyone in the future. But when a Calvinist insists that a Limited Atonement actually saves people, he means that the Atonement in and of itself is the ground of anyone's salvation even though he implies that the Atonement does not save men at the time it was made. But if the Atonement did not actually save anyone at the time it was made, then the Calvinists would have to admit that neither a universal atonement nor a Limited Atonement actually saves anyone. So, as the four-point Calvinist Chafer explains:

> Certainly Christ's death of itself forgives no sinner, nor does it render unnecessary the regenerating work of the Holy Spirit. Any one of the elect whose salvation is predetermined, and for whom Christ died, may live the major portion of his life in open rebellion against God and, during that time, manifest every feature of depravity and spiritual death. This alone should prove that men are not severally saved by the act of Christ in dying, but rather that they are saved by the divine application of that value when they believe.[120]

But secondly, even if no man ever availed himself of a universal atonement in the Church Age, the Bible says: **"And for this cause he is the mediator of the new testament, that by means of death, for the redemption of the transgressions *that were* under the first testament, they which are called might receive the promise of eternal inheritance"** (Heb. 9:15). The Calvinist would at least have to admit that Christ made an effectual atonement for the Old Testament saints.

As pertaining to the analogy between Adam and Christ, the Bible makes this perfectly clear:

> **But not as the offence, so also *is* the free gift. For if through the offence of one many be dead, much more the grace of God, and the gift by grace, *which is* by one man, Jesus Christ, hath abounded unto many (Rom. 5:15).**

> **Therefore as by the offence of one *judgment came* upon all men to condemnation; even so by the righteousness of one *the free gift came* upon all men unto justification of life**

(Rom. 5:18).

But instead of proving Limited Atonement, the analogy rather disproves it. Therefore, although Calvinists correctly interpret the **"many"** in the protasis of verse fifteen as "all," they transform the **"all"** in the apodosis of verse eighteen into "many" and restrict the apodosis of both verses.[121] There is no difference here in extent, but there is in execution. Paul's aim is to show that just as by *one man* came condemnation and death, so by *one man* came righteousness and life. The key to the verses is supplied in the context. Although Adam's sin was both universal and unrefuseable, Christ's **"free gift"** (Rom. 5:16, 18), the **"gift of righteousness,"** must be received (Rom 5:17). As acknowledged by Calvinists, verse eighteen is a summation even as verse nineteen is an explanation: **"For as by one man's disobedience many were made sinners, so by the obedience of one shall many be made righteous"** (Rom. 5:19).[122] The future tense points to the fact that the benefits of Christ's work apply only to those throughout history who receive it.

This is further confirmed in another passage: **"For as in Adam all die, even so in Christ shall all be made alive"** (1 Cor. 15:22). Although the sin of Adam was the ground of all men's condemnation, they were excused if they got "in Christ." And this is where the Calvinist goes astray. For although all men are "in Adam" by descent, Christ had no physical descent, those "in him" got in spiritually and therefore never at their birth, regardless of their being sprinkled into the covenant in a Reformed church. Furthermore, if Christ sustained the same relationship to the race as Adam (which he did), he couldn't possibly have made a limited atonement any more than the fall of Adam could have affected only *part* of his descendants. The simple reason that the Atonement had to be for all men is simple: Christ was the Son of Man (Mat. 8:20; Mark 9:12; Luke 19:10; John 3:13). By virtue of his relationship to mankind, it was impossible for him *not* to make an unlimited atonement. He was the second man (1 Cor. 15:47), and sustained the same relationship to the human race that Adam did; hence, he is also the second Adam (1 Cor. 15:45). The solution for the problem is the same as it was for Unconditional Election and will be the same throughout this book: everything depends on being "in Christ." Jesus Christ had eternal life (John 1:1), he was eternal life (1 John 1:2), and he gives eternal life (John 10:27). By getting "in him" (Eph. 1:4) one is connected intrinsically with eternal life.

Regarding Owen's often-copied, extreme argument about the sin of unbelief, there are two glaring inconsistencies in his reasoning. First of all, why does God demand that men believe if Christ died for, and thereby removed, the sin of unbelief? If **"he that believeth not is condemned already"** (John 3:18), and this sin is expiated and God is propitiated, then no one whom Christ died for could be held accountable for unbelief: they would already be saved. And what would happen if one of the "elect" did not believe? If all his sins were blotted out, which would necessarily include the sin of unbelief, how could he be "condemned already" for not believing? Secondly, if Christ did not die for certain men they cannot be condemned for unbelief. A man cannot reject what does not exist. The Gospel is that **"Christ died for our sins according to the scriptures; And that he was buried, and that he rose again the third day according to the scriptures"** (1 Cor. 15:3-4). If Christ did not die for a man then there is no Gospel for him to believe or not believe. According to the one who made the Atonement, the reason the Holy Spirit will **"reprove the world of sin"** (John 16:8) is **"because they believe not on me"** (John 16:9). So rather than proving the truth of Limited Atonement, the argument about the sin of unbelief does nothing but negate it. Not to be thwarted, Owen makes one last attempt to bludgeon his opponents:

> Doth it become the wisdom of God to send Christ to die for men that they might be saved, and never cause these men to hear of any such thing; and yet to purpose and declare that unless they do hear of it and believe it, they shall never be saved? What wise man would pay a ransom for the delivery of those captives which he is sure shall never come to the knowledge of any such payment made, and so never be the better for it? Is it answerable to the goodness of God, to deal thus with his poor creatures? to hold out towards them all in pretence the most intense love imaginable, beyond all compare and illustration,—as his love in sending his Son is set forth to be,—and yet never let them know of any such thing, but in the end to damn them for not believing it?[123]

To which we reply: doth it become the wisdom and goodness of God to elect billions to hell before their birth by a sovereign, eternal decree of Unconditional Election, and to make it certain, to render them with Total Depravity so that they will be unable to receive Irresistible Grace which will not even be offered to them in the first place since Christ did not make a Limited Atonement for them?

Proof Texts

In taking up the actual Scripture proof texts used to prove Limited Atonement, it will be seen that Calvinists defend the third point of the TULIP with a vigor equal to their defense of the other points. Gerstner begins: "We maintain that all texts dealing with this subject, properly understood, teach that Christ died only for the elect."[124] There are three types of Scripture passages used by Calvinists in an attempt to prove Limited Atonement: (1) Christ dying for the world. (2) Christ dying for all men. (3) Christ dying for a particular group. Since the first two types of Scriptures so obviously mitigate against their doctrine, Calvinists only use them to prove Limited Atonement in the course of defending themselves against the attacks of their opponents. The Calvinist dilemma is stated by Sproul: "The biggest problem with definite or limited atonement is found in the passages that the Scriptures use concerning Christ's death 'for all' or for the 'whole world.'"[125] Steele and Thomas concur, and explain:

> One reason for the use of these expression was to correct the false notion that salvation was for the Jews alone. Such phrases as "the world," "all men," "all nations," and "every creature" were used by the New Testament writers to emphatically correct this mistake. These expression are intended to show that Christ died for all men without *distinction* (i.e., He died for Jews and Gentiles alike) but they are not intended to indicate that Christ died for all men without *exception* (i.e., He did not die for the purpose of saving each and every lost sinner).[126]

Sproul also adds: "The world for whom Christ died cannot mean the entire human family. It must refer to the universality of the elect (people from every tribe and nation)."[127] The other group of verses advanced in support of Limited Atonement are used offensively by the Calvinists against their opponents, but these will found to be spurious as well.

The first type of Scriptures that concern Limited Atonement are those passages that present Christ as dying for the world. There are three groups of texts to be considered: those in the Gospel of John, those in the Pauline Epistles, and those in the First John. Although Calvinists confound the world with the so-called elect, the Bible plainly declares the universality of the Atonement for the world:

> **The next day John seeth Jesus coming unto him, and saith, Behold the Lamb of God, which taketh away the sin of the world (John 1:29).**
>
> **For God so loved the world, that he gave his only begotten Son, that whosoever believeth in him should not perish, but have everlasting life (John 3:16).**
>
> **And said unto the woman, Now we believe, not because of thy saying: for we have heard *him* ourselves, and know that this is indeed the Christ, the Saviour of the world (John 4:42).**
>
> **I am the living bread which came down from heaven: if any man eat of this bread, he shall live for ever: and the bread that I will give is my flesh, which I will give for the life of the world (John 6:51).**
>
> **To wit, that God was in Christ, reconciling the world unto himself, not imputing their trespasses unto them; and hath committed unto us the word of reconciliation (2 Cor. 5:19).**
>
> **And he is the propitiation for our sins: and not for ours only, but also for *the sins of* the whole world (1 John 2:2).**
>
> **And we have seen and do testify that the Father sent the Son *to be* the Saviour of the world (1 John 4:14).**

And what do the Calvinists do when confronted with a universal atonement? Custance admits the obvious implications: "Statements like these, and there are many others, appear to prohibit placing limitations upon the intrinsic worth of that sacrifice or upon its intention in application."[128]

Beginning with the Gospel of John, it is clear that the Lamb of God took away the sin of the world. Or did he? Pink explains: "As to *who's* 'sin' (i.e., *guilt*, as in 1 John 1:7, etc.) *has been* 'put away,' Scripture leaves us in no doubt—it was that of the elect, the 'world' (John 1:29) of God's people!"[129] Gunn adds: "Christ also will take away the sin of the world in the sense that He will totally remove sin and the curse from the world at His second coming."[130] Did Jesus Christ give his flesh for the life of the world? Not according to John Owen: "Because it was not for the Jews only, but also for all the elect of God everywhere, he calleth them 'the world.' That the *world* here cannot signify all and every one that ever were or should be, is as manifest as if it were written with the beams of the sun."[131] Pink adds: "We are *obliged* to understand the reference in John 6:33 as being to the 'world of the godly', i.e., God's own people."[132] Is Christ the Saviour of the world? Again, Owen gives us the Calvinist interpretation: "Because he saves all that are saved, even the people of God (not the Jews only), all over the world."[133] Regarding John 3:16, the most familiar verse in the Bible, Calvinists have worked overtime to nullify it. Homer Hoeksema claims that the word **"world"** in John 3:16 denotes "the sum total of the elect as an organic whole, the body of Christ, the church."[134] Incredibly, Ness claims that **"whosoever"** in John 3:16 "restrains this love of God to some and not to others."[135] Other Calvinists attempt to change the subject. Talbot and Crampton assert: "John 3:16 (and other passages like it) says nothing about who is *capable* of coming to Christ."[136] R. B. Kuiper (1886-1966) insists that "the emphasis of John 3:16 is on the sinfulness of the world, not on its size, and consequently on the sovereignty of God's love rather than its comprehensiveness."[137] Pink speaks for the majority of Calvinists when he declares: "The 'world' in John 3:16 must, in the final analysis, refer to the world of God's people. *Must* we say, for there is no other alternative *solution*."[138] But even five-point Calvinists posit another alternative. Although giving credence to Pink's view of John 1:29, the Presbyterian theologian Dabney remarks: "Make 'the world' which Christ loved, to mean 'the elect world;' and we reach the absurdity, that some of the elect may not believe, and perish."[139] And even Kuiper acknowledges: "It is doubtful whether anywhere in Scripture the world is identified with the elect."[140] Nevertheless, if one is a five-point Calvinist, the word *world* is generally taken to be a synonym for the "elect."

So everything hinges on the meaning of the word *world*. As Spencer says: "Much of what we think about the atoning death of

Christ will be tempered by what we understand the simple word 'world' to mean."[141] Calvinists are quick to point out that the word *world* is used in several different senses.[142] They also appeal to plainly hyperbolic phrases like **"behold, the world is gone after him"** (John 12:19) to prove that the world only means the "elect."[143] But no one is disputing that the word *world* is used in different senses. What is disputed, however, is that the term ever signifies the so-called elect.

The word *world* occurs eighty times in the Gospel of John in fifty-nine verses. And although it is used in different senses, it never refers to the "elect." The world knew not Christ (John 1:10). The world hates Christ (John 7:7). The world's works are evil (John 7:7). Unsaved Jews were of this world (John 8:23). Satan is the prince of this world (John 12:31, 14:30, 16:11). Christ's own are distinguished from the world (John 13:1, 14:19, 22). The world cannot receive the Holy Spirit (John 14:17). The world hates the disciples (John 15:18, 17:14). The disciples were not of the world (John 15:19, 17:16). The world brings tribulation (John 16:33). The disciples were out of the world (John 17:6). Christ prayed not for the world (John 17:9). Christ is not of the world (John 17:16). The disciples were sent into the world (John 17:18). The world did not know God (John 17:25). Christ's kingdom is not of this world (John 18:36). In arguing for Limited Atonement, Sproul inadvertently proves that the world does not refer to the "elect": "Jesus' atonement and his intercession are joint works of his high priesthood. He explicitly excludes the non-elect from his great high priestly prayer. 'I do not pray for the world but for those whom you have given Me' (John 17:9). Did Christ die for those for whom he would not pray?"[144] Herman Hoeksema also inadvertently admits that "when our Lord announces Himself as the light of the world it is evident that He speaks of the world of men, of the entire human race."[145] So not only does the word *world* never denote the "elect," it is unequivocally demeaned and condemned by God.

Although Kuiper maintains that "the term *world* as used in John 3:16 presents a serious difficulty of exegesis,"[146] the context makes it perfectly clear. To explain John 3:16 without making mention of what the context is referring to is to give evidence of a deceitful motive. A comparison is being made between an incident in the time of Moses and the death of Christ. What is true of the former is necessarily true of the latter. The passages seen together are as follows:

> And as Moses lifted up the serpent in the wilderness, even so must the Son of man be lifted up:
> That whosoever believeth in him should not perish, but have eternal life (John 3:14-15).

> And the LORD sent fiery serpents among the people, and they bit the people; and much people of Israel died.
> Therefore the people came to Moses, and said, We have spoken against the LORD, and against thee; pray unto the LORD, that he take away the serpents from us. And Moses prayed for the people.
> And the LORD said unto Moses, Make thee a fiery serpent, and set it upon a pole: and it shall come to pass, that every one that is bitten, when he looketh upon it, shall live.
> And Moses made a serpent of brass, and put it upon a pole, and it came to pass, that if a serpent had bitten any man, when he beheld the serpent of brass, he lived (Num. 21:6-9).

Just as the cure for being bitten was obtained by believing what God said and doing it (Num 21:8), so the cure for sin is obtained by believing what God said and doing it (John 3:15). Another reason it is obvious that the world in John 3:16 could not be the "elect" is that, in the Calvinistic system, the so-called elect have never been in danger of perishing and never can be. And not only does John 3:14-15 explain John 3:16, but John 3:19 defines the world as "men": **"And this is the condemnation, that light is come into the world, and men loved darkness rather than light, because their deeds were evil"** (John 3:19). That is why that when Christ comes as a light into the world, individual men must believe to get out of darkness (John 12:46). Likewise, although Christ gave his flesh for the life of the world, individual men must eat of it (John 6:51), which is defined as believing (John 6:27-29).

Turning now to the Pauline Epistles, we read: **"To wit, that God was in Christ, reconciling the world unto himself, not imputing their trespasses unto them; and hath committed unto us the word of reconciliation"** (2 Cor. 5:19). Sproul claims that "Semi-Pelagians" appeal to this verse.[147] So who was reconciled by Christ's death? Gary Long asserts: "It is concluded, therefore, that II Corinthians 5:19 does not teach that all men distributively (i.e., without exception) have been reconciled either provisionally or hypothetically. Rather it teaches that God is and has been reconciling His people (without distinction from the world in a relative sense) one by one throughout history and will continue so until the last one of His sheep is added to His fold."[148] Pink likewise rejoins in further detail: "Here again, 'the world' *cannot* mean 'the world of the ungodly,' for *their* 'trespasses' are 'imputed' to them, as the judgment of the Great White Throne will yet show. But 2 Cor. 5:19 plainly teaches there *is* a 'world' which *are* 'reconciled,' reconciled unto God, because their trespasses are *not* reckoned to their account, having been borne by their Substitute. Who then are they? Only one answer is fairly possible—the world of God's people!"[149] Two things, then, need to be determined: the identification of the world, and the nature of reconciliation.

In the Pauline Epistles, the word *world* occurs sixty-nine times in sixty-one verses. And like the Gospel of John, it is used in several different senses but never refers to the "elect." The world by wisdom knew not God (1 Cor. 1:21). The wisdom of this world is disparaged (1 Cor. 2:6, 3:19). The princes of this world crucified Christ (1 Cor. 2:8). The spirit of the world is disparaged (1 Cor. 2:12). The saints shall judge the world (1 Cor. 6:2). Satan is the God of this world (2 Cor. 4:4), the world is evil (Gal. 1:4). The elements of the world are warned against (Gal. 4:3). Christians shine as lights in the world (Phil. 2:15). The rudiments of the world are warned against (Col. 2:20). So not only does the word *world* never denote the "elect," it is unequivocally demeaned and condemned by God. That the world in 2 Corinthians 5:19 does not refer to the "elect" is confirmed by the Calvinist George Smeaton (1814-1889): "Here it does not mean the world of believers—a sense in which, so far as I know, it does not occur—but the world of mankind as one day standing out to view."[150]

As for the nature of reconciliation, and as mentioned previously, the Bible differentiates between the universal provision and the individual application of the different aspects of the Atonement. The context of 2 Corinthians 5:19 makes this evident as pertaining to reconciliation:

And all things *are* of God, who hath reconciled us to himself by Jesus Christ, and hath given to us the ministry of

> reconciliation;
> To wit, that God was in Christ, reconciling the world unto himself, not imputing their trespasses unto them; and hath committed unto us the word of reconciliation.
> Now then we are ambassadors for Christ, as though God did beseech *you* by us: we pray *you* in Christ's stead, be ye reconciled to God.
> For he hath made him *to be* sin for us, who knew no sin; that we might be made the righteousness of God in him (2 Cor. 5:18-21).

Owen maintains that "they who are called the world, verse 19, are termed 'us,' verse 18."[151] But the Apostle Paul elsewhere contrasts "us" with "the world":

> Now we have received, not the spirit of the world, but the spirit which is of God; that we might know the things that are freely given to us of God (1 Cor. 2:12).

> Who gave himself for our sins, that he might deliver us from this present evil world, according to the will of God and our Father (Gal. 1:4).

The "elect" could not have been reconciled at the cross—God **"not imputing their trespasses unto them"**—for the simple reason that they were not yet in existence. And secondly, the "elect" could not have been personally reconciled until they believed. The reason being that they were in their sins until they were saved (1 Cor. 15:17). The true nature of the reconciliation of the "elect" is confirmed by noting the context. If the "elect" were actually reconciled at the cross *like the Calvinists say they were,* then what is Paul doing with a ministry of reconciliation? What is Paul doing in 2 Corinthians 5:20 beseeching people to be reconciled to God? Obviously, he did not believe in Limited Atonement.

This two-fold differentiation of reconciliation is likewise observed in Colossians:

> And having made peace through the blood of his cross, by him to reconcile all things unto himself; by him, *I say,* whether *they be* things in earth, or things in heaven.
> And you, that were sometime alienated and enemies in *your*

LIMITED ATONEMENT

mind by wicked works, yet now hath he reconciled (Col. 1:20-21).

Because not even a Calvinist could say that the **"all things"** which are reconciled in Colossians 1:20 represent the "elect," Long invents a distinction between what he calls "cosmic reconciliation" (Col. 1:20) and "soteric reconciliation" (Col 1:21).[152] So although holding to Limited Atonement, Long recognized that there really is a two-fold distinction of reconciliation. Yet, he still assails the two-fold application of terms as set forth by those who hold to an unlimited atonement.[153]

Moving to First John, we find two verses which explicitly state that Christ died for the world:

And he is the propitiation for our sins: and not for ours only, but also for the sins of the whole world (1 John 2:2).

And we have seen and do testify that the Father sent the Son to be the Saviour of the world (1 John 4:14).

The Calvinists have a particular problem with 1 John 2:2, as they themselves acknowledge:

On the surface this text seems to demolish limited atonement.[154]

Perhaps no text in Scripture presents more plausible support to the doctrine of universal atonement than 1 John 2:2.[155]

There is one passage more than any other which is appealed to by those who believe in universal redemption, and which at first sight appears to teach that Christ died for the whole human race.[156]

Although Calvinists disagree among themselves as to the exact interpretation of this verse, they are all united in their denial that the Atonement of Christ was for the world.

Speaking for most Calvinists who have commented on 1 John 2:2, Pink gives the standard Calvinistic interpretation:

When John says, "He is the propitiation for *our* sins" he can only mean for the sins of *Jewish believers*.[157]

When John added, "And not for ours only, but also for *the whole world*" he signified that Christ was the propitiation for the sins of *Gentile* believers *too*, for, as previously shown, "the world" is a term *contrasted* from Israel.[158]

Pink insolently claims that "the above interpretation is confirmed by the fact that no other is consistent or intelligible."[159] He also adds that "to insist that 'the whole world' in 1 John 2:2 signifies the entire human race is to undermine the very foundations of our faith."[160] It is indeed strange how anti-dispensational, Reformed Calvinists, who minimize any distinction between Israel and the Church, suddenly become dispensationalists when trying to explain away 1 John 2:2. In his early book *The Sovereignty of God,* Pink states that "John also is writing *to* saved Israelites, but *for* saved Jews *and* saved Gentiles."[161] In a later work, however, Pink laments that certain "would-be super-expositors dogmatically assert that the four Gospels are Jewish, and that the epistles of James and Peter, John and Jude are designed for a 'godly Jewish remnant' in a future 'tribulation period,' that nothing but the Pauline epistles contain 'Church truth.'"[162] But as we have seen in the previous chapter, and will see again, when a Calvinist wishes to prove his doctrine, the distinction between Jews and Gentiles or Israel and the Church is regularly obliterated.

The majority of Calvinists agree with this *ethnological* interpretation,[163] but there is some dissension in the camp. Some take the **"whole world"** *geographically;* that is, the "elect" outside of Asia Minor.[164] Warfield takes the **"whole world"** *eschatologically*—the future world that is saved at the second coming of Christ.[165] Smeaton has it "the redeemed of every period, place, and people—that is, prospectively and retrospectively."[166] He then categorically insists: "This is the point of the distinction; it is not the distinction elsewhere expressed between Jew and Gentile."[167] And as Dabney maintains: "It is at least doubtful whether the express phrase, 'whole world,' can be restrained to the world of elect as including other than Jews. For it is indisputable, that the Apostle extends the propitiation of Christ beyond those whom he speaks of as 'we,' in verse first. The interpretation described obviously proceeds on the assumption that these are only Jewish believers. Can this be substantiated? Is this catholic epistle addressed only to Jews? This is more than doubtful."[168]

The question in 1 John 2:2 is two-fold: who are the **"our"** and what is meant by **"the world"**? John tells us who he is writing to: **"These things have I written unto you that believe on the name of the Son of God; that ye may know that ye have eternal life, and that ye may believe on the name of the Son of God"** (1 John 5:13). The **"our"** in 1 John 2:2 cannot be limited to just the Jews. The same group has **"fellowship with the Father, and with his Son Jesus Christ"** (1 John 1:3) and has **"an advocate with the Father, Jesus Christ the righteous"** (1 John 2:1). There is no Jew–Gentile distinction that John is here trying to remove, whether among the saved or the lost. In Christ there is no Jew and Gentile:

> **Give none offence, neither to the Jews, nor to the Gentiles, nor to the church of God (1 Cor. 10:32).**

> **There is neither Jew nor Greek, there is neither bond nor free, there is neither male nor female: for ye are all one in Christ Jesus (Gal. 3:28).**

In fact, the words *Jew* and *Gentile* do not even occur in First John, although Paul used them when describing the universality of sin (Rom. 3:9).

Regarding the word *world,* as we have seen in John's Gospel, although it is used in different senses, it never refers to the so-called elect. The word *world* occurs twenty-three times in First John in seventeen verses. We are commanded to **"love not the world"** (1 John 2:15). The world is full of lust (1 John 2:16) and will pass away (1 John 2:17). The world knows neither Christ nor the Christian (1 John 3:1). The **"spirit of antichrist"** is in the world (1 John 4:3). We have overcome the world (1 John 5:4). So not only does the word *world* never denote the "elect," it is unequivocally demeaned and condemned by God. And just as John contrasts Christians with the world in the first place in First John where the word *world* appears, so he delineates the same two groups in the last instance: **"*And* we know that we are of God, and the whole world lieth in wickedness"** (1 John 5:19). John only used the expression **"the whole world"** twice in his first epistle. Could **"the whole world"** that lies in wickedness possibly be "elect Gentiles"? And while it is true, albeit rarely, that in the Bible the word *world* sometimes means "Gentiles as contrasted with Jews" (Rom. 11:12, 15), rather than alleviate the problem, it rather amplifies it. If Christ is the propitiation for the sins of the whole world, meaning the Gentiles: are all Gentiles saved? No Calvinist would make such a foolish assertion. Yet, according to their definition of the extent of the Atonement, anyone whose sins are propitiated is saved.

Sometimes Calvinists make reference to a passage in John's Gospel when attempting to prove their doctrine of Limited Atonement in 1 John 2:2. Pink insists that "if the reader really desires to know the meaning of I John 2:2 let him compare John 11:51, 52."[169] He claims that this "is a strictly parallel passage."[170] In fact, Pink vaunts about proofs for Limited Atonement that "if there is one scripture more than any other upon which we should be willing to rest our case it is John 11:49-52."[171] Therefore, a look at this passage is in order:

> **And one of them, named Caiaphas, being the high priest that same year, said unto them, Ye know nothing at all, Nor consider that it is expedient for us, that one man should die for the people, and that the whole nation perish not. And this spake he not of himself: but being high priest that year, he prophesied that Jesus should die for that nation; And not for that nation only, but that also he should gather together in one the children of God that were scattered abroad (John 11:49-52).**

Pink makes the **"children of God"** the Church: "Is it not remarkable that the members of the Church are here called 'children of God' even before Christ died, and therefore before He commenced to build His Church! The vast majority of them had not then been born, yet were they regarded as 'children of God;' children of God because they had been chosen in Christ before the foundation of the world."[172] But is it not more remarkable how wrong TULIP Calvinism is? Although other Calvinists interpret likewise,[173] Pink's children are bastards (Heb. 12:8).

If Jesus Christ died for the whole Jewish nation like was prophesied by Caiaphas, then all Jews would have to be saved just like all Gentiles would have to be saved in 1 John 2:2 if it is referring to the Gentiles. The way the Calvinists get around this is to further limit the Jews and Gentiles to only the "elect" in each group. But was Caiaphas limiting his prophesy to just the "elect" Jews? Did he not say **"the whole nation"** (John 11:50)? Although Caiaphas equated **"the people"** with **"the whole nation,"** the Jews were now just a nation like the other nations of the earth. When John interprets the prophesy of Caiaphas he reiterates that Christ will die for the nation of the Jews but adds that he will also die for the Jews **"scattered abroad"** (John 11:52). Thus, this is related to the Jewish sheep discussed in the previous chapter. Outside of referring to Israel, the phrase "children of God" is never a reference to members of the Church until they are saved: **"For ye are all the children of God by faith in Christ Jesus"** (Gal. 3:26). Before salvation, the "elect" were **"children of wrath"** (Eph. 2:3) and **"children of disobedience"** (Col. 3:6). Furthermore, if a man was already a child of God in the New Testament sense, why would he need an atonement? Can a child of God go to hell? So regardless of Pink's claim that this "is a strictly parallel passage," John 11:49-52 does not interpret 1 John 2:2. So what is the import of the passage in 1 John 2:2? Simple, Christ was the propitiation for the sins of John and the believers he wrote to, but he was also the propitiation for the sins of the whole world.

The second type of Scriptures that concern Limited Atonement are those passages that present Christ as dying for all men. Like they do regarding the word *world,* Calvinists are quick to point out that the word *all* is used in several different senses.[174] They also appeal to plainly hyperbolic phrases like **"hated of all men"** (Mat. 10:22)[175] to prove that *all* only means the "elect." But just as was pointed out regarding the word *world,* no one is disputing that the word *all* is used in different senses. What is disputed, however, is that the term ever signifies the so-called elect. The Bible plainly declares that the Atonement of Christ was for all men:

> **All we like sheep have gone astray; we have turned every one to his own way; and the LORD hath laid on him the iniquity of us all (Isa. 53:6).**

> **For the love of Christ constraineth us; because we thus judge, that if one died for all, then were all dead (2 Cor. 5:14).**

> **Who gave himself a ransom for all, to be testified in due time (1 Tim. 2:6).**

> **For therefore we both labour and suffer reproach, because we trust in the living God, who is the Saviour of all men,**

> specially of those that believe (1 Tim. 4:10).
>
> But we see Jesus, who was made a little lower than the angels for the suffering of death, crowned with glory and honour; that he by the grace of God should taste death for every man (Heb. 2:9).

And what do the Calvinists do when confronted with a universal atonement? Owen boldly states: "The Scripture nowhere saith Christ died *for all men.*"[176] Pink is even stronger: "To affirm that Christ shed His blood for the sins of all mankind, is to be guilty of charging Him with rebellion against the sovereign will of God."[177]

The first passage to be examined is 2 Corinthians 5:14, where we read that **"one died for all."** As mentioned at the beginning of this section, Calvinists will use verses that obviously mitigate against their doctrine in their attempt prove Limited Atonement, but only in the course of defending themselves against the attacks of their opponents. This is no more apparent than on the verse in question. Calvinists ardently maintain that rather than this verse teaching an unlimited atonement, it is actually strongly in favor of Limited Atonement:

> This is another striking example of how a text may seem at first glance to support a universalistic theory of the atonement but in reality does just the opposite.[178]
>
> So far from lending support to the doctrine of universal atonement this text does the opposite.[179]
>
> If the entire verse and passage from which these words are quoted be carefully examined, it will be found that instead of teaching an unlimited atonement, it emphatically argues a limited design in the death of Christ.[180]

Because it is essential to a proper interpretation of the verse, the passage in full is here given:

> **For the love of Christ constraineth us; because we thus judge, that if one died for all, then were all dead:**
> **And *that* he died for all, that they which live should not henceforth live unto themselves, but unto him which died for them, and rose again (2 Cor. 5:14-15).**

Since they believe that if Christ dies for a man then that man will be saved, Calvinists have to limit the "all" to the "elect." While arriving at the same conclusion, there are two approaches taken by the Calvinists in doing so: one focusing on verse fourteen and the other on verse fifteen. Pink gives us the standard Calvinist interpretation:

> The "all" for which Christ died are the they which "live," and which are here bidden to live "unto Him." This passage then teaches three important truths, and the better to show its scope we mention them in their inverse order: certain ones are here bidden to live no more unto themselves but unto Christ; the some thus admonished are "they which live," that is live spiritually, hence, the children of God, for they alone of mankind possess spiritual life, all others being *dead* in trespasses and sins; those who *do* thus live are the ones, the "all," the "them," for whom Christ died and rose again. This passage therefore teaches that Christ died for *all His people,* the elect, those given to Him by the Father; that as the result of His death (and rising again *"for them"*) they "live"—and the elect are the *only* ones who *do* thus "live;" and this life which is theirs through Christ must be lived "unto Him," Christ's *love* must now "constrain" them.[181]

To reinforce their interpretation, some Calvinists amend the Scripture.[182]

That the **"all"** in verse fourteen really represents all men can be seen by noting that the "elect" are already represented in the verse by the expressions **"us"** and **"we."** But besides not understanding how a man whom Christ died for could not be saved, the mistake of the Calvinists is in assuming that all for whom Christ died will live. Following the restrictive **"us"** and **"we"** in the first part of verse fourteen, **"all"** is used three times in a universal sense. This is followed in verse fifteen by the restrictive phrase **"that they which live,"** implying that not everyone of the **"all"** for whom Christ died lives. Honest Calvinists like Dabney recognize this: "In 2 Cor. v:15, if we make the all for whom Christ died, mean only the all who live unto Him—i.e., the elect—it would seem to be implied that of those elect for whom Christ died, only a part will live to Christ."[183] To get around the universal aspects of the passage, Custance admits that Christ really died for all men, but then claims that Christ died "not for men's sinful actions but for man's sinful condition."[184]

Custance makes a distinction between Christ dying for *sin* and *sins,* the "non-elect" only getting their sin removed while the "elect" get both remitted.[185] But when the Bible declares that Christ was a propitiation for the sins of the whole world (1 John 2:2), Custance shifts gears and retreats back to the "sufficient for all" routine.[186] The teaching of 1 Corinthians 5:14 is clear: Christ died for all men indiscriminately.

In considering the next passage in question, 1 Timothy 2:6, the context is essential for a proper interpretation:

> **I exhort therefore, that, first of all, supplications, prayers, intercessions,** *and* **giving of thanks, be made for all men;**
> **For kings, and** *for* **all that are in authority; that we may lead a quiet and peaceable life in all godliness and honesty.**
> **For this** *is* **good and acceptable in the sight of God our Saviour;**
> **Who will have all men to be saved, and to come unto the knowledge of the truth.**
> **For** *there is* **one God, and one mediator between God and men, the man Christ Jesus;**
> **Who gave himself a ransom for all, to be testified in due time (1 Tim. 2:1-6).**

Since Calvinists confound the universal provision and the individual application of the Atonement, they maintain that **"a ransom for all"** has to be limited to "a ransom for the elect" because they are the only ones who get saved. Smeaton gives us the standard Calvinist interpretation:

> We cannot put a different sense upon the terms than the apostle employs throughout the context; that is, all ranks, conditions, and classes of men. He died for men of all conditions, high, low; for all nationalities, Jew and Gentile equally. But the text does not affirm that He gave Himself for all men indiscriminately—the elect of every rank, and tribe, and people. More particularly, THE ALL for whom He gave Himself a ransom, were they for whom He acted as a mediator in atonement and intercession.[187]

To back up this interpretation, Custance prefers the translation "for *all sorts of* men."[188] But in his attempt to enhance 1 Timothy 2:6, Pink almost overthrows his doctrine of Limited Atonement: "'For there is one God, and one Mediator, between God and men (not "man", for this would have been a generic term and signified mankind. O the accuracy of Holy Writ!), the Man Christ Jesus; who gave Himself *a ransom for all,* to be testified in due time' (1 Tim. 2:5,6)."[189] O the inaccuracy of TULIP Calvinism! Pink has just unwittingly proved an unlimited atonement in Hebrews 2:9 and John 3:16. If *man* is a generic term signifying "mankind," and *men* a particular term representing the ones for whom Christ died, then Christ really **"tasted death for every man"** in Hebrews 2:9, and we have the absurdity that the "elect" **"loved darkness rather than light, because their deeds were evil"** (John 3:19).

There are four reasons why **"a ransom for all"** should not be interpreted as "a ransom for the elect." First of all, the mediator is clearly between **"God and men,"** not "God and the elect." The other reasons concern the identity of the **"all men"** in the context. The **"all men"** of verses one and four do not refer to just classes of men. Classes of men are given in verse two. There would be no point in doing this if it had already been done in verse one. Additionally, the **"all that are in authority"** of verse two would be meaningless if the Calvinists consistently interpreted the **"all"** like they did in the previous verse. The men in authority in verse two already make up a class.

Furthermore, if Paul wanted to say "classes of men" he could have done so:

> **And when he had called unto *him* his twelve disciples, he gave them power *against* unclean spirits, to cast them out, and to heal all manner of sickness and all manner of disease (Mat. 10:1).**
>
> **For every kind of beasts, and of birds, and of serpents, and of things in the sea, is tamed, and hath been tamed of mankind (Jam. 3:7).**

When the Bible refers to what Sproul earlier called "the universality of the elect (people from every tribe and nation),"[190] it does so in unambiguous terms:

> **And they sung a new song, saying, Thou art worthy to take the book, and to open the seals thereof: for thou wast slain, and hast redeemed us to God by thy blood out of every**

448 THE OTHER SIDE OF CALVINISM

kindred, and tongue, and people, and nation (Rev. 5:9).

And finally, the attempt of the Calvinists to make the **"all"** and the **"all men"** of this passage refer to all classes of men does not alleviate their problem anyway. Whoever these men are, God desires their salvation (1 Tim. 2:4) and gave himself a ransom for them (1 Tim. 2:6). Therefore, since (in Calvinistic thought) only the "elect" will ever be saved and ransomed, it is not enough just to transform **"all"** and **"all men"** into all classes of men—it would have to be further limited to just the "elect" in these classes. Not all kings are of the "elect." And neither are all in authority. But this won't work either, because if there is a such thing as the "elect," then they are mentioned in conjunction with the reason prayers ought to be made: **"that we may lead a quiet and peaceable life"** (1 Tim. 2:2). The **"we"** are the "elect" in the passage, not the **"all men."**

The next verse in 1 Timothy provides irrefutable proof for an unlimited atonement by giving us the definitive Scripture definition of *all men* that destroys what is left of Limited Atonement: **"For therefore we both labour and suffer reproach, because we trust in the living God, who is the Saviour of all men, specially of those that believe"** (1 Tim. 4:10). The phrase **"all men"** is set in contrast to **"those that believe."** Therefore, the **"those that believe"** are the "elect." Consequently, the **"all men"** couldn't possibly be "all sorts of elect men" like the Calvinists made it in 1 Timothy 2:1-6. But since it is so obvious that the phrase **"all men"** cannot be limited to the "elect," the Calvinist has a solution to his dilemma: correct the Scripture when it doesn't line up with TULIP theology. Christ is not the Saviour of all men, he is only the "Preserver."[191] Gary North brazenly states: "Christ is indeed the savior of all people prior to the day of judgment."[192] In objection to the Calvinistic imprecations, it should be noted that the verse said **"Saviour,"** anything else is flagrant corruption of the word of God (2 Cor. 2:17). The Apostle Paul here calls God the **"Saviour"** exactly like he does in five other places in his epistles (1 Tim. 1:1, 2:3; Tit. 1:3, 2:10, 3:14). This contrast between **"all men"** and **"those that believe"** can also be found elsewhere in the Pauline Epistles: **"As we have therefore opportunity, let us do good unto all *men*, especially unto them who are of the household of faith"** (Gal. 6:10). It can also be found in different words: **"Even the righteousness of God, *which is* by faith of Jesus Christ unto all** and upon all them that believe: for there is no difference" (Rom. 3:22).

The next verse to be examined which says explicitly that Christ died for all men is worded even stronger than the previous three we have addressed: **"But we see Jesus, who was made a little lower than the angels for the suffering of death, crowned with glory and honour; that he by the grace of God should taste death for every man"** (Heb. 2:9). Short of altering the Scripture, there is no getting around the import of this verse. But that is exactly what the Calvinists do: alter the Scripture when it doesn't line up with their theology.[193] John Murray insists that it is "baseless" to appeal to this verse "in support of a doctrine of universal atonement."[194] Boettner gives us the standard Calvinist interpretation: "The original Greek, however, does not use the word 'man' here at all, but simply says, 'for every.'"[195] In taking advantage of the ignorance of his readers, Boettner has manifested his total lack of knowledge of simple Greek grammar. Like any other adjective, demonstrative, prepositional phrase, or participle, the word **"every"** is used substantively. Is Boettner supported by any Greek grammarian? Not Henry Alford (1810-1871).[196] Not Kenneth Wuest (1893-1961).[197] Not A. T. Robertson (1863-1934).[198] Pink violates every Greek grammar and text in the world and alters **"every man"** to "every son," conjecturing a reading out of thin air found in no extant Greek manuscript anywhere.[199] Other Calvinists simply maintain that the context concerns **"sons"** (Heb. 2:10), **"they who are sanctified"** (Heb. 2:11), **"brethren"** (Heb. 2:12), and **"children"** (Heb. 2:13).[200]

What the Calvinists are saying is true, but what they have failed to notice is that the context changes from the general to the particular. Verse nine is merely the end of the general section:

> **But one in a certain place testified, saying, What is man, that thou art mindful of him? or the son of man, that thou visitest him?**
> **Thou madest him a little lower than the angels; thou crownedst him with glory and honour, and didst set him over the works of thy hands:**
> **Thou hast put all things in subjection under his feet. For in that he put all in subjection under him, he left nothing *that is* not put under him. But now we see not yet all things put under him.**

> But we see Jesus, who was made a little lower than the angels for the suffering of death, crowned with glory and honour; that he by the grace of God should taste death for every man (Heb. 2:6-9).

The beginning thought in Hebrews 2:6 is **"what is man,"** not "what are the elect." This change from the general to the particular is also evident elsewhere:

> For the grace of God that bringeth salvation hath appeared to all men,
> Teaching us that, denying ungodliness and worldly lusts, we should live soberly, righteously, and godly, in this present world (Tit. 2:11-12).

Thus, the import of **"every man"** in Hebrews 2:9 is clear: Christ really did taste **"death for every man."** The **"every man"** is even stronger than all men, as Alford relates: "If it be asked, why *every man* rather than *all men*, we may safely say, that the singular brings out, far more strongly than the plural would, the applicability of Christ's death *to each individual man.*"[201]

There is one other verse to be considered which conclusively proves that Christ died for all men: **"All we like sheep have gone astray; we have turned every one to his own way; and the LORD hath laid on him the iniquity of us all"** (Isa. 53:6). Once again, we hear from the Calvinists: .... What? No Calvinists to speak up against unlimited atonement? The silence is deafening. The verse was "preteritioned" by all the Calvinists. Frank Beck (1917-1964) runs to Isaiah 53:11-12 and extracts the word **"many"** and claims that this is what **"us"** refers to.[202] John Murray almost overthrows his theology when he admits: "It would be easy to argue that the denotation of the 'all' in the last clause is just as extensive as the number of those who have gone astray and have turned every one to his own way. If so, the conclusion would be that the Lord laid on his Son the iniquity of all men and that he was made an offering for the sin of all."[203] Best interprets the **"all"** as "the whole flock of sheep that are given to Christ in the covenant of redemption."[204] But if words have any meaning, then all those who went astray had their iniquity laid on Jesus Christ. The Atonement is limited: it is limited to all those who **"have gone astray."** Have all men gone astray or only some of them? Although Isaiah 53 is not limited in the New Testament to just Jews (Acts 8:30-35; 1 Pet. 2:24-25), if Calvinists want to get dispensational and say that Isaiah was referring to Jews only (Isa. 53:8), then they still have the same problem. Are all Jews saved? If **"the LORD hath laid on him the iniquity"** of only Jews, then the sins of every one of them were borne by Jesus Christ. And according to the Calvinistic system, if Christ takes away any man's sin, that man is efficaciously reconciled to God. Are all Jews reconciled to God? Obviously not. Is the first **"all"** in Isaiah 53:6 the same as the last one. Obviously so.

When faced with such an indomitable body of evidence as to the universal nature of the Atonement, the Calvinist retreats to those Scriptures which speak of Christ dying for a particular group, as if that overthrows the doctrine of an unlimited atonement. Any class of people will do, as long as it expressly states that Christ died for them:

And she shall bring forth a son, and thou shalt call his name JESUS: for he shall save his people from their sins (Mat. 1:21).

Even as the Son of man came not to be ministered unto, but to minister, and to give his life a ransom for many (Mat. 20:28).

For this is my blood of the new testament, which is shed for many for the remission of sins (Mat. 26:28).

As the Father knoweth me, even so know I the Father: and I lay down my life for the sheep (John 10:15).

Take heed therefore unto yourselves, and to all the flock, over the which the Holy Ghost hath made you overseers, to feed the church of God, which he hath purchased with his own blood (Acts 20:28).

Husbands, love your wives, even as Christ also loved the church, and gave himself for it (Eph. 5:25).

So Christ was once offered to bear the sins of many; and unto them that look for him shall he appear the second time without sin unto salvation (Heb. 9:28).

In these passages the Calvinist insists that Christ died for a particular group to the exclusion of all mankind.[205] These are all taken to be one and the same group: the "elect." And if Christ died for the "elect," then he died for no one else, as Charles Hodge maintains: "Every assertion, therefore that Christ died for a people, is a denial of the doctrine that He died equally for all men."[206]

Typical Calvinist comments on these verses are as follows:

> When the Word declares that Christ "loved the Church and gave himself for it" (Eph. 5:25), all should see that such discriminative language is meaningless, if He also loved and gave Himself for the entire human race.[207]

> When He speaks of His "sheep" it is obvious that He is referring to those elect ones whom the Father gave Him for His Own.[208]

> Notice, this verse does not say that He gave His life a ransom for **all**, but for **many**.[209]

> The name "sheep" is synonymous with "elect," for such are "sheep" *before* they believe, yea, before they are born.[210]

> The persons for whom the atonement is offered are called His people—a name which indicates that they were already Christ's in the divine purpose.[211]

> Jesus plainly tells His disciples that His blood was not shed for all, but for many.[212]

Since these are the verses that Calvinists use in an offensive manner to prove the truth of Limited Atonement, comments like these are endless.

Perhaps the most abused verses of Scripture are those which claim that Christ died for **"many."** Every TULIP Calvinist who has ever lived makes **"many"** the "elect." But notice that the word *many* sometimes means "all":

> **But not as the offence, so also *is* the free gift. For if through the offence of one many be dead, much more the grace of God, and the gift by grace, *which is* by one man, Jesus Christ, hath abounded unto many (Rom. 5:15).**
> **For as by one man's disobedience many were made sinners,**

so by the obedience of one shall many be made righteous (Rom. 5:19).

Did the fall of Adam affect all of his posterity or just some of them? The word **"many"** is used here because it better expresses the contrast with "one." The word *all* would be in opposition to the word *some*. That the word **"many"** is here used in this respect is confirmed by the Calvinists Charles Hodge and John Murray:

> They are called *the many* because they are many, and for the sake of the antithesis to *the one*. The many died for the offence of one; the sentence of death passed on all for his offence.[213]

> When Paul uses the expression "the many", he is not intending to delimit the denotation. The scope of "the many" must be the same as the "all men" of verses 12 and 18. He uses "the many" here, as in verse 19, for the purpose of contrasting more effectively "the one" and "the many", singularity and plurality—it was the trespass of "the one", indeed "the one trespass" (vs. 18) of the one, but "the many" died as a result.[214]

Therefore, according to the Calvinists themselves, the fact that Christ died for **"many"** does not necessarily prove the truth of Limited Atonement.

The **"many"** that Christ died for are further identified by Calvinists as God's people: **"And she shall bring forth a son, and thou shalt call his name JESUS: for he shall save his people from their sins"** (Mat. 1:21). All five-point Calvinists (without distinction or exception) insist that Matthew 1:21 is a reference to the "elect." Pink claims that the **"his people"** are "not merely Israel, but all whom the Father had 'given' Him."[215] Scripture? He didn't give any. But by comparing Scripture with Scripture (1 Cor. 2:13) the identity of the **"his people"** in Matthew 1:21 can be determined. First of all, the Bible relates of the Lord Jesus Christ: **"He was in the world, and the world was made by him, and the world knew him not. He came unto his own, and his own received him not"** (John 1:10-11). Did the "elect" know him not? Did the "elect" receive him not? If the **"world"** and **"his own"** are synonyms for the "elect," which denotation Calvinists usually make, then the "elect" neither knew him nor received him. Obviously, **"his own"** has to refer to Israel, not "elect" Israel, but

Israel. Jesus Christ was a minister of the circumcision (Rom. 15:8), sent to the house of Israel (Mat. 15:24), God's people (Mat. 2:6). **"Salvation is of the Jews"** (John 4:22). The Scripture infallibly interprets itself: **"Blessed *be* the Lord God of Israel; for he hath visited and redeemed his people, And hath raised up an horn of salvation for us in the house of his servant David"** (Luke 1:68). So not only did the nation of Israel have a Saviour (Mat. 1:21), they had a Redeemer (Luke 1:68). But even though the verse explicitly identified **"his people"** as Israel, Owen still makes the redeemed people of Luke 1:68 the "elect."[216]

In the last chapter we saw clearly who the sheep of John chapter ten were. God's sheep are the equivalent of God's people: the nation of Israel. If Christ died for *all* of Israel and some of them were lost, then he had to have made an unlimited atonement. So when Pink says: "Nor did Aaron make any atonement for the sins of the Midianites and Ammonites!"[217] as he seeks to prove the truth of Limited Atonement, he is really saying too much. True, the atonement made by Aaron in the Old Testament was only for the nation of Israel. But were all Jews at that time counted among God's "elect"? No Calvinist would say that they were. Therefore, although Aaron's atonement was limited to Israel, it was still unlimited in its extent.

Regarding the death of Christ for these groups, it should first be noticed that the Scripture nowhere states that Christ died *only* for these various groups to the exclusion of all others. Secondly, these groups are not all one and the same; viz., Israel is not the Church (1 Cor. 10:32). But the main reason it is apparent that TULIP Calvinism has a bogus third point is because, by the same reasoning as the Calvinists, Christ died only for Paul and the churches of Galatia (Gal. 1:4), Paul and the church of Corinth (2 Cor. 5:21), Paul and the church of Rome (Rom. 5:8), John and the ones he wrote to (1 John 3:16), the disciples of Christ (Luke 22:19-20), Paul and Titus (Tit. 2:14), or those who are weak (1 Cor. 8:11). By just taking the revelation of one verse of Scripture it could be proven that Christ died only for one person on the face of the earth: **"I am crucified with Christ: nevertheless I live; yet not I, but Christ liveth in me: and the life which I now live in the flesh I live by the faith of the Son of God, who loved me, and gave himself for me"** (Gal. 2:20). So according to the philosophical speculations of Calvinism, it could be said that Christ died only for Paul. What the

Calvinists are doing is confounding the universal provision and the individual application of the Atonement.

As further proof that Christ didn't die exclusively for the aforementioned groups, there are other groups mentioned in the Scriptures whom Christ died for that the Calvinists neglected to mention. Out of these other groups there are two basic types. The first type concerns particular groups that Christ is said to die for yet who ultimately will perish in hell:

> **Of how much sorer punishment, suppose ye, shall he be thought worthy, who hath trodden under foot the Son of God, and hath counted the blood of the covenant, wherewith he was sanctified, an unholy thing (Heb. 10:29).**

> **But there were false prophets also among the people, even as there shall be false teachers among you, who privily shall bring in damnable heresies, even denying the Lord that bought them, and bring upon themselves swift destruction (2 Pet. 2:1).**

So not only is Jesus Christ the Saviour (1 Tim. 4:10) and Redeemer (1 Tim. 2:6) of the world, he is said to have sanctified and bought apostates and false prophets. Charles Bronson (1931-1995) insists that it "approaches blasphemy to say that Christ shed His precious blood for some and then, after all, they perished in Hell."[218] Dabney dismisses both verses because: "The language of Peter, and that of Hebrews x:24, may receive an entirely adequate solution, without teaching that Christ actually 'bought,' or 'sanctified' any apostate, by saying that the Apostles speak there *'ad hominem.'*"[219] But because of the diversity of interpretations put on these verses by Calvinists in their attempt to evade the clear teaching of Scripture, they cannot be disregarded so easily.

Concerning those who were sanctified in Hebrews 10:29, Calvinists try to get around the obvious implications in a variety of ways. Beck claims they were "sanctified, but not saved."[220] Gill maintains that Christ himself "is said here to be *sanctified.*"[221] Owen makes them "professors of the faith of the gospel," and adds the phrase "in the profession of the gospel" after **"sanctified."**[222] Other than a few isolated comments, Calvinists are strangely silent on this passage.[223] The context of the verse, however, is **"if we sin wilfully after that we have received the knowledge of the truth"**

(Heb. 10:26) and **"the Lord shall judge his people"** (Heb. 10:30).

Regarding those who were bought in 2 Peter 2:1, Calvinists are more elaborate in their denial that Christ bought false teachers. Smeaton admits that this verse "is not without its difficulties, and is variously expounded; being the passage in fact, in which the Lutheran and Arminian polemical writers uniformly intrench themselves and defy assault."[224] He concludes that these false teachers "gave themselves out as redeemed men, and were so accounted in the judgment of the church while they abode in her communion."[225] Shedd says that the false teachers "are described according to their profession, not as they are in the eye of God. They claim to have been bought by the blood of Christ, and yet by their damnable heresies nullify the atonement."[226] A. A. Hodge counts 2 Peter 2:1 as among those passages that "are just like those constant warnings which are addressed in Scripture to the elect, which are designed as means to carry out and secure that perseverance in grace which is the end of election."[227]

Besides these general statements, however, there are two words in the phrase **"even denying the Lord that bought them"** that Calvinists focus on in their attempt to disprove that the Atonement was for all men. Gill concisely summarizes the usual Calvinist interpretation: "Christ is not here at all spoken of; nor is there one syllable of his dying for any persons, in any sense whatever."[228] The first argument of the Calvinists is that **"Lord"** is here a reference to God the Father and not Christ because the underlying Greek word is not the usual word for "Lord."[229] And as Ness also adds: "And even though it could be proved to apply to Christ in the above text, it may be explained upon the principle that it is no unusual thing with the inspired writers to speak of things not as they actually are, but according to the profession of the party."[230] The next argument is that **"bought"** doesn't really mean "bought."[231] Owen alters **"bought"** to "delivered," maintaining that "their buying was only in respect of this separation from the world, in respect of the enjoyment of the knowledge of the truth."[232] But not only is the Scripture against these explanations, as has been proven on other occasions, it is the Calvinists themselves who regularly overthrow the opinions of other Calvinists.

If it is God the Father who is spoken of in 1 Peter 1:21 it wouldn't make any difference, for Paul instructed the Ephesian elders to **"feed the church of God, which he hath purchased with**

his own blood" (Acts 20:28). Some Calvinists explicitly assert that it is Christ who is spoken of in 1 Peter 2:1 *and not* God the Father.[233] Long, a Calvinist who makes this assertion, does not give up Limited Atonement, he merely insists that **"Lord"** refers to "God the Son as sovereign Lord and not to God the Son as mediator."[234] And regarding the meaning of the term **"bought,"** the same word is used elsewhere in the Scripture: **"For ye are bought with a price: therefore glorify God in your body, and in your spirit, which are God's"** (1 Cor. 6:20). Long likewise rejects the "deliverance" view of Owen and others, but himself corrects the Scripture, preferring "created" to **"bought,"** and interpreting the verse "non-redemptively as referring to the creation of the false teachers by Christ their sovereign Lord."[235] Smeaton rejects both of the standard Calvinistic interpretations and maintains that "these false teachers are described according to their own profession and the judgment of charity."[236] The Scripture is clear: Christ sanctified and bought apostates and false teachers.

The second type of group under consideration concerns general groups that Christ is said to die for. Because these groups are anything but ambiguous, these verses definitively prove that the Atonement of Christ is unlimited in extent:

> **For the Son of man is come to seek and to save that which was lost (Luke 19:10).**
>
> **For when we were yet without strength, in due time Christ died for the ungodly (Rom. 5:6).**
>
> **But when the fulness of the time was come, God sent forth his Son, made of a woman, made under the law, To redeem them that were under the law, that we might receive the adoption of sons (Gal. 4:4-5).**
>
> **This *is* a faithful saying, and worthy of all acceptation, that Christ Jesus came into the world to save sinners; of whom I am chief (1 Tim. 1:15).**
>
> **For Christ also hath once suffered for sins, the just for the unjust, that he might bring us to God, being put to death in the flesh, but quickened by the Spirit (1 Pet. 3:18).**

The reason these verses are never mentioned by the Calvinists is obvious. Are only the "elect" lost? Are only the "elect" ungodly? Are the "elect" the only ones who were under the law? Are only the "elect" sinners? Are only the "elect" unjust? If Christ died for and came to save the lost, the ungodly, those under the law, sinners, and the unjust, then he must have made an unlimited atonement, for that is the condition of all men—not just the "elect." Therefore, Jesus Christ is **"the Saviour of the world"** (John 4:42; 1 John 4:14), whether all men accept him or not.

Although not as general a group as the ones just mentioned, there is one other general group that Christ is said to die for: **"Greater love hath no man than this, that a man lay down his life for his friends"** (John 15:13). The question is: Who are Christ's friends? Well, on one occasion Jesus Christ said: **"The Son of man is come eating and drinking; and ye say, Behold a gluttonous man, and a winebibber, a friend of publicans and sinners!"** (Luke 7:34). But if it be objected that this was a statement said in error by the Pharisees, then what can be said against the word of Christ himself concerning Judas: **"And Jesus said unto him, Friend, wherefore art thou come? Then came they, and laid hands on Jesus, and took him"** (Mat. 26:50). Was Judas one of the "elect"?

As was pointed out at the beginning of this section, the first two types of Scriptures used by the Calvinists to prove Limited Atonement so obviously mitigate against their doctrine that Calvinists only use them to prove Limited Atonement in the course of defending themselves against the attacks of their opponents. The third type of Scriptures advanced in support of Limited Atonement—those which maintain that Christ died for a particular group—although used offensively by the Calvinists because they seem at first glance to prove their doctrine, substantiate the contrary when all the groups that Christ died for are examined. But in addition to the three types of Scripture passages used to prove the third point of Calvinism, Calvinists read Limited Atonement into every conceivable verse. A case in point is a verse in the Psalms that mentions redemption: **"The LORD redeemeth the soul of his servants: and none of them that trust in him shall be desolate"** (Psa. 34:22). The Sovereign Grace Baptist Jimmie Davis claims that "there are terms used in the verse which can definitely be supportive of the teaching of a limited atonement."[237] He makes the "servants" to be "none other than the elect."[238] So just as we saw regarding the previous two "points," Calvinists read their doctrine into every conceivable verse.

Although not mentioned in the body of this section, there are other verses which prove conclusively that the Atonement was for all men; namely, those verses which assert that "whosoever believeth" may avail himself of the Atonement and be saved:

> **To him give all the prophets witness, that through his name whosoever believeth in him shall receive remission of sins (Acts 10:43).**
>
> **For I am not ashamed of the gospel of Christ: for it is the power of God unto salvation to every one that believeth; to the Jew first, and also to the Greek (Rom. 1:16).**
>
> **For the scripture saith, Whosoever believeth on him shall not be ashamed (Rom. 10:11).**
>
> **For whosoever shall call upon the name of the Lord shall be saved (Rom. 10:13).**
>
> **Whosoever believeth that Jesus is the Christ is born of God: and every one that loveth him that begat loveth him also that is begotten of him (1 John 5:1).**
>
> **And the Spirit and the bride say, Come. And let him that heareth say, Come. And let him that is athirst come. And whosoever will, let him take the water of life freely (Rev. 22:17).**

There are no "whosoevers" with a doctrine of Limited Atonement.

Calvin's Calvinism

There is, as kind of an appendix to the subject, one more thing to be examined that pertains to Limited Atonement: the views of John Calvin himself. As bizarre as it sounds, Calvin, it is claimed by some, did not completely embrace the TULIP system of which his name is inseparably conjoined.[239] Following the lead of the theologian James Richards (1767-1843), Calvin is thought by some to have modified his doctrine of Limited Atonement as he got older and wiser until he finally reached the conclusion of an unlimited atonement.[240] Others claim that it was Beza and other followers of Calvin who developed the doctrine of Limited Atonement.[241] As is to be expected, most five-point Calvinists claim that Calvin held to Limited Atonement.[242] But before examining the evidence from Calvin's writings for or against Limited Atonement, it is of paramount importance to notice the scene of history during his time.

Theodore Beza, the successor of Calvin, and the acknowledged "chief theologian of the Reformed Church after Calvin,"[243] most definitely held to Limited Atonement.[244] No creed written before or just after Calvin's death either expressly affirms or denies Limited Atonement. However, article thirty-one of the Thirty-Nine Articles of the Church of England, adopted shortly before Calvin's death, states that "the offering of Christ once made is *the* perfect redemption, propitiation, and satisfaction, for all the sinnes of the whole worlde."[245] After the death of Calvin, the Saxon Visitation Articles of 1592, written by the Lutherans somewhat against the Calvinists, mention as the "false and erroneous doctrine of the Calvinists" that "Christ did not die for all men, but only for the elect."[246] This confirms two things: the doctrine of Limited Atonement, although not yet so-called, was the teaching of Calvinism, and that the appellation derived from Calvin's name was then in vogue. It is only after the Arminian controversy that we find the extent of the Atonement addressed in the creeds of the Calvinists. The Canons of Dort (1619) and the Westminster Confession of Faith (1646) expressly affirm the doctrine of Limited Atonement, as has already been pointed out. The original confession of the Particular Baptists, the London Confession of 1644, maintained Limited Atonement in article twenty-one: "That Christ Jesus by his death did bring forth salvation and reconciliation onely for the elect, which were those which God the Father gave him."[247] The Second London Confession of 1677, as related earlier, was based on the Westminster Confession. And from the time of these creeds until today, the overwhelming majority of all Calvinists have been outspoken on behalf of the doctrine of Limited Atonement. So the problem is simply that Calvin's views on Limited Atonement are anachronistic. It is not true as Lightner infers that Calvin was "carefully avoiding the issue."[248] As Robert Peterson affirms, "Frequently overlooked and yet most important is the fact that the extent of the Atonement was not an issue in Calvin's time."[249] Therefore, A. A. Hodge correctly ascertains: "Calvin does not appear to have given the question we are at present discussing a deliberate consideration, and has certainly not left behind him a clear and consistent statement of his views."[250] Therefore, the case of Calvin is unique, and demands a comprehensive study.

With this historical background in mind, consideration of Calvin's views can more accurately be determined. The main argument on behalf of Calvin holding to a universal atonement is his supposed comments on 1 John 2:2. But before examining what will be proved to be a spurious quotation from Calvin on the passage, we will first examine the relevant Scriptures on the Atonement as commented on by Calvin in his commentaries. Since the extent of the Atonement was not an issue in Calvin's day, he, contrary to his modern-day disciples, doesn't violently wrest certain passages which state that Christ died for a particular group; viz: Matthew 1:21, John 10:15, Acts 20:28, Ephesians 5:25. On the other passages which have thus far been examined, Calvin's comments on them will be considered here, but in reverse order. It should be noted that when Calvin wrote on the Synoptic Gospels he did so under the format of a harmony so his comments on a particular verse in Matthew are really made on the parallel verses in Mark and Luke also. The format to be followed throughout this section will be the citation of the Scripture and then Calvin's comments.

The first group of verses to be considered are those which state that Christ died for "many":

Even as the Son of man came not to be ministered unto, but to minister, and to give his life a ransom for many (Mat. 20:28).

'Many' is used, not for a definite number, but for a large number, in that He sets Himself over against all others, and this is its meaning also in Romans 5:15, where Paul is not talking of a part of mankind but of the whole human race.[251]

For this is my blood of the new testament, which is shed for many for the remission of sins (Mat. 26:28).

The word *many* does not mean a part of the world only, but the whole human race: he contrasts *many* with *one,* as if to say that he would not be the Redeemer of one man, but would meet death to deliver many of their cursed guilt. No doubt that in speaking to a few Christ wished to make His teaching available to a larger number. At the same time we must note that in Luke (saying *for you*) He addresses the disciples by name and encourages the faithful as individuals to apply the pouring-out of His blood to their benefit. So when we come to the holy table not only should the general idea come to our mind that the world is redeemed by the blood of Christ, but also each should reckon himself that his sins are covered.[252]

But not as the offence, so also *is* the free gift. For if through the offence of one many be dead, much more the grace of God, and the gift by grace, *which is* by one man, Jesus Christ, hath abounded unto many (Rom. 5:15).

Paul does not here contrast the larger number with the many, for he is not speaking of the great number of mankind, but he argues that since the sin of Adam has destroyed many, the righteousness of Christ will be no less effective for the salvation of many.[253]

So Christ was once offered to bear the sins of many; and unto them that look for him shall he appear the second time without sin unto salvation (Heb. 9:28).

He says many meaning all, as in Rom. 5.15. It is of course certain that not all enjoy the fruits of Christ's death, but this happens because their unbelief hinders them. That question is not dealt with here because the apostle is not discussing how few or how many benefit from the death of Christ, but means simply that He died for others, not for Himself. He therefore contrasts the many to the one.[254]

The next group of verses are those which mention particular groups that Christ is said to die for yet who ultimately will perish in hell:

Of how much sorer punishment, suppose ye, shall he be thought worthy, who hath trodden under foot the Son of God, and hath counted the blood of the covenant, wherewith

he was sanctified, an unholy thing (Heb. 10:29).

It is most unworthy to profane the blood of Christ which is the agent of our sanctification; and that is what those who depart from the faith do.[255]

But there were false prophets also among the people, even as there shall be false teachers among you, who privily shall bring in damnable heresies, even denying the Lord that bought them, and bring upon themselves swift destruction (2 Pet. 2:1).

Peter is here referring (in my opinion) to that which is expressed by Jude when he refers to the grace of God being turned into lasciviousness. Christ redeemed us to have us as a people separated from all the iniquities of the world, devoted to holiness and purity. Those who throw over the traces and plunge themselves into every kind of licence are not unjustly said to deny Christ, by whom they were redeemed.[256]

The third group of verses are those which state that Christ died for "all":

And I, if I be lifted up from the earth, will draw all *men* unto me (John 12:32).

When He says *all*, it must be referred to the children of God, who are of His flock. Yet I agree with Chrysostom, who says that Christ used the universal word because the Church was to be gathered from the Gentiles and Jews alike.[257]

Therefore as by the offence of one *judgment came* upon all men to condemnation; even so by the righteousness of one *the free gift came* upon all men unto justification of life (Rom. 5:18).

Paul makes grace common to all men, not because it in fact extends to all, but because it is offered to all. Although Christ suffered for the sins of the world, and is offered by the goodness of God without distinction to all men, yet not all receive Him.[258]

And *that* he died for all, that they which live should not henceforth live unto themselves, but unto him which died for them, and rose again (2 Cor. 5:15).

We should note the purpose of Christ's death—that He died for us that we might die to ourselves. We should also notice how he goes on to explain that to die to ourselves is to live to Christ, or to explain it more fully, it is to renounce ourselves that we may live to Christ who redeemed us that He might have us in His power as His peculiar possession.[259]

And, having made peace through the blood of his cross, by him to reconcile all things unto himself; by him, *I say*, whether *they be* things in earth, or things in heaven (Col. 1:20).

I say that men have been reconciled to God because they were previously alienated form Him by sin, and because they would have experienced Him as the Judge to their ruin, had not the grace of the Mediator interposed to appease His anger. Hence the nature of the peace-maker between God and men is that enmities have been abolished through Christ, and thus God from a Judge becomes a Father. . . . Should anyone, on the plea of the universality of the expression ask in reference to devils, whether Christ is their Peace-maker also, I answer, 'No; not even of the ungodly.' Though I confess that there is a difference, inasmuch as the benefit of redemption is offered to the ungodly, but not to the devils. This, however, has nothing to do with Paul's words, which only say that it is through Christ alone that all creatures who have any connexion at all with God cleave to Him.[260]

Who gave himself a ransom for all, to be testified in due time (1 Tim. 2:6).

The universal term 'all' must always be referred to classes of men but never to individuals. It is as if he had said, 'Not only Jews, but also Greeks, not only people of humble rank but also princes have been redeemed by the blood of Christ.' Since therefore He intends the benefit of His death to be common to all, those who hold a view that would exclude any from the hope of salvation do Him an injury.[261]

For therefore we both labour and suffer reproach, because

we trust in the living God, who is the Saviour of all men, specially of those that believe (1 Tim. 4:10).

His argument is that God's kindness extends to all men. And if there is no one without the experience of sharing in God's kindness, how much more of that kindness shall the godly know, who hope in Him.[262]

But we see Jesus, who was made a little lower than the angels for the suffering of death, crowned with glory and honour; that he by the grace of God should taste death for every man (Heb. 2:9).

When he says *for every man*, he does not mean that He should be an example to others, in the way that Chrysostom adduces the metaphor of a physician. He means that Christ died for us, because He took on Himself our lot, and redeemed us from the curse of death.[263]

The last group of verses to be considered are those which state that Christ died for the world:

The next day John seeth Jesus coming unto him, and saith, Behold the Lamb of God, which taketh away the sin of the world (John 1:29).

And when he says *the sin of the world* he extends this kindness indiscriminately to the whole human race, that the Jews might not think the Redeemer has been sent to them alone. From this we infer that the whole world is bound in the same condemnation; and that since all men without exception are guilty of unrighteousness before God, they have need of reconciliation.[264]

For God so loved the world, that he gave his only begotten Son, that whosoever believeth in him should not perish, but have everlasting life (John 3:16).

And He has used a general term, both to invite indiscriminately all to share in life and to cut off every excuse from unbelievers. Such is also the significance of the term 'world' which He had used before. For although there is nothing in the world deserving of God's favour, He nevertheless shows He is favourable to the whole world when He calls all without exception to the faith in Christ, which is indeed an entry into life. Moreover, let us remember that although life is promised generally to all who believe in Christ, faith is not common to all. Christ is open to all and displayed to all, but God opens the eyes only of the elect that they may seek Him by faith.[265]

And said unto the woman, Now we believe, not because of thy saying: for we have heard *him* ourselves, and know that this is indeed the Christ, the Saviour of the world (John 4:42).

Again, when they proclaim that Jesus is the Saviour of the world and the Christ, they have undoubtedly learned this from hearing Him. From this we infer that in two days Christ taught the sum of the Gospel more plainly there than He had so far done in Jerusalem. And He declared that the salvation He had brought was common to the whole world, so that they should understand more easily that it belonged to them also.[266]

To wit, that God was in Christ, reconciling the world unto himself, not imputing their trespasses unto them; and hath committed unto us the word of reconciliation (2 Cor. 5:19).

Why has God appeared to men in Christ: For reconciliation, in order that the hostility might be ended and we who were strangers might be adopted as sons. Although Christ's coming had its source in the overflowing love of God for us, yet, until men know that God has been propitiated by a mediator, there cannot but be on their side a separation which prevents them from having access to God.[267]

At the beginning of our examination of Calvin's views on the Atonement, reference was made to his comments on 1 John 2:2. Almost every writer who cites Calvin's remarks on the passage as proof that he rejected Limited Atonement refers, not to Calvin's commentaries, but to Strong's theology.[268] Strong acquiesces to Richards' opinion that Calvin acceded to the theory of universal atonement in his later years, and then spuriously quotes Calvin on 1 John 2:2.[269] In their zeal to make Calvin a four-point Calvinist, a quote of a quote is all the evidence given. This quotation by Strong is also acknowledged by Calvinists to be spurious.[270] Notice first of all Strong's citation of Calvin on 1 John 2:2 and then Calvin's comments as taken from his commentary:

> Christ suffered for the sins of the whole world, and in the goodness of God is offered unto all men without distinction, his blood being shed not for a part of the world only, but for the whole human race; for although in the world nothing is found worthy of the favor of God, yet he holds out the propitiation to the whole world, since without exception he summons all to the faith of Christ, which is nothing else than the door unto hope.[271]

> But here the question may be asked as to how the sins of the whole world have been expiated. I pass over the dreams of the fanatics, who make this a reason to extend salvation to all the reprobate and even to Satan himself. Such a monstrous idea is not worth refuting. Those who want to avoid this absurdity have said that Christ suffered sufficiently for the whole world but effectively only for the elect. This solution has commonly prevailed in the schools. Although I allow the truth of this, I deny that it fits this passage. For John's purpose was only to make this blessing common to the whole Church. Therefore, under the word 'all' he does not include the reprobate, but refers to all who would believe and those who were scattered through various regions of the earth. For, as is meet, the grace of Christ is really made clear when it is declared to be the only salvation of the world.[272]

That this is a true and accurate translation of Calvin's comments on 1 John 2:2 (he wrote in Latin) we give double proof. The edition of Calvin's commentaries in popular use before the one quoted above uses as its translation on 1 John 2:2 that of John Owen from 1855. The translations match as closely as can be expected.[273] Secondly, A. A. Hodge, in his book on the Atonement, which he wrote back in 1867, cites Calvin's comments on 1 John 2:2 as explicit proof that Calvin *did not* believe in a general atonement.[274]

Besides the commentaries of Calvin we have his *Institutes*. The only trouble is, as Peterson points out: "There is too little evidence in the *Institutes* to reach a conclusion on the extent of the atonement."[275] The reason for this has already been mentioned: the extent of the Atonement was not an issue in Calvin's time. In addition to Calvin's *Institutes* and commentaries, there are also various theological treatises of Calvin to be investigated. In his *A Treatise on the Eternal Predestination of God*, Calvin answered the aforementioned Pighius as follows:

> To this pretended difficulty of Pighius, therefore, I would briefly reply that Christ was *so* ordained the Saviour of the whole world, as that He might save those that were given unto Him by the Father out of the whole world, that He might be the eternal life of them of whom He is the Head; that He might receive into a participation of all the "blessings in Him" all those whom God adopted to Himself by His own unmerited good pleasure to be His heirs. . . . Hence we read everywhere that Christ diffuses life into none but the members of His own body. . . . Hereupon follows also a third important fact, that the virtue and benefits of Christ are extended unto, and belong to, none but the children of God.[276]

In the same treatise, Calvin replied to another detractor named Georgius Siculus (1500-1551) concerning the import of 1 John 2:2:

> John does indeed extend the benefits of the atonement of Christ, which was completed by His death, to all the elect of God throughout what climes of the world soever they may be scattered. . . . For our present question is, not what the power or virtue of Christ is, nor what *efficacy it has in itself*, but *who those are* to whom He gives Himself to be enjoyed. Now if the possession of Christ stands in faith, and if faith flows from the Spirit of adoption, it follows that he alone is numbered of God among His children who is designed of God to be a partaker of Christ. Indeed, the evangelist John sets forth the office of Christ to be none other than that of "gathering together all the children of God" in one by His death. From all which we conclude that although reconciliation is offered unto all men through Him, yet, that the great benefit belongs peculiarly to the elect, that they might be "gathered together" and be made "together" partakers of eternal life.[277]

In a tract on the Lord's Supper against Tileman Heshusius (1527-1588), Calvin declared what he really believed about the Atonement:

> The first thing to be explained is how Christ is present with unbelievers, to be the spiritual food of their souls, and in short

the life and salvation of the world. As he adheres so doggedly to the words, I should like to know how the wicked can eat the flesh of Christ which was not crucified for them, and how they can drink the blood which was not shed to expiate their sins?[278]

As a last resort, one ambiguous remark by Calvin on his deathbed is sometimes appealed to in order to establish that he held to a universal atonement: "I testify also and declare, that I suppliantly beg of Him, that He may be pleased so to wash and purify me in the blood which my Sovereign Redeemer has shed for the sins of the human race."[279] Some translations of Calvin's dying words read "shed for us poor sinners"[280] or "shed for all poor sinners."[281] Whatever the exact wording, it is still negated by other statements that Calvin made on the Atonement. And that is the problem: Calvin made statements that imply he believed in an unlimited Atonement, but he also made statements that imply he believed in Limited Atonement. In none of the passages examined does Calvin explicitly mention the extent of the Atonement. So as mentioned previously, because the extent of the Atonement was not an issue in Calvin's time, there is no evidence that he ever discussed the issue. It should be remembered, however, that Calvinists who believe in Limited Atonement often claim that Christ did die for all men. As has been pointed out already, Calvinists will talk about the benefits of Christ's death to the world in order to relate their doctrine of Limited Atonement to the "non-elect." Thus, when Christ is said to be the **"Saviour of all men"** in 1 Timothy 4:10, Calvin, like his modern-day counterparts, defines **"Saviour"** as "a general term, meaning one who guards and preserves."[282] So, by insisting that there is a certain sense in which Christ died for all men, Calvinists can make general statements about the nature of the Atonement.

So what did Calvin actually believe about the extent of the Atonement? Has there ever been a man who claimed that God has willed everything, including sin, the Fall, and reprobation, who *didn't* believe in Limited Atonement? If Calvin had lived a few years later he would have no doubt concurred with John Owen in arguing for Limited Atonement. Five-point Calvinists believe that Calvin held to Limited Atonement because of the very nature of his system:

> Calvin taught that God loved the elect and planned their holiness

and salvation while on the other hand, He hated the reprobate and planned their sin and damnation.[283]

When the advocates of a general atonement claim to stand by Calvin, they ought to be well prepared for the arduous undertaking. The entire analogy and spirit of Calvin's system was as a whole broadly characterized by the subjection of Redemption to election as a means to an end.[284]

But as has been maintained throughout this chapter, if only those eternally predestinated could possibly be saved, what difference does it make whom Christ died for? Therefore, what does it matter what Calvin believed about the extent of the Atonement? Would Calvin and Calvinism be vindicated if it could be proved that Calvin did not believe in Limited Atonement? Because the third point of Calvinism is not essential to the Calvinistic system as a whole, the answer is a resounding, "no!"

The Other Side of Limited Atonement

Although it is deemed by Calvinists to be their most objectional and controversial "point"—so much so that even some Calvinists reject it—Limited Atonement is still defended with a vengeance by traditional five-point Calvinists. But as we have seen throughout this chapter, the other side of Limited Atonement is its nonessentiality. Limited Atonement is simply adding insult to the injury of Unconditional Election. For if certain men are not of those elected to salvation, then what does it matter whether Christ died for them or not? In the Calvinistic system, it makes absolutely no difference whatsoever whether Christ died for the "non-elect"—they could not be saved if Christ died a thousand deaths for them. Calvinists do not hesitate to insist that the reason Christ's blood was shed only for the "elect" is because God did not want any others to be saved. This is another part of the other side of Limited Atonement, and brings us right back to Unconditional Election. Therefore, to make an issue out of Limited Atonement is a waste of time. And just as a denial of Unconditional Election is translated by Calvinists into a departure from salvation by grace, so the Calvinists imply that anyone who denies Limited Atonement rejects the true doctrine of the Atonement as found in the Bible. This is more of the other side of Limited Atonement.

Like the doctrines of Total Depravity and Unconditional Election, the Calvinist has a difficult time reconciling his third point with evangelism and responsibility. Custance bemoans: "One of the most common criticisms of those who hold the Augustinian-Calvinist position is that their theology of Limited Atonement tends to weaken the incentive to evangelism."[285] Really? I wonder why? John Murray laments: "It is frequently objected that this doctrine is inconsistent with the full and free offer of Christ in the gospel."[286] But not only is it inconsistent, it is in direct opposition to it. Wherefore Kuiper says: "The statement 'Christ died for you,' when addressed indiscriminately to the unconverted, is grossly ambiguous."[287] So to be consistent, the Gospel can only be offered to the "elect." Yet the Calvinists maintain: "Whoever the Lord Jesus died for is of necessity going to be saved."[288] So if no offer can be made to the "non-elect," and the "elect" are sure to be saved, all preaching is not only vain and useless, but an absolute, total, and complete waste of time. All the talk about the Atonement of Christ being sufficient for all and providing common grace is meaningless tripe. If only the "elect" will be saved, it makes no difference whom Christ died for.

Regarding the effect of Limited Atonement on evangelism, the Calvinists claim that it has none:

> This does not, in any wise, lessen the responsibility of God's people to witness, preach the gospel, evangelize and carry on missionary work.[289]

> Particular redemption must not prevent His servants from preaching the Gospel to every creature and announcing that there is a Saviour for every sinner out of hell who appropriates Him for his own.[290]

> The doctrine of limited atonement also does not contradict the sincere nature of God's gospel offer.[291]

Bronson claims that "some of the greatest of soul winners have believed in particular redemption."[292] Palmer insists that "instead of being a hindrance to evangelism," Limited Atonement "is a great encouragement to it."[293] So even though Christ died only for the "elect," thereby securing their salvation, the Gospel must be taken by soul winners to all men, not just the "elect." This is yet more of the other side of Limited Atonement. But we repeat, if only the "elect" will be saved, it makes no difference whom Christ died for.

The precarious doctrine of Limited Atonement renders the salvation of any man doubtful and uncertain. The Calvinists Steele and Thomas correctly state that "election itself saved no one; it only marked out particular sinners for salvation."[294] Yet Custance says: "We ought not to use such a misleading appeal as 'Christ died for you' because we cannot apply this to any man indiscriminately unless we know he is to be counted among the elect, a knowledge which we cannot have with certainty."[295] So, in the Calvinistic system, election itself doesn't guarantee anyone's salvation until Christ dies for that person, yet, one cannot tell anyone that Christ died for him unless he is one of the "elect," which cannot be determined for certain unless Christ died for him. So how does one know whether anyone is saved or not? As we shall see in the last chapter, the only proof, if you can call it that, is that they persevere in holiness in their profession of faith to the end.

Limited Atonement is a Reformed, Calvinistic doctrine; it should not to be equated with biblical Christianity. This is inadvertently stated by Calvinists:

> There is a further class of passages which seem to belong together and which may indeed be interpreted to signify a certain universalistic aspect of the Lord's death which cannot be denied but which in no way conflicts with the doctrine of Limited Atonement as formulated by the Reformers.[296]
>
> There are a number of biblical passages which teach the Calvinist doctrine of Christ's limited atonement.[297]

But once again we hasten to assert that if only the "elect" can and will be saved, who cares whether Christ died for the "elect," the "non-elect," angels, or devils: it makes absolutely no difference. The debate among the Calvinists about Limited Atonement is a smoke screen to conceal the true nature of Calvinism: God by a sovereign, eternal decree of Unconditional Election has consigned billions to hell before their birth, and to make it certain, he has rendered them with Total Depravity so that they will be unable to receive Irresistible Grace which will not even be offered to them in the first place since Christ did not make a Limited Atonement for them. But like the other "points," the word of God is not bound by the philosophical speculations and theological implications of Limited Atonement.

Chapter 9
IRRESISTIBLE GRACE

The fourth stem of the TULIP is Irresistible Grace. Like the previous three points, the problem with the name Irresistible Grace is that it suffers from the prefixing of a bogus addition to an otherwise scriptural term. The depravity of man is a biblical doctrine, but the transformation of man's depravity into inability as found in the teaching of Total Depravity is another story. Likewise, the doctrine of election is also scriptural, but to maintain that the Calvinistic doctrine of Unconditional Election, and all the baggage that goes with it, can be found in the Bible is a little far-fetched. The Atonement of Christ is certainly a crucial doctrine, but to insist that the Limited Atonement of Calvinism is connected with it is a different matter. Now, regarding the fourth point of Calvinism, it is undeniably true that any man who was ever saved was saved by the grace of God. But although the word *grace* occurs 170 times in the Bible, not only is it never found prefixed by the term *irresistible*, no form of the word *irresistible* even occurs. Naturally, the Calvinist counters that although the term Irresistible Grace is not mentioned in the Bible, the teaching of Irresistible Grace is. This, however, remains to be seen.

Although it is one of the three essential points of Calvinism, Irresistible Grace has been said by Calvinists to be "the most telltale evidence of the presence or absence of Calvinism."[1] And because it is one of the three essential points, Irresistible Grace stands or falls very much with Total Depravity. In fact, as was pointed out in chapter 6, Total Depravity necessitates Irresistible Grace. As the Dutch Reformed Gise Van Baren insists: "One cannot maintain total depravity, yet deny irresistible grace."[2] Because of this, the Canons of Dort treated the two subjects under one heading: "Of the Corruption of Man, His Conversion to God, and the Manner Thereof." Therefore, there will of necessity be some overlap with Total Depravity in any treatment of Irresistible

Grace, for in the Calvinistic system: "Total depravity implies that an *irresistibly* powerful grace of God is the only hope for the dead sinner."[3] This was brought out in our analysis of Total Depravity. There Pink acknowledged what he and all Calvinists really believe about Total Depravity: "Freedom of the will defines our conception of human depravity."[4] We saw that Total Depravity was really Total Inability and had nothing to do with depravity at all: it concerned the question of the free will of man to accept or reject the grace of God. And as we also saw, Total Depravity, as the foundation of the TULIP system, consigned all men to the following lot in life:

It is good that a man should both hope and quietly wait for the salvation of the LORD (Lam. 3:26).

So like the doctrine of Unconditional Election, Irresistible Grace is built upon a false premise. It is here that we see the real plan of salvation according to the Calvinistic system. If men are unable to believe on Jesus Christ, yet God has elected some to salvation and atoned for their sin, then the only way any of them can and will be saved is by quietly waiting for God to overpower their will so they can believe the Gospel. This is the purpose of Irresistible Grace according to the Calvinists, and is only the logical result of believing the other "points." As Seaton explains: "If men are unable to save themselves on account of their fallen nature, and if God has purposed to save them and Christ has accomplished their salvation, *then* it logically follows that God must also provide the means for calling them into the benefits of that salvation which He has procured for them."[5] Tom Ross insists that "if every man is totally depraved, corrupt, and naturally unwilling to come to Christ, God must do a powerful inward work to change the sinner's disposition and draw him to a saving knowledge of Jesus Christ."[6] Gunn maintains that "grace must be irresistible if any are to be saved."[7]

As one of the three essential points of Calvinism, Irresistible Grace is also directly related to Unconditional Election. Tom Ross explains that "the effectual call" of Irresistible Grace "is the consequence of God's eternal election."[8] This makes sense because if grace is truly irresistible, it can only be given to the "elect," lest one of the "non-elect" get saved. Bruce Ware regards the fourth point of Calvinism as "a necessary complement to its doctrine of unconditional election, each of which entails and is entailed by the other."[9] And even though Limited Atonement is not essential to Calvinism, and is actually denied by some Calvinists, Van Baren insists that "one who believes that Christ died for *all* sinners, can not believe the truth of irresistible grace."[10] Gerstner maintains that "irresistible grace is implicitly denied by the explicit denial of limited Atonement."[11] But as we saw back in chapter 6, the spurious nature of Total Depravity renders not only Unconditional Election unnecessary, but Irresistible Grace as well. If man does not have inability, then he can be saved without Unconditional Election and Irresistible Grace. This in and of itself, however, does not automatically render Irresistible Grace a false doctrine. If Irresistible Grace is true, God could still "irresistibly" come upon a sinner in spite of his ability to be saved without it. Therefore, it is still necessary to examine the claims of the Calvinists on their fourth point.

Definitions

How do the Calvinists define Irresistible Grace? Palmer replies: "All that irresistible grace means is that God sends his Holy Spirit to work in the lives of people so that they will definitely and certainly be changed from evil to good people."[12] Spencer adds: "Since it is the will of God that those whom He gave to His dear Son in eternity past should be saved. He will surely act in sovereign grace in such a way that the elect will find Christ irresistible."[13] Perhaps it would be better to ascertain *how* this grace operates. These sections from chapter X of the Westminster Confession of Faith are often quoted:

> I. All those whom God hath predestinated unto life, and those only, he is pleased, in his appointed and accepted time, effectually to call, by his Word and Spirit, out of that state of sin and death, in which they are by nature, to grace and salvation, by Jesus Christ; enlightening their minds spiritually and savingly to understand the things of God, taking away their heart of stone, and giving unto them a heart of flesh; renewing their wills, and, by his almighty power, determining them to that which is good, and effectually drawing them to Jesus Christ: yet so, as they come most freely, being made willing by his grace.

> II. This effectual call is of God's free and special grace alone, not from anything at all foreseen in man, who is altogether passive therein, until, being quickened and renewed by the Holy Spirit, he is thereby enabled to answer this call, and to embrace the grace offered and conveyed in it.

The Canons of Dort concur with this description of Irresistible Grace:

> But that others who are called by the gospel, obey the call, and are converted, is not to be ascribed to the proper exercise of free will, whereby one distinguishes himself above others equally furnished with grace sufficient for faith and conversions, as the proud heresy of Pelagius maintains; but it must be wholly ascribed to God, who as he has chosen his own from eternity in Christ, so he confers upon them faith and repentance, rescues them from the power of darkness, and translates them into the kingdom of his own Son, that they may show forth the praises of him, who hath called them out of darkness into his marvelous light; and may glory not in themselves, but in the Lord according to the testimony of the apostles in various places.[14]

So Irresistible Grace is what actually saves a man, believing on Christ is only the result of this "grace." It is for this reason that Warfield called Irresistible Grace "the hinge of Calvinistic soteriology."[15]

That the Calvinists actually believe a man must be regenerated *before* exercising faith in Christ will be demonstrated from the Calvinists themselves. To those Calvinists who sense you recognize the connotations of it, Irresistible Grace is toned down to lessen its harshness to non-Calvinists. Palmer suggests that if the word *irresistible* "causes misunderstanding, then another word may be chosen. For example, *efficacious,* or *effectual,* or *unconquerable,* or *certain.*"[16] Because Sproul believes that "the term *irresistible grace* is misleading," he uses the phrase "effectual grace" to "avoid some confusion."[17] Although Gunn likewise prefers "effectual grace,"[18] others choose "efficacious"[19] or "invincible"[20] grace. The preferred term is "effectual calling,"[21] derived from chapter X in the Westminster Confession of Faith. But just like the term Irresistible Grace, when a Calvinist uses the phrase "effectual calling," he insists that "the stress is on the word *effectual.*"[22] So once again the meaning of a scriptural term is altered by the Calvinists with a prefix. But calling Irresistible Grace by these other designations can never change the fact of what it really is.

God's Will

Not only is Irresistible Grace built on the false premise of Total Depravity, it too has an underlying theory. The theory behind Irresistible Grace is that God's will is always done. The reason God's will is always done is, according to Calvinists, because God wills every event that takes place. Thus, Steven Houck can say: "God sovereignly works in all things in such a way that He makes all things do what He has willed in His eternal counsel."[23] And as we saw in chapter 7, when a Calvinist talks about God willing something he means God decreeing something. So the reason a Calvinist can claim that God's will is always done is because the will of God is founded on his decree. It is to be remembered that by God's decree the Calvinists mean a sovereign, singular, eternal, all-encompassing decree. Thus, if God decreed all things in an absolute sense, then nothing could ever happen that went against God's will because "God's decree is synonymous with God's will."[24]

Calvinists frequently divide God's will into his secret will and his revealed will. Best terms these God's "will of purpose" and "will of command."[25] In keeping with the propensity of the Calvinists to exhaust their detractors with theological terminology, these two wills have also been referred to as "sovereign will and moral will," "efficient will and permissive will," and "decretive will and perceptive will."[26] According to Pink: "The secret will of God is His eternal, unchanging purpose concerning all things which He hath made, to be brought about by certain means to their appointed ends."[27] This secret will is "always effected, always fulfilled."[28] On the other hand, the revealed will of God "contains not His purpose and decree but our duty,—not what *He* will do according to His eternal counsel, but what *we* should do if we would please Him."[29] God's secret will is, as the name implies, secret, but man is responsible to obey God's revealed will because it is in fact revealed.[30] On this point—the secret/revealed dichotomy—we can agree with the Calvinists, for the idea is certainly scriptural: **"The secret *things belong* unto the LORD our God: but those *things which are* revealed *belong* unto us and to our children for ever,** that *we* may do all the words of this law" (Deu. 29:29). But as usual, there is another side of Calvinism that must here be explored.

To begin with, the Calvinists are correct in asserting that God has a "secret will" that shall be carried out:

> **The LORD of hosts hath sworn, saying, Surely as I have thought, so shall it come to pass; and as I have purposed, *so* shall it stand (Isa. 14:24).**

> **And all the inhabitants of the earth *are* reputed as nothing: and he doeth according to his will in the army of heaven, and *among* the inhabitants of the earth: and none can stay his hand, or say unto him, What doest thou? (Dan. 4:35).**

So there is a sense in which "the Scriptures make it very clear that no one can frustrate the eternal counsel and will of God."[31] But no one who believed what the Bible said about God would disagree with this. Secondly, the Calvinists are again accurate when they maintain that God has a "revealed will" that man is responsible to obey:

> **For this is the will of God, *even* your sanctification, that ye should abstain from fornication (1 Thes. 4:3).**

> **In every thing give thanks: for this is the will of God in Christ Jesus concerning you (1 Thes. 5:18).**

The problem with the Calvinistic concept of the will of God concerns what happens when man does not obey God's revealed will.

How many Christians from the first century until the present day have either committed fornication (1 Thes. 4:3) or been unthankful (1 Thes. 5:18)? How many hundreds? How many thousands? Obviously, man does not always obey the will of God. But because the Calvinist believes that God's will is based on his decree and is therefore always done, the fact that a man commits fornication or is unthankful is not actually contrary to God's will at all. Pink explains further:

> God's revealed will is never done perfectly or fully by any of us, but His secret will never fails of accomplishment even in the

minutest particular.[32]

> But, God knowing that we should fail to perfectly do His revealed will ordered His eternal counsels accordingly, and these eternal counsels, which make up His secret will, though unknown to us are, though unconsciously, fulfilled in and through us.[33]

Thus, Beza can say: "Nothing falls outside of the divine willing, even when certain events are clearly contrary to God's will."[34] That fornication and unthankfulness are actually part of God's "secret will" should come as no surprise in light of what we saw in chapter 7 about the Calvinistic concept of God's all-encompassing decree.

The fact that God allows things to happen that are evil and contrary to his nature further necessitates the idea of the permissive will of God. This is abhorrent to most Calvinists, and is consequently made into foreordination: "God can foreordain things in different ways. But everything that happens must at least happen by his permission. If he permits something, then he must decide to allow it. If He decides to allow something, then in a sense He is foreordaining it."[35] We saw in chapter 7 that Calvinists who deny God's permissive will make him the author of sin. To escape this charge, some Calvinists do acknowledge the permissive will of God but found it on God's decree. This would give us the oxymoron of "sovereign permission." But this contradiction makes permission null and void, for Pink maintains that "God only permits that which is according to His will."[36] If a Calvinist is going to deny that fornication and unthankfulness are really God's will and part of his decree then there is no other alternative than the permissive will of God. How else could one account for man ignoring and rejecting God's will beside the idea that sometimes God's will is ideal and commanded yet unrealized and disobeyed? God's will can refer to what he performs, what he prefers, as well as what he permits. Failure to distinguish between all aspects of God's will has led many Calvinists to ridiculous extremes:

> Because God's will is always done, the will of every creature must conform to the sovereign will of God.[37]

> God is the absolute sovereign Ruler of heaven and earth, and we are never to think of Him as wishing or striving to do what He

knows He will not do. For Him to do otherwise would be for Him to act foolishly.[38]

These two Calvinistic ideas—man must always do God's will and God cannot will what never takes place—must be examined further to see the utter fallacy of the Calvinist position.

That the will of God is not necessarily synonymous with God's "decree" is evident by what the Bible says about God's will. The Christian is commanded: **"Be ye not unwise, but understanding what the will of the Lord is"** (Eph. 5:17). This will is to be proved (Rom. 12:2) and done from the heart (Eph. 6:6). Paul submitted to the will of God as an apostle (2 Tim. 1:1), and prayed for Christians to be **"filled with the knowledge of"** (Col. 1:9) and **"stand perfect and complete in all the will of God"** (Col. 4:12). He expressed the desire that his plans would be accomplished **"by the will of God"** (Rom. 1:10, 15:32). Just as James declared: **"If the Lord will, we shall live, and do this, or that"** (Jam. 4:15), so Paul likewise said:

> **But I will come to you shortly, if the Lord will, and will know, not the speech of them which are puffed up, but the power (1 Cor. 4:19).**
>
> **For I will not see you now by the way; but I trust to tarry a while with you, if the Lord permit (1 Cor. 16:7).**

Doing the will of God is not automatic. Not only does it take a conscious effort, these verses show that it is not a certainty:

> **For whosoever shall do the will of my Father which is in heaven, the same is my brother, and sister, and mother (Mat. 12:50).**
>
> **If any man will do his will, he shall know of the doctrine, whether it be of God, or *whether* I speak of myself (John 7:17).**

The idea that man must always do God's will is a cornerstone of Calvinism. If God's will is what he has decreed and is therefore always done, then no one (including the Apostle Paul) should ever be concerned about whether God's will is being carried out or not—it could never *not* be carried out.

The idea that God cannot will what never takes place is another foundational principle of Calvinism. But although the Calvinist cannot conceive of God desiring something to take place which never does, the Scripture makes it clear that God can:

> **O that there were such an heart in them, that they would fear me, and keep all my commandments always, that it might be well with them, and with their children for ever! (Deu. 5:29).**

> **O Jerusalem, Jerusalem, *thou* that killest the prophets, and stonest them which are sent unto thee, how often would I have gathered thy children together, even as a hen gathereth her chickens under *her* wings, and ye would not! (Mat. 23:37).**

Of this latter verse Gill laments: "Nothing is more common in the mouths and writings of the Arminians than this Scripture."[39] And although he correctly points out that the ones Christ would have gathered are not the ones who resisted,[40] as it is sometimes interpreted by non-Calvinists,[41] the fact remains that someone was able to thwart what Christ desired to accomplish. Thus, it is evident that men can and do resist the grace of God in various ways. They refuse to receive God's instruction (Jer. 5:3), hear God's words (Jer. 13:10), obey God (Neh. 9:16), and choose what God delights in (Isa. 65:12). Many times God calls and man refuses to answer (Pro. 1:24; Jer. 7:13). God's "elect" nation, the Jews, even rejected him:

> **Yea, they turned back and tempted God, and limited the Holy One of Israel (Psa. 78:41).**

> **But my people would not hearken to my voice; and Israel would none of me (Psa. 81:11).**

It is possible for man to **"set at nought"** God's counsel (Pro. 1:25). The Pharisees and lawyers **"rejected the counsel of God against themselves"** (Luke 7:30). The principle evident in the statement of Jesus Christ to Pilate, **"Thou couldest have no power at all against me, except it were given thee from above"** (John 19:11), is not the issue. Man could not breathe but for the grace of God.

The issue is whether God will let a man resist him.

Because the Calvinist believes that man must always do God's will and God cannot will what never takes place, there are two verses in particular that cause him great vexation:

> **Who will have all men to be saved, and to come unto the knowledge of the truth (1 Tim. 2:4).**

> **The Lord is not slack concerning his promise, as some men count slackness; but is longsuffering to us-ward, not willing that any should perish, but that all should come to repentance (2 Pet. 3:9).**

These passages intimidate Calvinists so much that Boettner considers them as "probably the most plausible defense for Arminianism."[42] Piper counts these two verses as "Arminian pillar texts concerning the universal saving will of God."[43] R. K. Wright acknowledges that these verses "are the two often thought to be decisively against Calvinism."[44] The same idea is evident in these two passages, it is just considered two different ways. In the former we have God willing for something to take place that never does, since obviously some men never get saved. In the latter we have God not willing for something to take place that does, since obviously some men perish.

In considering the first passage in question, the context is essential for a proper interpretation:

> **I exhort therefore, that, first of all, supplications, prayers, intercessions, *and* giving of thanks, be made for all men;**
> **For kings, and *for* all that are in authority; that we may lead a quiet and peaceable life in all godliness and honesty.**
> **For this *is* good and acceptable in the sight of God our Saviour;**
> **Who will have all men to be saved, and to come unto the knowledge of the truth.**
> **For *there is* one God, and one mediator between God and men, the man Christ Jesus (1 Tim. 2:1-5).**

Pink insists that verse four "*cannot* teach that God wills the salvation of all mankind, or otherwise all mankind *would* be saved."[45] Calvin considers it a "childish illusion" to think that this passage contradicts predestination.[46] As we saw in the previous chapter on Limited Atonement, the **"all men"** is defined for us in the context. But for the standard Calvinist position, we cite Calvin himself:

> For the apostle's meaning here is simply that no nation of the earth and no rank of society is excluded from salvation, since God wills to offer the Gospel to all without exception. Since the preaching of the Gospel brings life, he rightly concludes that God regards all men as being equally worthy to share in salvation. But he is speaking of classes and not of individuals and his only concern is to include princes and foreign nations in this number.[47]

Most Calvinists use this "all men without distinction" explanation.[48] Wright even asserts that "ever since Augustine this has been the preferred Calvinistic understanding of the verse."[49] Gill, however, interprets the **"all men"** as the Gentiles, exactly like the Calvinists do on other passages when seeking to maintain Limited Atonement.[50] But this really doesn't change anything, for to do this, Gill would have to make it "all Gentiles without distinction," since not all Gentiles get saved. Recognizing that the "case for this limitation on God's universal saving will has never been convincing to Arminians,"[51] the Calvinist Piper affirms that God really does love "the world with a deep compassion that desires the salvation of all men."[52] However, this desire is tempered by God's secret will, by which he "has chosen from before the foundation of the world whom he will save from sin."[53] This was also the position of Spurgeon,[54] for which he has been castigated by other Calvinists for "an atrocious piece of exegesis."[55]

As was pointed out in the previous chapter, there are four reasons why the **"all men"** of verses one and four do not refer to just classes of men. First of all, classes of men are given in verse two. There would be no point in doing this if it had already been done in verse one. Secondly, the **"all that are in authority"** of verse two would be meaningless if the Calvinists consistently interpreted the **"all"** like they did in the previous verse. The men in authority in verse two already make up a class. Furthermore, if the Apostle Paul wanted to say "classes of men" he could have done so:

And when he had called unto *him* his twelve disciples, he

> gave them power *against* unclean spirits, to cast them out, and to heal all manner of sickness and all manner of disease (Mat. 10:1).

> For every kind of beasts, and of birds, and of serpents, and of things in the sea, is tamed, and hath been tamed of mankind (Jam. 3:7).

When the Bible refers to what Sproul calls "the universality of the elect (people from every tribe and nation),"[56] it does so in unambiguous terms:

> And they sung a new song, saying, Thou art worthy to take the book, and to open the seals thereof: for thou wast slain, and hast redeemed us to God by thy blood out of every kindred, and tongue, and people, and nation (Rev. 5:9).

And finally, the attempts of the Calvinists to make the **"all men"** of this passage refer to all classes of men does not alleviate their problem anyway. Whoever these men are, God desires their salvation. Therefore, since (in Calvinistic thought) only the "elect" will ever be saved, it is not enough just to transform the **"all men"** into all classes of men—it would have to be further limited to just the "elect" in these classes. Not all kings are of the "elect." And neither are all in authority. But this won't work either, because if there is a such thing as the "elect," then they are mentioned in conjunction with the reason prayers ought to be made **"that we may lead a quiet and peaceable life"** (1 Tim. 2:2). The **"we"** are the "elect" in the passage, not the **"all men."**

But Calvin's error is two-fold. His other blunder was in stating that "God wills to offer the Gospel to all." The offer of the Gospel wasn't even under consideration. And as we shall presently see, Calvinists don't really believe that God wills to offer the Gospel to all men anyway. The verse in question says that God **"will have all men to be saved."** God wills that all men be saved. The only reason all men aren't saved was given by the Saviour: **"And ye will not come to me, that ye might have life"** (John 5:40). The provision of **"one mediator between God and men"** (1 Tim. 2:5) confirms that God desires the salvation of all men.

The companion passage to 1 Timothy 2:4 likewise causes Calvinists indigestion:

> **The Lord is not slack concerning his promise, as some men count slackness; but is longsuffering to us-ward, not willing that any should perish, but that all should come to repentance (2 Pet. 3:9).**

Best maintains that those who see in this verse God's "desire that all men be saved" either believe in universalism, deny Christ's second coming, or believe God must conform to the will of man.[57] And because he believes that God's will is always done and God cannot will what never takes place, Boettner remarks: "Since Scripture tells us that some men are going to be lost, II Peter 3:9 cannot mean that God is earnestly wishing or striving to save all individual men. For if it were His will that every individual of mankind should be saved, then not one soul could be lost."[58] Clark insists that "God does not will the salvation of every member of the human race. It is not his will that every man without exception should repent."[59] Who then does God will should repent? Pink replies: "His decreed purpose is that *all* His elect will come to repentance, and repent they *shall*."[60] So according to most Calvinists, God is not willing that any of the "elect" should perish.[61] But not all Calvinists swallow this TULIP whole. Berkouwer relates of a fellow theologian: "But then he speaks of 'all elect,' although the text does not mention the word 'elect' at all."[62] Just like we saw regarding 1 Timothy 2:4, there are some Calvinists who accept God's "universal saving will" as it is revealed in 2 Peter 3:9.[63] These Calvinists include Calvin himself:

> This is His wondrous love towards the human race, that He desires all men to be saved, and is prepared to bring even the perishing to safety. We must notice the order, that God is prepared to receive all men into repentance, so that none may perish. These words indicate the means of obtaining salvation, and whoever of us seeks salvation must learn to follow in this way.[64]

But after advancing this interpretation, the Calvinists are forced, like they were on 1 Timothy 2:4, to balance it with God's secret will. Thus, in answer to the question of why so many perish, Calvin replies: "No mention is made here of the secret decree of God by which the wicked are doomed to their own ruin."[65]

If the **"us-ward"** in this verse is limited to just the "elect" then the Calvinist is faced with several problems. First of all, and most importantly, like we saw in chapter 7 on Unconditional Election, there is no such thing as a group of people termed the "elect" who have not yet been saved. Therefore, if the **"us-ward"** is limited to those who are really "elect," then there results the absurdity that the "elect" are in danger of perishing and need to repent. Secondly, how could God be longsuffering to the "elect"? The "elect" couldn't perish if they tried! Pink even admits that "repent they shall." If an omnipotent God made an eternal, sovereign decree electing the "elect" to salvation—how could it be otherwise that they could perish? The **"us-ward"** is simply a reference to the **"men"** in the previous phrase. Because the longsuffering of God delays his coming, scoffers consider it slackness but believers count it **"salvation"** (2 Pet. 3:15) because by it they were given time to repent. In his first epistle the Apostle Peter likewise spoke of the longsuffering of God: **"Which sometime were disobedient, when once the longsuffering of God waited in the days of Noah, while the ark was a preparing, wherein few, that is, eight souls were saved by water"** (1 Pet. 3:20). During this time, God said: **"My spirit shall not always strive with man, for that he also *is* flesh: yet his days shall be an hundred and twenty years"** (Gen. 6:3). The Lord is longsuffering to all men, not just the "elect." And finally, when God wants to limit *us-ward* to just the "elect," he does so: **"And what *is* the exceeding greatness of his power to us-ward who believe, according to the working of his mighty power"** (Eph. 1:19). So despite the teachings of Calvinism, God can be not willing for something to take place that does, since obviously some men perish.

It should be obvious by now that a man can resist the work of Holy Spirit. This is clearly brought out in Stephen's address before the council of the Jews: **"Ye stiffnecked and uncircumcised in heart and ears, ye do always resist the Holy Ghost: as your fathers *did*, so *do* ye"** (Acts 7:51). Tom Ross laments: "The Arminians loudly assert that this verse teaches that men can and do resist the power of the Holy Spirit in salvation."[66] Clark misrepresents the position of his opponents: "This verse is supposed to be inconsistent with irresistible grace, and to imply therefore that man has ability to convert himself."[67] Van Baren has a unique, deceptive interpretation to get rid of the obvious implication:

> Does it not from this appear that God's grace is after all resistible? Other passages of Scripture apparently speak in this same vein. But remember: in Acts 7 Stephen is speaking to the Jews concerning the words of the prophets which came to the Jews in the past. In resisting the words of these prophets, the Jews had resisted the Holy Ghost. How did they do that? The Holy Ghost reveals God's Word to holy men: prophets and apostles. The Holy Ghost uses ministers of the Word to proclaim the Word of God throughout all ages: to the Jew of the Old Dispensation, and to every tribe and tongue and language in the New. And what do these who hate the Word do? They resist; they rebel; they show scorn. They take those whom the Holy Ghost uses to proclaim the Word, and kill them. Of all this Stephen is speaking. He is not telling them that the Spirit of God was given to all to lead all to repentance—but many resisted. Certainly not. But the Spirit is resisted when these resist the holy men whom the Spirit sends.[68]

Wouldn't it just be easier to say that Stephen lied? After admitting that "the grace of God can be resisted," Beck has to add "successfully" to the text to get rid of the fact that the Holy Ghost can be resisted.[69]

The Calvinist not only cannot conceive of God willing something that never takes place, he also cannot fathom that God would let a man resist him. Back in the chapter on Total Depravity, we saw that Calvinists believe that for God to get the glory for salvation, man must be *unable* to accept or reject. Because they feel this way, the Calvinists essentially charge their opponents with holding contemptible views of God:

> If God's grace can be *successfully* resisted then *God* can be overcome.[70]

> God is not omnipotent if he can be resisted and rejected.[71]

> If every man possesses a free will that is powerful enough to resist the will of God in salvation, what would prevent that same man from choosing to resist the will of God in damnation at the great white throne of judgment?[72]

But according to the Bible, the grace of God and the Holy Spirit cannot only be resisted, but frustrated (Gal. 2:21), done despite to

(Heb. 10:29), received in vain (2 Cor. 6:1), fallen from (Gal. 5:4), failed (Heb. 12:15), and turned into lasciviousness (Jude 4). It is as simple as Arminius once said: "Grace is not an omnipotent act of God, which cannot be resisted by the free-will of men."[73] When faced with such clear evidence that man can resist God, the Calvinist invents a new facet of TULIP theology with the resultant terminology to confuse the reader: a system of two calls to salvation—one resisted by the "non-elect" and one accepted by the "elect." Therefore, Ness can claim that the Jews in Acts 7:51 merely "resisted the preaching of the gospel (outward means of grace)."[74] So Acts 7:51 was just an outward call only: the inward call being Irresistible Grace but in this case not given. Thus, as Tom Ross explains: "What Stephen was referring to was the rejection of the general call of God to repentance, not the effectual call to salvation."[75]

Effectual Calling

By formulating a system of two calls, the Calvinists are able to consign all resistance to God to resistance to a general call. This enables them to still maintain the teaching of Irresistible Grace by making it synonymous with an effectual call. Thus, as we have seen, the preferred alternate term for Irresistible Grace is "effectual calling." We also saw that this term was derived from chapter X in the Westminster Confession of Faith:

> I. All those whom God hath predestinated unto life, and those only, he is pleased, in his appointed and accepted time, effectually to call, by his Word and Spirit, out of that state of sin and death, in which they are by nature, to grace and salvation, by Jesus Christ; enlightening their minds spiritually and savingly to understand the things of God, taking away their heart of stone, and giving unto them a heart of flesh; renewing their wills, and, by his almighty power, determining them to that which is good, and effectually drawing them to Jesus Christ: yet so, as they come most freely, being made willing by his grace.

Although the Calvinists refer to these calls by different names, they all signify the same thing. Besides the nomenclature of "general" and "effectual,"[76] the common terms are "external" and "internal"[77] "outer" and "inner,"[78] "outward" and "inward,"[79] and "general" and "special."[80] Some Calvinists use all the terms interchangeably.[81] There is one other set of terms that is perhaps more accurate, but this set is only used by non-Calvinists: "insincere" and "sincere."[82]

According to Calvinists, the general call is "extended throughout the world, through the proclamation of the gospel, telling all sinners everywhere that through faith in Christ they may receive forgiveness of their sins and have eternal life."[83] The three elements that make up the general call are explained by Talbot and Crampton: (1) A biblical presentation of Jesus Christ as the Son of God incarnate. (2) A sincere invitation to repent of sin, and by faith to accept Christ as Savior and Lord. (3) The promise of the forgiveness of sins in Him alone.[84] But as is admitted by Calvinists, this is a mock invitation, for the general call "will not work a work of salvation in a sinner's soul."[85] Gunn even confesses that "the general call, like sheet lightning, is grand and beautiful but never strikes anything."[86] Storms concedes that "the Bible does not use the word *external* with reference to a call of God," but insists that because "God issues an invitation which is universal, yet ultimately ineffective," Calvinists are justified in using the term anyway.[87]

On the other hand, by the effectual call "the Spirit graciously causes the elect sinner to cooperate, to believe, to repent, to come freely and willingly to Christ."[88] Tom Ross terms the effectual call "one of the most important truths taught in the Holy Scriptures."[89] For anyone to be saved, "the outward call must be accompanied by the inward call of God's Holy Spirit."[90] But as Berkhof relates of these two calls: "God is the author of both; the Holy Spirit operates in both; and in both the Word of God is employed."[91] So even though these two calls appear to be the same, Calvinists insist that "a failure to see the difference between the general and effectual call brings reproach upon the power and majesty of God."[92] Some Calvinists insist that the effectual call can never be resisted,[93] while others emphasize that, although it can be resisted, it "is irresistible in the sense that it is invincible."[94] But what is important to note about the effectual call is that it is "ultimately persuasive" or "ultimately irresistible."[95] So, if this effectual call always eventually results in the salvation of a sinner, then why doesn't God just give everyone an effectual call? Does not God desire the salvation of all men? As we shall see in the next section, the reason why God can't indiscriminately give an effectual call is because he only wants the "elect" to be saved. If an effectual call was given to someone who was one of the "non-elect" it would result in a regenerated "reprobate" whom Christ did not die for. But suppose one of the "elect" doesn't want to receive the word of God and be saved? Never fear: "Christ will not let him reject Him."[96] Yet, Rose maintains that "God does not bring anyone into the kingdom against his or her will."[97]

But to further complicate matters, some Calvinists imply that the general call can be accepted. First, Tom Ross states the standard Calvinist position: "The general call is further distinguished from the effectual call by the fact that it is always resisted, whereas the effectual call is never resisted."[98] After all the Calvinists have said about the general and effectual call, this is to be expected. But other Calvinists say that the general outward "can be" or "may be" resisted.[99] This implies that the general call can be accepted. If the general call is often rejected but not always rejected then this proves from the Calvinists themselves that there is no difference between the general and effectual call because the "elect" can accept the general call. Gerstner himself even disdains this distinction: "The traditional Reformed distinction between the internal and external call can be a source of confusion. There are not two different calls. They are one and the same call. The internal spiritual call is to the regenerate. The external audible call is to the regenerate. This one call to the regenerate is heard by the ears of many unregenerate. But what they hear is not a call to them but to the regenerate."[100]

Although the Bible does distinguish between types of calls, this in no way proves the general/effectual dichotomy of the Calvinists. Pink insists that "the word 'called' in the New Testament Epistles is never applied to those who are recipients of a mere external invitation of the Gospel. The term always signifies an inward and effectual call."[101] The problem with this statement is two-fold. Not only is there no distinction in the Bible between a general and an effectual call to salvation, the word *call* (and its derivatives) does not necessarily refer to a call to salvation. In fact, the primary designations to calling are not to salvation at all. Paul was **"called *to be* an apostle"** (Rom. 1:1). Peter was **"called Cephas"** (John 1:24). Herod **"called the wise men"** (Mat. 2:7). James and John, while mending their nets, were **"called"** by Jesus Christ (Mat. 4:21). Aaron was **"called of God"** to the priest's office (Heb. 5:4). Jerusalem is spiritually **"called Sodom and Egypt"** (Rev. 11:8).

Christians are **"called *to be* saints"** (1 Cor. 1:2), and are both **"called the children of the living God"** (Rom. 9:26) and **"called the sons of God"** (1 John 3:1). Calling is a vocation (Eph. 4:1), a call to holiness (1 Thes. 4:7), a call to peace (1 Cor. 7:15), a call to liberty (Gal. 5:13). It can also be a call related to salvation (1 Cor. 1:9; Gal. 1:6; 2 Thes. 2:14; 1 Pet. 2:9), but Irresistible Grace should not be confused with calling or salvation.

Although the following verses in Matthew were used by Calvinists to prove Unconditional Election, because they also contain the word *called,* some Calvinists consider them proof texts for the two-call system of Irresistible Grace:

> **So the last shall be first, and the first last: for many be called, but few chosen (Mat. 20:16).**
>
> **For many are called, but few are chosen (Mat. 22:14).**

Surprisingly, Rose considers this the inner, effectual call.[102] But recognizing that this would entail a different number of those "effectually called" and those "elected," other Calvinists maintain that this is an example of a general call.[103] Best sees both calls evident: "The calling of the many is the general call. The choosing of the few is the effectual call."[104] To relate these verses to Irresistible Grace, Calvinists have to add "to salvation" after each occurrence of the word **"called."** But as we saw in chapter 7, the context of both passages had nothing to do with **"the gospel of the grace of God"** (Acts 20:24). Both passages concern **"the kingdom of heaven"** (Mat. 20:1, 22:2), not heaven or salvation. And both passages are parables, not doctrinal statements on the plan of salvation. The first verse in question had to do with laborers (Mat. 20:1); salvation is a gift (Rom. 6:23; Eph. 2:8). In Matthew 22:14 the ones called were **"bid to the marriage"** (Mat. 22:9), not irresistibly forced to go. The ones called were **"good and bad"** (Mat. 22:10), not just the "elect." And finally, the ones said to be chosen responded to what the Calvinists admit is a general call (Mat. 22:9). The "effectual" call to a particular group was refused (Mat. 22:3). Therefore, the ones chosen and the ones rejected received the same call. If it was "effectual" for the one group, it had to be for the other. And although it has been amply pointed out in our study of Unconditional Election, it is worth noticing again that the calling here comes before the choosing. This completely overthrows the Calvinistic *ordo salutis,* for the choosing supposedly took place before the foundation of the world.

Another passage presented as a proof text for Irresistible Grace was also used by the Calvinists to prove Unconditional Election:

> **And we know that all things work together for good to them that love God, to them who are the called according to *his* purpose.**
> **For whom he did foreknow, he also did predestinate *to be* conformed to the image of his Son, that he might be the firstborn among many brethren.**
> **Moreover whom he did predestinate, them he also called: and whom he called, them he also justified: and whom he justified, them he also glorified (Rom. 8:28-30).**

Ware terms this one of "the most straightforward" expressions of "God's effectual call."[105] The Hardshell Baptist Eddie Garrett calls verse thirty "one of the classic passages on irresistible grace."[106] In explaining the phrase "them he also called," Johns says: "Then in proper time He called them and made them willing to come to Christ."[107] To ensure that this call is limited to the "elect," some Calvinists add "all" before each of the phrases in this "golden chain" of salvation.[108] Ware concludes: "If in Romans 8:30 all those called are justified and glorified, but if many who hear God's general gospel call to believe instead resist and so are neither justified nor glorified, then it follows that the 'call' of 8:30 is the effectual call."[109]

There are four problems with making **"called"** in this passage refer to Irresistible Grace. First, as was mentioned in chapter 7 on Unconditional Election, Romans 8 does not contain the elusive *ordo salutis,* as is evident by the glaring omission of regeneration (Tit. 3:5) and sanctification (Jude 1). Second, a contrary order of these terms is given, not once, but several times. In Matthew 20:16 and 22:14, calling comes before "election," but in Romans 8:29 it is after predestination. In Acts 2:23 foreknowledge comes after the supposed predestination, but in 1 Peter 1:2 and Romans 8:29 it doesn't. In 2 Thessalonians 2:13 and 1 Peter 1:2, sanctification follows "election," but in Jude 1 it precedes calling. According to 2 Timothy 1:9 and 2 Pet 1:10, the order is salvation, calling, and then election. In Jude 1, however, one is sanctified, preserved, and then called. But in 1 Corinthians 6:11, the believer is washed, sanctified, and then justified. Third, that believers are in Scripture described as being **"called"** there is no doubt:

> **I marvel that ye are so soon removed from him that called you into the grace of Christ unto another gospel (Gal. 1:6).**
>
> **That ye would walk worthy of God, who hath called you unto his kingdom and glory (1 Thes. 2:12).**
>
> **But ye *are* a chosen generation, a royal priesthood, an holy nation, a peculiar people; that ye should shew forth the praises of him who hath called you out of darkness into his marvellous light (1 Pet. 2:9).**

But this is merely a technical description of believers—because they have answered the call. Paul said to the Thessalonians about their salvation: **"Whereunto he called you by our gospel, to the obtaining of the glory of our Lord Jesus Christ"** (2 Thes. 2:14). The gospel preached by Paul to the Thessalonians was certainly not limited to just the "elect." Therefore, even though both the "elect" and "reprobate" might be called, only those who respond to the call are termed **"the called"** (Rom. 8:28) and are said to be "called" (Rom. 8:30). And finally, the whole idea of Irresistible Grace in this passage (and any other) is based on the Calvinistic doctrine of Unconditional Election. As Haldane says: "Effectual calling, then, is the proper and necessary consequence and effect of election."[110] But as we saw in chapter 7, there is no such thing as God's "elect" and "reprobate" unconditionally chosen to heaven or hell before the foundation of the world. God has made all men the same in a certain sense (Psa. 33:13-15). Therefore, since Unconditional Election has been proved to be spurious, then Irresistible Grace is as well.

Another passage that supposedly proves the two-call system of Irresistible Grace is also in the Pauline Epistles:

> **For the Jews require a sign, and the Greeks seek after wisdom:**
> **But we preach Christ crucified, unto the Jews a stumblingblock, and unto the Greeks foolishness;**
> **But unto them which are called, both Jews and Greeks,**

Christ the power of God, and the wisdom of God (1 Cor. 1:22-24).

Ware insists that verse twenty-four "presents to us a powerful and God-honoring instance of God's calling that is at once effectual, irresistible, and selective."[111] To increase the Calvinistic connotations, Clark alters **"them which are called"** to "the elect themselves."[112] The reason Calvinists limit the calling here to an effectual, irresistible call is because of the contrast between Jews and Greeks generally (1 Cor. 1:22, 23) and Jews and Greeks who are called (1 Cor. 1:24). The response of these three groups to the Gospel is given here. The preaching of **"Christ crucified"** is to the Jews **"a stumblingblock,"** to the Greeks **"foolishness,"** and to them which are called **"the power of God, and wisdom of God."** Therefore, the call mentioned here must be an effectual one (so the Calvinists say) because "the called actually see and believe in Christ as God's power and wisdom. It results in their actual salvation."[113]

The problem with this conclusion is that it ignores both the previous and ensuing context. The **"them which are called"** (1 Cor. 1:24) are the same as **"us which are saved"** (1 Cor. 2:18), **"them that believe"** (1 Cor. 1:21), and **"brethren"** (1 Cor. 1:26). The **"them which are called"** are so designated because they answered the call. Although they would term it a general call, Calvinists would still have to admit that the unregenerate have been called. So even in the Calvinistic system of two calls, only those who answer the call are denominated **"them which are called."** But the call in the context is one: **"the preaching of the cross."** Some reject it and some accept it. This one and the same call is considered both **"foolishness"** and **"the power of God"** (1 Cor. 1:18). This dichotomy can be seen elsewhere in the Pauline Epistles:

> For we are unto God a sweet savour of Christ, in them that are saved, and in them that perish:
> To the one *we are* the savour of death unto death; and to the other the savour of life unto life. And who *is* sufficient for these things? (2 Cor. 2:15-16).

Another verse in the context of 1 Corinthians also makes it clear that the calling in verse twenty-four is not Irresistible Grace: **"For ye see your calling, brethren, how that not many wise men after the flesh, not many mighty, not many noble, *are called*" (1 Cor. 1:26). It is to be remembered that in the Calvinistic system the only ones called with an effectual calling are those who were elected to salvation before the foundation of the world. Furthermore, this election is supposed to be unconditional. Therefore, if not many wise men, mighty men, or noble men are called, it is because not many of them were elected. And contrariwise, many men who are not wise, mighty, or noble were elected. But if this be the case, then election would not be unconditional it would be conditional. So on the basis of what the Calvinists claim to believe about their system, the calling in 1 Corinthians could not be related to Irresistible Grace.

The whole purpose in the Calvinist building an elaborate system of two calls is because he believes that God's will is always done and God cannot will what never takes place. In the Calvinistic system, God cannot desire the salvation of a sinner and call him by the Gospel without irresistibly overcoming his will. Contrast this with how the Lord Jesus Christ operated: **"But go ye and learn what *that* meaneth, I will have mercy, and not sacrifice: for I am not come to call the righteous, but sinners to repentance"** (Mat. 9:13). The Lord Jesus Christ did not come to call "elect sinners," and neither did he come to mock the "non-elect," he came to call **"sinners to repentance."** All sinners are called with the same call.

The Calvinistic dichotomy of general and effectual calling is also spoken of in corresponding terms of grace: "common," "cooperative," "general," or "prevenient," grace and "special," "operative," "saving," "efficacious," or "effectual" grace.[114] The characteristics of and differences between common and special grace are the same as those given for the general and effectual call. Boettner maintains that common grace "is not capable of producing a genuine conversion."[115] Therefore, common grace "is *not* irresistible"[116] because it is "a lower degree of grace than special."[117] On the other hand, special grace "succeeds in overcoming the enmity of the carnal mind and the opposition of the sinful will."[118] The contrast between common and special grace is explained by the Presbyterian theologian William Shedd:

> In common grace God demands faith in Christ, but does not

give it; in special grace God both demands and gives faith.[119]

In common grace man must of himself fulfil the condition of salvation, namely, believe and repent; in special grace God persuades and enables him to fulfil it.[120]

In common grace the call to believe and repent is invariably ineffectual, because man is averse to faith and repentance and in bondage to sin; in special grace the call is invariably effectual, because his aversion and bondage are changed into willingness and true freedom by the operation of the Holy Spirit.[121]

So special grace, like effectual calling, is equivalent to Irresistible Grace, and is therefore irresistible: "When saving grace worked faith in our hearts and brought us to salvation, we had neither the will nor the power nor the wish to resist."[122]

The nature of common grace has been the cause of much debate among the Reformed Calvinists. The common grace of God which he universally bestows on man is supposed to include things like fruitful seasons, health, material prosperity, general intelligence, talents, culture, and common virtue.[123] But because some Calvinists included in this some spiritual things concerning God and the "non-elect," controversy broke out. Back in 1924 the Christian Reformed Church issued its famous "three points" of common grace, the main point of each being:[124]

1. Concerning *the favorable attitude of God toward mankind in general and not only toward the elect,* the Synod declares that according to Scripture and the Confession it is certain that, besides the saving grace of God bestowed only upon those chosen unto eternal life, there is also a certain favor or grace of God manifested to His creatures in general.

2. Concerning *the restraint of sin in the life of the individual and of society,* the Synod declares that according to Scripture and the Confession there is such a restraint of sin.

3. Concerning *the performance of so-called civic righteousness by the unregenerate,* the Synod declares that according to Scripture and the Confession the unregenerate, although incapable of any saving good (Canons of Dort, III, IV:3), can perform such civic good.

Because some Calvinists disagreed with these sentiments, a split occurred in the Christian Reformed Church and, under the leadership of Herman Hoeksema, the Protestant Reformed Church was formed.[125]

The controversy over common grace is a non-issue to those who are not Calvinists. As North relates: "The concept of common grace is seldom discussed outside of Calvinistic circles."[126] Shedd states why this is so: "The distinction between common and special grace is closely connected with the Calvinistic doctrine of election and preterition."[127] Therefore, once the Calvinistic doctrine of election is seen to be spurious, the debate over common grace quickly fades away. The problem originated because God was said to hate the "non-elect" and yet at the same time appear to show them favor. Thus, two kinds of grace were invented to explain the dilemma. This also enabled the Calvinists to consign any and all Scriptures dealing with man's resistance to God as merely resistance to God's common grace.

The Calvinistic distortion of the grace of God does not stand the scrutiny of Scripture, for it is built on a false premise: the imaginary distinction between the "elect" and the "non-elect." God is **"no respecter of persons"** (Acts 10:34), and of the inhabitants of the earth, **"he fashioneth their hearts alike"** (Psa. 33:15). God **"maketh his sun to rise on the evil and on the good, and sendeth rain on the just and on the unjust"** (Mat. 5:45). God is **"kind unto the unthankful and *to* the evil"** (Luke 6:35). But at the same time: **"He that believeth not the Son shall not see life; but the wrath of God abideth on him"** (John 3:36). So in order to rectify this problem: **"The kindness and love of God our Saviour toward man appeared"** (Tit. 3:4). Regardless of how many different types of grace the Calvinist wants to invent, "special" grace is available to every man: **"For the grace of God that bringeth salvation hath appeared to all men"** (Tit. 2:11). To enable man to accept this grace, the Holy Spirit **"will reprove the world of sin, and of righteousness, and of judgment"** (John 16:8), not just the "elect." It is the word of God, not an effectual call or an outpouring of special grace, that brings conviction: **"For this cause also thank we God without ceasing, because, when ye received the word of God which ye heard of us, ye received *it* not *as* the word of men, but as it is in truth, the word of God, which effectually worketh also in you that believe"** (1 Thes.

2:13).

Proof Texts

Surely such an important doctrine as Irresistible Grace has some examples in the Bible by which the skeptic can see it in operation. Clark affirms that "the Bible speaks many, many, times about irresistible grace."[128] Then follows a list of verses where the term *irresistible* nor *grace* not only doesn't occur, but couldn't be inferred from the passage.[129] Other Calvinists likewise list "key verses" that supposedly prove Irresistible Grace,[130] but once again, neither of the terms can be found in any of the verses. There are a handful of verses abused by all Calvinists in an attempt to prove the mechanics of Irresistible Grace. Beginning in the Old Testament, we first see what Clark calls "the most powerful and certainly the most picturesque assertion of grace unconditional and irresistible."[131] He then claims that "in this passage every one of the five points of Calvinism fulfills its function."[132]

> **The hand of the LORD was upon me, and carried me out in the spirit of the LORD, and set me down in the midst of the valley which** *was* **full of bones,**
> **And caused me to pass by them round about: and, behold,** *there were* **very many in the open valley; and, lo,** *they were* **very dry.**
> **And he said unto me, Son of man, can these bones live? And I answered, O Lord GOD, thou knowest.**
> **Again he said unto me, Prophesy upon these bones, and say unto them, O ye dry bones, hear the word of the LORD.**
> **Thus saith the Lord GOD unto these bones; Behold, I will cause breath to enter into you, and ye shall live:**
> **And I will lay sinews upon you, and will bring up flesh upon you, and cover you with skin, and put breath in you, and ye shall live; and ye shall know that I** *am* **the LORD (Eze. 37:1-6).**

Clark considers this chapter in Ezekiel to be "the culmination of the Old Testament's teaching on predestination or foreordination. The TULIP is there in all its beauteous glory."[133] He also comments: "Could the dry bones, by their own free will, have frustrated God's intention to save them?"[134] But who are the **"dry bones"**? The "elect" who are waiting to be saved by Irresistible Grace? The context identifies without dispute who the **"dry bones"** are:

> **Then he said unto me, Son of man, these bones are the whole house of Israel: behold, they say, Our bones are dried, and our hope is lost: we are cut off for our parts.**
> **Therefore prophesy and say unto them, Thus saith the Lord GOD; Behold, O my people, I will open your graves, and cause you to come up out of your graves, and bring you into the land of Israel (Eze. 37:11-12).**

The restoration of Israel is clearly in view, not the salvation of an "elect" sinner. Like any amillennialist, Clark has spiritualized the promises to Israel and applied them to the Church.

A similar misapplication of Scripture is made in the writings of another Old Testament prophet: **"The LORD hath appeared of old unto me,** *saying,* **Yea, I have loved thee with an everlasting love: therefore with lovingkindness have I drawn thee"** (Jer. 31:3). Because it contains a form of the word *draw,* this verse is interpreted by Calvinists as Irresistible Grace applied to the "elect."[135] But once again we ask: to whom is God speaking? Several verses in the context make it perfectly clear:

> **At the same time, saith the LORD, will I be the God of all the families of Israel, and they shall be my people.**
> **Thus saith the LORD, The people** *which were* **left of the sword found grace in the wilderness;** *even* **Israel, when I went to cause him to rest (Jer. 31:1-2).**

> **Again I will build thee, and thou shalt be built, O virgin of Israel: thou shalt again be adorned with thy tabrets, and shalt go forth in the dances of them that make merry (Jer. 31:4).**

> **For thus saith the LORD; Sing with gladness for Jacob, and shout among the chief of the nations: publish ye, praise ye, and say, O LORD, save thy people, the remnant of Israel (Jer. 31:7).**

The whole chapter concerns the future of Israel. The context has once again been sacrificed on the altar of TULIP theology.

The two straws grasped at by the Calvinists in the Psalms that are used to teach Irresistible Grace serve only to show how violently Scripture can be wrested:

> **Blessed** *is* **the man** *whom* **thou choosest, and causest to approach** *unto thee, that* **he may dwell in thy courts: we shall be satisfied with the goodness of thy house,** *even* **of thy holy temple (Psa. 65:4).**
>
> **Thy people** *shall be* **willing in the day of thy power, in the beauties of holiness from the womb of the morning: thou hast the dew of thy youth (Psa. 110:3).**

Because it mentions someone being chosen, the first verse was also facetiously used to prove Unconditional Election. These verses are carelessly employed as proof of Irresistible Grace by all Calvinists on a continual basis.[136] A typical example of how this is done can be seen in the Sovereign Grace Baptist, Joseph Wilson. After making the statement that "the Holy Spirit will effectually and irresistibly work the salvation experience in all those chosen by the Father and redeemed by the Son," he quotes Psalm 65:4 and 110:3 as his proof texts.[137]

Regarding the first verse in question, Clark says that it "seems at first sight to be as explicit as any Calvinist could wish."[138] He further claims that it is "entirely too Calvinistic for the Arminian."[139] But Clark and the others who present this as proof of Irresistible Grace are somewhat deficient in basic punctuation skills, for every time a Calvinist quotes this verse he stops at the comma, omitting the purpose for the choosing and the approaching: **"That he may dwell in thy courts."** The verse speaks of God's courts, God's house, and God's temple. New Testament salvation is not even remotely connected with the verse, the Psalm, nor the Psalm before or after it. The second verse in question is likewise applied to God making a sinner willing to receive Christ. Once again, Wilson furnishes us with an example of a Calvinist in action. In discussing salvation, he says: "God is determined to have some men saved. He chose them to salvation. He predestinated them to salvation. How is He to accomplish His purpose in their salvation?"[140] His answer? "There is the effectual call given only to the elect."[141] His proof text: **"Thy people** *shall be* **willing in the day of thy power."**[142] This incredible misuse of Scripture is accomplished by totally disregarding the context of the Psalm: the Second Advent of Jesus Christ. Once again, New Testament salvation is not even remotely connected with the verse.

The New Testament proof texts for Irresistible Grace are as equally misunderstood, misinterpreted, and misapplied as those for the Old. The first two are similar in that they both concern what the Calvinist would term "God's sovereign will":

For as the Father raiseth up the dead, and quickeneth *them;* even so the Son quickeneth whom he will (John 5:21).

Of his own will begat he us with the word of truth, that we should be a kind of firstfruits of his creatures (Jam. 1:18).

These two verses are normally just listed by Calvinists in a string of proof texts for Irresistible Grace.[143] No exegesis is ever attempted, and little comment is made beside the standard Calvinistic cliches. These verses are analogous to the foundational proof texts for Total Depravity: John 1:13 and Romans 9:16. The idea read into all of them by the Calvinists is that we are saved if and when God wills it, our own free will in receiving being completely passive.

Regarding the passage in John, Clark comments: "Who is to be reborn or resurrected depends totally on the will of God. The Son quickens whom he will. No one can stay his hand; no one can resist his will. The matter lies entirely in God's hands. God is irresistible."[144] Just like he seizes upon the words *choose* and *ordain*, the Calvinist forces his TULIP theology into every occurrence of the word *quicken* as well. But notice in John 5:21 that physical death is what is in view. The raising of the dead is part of the **"greater works than these"** mentioned in the previous verse (John 5:20). Just as God the Father has the power of life and death (Deu. 32:39; 1 Sam. 2:6; 2 Kgs. 5:7), so the Lord Jesus Christ would later raise the son of the widow of Nain (Luke 7:14), the daughter of Jairus (Luke 8:54), and Lazarus (John 11:43). The notion of a spiritual quickening is found later in the context (John 5:24-25).

Concerning the sister passage in James, Clark again gives the Calvinist interpretation: "We were begotten by God's will. Can a child not yet begotten prevent the begetter from begetting him? A plain question like this shows what nonsense is involved in denying irresistible grace and predestination."[145] After saying that "salvation is conferred upon a select number who are conceived by the Holy Spirit and born again by the will of God alone," Custance lists

James 1:18 as a proof text for his statement.[146] But as if that weren't Calvinistic enough, he further adds: "Whoever thus comes to birth does not by this dramatic experience become a child of God, but actually has already become a child of God (John 17:6) by a prior experience of supernatural conception. When he comes to birth, he has already been introduced into the family of God."[147] But once again, the interpretation can be found in the context. Three contrasts should be noted. God not only does not tempt **"any man"** (Jam. 1:13), he is the author of **"every good gift and every perfect gift"** (Jam. 1:17). Man is **"drawn away of his own lust"** (Jam. 1:14), but God does things **"of his own will"** (Jam. 1:18). Lust **"bringeth forth sin"** (Jam. 1:15), but God **"begat"** believers (Jam. 1:18). And if salvation is by Irresistible Grace as the Calvinists say, then why is there an injunction to **"receive with meekness the engrafted word, which is able to save your souls"** (Jam. 1:21).

One of the few actual examples given by Calvinists of an individual in the Bible being saved by Irresistible Grace is the conversion of Lydia: **"And a certain woman named Lydia, a seller of purple, of the city of Thyatira, which worshipped God, heard *us:* whose heart the Lord opened, that she attended unto the things which were spoken of Paul"** (Acts 16:14). Besides the usual listing of this verse as a proof text,[148] Calvinists explicitly state that Lydia was saved by Irresistible Grace:

> The Lord opened Lydia's heart—then she listened and believed. That is the irresistible power of the grace of our God. He breaks open the closed heart; and the child of God believes.[149]

> Without that opening of the heart, Lydia could not have believed. That is irresistible grace.[150]

> Paul, the preacher, spoke to Lydia's ear—the outward call; but the Lord spoke to Lydia's heart—the inward call of irresistible grace.[151]

The question of the two calls has already been dealt with. Garrett dispenses with the calls altogether, and insists that Lydia was already regenerate when Paul preached to her.[152]

The trouble with the Calvinists' arguments is that they have just enough truth in them to be palatable. No one is disputing the fact that salvation is by God's grace and God's grace alone. And as we have seen throughout this work, salvation is by God's initiative:

> **For God so loved the world, that he gave his only begotten Son, that whosoever believeth in him should not perish, but have everlasting life (John 3:16).**
>
> **But God commendeth his love toward us, in that, while we were yet sinners, Christ died for us (Rom. 5:8).**
>
> **We love him, because he first loved us (1 John 4:19).**

But to maintain from all this that a sinner cannot believe the Gospel unless God overcomes him by Irresistible Grace is a TULIP of another color. Unless God opens the **"eyes"** (Acts 26:18) and **"heart"** (Acts 16:14) of a lost man, he will never see his true condition. But God opening Lydia's heart didn't guarantee her salvation any more than all Gentiles being saved because God **"opened the door of faith unto the Gentiles"** (Acts 14:27). The Psalmist prayed **"Open thou mine eyes, that I may behold wondrous things out of thy law"** (Psa. 119:18). Notice that after conversion one still needs his understanding opened by the Lord (Luke 24:45; Eph. 1:17-18). And as mentioned previously, suppose that God did overcome Lydia with Irresistible Grace, how does that prove he does the same for every sinner? The opening of Lydia's heart was God's work; the attending to the things Paul spoke was hers. And what were the things Paul spoke? Paul's sole purpose in going to Macedonia was **"to preach the gospel"** (Acts 16:10). The fact that Lydia responded to the Gospel preached by Paul does not in any way prove that God's grace was irresistible. It proves that Lydia responded to the Gospel.

As has been demonstrated in previous chapters, Calvinists often seize upon a particular word or phrase in a verse and make it say whatever they want. But as mentioned previously, a word or phrase can be used to prove anything if it is divorced from its context. Such is the case with the next Calvinistic proof text for Irresistible Grace: **"Thou wilt say then unto me, Why doth he yet find fault? For who hath resisted his will?"** (Rom. 9:19). The phrase **"for who hath resisted his will?"** is incessantly extracted from this verse and applied to man not being able to resist God's Irresistible Grace.[153] The Calvinists' foundational error is in mistaking Romans

9:19 for a doctrinal statement of the Apostle Paul. **"For who hath resisted his will?"** is a false deduction by one of Paul's critics, which is apparent by reading the entire verse and not extracting a portion of the verse to use as a proof text. There is a striking parallel between the controversialist of Paul in Romans 9 and Romans 3. The underlying objection concerned God being unrighteous. The reply: **"God forbid"** (Rom. 3:6, 9:14). Paul often alluded to his opponents, both actual (Rom. 3:8) and allegorical (Rom. 3:1), and anticipated their criticisms. The objection in Romans 9:19 is part of the third pair in Romans that begins with: **"What shall we say then?"** (Rom. 6:1–6:15; 7:7–7:13; 9:14–9:19).

Because it too mentions God's will, another passage in the Pauline Epistles is sometimes given by Calvinists as a proof text for Irresistible Grace:

> **Wherefore, my beloved, as ye have always obeyed, not as in my presence only, but now much more in my absence, work out your own salvation with fear and trembling.**
> **For it is God which worketh in you both to will and to do of** *his* **good pleasure (Phil. 2:12-13).**

This verse has been interpreted by many Calvinists to teach that God works in an unsaved man to regenerate him so he can respond to the Gospel. Clark finds it strange and incomprehensible "that some commentators use this verse to attack Calvinism" when he himself considers it "among the strongest supports for Calvinism."[154] He further claims that "among the many biblical passages that deny free will," this one "is one so clear and so pointed that I do not see how anyone could possibly misunderstand it."[155]

Although many Calvinists likewise apply this passage to God working salvation in the unregenerate,[156] some realize that this is not the case. The Dutch Reformed, supralapsarian Calvinist Herman Hoeksema correctly points out that the ones written to are already saved, salvation is already theirs, and receiving or obtaining salvation is not even in view.[157] One cannot work out what he does not have. So although a man cannot work *for* his salvation or *at* his salvation (Rom. 4:5; Eph. 2:9), he can **"work out"** his salvation. The Philippian Christians can work out their salvation because God works in them. Paul was not telling them to do anything different than he himself did. Paul worked because God worked in him: **"Whereunto I also labour, striving according to his working,**

which worketh in me mightily" (Col. 1:29). The two-fold purpose of God working is given in verse thirteen. Contrary to **"the spirit that now worketh in the children of disobedience"** (Eph. 2:2), God works in the Christian **"to will"** his good pleasure and **"to do"** his good pleasure. Because he believes that God's will is always done and God cannot will what never takes place, Clark contends that nobody "could miss the statement that God controls a man's will as well as his actions."[158] But there are two problems with this analysis. If God worked in a man to do his sovereign irresistible will then what would be the purpose of Paul's command to work? And secondly, this would make synonymous the **"to will"** and the **"to do."** We are God's **"workmanship"** (Eph. 2:20), for he is at work in us:

> **Now unto him that is able to do exceeding abundantly above all that we ask or think, according to the power that worketh in us (Eph. 3:20).**
>
> **For this cause also thank we God without ceasing, because, when ye received the word of God which ye heard of us, ye received** *it* **not** *as* **the word of men, but as it is in truth, the word of God, which effectually worketh also in you that believe (1 Thes. 2:13).**

The reason for God working in the Christian is expanded upon in another Scripture: **"Make you perfect in every good work to do his will, working in you that which is wellpleasing in his sight, through Jesus Christ; to whom** *be* **glory for ever and ever. Amen"** (Heb. 13:21).

The cornerstone of the doctrine of Irresistible Grace is part of the Calvinistic trilogy in John chapter six: **"No man can come to me, except the Father which hath sent me draw him: and I will raise him up at the last day"** (John 6:44). Carson terms this one of the "predestination passages" in John's Gospel.[159] It is to be remembered that the sixth chapter of John contains what the Calvinists perceive as the foundation for the trilogy of Total Depravity, Unconditional Election, and Irresistible Grace. The matter of election has been dealt with sufficiently in chapter 7, but as we saw in chapter 6, the connection between Total Depravity and Irresistible Grace is no where more manifest than in John 6:44. So although John 6:44 is also a Calvinistic proof text for Total

Depravity, because it gives as a reason for the sinner's "inability" to come to Christ the lack of what the Calvinists consider to be an irresistible call by God the Father, it is here examined in the chapter on Irresistible Grace.

Calvinists of every stripe are united in referring to John 6:44 as a proof text for Irresistible Grace.[160] Pink comments on the passage:

> To predicate the freedom of the will is to *deny* that man is totally depraved. To say that man *has* the power within himself to either reject or accept Christ, is to *repudiate* the fact that he is the captive of the Devil. It is to say *there is* at least one good thing in the flesh. It is to flatly contradict this word of the Son of God—"No man *can* come to me, *except* the Father which hath sent me draw him."[161]

Herman Hoeksema adds: "Every man that will come has been taught to will and to come by the efficacious drawing power of the grace of God."[162] Pink terms this drawing the "secret and effectual operation of the Spirit" by which "the Father brings each of His elect to a saving knowledge of Christ."[163]

Now, spiritually speaking, one can certainly say in this age that no man can come to Christ except the Father draw him. As has been mentioned throughout this work, salvation is by God's initiative (John 3:16; Rom. 5:8; 1 John 4:19). But any man can ask God to draw him to Jesus Christ without waiting for Irresistible Grace. Pink even asserts that "if I cannot come to Christ except the Father 'draws' me, then my responsibility is to *beg* the Father *to* 'draw' me."[164] And not only can a man be drawn, we are even instructed: **"Draw nigh to God, and he will draw nigh to you"** (Jam. 4:8). But God drawing a man should not be equated with God saving a man. The drawing of God is not irresistible. As we saw in chapter 7, God can influence, guide, lead, or direct a man without ordaining that he do something. Furthermore, as pictured in the Song of Solomon, the Church still prays to be drawn. Solomon the son of David (Song 1:1), a type of Christ the son of David (Mat. 1:1), has a woman he loves (Song 1:2), like the Lord Jesus Christ loves the Church (Eph. 5:25). The woman here, in praying, **"draw me, we will run after thee"** (Song 1:4), is, in the words of John Gill, "desirous of nearer and more intimate communion with Christ."[165]

But as usual, the Calvinists read into this verse a great deal more than meets the eye. Because he believes that "this drawing of men by the Father to the Son is always efficacious,"[166] Storms claims that "just as it is impossible for a man to come to Christ apart from the Father drawing him, so also is it impossible for a man not to come to Christ if the Father does draw him."[167] Pink explains in what this drawing consists: "The word used is a strong one, signifying, the putting forth of power and *obliging* the object seized to respond."[168] He equates this drawing to that "Divine power overcoming the sinner's innate enmity which makes him *willing to come* to Christ that he might have life."[169] Hoeksema maintains that salvation does not "wait for the determination of" man's will because "the sinner is of himself neither capable nor willing to receive that salvation."[170] However, Spencer insists that this "does *not* mean that God does violence to man's spirit by forcing him to do something he does not want to do."[171] Palmer explains further: "If someone has a desire to ask God for help, it is God working in him, God always does this in a way that man likes."[172] But it is at this point that some Calvinists begin to get nervous. Boettner confesses that the word *irresistible* is "somewhat misleading since it does suggest that a certain overwhelming power is exerted upon the person, in consequence of which he is compelled to act contrary to his desires, whereas the meaning intended, as we have stated before, is that the elect are so influenced by divine power that their coming is an act of voluntary choice."[173]

For proof of what the Calvinists really mean by God drawing a sinner, recourse to what they say about the word *draw* is all that is necessary. In spite of what he just said about the "elect" just being "influenced," Boettner enhances the word *draw* when he quotes this verse: "No man can come unto me except the Father that sent me draw [literally, *drags*] him."[174] Other Calvinists do likewise, referring to select verses that contain a form of the word *draw* (John 18:10, 21:6)[175] while ignoring others (Acts 5:37, 20:30). Instead of the word *draw*, Sproul prefers "compel,"[176] while Pink settles for "impel."[177] So what the Calvinists are teaching is that the "drawing" in John 6:44 is Irresistible Grace. By misapplying the verse to salvation in this age, the claim can then be made that if God draws all men then all men will be saved; therefore, he only draws the "elect," those whom he has given to the Son (John 6:37).

There are two passages in the context which amplify and explain this drawing:

> **It is written in the prophets, And they shall be all taught of God. Every man therefore that hath heard, and hath learned of the Father, cometh unto me (John 6:45).**
>
> **And he said, Therefore said I unto you, that no man can come unto me, except it were given unto him of my Father (John 6:65).**

In support of his statement in verse forty-four, our Lord appeals to a verse in Isaiah: **"And all thy children *shall be* taught of the LORD; and great *shall be* the peace of thy children"** (Isa. 54:13). Best insists that "the elect shall be taught of God."[178] Pink says that those taught are "God's children."[179] But rather than being a reference to the "elect," the verse in Isaiah has reference to restored Israel in the millennium, as the whole chapter shows. We have already seen in our study of election that there is no such thing as the "elect" given to Christ in eternity. As was pointed out in chapter 7, we have here the separation of the Jewish sheep from the goats and the drawing of them to the Messiah. The ones given are Jewish disciples. They are said to be his sheep (John 10:27). John baptized that Christ should be manifest to Israel (John 1:31). Although Israel as a whole received him not (John 1:11), he was known of his sheep (John 10:14), the epitome of which can be seen in Simeon, who was **"just and devout, waiting for the consolation of Israel: and the Holy Ghost was upon him"** (Luke 2:25). Doctrinally, however, we are still before Calvary. The New Testament has not yet been instituted (Mat. 26:28; Heb. 9:17), and the Holy Spirit has not yet been given (John 7:39). Of those taught of God (John 6:45), only those who hear (**"He that hath ears to hear, let him hear"** [Mark 4:9]) and learn of the Father (Mat. 11:27, 16:17; John 6:65) come to Christ. Even after salvation, Christians need to be taught of God:

> **But as touching brotherly love ye need not that I write unto you: for ye yourselves are taught of God to love one another (1 Thes. 4:9).**
> **Let us therefore, as many as be perfect, be thus minded: and if in any thing ye be otherwise minded, God shall reveal even**

this unto you (Phil. 3:15).

The error of the Calvinists on John 6:44 is two-fold. First and foremost is the misapplication of a verse with a decidedly Jewish context as a doctrinal statement on salvation in this age. And secondly, in a spiritual sense, there is the fallacy of making the drawing of God irresistible and equating it with salvation.

That John 6:44 is in a pre-crucifixion passage directly relating to God's true "elect"—the Jews—can also be seen by the change that takes place at the end of Christ's public ministry after the Jews rejected him:

> **Now is the judgment of this world: now shall the prince of this world be cast out.**
> **And I, if I be lifted up from the earth, will draw all *men* unto me.**
> **This he said, signifying what death he should die (John 12:31-33).**

It seems to have been forgotten by Calvinists that in John 6:44 it is the Father who draws but in John 12:32 it is Christ who draws. No longer would some men be drawn to him by the Father, but Jesus Christ himself would draw all men to himself. But because of their insistence that God's drawing is to be equated with salvation in this age by Irresistible Grace, Calvinists are forced to modify the phrase **"all men"** found in verse thirty-two:

> He received the promise of the Spirit, in order that by that Spirit He might draw all His own unto Him into glory.[180]

> When He says *all,* it must be referred to the children of God, who are of His flock.[181]

> The "all" plainly refers to all of *God's elect.*[182]

To claim that this drawing is one and the same as the Father's drawing in John 6:44 is to ignore the context. And even though Calvinists err in equating the drawing with the act of salvation itself; nevertheless, some Calvinists are on the right track:
> The drawing does not refer to all people individually but the means by which Gentiles will be included in the people of

God.[183]

Christ's design was to show that His grace would not be confined to Israel.[184]

Not only did the death of Christ have reference to more than just the "elect," but his birth did likewise: **"That was the true Light, which lighteth every man that cometh into the world"** (John 1:9). Calvin had some "universalist" remarks on this verse: "Beams from this light are shed upon the whole race of men, as I said before. For we know that men have this unique quality above the other animals, that they are endowed with reason and intelligence and that they bear the distinction between right and wrong engraved in their conscience. Thus there is no man to whom some awareness of the eternal light does not penetrate."[185]

This is the third time in John's Gospel that the idea of Christ being **"lifted up"** has been put forth (John 3:14, 8:28, 12:32). Satan was to be **"cast out"** (John 12:31), but Christ was to be **"lifted up"** (John 12:32). The Lord being **"lifted up"** is said to be parallel to an event in the Old Testament.

> **And as Moses lifted up the serpent in the wilderness, even so must the Son of man be lifted up:**
> **That whosoever believeth in him should not perish, but have eternal life (John 3:14-15).**

Just as those bitten had to look on the serpent for it to be effectual (Num. 21:8), so the lifting up of the Lord Jesus Christ on the cross does not in itself constitute an irresistible draw to salvation—one must still appropriate it. Recognizing the fallacy of limiting this drawing to just the "elect," Spencer admits that all men are really drawn to Christ, but to keep the "non-elect" from salvation, he claims that the "elect" are drawn for salvation and the "non-elect" for condemnation.[186]

But not only does a change take place at the end of Christ's public ministry, another shift is made after the departure of Christ back to heaven. Instead of the Father drawing men during the ministry of Christ, the lifting up of our Lord on the cross is followed by the work of the Holy Spirit in this age:

> **Nevertheless I tell you the truth; It is expedient for you that**

> I go away: for if I go not away, the Comforter will not come unto you; but if I depart, I will send him unto you.
> And when he is come, he will reprove the world of sin, and of righteousness, and of judgment:
> Of sin, because they believe not on me;
> Of righteousness, because I go to my Father, and ye see me no more;
> Of judgment, because the prince of this world is judged (John 16:7-11).

The Holy Spirit will **"reprove the world of sin,"** not the "elect."

Repentance and Faith

When faced with the absolute necessity of a man repenting and believing on Christ of his own free will, the Calvinist reaches way down into his sovereign grace trough and extracts his last defense for Irresistible Grace: repentance and faith must be given to a man before he can be saved:

> The Bible portrays faith and repentance as God's gifts to his elect.[187]

> He must have the power of faith before he can believe, the gift of repentance before he can repent.[188]

> The once dead sinner is drawn to Christ by the inward supernatural call of the Spirit who through regeneration makes him alive and creates within him faith and repentance.[189]

So like an effectual call and special grace, not only must repentance and faith be given to a man before he can be saved, only the "elect" are eligible. This does not mean that a man can be saved without repentance and faith—to the contrary—Paul testified **"both to the Jews, and also to the Greeks, repentance toward God, and faith toward our Lord Jesus Christ"** (Acts 20:21). Christ preached: **"repent ye, and believe the gospel"** (Mark 1:15). The issue is whether repentance and faith are irresistible gifts that God gives only to the "elect."

There are three texts used by Calvinists to prove that repentance must be given to a man before he can be saved:

> **Him hath God exalted with his right hand *to be* a Prince and a Saviour, for to give repentance to Israel, and forgiveness of sins (Acts 5:31).**
>
> **When they heard these things, they held their peace, and glorified God, saying, Then hath God also to the Gentiles granted repentance unto life (Acts 11:18).**
>
> **In meekness instructing those that oppose themselves; if God peradventure will give them repentance to the acknowledging of the truth (2 Tim. 2:25).**

It is incredible that these verses are even cited to back up the Calvinists' suppositions. But because they mention God giving or granting repentance, they are regularly listed as proof texts.[190] If God granting repentance to a man is what the Calvinists say it is then all Jews would be saved because God gave **"repentance to Israel"** (Acts 5:31). Pink gets around the text by altering it to "spiritual Israel."[191] But that won't work either because then all Gentiles would have to be saved as well because **"God also to the Gentiles granted repentance unto life"** (Acts 11:18). Calvinists would have to make it "elect" Gentiles in order to use this verse as a proof text for Irresistible Grace. Both statements are referring to national privileges, as in Romans 9–11, not God irresistibly saving the unconditionally elected sinner. The other text falls under Paul's personal ministerial instructions to Timothy concerning certain individuals. As can be seen from the two other passages, God could give a man repentance all day long and he could still go to hell. And besides, if repentance was God's irresistible gift to his "elect," then Paul would not be concerned about **"if God peradventure"** would do something, for in the Calvinistic system, not only do only the "elect" get repentance, they get it exactly when God decreed to give it to them.

The next thing to be considered is the idea that faith must be irresistibly given to a man so he can get saved. Rose calls this "a disputed element of Calvinism" because "some Christians have not grasped" this teaching.[192] Although there is really only one verse that could be used by Calvinists to prove that faith must be given to a man before he can be saved, this does not mean that they do not attempt to employ others. The procedure utilized here by the Calvinists is the same that we have seen before: a statement is made in support of some particular facet of Calvinistic doctrine followed by a string of "proof texts" that prove nothing related to the statement that was made. A perfect example of how this is done can be seen in the writings of two Calvinists. First is Mathison:

> Saving faith is a gift of God, a result of the regenerating work of the Holy Spirit (John 6:44-45; Acts 13:48; 16:14; 18:27; 1 Cor. 2:4-5; 2 Cor 4:6; Eph. 1:17-18; 2:8; Phil. 1:29).[193]

Of these nine passages listed as proof texts, seven of them do not mention the word *faith* and only one of them has the word *gift*. Two passages contain a form of the word *give*, but neither one of them have the word *faith*. Only one verse contains both the word *faith* and the word *gift*. Another example is C. Samuel Storms:

> Numerous texts assert that such faith is God's own gracious gift (see especially Eph. 2:8-9; Phil. 1:29; 2 Pet. 1:1; 2 Tim. 2:24-26; Acts 5:31; 11:18).[194]

Of these six passages, only two of them contain the word *faith*. The last three are actually the Calvinistic proof texts for repentance being a gift of God to his "elect." One verse has a form of the word *give,* but does not mention faith. Once again, only one passage given as a proof text contains both the word *faith* and the word *gift*.

Because it is intrinsically connected with the following verse, these two verses together are capstone of the Calvinist "faith-gift" theory:

> **For by grace are ye saved through faith; and that not of yourselves:** *it is* **the gift of God:**
> **Not of works, lest any man should boast (Eph. 2:8-9).**

Clark gives us the standard Calvinist interpretation:

> A dead man cannot seek God; he cannot exercise faith in Jesus Christ. Faith is an activity of spiritual life, and without the life there can be no activity. Furthermore, faith is not the result of man's so-called free will. Man, all by himself, cannot produce faith. It does not come by any independent decision. The Scripture is explicit, plain, and unmistakable: "For by grace are ye saved through faith, and that not of yourselves, it is the gift of God" (Eph. 2:8). Look at the words again, "It is the gift of

God." If God does not give a man faith, no amount of will power and decision can manufacture it for him.[195]

In reply to the Calvinists, our first recourse is naturally to Scripture. To begin with, the little word **"for"** at the beginning of Ephesians 2:8 has been overlooked with disastrous consequences, for this refers us to the immediate context which is God saving the dead sinner, not irresistibly granting faith. Salvation is by grace, through faith, not of ourselves, God's gift, and not of works. There are two parallels in the passage: for by grace are ye saved—it is the gift of God; not of yourselves—not of works. Grace is God's unmerited favor and is therefore **"not of yourselves."** Paul reiterates this by stating that **"*it is* the gift of God"** and consequently is **"not of works."** Faith is but the medium of reception. Faith is never spoken of as a gift given to unsaved men. The closest thing to this idea is faith being given to a man as a spiritual gift along with **"the gifts of healing"** (1 Cor. 12:9), but this is only to a man who is already saved. There is no other place in the Bible where faith is ever said to be a gift, but there are places that expand upon the gift of God:

> **But not as the offence, so also *is* the free gift. For if through the offence of one many be dead, much more the grace of God, and the gift by grace, *which is* by one man, Jesus Christ, hath abounded unto many.**
> **And not as *it was* by one that sinned, *so is* the gift: for the judgment *was* by one to condemnation, but the free gift *is* of many offences unto justification.**
> **For if by one man's offence death reigned by one; much more they which receive abundance of grace and of the gift of righteousness shall reign in life by one, Jesus Christ.)**
> **Therefore as by the offence of one *judgment came* upon all men to condemnation; even so by the righteousness of one *the free gift came* upon all men unto justification of life (Rom. 5:15-18).**
>
> **For the wages of sin *is* death; but the gift of God *is* eternal life through Jesus Christ our Lord (Rom. 6:23).**

Salvation is God's gift, God's free gift. Yet, in spite of these clear verses, Coppes has the audacity to say that "Arminianism conceives salvation as a gift to be received or rejected by men."[196] But by its very nature a gift has to be received or rejected. There is no such thing as an irresistible gift.

A witness to the truth of the Scriptures against the Calvinist "faith-gift" interpretation can be found in the Greek grammarians.[197] Because it so mitigates against their position, honest Calvinists are forced to recognize that the demonstrative pronoun **"that"** in Ephesians 2:8 is neuter while the word for **"faith"** is feminine; however, this does not prevent them from making the connection anyway.[198] That the neuter demonstrative **"that"** refers to the whole concept of salvation by grace is evident by noting its similar use in some other passages:

> **But brother goeth to law with brother, and that before the unbelievers (1 Cor. 6:6).**
>
> **Nay, ye do wrong, and defraud, and that *your* brethren (1 Cor. 6:8).**

In both of these verses the usage of **"that"** parallels Ephesians 2:8. A knowledge of Greek grammar is not even necessary. The Scriptures interpret themselves.

As a further witness to the truth of the Scriptures, some of the most respected Calvinists expressly deny this "faith-gift" interpretation. The Dutch Reformed Homer Hoeksema acknowledges that the "whole idea of salvation-by-grace-through-faith" is what is in view.[199] The "impenitent Augustinian and Calvinist"[200] F. F. Bruce concedes that "it is probably best to understand 'and this' as referring to salvation as a whole, not excluding the faith by which it is received."[201] Yet, the greatest witness against the Calvinists is Calvin himself: "But they commonly misinterpret this text, and restrict the word 'gift' to faith alone. But Paul is only repeating his earlier statement in other words. He does not mean that faith is the gift of God, but that salvation is given to us by God, or, that we obtain it by the gift of God."[202] In this respect Calvin rightly departed from Augustine, who changed his original view and made faith an irresistible gift of God given to the elect.[203]

But supposing for a minute that faith "is the gift of God which God grants to His chosen people out of grace,"[204] what does this actually prove? Taking **"faith"** in Ephesians 2:8 in this manner really proves very little. If the Calvinistic "faith-gift" interpretation of Ephesians 2:8 is adopted then there are several things it doesn't say that Calvinists must read into it. If faith is a gift then (1) it doesn't say that only the "elect" can get it, (2) it doesn't say what the requirements are to get it, (3) it doesn't say that if a man received it he would get saved, and (4) it doesn't say that it is an irresistible gift. As usual, because of their influence on theology, the Calvinists are counting on their opponents reading these things into the verse along with the "faith-gift" interpretation.

The underlying cause for making faith an irresistible gift of God is the false notion of faith being a work.[205] Herman Hoeksema argues that "it cannot even be said that faith is the hand whereby we take hold of the salvation that is offered us."[206] Paul places grace and works in antithesis, as well as faith and works, but faith is never opposed to grace, which it would have to be if it were a work. If salvation is by grace then it could never be by works: **"And if by grace, then *is it* no more of works: otherwise grace is no more grace. But if *it be* of works, then is it no more grace: otherwise work is no more work"** (Rom. 11:6). But not only is salvation not of works, it is **"of faith, that *it might be* by grace"** (Rom. 4:16). The Apostle Paul mentions many things that are **"not of works"** (Eph. 2:9) but faith is not one of them. Justification is not of works (Rom. 3:20). Righteousness is not of works (Rom. 9:32). Election is not of works (Rom. 9:11). Receiving the Holy Spirit is not of works (Gal. 3:2). Salvation and calling are not of works (2 Tim. 1:9). Salvation is not even by **"works of righteousness"** (Tit. 3:5). To make faith the gift of God would mean that Paul was saying that faith is **"not of works"** (Eph. 2:9). Recognizing this, Charles Hodge, who dismisses Calvin's interpretation as "tautological," makes the phrase **"and that not of yourselves: *it is* the gift of God"** a parenthetical statement.[207] But to say that faith is not of works, as most Calvinists do, is not only redundant, it is completely unnecessary. The Bible mentions repeatedly that we are not saved by works but that we are saved by faith. Therefore, if a man is not saved by works then faith could not be a work. According to the Scripture, the man who believes or has faith is the man who does not work:

> **Now to him that worketh is the reward not reckoned of grace, but of debt. But to him that worketh not, but believeth on him that justifieth the ungodly, his faith is counted for righteousness (Rom. 4:4-5).**

The Lord Jesus Christ himself commended the exercise of faith (Mat. 8:10, 9:2, 22, 15:28; Mark 10:52; Luke 7:50).

As mentioned previously, faith is but the medium of reception. It is the God appointed means of appropriation:

> **Therefore being justified by faith, we have peace with God through our Lord Jesus Christ (Rom. 5:1).**

> **For ye are all the children of God by faith in Christ Jesus (Gal. 3:26).**

> **And be found in him, not having mine own righteousness, which is of the law, but that which is through the faith of Christ, the righteousness which is of God by faith (Phil. 3:9).**

This is recognized by honest Calvinists. The aforementioned Hodge acknowledged that "there is no merit in believing. It is only the act of receiving a proffered favour."[208] Machen explains this further:

> Faith means not doing something but receiving something; it means not the earning of a reward but the acceptance of a gift. A man can never be said to obtain a thing for himself if he obtains it by faith; indeed to say that he obtains it by faith is only another way of saying that he does not obtain it for himself but permits another to obtain it for him. Faith, in other words, is not active but passive; and to say that we are saved by faith is to say that we do not save ourselves but are saved only by the one in whom our faith is reposed.[209]

But not only do modern Presbyterian theologians recognize the true nature of faith, Calvin himself stated that salvation "is received by faith alone, without the merit of works."[210] So it is certainly proper to speak of God providing salvation and man receiving it of his own free will. Calvin spoke of two sides to salvation:

> On one side, we must look at God; and, on the other, at men. God declares that he owes us nothing; so that salvation is not a reward or recompense, but mere grace. Now it may be asked how men receive the salvation offered to them by the hand of God? I reply, by faith. Hence he concludes that here is nothing of our own. If, on the part of God, it is grace alone, and if we bring nothing but faith, which strips us of all praise, it follows

that salvation is not of us.[211]

Pink likewise overthrows his TULIP theology, for after claiming that both faith and repentance were gifts,[212] he slips up later and says: "The human side of our salvation from the penalty of sin respects our repentance and faith. Though these possess no merits whatever, and though they in no sense purchase our pardon, yet according to the order which God has appointed, they are (instrumentally) essential."[213]

It should be apparent by now that saving faith is available to any man:

> **But what saith it? The word is nigh thee, *even* in thy mouth, and in thy heart: that is, the word of faith, which we preach (Rom. 10:8).**
>
> **So then faith *cometh* by hearing, and hearing by the word of God (Rom. 10:17).**

And on a practical note, if the "faith-gift" theory of Calvinism is true, why does God give the gift of faith and repentance to so many Americans and so few Albanians, Turks, Japanese, and Sudanese? And on a lighter note: **"God hath dealt to every man the measure of faith"** (Rom. 12:3).

The whole debate over whether faith is God's gift to his "elect" is really immaterial, for as Houck says: "If a man has faith it is because God has already regenerated him."[214] If this is true, then the issue is not really the source of faith at all. The previous discussion is actually a moot point if faith and repentance are not given to a man until after God regenerates him by Irresistible Grace. And if God does regenerate a man, he has no choice but to repent and believe, as Houck again asserts: "Since in regeneration God gives him spiritual life and since by the saving call God irresistibly calls him to faith, he **must** believe."[215] But it is not just Presbyterian and Reformed Calvinists who believe this, it is also premillennial, Sovereign Grace Baptists: "Baptists have always believed that it was the new birth that caused repentance and faith, and not vice versa."[216] What he should have said is that "*Calvinistic* Baptists have always believed . . . ," for not all Baptists have subscribed to Calvinism. Another Sovereign Gracer concludes that the only way salvation can be by grace is if it comes before faith in Christ: "In a previous work, I indicated that Grace is defined as unmerited favor, and that a consistent application of this definition absolutely precludes any possibility that salvation (by grace) could require our act of faith before it was allocated."[217] So once again, the whole preceding debate is immaterial when seen in the light of what a Calvinist really believes about New Testament salvation.

New Testament Salvation

Although is has been intimated several times in this chapter, it is here that we see the real plan of salvation according to the Calvinistic system. If men are dead in sin to the extent that they are unable to believe on Jesus Christ of their own free will, yet God has elected some to salvation, atoned for their sin, and wills for them to be saved, then the only way any of them can and will be saved is by quietly waiting for God to overpower their will and regenerate them so they can repent and believe the Gospel. For them to do otherwise, God's will would be thwarted. Therefore, in the Calvinistic system, believing on Christ becomes the result of salvation, not the cause of it, as Sproul plainly says: "The Reformed view of predestination teaches that before a person can choose Christ his heart must be changed. He must be born again."[218] He then goes on to point out that the maxim "Regeneration precedes faith" is "a cardinal point of Reformed theology."[219] To convince the skeptic that Calvinists really do transpose the order of salvation, we cite the Calvinists directly:

> A person is regenerated before he believes.[220]
>
> A man is not saved because he believes in Christ; he believes in Christ because he is saved.[221]
>
> A man is not regenerated because he has first believed in Christ, but he believes in Christ because he has been regenerated.[222]
>
> When a man savingly believes, the saving power of Christ has already delivered him from his state of spiritual death.[223]
>
> We do not believe in order to be born again; we are born again in order that we may believe.[224]

This is also taught in chapter X of the Westminster Confession of Faith:

> II. This effectual call is of God's free and special grace alone, not from anything at all foreseen in man, who is altogether passive therein, until, being quickened and renewed by the Holy Spirit, he is thereby enabled to answer this call, and to embrace the grace offered and conveyed in it.

Pink claims that if one believes that "the Holy Spirit quickens those who believe" then "this is to put the cart before the horse. Faith is not the cause of the new birth, but the consequence of it."[225] But because of this reversal of the plan of salvation, it is Calvinism, as a non-Calvinist writer put it, that "has its theological cart before the biblical horse."[226] This is why it was maintained at the beginning of this chapter that in the Calvinistic system Irresistible Grace is what actually saves a man, believing on Christ is only the result of this "grace."

To bolster their position, Calvinists frequently misrepresent the views of non-Calvinists. This is done in two ways. First of all, Calvinists imply that their opponents teach that a man can, with God's help, save himself:

> Regeneration is a change wrought in us by God, not an autonomous act performed by us for ourselves.[227]

> In the eyes of the Calvinist, sinful man stands in need, not of inducements or of assistance to save himself, but precisely of saving. He holds that Jesus Christ has come, not to advise, urge or woo, or to help a man to save himself, but to save him, to save him through the prevalent working in him of the Holy Spirit. This is the root of the Calvinistic soteriology.[228]

The trouble with these statements is that no one opposed to Calvinism who believed the Bible would ever teach that a man could in any way regenerate or save himself. So the next thing the Calvinists insinuate is that their opponents teach that a man can assist God with his salvation. In keeping with their proclivity to exhaust their adversaries with theological terminology, Calvinists claim that their doctrine of salvation is "monergism" while that of their opponents is "synergism."[229] Sproul also terms these "operative grace" and "cooperative grace."[230] Now, according to the etymology of these words, monergism would be "working alone" and synergism would be "working together." And this is exactly how the Calvinist uses these terms. The problem, however, is that Calvinists apply them to salvation in such a way as to denigrate their opponents. According to Calvinists: "Monergism is something that operates by itself or works alone as the sole active party."[231] Therefore: "Since the grace of regeneration is monergistic and requires no cooperation from us, its efficacy lies in itself and not in us. We can do nothing to make it effective; we can do nothing to make it ineffective. We are passive with respect to our own regeneration."[232] Synergism, on the other hand, "is a cooperative venture, a working together of two or more parties."[233] Therefore: "Synergism is fatal to any sound Christian soteriology, for it is a denial of man's total bondage in sin and a claim to some remaining will to absolute good."[234] What the Calvinists are saying is that their system alone teaches that salvation is solely the work of God. In any teaching but Calvinism salvation is made to be the joint effort of God and man. Custance insists that "the only defence against Synergism is an unqualified Calvinism ascribing all the glory to God."[235] So once again the idea surfaces that for God to get the glory for salvation, man must be *unable* to accept or reject.

Not only do those opposed to Calvinism deny that a man can in any way regenerate or save himself, they also deny that man works together with God to bring about his salvation. So what is the issue? Sproul replies: "The classic dispute over monergism and synergism is not over the question of who does the regenerating. Virtually everyone agrees that only God can do the work of regeneration proper."[236] So what then is the issue? Sproul again replies: "The issue focuses instead on what the unregenerate person can do to evoke the divine work of regeneration. Synergists hold that one can 'choose Christ' or 'believe in Christ' prior to regeneration.[237] Custance goes even further: "If man contributes any essential part towards his salvation, he effectively becomes his own saviour, even if that contribution takes no more concrete form than that of merely allowing God to act by non-resistance."[238] So according to Calvinism, if a man believes in Christ and therefore no longer resists the Holy Spirit, he is stealing glory from God and assisting God with his salvation. So once again it bears repeating: In the Calvinistic system Irresistible Grace is what actually saves a man, believing on Christ is only the result of this "grace."

After bitterly attacking dispensationalists for holding what they consider to be erroneous views on salvation,[239] Calvinists have the audacity to insist that it is their opponents who distort the Gospel and the plan of salvation:

> In truth there is no "Gospel" that is not entirely rooted in the sovereignty of God's grace in salvation, which is the sum and substance of Calvinism.[240]

> Arminianism reverses the order of salvation.[241]

Homer Hoeksema explains the Reformed view of salvation: "The Reformed faith maintains that when the gospel of Christ crucified is proclaimed, the gift of faith is sovereignly bestowed only upon the elect through regeneration and the efficacious calling, that then the elect repent and believe and have everlasting life."[242] Although this is how most Calvinists would describe the salvation of a soul, some Calvinists, including Herman Hoeksema, distinguish between regeneration and effectual calling. Hoeksema argues that a man is *first* regenerated and *then* called with an effectual call.[243] He says of the change wrought in man by regeneration that a man "may not at once become conscious of the profound change that is wrought within him. Perhaps he does not come immediately to repentance and conscious faith."[244] Berkhof explains further: "In the case of those who live under the administration of the gospel the possibility exists that they receive the seed of regeneration long before they come to years of discretion and therefore also long before the effectual calling penetrates to their consciousness."[245] So according to Hoeksema and Berkhof, it is not the dead who **"hear the voice of the Son of God"** (John 5:25), it is the regenerate who hear.

This peculiar teaching is also the position of the Primitive or Hardshell Baptists. One of their most prominent preachers is Eddie Garrett, the editor of the now defunct publication *The Hardshell Baptist*. Because he believes that "regeneration must precede the hearing or understanding of the gospel. Life must precede action,"[246] Elder Garrett postulates two kinds of faith and two kinds of salvation:

> Now we must understand that there is more than one kind of faith. There is the faith that is implanted in us in regeneration

> and there is BELIEF. We are not saved eternally by our belief in the gospel; but our believing the gospel is a result of our having been born of God.[247]
>
> We have the ETERNAL phase of salvation, over which we have nothing to do and then the GOSPEL salvation or the TIME phase of salvation, with which we do have something to do. The eternal phase secures a place for us in the family of God and the time phase concerns our conduct after we have entered the family of God.[248]

If this is true then how much time is there between the first application of faith and salvation and the second? To see Garrett's response, consider the salvation of five well-known individuals:

> *Paul:* "The calling (regeneration) was done before he was born."[249]
> *Jeremiah:* "Paul is not unique in this regard. It was also true in Jeremiah's case."[250]
> *Cornelius:* "He was already regenerated before Peter ever went over to preach to him."[251]
> *John the Baptist:* "John the Baptist was born again while in his mother's womb."[252]
> *Lydia:* "Lydia was already a child of God, born again."[253]

Incredibly, Garrett is saying that Paul, Jeremiah, Cornelius, John the Baptist, and Lydia were regenerated long before they were saved. Best agrees, and claims that "as there is time between implanting seed in the womb and bringing forth a child in birth, so is it in the spiritual realm with this important difference—no one knows when the work of regeneration takes place."[254]

The radical position of the Primitive Baptists and the Reformed theologians raises some important questions. And actually, these same questions would apply to any Calvinist who averred that regeneration preceded faith and repentance. If those who come to Christ are already regenerated then why do they come to Christ? If they are regenerated before they believe then are they not saved? Can a man be regenerated by God and still be lost? What happens if a man dies after he is regenerated but before he believes on Christ? Can a regenerated man go to hell? Can a non-believer go to heaven? Is there a such thing as a regenerated, unconsciously saved potential believer?

So after adamantly insisting that regeneration precedes faith, some Calvinists, even those who would not go as far as Hoeksema, Berkhof, and the Primitive Baptists, sensing that their views will not stand the test of Scripture, attempt to palliate their maxim. After stating that the new birth is the cause of repentance and faith, Keener regresses and says: "I am not telling you that you are born again, and you begin to believe and to repent later."[255] Sproul, after terming regeneration "the necessary condition of faith," claims that "Reformed theology grants that God's act of regeneration and the believer's act of faith are simultaneous, not separated, with respect to time."[256] He posits that regeneration precedes faith "with respect to *logical priority,* not *temporal priority.*"[257] After stating that conversion embraces both repentance and faith, the Baptist theologian Strong maintains that "regeneration and conversion are not chronologically separate."[258] They are "but the divine and human sides or aspects of the same fact."[259]

Contrary to any variety of Calvinism, the Bible is perfectly clear that the imputed righteousness of Christ, which is the basis of our justification and spiritual blessings, is given *after* a man believes:

> **And therefore it was imputed to him for righteousness.**
> **Now it was not written for his sake alone, that it was imputed to him;**
> **But for us also, to whom it shall be imputed, if we believe on him that raised up Jesus our Lord from the dead (Rom. 4:22-24).**

In the Bible a man has life because he believes; he does not believe because he has life:

> **But as many as received him, to them gave he power to become the sons of God, *even* to them that believe on his name (John 1:12).**

> **But these are written, that ye might believe that Jesus is the Christ, the Son of God; and that believing ye might have life through his name (John 20:31).**

> **For I am not ashamed of the gospel of Christ: for it is the power of God unto salvation to every one that believeth; to the Jew first, and also to the Greek (Rom. 1:16).**

> For after that in the wisdom of God the world by wisdom knew not God, it pleased God by the foolishness of preaching to save them that believe (1 Cor. 1:21).

> For ye are all the children of God by faith in Christ Jesus (Gal. 3:26).

According to Calvinism, God does not **"save them that believe."** Instead, as Warren sees it: "It is by the foolishness of preaching that God saves those who are ordained to eternal life."[260] In Calvinism, one has to have life to get life. Gerstner makes it plain that those who come to Christ are already saved: "We must not get the notion that people come to Jesus and as a result of that they are 'born again' by God. On the contrary, we see what people do when they are left to themselves: they do not believe; they do not come to Jesus. Those who do come to Jesus are not therefore born again, but on the contrary indicate that they have been born again. In other words, they are not born again because they come to Jesus but they come to Jesus because they have been born again."[261] But if a man comes to Christ because he is already born again then Irresistible Grace has to be what actually saves him.

In the Bible, God saves those who believe:

> For God so loved the world, that he gave his only begotten Son, that whosoever believeth in him should not perish, but have everlasting life (John 3:16).

> Verily, verily, I say unto you, He that believeth on me hath everlasting life (John 6:47).

> And they said, Believe on the Lord Jesus Christ, and thou shalt be saved, and thy house (Acts 16:31).

> That if thou shalt confess with thy mouth the Lord Jesus, and shalt believe in thine heart that God hath raised him from the dead, thou shalt be saved (Rom. 10:9).

Contrariwise, a man who refuses to believe is lost:

> He that believeth on him is not condemned: but he that believeth not is condemned already, because he hath not believed in the name of the only begotten Son of God (John

3:18).

He that believeth on the Son hath everlasting life: and he that believeth not the Son shall not see life; but the wrath of God abideth on him (John 3:36).

I said therefore unto you, that ye shall die in your sins: for if ye believe not that I am he, ye shall die in your sins (John 8:24).

The problem is with man's sin, not God willingness to apply Irresistible Grace only to the "elect":

**Behold, the LORD's hand is not shortened, that it cannot save; neither his ear heavy, that it cannot hear:
But your iniquities have separated between you and your God, and your sins have hid *his* face from you, that he will not hear (Isa. 59:1-2).**

God is **"ready to forgive; and plenteous in mercy"** (Psa. 86:5), but must **"be just, and the justifier of him which believeth in Jesus"** (Rom. 3:26). Salvation is free—but only because Jesus paid it all. Since God doesn't force himself on anyone, it is left up to man to either accept or reject: **"Death and life *are* in the power of the tongue"** (Pro. 18:21). Therefore, salvation by Irresistible Grace is **"another gospel"** (Gal. 1:6). And as Paul said: **"If any *man* preach any other gospel unto you than that ye have received, let him be accursed"** (Gal. 1:9).

Closely connected with the dispute among the Calvinists over the extent that regeneration precedes faith and repentance is the conflict over the use of means in the regeneration of a sinner. This has been the subject of much controversy among the Calvinists, and especially the Baptists. When Calvinists argue over the use of means in regeneration they are not quibbling over evangelistic methods. The question of the use of means in regeneration is a separate issue from that of evangelism, although it is true that those who disdain means likewise disparage evangelism. As we have seen throughout this work, it is the Baptists—not the Presbyterian and Reformed—who are the militant Calvinists. And this is no more evident than in the subject at hand.

The five-point Calvinists among the Baptists are *generally* denominated as either Sovereign Grace Baptists or Primitive Baptists. In addition to their other differences (which are many), the Sovereign Grace Baptists (also called Missionary Baptists) and the Primitive Baptists disagree over the subject of whether God uses means to bring about the salvation of a sinner. As a consequence, both groups regularly anathematize each other as heretics.[262] The epitome of consistent Calvinism is the unabashed Primitive Baptist, Eddie Garrett, who relates of his denomination:

> Primitive Baptists are still standing on the same old proposition that the apostles stood on—that God gives life to dead, alien, sinners independent of the preached word.[263]
>
> Primitive Baptists believe that the scriptures teach that sinners are regenerated, or born again, independently of, or without, the gospel as a means.[264]

Because they deny means in regeneration, Primitive Baptists can make extraordinary statements like:

> The population of heaven after the end of the world will not be determined by those who have accepted the Lord Jesus Christ, but by those whom the Lord Jesus Christ accepted before the beginning.[265]
>
> God has an elect people and Christ died for them and they all will be born again and will live in heaven; all due to his sovereign grace. Many of them will have never heard the gospel.[266]
>
> Salvation is NOT dependent upon gospel faith. Indeed, it could not be so, for millions of children of God have never heard the gospel preached. Only a very small percentage of humans heard the gospel before they died. Consequently, they did not and could not have had gospel faith.[267]

Contrary to this, the Sovereign Grace Baptists insist that "one must and will go to hell if he never hears and believes the precious gospel of Jesus Christ."[268] But the Primitive Baptists are so adamant about this point that they regard the teaching that God uses means in bringing about the regeneration of a sinner as not only a "fable,"[269] but as "free willism,"[270] "Arminianism,"[271] and "a pure denial of the doctrine of Total Depravity."[272] After all that the Sovereign Gracer Bob Ross has said about Arminianism, it is indeed humorous that Eddie Garrett regards him as "nothing but an Arminian posing as a Calvinist."[273] If it is Irresistible Grace that actually saves a man, as has been maintained and proved throughout this chapter, then common sense dictates the conclusion that the Primitive Baptists are the consistent Calvinists.

Although the Primitive Baptists are the consistent Calvinists, this certainly does not mean that they are in agreement with the Scripture. Indeed, the more consistent a Calvinist is, the further away from Scripture he departs. It therefore goes without saying that the word of God is the necessary means whereby anyone is saved:

> **So then faith *cometh* by hearing, and hearing by the word of God (Rom. 10:17).**
>
> **For though ye have ten thousand instructors in Christ, yet *have ye* not many fathers: for in Christ Jesus I have begotten you through the gospel (1 Cor. 4:15).**
>
> **Being born again, not of corruptible seed, but of incorruptible, by the word of God, which liveth and abideth forever (1 Pet. 1:23).**
>
> **Wherefore lay apart all filthiness and superfluity of naughtiness, and receive with meekness the engrafted word, which is able to save your souls (Jam. 1:21).**

The result of denying means in regeneration is the teaching that many of the "elect" whom God regenerates never do hear the Gospel before they die and go to heaven. Garrett concludes: "Hearing and believing the gospel is one thing and being born again is quite another. The sum total of God's elect is greater than what ever hear and believe the gospel."[274]

Infant Salvation

That Irresistible Grace is actually what saves a man can be seen in what the Calvinists believe about the manner of the salvation of infants, imbeciles, and the heathen. Here we will see the Calvinists completely overthrow the plan of salvation: both the Bible's as well as their own. After denominating you as an Arminian believing in salvation by works if you reject salvation by Irresistible Grace, the Calvinists have the arrogance to repudiate everything they have said heretofore about faith, repentance, and the means necessary for salvation. The question here is not whether some or all of the members of these classes are numbered among the "elect," for as we saw in chapter 7, Calvinists believe that at least some of them are. The issue here is the manner in which those that are "elect" get saved.

To begin with, Calvinists insist that only their system provides the necessary answers to the subject at hand:

> Calvinism, instead of implicating the damnation of any dead child, is the *only* system of theology, which does, fairly and fully, give a biblical, rational, and theological basis for the doctrine of the salvation of all dead infants, idiots, and incapables, living and dying in moral incompetency.[275]

> Only in Calvinism, with its doctrine of the guilt and corruption of all mankind through the fall, and its doctrine of grace through which some are sovereignly rescued and brought to salvation while others are passed by, do we find an adequate explanation of the phenomenon of the heathen world.[276]

And what is this explanation? If one carefully reads what the Calvinists have written about Irresistible Grace, some clues can be found. After discussing the regeneration of a sinner by means of an effectual call, Talbot and Crampton mention, almost in passing, that "God has chosen this means as the normal way that people are drawn to Christ."[277] Shedd does the same thing, but adds a critical additional statement: "This is the ordinary divine method, except in the case of infants."[278] These statements imply that God has two methods of salvation: ordinary and extraordinary. Confirmation of this implication can be seen in the Westminster Confession of Faith: "Elect infants, dying in infancy, are regenerated, and saved by Christ, through the Spirit, who worketh when, and where, and how he pleaseth: so also are all other elect persons who are uncapable of being outwardly called by the ministry of the Word."[279] The Philadelphia Confession of Faith, accepted by the Sovereign Grace Baptists, reads exactly the same but for the spelling of one word.[280]

Regarding the salvation of the heathen, an admirable defender of the Westminster Confession, William G. T. Shedd, offers his comments on the Confession:

> The Confession, in this section, intends to teach that there are some unevangelized men who are "regenerated and saved by Christ through the Spirit" without "the ministry of the written word," and who differ in this respect from evangelized men who are regenerated in connection with it. There are these two classes of regenerated persons among God's elect. They are both alike in being born, "not of blood, nor of the will of the flesh, nor of the will of man, but of God." They are both alike in respect to faith and repentance, because these are the natural and necessary effects of regeneration. Both alike feel and confess sin; and both alike hope in the Divine mercy, though the regenerate heathen has not yet had Christ presented to him.[281]

Shedd claims that "a regenerate heathen is both a believer and a penitent. He feels sorrow for sin, and the need of mercy."[282] He then explains how this is possible: "For although the Redeemer has not been presented to him historically and personally as the object of faith, yet the Divine Spirit by the new birth has wrought in him the sincere and longing *disposition* to believe in him."[283] Incredibly, Shedd claims that the heathen's "need of mercy" is "potentially and virtually faith in the Redeemer."[284] So what we have is a regenerate, *potential* believer. Computers may have given us virtual reality, but Calvinism has given us virtual believers. Yet, after all this virtual theology about God's extraordinary work, Shedd concedes that (1) "little is said bearing upon it in Scripture," (2) "the Church is not to expect and rely upon" it, and (3) "the number of saved unevangelized adults" cannot be confirmed.[285] And what is Shedd's proof text? **"And I say unto you, That many shall come from the east and west, and shall sit down with Abraham, and Isaac, and Jacob, in the kingdom of heaven"** (Mat. 8:11).[286] But Shedd is not alone, Zwingli held that God had "elect" heathen who were our future neighbors in heaven.[287] Zanchius likewise concluded: "It is not indeed improbable, but some individuals in these unenlightened countries might belong to the secret election of grace, and the habit of faith might be wrought in these."[288] This heresy is still held by modern Calvinists, for even

Boettner acknowledges: "We do not deny that God can save some even of the adult heathen people if he chooses to do so, for His Spirit works when and where and how He pleases, with means or without means. If any such are saved, however, it is by a miracle of pure grace. Certainly God's ordinary method is to gather His elect from the evangelized portion of mankind, although we must admit the possibility that by an **extraordinary** method some few of His elect may be gathered from the unevangelized portion."[289]

That any man in the Church Age could be eternally saved without believing on Jesus Christ is a direct contradiction and overturn of Scripture:

> **I said therefore unto you, that ye shall die in your sins: for if ye believe not that I am** *he,* **ye shall die in your sins (John 8:24).**

> **Jesus saith unto him, I am the way, the truth, and the life: no man cometh unto the Father but by me (John 14:6).**

> **Neither is there salvation in any other: for there is none other name under heaven given among men, whereby we must be saved (Acts 4:12).**

A similar heresy held by some Calvinistic Baptists is that a man in the Church Age can be eternally lost but not for the sin of unbelief:

> A person who is born in a primitive land and has never heard the Gospel will not be guilty of rejecting what he has never heard, but he is still a sinner and deserving of hell, and guilty of sinning against God.[290]

> Those who have died without hearing the Gospel will not be charged with the specific sin of rejecting the Gospel yet they will still be judged for all their sins.[291]

But contrary to Calvinism, the Bible explicitly states: **"He that believeth on him is not condemned: but he that believeth not is condemned already, because he hath not believed in the name of the only begotten Son of God"** (John 3:18). The Lord Jesus Christ said that the Holy Spirit would **"reprove the world of sin, and of righteousness, and of judgment"** (John 16:8) because **"they believe not on me"** (John 16:9).

If there is still any doubt about what Calvinists really believe about salvation by Irresistible Grace then the case of infants should make it perfectly clear. Boettner declares that "the doctrine of infant salvation finds a logical place in the Calvinistic system; for the redemption of the soul is thus infallibly determined irrespective of any faith, repentance, or good works, whether actual or foreseen."[292] Shedd further explains: "The only form of grace that is possible to the dying infant is regenerating grace, and the only call possible is the effectual call. If therefore God manifests any grace at all to the dying infant, it must be special and saving; and if he call him at all, he must call him effectually."[293] This is truly Irresistible Grace in action. All the talk about the order and necessity of faith, repentance, and means is immaterial. R. A. Webb (1856-1919), a Calvinist who wrote a whole book on the subject of infant salvation, explains what happens when an infant is saved:

> The infant, therefore, though incapable of "works" of any kind, may be a subject of grace—may be operated upon by the influence of the Holy Spirit, and changed and fitted, as an infant, for a life in heaven. Its heart may be regenerated; to it the atoning righteousness of Christ may be divinely imputed, as the ground of its justification; a child may be adopted into the family of God, even as it is adopted into a human family; its infantile life may be cleansed by the same purifying grace, which purges away the pollution of an adult sinner.[294]

This enables Warfield to claim that "the majority of the human race have up to the present, at least, been saved after the manner taught by the Calvinists."[295]

It is understandable that Calvinists would insist on the regeneration of "elect" heathen, but it is indeed peculiar that Calvinists maintain that infants must be regenerated to be saved. And it is not just Presbyterian and Reformed Calvinists who believe this, for Sovereign Grace Baptists affirm the same thing: "I cannot explain how God regenerated His elect infants or imbeciles except it is by the Holy Spirit. God does as it pleases Him without having to explain everything to us. I do believe they are regenerated by the Holy Spirit."[296] But since he posits that all men must hear the Gospel to be saved, one Sovereign Gracer has infants being more than just regenerated: "If God preached the gospel unto Abraham, and He did according to Galatians 3:8, then we should not think it to be a strange thing to have Him open an infant's understanding to the death, burial, and resurrection of His Son."[297] Tom Ross informs us that "it would not be any more difficult for the Holy Spirit to regenerate a baby that is spiritually dead, than it would be for Him to regenerate a fully grown man who is dead in sins."[298] But does not this prove once again that it is Irresistible Grace that saves a man? This teaching is a direct result of the Calvinists' teaching on repentance and faith being gifts to God's "elect," for as Webb acknowledges, repentance and faith merely bring into consciousness "the benefits of the atonement of Christ."[299]

Even worse than this is the teaching that some of the "elect" are saved after their death. Because he believes that "elect" infants must be regenerated, Strong posits a novel idea as to when these "elect" infants get saved: "Since there is no evidence that children dying in infancy are regenerated prior to death, either with or without the use of external means, it seems most probable that the work of regeneration may be performed by the Spirit in connection with the infant soul's first view of Christ in the other world."[300] But as the Primitive Baptist Garrett commented: "This is akin to Roman Catholic doctrine and Mormon doctrine."[301] The salvation of infants has nothing to do with whether they are "elect," regenerated, or innocent. They are none of these. Although **"dead in trespasses and sins"** (Eph. 2:1), God doesn't hold them accountable. This principle is illustrated in the Old Testament:

> **Moreover your little ones, which ye said should be a prey, and your children, which in that day had no knowledge between good and evil, they shall go in thither, and unto them will I give it, and they shall possess it (Deu. 1:39).**
>
> **And should not I spare Nineveh, that great city, wherein are more than sixscore thousand persons that cannot discern between their right hand and their left hand; and *also* much cattle? (Jon. 4:11).**

Infants alone have a scriptural case of Total Inability.

The Calvinistic teaching that regeneration precedes faith should in and of itself prove that Irresistible Grace is what saves a man. But the admission by the Calvinists of the possibility of some of the "elect" being saved without the Gospel—whether infants, heathen, or anyone else—shows us the real plan of salvation according to the

Calvinistic system. Irresistible Grace is actually what saves a man, believing on Christ is only the result of salvation, not the cause of it. It is indeed incredible that Calvinists would attack dispensationalism for teaching two plans of salvation[302] when it is the Calvinists themselves who have two plans of salvation: an ordinary plan for the regular "elect" and an extraordinary one for the infant and heathen "elect." Sovereign Grace Baptists who hesitate to wholeheartedly accept Irresistible Grace for what it really is have come under criticism from their Reformed "cousins":

> There are many who maintain the truths of sovereign predestination, of irresistible calling, of perseverance of the saints, and especially the truth of sovereign grace in the work of salvation, but who nevertheless deny that God can and does save children from infancy on and before they arrive at years of discretion. Cannot God, the sovereign God of all grace, save children if He saves without the cooperation of the will of man? Cannot God, Who alone works the work of salvation through the Spirit of Christ also apply the blessings of the cross to the hearts of children? This has indeed been the dilemma of Baptists. And exactly because of this, Baptists have as often as not departed from the truth of sovereign grace.[303]

The Calvinists who adamantly insist that regeneration precedes faith—both logically and temporally—and who deny the use of means in regeneration are truly the consistent Calvinists. But if these things are true, then how does this affect the subject of evangelism?

Evangelism

After all the talk about Irresistible Grace, effectual calling, and salvation by sovereign grace alone, the Calvinist repudiates his entire system of theology when the question of evangelism is examined. Anticipating the objections to TULIP evangelism, McFetridge attempts to awe his opponents: "There is no other system which has displayed so powerful an evangelizing force as Calvinism."[304] Engelsma insists that Reformed preaching is "Biblical gospel-preaching."[305] "The Reformed Faith," he argues, "is perfectly compatible" with evangelism.[306] Bastian Kruithof (1902-1990) believes that "Calvinism has sparked the missionary drive in its deepest and widest meaning."[307] The Baptist Kenneth Good contends that "a commitment to the Doctrines of Grace is not incompatible with dedication to the work of evangelism."[308] If these statements are true then one would expect to find no difference in the evangelistic methods employed by Calvinists and non-Calvinists. But this is not the case, for as Kober acknowledges: "One's view of election determines one's method of evangelism."[309] Knowing the glaring inconsistency that exists between evangelism and his theology, the Calvinist does ask the right questions:

> Supposing that all things do in fact happen under the direct dominion of God, and that God has already fixed the future by His decree, and resolved whom He will save, and whom not—how does this bear on our duty to evangelize?[310]

> If Election guarantees the salvation of all that are predestinated to be saved, why should we be bothered with evangelism, personal or missionary? What possible difference can it make whether we speak to men or not?[311]

Realizing the genuine nature of such queries, the Calvinist contradicts his very system by his attempts to give credence to evangelism in light of his theology.

The antinomy resulting from this justification can be seen in statements like:

> Our zeal for the doctrine of election must not suffer us to ignore the necessity of using means. They who reason, If I be elected, I shall be saved whether or not I repent and trust in Christ, are fatally deceiving themselves.[312]

> One could argue from John 6:37 that the elect will be saved regardless of whether we go and preach or stay home and sew. Some have certainly taken that position. But that conclusion is wrong. It may be logical; but it is carnal neglect.[313]

> Some fear that belief in the sovereign grace of God leads to the conclusion that evangelism is pointless, since God will save His elect anyway, whether they hear the gospel or not. This, as we have seen, is a false conclusion based on a false assumption.[314]

But if a man really believes in the Five Points of Calvinism, the "elect" will be overcome with Irresistible Grace no matter what:

> No man elected to salvation could possibly die or be killed unsaved.[315]

> Not one of the elect can perish, but they must all necessarily be saved.[316]

> His decreed purpose is that *all* His elect will come to repentance, and repent they *shall*.[317]

Pink unwittingly sums up our position: "Those who refuse to receive the truth of divine election are fond of saying that the idea of God having eternally chosen one and passed by another of His creatures would reduce evangelical preaching to a farce. They argue that if God has foreordained a part of the human race to destruction, it can contain no bona fide offer of salvation to them."[318] What we are concerned with is the abovementioned offer, for if the offer is legitimate, TULIP theology is overthrown, but if the offer is not genuine, then all the injunctions in the Bible to repent and believe are fraudulent.

On the subject of evangelism, it should first be noted that Calvinists do raise some genuine concerns. Tom Ross accurately relates that "one of the reasons why false professions are abundant and church memberships are loaded with lost people is because men have resorted to false and unscriptural methods of evangelism attempting to help God out."[319] Much of what passes for evangelism today is not biblical evangelism at all. Therefore, what Pink said about evangelism in his day is even more applicable to today:

> Most of the so-called evangelism of our day is a grief to genuine Christians, for they feel that it lacks any scriptural warrant, that it is dishonoring unto God, and that it is filling the churches with empty professors. They are shocked that so much frothy superficiality, fleshly excitement and worldly allurement should be associated with the holy name of the Lord Jesus Christ.[320]

Calvinists are certainly correct in deploring the substitution of the phrases "give your life to Christ," "open your heart to Christ," "make your decision for Christ," "decide for Christ," "let Christ come into your life," and similar expressions, for the biblical injunctions to repent and believe.[321] Calvinists also justly criticize the shallow evangelistic methods of Billy Graham.[322]

On the definition of evangelism, we are also in agreement with the Calvinists:

> Evangelism, therefore, is the activity of preaching the gospel to those outside the congregation already established in the truth, in order to bring them to Christ.[323]

> Evangelism is to be defined as the setting forth of the good news of the Gospel of Christ.[324]

The free offer of salvation in the Gospel is the heart of evangelism. And like the disputes among the Calvinists over the extent that regeneration precedes faith and the use of means in regeneration, the nature of this offer has occasioned much controversy among the Calvinists.

So just what do Calvinists believe about the offer of salvation in the Gospel? Is it serious and genuine? Packer asserts that it is: "The belief that God is sovereign in grace does not affect the *genuineness* of the gospel invitations or the *truth* of the gospel promises. Whatever we may believe about election, and, for that matter, about the extent of the atonement, the fact remains that God in the gospel really does offer Christ and promise justification and life to 'whosoever will.'"[325] Morton Smith maintains that the Gospel call is both universal and sincere: "The offer of the Gospel is to be made to all men, and it is to be understood as a sincere offer."[326] John Murray and Ned Stonehouse (1902-1962) give us God's perspective: "The gospel is not simply an offer or invitation but also implies that God delights that those to whom the offer comes would enjoy what is offered in all its fullness."[327] Smith even avows that to exclude "the free offer of the Gospel to all men" is "hyper-Calvinism."[328] But if the "free offer of the Gospel" is an unfeigned offer, then it logically follows that it can be accepted or rejected—by anyone. But as we have seen in abundance throughout this work, the essence of Calvinism is that only the "elect" can actually receive it.

Some Calvinists—those who are a little more consistent than their brethren—would disagree with Packer and company. David

Engelsma, the Protestant Reformed supralapsarian, contends that "the well-meant offer is nothing but a variation of the Pelagian-Arminian 'whosoever will gospel.'"[329] Custance maintains that although "Christ is offered" in the Gospel, "salvation is *not* offered."[330] Therefore, the offer is merely a declaration: a declaration that only the "elect" hear "as an invitation."[331] To the "non-elect" this declaration comes "as a judgment which leaves them without excuse."[332] Engelsma, after stating that the call is a serious one, elucidates the relation of the supposedly genuine call to the "reprobate": "The call does not express God's love for them, nor does it imply what Jesus did for them. By the call, God confronts them with their duty and shows them what will be pleasing to Him. But His purpose with the call to them is not a saving purpose. On the contrary, it is His purpose to render them inexcusable and to harden them."[333] The idea that the Gospel "actualizes the salvation of the elect and the damnation of the reprobate" is said by another Calvinist to be "a dualistic, schizophrenic gospel."[334] Therefore, Engelsma further insists that the word *offer,* since it is "loaded with Arminian connotations," be replaced with "the call of the gospel."[335] Herman Hoeksema likewise rejects the Gospel as an offer or invitation, claiming that it is a demand.[336] Now, it is true that God **"commandeth all men every where to repent"** (Acts 17:30), but this doesn't change anything except the terminology: a command must still be either obeyed or disobeyed. In keeping with the true nature of Irresistible Grace, Hoeksema asserts that "salvation is not an offer, but a wonder work of God; and the sinner has no hand to accept it."[337]

How then can a man be condemned for rejecting an offer that isn't really an offer? Again Engelsma explains: "Those who do not believe the gospel sin against the grace of God, not as if they resist and frustrate God's grace directed to them personally in an attempt to save them—which is the heresy of the well-meant offer—but in the sense that they say 'No' to the Christ presented to them in the gospel."[338] Although sometimes called *hyper-Calvinists* themselves, these Calvinists who believe that Christ is presented in the Gospel but no genuine offer of salvation is made have the audacity to accuse some of their "brethren" of being hyper-Calvinists if they forgo preaching to sinners altogether.[339] This proves once again that the term *hyper-Calvinism* is relative. As we saw in chapter 1, it is used by Calvinists to make themselves look orthodox much the same as they use the label *Arminian*. By crusading against the errors of both hyper-Calvinism and Arminianism, the Calvinist can take the middle road and appear to be orthodox. But if a Calvinist really believes his TULIP theology, he not only must reject the "well-meant offer," but any offer, period. So just like we saw regarding the denial of the use of means in regeneration, the denial of any offer of salvation is the only logical position for a Calvinist to take.

The controversy among the Calvinists concerning the free offer of the Gospel is actually much ado about nothing. The aforementioned Calvinists Murray and Stonehouse, who have been castigated by other Calvinists for believing in it,[340] recognized the root of the issue: "It would appear that the real point in dispute in connection with the free offer of the gospel is whether it can properly be said that God **desires** the salvation of all men."[341] But even though they maintain that God desires the salvation of all men, Murray and Stonehouse, together with all other Calvinists who would agree with them, really don't mean what they are saying. It turns out that this desire of God is only part of his revealed will—the damnation of the reprobate "non-elect" is still part of God's secret will.[342] So regardless of what a Calvinist claims to believe about the free offer of the Gospel, because he believes that God's will is always done and God cannot will what never takes place, any serious discussion about the offer of salvation in the Gospel is precluded.

In light of the teaching of Irresistible Grace, there is nothing more tragic than a Calvinist trying to justify soul winning and preaching the Gospel to the "non-elect." Spurgeon insists that "soul-winning is the chief business of the Christian minister."[343] Wilson adds that not only is there "absolutely no conflict between soul winning and the doctrines of grace," there is a "close connection" between them.[344] In fact, he asserts that "the doctrines of grace encourage soul winning."[345] Packer contends that "we should not be held back by the thought that if they are not elect, they will not believe us, and our efforts to convert them will fail. That is true; but it is none of our business, and should make no difference to our action."[346] Calvinists talk out of both sides of their mouth when they try to uphold both Calvinism and the importance of preaching the Gospel. Several examples should make this perfectly evident. First is Engelsma: "It is clear, then, that the Reformed preacher, although he repudiates the well-meant offer, can call sinners, any sinner and all sinners, to repentance and faith and that he can do this with all seriousness and urgency."[347] Next, Jay Adams makes two contradictory statements:

> Repentance and faith are the acts of *regenerated* men, not of men *dead in sins*.[348]

> Nor are we saying that preachers should not urge, yea, plead with men to repent and believe.[349]

This double-talk is also found in the Westminster Confession:

> Man, by his fall, having made himself uncapable of life by that covenant, the Lord was pleased to make a second, commonly called the *covenant of grace;* wherein he freely offereth unto sinners life and salvation by Jesus Christ; requiring of them faith in him, that they may be saved, and promising to give unto all those that are ordained unto eternal life his Holy Spirit, to make them willing, and able to believe.[350]

But in spite of both Spurgeon's maxim and his own attempt at the reconciliation of Calvinism and soul winning, Wilson acknowledges that some Sovereign Grace Baptist preachers "think that the doctrines of grace are contrary to soul winning."[351] And not only does he admit that "many Sovereign Gracers are not soul winners,"[352] he laments that "many who are Missionary Baptist in doctrine are Hardshell in practice."[353] Seemingly oblivious to his theology, Wilson says of the Sovereign Grace Baptists:

> We do not win many souls. A few of our kind of churches win a soul now and then, but most of us do very, very little of this. We do not have a real and continuing and successful visitation program. Our preachers are not soul winning men. We do not have soul winning members. We do not preach much on soul winning. We rarely preach on it as a duty, and we almost never give any instructions on why and how to win souls. We do not really work at winning souls in our churches. We make almost no effort at winning souls in the conclusions of our sermons or in our invitations at the close of our sermons.[354]

Contrary to Wilson's diatribe, one practice that Calvinists especially dislike is the altar call or public invitation. The easiest way to condemn proponents of the public invitation is to trace it back to the ministry of Charles G. Finney.[355] This implies that any preacher who gives a public invitation accepts everything else that Finney taught. But it is not just the misuse of the altar call that upsets Calvinists. Talbot and Crampton dismiss it as "unbiblical."[356] Engelsma is bolder: "The Reformed faith condemns, indeed despises, the altar call."[357] The Sovereign Grace Baptists likewise reject the public invitation: "Should sovereign grace preachers use the invitation system? I believe not. As I see it, grace preachers calling on sinners to walk an aisle to accept Christ are contradicting their theology with Arminian practice. People who are regenerated by the Holy Spirit will repent and believe. They do not have to be forced into it by a public invitation."[358] So what should Calvinistic preachers do? Pink says that "when praying for the salvation of others, it should always be with the proviso 'If they be thine elect.'"[359] After everything that he has said about election and predestination, Boettner still maintains that it is the duty of the preacher toward his audience "to pray for them that they may each be among the elect."[360] But if election is by an unconditional, sovereign, eternal decree, and salvation is by the application of Irresistible Grace, then what would be the point of praying for someone to be one of the "elect" or to be saved? Pink admits that "the elect are usually to be found where the ministers of Christ labor much."[361] But why is that? Obviously, it appears that the "elect" are saved through the Gospel, not Calvinism. It is also ironic that Reformed Calvinists who object to the public invitation don't object to synods, classes, ruling elders, stated clerks, general assemblies, presbyteries, and denominations. Adams calls responding to an invitation "decisional regeneration," and equates it with the heresy of baptismal regeneration.[362] But this is ridiculous, for infinitely more people have gone to hell trusting in their infant baptism than ever went to hell because they died trusting their response to a public invitation. Surprisingly, however, Clark says: "Possibly even inviting the audience to walk down to the front could be a good thing."[363]

With all that the Calvinists have said about the order of salvation, the use of means in regeneration, the salvation of infants and the heathen, and evangelism, it remains to be seen what the Calvinists actually believe about the nature and purpose of the Gospel. Engelsma claims that "the Reformed Faith can do evangelism, because it has the gospel to preach."[364] But does it? The Bible clearly defines what the Gospel is:

> **Moreover, brethren, I declare unto you the gospel which I preached unto you, which also ye have received, and wherein ye stand;**
> **By which also ye are saved, if ye keep in memory what I preached unto you, unless ye have believed in vain.**
> **For I delivered unto you first of all that which I also received, how that Christ died for our sins according to the scriptures;**
> **And that he was buried, and that he rose again the third day according to the scriptures (1 Cor. 15:1-4).**

The Gospel is the good news that Jesus Christ has done something about sin. It is not, as Pink points out: "An announcement that God has relaxed His justice or lowered the standard of His holiness."[365] It is a proposition, yes, but a proposition that demands an appropriation. Calvinists are correct in pointing out that the Gospel is not "You must be born again," "You must be saved," "Repent," or similar phrases, even though these things are true.[366]

So what is the problem? Don't Calvinists believe in the same Gospel as non-Calvinists? It is not the Gospel per se that is the problem, but what the Calvinists read into it. Good maintains that "true gospel teaching and preaching must include the Doctrines of Grace if it is to be faithful to its calling."[367] He further insists that "apart from these revealed truths any 'gospel' that is preached publicly or taught privately must be seriously defective."[368] And as we saw in chapter 1, Calvinists go so far as to identify Calvinism with the Gospel itself:

> Calvinism is the Gospel and to teach Calvinism is in fact to preach the Gospel.[369]

> Calvinism is the Gospel. Its outstanding doctrines are simply the truths that make up the Gospel.[370]

But as we also saw in chapter 1: "The elect alone are the object of grace; for them alone the gospel is good news."[371] So is it really true that Calvinists believe in the same Gospel as non-Calvinists? Custance claims that "it must always be borne in mind that there is no difference between the Gospel preached to those who are not among the elect and those who are."[372] Yet Adams says: "What is the gospel (i.e., 'good news')? Simply this: that Jesus Christ died on the cross for elect sinners, taking the punishment they deserved for all their sins."[373] So regarding the nature of the Gospel, Calvinists do not preach the same Gospel as their opponents.

Regarding the purpose of the Gospel, it has already been proved that, according to Calvinism, it is Irresistible Grace that saves a man and not his believing on Christ. This reduces the Gospel to an afterthought, as is evident by the attitude expressed toward the Gospel by a Primitive Baptist:

> I do not want anyone to think I am selling the gospel short. It has its place in God's scheme of things.[374]

> For us to say that one must hear the gospel in order to be saved for heaven, it would severely limit the Holy One of Israel.[375]

And since it is Irresistible Grace that actually saves a man, Shedd counsels sinners not to **"believe on the Lord Jesus Christ, and thou shalt be saved"** (Acts 16:31), but to pray for regeneration.[376]

So what is the purpose of the Gospel? Best replies:

> The gospel makes disciples, but it does not make children of God.[377]

> The word of the gospel is to effect conversion and practical sanctification, not regeneration.[378]

If God regenerates sinners without the preaching of the Gospel then who should the Gospel be preached to? Garrett instructs us: "The Gospel is not a means in regeneration. The Gospel is for the man who already has life."[379] His proof text? **"But is now made manifest by the appearing of our Saviour Jesus Christ, who hath abolished death, and hath brought life and immortality to light through the gospel"** (2 Tim. 1:10). He follows the reasoning that "it would be impossible to bring life to light where there was no life."[380] Therefore, the Gospel merely "brings life to light."[381] But the verse said that Jesus Christ **"abolished death, and hath brought life and immortality to light."** This was accomplished **"through the gospel."** The context was grace, which although in existence, was obscured until Jesus Christ showed up to manifest it:

"For the law was given by Moses, but grace and truth came by Jesus Christ" (John 1:17). The Gospel itself was not under discussion. God the Father was said to save and call us (2 Tim. 1:9), while God the Son abolished death and **"brought life and immortality to light"** (2 Tim. 1:10). Life is the **"promise of life that now is"** and immortality is **"that which is to come"** (1 Tim. 4:8). But if the Gospel is **"the power of God unto salvation"** (Rom. 1:16), yet is only to be preached to the regenerate, then what is the purpose in preaching it? Garrett again advises us: "We preach out to the children of God what they ought to do; not to dead alien sinners. We can only preach to save God's people."[382] To save God's people? Are God's people lost? Salvation presupposes a danger or peril, but not according to Garrett: "Who is it that believes? Not the dead sinner. The gospel saves the child of God,—it saves him to the truth."[383] So the **"gospel of your salvation"** (Eph. 1:13), by which you are called **"to the obtaining of the glory of our Lord Jesus Christ"** (2 Thes. 2:14), has nothing to do with salvation after all. When a man is converted, it is "not in the sense of regeneration," but merely conversion "to the truth."[384] Now, not all Calvinists would go this far, but once the teaching is adopted that regeneration precedes faith, this is only the logical result.

There are four reasons, as stated by the Calvinists themselves, why no rational, thinking, sane person would ever associate such diametrically opposed ideals as evangelism and Calvinism:

> The Scripture teaches that the ultimate destiny of every individual is decided by the will of God.[385]

> It follows that He never did, nor does He now, will that every individual of mankind should be saved.[386]

> God's purpose with the call to those whom He has not elected is not their salvation, but their damnation. Hence, He does not give them the faith which He demands and, instead, hardens them by the preaching of the gospel.[387]

> A Calvinist will not use gimmicks or tricks to coax men to Christ. He realizes that the Holy Spirit will effectively draw those to the Savior whose names are written in heaven.[388]

A look at true biblical evangelism should confirm this thesis.

The best example of biblical evangelism is the work of the Apostle Paul. A look at his ministry should confirm whether his theology of evangelism was of the TULIP variety. Naturally, the Calvinist claims it was: "Paul did not regard the preaching of the gospel as an offer of salvation."[389] It therefore behooves us to examine Paul's teaching on the Gospel's relation to salvation. Paul was committed with the Gospel (Gal. 2:7), made a minister of the Gospel (Eph. 3:7), and sent to preach the Gospel (1 Cor. 1:7). He even designated the Gospel committed to him as **"my gospel"** (Rom. 2:16). Rather than believing in Unconditional Election and Irresistible Grace, Paul strove to preach the Gospel (Rom. 15:20), and declared: **"Woe is unto me, if I preach not the gospel"** (1 Cor. 9:16), because he knew that salvation was conditioned on a man first hearing the Gospel:

> **How then shall they call on him in whom they have not believed? and how shall they believe in him of whom they have not heard? and how shall they hear without a preacher? (Rom. 10:14).**

> **So then faith** *cometh* **by hearing, and hearing by the word of God (Rom. 10:17).**

> **Forbidding us to speak to the Gentiles that they might be saved, to fill up their sins alway: for the wrath is come upon them to the uttermost (1 Thes. 2:16).**

Rather than believing that all the "elect" would be overcome with Irresistible Grace, Paul relied on the power of the word of God:

> **Holding forth the word of life; that I may rejoice in the day of Christ, that I have not run in vain, neither laboured in vain (Phil. 2:16).**

> **Finally, brethren, pray for us, that the word of the Lord may have** *free* **course, and be glorified, even as** *it is* **with you (2 Thes. 3:1).**

He therefore sought for opportunity to preach:

> **To preach the gospel in the** *regions* **beyond you,** *and* **not to**

> boast in another man's line of things made ready to our hand (2 Cor. 10:16).

> Withal praying also for us, that God would open unto us a door of utterance, to speak the mystery of Christ, for which I am also in bonds (Col. 4:3).

He rejoiced, not that his converts were recipients of Irresistible Grace, but that they put their faith in Jesus Christ:

> Wherefore I also, after I heard of your faith in the Lord Jesus, and love unto all the saints (Eph. 1:15).

> Since we heard of your faith in Christ Jesus, and of the love *which ye have* to all the saints (Col. 1:4).

Although Paul credited God with his results (1 Cor. 3:6), he realized the part he had in bringing the Gospel to people. The theology and ministry of the Apostle Paul was rather unlike the theology and ministries of modern Calvinists. Custance alleges that "when we depart from Calvinism with its emphasis upon the sovereignty of God's grace and the total helplessness of man, we tend to constitute ourselves not merely sowers but germinations, with the power to give life."[390] But this merely confirms that the Apostle Paul departed from Calvinism:

> If by any means I may provoke to emulation *them which are* my flesh, and might save some of them (Rom. 11:14).

> For though ye have ten thousand instructors in Christ, yet *have ye* not many fathers: for in Christ Jesus I have begotten you through the gospel (1 Cor. 4:15).

> To the weak became I as weak, that I might gain the weak: I am made all things to all *men*, that I might by all means *save* some (1 Cor. 9:22).

> I beseech thee for my son Onesimus, whom I have begotten in my bonds (Phile. 10).

All those who aspire to practice biblical evangelism will do likewise.

Evangelism and Calvinism—polar opposites. Is it any wonder that "opponents of Calvinism have a way of pointing to distinctively Reformed doctrines which, they say, are bound to deter evangelistic effort."[391] Yet Kuiper still contends: "If Calvinists are not as zealous for evangelism as they ought to be, the difficulty lies not in their being Calvinists but in their not being Calvinistic enough."[392] Although it is ludicrous to think that the increase in one's evangelistic activity corresponds with an increase in one's adherence to Calvinism, it should be pointed out that no defense is here being made for the evangelistic methods of Billy Graham, Charles G. Finney, or any other evangelist—whether criticized by Calvinists or not. But in the Calvinistic system, there is no need for any evangelist at all. Custance even admits that our responsibility to "warn men of their position before God" is essential only for obedience to God.[393] Pink claims that we "do not preach the Gospel *because we* believe that men are free moral agents, and therefore capable of receiving Christ, but we preach it *because we are commanded to do so.*"[394] Now, it is certainly true that we preach because we are commanded to do so. Like Ezekiel of old, we preach **"whether they will hear, or whether they will forbear"** (Eze. 2:7). But the fact remains that men have the ability to hear or not hear without Irresistible Grace. This does not mean that Calvinists do not raise some important issues. Praying a prayer, signing a card, joining a church, walking an aisle, or responding to an altar call does not save anyone. But neither does infant baptism in a Reformed church. And one thing the Calvinistic Baptists should consider is what happens when someone is genuinely converted under Calvinistic evangelism. Engelsma instructs us that "it is also essential in the work of evangelism that those brought to the saving knowledge of the truth be directed to join a true church, a soundly Reformed church."[395] What do the Calvinistic Baptists think of this? Is Calvinism thicker than "church truth"?

When all else fails, Calvinists will appeal to the ministry of Charles Spurgeon as proof that one can be both evangelistic and Calvinistic. But the fact that Spurgeon had such a large church and a fruitful ministry is not due to the fact that he was a Calvinist, it is because he was inconsistent in the practice of his Calvinism. If the things Spurgeon preached in his sermons were written in a theology book, Calvinists would consider them to be the writings of an Arminian:

> And, oh, dear friends, you that are not saved, take care that you receive this message. Believe it. Go to God with this on your tongue—"Lord save me, for Christ died for the ungodly, and I am one of them." Fling yourself right on to this as a man commits himself to his lifebelt amid the surging billows. . . . Accept this truth, my dear hearer, and you are saved.[396]
>
> Are you a sinner? That felt, that known, that professed, you are now invited to believe that Jesus Christ died for you, because you are a sinner; and you are bidden to cast yourself upon this great immovable rock, and find eternal security in the Lord Jesus Christ.[397]

It is an undeniable axiom that the more *consistently* a man practices his Calvinism, the less evangelistic he becomes. But contrariwise, those who reject Calvinism ought to be more earnest in their evangelistic efforts.

The Other Side of Irresistible Grace

After all the talk about Irresistible Grace, effectual calling, and salvation by sovereign grace alone, it is apparent that the Calvinist repudiates his entire system of theology when the question of evangelism is examined. But this is just the beginning of the other side of Irresistible Grace. And not only do Calvinists backslide on this critical point, they relapse on another cardinal point of their theology as well. It is to be remembered that Calvinists feel so strongly about Irresistible Grace that "to deny that man is wholly passive in regeneration is to deny the depravity of man."[398] But after insisting that man is wholly passive in regeneration, some Calvinists argue that man cannot wholly just wait on God to save him: "Although it is true that none would be saved were it not for the irresistible grace of God, no one may ever fall into the rationalistic trap of saying that he has nothing to do. He may not reason that since all depends on the Holy Spirit, he does not need to believe; or that he must simply wait for the Spirit to move him, and there is nothing that he can do to be saved."[399] But is this not exactly what Calvinists believe? Is it not as simple as Sproul says: "Those whom he regenerates come to Christ. Without regeneration no one will ever come to Christ. With regeneration no one will ever reject him"?[400] And in spite of the fact that every Calvinist believes in a sovereign, eternal, unconditional election to salvation actuated by Irresistible Grace, Boettner adamantly interjects: "No one is to assume his salvation as a matter of course."[401] But if one could not assume his salvation after a sovereign, eternal, unconditional decree by an omnipotent, omniscient, omnipresent God, then a change in theology is in order.

Another part of the other side of Irresistible Grace, as maintained throughout this chapter, is not just that a man cannot resist the grace of God, but that without an "effectual call" of Irresistible Grace a sinner cannot be saved, period. Calvinists would like everyone to think that it is either their doctrine of Irresistible Grace or no salvation at all. Van Baren claims that "it is only by the irresistible grace of God that one is born again."[402] If one believes that the grace of God can be resisted, then he is charged with holding "the Arminian doctrine of resistible grace,"[403] with all the implications inherent in the term. When confronted with the fact that **"whosoever will"** (Rev. 22:17) or **"whosoever believeth"** (John 3:15, 16; Acts 10:43; Rom. 10:11) can be saved, the Calvinist explains it away by arguing something to the effect that "the saving grace of God, changing the heart of the sinner, precedes the will to come to Christ."[404] Boettner reiterates: "Only those who are quickened (made spiritually alive) by the Holy Spirit ever have that will or that desire."[405] Thus, the main facet of the other side of Irresistible Grace is that a sinner must be regenerated by God *before* he can believe on Christ for salvation. So as we have seen, Total Depravity, as the foundation of the TULIP system, consigned all men to the following lot in life until such time as Irresistible Grace is applied:

> ***It is* good that *a man* should both hope and quietly wait for the salvation of the LORD (Lam. 3:26).**

But even though a man must wait for God to regenerate him by Irresistible Grace before he can believe, Calvinists still insist that men are responsible for their not believing. Custance asserts that "men are condemned because of their own free will" because "they have refused his offer of salvation."[406] But on the other hand: "Men, who would otherwise refuse, accept his salvation because He gives them the power to do so."[407] So although a man can reject Christ of his own free will, he cannot accept Christ of his own free will. This is yet another part of the other side of Irresistible Grace.

Although it is sometimes used by Calvinists to prove the doctrine of Total Depravity,[408] the story of the healing of the paralytic man in John chapter five not only disproves the first point of Calvinism, but the teaching of Irresistible Grace as well. By the pool of Bethesda there **"lay a great multitude of impotent folk, of blind, halt, withered, waiting for the moving of the water"** (John 5:3). This pictures the condition of the lost sinner: impotent (Rom. 5:6), blind (2 Cor. 4:4), halt (Eph. 2:12), withered (Isa. 1:6). Yet: **"When Jesus saw him lie, and knew that he had been now a long time *in that case,* he saith unto him, Wilt thou be made whole?"** (John 5:6). Was the man with Total Depravity saved by Irresistible Grace because of God's Unconditional Election and Christ's Limited Atonement? The man had to freely accept or reject Christ's offer: **"Wilt thou be made whole?"** (John 5:6). Salvation by Irresistible Grace requires neither man's knowledge nor consent. So when R. C. Sproul wrote a book about Reformed theology entitled *Grace Unknown,* he inadvertently revealed the Calvinists' true position: the grace of God is not only *unknown* to the "non-elect," it is *unknown* to the "elect" as well since they are "wholly passive" when God applies Irresistible Grace.

Since the doctrines of Total Depravity and Unconditional Election have been proven to be false, the teaching of Limited Atonement has been proven to be not only bogus but irrelevant and nonessential, and the doctrine of Irresistible Grace has been proven to be spurious as well, it is apparent that what makes the word of God effectual is not an Irresistible Grace necessitated by the previous three points of the TULIP, but simply believing it: **"For this cause also thank we God without ceasing, because, when ye received the word of God which ye heard of us, ye received *it* not *as* the word of men, but as it is in truth, the word of God, which effectually worketh also in you that believe"** (1 Thes. 2:13). Although it should be remembered that all non-Calvinists are not Arminians, Palmer nevertheless states the real issue: "Thus according to the Arminian, the reason one accepts and another rejects the gospel is that *man* decides; but according to the Calvinist, it is that *God* decides."[409] In this respect the Calvinists do have a point.

The Bible believing position on the ministry of the Holy Spirit is clear. The Lord Jesus Christ related of the Holy Spirit:

> And when he is come, he will reprove the world of sin, and of righteousness, and of judgment:
> Of sin, because they believe not on me;
> Of righteousness, because I go to my Father, and ye see me no more;
> Of judgment, because the prince of this world is judged (John 16:8-11).

The Holy Spirit will **"reprove the world of sin,"** not just the "elect." Irresistible Grace has nothing to do with any man's salvation. One either believes or doesn't: **"And some believed the things which were spoken, and some believed not"** (Acts 28:24). Calvinists are forever wondering *why* men come to Christ.[410] Their conclusion: Unconditional Election and Irresistible Grace. Those who believe the Bible, however, wonder just the opposite: *why don't* men come? The reason: only the depravity of man can explain his refusal to accept God's free gift of eternal life. The Lord Jesus Christ made it perfectly clear why men don't come to him: **"And ye will not come to me, that ye might have life"** (John 5:40). Not being overcome with Irresistible Grace is never the reason.

The other side of Irresistible Grace reveals the closing act of a divine puppet show. Calvinism, according to John Wesley, "represents our Lord as a hypocrite, a deceiver of the people, a man void of common sincerity, as mocking his helpless creatures by offering what he never intends to give, by saying one thing and meaning another."[411] It is no wonder that Arminius stated about Irresistible Grace: "I am fully persuaded, that the doctrine of Irresistible Grace is repugnant to the Sacred Scriptures, to all the Ancients, and to our own Confession and Catechism."[412] This does not mean that he, or any non-Calvinist, rejected salvation by grace. Even the Calvinist John Leith admits that although "Arminius was especially concerned to refute any doctrine of irresistible grace," "he always insisted that no person can turn to God at all except by the grace of God."[413] So needless to say, the word of God is not bound by the other side of Calvinism: the philosophical speculations and theological implications of Irresistible Grace.

Chapter 10
PERSEVERANCE OF THE SAINTS

The fifth and last point of the Calvinistic system is Perseverance of the Saints. Unlike the four previous points, however, the problem with the term Perseverance of the Saints is that it is ambiguous. The depravity of man is a biblical doctrine, but as we have seen, the Calvinistic doctrine of Total Depravity is not. Likewise, although the doctrine of election is also scriptural, the Calvinistic doctrine of Unconditional Election is certainly not. The third point of Calvinism, Limited Atonement, is so controversial and difficult to defend that many Calvinists reject it. Although salvation is unquestionably by grace, the Calvinistic doctrine of Irresistible Grace, as proved in the previous chapter, teaches salvation by another Gospel. Regarding the expression Perseverance of the Saints, the meaning of the final word is perfectly clear. Only the Roman Catholic Church has misinterpreted it. Calvinists and their opponents would each equate a saint with a born-again child of God. The meaning of the word *perseverance* is what is obscure. Therefore, and because of the overwhelming influence of Calvinism on theology, many men who claim to believe in "eternal security" will avouch to be one-point Calvinists: they will grant that 20 percent of the Five Points of Calvinism are scriptural. Yet, a total disregard for the Five Points of Calvinism as a whole has been maintained throughout this work. This may have led some to believe that the doctrine of eternal security would in the end be rejected. But rather than rejecting the eternal security of the believer, this chapter will prove that it is the Calvinists who reject the biblical teaching of eternal security. The fifth point of the TULIP, *as it was originally formulated and commonly interpreted,* is at enmity with eternal security. This will be demonstrated at length, not only from the Bible, but from the Calvinists themselves.

Although Boettner maintains that "this doctrine does not stand alone but is a necessary part of the Calvinistic system of theology,"[1] Perseverance of the Saints is actually one of the two non-essential points of Calvinism. Just as we saw that Limited Atonement was not requisite to the carrying out of the TULIP system, so we will see that Perseverance of the Saints falls in the same category. Total Depravity *demands* that God must elect and irresistibly save any man who will ever be saved. But whether the Atonement was limited or unlimited is immaterial. Likewise, whether the "elect" persevere, *as defined by the Calvinists,* is also of no consequence. Nevertheless, Kruithof asserts that Perseverance of the Saints, like the other four points, rests on the "Absolute Sovereignty of God."[2] Spencer relates this fifth point of Calvinism with the other points: *"Perseverance of the saints* is dependent upon *irresistible grace,* granted us because Christ died for us since the atonement we have by His blood was *limited* to the elect. That election, praise the Lord, was not based upon some *condition* of good foreknown to be in us since 'there is none good, no not one.' By the grace of God it was an *unconditional election* because no condition could be found! No condition could be found because man is *totally depraved.*"[3] And although Gunn claims that Perseverance of the Saints is "perhaps the most misused of the five points,"[4] it is actually the one most misunderstood by non-Calvinists and therefore requires extensive scrutiny.

Definitions

According to Berkhof, this doctrine "requires careful statement, especially in view of the fact that the term 'perseverance of the saints' is liable to misunderstanding."[5] Like the other points of Calvinism, Perseverance of the Saints is sometimes called by other names to add to the confusing labyrinth of Calvinistic terminology. The most popular other term is "final perseverance,"[6] hinting at the underlying meaning of the fifth point. Beck prefers "preservation of the saved."[7] Others recommend "perseverance of God,"[8] since "the perseverance of the saints depends on the perseverance of God."[9] Rose considers the term Perseverance of the Saints to be "misleading," and says that "it should be called the 'Preservation of the Saints,' for it is God who preserves us to the end."[10] Other Calvinists, recognizing the Arminian implications of the term *perseverance,* also change it to "preservation."[11] As to which is the better title—preservation or perseverance—Pink admits that although "at first sight the former seems preferable, as being more honoring to God," he himself prefers "the latter because rightly understood it includes the former, while at the same time pressing the believer's responsibility."[12] Thus, there are two ideas inherent in the Calvinists' definitions of Perseverance of the Saints.

The first thing that some Calvinists emphasize is that it is God who perseveres in keeping the believer saved:

> Perseverance may be defined as *that continuous operation of the Holy Spirit in the believer, by which the work of divine grace that is begun in the heart, is continued and brought to completion.*[13]

> The doctrine declares that once God has begun the work of salvation in any person, He will persevere therein to the end and will never let any of His own be lost.[14]

If this is how all Calvinists defined Perseverance of the Saints then we would have no argument with them on their fifth point.

The great majority of Calvinists, however, do not accentuate this truth. Rather, they emphasize that the believer perseveres outwardly in the faith:

> This doctrine teaches that those who truly have come to saving faith in Christ will persevere in the faith.[15]

> The new life bestowed by irresistible grace is lived out the rest of the regenerate person's life.[16]

> They whom God has regenerated by the Holy Spirit and effectually called to a state of grace will persevere in progressive sanctification until they are brought finally to glory.[17]

> But let us appreciate the doctrine of the perseverance of the saints and recognize that we may entertain the faith of our security in Christ only as we persevere in faith and holiness to the end.[18]

Obviously, these explanations for perseverance are quite different than the previous ones.

Sometimes Calvinists combine both ideas:

> One always perseveres because he is preserved by the living God—and there is no other possible reason for perseverance.[19]
>
> Perseverance is what we do. Preservation is what God does. We persevere because God preserves.[20]
>
> The converted sinner is made to **persevere in the faith** by the **preserving** grace of God. The true believer who is saved by God's sovereign grace can not lose that salvation. God, by His sovereign power, keeps the believer so that he can not fall totally and absolutely from the state of grace.[21]
>
> The Reformed doctrine of perseverance says that all who were chosen, redeemed, and regenerated by God are eternally saved and are kept in faith by the power of God. They must and will, therefore, persevere in holiness to the end.[22]

In combining both of these ideas, Pink further explains: "The twin truths of Divine preservation and Christian perseverance must not be parted, for the former is accomplished via the latter and not without it."[23]

As on the other points, the descriptions given to the Perseverance of the Saints in the Westminster Confession of Faith and the Canons of Dort are pertinent to the subject at hand:

> They whom God hath accepted in his Beloved, effectually called, and sanctified by his Spirit, can neither totally nor finally fall away from the state of grace, but shall certainly persevere therein to the end, and be eternally saved.[24]
>
> By reason of these remains of indwelling sin, and the temptations of sin and of the world, those who are converted could not persevere in a state of grace, if left to their own strength. But God is faithful, who having conferred grace, mercifully confirms, and powerfully preserves them therein, even to the end.[25]

In spite of the attempts of the Calvinists to connect both of them, the two ideas inherent in the Calvinists' definitions of Perseverance of the Saints are actually completely unrelated. God's *preserving* is not the same thing as the saint's *persevering;* being *preserved* in salvation is not the same thing as outwardly *persevering* in the faith. But what is even more disturbing is what is entailed in a man persevering. In defining perseverance, Calvinists emphasize continuance in believing and living in holiness to the end of one's life much like an Arminian would do. There are also a number of conclusions which can be drawn from the above definitions for perseverance.

Conclusions

There are five conclusions which can be drawn from the Calvinists' definitions for perseverance. The first is that the saints *will* persevere in the faith. This is confirmed by Calvinists:

> The saints will persevere, and those who persevere are the saints.[26]

> The Christian shall persevere.[27]

> The term *perseverance of the saints* emphasizes that Christian's—saints, as Paul calls them in his letters—will persevere in trusting in Christ as their Savior. They will not turn on and then turn off, but they will continue believing forever.[28]

> Those whom the Father chose, and the Son died for, and the Holy Spirit regenerated, will persevere in holiness and faith until the end and will surely be saved for all eternity.[29]

If the saints will persevere in the faith, then the second conclusion that can be drawn from the Calvinists' definitions for perseverance is that only those who persevere in the faith are *true* Christians. This is also confirmed by Calvinists:

> The perseverance of the saints reminds us very forcefully that only those who persevere to the end are truly saints.[30]

> There are many who profess to be Christians but are not. They fall from their profession. The true child of God, however, perseveres in the faith.[31]

> By the term "perseverance" we mean that true saints do continue in faith.[32]

We teach that all true saints will continue in a state of holiness and righteousness through this life on earth until they are brought to Heaven at last.[33]

If only those who persevere in the faith are true Christians, then the third conclusion that can be drawn from the Calvinists' definitions for perseverance is that those who do not persevere in the faith are *lost,* no matter what they once professed. Again, this is confirmed by Calvinists:

> Those who do not persevere unto the end, belong not to the calling of God, which is always effectual.[34]

> No one who denies God should be deceived into thinking that because he once professed faith in Christ he is eternally secure.[35]

> We further hold that a person who does not persevere is a hypocrite, not a saint.[36]

> Those who persevere not in faith and holiness, love and obedience, will assuredly perish.[37]

Since it is obvious that all Christians do not persevere in the faith, the Calvinist is faced with a formidable problem. Thus, the fourth conclusion that can be drawn from the Calvinists' definitions for perseverance is that the solution to Christians not persevering is that real Christians will *return* to the faith before their demise. Again, this is also confirmed by Calvinists:

> We believe that those who once become true Christians cannot totally fall away and be lost,—that while they may fall into sin temporarily, they will eventually return and be saved.[38]

> True Christians will eventually turn back to God, and have restored fellowship with Him.[39]

> We believe that true Christians can fall seriously and radically. We do not believe that they can fall *totally* and *finally*.[40]

> Though the true believer may slip into grievous sin, he does not fall absolutely. God brings him back so that by faith he walks in

the ways of God. He is preserved **in the way of faith**—a faith that results in godly living.[41]

When confronted with the fact that some Christians never return to the faith, the Calvinist is confronted with another dilemma. Thus, the fifth conclusion that can be drawn from the Calvinists' definitions for perseverance is that the solution to Christians not returning to the faith is that such were *never saved* in the first place. This is yet once again confirmed by Calvinists:

> If they persist in apostasy until death, then theirs is a full and final fall from grace, which is evidence that they were not genuine believers in the first place.[42]

> Many who profess to believe fall away, but they do not fall from grace for they were never in grace.[43]

> There are those who profess faith in Christ and join the church who later abandon the faith and return to worldly living. A person who does that is giving evidence that he is not a Christian and never has been a Christian.[44]

> Falling away from the Faith, doesn't mean that one loses his salvation, it means that one never had any salvation from the beginning.[45]

Because Perseverance of the Saints is the one point of Calvinism most understood by non-Calvinists, this litany of evidence has been presented to clearly establish, from a wide variety of Calvinists, precisely what a belief in Perseverance of the Saints entails. So according to the Calvinists themselves:

1. The saints *will* persevere in the faith
2. Only those who persevere in the faith are *true* Christians
3. Those who do not persevere in the faith are *lost*
4. Real Christians will *return* to the faith before their demise
5. Those who do not return to the faith were *never saved*

Although these conclusions are interrelated, they are distinct and clearly evident. But one conclusion that could never be drawn from the Calvinists' definitions for perseverance is that Perseverance of the Saints is the same thing as eternal security.

Eternal Security

This last point of Calvinism is often mistaken for the doctrine of eternal security or "once saved, always saved." But in reality, such is not the case, for as seen by the above definitions, the two ideas have no connection whatsoever. Although some Calvinists do term Perseverance of the Saints "eternal security,"[46] others take offence at this or similar terms.[47] Mathison claims that eternal security "is neither Calvinistic nor Arminian."[48] Talbot and Crampton consider it a "pseudo-Christian doctrine."[49] Gerstner describes eternal security as "antinomian."[50] Regarding the similar expression, "once saved, always saved," Calvinists are likewise divided. Palmer insists that the doctrine of "once saved, always saved" is one of the grandest of Biblical teachings.[51] Other Calvinists, however, disagree:

> We have no sympathy whatever with the bald and unqualified declaration "Once saved always saved."[52]

> I have never liked that definition because it leaves God out of the process, and makes the security of the believer automatic.[53]

> It should be obvious that the Calvinist doctrine of the perseverance of the saints is not one and the same thing with *"once saved, always saved."*[54]

Pink further claims that "many have been lulled into a fatal sleep by the soothing lullaby 'once saved, always saved.'"[55] Anthony Hoekema (1913-1988), former professor of systematic theology at Calvin Theological Seminary, after stating that "no Protestant creed has a better or more complete statement of the doctrine of the perseverance of true believers than the Canons of Dort," adds that "the Canons of Dort do not in any way support the erroneous understanding of this doctrine that some seem to have: namely, 'Once saved, always saved, regardless of how we live.'"[56] But whether Calvinists call Perseverance of the Saints "eternal security" is irrelevant, for when it is examined what the fifth point of Calvinism really entails, it will be seen that it is not the same thing as eternal security no matter what it is called. Yet, even though the Calvinists themselves for the most part repudiate eternal security, genuine Arminians (those who would claim the title) regularly associate eternal security with Calvinism.[57] Gerstner terms John Walvoord's defense of eternal security against Arminianism as a defense, "not of the orthodox doctrine, but of a travesty of it worse than the Arminian doctrine itself."[58]

Because the doctrine of eternal security is so often equated with the Calvinistic fifth point of Perseverance of the Saints, Calvinists can coerce Christians into accepting the Five Points of Calvinism in their entirety by capitalizing on their opponents' belief in eternal security. This is done by implying that a slighting of election and predestination, *as taught by the Calvinists,* negates any belief in eternal security. Mason begins the refrain: "If unconditional election is not true, then the DOCTRINE of 'ONCE IN GRACE, ALWAYS IN GRACE' is not true. It is interesting to note that strong views concerning election and predestination, always go along with belief in the Security of the Believer. The two cannot be consistently separated."[59] Palmer adds: "All the Five Points of Calvinism hang or fall together. The doctrine of the perseverance of the saints naturally follows from the Biblical fact of unconditional election. If the doctrine of election is false, then this doctrine is false, too; but if the doctrine of election is true, then this doctrine necessarily follows."[60] Because he believes that "the five points of Calvinism are closely related. One point presupposes the others," Van Baren rejoins: "Deny perseverance and preservation, and election means nothing. Or reverse it: deny election, and perseverance has no meaning."[61] Sometimes other points of the TULIP are used as well: "If Christ died for the elect, for God's sheep, then the perseverance of the saints naturally follows."[62] Tom Ross connects Perseverance of the Saints with all of the previous points: "Arminian Baptists find themselves on two horns of a dilemma. If they deny total depravity, unconditional election, particular redemption, and effectual calling, they must of necessity also deny the saint's final perseverance. All of the doctrines of grace form a harmonious whole. They stand or fall together. It is inconsistent to embrace one of the five points and not all."[63] It is only because the doctrine of eternal security is often equated with the Perseverance of the Saints that many think they are Calvinists because they hold to this teaching. But when it comes to "the Reformed view of eternal security,"[64] we will see immediately (and throughout this chapter) that the idea of security is not even in view.

Arminianism

As we saw back in the first chapter of this work, Calvinists insist that there are really only two tenable schemes among real Christians: Calvinism and Arminianism. But as we have seen throughout this work, Arminianism is not limited to the supposed doctrines of Arminius, for according to Calvinists, Arminianism is anything contrary to Calvinism. It cannot be emphasized enough that this arbitrary division of men into either Calvinist or Arminian is the strength of the Calvinistic system. After making disdainful contrasts between Calvinism and Arminianism, Calvinists make such shocking statements about Arminianism that no one would dare claim to be an Arminian. And if there are only two theological systems, then it is apparent that most men who desire to appear orthodox would claim to be a Calvinist. Besides these contrasts with Calvinism and general attacks against Arminianism, the Calvinists further misrepresent their opponents by using the guilt by association argument—classifying Arminians with everything under the sun which is unorthodox or heretical. Calvinists then attempt to denigrate Arminianism by the implication that Arminians believe in salvation by works. The Calvinist maintains that only in Calvinism can we find the teaching of salvation by grace. But to maintain that only in Calvinism can the teaching of salvation by grace be found is to charge anyone who is not a Calvinist with believing in salvation by works. This accusation by itself is often enough to make Calvinists out of men who otherwise would not claim any title. So once again it cannot be emphasized enough that this arbitrary division of men into either Calvinists or Arminians is the strength of the Calvinistic system. When everything contrary to Calvinism is labeled Arminianism, and Arminianism is presented in the worst possible light, it is no wonder that so many men have claimed to be Calvinists. Most just know they are not an Arminian and take the name of Calvin by default.

There is no question that the Calvinists have misused the term *Arminianism*. However, this does not mean that Arminianism is to be equated with orthodoxy. Mention the label *Arminianism* today and the first thing that comes to mind (and rightly so) is the doctrine of *conditional* security; that is, the teaching that salvation is conditioned on whether a man perseveres in the faith. But in view of the definitions given by the Calvinists for their doctrine of

Perseverance of the Saints, as well as the conclusions that have been reached (and confirmed by Calvinists) about this teaching, it is apparent that Perseverance of the Saints is not only not eternal security, it is not Calvinism either. It is rather just the opposite: Arminianism. This will be proved by a comparison between the sentiments of Calvinists and *real* Arminians on the subject of perseverance.

The first true Arminian to be examined is Guy Duty, author of a work against eternal security entitled *If Ye Continue*.[65] Like most Arminians, Duty equates eternal security with Calvinism.[66] With help from the testimony of "leading Greek authorities,"[67] except when his disagrees with them,[68] Duty presents us with perseverance from his Arminian viewpoint:

> True faith reveals itself in continual obedience to Christ's conditions for salvation.[69]
>
> We have seen that God's salvation covenant is a *Continuing Covenant*. And it is a monstrous deception to teach that the continual sinner will be saved by a continuing covenant that demands his continual obedience.[70]
>
> There is no cleansing from sin, and no salvation, without a continual walking in God's light.[71]

The next Arminian to assist us in this comparison is Robert Shank. His major work on the subject of perseverance is *Life in the Son*.[72] Like his fellow Arminian, Guy Duty, Shank confounds eternal security with Calvinism.[73] He constantly refers to eternal security as perseverance.[74] He also refers to the same Greek authorities as Duty,[75] but likewise corrects them when he disagrees.[76] Shank presents us with perseverance from another Arminian perspective:

> Keeping His commandments is not optional for men who would enter into life. It is an essential aspect of saving faith.[77]
>
> There is no saving faith apart from obedience.[78]
>
> There is no valid assurance of election and final salvation for any man, apart from deliberate perseverance in faith.[79]

Shank gives us seven principles that we may know whether we are actually persevering:[80]

1. Sincere faith in Jesus Christ
2. Honoring Christ as Lord and keeping his commandments
3. Walking after the example of Christ
4. Loving the Father and his will rather than the world
5. Habitually practicing righteousness rather than sin
6. Love for the brethren
7. Consciousness of the indwelling presence of the Holy Spirit

Shank's conclusion: "Objectively, the elect will persevere, and they who persevere are elect. Subjectively, the individual is elect *only as he perseveres*."[81]

The purpose in going into such detail on the views of Arminians is two-fold. First, to show that Arminianism is not an acceptable alternative to Calvinism. Anyone who has digested much Calvinistic literature knows that according to the Calvinist, if one takes exception to Calvinism then he is an Arminian. But to this we vehemently object. Second, to prove that Calvinists have a false notion of eternal security, as seen by the fact that they have exactly the same sentiments on perseverance as the Arminians. So lurking behind the other side of Calvinism is Arminianism. If Calvinism is true, then one would think that a sinner with Total Depravity, whom God has chosen before the foundation of the world by Unconditional Election, whom Christ has made a Limited Atonement for, and whom God has regenerated by Irresistible Grace, would be saved whether he persevered or not. But by confounding God's *preservation* of the believer with the believer's *perseverance* in the faith, Calvinists have contradicted their entire system of theology.

Keeping in mind the sentiments of Arminianism on the subject of perseverance, we now turn to the Calvinists. Pink begins with an incredible statement: "There is a deadly and damnable heresy being widely propagated today to the effect that, if a sinner truly accepts Christ as his personal Saviour, no matter how he lives afterwards, he cannot perish. That is a satanic lie, for it is at direct variance with the teaching of the Word of truth. Something more than believing in Christ is necessary to ensure the soul's reaching heaven."[82] And what could possibly be more important than obeying the command: **"Believe on the Lord Jesus Christ, and**

thou shalt be saved, and thy house" (Acts 16:31)? Sometimes these acts of perseverance encompass negative injunctions, like those given by John Otis:

> Those who do not love their neighbor, especially those of the household of faith, are yet lost in their sins.[83]

> It is impossible for a racist to be a genuine Christian![84]

> There are several ways in which we hate our brother. One of the most common ways is by harbouring bitterness in our hearts and by maintaining an unforgiving spirit. Not only do these traits destroy us physically, but they will surely destroy our souls in Hell.[85]

Pink adds: "Reader, if there is a reserve in your obedience, you are on the way to hell."[86]

These prohibitions are also joined by positive directives:

> Holiness in this life is such a part of our "salvation" that it is a *necessary means* to make us meet to be partakers of the inheritance of the saints in heavenly light and glory.[87]

> Neither the members of the church nor the elect can be saved unless they persevere in holiness; and they cannot persevere in holiness without continual watchfulness and effort.[88]

> Endurance in faith is a condition for future salvation. Only those who endure in faith will be saved for eternity.[89]

Pink concludes: "Holiness in this life is *absolutely necessary to salvation,* not only as a means to the end, but by a nobler kind of necessity—as part of the end itself."[90]

If one did not know better, he would adamantly insist that the above citations were taken from Arminians like John Wesley, Richard Watson, or the aforementioned Duty and Shank. But upon being informed that every quotation given was the words of a Calvinist, can there be any doubt that Calvinists have exactly the same sentiments on perseverance as Arminians? The confounding of God's *preservation* of the believer with the believer's *perseverance* in the faith makes salvation possible only with a holy life and without the slightest blemish. Therefore, we reiterate: the other side of Perseverance of the Saints is Arminianism, for if any works are required in addition to faith, then as Joseph Dillow relates: "Requirements which must be met in order to secure a certain result, going to heaven, are in fact conditions necessary for the attainment of that result. And if a life of works is a necessary condition for obtaining the result of heaven, then salvation is ultimately conditioned upon works and not faith alone."[91] The Bible, however, is clear—salvation is not of works:

> **But to him that worketh not, but believeth on him that justifieth the ungodly, his faith is counted for righteousness (Rom. 4:5).**
>
> **For by grace are ye saved through faith; and that not of yourselves:** *it is* **the gift of God:**
> **Not of works, lest any man should boast (Eph. 2:8-9).**
>
> **Not by works of righteousness which we have done, but according to his mercy he saved us, by the washing of regeneration, and renewing of the Holy Ghost (Tit. 3:5).**

For a Calvinist to say otherwise is to teach another Gospel (Gal. 1:6).

Contrary to salvation through perseverance as taught by Calvinism, the Bible presents salvation as a result of one thing (as far as man is concerned)—believing, as the Calvinist Chafer explains: "This one word 'believe' represents all a sinner can do and all a sinner must do to be saved."[92] As was pointed out in the previous chapter, according to the Bible, God saves those who believe:

> **For God so loved the world, that he gave his only begotten Son, that whosoever believeth in him should not perish, but have everlasting life (John 3:16).**
>
> **Verily, verily, I say unto you, He that believeth on me hath everlasting life (John 6:47).**
>
> **And they said, Believe on the Lord Jesus Christ, and thou shalt be saved, and thy house (Acts 16:31).**
>
> **That if thou shalt confess with thy mouth the Lord Jesus,**

and shalt believe in thine heart that God hath raised him from the dead, thou shalt be saved (Rom. 10:9).

Contrariwise, a man who refuses to believe is lost:

He that believeth on him is not condemned: but he that believeth not is condemned already, because he that not believed in the name of the only begotten Son of God (John 3:18).

He that believeth on the Son hath everlasting life: and he that believeth not the Son shall not see life; but the wrath of God abideth on him (John 3:36).

I said therefore unto you, that ye shall die in your sins: for if ye believe not that I am he, ye shall die in your sins (John 8:24).

The requirement of the Calvinists that the believer must persevere in good works as a condition of his salvation has been referred to as "back loading" the Gospel.[93] Obviously, Calvinists do not come right out and say what they really believe. Their requirements for perseverance are usually masked by remarks about the believer being saved by a faith that results in works. Although they may claim that salvation is entirely by grace, their "back loading" of the Gospel, by attaching negative injunctions and positive directives, renders Perseverance of the Saints salvation by another Gospel (Gal. 1:6). But to further prove conclusively that all Calvinists are Arminians when it comes to eternal security, we will simply examine the respective comments of Calvinists and Arminians on certain passages of Scripture. Here we will once again find no perceivable difference in the conclusions of the Calvinists and the Arminians.

Proof Texts

Although there are an abundance of proof texts to show that believers are preserved by God, there are none which affirm that believers will always or finally persevere in the faith. Therefore, unlike the previous four chapters, the examination of proof texts in this chapter will focus on those texts which demonstrate that

Calvinists are Arminians when it comes to the fifth point of the TULIP. This will be done by examining their respective interpretations of certain key verses of Scripture. For the Calvinistic interpretation of these verses, the comments of three Calvinists with impeccable credentials will be presented: Charles Hodge, Arthur W. Pink, and the quintessential Calvinist—John Calvin himself. The comments of the Arminians will be provided by the aforementioned Guy Duty and Robert Shank, in addition to Richard Lenski (1864-1936), the noted Lutheran expositor.

The first passage on perseverance concerns an example used by the Apostle Paul:

> **Know ye not that they which run in a race run all, but one receiveth the prize? So run, that ye may obtain.**
> **And every man that striveth for the mastery is temperate in all things. Now they** *do it* **to obtain a corruptible crown; but we an incorruptible.**
> **I therefore so run, not as uncertainly; so fight I, not as one that beateth the air:**
> **But I keep under my body, and bring** *it* **into subjection: lest that by any means, when I have preached to others, I myself should be a castaway (1 Cor. 9:24-27).**

For the Calvinist interpretation of the passage, we cite Calvin himself and the admired Presbyterian theologian, Charles Hodge:

> He has finished what he wanted to teach. Now, in order to impress it on the minds of the Corinthians, he adds an exhortation. In short, he says that what they had attained so far is nothing, unless they keep steadily on; because it is not enough that they once started off on the way of the Lord, if they do not make an effort to reach the goal. This corresponds to the word of Christ in Matt. 10.22: "He that endureth to the end, the same shall be saved."[94]

> What an argument and what a reproof is this! The reckless and listless Corinthians thought they could safely indulge themselves to the very verge of sin, while this devoted apostle considered himself as engaged in a lifestruggle of his salvation.[95]

Since this is one of the Arminians' standard passages, we will look at the comments of three Arminians: Duty, Shank, and Lenski:

After all his preaching and labor for Christ he feared being a castaway.... The combined weight of leading New Testament Greek authorities support the view that Paul referred to his salvation when he used the word "castaway" in I Corinthians 9:27.... This is what Paul feared would happen to him at the Judgment. He would not let the power of sin get its mastery over him.[96]

Many have contended that Paul's fear was not that he might fail of salvation, but rather that he might find himself disqualified for further service as an apostle and that he might fail to receive the full reward which faithfulness secures.... Influence of the immediate context establishes the fact that Paul's fear was the possibility of losing, not opportunities or rewards for service, but the salvation of his own soul.[97]

What a calamity when a professing Christian finds himself "rejected" in the end! How much worse when one of the Lord's own heralds has this experience! Paul regards his work with extreme seriousness. The fact that he is an apostle is not yet proof to him that he will be saved. He knows the test that he must face.[98]

If there any difference between the remarks of the Calvinists and Arminians? Was the Apostle Paul worried about losing his salvation? This is the same Paul who exclaimed:

For I am persuaded that neither death, nor life, nor angels, nor principalities, nor powers, nor things present, nor things to come,
Nor height, nor depth, nor any other creature, shall be able to separate us from the love of God, which is in Christ Jesus our Lord (Rom. 8:38-39).

The obtaining is a prize or reward, signified by a crown. We have already obtained (2 Pet. 1:1); we have eternal life (1 John 5:11). The error of both the Calvinists and Arminians is in discounting the judgment seat of Christ (Rom. 14:10; 1 Cor. 3:13-15; 2 Cor. 5:10), where crowns are given (1 Cor. 9:25; 1 Thes. 2:19; 2 Tim. 4:8; Jam. 1:12; 1 Pet. 5:4). The lost are promised salvation (John 3:18); the saved are promised rewards (1 Cor. 3:14). Salvation is a free gift (Eph. 2:8); rewards are earned by works (1 Cor. 9:25). Salvation is a present possession (John 5:24); rewards are a future possibility (2 Tim. 4:8).

The next verse in question concerns the Apostle Paul's instructions to Timothy: **"Take heed unto thyself, and unto the doctrine; continue in them: for in doing this thou shalt both save thyself, and them that hear thee"** (1 Tim. 4:16). Once again the namesake of Calvinism speaks:

> The zeal of pastors will be greatly increased when they are told that both their own salvation and that of their people depends upon their serious and earnest devotion to their office.[99]

For the Arminian contribution we turn to Duty:

> Paul told Timothy to do something for his salvation and the salvation of others. . . . It was by continuing in the doctrines of Christ and by doing them that Timothy and his hearers would be saved. We agree with Calvin's comment on this text.[100]

The problem with both the Calvinist and the Arminian is in taking the word *salvation* as always referring to salvation from hell. No one is saved from hell in 2 Corinthians 1:6 or 1 Timothy 2:15. No Calvinist would say that salvation was from hell in Luke 1:71 or Acts 27:31. As Paul was concerned about his ministry (1 Tim. 1:12) in 1 Corinthians 9:27, so he here admonishes Timothy.

The last verse to be examined is probably one of the most misapplied in the entire Bible: **"But he that shall endure unto the end, the same shall be saved"** (Mat. 24:13). This time we have Calvin joined by Pink:

> When the love of many should fail to support the weight of iniquity Christ tells them that this barrier too must be overcome in case the faithful should break under bad example and defect. So He repeats the sentence, that no man can be saved unless he strive lawfully to persevere to the end of the course.[101]

> Sad indeed is it to witness so many young professing Christians just starting out on their arduous journey to Heaven, being told that the words "He that endureth to the end shall be saved" apply not to them, but only to the Jews; and that while unfaithfulness on their part will forfeit some "millennial" crown, yet so long as they have accepted Christ as their personal Saviour, no matter how they must indulge the flesh or fraternize

with the world, Heaven itself cannot be missed.[102]

Modern Calvinists still appeal to this verse in the same manner.[103] For the same viewpoint, but as stated from an Arminian perspective, we present Lenski and Shank:

> To endure means to bear whatever a true confession of Christ brings upon us. Jesus himself says that in the case of some this will mean *death*. . . . Back of the passive is Christ, the Savior; he will at that moment bestow the heavenly salvation.[104]

> Some have interpreted v. 13 to mean only that he who survives the tribulation will be saved physically by the appearing of the Lord. Such interpretation completely ignores the context (cf. vv. 11, 12—clearly a spiritual peril) and amounts to no more than a declaration that he who does not perish bodily will survive physically—a meaningless statement of the obvious.[105]

Other Arminians also appeal to this verse in the same manner.[106] But since the expression **"unto the end"** is only defined one time (Mat. 28:20), the context must be the determining factor on the other occasions when this phrase occurs. The context here obviously concerns a future tribulation period (Mat. 24:21, 29)—a period of time—not the end of one's life. And as we saw in our study of Unconditional Election, those addressed are not "elect sinners" waiting to be saved by Irresistible Grace, but Jewish saints. Matthew 24:13 has nothing to do—directly or indirectly—with the salvation of anyone in the Church age under grace. We are already confirmed to the end (1 Cor. 1:7-8).

So just as was true in the previous section, if one did not know better, he would adamantly insist that all of the above citations were the comments of Arminians. But the fact that some of these quotations were the words of Calvinists proves that Calvinists have exactly the same sentiments on perseverance as Arminians. The confounding of God's *preservation* of the believer with the believer's *perseverance* in the faith contradicts not only the Bible, but the Calvinists' entire system of theology as well.

Perseverance

It should be obvious by now that there is a difference between the saints persevering in the faith and their being preserved in salvation by God. But anyone with a dictionary would have known that *perseverance* is not the same as *preservation*. The Baptist Curtis Hutson (1934-1995) perceived this fact and correctly surmised: "The Bible teaches, and I believe in, the eternal security of the born-again believer. The man who has trusted Jesus Christ has everlasting life and will never perish. But the eternal security of the believer does not depend upon his perseverance."[107] For statements like this he has been called "an Arminian Baptist evangelist"[108] This rhetoric should come as no surprise to anyone familiar with Calvinism, for any opponent is an Arminian no matter what he believes. There is some dissension among the Calvinists, however. The Hardshell Baptist Eddie Garrett, who certainly could never be accused of Arminianism, stated that he believed "that the Bible does not teach the **Perseverance** of the saints but that it teaches the **Preservation** of the saints."[109] So even according to some Calvinists, there is a difference between the two words, and consequently the doctrines which follow.

It was mentioned earlier in this chapter that although there are an abundance of proof texts to show that believers are preserved by God, there are none which affirm that believers will always or finally persevere in the faith. The word *perseverance* is used but once in the Scriptures: **"Praying always with all prayer and supplication in the Spirit, and watching thereunto with all perseverance and supplication for all saints"** (Eph. 6:18). This obviously has reference to prayer and not anyone's eternal salvation. The standard Calvinist reply is given by Van Baren: "And though the word, 'perseverance,' is used only once in the Bible, the idea is found throughout Scripture."[110] But is "the idea" that all of the saints *will* persevere found throughout Scripture?

The New Testament is abundantly clear in its declaration that Christians may not persevere. It is possible to depart from the faith (1 Tim. 4:1), err from the faith (1 Tim. 6:10), err concerning the faith (1 Tim. 6:20), deny the faith (1 Tim. 5:8), make shipwreck of the faith (1 Tim. 1:19), cast off one's first faith (1 Tim. 5:12), swerve from the faith (1 Tim. 1:6), and not continue in the faith (Col. 1:23). Believers can fall from their own stedfastness (2 Pet. 3:17), become barren and unfruitful (2 Pet. 1:8), deny Christ (2 Tim. 2:12), and be ashamed when Christ returns (1 John 2:28). Hymenaeus and Alexander did not persevere—they were delivered by Paul **"unto Satan"** (1 Tim. 1:20). But this could not mean that they were never saved, like some Calvinists claim, because the fornicator among the Corinthians was also delivered to Satan (1 Cor. 5:5) and consequently restored (2 Cor. 2:6-8). Demas forsook Paul because of his love for the world (2 Tim. 4:10). Yet of Mark, who also deserted him (Acts 13:13), Paul later said **"He is profitable to me for the ministry"** (2 Tim. 4:11). If the Calvinist claims that only the Corinthian fornicator and Mark were regenerate because they alone returned to the faith before their death, then what about Lot? The Bible calls Lot **"just"** (2 Pet. 2:7) and **"righteous"** (2 Pet. 2:8). But the last time we hear of him he is drunk in a cave committing incest with his two daughters (Gen. 19:33-36). Did he persevere in the faith? A righteous man can turn from his righteousness and never turn back (Eze. 18:24).

The fact that Christians may not persevere does not mean that they should not strive to do so. There are numerous exhortations in the Bible for believers to persevere:

> **Therefore, my beloved brethren, be ye stedfast, unmoveable, always abounding in the work of the Lord, forasmuch as ye know that your labour is not in vain in the Lord (1 Cor. 15:58).**

> **Wherefore, my beloved, as ye have always obeyed, not as in my presence only, but now much more in my absence, work out your own salvation with fear and trembling (Phil. 2:12).**

> **Keep yourselves in the love of God, looking for the mercy of our Lord Jesus Christ unto eternal life (Jude 1:21).**

These passages have no meaning if all Christians will automatically persevere. It is amazing how a Calvinist who professes to believe in Total Depravity can deny that a saved man could not persevere in the faith. The problem is simple:

> **Watch and pray, that ye enter not into temptation: the spirit indeed *is* willing, but the flesh *is* weak (Mat. 26:41).**

> **For I know that in me (that is, in my flesh,) dwelleth no good thing: for to will is present with me; but *how* to perform that which is good I find not (Rom. 7:18).**

Is the old sinful nature eradicated at the point of salvation? Is perfect holiness attainable in this life? Can a Christian not sin worse than a non-Christian? As was pointed out in chapter 7, God's elect people—the nation of Israel—did worse than the heathen (2 Chr. 33:9). If it wasn't for God's preservation no one would persevere, whether they were one of the "elect" or not.

Although good works are not necessary for salvation, which every Calvinist would acknowledge, the Christian is enjoined to practice them, but never in order to keep his salvation:

> **For we are his workmanship, created in Christ Jesus unto good works, which God hath before ordained that we should walk in them (Eph. 2:10).**
>
> **That ye might walk worthy of the Lord unto all pleasing, being fruitful in every good work, and increasing in the knowledge of God (Col. 1:10).**
>
> **This *is* a faithful saying, and these things I will that thou affirm constantly, that they which have believed in God might be careful to maintain good works. These things are good and profitable unto men. (Tit. 3:8).**
>
> **And let us consider one another to provoke unto love and to good works (Heb. 10:24).**

Although the Christian will one day be judged for his works, this has nothing to do with his salvation (1 Cor. 3:13-15).

There are plenty of instructions given to the Christian on how to live, but never on how to confirm or maintain his salvation:

> **Whether therefore ye eat, or drink, or whatsoever ye do, do all to the glory of God (1 Cor. 10:31).**
>
> **And whatsoever ye do in word or deed, *do* all in the name of the Lord Jesus, giving thanks to God and the Father by him (Col. 3:17).**
>
> **Finally, brethren, whatsoever things are true, whatsoever things *are* honest, whatsoever things *are* just, whatsoever things *are* pure, whatsoever things *are* lovely, whatsoever things *are* of good report; if *there be* any virtue, and if *there***

***be* any praise, think on these things (Phil. 4:8).**

Abstain from all appearance of evil (1 Thes. 5:22).

Although the Christian will be judged for **"the things *done* in *his* body, according to that he hath done, whether *it be* good or bad"** (2 Cor. 5:10), this has nothing to do with his salvation.

So if it is true that there is a difference between the saints persevering in the faith and their being preserved in salvation by God, and if it is true that saints will be judged in the future, what, if anything, can happen to them in this life if they do not persevere? Plenty. A Christian who fails to persevere can lose his joy, assurance, fellowship, rewards, and his life, but he cannot lose his salvation. The reason Calvinists get so upset about Christians who do not persevere is pride and envy. Why should a carnal Christian who fails to persevere end up in heaven? After all, I have put down my flesh, I have done good works, I have persevered. Why does God let that carnal Christian live his life in such a condition? How could he possibly be one of the "elect"?

Lordship Salvation

The Calvinistic teaching of Perseverance of the Saints has only recently surfaced among modern Fundamentalists and Evangelicals under the synonym of lordship salvation. The emphasis of lordship salvation, however, is more on the act of salvation itself. In addition to "back loading" the Gospel by requiring the believer to persevere in good works as a condition of his salvation, lordship salvation is guilty of "front loading" the Gospel by requiring works of submission and obedience as conditions for salvation.[111] Much has been written of late on the subject of lordship salvation, both pro[112] and con,[113] so little attempt will be made here to continue the debate other than to show the connection between lordship salvation and Calvinism.

The issue in lordship salvation is not whether Jesus Christ is the Lord, for he is whether accepted as the Lord or not. Neither is the issue whether Christ should be the Lord of the Christian's life, all parties agree that he should be. The real issue is whether a sinner must make Christ the Lord of his life at the time he believes on Jesus Christ for salvation. Lordship advocates have explained their position as follows:

> The Gospel calls upon us to obey, to surrender ourselves fully to the Lordship of Christ, to take His yoke upon us, to walk even as He walked.[114]
>
> Friend, if Jesus Christ isn't the Lord of your life, then you are yet lost in your sins.[115]
>
> Lordship advocates teach that believing in Christ and resolving to obey Him are not two acts but one.[116]

Pink even uttered the same trite sayings we hear today: "No one can receive Christ as his Savior while he rejects Him as Lord."[117] Kenneth Gentry appeals to "noteworthy scholars" like John Gerstner, Arthur W. Pink, R. C. Sproul, J. I. Packer, and John MacArthur for proof that lordship salvation is biblical.[118]

One of the most notable propagators of the lordship salvation teaching is the abovementioned John MacArthur. Although claiming that he doesn't like the term *lordship salvation* because "it implies that Jesus' lordship is a false addition to the gospel," MacArthur maintains that lordship salvation is simply "the biblical and historic doctrine of soteriology."[119] He has written extensively on the issue at hand:

> There is no salvation except "lordship salvation."[120]
>
> The signature of saving faith is surrender to the lordship of Jesus Christ.[121]
>
> Those who deny the lordship of Christ are damned.[122]
>
> The call to Calvary must be recognized for what it is: a call to discipleship under the Lordship of Jesus Christ. To respond to that call is to become a believer. Anything less is simply unbelief.[123]

He also injuriously describes the non-lordship position in the following terms:

> It warps and sometimes completely destroys the gospel.[124]
>
> It is a distinctly different view of salvation than the Biblical one.[125]

To prove that lordship salvation is biblical, MacArthur uses the historical argument.[126]

Before examining some of the errors of lordship salvation, the connection between this doctrine and Calvinism will be proved from the lordship adherents themselves. Keith Mathison and Curtis Crenshaw term lordship salvation "the Reformed position."[127] Others have simply said:

> Lordship salvation flows from a Calvinistic foundation.[128]

> It is largely associated with Reformed or Calvinistic theology.[129]

In typical Calvinist fashion, opposition to lordship salvation is called Arminian.[130] Kenneth Gentry, who acknowledges that much of his "early theological development was fed by publications from Presbyterian and Reformed," states that lordship salvation "has largely suffered, not from its connection with Calvinism, but from its misrepresentation by Arminian and Pelagian writers."[131] There is no doubt at all about MacArthur's Calvinism. Besides using the standard Calvinistic term "sovereign grace,"[132] he reverses the plan of salvation,[133] and prefers the term Perseverance of the Saints to "eternal security."[134]

But not only is lordship salvation connected with Calvinism, it also concurs with Arminianism, as can be seen by the sentiments of Robert Shank:

> No man can accept Jesus as Saviour of his soul without accepting Him as Lord of his life.[135]

> The lordship of Jesus over self, life, and possessions must be acknowledged if we are to know Him as Saviour.[136]

> It is vain for one to speak of his faith in Christ as Saviour who is not definitely committed to the lordship of Christ and positively opposing the dominion of sin in his personal life.[137]

> The commitment of oneself to Christ in accepting Him as Saviour and Lord is the necessary starting point. But the initial decision must be reaffirmed and implemented in the life which follows. We must continue to choose between the lordship of Christ and the dominion of sin.[138]

So just like the subject of perseverance, there is no difference Calvinism and Arminianism when it comes to lordship salvation.

Although the adherents of lordship salvation routinely emphasize the differences among their opponents,[139] they are not as united as they would have us believe. Nevertheless, there are some basic errors that all advocates of lordship salvation espouse. The first is their contempt for dispensationalism.[140] Even MacArthur, who calls himself a "traditional premillennial dispensationalist,"[141] assails Clarence Larkin (1850-1924), E. Schuyler English (1899-1991), Charles Ryrie, and Lewis Sperry Chafer for holding traditional dispensational views like the Sermon on the Mount is not the Gospel and **"the gospel of the kingdom"** (Mat. 24:14) is not the same as **"the gospel of the grace of God"** (Acts 20:24).[142] Closely allied with this aversion to dispensationalism is the charge of antinomianism laid at the feet of non-lordship proponents.[143]

Other errors of lordship salvation include the denial that there can be a carnal Christian,[144] the denial that the believer has two natures,[145] a blurring of the distinction between the believer's standing and state,[146] the accusation that their opponents believe in "cheap grace" or "easy believism,"[147] the confounding of salvation and discipleship,[148] a blurring of the different aspects of sanctification,[149] a distorted view of faith and repentance,[150] the reliance on modern versions of the Bible as proof texts for lordship salvation,[151] and finally, a lack of definite statements on just what lordship really is. But in replying to the Calvinist advocates of lordship salvation, refutation will for the most part be provided by the Calvinists themselves.

The first three of the abovementioned errors are directly contradicted by other Calvinists. Because it so directly goes against the Calvinistic teaching of Perseverance of the Saints, lordship advocates are adamant in their denial that there can be a carnal Christian. But those who speak of a carnal Christian are only using the terminology of Scripture: **"And I, brethren, could not speak unto you as unto spiritual, but as unto carnal, *even* as unto babes in Christ"** (1 Cor. 3:1). For the word of a Calvinist, we cite the Hardshell Baptist Eddie Garrett: "Whether we like it or not there is such a thing as a **carnal** Christian."[152] Regarding the two natures in the believer, Arthur W. Pink, certainly a Calvinist with impeccable credentials, maintained that "in the Christian there are two distinct and diverse 'natures,' namely, the 'flesh' and the 'spirit.'"[153] It is interesting to note that Shank the Arminian, whom we have heard from several times already, also rejects the two natures in the believer as causing a carnal Christian.[154] And finally, in reply to the proponents of lordship salvation who blur the distinction between the believer's standing (Rom. 5:1; Eph. 1:6) and state (Phil. 4:7; 2 Cor. 5:9), Garrett again explains: "I would remind the reader just how important it is to understand the distinction between **standing** and **state**. **Standing** has reference to what I am as viewed by God through the work of His Son. **State** is my actual condition of soul."[155]

For lordship salvation adherents to charge their opponents with believing in cheap grace is ludicrous. In the Bible grace is not only cheap, it is free: **"But not as the offence, so also *is* the free gift. For if through the offence of one many be dead, much more the grace of God, and the gift by grace, *which is* by one man, Jesus Christ, hath abounded unto many"** (Rom. 5:15). This is confirmed by a Calvinist: "The Biblical teaching is that grace is not only cheap, it is completely free; otherwise it would not be grace."[156] Likewise the charge of easy believism. The Scripture nowhere presents believing on Christ for salvation as something hard to do. In fact, it is the only thing that one can possibly do: **"But to him that worketh not, but believeth on him that justifieth the ungodly, his faith is counted for righteousness"** (Rom. 4:5). It might be hard to admit that one is a sinner and deservedly on his way to hell. It might be hard to acknowledge that trusting in religion and good works will land a man in the lake of fire. But once these things are conceded, believing is easy. Salvation is pictured as looking (Isa. 45:22), coming (Mat. 11:28), receiving (John 1:12), eating (John 6:51), drinking (John 7:37), trusting (Eph. 1:13), and taking (Rev. 22:17). A departure from the biblical plan of salvation is the only way that believing on Christ can be made difficult. And once again it should be mentioned that Shank the Arminian also assails easy believism.[157]

Regarding the confounding of salvation and discipleship, it should be apparent that while salvation is obtained in an instant of time, discipleship is an ongoing process. Some men were disciples first and then Christians (John 2:11). Judas was a disciple but obviously not saved (John 12:4). Joseph and Nicodemus were saved, but were secret disciples (John 19:38-39). Some of Christ's disciples **"went back, and walked no more with him"** (John

6:66). Salvation is one thing; discipleship is another. If discipleship is salvation then the disciples of Christ, who acknowledged him as Lord (Mat. 8:25), lost their salvation, because **"all the disciples forsook him and fled"** (Mat. 26:56). Salvation costs nothing; discipleship costs everything.

The blurring of the different aspects of sanctification is another problem with lordship salvation. In the Bible sanctification is three-fold: positional (1 Cor. 6:11; Heb. 10:10), progressive (John 17:17; 1 Thes. 4:3), and future (Phil. 3:21; 1 John 3:2). The failure to distinguish these three aspects of sanctification contributes not only to lordship salvation, but to perfectionism as well. The sanctification necessary for the salvation of any Christian has already been attained.

Because they are for the most part Calvinists, advocates of lordship salvation usually make faith and repentance God's gifts to his "elect." But this is not the only way they distort these doctrines. Faith is customarily redefined as obedience.[158] But obedience of the Gospel (Rom. 10:16) is an **"obedience of faith"** (Rom. 16:26). It is even acknowledged by Calvinists that one of their own, J. Gresham Machen, taught that obedience is not a part of faith and that one is not justified by "obedient faith."[159] Even some lordship salvation proponents condemn MacArthur for his redefinition of faith.[160] The proclivity of Calvinists and lordship salvation adherents to redefine repentance as turning from sin, repudiation of the old life, turning to God, remorse, conversion, or changing one's life has been referred to as an "illegitimate totality transfer," that is, the transferring of these ideas into the meaning of the word.[161] Yet, the idea that repentance is basically a change of mind is acknowledged not only by Calvinists like Gordon Clark,[162] but by those who espouse lordship salvation as well.[163] As proof that this is indeed the true denotation of the term, a simple look at how the Bible uses the term is all that is required. In the Bible, the word *repentance* is used in reference to salvation, it is used of God repenting, it is used in non-salvation contexts, and it is said to be done by those who are already Christians:

> **Testifying both to the Jews, and also to the Greeks, repentance toward God, and faith toward our Lord Jesus Christ (Acts 20:21).**

> **And God sent an angel unto Jerusalem to destroy it: and as**

PERSEVERANCE OF THE SAINTS

> he was destroying, the LORD beheld, and he repented him of the evil, and said to the angel that destroyed, It is enough, stay now thine hand. And the angel of the LORD stood by the threshingfloor of Ornan the Jebusite (1 Chr. 21:15).

> But what think ye? A *certain* man had two sons; and he came to the first, and said, Son, go work to day in my vineyard.
> He answered and said, I will not: but afterward he repented, and went (Mat. 21:28-29).

> For though I made you sorry with a letter, I do not repent, though I did repent: for I perceive that the same epistle hath made you sorry, though *it were* but for a season (2 Cor. 7:8).

Paul preached repentance but in distinction from turning to God and doing works: **"But showed first unto them of Damascus, and at Jerusalem, and throughout all the coasts of Judaea, and *then* to the Gentiles, that they should repent and turn to God, and do works meet for repentance"** (Acts 26:20).

In seeking to justify their position, lordship salvation advocates do appeal to the Scripture for support. The problem, however, is that they rely almost exclusively on modern versions of the Bible for their proof texts. Instead of the familiar readings of the Authorized Version, subtle changes have been made in the following verses:

> That if thou shalt confess with thy mouth the Lord Jesus, and shalt believe in thine heart that God hath raised him from the dead, thou shalt be saved (Rom. 10:9).

> Wherefore I give you to understand, that no man speaking by the Spirit of God calleth Jesus accursed: and *that* no man can say that Jesus is the Lord, but by the Holy Ghost (1 Cor. 12:3).

> For we preach not ourselves, but Christ Jesus the Lord; and ourselves your servants for Jesus' sake (2 Cor. 4:5).

> As ye have therefore received Christ Jesus the Lord, *so* walk ye in him (Col. 2:6).

Instead of reading "the Lord," most modern versions read "as Lord" or "is Lord." But if one can simply go to the version of the Bible he chooses to substantiate his doctrine, then one can prove anything.

The last problem with lordship salvation is the lack of definite statements on just what lordship really is. Otis maintains that "obedience to God's commandments is submission to Christ's Lordship."[164] And what should the extent of our obedience be? Otis again explains: "Submitting to Christ's Lordship is the constant obedience to God's commandments."[165] If this is true then no Calvinist has ever submitted to the lordship of Christ. To "walk as Christ walked"—to really submit to his lordship—entails nothing short of sinless perfection. God demands absolute perfection at all times: anything less is a rejection of the lordship of Christ. Now, no lordship salvation advocate would say that a man must live absolutely sinless to be a genuine believer. But just what level of lordship is required to be counted among God's "elect"? Does smoking disqualify one from practicing lordship? What about drinking, gambling, adultery, fornication, lying, cheating, stealing, coveting, pride, or evil thoughts? The Calvinist would reply that it is the habitual practice of these things that proves one is lost. But how does one define "habitual practice"? And what if a man surrendered to quitting all of these things at the moment he was saved but was not able to accomplish it completely? Is his salvation now questionable? Zane Hodges clearly recognized the real problem:

> The problem is that lordship teachers have set up their own standards by which to measure God's saving work in an individual life. If these standards are not met, lordship thought insists that God cannot be involved. Only if the professing believer meets the level of attainment required by lordship thinkers—only then will lordship theologians admit that such a believer may be truly saved.[166]

Holiness is certainly what the Bible commands for a Christian (1 Pet. 1:16), but the Gospel **"is the power of God unto salvation to every one that believeth"** (Rom. 1:16), not to everyone who surrenders to the lordship of Christ. Every devil in hell will surrender to the lordship of Christ (Phil. 3:10-11).

The difference between salvation and lordship can be seen in the Apostle Paul's distinctive exhortations to unsaved men and saved men:

> And they said, Believe on the Lord Jesus Christ, and thou shalt be saved, and thy house (Acts 16:31).
>
> I beseech you therefore, brethren, by the mercies of God, that ye present your bodies a living sacrifice, holy, acceptable unto God, *which is* your reasonable service (Rom. 12:1).

No unsaved man could possibly be expected to meet the demands for surrendering to Christ's lordship: **"But the natural man receiveth not the things of the Spirit of God: for they are foolishness unto him: neither can he know *them*, because they are spiritually discerned"** (1 Cor. 2:14). One would think that a Calvinist who believed in Total Depravity would recognize this fact.

In spite of the affinity that lordship salvation has with both Calvinism and Arminianism, it is not just non-Calvinists who reject lordship salvation. Since MacArthur is one of the foremost propagators of this teaching, we will use his book on the subject as an example. Reviewers of MacArthur's book *The Gospel According to Jesus* who term his view "The Gospel According to John MacArthur" include both Calvinists and non-Calvinists.[167] John Robbins, another Calvinist with impeccable credentials, and one who doesn't hesitate to criticize other Calvinists, calls MacArthur a "semi-Arminian,"[168] and comments:

> MacArthur attacks justification by faith alone and suggests that works be understood as part of faith.[169]
>
> Rather than discussing the Gospel, MacArthur discusses psychology.[170]
>
> MacArthur has offered an un-Scriptural definition of faith.[171]
>
> In his stress on "total commitment," MacArthur has strayed into the heresy of perfectionism.[172]
>
> MacArthur's book is very confused and dangerous. It does not present the Gospel according to Jesus, but another gospel, which is not a gospel at all, similar to that of the Roman church.[173]

So, if even Calvinists reject the doctrine of Lordship salvation, why do most Calvinists cling to it? The lethargy and moral laxity of many Christians is obviously a significant cause for the propagation of this teaching. Two wrongs, however, never make a right. Besides being just plain wrong, lordship salvation is dangerous because it teaches that assurance of salvation is obtained by our own works as manifested in our lives instead of the finished work of Christ as revealed in the Scripture. It also gives false assurance of salvation to those who are trusting in their works to save them. But as the Lord Jesus Christ related:

> **Not every one that saith unto me, Lord, Lord, shall enter into the kingdom of heaven; but he that doeth the will of my Father which is in heaven.**
> **Many will say to me in that day, Lord, Lord, have we not prophesied in thy name? and in thy name have cast out devils? and in thy name done many wonderful works?**
> **And then will I profess unto them, I never knew you: depart from me, ye that work iniquity (Mat. 7:21-23).**

And what is the will of the Father: **"And this is the will of him that sent me, that every one which seeth the Son, and believeth on him, may have everlasting life: and I will raise him up at the last day"** (John 6:40).

Preservation

Regarding the actual preservation of the saints—their eternal security—there couldn't possibly be any doubt about the saints being preserved. If salvation is all of grace and entirely the work of God, it could never depend on whether a man persevered. And as has been maintained throughout this work, there is a difference between the saints persevering in the faith and their being preserved in salvation by God. According to both the dictionary and the definitions given by the Calvinists, perseverance implies persistence, continuance, and effort. It is the work of man. Does this mean that the grace of God is not sufficient to help man to persevere in holiness and maintain good works? To the contrary, the Lord told Paul: **"My grace is sufficient for thee"** (2 Cor. 12:9). The problem is the sinful nature of man. On the other hand, when something is preserved—whether a Christian or a piece of fruit—it contributes nothing to is own preservation. The preservation depends entirely on an outside party. But unlike a piece of fruit, which can be improperly preserved by human hands, Christ said of believers: **"And I give unto them eternal life; and they shall never perish, neither shall any *man* pluck them out of my hand"** (John 10:28).

The word *perseverance,* as we have seen, is used but once in the Scriptures, and that in reference to prayer, not salvation. Forms of the word *preservation,* however, do occur in the Scripture:

> **And the very God of peace sanctify you wholly; *and I pray God* your whole spirit and soul and body be preserved blameless unto the coming of our Lord Jesus Christ (1 Thes. 5:23).**

> **And the Lord shall deliver me from every evil work, and will preserve *me* unto his heavenly kingdom: to whom *be* glory for ever and ever. Amen (2 Tim. 4:18).**

> **Jude, the servant of Jesus Christ, and brother of James, to them that are sanctified by God the Father, and preserved in Jesus Christ, *and* called (Jude 1).**

To get rid of the plain truth of Scripture, Pink relates this preservation to *"temporal preservation prior to salvation."*[174] He insists that although the "elect" sinner was in Christ before the foundation of the world, he was still in his sins and needed to be preserved until Irresistible Grace could be applied to him.[175]

Not only are Christians preserved, they are united with Christ. They belong to Christ and he to God (1 Cor. 3:23), they are in the Father (1 Cor. 8:6), and in Jesus Christ (Eph. 1:1), and he in them (Col. 1:27). The solution is to get out of Adam and into Jesus Christ: **"For as in Adam all die, even so in Christ shall all be made alive"** (1 Cor. 15:22). Believers are not just in him, they are **"joined unto the Lord"** (1 Cor. 6:17), **"members of his body, of his flesh, and of his bones"** (Eph. 5:30), **"partakers of the divine nature"** (2 Pet. 1:4), and of **"the glory that shall be revealed"** (1 Pet. 5:1). We are crucified with Christ (Gal. 2:20), dead with Christ (Col. 2:20), buried with Christ (Rom. 6:4), quickened with Christ (Eph. 2:5), risen with Christ (Col. 3:1), alive with Christ (Col 3:3-4), and seated **"together in heavenly places in Christ Jesus"** (Eph. 2:6), blessed **"with all spiritual blessings in heavenly *places* in Christ"** (Eph. 1:3). This union with Christ is pictured in a number of ways:

> Building and foundation (Eph. 2:20-22)
> Vine and branches (John 15:5)
> Husband and wife (Eph. 5:23, 30-32)
> Body and members (1 Cor. 12:12)
> Shepherd and sheep (John 10:14)
> Adam and the race (1 Cor. 15:22)

And as the Calvinist John Murray explains: "Union with Christ is really the central truth of the whole doctrine of salvation."[176]

To further confirm that believers are preserved whether they persevere or not, the very nature of salvation should be considered. Is salvation an instantaneous act of God that fixes the present position and eternal destiny of the individual or is it a process that depends on man's perseverance? Both Arminianism and the Calvinistic teaching of Perseverance of the Saints results in the latter. The nature of salvation is not only a spiritual union (1 Cor. 6:17), but a spiritual birth (1 Pet. 1:23), a spiritual resurrection (John 5:24), a spiritual translation (Col. 1:13), a spiritual creation (2 Cor. 5:17), and a spiritual circumcision (Col. 2:11). Believers have been regenerated (Tit. 3:5), justified (Rom. 5:1), forgiven (Eph. 4:32), accepted (Eph. 1:6), washed (1 Cor. 6:11), indwelt by the Holy Spirit (John 14:17), sealed with the Holy Spirit (Eph. 4:30), adopted (Gal. 4:5), purified (1 Pet. 1:22), anointed (2 Cor. 1:21), reconciled (2 Cor. 5:18), redeemed (Col. 1:14), sanctified (Heb. 10:10), purged (2 Pet. 1:9), and saved (2 Tim. 2:9). We have obtained an inheritance (Eph. 1:11) that is incorruptible, undefiled, and reserved in heaven for us (1 Pet. 1:4). We have eternal life (1 John 5:13). We have passed from death to life (John 5:24). We have been called from darkness to light (1 Pet. 2:9). We have the righteousness of Christ (Rom. 3:22). We have obtained mercy (1 Pet. 2:10) and received grace (Rom. 5:17). We are **"kept by the power of God"** (1 Pet. 1:5), confirmed unto the end (1 Cor. 1:8). We are confident that he who began a work in us will perform it (Phil. 1:6) until we are presented faultless (Jude 24), without spot or wrinkle, holy and without blemish (Eph. 5:27).

The final reason that all born-again believers are preserved is predestination—the Bible variety, not that espoused by Calvinism. As we saw in chapter 7, Calvinism has falsely connected predestination with a sovereign, eternal decree to salvation. But the subject of predestination properly belongs here, rather than under Unconditional Election, since predestination concerns only saved men—not "elect sinners." Predestination is one of the greatest promises and surest proofs of eternal security. Any man who is saved is predestinated by God **"to be conformed to the image of his Son"** (Rom. 8:29):

> **And as we have borne the image of the earthy, we shall also bear the image of the heavenly (1 Cor. 15:49).**
>
> **Who shall change our vile body, that it may be fashioned like unto his glorious body, according to the working whereby he is able even to subdue all things unto himself (Phil. 3:21).**
>
> **Beloved, now are we the sons of God, and it doth not yet appear what we shall be: but we know that, when he shall appear, we shall be like him; for we shall see him as he is (1 John 3:2).**

Predestination is a biblical doctrine, it has just been misapplied by the Calvinists—with dreadful consequences.

In spite of the monumental abundance of evidence for eternal security, both Arminians and Calvinists claim that a man must continue believing throughout his life in order to be saved.[177] Both hastily refer to 2 Timothy 2:12: **"If we suffer, we shall also reign with *him:* if we deny *him,* he also will deny us"** (2 Tim. 2:12).[178] But the verse clearly refers to a millennial reign with Christ. The next verse, however, is devastating to both the Calvinistic and Arminian views of eternal security: **"If we believe not, *yet* he abideth faithful: he cannot deny himself"** (2 Tim. 2:13). Our preservation depends on the faithfulness of Jesus Christ, not our perseverance. Jesus Christ would have to deny himself to change our present position, for we are in him (Phil. 1:1), and not only can no man pluck us out of his hand (John 10:28), we are part of his hand (Eph. 5:30). Since Jesus Christ **"is our life"** (Col. 3:4), our everlasting life is intrinsically connected with the eternal life of Jesus Christ: **"Yet a little while, and the world seeth me no more; but ye see me: because I live, ye shall live also"** (John 14:19). But if salvation is secure regardless of a man's perseverance in the faith, will not men turn **"the grace of our God into**

lasciviousness," (Jude 14)? Doesn't this teaching lead to antinomianism? Although modern Calvinists are always quick to charge their opponents with antinomianism, as we saw in chapter 1, it is the Calvinists themselves who have historically been identified with this teaching, not their opponents.

Arminius

As we have seen throughout this work, Arminius was an orthodox Dutch Reformed theologian whose only real fault (if it be considered a fault) was to disagree with the established doctrines of Calvinism. But as we have seen in chapter 1 of this work, Arminianism has been charged with every heresy imaginable. So what has particularly given Arminius a bad name is not necessarily his theology but the theology of some of his so-called followers. Mention the term *Arminianism* today and the first thing that comes to mind is the doctrine of conditional security; that is, the teaching that one can lose his salvation unless he does something. But as admitted by honest Calvinists, Arminius did not believe this teaching.[179] And contrary to what Calvinists would have us believe, this is in many cases the only thing that would render an "Arminian" unorthodox. So because Arminius has been so misrepresented by both Calvinists and Arminians, a look will be necessary at the teachings of Arminius on the subject of perseverance. And although Arminius' sentiments may not be exactly in accord with what is today referred to as eternal security, upon further examination it will be seen that Arminius held precisely the same views of perseverance as any Calvinist of his day.

To begin with, Arminius gives a historical summation of the doctrine of perseverance:

> The opinion which DENIES, "that true believers and regenerate persons are either capable of falling away, or actually do fall away, from the faith totally and finally," was never, from the very times of the Apostles down to the present day, accounted by the church as a catholic verity: Neither has that which AFFIRMS the contrary ever been reckoned as an heretical opinion; nay, that which affirms it possible for believers to fall away from the faith, has always had more supporters in the church of Christ, than that which denies its possibility or its

actually occurring.[180]

Next, he give his sentiments on assurance:

> Since God promises eternal life to all who believe in Christ, it is impossible for him who believes, and who knows that he believes, to doubt of his own salvation, unless he doubts of this willingness of God. But God does not require *him to be better assured of his individual salvation* as a duty which must be performed to himself or to Christ; but it is a consequence of that promise, by which God engages to bestow eternal life on him who believes.[181]

> With regard to the certainty of salvation, my opinion is, that it is possible for him who believes in Jesus Christ to be certain and persuaded, and, *if his heart condemn him not*, that he is now in reality assured, *that he is a Son of God, and stands in the grace of Jesus Christ.* Such a certainty is wrought in the mind, as well by the action of the Holy Spirit inwardly actuating the believer and by the fruits of faith,—as from his own conscience, and the testimony of God's Spirit witnessing together with his conscience. I also believe, that it is possible for such a person, with an assured confidence in the grace of God and his mercy in Christ, to depart out of this life, and to appear before the throne of grace, without any anxious fear or terrific dread.[182]

Concerning actual perseverance, Arminius stated:

> My sentiments respecting the Perseverance of the Saints are, That those persons who have been grafted into Christ by true faith, and have thus been made partakers of his life-giving Spirit, possess *sufficient powers* to fight against Satan, sin, the world and their own flesh, and to gain the victory over these enemies,—yet not without the assistance of the grace of the same Holy Spirit.—Jesus Christ also by his Spirit assists them in all their temptations, and affords them the ready aid of his hand; and, provided they stand prepared for the battle, implore his help, and be not wanting to themselves, Christ preserves them from falling: So that it is not possible for them, by any of the cunning craftiness or power of Satan, to be either seduced or dragged out of the hands of Christ. But I think it is useful and will be quite necessary in our first convention, to institute a diligent enquiry from the Scriptures, Whether it is not possible

> for some individuals through negligence to desert the commencement of their existence in Christ, to cleave again to the present evil world, to decline from the sound doctrine which was once delivered to them, to lose a good conscience, and to cause Divine grace to be ineffectual. Though I here openly and ingenuously affirm, I never taught that a *true believer can either totally or finally fall away from the faith, and perish*; yet I will not conceal, that there are passages of Scripture which seem to me to wear this aspect; and those answers to them which I have been permitted to see, are not of such a kind as to approve themselves on all points to my understanding. On the other hand, certain passages are produced for the contrary doctrine which are worthy of much consideration.[183]

So Arminius, rather than wresting the Scripture to prove a preconceived notion, very correctly admits that there are certain passages of Scripture which *seem* to teach that a man could lose his salvation.

The followers of Arminius, to offset the superstitions of Calvinism, departed slightly from the views of Arminius, as can be seen by the fifth article of the Remonstrance:

> That those who are incorporated into Christ by a true faith, and have thereby become partakers of his life-giving Spirit, have thereby full power to strive against Satan, sin, the world, and their own flesh, and to win the victory; it being well understood that it is ever through the assisting grace of the Holy Ghost; and that Jesus Christ assists them through his Spirit in all temptations, extends to them his hand, and if only they are ready for the conflict, and desire his help, and are not inactive, keeps them from falling, so that they, by no craft or power of Satan, can be misled nor plucked out of Christ's hands, according to the Word of Christ, John x. 28: 'Neither shall any man pluck them out of my hand.' But whether they are capable, through negligence, of forsaking again the first beginnings of their life in Christ, of again returning to this present evil world, of turning away from the holy doctrine which was delivered them, of losing a good conscience, of becoming devoid of grace, that must be more particularly determined out of the Holy Scripture, before we ourselves can teach it with the full persuasion of our minds.

By the time of the Synod of Dort, the Arminians had further

departed from the position of Arminius, as seen by a selection from the fourth article of their Opinions presented at the synod:

> 3. True believers can fall from true faith and fall into such sins as cannot be consistent with true and justifying faith; and not only can this happen, but it also not infrequently occurs.
> 4. True believers can through their own fault fall into horrible sins and blasphemies, persevere and die in the same: and accordingly they can finally fall away and go lost.

Unfortunately, the term *Arminianism* is today intrinsically connected with the doctrine of conditional security. So what has given Arminius a bad name is not his theology but the theology of his so-called followers. And as concluded in chapter 4, they have forfeited the privilege of wearing the name *Arminian*. They have departed much further from him than he would ever condone.

The Other Side of Perseverance of the Saints

Pink laments that present-day evangelists tell their hearers that "salvation is by grace and is received as a free gift; that Christ has done everything *for the sinner,* and nothing remains but for him to 'believe'—to trust in the infinite merits of His blood."[184] Pink is implying that salvation is some kind of process instead of an instantaneous act. But this is exactly what Shank the Arminian says: "To think of the new birth exclusively as a transformation wrought by the Spirit at the moment of conversion is to have an inadequate concept of the doctrine."[185] The argument is made by both Calvinists and Arminians that we are saved "from our sins" not "in our sins."[186] Gerstner claims this would be "perseverance of the sinners, not perseverance of the saints."[187] This makes salvation an ongoing process. But in the Bible, God, **"even when we were dead in sins, hath quickened us together with Christ"** (Eph. 2:5). This establishes once again that the other side of Perseverance of the Saints is Arminianism. Another facet of the other side of Perseverance of the Saints is a distortion of the true doctrine of the Saint's preservation by God. Calvinists not only reject the idea that the Christian is preserved in salvation regardless of his perseverance, they apply the term *preservation* in an unscriptural manner, as demonstrated by Best: "The chosen one will be preserved by God's providence until he does believe."[188] God doesn't preserve the "elect" for the simple reason that there is no such thing as God's "elect" chosen by a sovereign, eternal decree.

One reason for this misconception about eternal security is that the Calvinist feels that if a man does not persevere then he somehow infringes on the sovereignty and faithfulness of God. Even Shank the Arminian recognized this, as seen in his response to a Calvinist: "Berkouwer's difficulty stems from his erroneous assumption that the faithfulness of God ensures that we, too, must inevitably prove faithful."[189] But in spite of the other four points of Calvinism, Calvinists make perseverance depend on something a man does:

> God preserves His people in this world through their perseverance.[190]
>
> We hold that perseverance is a duty incumbent upon the saints, and that they perform this duty through Divine Grace.[191]
>
> There is no perseverance without man's working out His own salvation.[192]
>
> The only proof I have that he preserves me is that by his grace, I am enabled to persevere.[193]

To say at the same time that salvation depends on a man's perseverance and that this perseverance is something he does is nothing but the very doctrine that Calvinists rail against: Arminianism. But as the Calvinist Eddie Garrett related about perseverance: "We are to 'work out' our salvation. See Phil. 2:12. But how can you 'work out' something you do not have? But this can be neglected! All of this implies clearly that there is the possibility that some children of God may not persevere in the truth. If these verses do not teach this then words have no meaning."[194]

Just like the denial of free will, Perseverance of the Saints is an outgrowth of the Reformation concern that it would produce moral laxity. Calvinists are correct in maintaining that "a mere profession of faith saves no one."[195] It is also certainly true that "mere church membership, of course, is no guarantee that the persons are real Christians."[194] But according to Pink, even the salvation of Calvinists is questionable: "To be a staunch and sound 'Calvinist' is NO evidence one is regenerate."[197] The Calvinists' response to moral laxity in the Church is to maintain that only those who persevere are truly saved: "One of the proofs that we are genuinely saved is that our faith will persevere to the end of our lives."[198] The other side of Perseverance of the Saints contains a dearth of Bible doctrine on subjects like the Judgment Seat of Christ, God's discipline of the believer in this life, and the gain or loss of rewards in the next. Although Christians who are justified cannot be condemned (Rom. 8:33-34), and Christians who are born again cannot be unborn (John 3:4), they are still commanded:

> **Wherefore let him that thinketh he standeth take heed lest he fall (1 Cor. 10:12).**
>
> **Nevertheless the foundation of God standeth sure, having this seal, The Lord knoweth them that are his. And, Let every one that nameth the name of Christ depart from iniquity (2 Tim. 2:19).**

The error of the Calvinists is in equating God's *preserving* with the saint's *persevering*. But being *preserved* in salvation is not the same thing as outwardly *persevering* in the faith. **"Man looketh on the outward appearance, but the LORD looketh on the heart"** (1 Sam. 16:7).

The other side of Perseverance of the Saints also contains a false view of assurance of salvation, for it makes salvation dependent on election, not receiving Jesus Christ. Coppes elucidates: "The only proper fount of the assurance of getting to heaven (glorification) is the doctrine of predestination."[199] And how does one know he is one of the "elect"?

> The only evidence of election is effectual calling, that is, the production of holiness. And the only evidence of the genuineness of this call and the certainty of our perseverance, is a patient continuance in well-doing.[200]
>
> We can never know that we are elected of God to eternal life except by manifesting in our lives the fruits of election—faith and virtue, knowledge and temperance, patience and godliness, love of brethren. It is idle to seek assurance of election outside of holiness of life.[201]
>
> Holiness, because it is the necessary product, is therefore the

sure sign of election.[202]

This is pure Arminianism. Shank the Arminian says the same thing: "There is no valid assurance of election and final salvation for any man, apart from deliberate perseverance in faith."[202] He also recognized that Calvin and Charles Hodge reached the same conclusion.[203] So the only perceivable difference between a Calvinist and an Arminian when it comes to assurance is that the Arminian requires holiness to prove salvation while the Calvinist demands holiness to demonstrate election, which then substantiates salvation.

The Perseverance of the Saints defoliates the entire TULIP. If a man's salvation depends on his perseverance then his Total Depravity would only be partial, or else he might have the Total Inability to persevere. If a man's salvation depends on his perseverance then he could never be the subject of Unconditional Election, for salvation would be conditional. If a man's salvation depends on his perseverance, a Limited Atonement was a failure, for some of the "elect" may not persevere long enough to benefit from it. If a man's salvation depends on his perseverance, Irresistible Grace could never have been applied, for the grace of God would prove to be resistible. If a man's salvation depends on his perseverance, Perseverance of the Saints is impossible, for no one *will* or *can* ever persevere in the absolute holiness which God requires. We have seen that the word of God is not bound by Total Depravity, Unconditional Election, Limited Atonement, and Irresistible Grace. We can now add Perseverance of the Saints to the list of the philosophical speculations and theological implications of the other side of Calvinism.

Appendix 1
THE REMONSTRANCE

Article I

That God, by an eternal, unchangeable purpose in Jesus Christ his Son, before the foundation of the world, hath determined, out of the fallen, sinful race of men, to save in Christ, for Christ's sake, and through Christ, those who, through the grace of the Holy Ghost, shall believe on this his Son Jesus, and shall persevere in this faith and obedience of faith, through this grace, even to the end; and, on the other hand, to leave the incorrigible and unbelieving in sin and under wrath, and to condemn them as alienate from Christ, according to the word of the gospel in John iii. 36: 'He that believeth on the Son hath everlasting life: and he that believeth not the Son shall not see life; but the wrath of God abideth on him,' and according to other passages of Scripture also.

Article II

That, agreeably thereunto, Jesus Christ, the Saviour of the world, died for all men and for every man, so that he has obtained for them all, by his death on the cross, redemption and the forgiveness of sins; yet that no one actually enjoys this forgiveness of sins except the believer, according to the word of the gospel of John iii. 16: 'God so loved the world that he gave his only-begotten Son, that whosoever believeth in him should not perish, but have everlasting life.' And in the First Epistle of John ii. 2: 'And he is the propitiation for our sins; and not for ours only, but also for the sins of the whole world.'

Article III

That man has not saving grace of himself, nor of the energy of his free will, in as much as he, in the state of apostasy and sin, can of and by himself neither think, will, nor do any thing that is truly good (such as saving faith eminently is); but that it is needful that he be born again of God in Christ, through his Holy Spirit, and renewed in understanding, inclination, or will, and all his powers, in order that he may rightly understand, think, will, and effect what is truly good, according to the Word of Christ, John xv. 5: 'Without me ye can do nothing.'

Article IV

That this grace of God is the beginning, continuance, and accomplishment of all good, even to this extent, that the regenerate man himself, without prevenient or assisting, awakening, following and co-operative grace, can neither think, will, nor do good, nor withstand any temptations to evil; so that all good deeds or movements, that can be conceived, must be ascribed to the grace of God in Christ. But as respects the mode of the operation of this grace, it is not irresistible, in as much as it is written concerning many, that they have resisted the Holy Ghost, Acts vii., and elsewhere in many places.

Article V

That those who are incorporated into Christ by a true faith, and have thereby become partakers of his life-giving Spirit, have thereby full power to strive against Satan, sin, the world, and their own flesh, and to win the victory; it being well understood that it is ever through the assisting grace of the Holy Ghost; and that Jesus Christ assists them through his Spirit in all temptations, extends to them his hand, and if only they are ready for the conflict, and desire his help, and are not inactive, keeps them from falling, so that they, by no craft or power of Satan, can be misled nor plucked out of Christ's hands, according to the Word of Christ, John x. 28: 'Neither shall any man pluck them out of my hand.' But whether they are capable, through negligence, of forsaking again the first beginnings of their life in Christ, of again returning to this present evil world, of turning away from the holy doctrine which was delivered them, of losing a good conscience, of becoming devoid of grace, that must be more particularly determined out of the Holy Scripture, before we ourselves can teach it with the full persuasion of our minds.

Appendix 2
THE COUNTER-REMONSTRANCE

1. As in Adam the whole human race, created in the image of God, has with Adam fallen into sin and thus become so corrupt that all men are conceived and born in sin and thus are by nature children of wrath, lying dead in their trespasses so that there is within them no more power to convert themselves truly unto God and to believe in Christ than a corpse has power to raise itself from the dead; so God draws out of this condemnation and delivers a certain number of men who in his eternal and immutable counsel He has chosen out of mere grace, according to the good pleasure of his will, unto salvation in Christ, passing by the others in his just judgment and leaving them in their sins.

2. that not only adults who believe in Christ and accordingly walk worthy of the gospel are to be reckoned as God's elect children, but also the children of the covenant so long as they do not in their conduct manifest the contrary; and that therefore believing parents, when their children die in infancy, have no reason to doubt the salvation of these their children.

3. that God in his election has not looked to the faith or conversion of his elect, nor to the right use of his gifts, as the grounds of election; but that on the contrary He in his eternal and immutable counsel has purposed and decreed to bestow faith and perseverance in godliness and thus to save those whom He according to his good pleasure has chosen to salvation.

4. that to this end He has first of all presented and given to them his only-begotten Son Jesus Christ, whom He delivered up to the death of the cross in order to save his elect, so that, although the suffering of Christ as that of the only-begotten and unique Son of God is sufficient unto the atonement of the sins of all men, nevertheless the same, according to the counsel and decree of God, has its efficacy unto reconciliation and forgiveness of sins only in the elect and true believer.

5. that furthermore to the same end God the Lord has his holy gospel preached, and that the Holy Spirit externally through the preaching of that same gospel and internally through a special grace works so powerfully in the hearts of God's elect, that He illumines their minds, transforms and renews their wills, removing the heart of stone and giving them a heart of flesh, in such a manner that by these means they not only receive power to

convert themselves and believe but also actually and willingly do repent and believe.

6. that those whom God has decreed to save are not only once so enlightened, regenerated and renewed in order to believe in Christ and convert themselves to God, but that they by the same power of the Holy Spirit by which they were converted to God without any contribution of themselves are in like manner continually supported and preserved; so that, although many weaknesses of the flesh cleave to them as long as they are in this life and are engaged in a continual struggle between flesh and Spirit and also sometimes fall into grievous sins, nevertheless this same Spirit prevails in this struggle, nor permitting that God's elect by the corruption of the flesh should so resist the Spirit of sanctification that this would at any time be extinguished in them, and that in consequence they could completely or finally lose the true faith which was once bestowed on them and the Spirit of adoption as God's children which they had once received.

7. that nevertheless the true believers find no excuse in this teaching to pursue carelessly the lusts of the flesh, since it is impossible that those who by a true faith are ingrafted into Christ should not produce the fruits of thankfulness; but on the contrary the more they assure themselves and feel that God works in them both to will and to do according to his good pleasure, the more they persist in working their own salvation with fear and trembling, since they know that this is the only means by which it pleases God to keep them standing and to bring them to salvation. For this reason He also employs in his Word all manner of warnings and threatenings, not in order to cause them to despair or doubt their salvation but rather to awaken in them a childlike fear by observing the weakness of their flesh in which they would surely perish, unless the Lord keep them standing in his undeserved grace, which is the sole cause and ground of their perseverance; so that, although He warns them in his Word to watch and pray, they nevertheless do not have this of themselves that they desire God's help and lack nothing, but only from the same Spirit who by a special grace prepares them for this and thus also powerfully keeps them standing.

Appendix 3
THE OPINIONS OF THE REMONSTRANTS

I. The opinion of the Remonstrants, which they in conscience have thus far considered and still consider to be in harmony with the Word of God, concerning the first Article, of the decree of Predestination, is this:

1. God has not decided to elect anyone to eternal life, or to reject anyone from eternal life, earlier in order than he has decreed to create them, without respect to any preceding obedience or disobedience, according to His good pleasure, in order to demonstrate the glory of His mercy and justice, or His absolute might and dominion.

2. Since God's decree, both concerning the salvation and the perdition of every man is not a decree of the end which He absolutely intended, therefore it follows also that the same decrees are not subordinate to such means by which the elect and the reprobate are efficaciously and inevitably led to their ordained end.

3. Therefore God has also with this purpose not created in the one Adam all men in the state of rectitude, has not ordained the fall and the permission of it, has not deprived Adam of the necessary and sufficient grace, does also not cause the Gospel to be preached and call men externally, and does not give them certain gifts of the Holy Spirit, in order that these should be means by which He should bring some of them unto life, but deprive others of the benefit of life. Christ, the Mediator, is not only the executor of election, but also the foundation of this same decree of election. The cause that some are effectually called, justified, persevere in the faith, and are glorified, is not that they have been absolutely chosen unto eternal life. That also others are left in the fall, that Christ is not given to them, that they are either not called at all or ineffectually called, are hardened and condemned is not the reason why they are absolutely rejected from eternal salvation.

4. God has not decreed without intervening actual sins to leave by far the greater part of men, excluded from all hope of salvation, in the fall.

5. God has ordained that Christ should be the atonement for the sins of the whole world, and by virtue of this decree He has decided to justify and to save those who believe in Him, and to provide men with the means

necessary and sufficient unto faith, in such a way as He knows to be befitting of His wisdom and righteousness. But He has in no wise determined, by virtue of an absolute decree, to give Christ, the Mediator, to the elect alone, and through an effectual calling to bestow faith upon, to justify, to preserve in the faith, and to glorify them alone.

6. No one is rejected from eternal life nor from the means sufficient thereto by any absolute antecedent decree, so that the merits of Christ, the calling, and all gifts of the Spirit can be profitable unto salvation for all, and indeed are beneficial, unless they through the abuse of the same turn them unto their perdition; but to unbelief, godlessness, and sins, as means and causes of damnation, no one is ordained

7. The election of particular persons is with regard to the end out of consideration of faith in Jesus Christ and perseverance; but not apart from consideration of faith and of perseverance in the true faith, as a condition required beforehand in the electing.

8. Rejection from eternal life took place after consideration of preceding unbelief and perseverance in unbelief, but not apart from consideration of preceding unbelief and perseverance in unbelief.

9. All children of believers are sanctified in Christ, so that none of them, departing this life before the use of understanding, goes lost. But in no wise are to be reckoned among the number of the reprobate some children of believers who leave this life in their infancy before they have committed any actual sin in their own persons, so that neither the holy bath of baptism nor the prayers of the church could be profitable for them unto salvation.

10. No children of believers who are baptized in the Name of the Father, the Son, and the Holy Spirit, living in the state of their infancy, are reckoned among the reprobate by a complete decree.

II. The opinion of the Remonstrants concerning the second Article, which deals with the universality of the merit of the death of Christ, is this:

1. The price of salvation, which Christ offered to God, His Father, is not only in and by itself sufficient for the redemption of the whole human race, but was also paid for all and every man, according to the decree, the will, and the grace of God the Father; and therefore no one is definitely excluded from the communion of the benefits of the death of Christ by an absolute and antecedent decree of God.

2. Christ, through the merit of His death, has so far reconciled the entire human race to God the Father, that the Father, because of that merit, without prejudice to His righteousness and truth, might make and was willing to make and to establish a new covenant of grace with sinners and damnworthy men.

3. Although Christ has merited reconciliation with God and the forgiveness of sins for all men and every man, nevertheless, according to the new covenant of grace, no one becomes an actual partaker of the benefits by the death of Christ except by faith; nor are sins forgiven to sinners before they actually and truly believe in Christ.

4. Only those are obligated to believe that Christ has died for them for whom Christ has indeed died. But the reprobate, as they are called, for whom Christ has not died, are not obligated to this faith, and can, by reason of their contrary unbelief, not be justly condemned; in fact, if there were such reprobates, they would be obligated to believe that Christ has not died for them.

III. The opinion of the Remonstrants concerning the third and fourth Article, regarding the grace of God and the conversion of man, is this:

1. Man does not have saving grace of himself, nor from the powers of his free will, seeing that he, in the state of sin, can of and by himself neither think, will, or do any good (at least that which is saving good, which is chiefly saving faith); but it is necessary that he be of God, in Christ, through His Holy Spirit, reborn and renewed in understanding, affections, will, and all his powers, in order that he may rightly understand, observe, will and accomplish saving good.

2. Now we hold that the grace of God is not only the beginning, but also the continuance and the completion of everything good, in such a manner that even the regenerate, without this preceding or prevenient, awakening, following and cooperating grace, can neither will nor accomplish the good, nor resist any temptations to evil; all good works and actions which anyone would be able to conceive are to be ascribed to the grace of God.

3. Nevertheless we do not believe that all zeal, care, and diligence exerted to obtain salvation before faith itself and the Spirit of regeneration, are idle and in vain, yea, even much rather harmful to man, but useful and profitable; on the contrary, we hold that to hear God's Word, to be sorry for sins committed, to desire the saving grace of God and the Spirit of regeneration (with which things nevertheless man is able to do nothing without grace) not only are not harmful and unprofitable, but much rather altogether useful and highly necessary in order to obtain faith and the Spirit of renewal.

4. The will, in the state of the fall, before the calling, has no power and freedom to will any good which is saving. Therefore we deny that the freedom to will saving good as well as to will evil belongs to the will in every state.

5. The efficacious grace by which anyone is converted is not

irresistible, and although God through the Word and the inner operation of His Spirit so influences the will that He both bestows the power to believe, or supernatural powers, and indeed causes man to believe; nevertheless man is able of himself to despise this grace, not to believe, and thus to perish through his own fault.

6. Although according to the altogether free will of God the disparity of divine grace may be very great, nevertheless the Holy Spirit bestows, or is ready to bestow, as much grace upon all men and every man to whom God's Word is preached as is sufficient for the furtherance of the conversion of men in its steps; and therefore not only do they obtain sufficient grace unto faith and conversion whom God is said to be willing to save according to the decree of absolute election, but also they who are not actually converted.

7. Man can through the grace of the Holy Spirit do more good than he actually does, and leave undone more evil than he actually leaves undone; and we do not believe that God simply does not will that man do more good than he does, and avoid more evil than he does avoid; and that from eternity it should be precisely decreed by Him that both of these should so take place.

8. All those whom God calls unto salvation, those He calls seriously, that is, with an upright and altogether unfeigned purpose and will to save. And we do not agree with those who hold that God externally calls some whom He does not will to call internally, that is, does not will that they be actually converted, even before they have rejected the grace of the calling.

9. There is not in God such a hidden will which stands over against His will which is revealed in the Word, that He according to that will (that is, the hidden will) does not will the conversion and the salvation of the greater part of those whom He through the Word of the gospel, and according to the revealed will, is seriously calling and inviting unto faith and salvation; neither do we here acknowledge, as some speak, a holy dissimulation, or a double person in God.

10. Nor do we believe that God calls the reprobate, as they are called, to these ends: in order that He should the more harden them, or deprive them of excuse, in order that He should punish them more severely, in order that He should make known their inability, but not in order that they should be converted, believe, and be saved.

11. It is not true that from the power and operation of the secret will, or of the divine decree, everything, not only the good but also the evil, necessarily occurs; so that all those who sin, in consideration of the divine decree, can do nothing but sin; that God would will to decree or to cause the sins of men, their mad, foolish, cruel works, and the sacrilegious blasphemy of His Name; and move the tongues of men to blasphemy, etc.

12. We also hold to be false and horrible that God should in a hidden manner incite men to the sin which He openly forbids; that those who sin

do not act contrary to the true will of God, properly so-called, that what is unrighteous (that is, that which conflicts with His commandment) is in harmony with the will of God, yea, also, that it is according to justice a crime worthy of death to do God's will.

IV. The opinion of the Remonstrants concerning the fifth Article, which speaks of perseverance, is this:

1. The perseverance of believers in the faith is not the outworking of an absolute decree by which God is said to have chosen particular persons, not circumscribed by any condition of obedience.

2. God, the Lord, bestows upon true believers as much grace and powers as He, according to His infinite wisdom deems to be sufficient for perseverance and for overcoming the temptations of the devil, the flesh, and the world; and it is never to be charged to God that they do not persevere.

3. True believers can fall from true faith and fall into such sins as cannot be consistent with true and justifying faith; and not only can this happen, but it also not infrequently occurs.

4. True believers can through their own fault fall into horrible sins and blasphemies, persevere and die in the same: and accordingly they can finally fall away and go lost.

5. Nevertheless we do not believe, though true believers sometimes fall into grave and conscience-devastating sins, that they immediately fall from all hope of conversion, but we acknowledge that it can happen that God according to His abundant mercy, again calls them to conversion through His grace; yea, we believe that this happens not infrequently, although they cannot know with certainty that this surely and indubitably will happen.

6. Therefore we heartily reject the following doctrines, which are daily spread abroad among the people in public writings, as being harmful to piety and good morals; namely: 1) That true believes cannot sin deliberately, but only out of ignorance and weakness. 2) That true believers through no sins can fall from the grace of God. 3) That a thousand sins, yea, all the sins of the whole world, cannot render election invalid; when it is added to this that all men are obligated to believe that they are chosen unto salvation, and therefore cannot fall from election, we present for consideration what a wide door that opens for carnal certainty. 4) That to believers and to the elect no sins, however great and grave they may be, are imputed; yea, that all present and future sins are now forgiven. 5) That true believers, having fallen into corrupt heresies, into grave and shameful sins, such as adultery and murder, on account of which the Church, according to the institution of Christ, is obligated to testify that she cannot tolerate them in her external fellowship, and that they shall

have no part in the kingdom of Christ, unless they repent, nevertheless cannot totally and finally fall from the faith.

7. A true believer, as for the present time he can be assured of the uprightness of his faith and of his conscience, so he can and must for that time also be assured of his salvation and of the saving favor of God toward him; and here we reject the opinion of the papists.

8. A true believer can and must be certain for the future that he, granted intervening, watching, praying, and other holy exercises, can persevere in the true faith, and that the grace of God to persevere will never be lacking to him; but we do not see how he may be assured that he will never neglect his duty in the future, but in the works of faith, piety, and love, as befits a believer, persevere in this school of christian warfare. Neither do we deem it necessary that the believer should be certain of this.

Appendix 4

THE CANONS OF DORT

I. OF DIVINE PREDESTINATION

1. As all men have sinned in Adam, lie under the curse, and are deserving of eternal death, God would have done no injustice by leaving them all to perish, and delivering them over to condemnation on account of sin, according to the words of the apostle, Rom. 3:19, "that every mouth may be stopped, and all the world may become guilty before God." And verse 23: "for all have sinned, and come short of the glory of God." And Rom. 6:23: "for the wages of sin is death."

2. But in this the love of God was manifested, that he sent his only begotten Son into the world, that whosoever believeth on him should not perish, but have everlasting life. 1 John 4:9. John 3:16.

3. And that men may be brought to believe, God mercifully sends the messengers of these most joyful tidings, to whom he will and what time he pleaseth; by whose ministry men are called to repentance and faith in Christ crucified. Rom 10:14,15. "How then shall they call on him in whom they have not believed? And how shall they believe in him of whom they have not heard? And how shall they hear without a preacher? And how shall they preach except they be sent?"

4. The wrath of God abideth upon those who believe not this gospel. But such as receive it, and embrace Jesus the Savior by a true and living faith, are by him delivered from the wrath of God, and from destruction, and have the gift of eternal life conferred upon them.

5. The cause or guilt of this unbelief as well as of all other sins, is no wise in God, but in man himself; whereas faith in Jesus Christ, and salvation through him is the free gift of God, as it is written: "By grace ye are saved through faith, and that not of yourselves, it is the gift of God," Eph. 2:8. "And unto it is given in the behalf of Christ, not only to believe on him," etc. Phil. 1:29.

6. That some receive the gift of faith from God, and others do not receive it proceeds from God's eternal decree, "For known unto God are all his works from the beginning of the world," Acts 15:18. "Who worketh all things after the counsel of his will," Eph. 1:11. According to which decree, he graciously softens the hearts of the elect, however obstinate, and inclines them to believe, while he leaves the non-elect in his just judgment to their own wickedness and obduracy. And herein is especially

displayed the profound, the merciful, and at the same time the righteous discrimination between men, equally involved in ruin; or that decree of election and reprobation, revealed in the Word of God, which though men of perverse, impure, and unstable minds wrest to their own destruction, yet to holy and pious souls affords unspeakable consolation.

7. Election is the unchangeable purpose of God, whereby, before the foundation of the world, he hath out of mere grace, according to the sovereign good pleasure of his own will, chosen, from the whole human race, which had fallen through their own fault, from their primitive state of rectitude, into sin and destruction, a certain number of persons to redemption in Christ, whom he from eternity appointed the Mediator and Head of the elect, and the foundation of Salvation. This elect number, though by nature neither better nor more deserving than others, but with them involved in one common misery, God hath decreed to give to Christ, to be paid by him and effectually to call and draw them to his communion by his Word and Spirit, to bestow upon them true faith, justification and sanctification; and having powerfully preserved them in the fellowship of his Son, finally, to glorify them for the demonstration of his mercy, and for the praise of his glorious grace; as it is written: "According as he hath chosen us in him, before the foundation of the world that we should be holy, and without blame before him in love; having predestinated us unto the adoption of children by Jesus Christ to himself, according to the good pleasure of his will, to the praise of the glory of his grace, wherein he hath made us accepted in the beloved." Eph. 1:4, 5, 6. And elsewhere: "Whom he did predestinate, them he also called, and whom he called, them he also justified, and whom he justified them he also glorified." Rom. 8:30

8. There are not various decrees of election, but one and the same decree respecting all those, who shall be saved, both under the Old and New Testament: since the Scripture declares the good pleasure, purpose and counsel of the divine will to be one, according to which he hath chosen us from eternity, both to grace and glory, to salvation and the way of salvation, which he hath ordained that we should walk therein.

9. This election was not founded upon foreseen faith, and the obedience of faith, holiness, or any other good quality or disposition in man, as the pre-requisite, cause or condition on which it depended; but men are chosen to faith and to the obedience of faith, holiness, etc., therefore election is the fountain of every saving good; from which proceed faith, holiness, and the other gifts of salvation, and finally eternal life itself, as its fruits and effects, according to that of the apostle: "He hath chosen us (not because we were) but that we should be holy, and without blame, before him in love," Eph 1:4.

10. The good pleasure of God is the sole cause of this gracious election; which does not consist herein, that out of all possible qualities and actions of men God has chosen some as a condition of salvation; but that he was pleased out of the common mass of sinners to adopt some certain persons as a peculiar people to himself, as it is written, "For the

children being not yet born neither having done any good or evil," etc., it was said (namely to Rebecca): "the elder shall serve the younger; as it is written, Jacob have I loved, but Esau have I hated." Rom. 9:11, 12, 13. "And as many as were ordained to eternal life believed." Acts 13:48.

11. And as God himself is most wise, unchangeable, omniscient and omnipotent, so the election made by him can neither be interrupted nor changed, recalled or annulled; neither can the elect be cast away, nor their number diminished.

12. The elect in due time, though in various degrees and in different measures, attain the assurance of this their eternal and unchangeable election, not by inquisitively prying into the secret and deep things of God, but by observing in themselves with a spiritual joy and holy pleasure, the infallible fruits of election pointed out in the Word of God—such as a true faith in Christ, filial fear, a godly sorrow for sin, a hungering and thirsting after righteousness, etc.

13. The sense and certainty of this election afford to the children of God additional matter for daily humiliation before him, for adoring the depth of his mercies, for cleansing themselves, and rendering grateful returns of ardent love to him, who first manifested so great love towards them. The consideration of this doctrine of election is so far from encouraging remission in the observance of the divine commands, or from sinking men in carnal security, that these, in the just judgement of God, are the usual effects of rash presumption, or of idle and wanton trifling with the grace of election, in those who refuse to walk in the ways of the elect.

14. As the doctrine of divine election by the most wise counsel of God, was declared by the prophets, by Christ himself, and by the apostles, and is clearly revealed in the Scriptures, both of the Old and New Testament, so it is still to be published in due time and place in the Church of God, for which it was peculiarly designed, provided it be done with reverence, in the spirit of discretion and piety, for the glory of God's most holy name, and for enlivening and comforting his people, without vainly attempting to investigate the secret ways of the Most High. Acts 20:27; Rom. 11:33, 34; 12:3; Heb. 6:17, 18.

15. What peculiarly tends to illustrate and recommend to us the eternal and unmerited grace of election, is the express testimony of sacred Scripture, that not all, but some only are elected, while others are passed by in the eternal election of God; whom God, out of his sovereign, most just, irreprehensible and unchangeable good pleasure, hath decreed to leave in the common misery into which they have willfully plunged themselves, and not to bestow upon them saving faith and the grace of conversion; but leaving them in his just judgement to follow their own ways, at last for the declaration of his justice, to condemn and perish them forever, not only on account of their unbelief, but also for all their other sins. And this is the decree of reprobation which by no means makes God the author of sin (the very thought of which is blasphemy), but declares him to be an awful,

irreprehensible, and righteous judge and avenger thereof.

16. Those who do not yet experience a lively faith in Christ, and an assured confidence of soul, peace of conscience, an earnest endeavor after filial obedience, and glorying in God through Christ, efficaciously wrought in them, and do nevertheless persist in the use of the means which God has appointed for working these graces in us, ought not to be alarmed at the mention of reprobation, nor to rank themselves among the reprobate, but diligently to persevere in the use of means, and with ardent desires, devoutly and humbly to wait for a season of richer grace. Much less cause have they to be terrified by the doctrine of reprobation, who, though they seriously desire to be turned to God, to please him only, and to be delivered from the body of death, cannot yet reach that measure of holiness and faith to which they aspire; since a merciful God has promised that he will not quench the smoking flax, nor break the bruised reed. But this doctrine is justly terrible to those, who, regardless of God and of the Savior Jesus Christ, have wholly given themselves up to the cares of the world, and the pleasures of the flesh, so long as they are not seriously converted to God.

17. Since we are to judge of the will of God from his Word, which testifies that the children of believers are holy, not by nature, but in virtue of the covenant of grace, in which they, together with the parents, are comprehended, godly parents have no reason to doubt of the election and salvation of their children, whom it pleaseth God to call out of this life in their infancy.

18. To those who murmur at the free grace of election, and just severity of reprobation, we answer with the apostle: "Nay, but, O man, who art thou that repliest against God?" Romans 9:30, and quote the language of our Savior: "Is it not lawful for me to do what I will with mine own?" Matthew 20:15. And therefore with holy adoration of these mysteries, we exclaim in the words of the apostle: "O the depth of the riches both of the wisdom and knowledge of God! how unsearchable are his judgements, and his ways past finding out! For who hath known the mind of the Lord, or who hath been his counsellor? or who hath first given to him, and it shall be recompensed to him again? For of him, and through him, and to him are all things: to whom be glory for ever.—Amen."

> The true doctrine concerning *Election* and *Rejection* having been explained, the Synod *rejects* the errors of those:

1. Who teach: That the will of God to save those who would believe and persevere in faith and in the obedience of faith, is the whole and entire decree of election unto salvation, and that nothing else concerning this decree has been revealed in God's Word. For these deceive the simple and plainly contradict the Scriptures, which declare that God will not only save those who will believe, but that he has also from eternity chosen certain particular persons to whom above others he in time will grant both faith in

Christ and perseverance; as it is written: "I manifested thy name unto the men whom thou gavest me out of the world," John 17:6. "And as many as were ordained to eternal life believed," Acts 13:48. And: "Even as he chose us in him before the foundation of the world, that we should be holy and without blemish before him in love," Eph. 1:4.

2. Who teach: That there are various kinds of election of God unto eternal life: the one general and indefinite, the other particular and definite; and that the latter in turn is either incomplete, revocable, non-decisive and conditional, or complete, irrevocable, decisive and absolute. Likewise: that there is one election unto faith, and another unto salvation, so that election can be unto justifing faith, without being a decisive election unto salvation. For this is a fancy of men's minds, invented regardless of the Scriptures, whereby the doctrine of election is corrupted, and this golden chain of our salvation is broken: "And whom he foreordained, them he also called; and whom he called, them he also justified; and whom he justified, them he also glorifed." Rom. 8:30.

3. Who teach: That the good pleasure and purpose of God, of which Scripture makes mention in the doctrine of election, does not consist in this, that God chose certain persons rather than others, but in this that he choose out of all possible conditions (among which are also the works of the law), or out of the whole order of things, the act of faith which from its very nature is undeserving, as well as its incomplete obedience, as a condition of salvation, and that he would graciously consider this in itself as a complete obedience and count it worthy of the reward of eternal life. For by this injurious error the pleasure of God and the merits of Christ are made of none effect, and men are drawn away by useless questions from the truth of gracious justification and from the simplicity of Scripture, and this declaration of the Apostle is charged as untrue: "Who saved us, and called us with a holy calling, not according to our works, but according to his own purpose and grace, which was given us in Christ Jesus before times eternal." 2 Tim. 1:9.

4. Who teach: That in the election unto faith this condition is beforehand demanded, viz., that man should use the light of nature aright, be pious, humble, meek, and fit for eternal life, as if on these things election were in any way dependent. For this savors of the teaching of Pelagius, and is opposed to the doctrine of the apostle, when he writes: "Among whom we also all once lived in the lust of our flesh, doing the desires of the flesh and of the mind, and were by nature children of wrath, even as the rest; but God being rich in mercy, for his great love wherewith he loved us, even when we were dead through our trespasses, made us alive together with Christ (by grace have ye been saved), and raised us up with him, and made us to sit with him in heavenly places, in Christ Jesus; that in the ages to come he might show the exceeding riches of his grace in kindness towards us in Christ Jesus; for by grace have ye been saved through faith; and that not of yourselves, it is the gift of God; not of works, that no man should glory," Eph. 2:3-9.

5. Who teach: That the incomplete and non-decisive election of particular persons to salvation occurred because of a foreseen faith, conversion, holiness, godliness, which either began or continued for some time; but that the complete and decisive election occurred because of foreseen perseverance unto the end in faith, conversion, holiness and godliness; and that this is the gracious and evangelical worthiness, for the sake of which he who is chosen, is more worthy than he who is not chosen; and that therefore faith, the obedience of faith, holiness, godliness and perseverance are not fruits of the unchangeable election unto glory, but are conditions, which, being required beforehand, were foreseen as being met by those who will be fully elected, and are causes without which the unchangeable election to glory does not occur. This is repugnant to the entire Scripture, which constantly inculcates this and similar declaration: Election is not out of works, but of him that calleth. Rom. 9:11. "And as many as were ordained to eternal life believed," Acts 13:48. "He chose us in him before the foundation of the world, that we should be holy," Eph. 1:4. "Ye did not choose me, but I chose you," John 15:16. "But if it be of grace, it is no more of works," Rom. 11:6. "Herein is love, not that we loved God, but that he loved us, and sent his Son," 1 John 4:10.

6. Who teach: That not every election unto salvation is unchangeable, but that some of the elect, any decree of God notwithstanding, can yet perish and do indeed perish. By which gross error they make God to be changeable, and destroy the comfort which the godly obtain out of the firmness of their election, and contradict the Holy Scripture which teaches, that the elect can not be led astray. Matt. 24:24; that Christ does not lose those whom the Father gave him. John 6:39; and that God hath also glorified those whom he foreordained, called and justified. Rom. 8:30.

7. Who teach: That there is in this life no fruit and no consciousness of the unchangeable election to glory, nor any certainty, except that which depends on a changeable and uncertain condition. For not only is it absurd to speak of an uncertain certainty, but also contrary to the experience of the saints, who by virtue of the consciousness of their election rejoice with the Apostle and praise this favor of God, Eph. 1; who according to Christ's admonition rejoice with his disciples that their names are written in heaven, Luke 10:20; who also place the consciousness of their election over against the fiery darts of the devil, asking: "Who shall lay anything to the charge of God's elect?" Rom. 8:33.

8. Who teach: That God, simply by virtue of his righteous will, did not decide either to leave anyone in the fall of Adam and in the common state of sin and condemnation, or to pass anyone by in the communication of grace which is necessary for faith and conversion. For this is firmly decreed: "He hath mercy on whom he will, and whom he will he hardeneth," Rom. 9:18. And also this: "Unto you it is given to know the mysteries of the kingdom of heaven, but to them it is not given," Matt. 13:11. Likewise: "I thank thee, O Father, Lord of heaven and earth, that

thou didst hide these things from the wise and understanding, and didst reveal them unto babes; yea, Father, for so it was well-pleasing in thy sight," Matt. 11:25, 26.

9. Who teach: That the reason why God sends the gospel to one people rather than to another is not merely and solely the good pleasure of God, but rather the fact that one people is better and worthier than another to whom the gospel is not communicated. For this Moses denies, addressing the people of Israel as follows: "Behold unto Jehovah thy God belongeth heaven and the heaven of heavens, the earth, with all that is therein. Only Jehovah had a delight in thy fathers to love them, and he chose their seed after them, even you above all peoples, as at this day," Deut. 10:14, 15. And Christ said: "Woe unto thee, Chorazin! woe unto thee, Bethsaida! for if the mighty works had been done in Tyre and Sidon which were done in you, they would have repented long ago in sackcloth and ashes," Matt 11:21.

II. OF THE DEATH OF CHRIST, AND THE REDEMPTION OF MEN THEREBY

1. God is not only supremely merciful, but also supremely just. And his justice requires (as he hath revealed himself in his Word), that our sins committed against his infinite majesty should be punished, not only with temporal, but with eternal punishment, both in body and soul; which we cannot escape, unless satisfaction be made to the justice of God.

2. Since therefore we are unable to make that satisfaction in our own persons, or to deliver ourselves from the wrath of God, he hath been pleased in his infinite mercy to give his only begotten Son, for our surety, who was made sin, and become a curse for us and in our stead, that he might make satisfaction to divine justice on our behalf.

3. The death of the Son of God is the only and most perfect sacrifice and satisfaction for sin; and is of infinite worth and value, abundantly sufficient to expiate the sins of the whole world.

4. This death derives its infinite value and dignity from these considerations, because the person who submitted to it was not only really man, and perfectly holy, but also the only begotten Son of God, of the same eternal and infinite essence with the Father and the Holy Spirit, which qualifications were necessary to constitute him a Savior for us; and because it was attended with a sense of the wrath and curse of God due to us for sin.

5. Moreover, the promise of the gospel is, that whosoever believeth in Christ crucified, shall not perish, but have everlasting life. This promise, together with the command to repent and believe, ought to be declared and published to all nations, and to all persons promiscuously and without distinction, to whom God out of his good pleasure sends the gospel.

6. And, whereas many who are called by the gospel, do not repent, nor believe in Christ, but perish in unbelief; this is not owing to any defect

or insufficiency in the sacrifice offered by Christ upon the cross, but is wholly to be imputed to themselves.

7. But as many as truly believe, and are delivered and saved from sin and destruction through the death of Christ, are indebted for this benefit solely to the grace of God, given them in Christ from everlasting, and not to any merit of their own.

8. For this was the sovereign counsel, and most gracious will and purpose of God the Father, that the quickening and saving efficacy of the most precious death of his Son should extend to all the elect, for bestowing upon them alone the gift of justifying faith, thereby to bring them infallibly to salvation: that is, it was the will of God, that Christ by the blood of the cross, whereby he confirmed the new covenant, should effectually redeem out of every people, tribe, nation, and language, all those, and those only, who were from eternity chosen to salvation, and given to him by the Father; that he should confer upon them faith, which together with all the other saving gifts of the Holy Spirit, he purchased for them by his death; should purge them from all sin, both original and actual, whether committed before or after believing; and having faithfully preserved them even to the end, should at last bring them free from every spot and blemish to the enjoyment of glory in his own presence forever.

9. This purpose proceeding from everlasting love towards the elect, has from the beginning of the world to this day been powerfully accomplished, and will henceforward still continue to be accomplished, notwithstanding all the ineffectual opposition of the gates of hell, so that the elect in due time may be gathered together into one, and that there never be wanting a church composed of believers, the foundation of which is laid in the blood of Christ, which may steadfastly love, and faithfully serve him as their Savior, who as a bridegroom for his bride, laid down his life for them upon the cross, and which may celebrate his praises here and through all eternity.

The true doctrine having been explained, the Synod *rejects* the errors of those:

1. Who teach: That God the Father has ordained his Son to the death of the cross without a certain and definite decree to save any, so that the necessity, profitableness and worth of what Christ merited by his death might have existed, and might remain in all its parts complete, perfect and intact, even if the merited redemption had never in fact been applied to any person. For this doctrine tends to the despising of the wisdom of the Father and the of the merits of Jesus Christ, and is contrary to Scripture. For thus saith our Savior: "I lay down my life for the sheep, and I know them," John 10:15, 27. And the prophet Isaiah saith concerning the Savior: "When thou shalt make his soul an offering for sin, he shall see his seed, he shall prolong his days, and the pleasure of Jehovah shall prosper in his hand," Is. 53:10. Finally, this contradicts the article of faith according to which we believe the catholic Christian church.

2. Who teach: That it was not the purpose of the death of Christ that he should confirm the new covenant of grace through his blood, but only that he should acquire for the Father the mere right to establish with man such a covenant as he might please, whether of grace or of works. For this is repugnant to Scripture which teaches that Christ has become the Surety Mediator of a better, that is, the new covenant, and that a testament is of force where death has occurred. Heb. 7:22; 9:15, 17.

3. Who teach: That Christ by his satisfaction merited neither salvation itself for anyone, nor faith, whereby this satisfaction of Christ unto salvation is effectually appropriated; but that he merited for the Father only the authority or the perfect will to deal again with man, and to prescribe new conditions as he might desire, obedience to which, however, depended on the free will of man, so that it therefore might have come to pass that either none or all should fulfill these conditions. For these adjudge too contemptuously of the death of Christ, do in no wise acknowledge the most important fruit or benefit thereby gained, and bring again out of hell the Pelagian error.

4. Who teach: That the new covenant of grace, which God the Father, through the mediation of the death of Christ, made with man, does not herein consist that we by faith, in as much as it accepts the merits of Christ, are justified before God and saved, but in the fact that God having revoked the demand of perfect obedience of the law, regards faith itself and the obedience of faith, although imperfect, as the perfect obedience of the law, and does esteem it worthy of the reward of eternal life through grace. For these contradict the Scriptures: "Being justified freely by his grace through the redemption that is in Christ Jesus: whom God set forth to be a propitiation through faith in his blood," Rom. 3:24, 25. And these proclaim, as did the wicked Socinus, a new and strange justification of man before God, against the consensus of the whole church.

5. Who teach: That all men have been accepted unto the state of reconciliation and unto the grace of the covenant, so that no one is worthy of condemnation on account of original sin, and that no one shall be condemned because of it, but that all are free from the guilt of original sin. For this opinion is repugnant to Scripture which teaches that we are by nature children of wrath. Eph. 2:3.

6. Who use the difference between meriting and appropriating, to the end that they may instill into the minds of the imprudent and inexperienced this teaching that God, as far as he is concerned, has been minded of applying to all equally the benefits gained by the death of Christ; but that, while some obtain the pardon of sin and eternal life, and others do not, this difference depends on their own free will, which joins itself to the grace that is offered without exception, and that it is not dependent on the special gift of mercy, which powerfully works in them, that they rather than others should appropriate unto themselves this grace. For these, while thy feign that they present this distinction, in a sound sense, seek to instill into the people the destructive poison of the Pelagian

errors.

7. Who teach: That Christ neither could die, needed to die, nor did die for those whom God loved in the highest degree and elected to eternal life, and did not die for these, since those do not need the death of Christ. For they contradict the Apostle, who declares: "Christ loved me, and gave himself for me," Gal. 2:20. Likewise: "Who shall lay any thing to the charge of God's elect? It is God that justifieth; who is he that condemneth? It is Christ Jesus that died," Rom. 8:33, 34, viz., for them; and the Savior who says: "I lay down my life for the sheep," John 10:15. And: "This is my commandment, that ye love one another, even as I have loved you. Greater love hath no man than this, that a man lay down his life for his friends," John 15:12, 13.

III., IV. OF THE CORRUPTION OF MAN, HIS CONVERSION TO GOD, AND THE MANNER THEREOF

1. Man was originally formed after the image of God. His understanding was adorned with a true and saving knowledge of his creator, and of spiritual things; his heart and will were upright; all his affections pure; and the whole man was holy; but revolting from God by the instigation of the devil, and abusing the freedom of his own will, he forfeited these excellent gifts; and on the contrary entailed on himself blindness of mind, horrible darkness, vanity and perverseness of judgement, became wicked, rebellious, and obdurate in heart and will, and impure in his affections.

2. Man after the fall begat children in his own likeness. A corrupt stock produced a corrupt offspring. Hence all the posterity of Adam, Christ only excepted, have derived corruption from their original parents, not by imitation, as the Pelagians of old asserted, but by the propagation of a vicious nature.

3. Therefore all men are conceived in sin, and by nature children of wrath, incapable of saving good, prone to evil, dead in sin, and in bondage thereto, and without the regenerating grace of the Holy Spirit, they are neither able nor willing to return to God, to reform the depravity of their nature, nor to dispose themselves to reformation.

4. There remain, however, in man since the fall, the glimmering of natural light, whereby he retains some knowledge of God, of natural things, and of the differences between good and evil, and discovers some regard for virtue, good order in society, and for maintaining an orderly external deportment. But so far is this light of nature from being sufficient to bring him to a saving knowledge of God, and to true conversion, that he is incapable of using it aright even in things natural and civil. Nay further, this light, such as it is, man in various ways renders wholly polluted, and holds it in unrighteousness, by doing which he becomes inexcusable before God.

5. In the same light are we to consider the law of the decalogue,

delivered by God to his peculiar people the Jews, by the hands of Moses. For though it discovers the greatness of sin, and more and more convinces man thereof, yet as it neither points out a remedy, nor imparts strength to extricate him from misery, and thus being weak through the flesh, leaves the transgressor under the curse, man cannot by this law obtain saving grace.

6. What therefore neither the light of nature, nor the law could do, that God performs by the operation of the Holy Spirit through the word or ministry of reconciliation: which is the glad tidings concerning the Messiah, by means whereof, it hath pleased God to save such as believe, as well under the Old, as under the New Testament.

7. This mystery of his will God discovered to but a small number under the Old Testament; under the New, (the distinction between various peoples having been removed), he reveals himself to many, without any distinction of people. The cause of this dispensation is not to be ascribed to the superior worth of one nation above another, nor to their making a better use of the light of nature, but results wholly from the sovereign good pleasure and unmerited love of God. Hence they, to whom so great and so gracious a blessing is communicated, above their desert, or rather notwithstanding their demerits, are bound to acknowledge it with humble and grateful hearts, and with the apostle to adore, not curiously to pry into the severity and justice of God's judgments displayed to others, to whom this grace is not given.

8. As many as are called by the gospel, are unfeignedly called. For God hath most earnestly and truly declared in his Word, what will be acceptable to him, namely, that those who are called, should come to him. He, moreover, seriously promises eternal life, and rest, to as many as shall come to him and believe on him.

9. It is not the fault of the gospel, nor of Christ, offered therein, nor of God, who calls men by the gospel, and confers upon them various gifts, that those who are called by the ministry of the word, refuse to come, and be converted: the fault lies in themselves; some of whom when called, regardless of their danger, reject the word of life; others, though they receive it, suffer it not to make a lasting impression on their heart; therefore, their joy, arising only from a temporary faith, soon vanishes, and they fall away; while others choke the seed of the word by perplexing cares, and the pleasures of this world, and produce no fruit.—This our Savior teaches in the parable of the sower. Matt. 13.

10. But that others who are called by the gospel, obey the call, and are converted, is not to be ascribed to the proper exercise of free will, whereby one distinguishes himself above others, equally furnished with grace sufficient for faith and conversions, as the proud heresy of Pelagius maintains; but it must be wholly ascribed to God, who as he has chosen his own from eternity in Christ, so he confers upon them faith and repentance, rescues them from the power of darkness, and translates them into the kingdom of his own Son, that they may show forth the praises of

him, who hath called them out of darkness into his marvelous light; and may glory not in themselves, but in the Lord according to the testimony of the apostles in various places.

11. But when God accomplishes his good pleasure in the elect, or works in them true conversion, he not only causes the gospel to be externally preached to them, and powerfully illuminates their minds by his Holy Spirit, that they may rightly understand and discern the things of the Spirit of God; but by the efficacy of the same regenerating Spirit, pervades the inmost recesses of the man; he opens the closed, and softens the hardened heart, and circumcises that which was uncircumcised, infuses new qualities into the will, which though heretofore dead, he quickens; from being evil, disobedient, and refractory, he renders it good, obedient, and pliable; actuates and strengthens it, that like a good tree, it may bring forth the fruits of good actions.

12. And this is the regeneration so highly celebrated in Scripture, and denominated a new creation: a resurrection from the dead, a making alive, which God works in us without our aid. But this is in no wise effected merely by the external preaching of the gospel, by moral suasion, or such a mode of operation, that after God has performed his part, it still remains in the power of man to be regenerated or not, to be converted, or to continue unconverted; but it is evidently a supernatural work, not powerful, and at the same time most delightful, astonishing, mysterious, and ineffable; not inferior in efficacy to creation, or the resurrection from the dead, as the Scripture inspired by the author of this work declares; so that all in whose heart God works in this marvelous manner, are certainly, infallibly, and effectually regenerated, and do actually believe.—Whereupon the will thus reviewed is not only actuated and influenced by God, but in consequence of this influence, becomes itself active. Wherefore also, man is himself rightly said to believe and repent, by virtue of that grace received.

13. The manner of this operation cannot be fully comprehended by believers in this life. Not withstanding which, they rest satisfied with knowing and experiencing, that by this grace of God they are enabled to believe with the heart, and love their Savior.

14. Faith is therefore to be considered as the gift of God, not on account of its being offered by God to man, to be accepted or rejected at his pleasure; but because it is in reality conferred, breathed, and infused into him; or even because God bestows the power or ability to believe, and then expects that man should by the exercise of his own free will, consent to the terms of salvation, and actually believe in Christ; but because he who works in man both to will and to do, and indeed all things in all, produces both the will to believe, and the act of believing also.

15. God is under no obligation to confer this grace upon any; for how can he be indebted to man, who had no previous gifts to bestow, as a foundation for such recompense? Nay, who has nothing of his own but sin and falsehood? He therefore who becomes the subject of this grace, owes

eternal gratitude to God, and gives him thanks forever. Whoever is not made partaker thereof, is either altogether regardless of these spiritual gifts, and satisfied with his own condition; or is in no apprehension of danger, and vainly boasts the possession of that which he has not. With respect to those who make an external profession of faith, and live regular lives, we are bound, after the example of the apostle, to judge and speak of them in the most favorable manner. For the secret recesses of the heart are unknown to us. And as to others, who have not yet been called, it is our duty to pray for them to God, who calls the things that are not, as if they were. But we are in no wise to conduct ourselves towards them with haughtiness, as if we had made ourselves to differ.

16. But as man by the fall did not cease to be a creature, endowed with understanding and will, nor did sin which pervaded the whole race of mankind, deprive him of the human nature, but brought upon him depravity and spiritual death; so also the grace of regeneration does not treat man as senseless stocks and blocks, nor takes away their will and its properties, neither does violence thereto; but spiritually quickens, heals, corrects, and at the same time sweetly and powerfully bends it; that where carnal rebellion and resistance formerly prevailed, a ready and sincere spiritual obedience begins to reign; in which the true and spiritual restoration and freedom of our will consist. Wherefore unless the admirable author of every good work wrought in us, man could have no hope of recovering from his fall by his own free will, by the abuse of which, in a state of innocence, he plunged himself into ruin.

17. As the almighty operation of God, whereby he prolongs and supports this our natural life, does not exclude, but requires the use of means, by which God of his infinite mercy and goodness hath chosen to exert his influence, so also the before mentioned, supernatural operation of God, by which we are regenerated, in no wise excludes, or subverts the use of the gospel, which the most wise God has ordained to be the seed of regeneration, and food of the soul. Wherefore, as the apostles, and teachers who succeeded them, piously instructed the people concerning this grace of God, to his glory, and the abasement of all pride, and in the meantime, however, neglected not to keep them by the sacred precepts of the gospel in the exercise of the Word, sacraments and discipline; so even to this day, be it far from either instructors or instructed to presume to tempt God in the church by separating what he of his good pleasure hath most intimately joined together. For grace is conferred by means of admonitions; and the more readily we perform our duty, the more eminent usually is this blessing of God working in us, and the more directly is his work advanced; to whom alone all the glory both of means, and of their saving fruit and efficacy is forever due. Amen.

The true doctrine having been explained, the Synod *rejects* the errors of those:

1. Who teach: That it cannot properly be said, that original sin in itself suffices to condemn the whole human race, or to deserve temporal and eternal punishment. For these contradict the Apostle, who declares: "Therefore as through one man sin entered into the world, and death through sin, and so death passed unto all men, for that all sinned," Rom. 5:12. And: "The judgment came of one unto condemnation," Rom. 5:16. And: "The wages of sin is death," Rom 6:23.

2. Who teach: That the spiritual gifts, or the good qualities and virtues, such as: goodness, holiness, righteousness, could not belong to the will of man when he was first created, and that these, therefore, could not have been separated therefrom in the fall. For such is contrary to the description of the image of God, which the Apostle gives in Eph. 4:24, where he declares that it consists in righteousness and holiness, which undoubtedly belong to the will.

3. Who teach: That in spiritual death spiritual gifts are not separate from the will of man, since the will in itself has never been corrupted, but only hindered through the darkness of the understanding and the irregularity of the affections; and that, these hindrances having been removed, the will can then bring into operation its native powers, that is, that the will of itself is able to will and to choose, or not to will and not to choose, all manner of good which may be presented to it. This is an innovation and an error, and tends to elevate the powers of the free will, contrary to the declaration of the Prophet: "The heart is deceitful above all things, and it is exceedingly corrupt," Jer 17:9; and of the Apostle: "Among whom (sons of disobedience) we also all once lived in the lusts of the flesh, doing the desires of the flesh and of the mind," Eph 2:3.

4. Who teach: That the unregenerate man is not really nor utterly dead in sin, nor destitute of all powers unto spiritual good, but that he can yet hunger and thirst after righteousness and life, and offer the sacrifice of a contrite and broken spirit, which is pleasing to God. For these are contrary to the express testimony of Scripture. "Ye were dead through trespasses and sins," Eph. 2:1, 5; and: "Every imagination of the thought of his heart are only evil continually," Gen. 6:5; 8:21. Moreover, to hunger and thirst after deliverance from misery, and after life, and to offer unto God the sacrifice of a broken spirit, is peculiar to the regenerate and those that are called blessed. Ps. 51:10, 19; Matt. 5:6.

5. Who teach: That the corrupt and natural man can so well use the common grace (by which they understand the light of nature), or the gifts still left him after the fall, that he can gradually gain by their good use a greater, viz., the evangelical or saving grace and salvation itself. And that in this way God on his part shows himself ready to reveal Christ unto all men, since he applies to all sufficiently and efficiently the means necessary to conversion. For the experience of all ages and the Scriptures do both testify that this is untrue. "He showeth his Word unto Jacob, his statutes and his ordinances unto Israel. He hath not dealt so with any nation: and as for his ordinances they have not known them," Ps. 147:19,

20. "Who in the generations gone by suffered all the nations to walk in their own way," Acts 14:16. And: "And they (Paul and his companions) having been forbidden of the Holy Spirit to speak the word in Asia, when they were come over against Mysia, they assayed to go into Bithynia, and the Spirit suffered them not," Acts 16:6, 7.

6. Who teach: That in the true conversion of man no new qualities, powers, or gifts can be infused by God into the will, and that therefore faith through which we are first converted, and because of which we are called believers, is not a quality or gift infused by God, but only an act of man, and that it can not be said to be a gift, except in respect of the power to attain to this faith. For thereby they contradict the Holy Scriptures, which declare that God infused new qualities of faith, of obedience, and of the consciousness of his love into our hearts: "I will put my law in their inward parts, and in their hearts will I write it," Jer. 31:33. And: "I will pour water upon him that is thirsty, and streams upon the dry ground; I will pour my Spirit upon thy seed," Is. 44:3. And: "The love of God hath been shed abroad in our hearts through the Holy Spirit which hath been given us," Rom 5:5. This is also repugnant to the continuous practice of the Church, which prays by the mouth of the Prophet thus: "Turn thou me, and I shall be turned," Jer. 31:18.

7. Who teach: That the grace whereby we are converted to God is only a gentle advising, or (as others explain it), that this is the noblest manner of working in the conversion of man, and that this manner of working, which consists in advising, is most in harmony with man's nature; and that there is no reason why this advising grace alone should not be sufficient to make the natural man spiritual, indeed, that God does not produce the consent of the will except through this manner of advising; and that the power of the divine working, whereby it surpasses the working of Satan, consists in this, that God promises eternal, while Satan promises only temporal goods. But this is altogether Pelagian and contrary to the whole Scripture which, besides this, teaches yet another and far more powerful and divine manner of the Holy Spirit's working in the conversion of man, as in Ezekiel: "A new heart also will I give you, and a new spirit will I put within you: and I will take away the stony heart out of your flesh, and I will give you a heart of flesh," Ezek. 36:26.

8. Who teach: That God in the regeneration of man does not use such powers of his omnipotence as potently and infallibly bend man's will to faith and conversion; but that all the works of grace having been accomplished, which God employs to convert man, man may yet so resist God and the Holy Spirit, when God intends man's regeneration and wills to regenerate him, and indeed that man often does so resist that he prevents entirely his regeneration, and that it therefore remains in man's power to be regenerated or not. For this is nothing less than the denial of all the efficiency of God's grace in our conversion, and the subjecting of the working of almighty God to the will of man, which is contrary to the Apostles who teach: "That we believe according to the working of the

strength of his power," Eph. 1:19. And: "That God fulfills every desire of goodness and every work of faith with power," 2 Thess. 1:11. And: "That his divine power hath given unto us all things that pertain unto life and godliness," 2 Peter 1:3.

9. Who teach: That grace and free will are partial causes, which together work the beginning of conversion, and that grace, in order of working, does not precede the working of the will; that is, that God does not efficiently help the will of man unto conversion until the will of man moves and determines to do this. For the ancient Church has long ago condemned this doctrine of the Pelagians according to the words of the Apostle: "So then it is not of him that willeth, nor of him that runneth, but of God that hath mercy," Rom. 9:16. Likewise: "For who maketh thee to differ? and what hast thou that thou didst not receive?" 1 Cor. 4:7. And: "For it is God who worketh in you both to will and to work, for his good pleasure," Phil. 2:13.

V. OF THE PERSEVERANCE OF THE SAINTS

1. Whom God calls, according to his purpose, to the communion of his Son, our Lord Jesus Christ, and regenerates by the Holy Spirit, he delivers also from the dominion and slavery of sin in this life; though not altogether from the body of sin, and from the infirmities of the flesh, so long as they continue in this world.

2. Hence spring daily sins of infirmity, and hence spots adhere to the best works of the saints; which furnish them with constant matter for humiliation before God, and flying for refuge to Christ crucified; for mortifying the flesh more and more by the spirit of prayer, and by holy exercises of piety; and for pressing forward to the goal of perfection, till being at length delivered from this body of death, they are brought to reign with the lamb of God in heaven.

3. By reason of these remains of indwelling sin, and the temptations of sin and of the world, those who are converted could not persevere in a state of grace, if left to their own strength. But God is faithful, who having conferred grace, mercifully confirms, and powerfully preserves them therein, even to the end.

4. Although the weakness of the flesh cannot prevail against the power of God, who confirms and preserves true believers in a state of grace, yet converts are not always so influenced and actuated by the Spirit of God, as not in some particular instances sinfully to deviate from the guidance of divine grace, so as to be seduced by, and comply with the lusts of the flesh; they must, therefore, be constant in watching and prayer, that they be not led into temptation. When these are neglected, they are not only liable to be drawn into great and heinous sins, by Satan, the world and the flesh, but sometimes by the righteous permission of God actually fall into these evils. This, the lamentable fall of David, Peter, and other saints described in Holy Scripture, demonstrates.

5. By such enormous sins, however, they very highly offend God, incur a deadly guilt, grieve the Holy Spirit, interrupt the exercise of faith, very grievously wound their consciences, and sometimes lose the sense of God's favor, for a time, until on their returning into the right way of serious repentance, the light of God's fatherly countenance again shines upon them.

6. But God, who is rich in mercy, according to his unchangeable purpose of election, does not wholly withdraw the Holy Spirit from his own people, even in their melancholy falls; nor suffers them to proceed so far as to lose the grace of adoption, and forfeit the state of justification, or to commit the sin unto death; nor does he permit them to be totally deserted, and to plunge themselves into everlasting destruction.

7. For in the first place, in these falls he preserves in them the incorruptible seed of regeneration from perishing, or being totally lost; and again, by his Word and Spirit, certainly and effectually renews them to repentance, to a sincere and godly sorrow for their sins, that they may seek and obtain remission in the blood of the Mediator, may again experience the favor of a reconciled God, through faith adore his mercies, and henceforward more diligently work out their own salvation with fear and trembling.

8. Thus, it is not in consequence of their own merits, or strength, but of God's free mercy, that they do not totally fall from faith and grace, nor continue and perish finally in their backslidings; which, with respect to themselves, is not only possible, but would undoubtedly happen; but with respect to God, it is utterly impossible, since his counsel cannot be changed, nor his promise fail, neither can the call according to his purpose be revoked, nor the merit, intercession and preservation of Christ be rendered ineffectual, nor the sealing of the Holy Spirit be frustrated or obliterated.

9. Of this preservation of the elect to salvation, and of their perseverance in the faith, true believers for themselves may and do obtain assurance according to the measure of their faith, whereby they arrive at the certain persuasion, that they ever will continue true and living members of the church; and that they experience forgiveness of sins, and will at last inherit eternal life.

10. This assurance, however, is not produced by any peculiar revelation contrary to, or independent of the Word of God; but springs from faith in God's promises, which he has most abundantly revealed in his Word for our comfort; from the testimony of the Holy Spirit, witnessing with our spirit, that we are children and heirs of God, Rom. 8:16; and lastly, from a serious and holy desire to preserve a good conscience, and to perform good works. And if the elect of God were deprived of this solid comfort, that they shall finally obtain the victory, and of this infallible pledge or earnest of eternal glory, they would be of all men the most miserable.

11. The Scripture moreover testifies, that believers in this life have to

struggle with various carnal doubts, and that under grievous temptations they are not always sensible of this full assurance of faith and certainty of persevering. But God, who is the Father of all consolation, does not suffer them to be tempted above that they are able, but will with the temptation also make a way to escape, that they may be able to bear it, 1 Cor. 10:13, and by the Holy Spirit again inspires them with the comfortable assurance of persevering.

12. This certainty of perseverance, however, is so far from exciting in believers a spirit of pride, or of rendering them carnally secure, that on the contrary, it is the real source of humility, filial reverence, true piety, patience in every tribulation, fervent prayers, constancy in suffering, and in confessing the truth, and of solid rejoicing in God: so that the consideration of this benefit should serve as an incentive to the serious and constant practice of gratitude and good works, as appears from the testimonies of Scripture, and the examples of the saints.

13. Neither does renewed confidence of persevering produce licentiousness, or a disregard to piety in those who are recovering from backsliding; but it renders them much more careful and solicitous to continue in the ways of the Lord, which he hath ordained, that they who walk therein may maintain an assurance of persevering, lest by abusing his fatherly kindness, God should turn away his gracious countenance from them, to behold which is to the godly dearer than life: the withdrawing whereof is more bitter than death, and they in consequence hereof should fall into more grievous torments of conscience.

14. And as it hath pleased God, by the preaching of the gospel, to begin this work of grace in us, so he preserves, continues, and perfects it by the hearing and reading of his Word, by meditation thereon, and by the exhortations, threatenings, and promises thereof, as well as by the use of the sacraments.

15. The carnal mind is unable to comprehend this doctrine of the perseverance of the saints, and the certainty thereof; which God hath most abundantly revealed in his Word, for the glory of his name, and the consolation of pious souls, and which he impresses upon the hearts of the faithful. Satan abhors it; the world ridicules it; the ignorant and hypocrite abuse, and heretics oppose it; but the spouse of Christ hath always most tenderly loved and constantly defended it, as an inestimable treasure; and God, against whom neither counsel nor strength can prevail, will dispose her to continue this conduct to the end. Now, to this one God, Father, Son, and Holy Spirit, be honor and glory, for ever. AMEN.

>The true doctrine having been explained, the Synod *rejects* the errors of those:

1. Who teach: That the perseverance of the true believers is not a fruit of election, or a gift of God, gained by the death of Christ, but a condition of the new covenant, which (as they declare) man before his decisive election and justification must fulfill through his free will. For the Holy

Scripture testifies that this follows out of election, and is given the elect in virtue of the death, the resurrection and intercession of Christ: "But the elect obtained it and the rest were hardened," Rom. 11:7. Likewise: "He that spared not his own Son, but delivered him up for us all, how shall he not also with him freely give us all things? Who shall lay anything to the charge of God's elect? It is God that justifieth; who is he that condemneth? It is Christ Jesus that died, yea rather, that was raised from the dead, who is at the right hand of God, who also maketh intercession for us. Who shall separate us from the love of Christ?" Rom 8:32-35.

2. Who teach: That God does indeed provide the believer with sufficient powers to persevere, and is ever ready to preserve these in him, if he will do his duty; but that though all things, which are necessary to persevere in faith and which God will use to preserve in faith, are made use of, it even then ever depends on the pleasure of the will whether it will persevere or not. For this idea contains an outspoken Pelagianism, and while it would make men free, it makes them robbers of God's honor, contrary to the prevailing agreement of the evangelical doctrine, which takes from man all cause of boasting, and ascribes all the praise for this favor to the grace of God alone; and contrary to the Apostle, who declares: "That it is God, who shall also confirm you unto the end, that ye be unreprovable in the day of our Lord Jesus Christ." 1 Cor. 1:18.

3. Who teach: That the true believers and regenerate not only can fall from justifying faith and likewise from grace and salvation wholly and to the end, but indeed often do fall from this and are lost forever. For this conception makes powerless the grace, justification, regeneration, and continued keeping by Christ, contrary to the express words of the Apostle Paul: "That while we were yet sinners Christ died for us. Much more then, being justified by his blood, shall we be saved from the wrath of God through him," Rom. 5:8, 9. And contrary to the Apostle John: "Whosoever is begotten of God doeth no sin, because his seed abideth in him; and he can not sin, because he is begotten of God," 1 John 3:9. And also contrary to the words of Jesus Christ: "I give unto them eternal life; and they shall never perish, and no one shall snatch them out of my hand. My father who hath given them to me, is greater than all; and no one is able to snatch them out of the Father's hand," John 10:28, 29.

4. Who teach: That true believers and regenerate can sin the sin unto death or against the Holy Spirit. Since the same Apostle John, after having spoken in the fifth chapter of his first epistle, vss. 16 and 17, of those who sin unto death and having forbidden to pray for them, immediately adds to this in vs. 18: "We know that whosoever is begotten of God sinneth not (meaning a sin of that character), but he that is begotten of God keepeth himself, and the evil one toucheth him not," 1 John 5:18.

5. Who teach: That without a special revelation we can have no certainty of future perseverance in this life. For by this doctrine the sure comfort of the true believers is taken away in this life, and the doubts of the papist are again introduced into the church, while the Holy Scriptures

constantly deduce this assurance, not from a special and extraordinary revelation, but from the marks proper to the children of God and from the constant promises of God. So especially the Apostle Paul: "No creature shall be able to separate us from the love of God, which is in Christ Jesus our Lord," Rom. 8:39. And John declares: "And he that keepeth his commandments abideth in him, and he in him. And hereby we know that he abideth in us, by the Spirit which he gave us." 1 John 3:24.

6. Who teach: That the doctrine of the certainty of perseverance and of salvation from its own character and nature is a cause of indolence and is injurious to godliness, good morals, prayers and other holy exercises, but that on the contrary it is praiseworthy to doubt. For these show that they do not know the power of divine grace and the working of the indwelling Holy Spirit. And they contradict the Apostle John, who teaches the opposite with express words in his first epistle: "Beloved, now are we the children of God, and it is not yet make manifest what we shall be. We know that, if he shall be manifested we shall be like him; for we shall see him even as he is. And every one that hath this hope set on him purifieth himself, even as he is pure," 1 John 3:2, 3. Furthermore, these are contradicted by the example of the saints, both of the Old and the New Testament, who though they were assured of their perseverance and salvation, were nevertheless constant in prayers and other exercises of godliness.

7. Who teach: that the faith of those, who believe for a time, does not differ from justifying and saving faith except only in duration. For Christ Himself, in Matt. 13:20, Luke 8:13, and in other places, evidently notes, besides this duration, a threefold difference between those who believe only for a time and true believers, when he declares that the former receive the seed in stony ground, but the latter in the good ground or heart; that the former are without root, but the latter have a firm root; that the former are without fruit, but that the latter bring forth their fruit in various measure, with constancy and steadfastness.

8. Who teach: That it is not absurd that one having lost his first regeneration, is again and even often born anew. For these deny by this doctrine the incorruptibleness of the seed of God, whereby we are born again. Contrary to the testimony of the Apostle Peter: "Having been begotten again, not of corruptible seed, but of incorruptible," 1 Peter 1:23.

9. Who teach: That Christ has in no place prayed that believers should infallibly continue in faith. For they contradict Christ himself, who says: "I have prayed for thee (Simon), that thy faith fail not," Luke 22:32; and the Evangelist John, who declares, that Christ has not prayed for the Apostles only, but also for those who through their word would believe: "Holy Father, keep them in thy name," and: "I pray not that thou shouldest take them out of the world, but that thou shouldest keep them from the evil one," John 17:11, 15, 20.

Appendix 5
THE LAMBETH ARTICLES

1. God from eternity hath predestinated certain men unto life; certain men he hath reprobated.

2. The moving or efficient cause of predestination unto life is not the foresight of faith, or of perseverance, or of good works, or of any thing that is in the person predestinated, but only the good will and pleasure of God.

3. There is predetermined a certain number of the predestinate, which can neither be augmented nor diminished.

4. Those who are not predestinated to salvation shall be necessarily damned for their sins.

5. A true, living, and justifying faith, and the Spirit of God justifying [sanctifying], is not extinguished, falleth not away; it vanisheth not away in the elect, either finally or totally.

6. A man truly faithful, that is, such a one who is endued with a justifying faith, is certain, with the full assurance of faith, of the remission of his sins and of his everlasting salvation by Christ.

7. Saving grace is not given, is not granted, is not communicated to all men, by which they may be saved if they will.

8. No man can come unto Christ unless it shall be given unto him, and unless the Father shall draw him; and all men are not drawn by the Father, that they may come to the Son.

9. It is not in the will or power of every one to be saved.

Appendix 6

THE WESTMINSTER CONFESSION OF FAITH

III. Of God's Eternal Decree

I. God, from all eternity, did, by the most wise and holy counsel of his own will, freely, and unchangeably ordain whatsoever comes to pass: yet so, as thereby neither is God the author of sin, nor is violence offered to the will of the creatures; nor is the liberty or contingency of second causes taken away, but rather established.

II. Although God knows whatsoever may or can come to pass upon all supposed conditions, yet hath he not decreed anything because he fore-saw it as future, or as that which would come to pass upon such conditions.

III. By the decree of God, for the manifestation of his glory, some men and angels are predestinated unto everlasting life; and others foreordained to everlasting death.

IV. These angels and men, thus predestinated, and foreordained, are particularly and unchangeably designed, and their number so certain and definite, that it cannot be either increased or diminished.

V. Those of mankind that are predestinated unto life, God, before the foundation of the world was laid, according to his eternal and immutable purpose, and the secret counsel and good pleasure of his will, hath chosen, in Christ, unto everlasting glory, out of his mere free grace and love, without any foresight of faith, or good works, or perseverance in either of them, or any other thing in the creature, as conditions, or cause moving him thereunto; and all to the praise of his glorious grace.

VI. As God hath appointed the elect unto glory, so hath he, by the eternal and most free purpose of his will, foreordained all the means thereunto. Wherefore, they who are elected, being fallen in Adam, are redeemed by Christ, are effectually called unto faith in Christ by his Spirit working in due season, are justified, adopted, sanctified, and kept by his power, through faith, unto salvation. Neither are any other redeemed by Christ, effectually called, justified, adopted, sanctified, and saved, but the elect only.

VII. The rest of mankind, God was pleased, according to the unsearchable counsel of his own will, whereby he extendeth or withholdeth mercy, as he pleaseth, for the glory of his sovereign power over his creatures, to pass by; and to ordain them to dishonor and wrath for their sin, to the praise of his glorious justice.

VIII. The doctrine of this high mystery of predestination is to be handled with special prudence and care, that men, attending to the will of God revealed in his Word, and yielding obedience thereunto, may, from the certainty of their effectual vocation, be assured of their eternal election. So shall this doctrine afford matter of praise, reverence, and admiration of God; and of humility, diligence, and abundant consolation to all that sincerely obey the gospel.

V. Of Providence

I. God the great Creator of all things doth uphold, direct, dispose, and govern all creatures, actions, and things, from the greatest even to the least, by his most wise and holy providence, according to his infallible foreknowledge, and the free and immutable counsel of his own will, to the praise of the glory of his wisdom, power, justice, goodness, and mercy.

II. Although in relation to the foreknowledge and decree of God, the first Cause, all things come to pass immutably, and infallibly; yet, by the same providence, he ordereth them to fall out, according to the nature of second causes, either necessarily, freely, or contingently.

III. God, in his ordinary providence, maketh use of means, yet is free to work without, above, and against them, at his pleasure.

IV. The almighty power, unsearchable wisdom, and infinite goodness of God so far manifest themselves in his providence, that it extendeth itself even to the first fall, and all other sins of angels and men; and that not by a bare permission, but such as hath joined with it a most wise and powerful bounding, and otherwise ordering, and governing of them, in a manifold dispensation, to his own holy ends; yet so, as the sinfulness thereof proceedeth only from the creature, and not from God, who, being most holy and righteous, neither is nor can be the author or approver of sin.

V. The most wise, righteous, and gracious God doth oftentimes leave for a season, his own children to manifold temptations, and the corruption of their own hearts, to chastise them for their former sins, or to discover unto them the hidden strength of corruption and deceitfulness of their hearts, that they may be humbled; and, to raise them to a more close and constant dependence for their support upon himself, and to make them more watchful against all future occasions of sin, and for sundry other just and holy ends.

VI. As for those wicked and ungodly men whom God, as a righteous Judge, for former sins, doth blind and harden, from them he not only withholdeth his grace whereby they might have been enlightened in their understandings, and wrought upon in their hearts; but sometimes also withdraweth the gifts which they had, and exposeth them to such objects as their corruption makes occasion of sin; and, withal, gives them over to their own lusts, the temptations of the world, and the power of Satan, whereby it comes to pass that they harden themselves, even under those means which God useth for the softening of others.

VII. As the providence of God doth, in general, reach to all creatures; so, after a most special manner, it taketh care of his church, and disposeth all things to the good thereof.

VI. Of the Fall of Man, of Sin, and of the Punishment thereof

I. Our first parents, begin seduced by the subtlety and temptation of Satan, sinned, in eating the forbidden fruit. This their sin, God was pleased, according to his wise and holy counsel, to permit, having purposed to order it to his own glory.

II. By this sin they fell from their original righteousness and communion with God, and so became dead in sin, and wholly defiled in all the faculties and parts of soul and body.

III. They being the root of mankind, the guilt of this sin was imputed, and the same death in sin and corrupted nature conveyed to all their posterity descending from them by original generation.

IV. From this original corruption, whereby we are utterly indisposed, disabled, and made opposite to all good, and wholly inclined to all evil, do proceed all actual transgressions.

V. This corruption of nature, during this life, doth remain in those that are regenerated; and although it be, through Christ, pardoned, and mortified; yet both itself, and all the motions thereof, are truly and properly sin.

VI. Every sin, both original and actual, being a transgression of the righteous law of God, and contrary thereunto, doth, in its own nature, bring guilt upon the sinner, whereby he is bound over to the wrath of God, and curse of the law, and so made subject to death, with all miseries spiritual, temporal, and eternal.

VII. Of God's Covenant with Man

I. The distance between God and the creature is so great, that although reasonable creatures do owe obedience unto him as their Creator, yet they could never have any fruition of him as their blessedness and reward, but by some voluntary condescension on God's part, which he hath been pleased to express by way of covenant.

II. The first covenant made with man was a *covenant of works,* wherein life was promised to Adam; and in him to his posterity, upon condition of perfect and personal obedience.

III. Man, by his fall having made himself incapable of life by that *covenant,* the Lord was pleased to make a second, commonly called the *covenant of grace;* wherein he freely offered unto sinners life and salvation by Jesus Christ: requiring of them faith in him, that they may be saved, and promising to give unto all those that are ordained unto eternal life his Holy Spirit, to make them willing, and able to believe.

IV. This covenant of grace is frequently set forth in the Scripture by the name of a testament, in reference to the death of Jesus Christ the Testator, and to the everlasting inheritance, with all things belonging to it, therein bequeathed.

V. This covenant was differently administered in the time of the law, and in the time of the gospel: under the law, it was administered by promises, prophecies, sacrifices, circumcision, the paschal lamb, and other types and ordinances delivered to the people of the Jews, all fore-signifying Christ to come; which were, for that time, sufficient and efficacious, through the operation of the Spirit, to instruct and build up the elect in faith in the promised Messiah, by whom they had full remission of sins, and eternal salvation; and is called the old testament.

VI. Under the gospel, when Christ, the substance, was exhibited, the ordinances in which this covenant is dispensed are the preaching of the Word, and the administration of the sacraments of Baptism and the Lord's Supper: which, though fewer in number, and administered with more simplicity, and less outward glory, yet, in them, it is held forth in more fulness, evidence and spiritual efficacy, to all nations, both Jews and Gentiles; and is called the new testament. There are not therefore two covenants of grace differing in substance, but one and the same, under various dispensations.

VIII. Of Christ the Mediator

I. It pleased God, in his eternal purpose, to choose and ordain the Lord Jesus, his only begotten Son, to be the Mediator between God and man, the Prophet, Priest, and King; the Head and Savior of his Church, the Heir or all things, and Judge of the world: unto whom he did from all eternity give a people, to be his seed, and to be by him in time redeemed, called, justified, sanctified, and glorified.

II. The Son of God, the second Person in the Trinity, being very and eternal God, of one substance and equal with the Father, did, when the fullness of time was come, take upon him man's nature, with all the essential properties, and common infirmities thereof, yet without sin; being conceived by the power of the Holy Ghost, in the womb of the virgin Mary, of her substance. So that two whole, perfect, and distinct natures, the Godhead and the manhood, were inseparably joined together in one person, without conversion, composition, or confusion. Which person is very God and very man, yet one Christ, the only Mediator between God and man.

III. The Lord Jesus, in his human nature thus united to the divine, was sanctified, and anointed with the Holy Spirit, above measure, having in him all the treasures of wisdom and knowledge; in whom it pleased the Father that all fullness should dwell; to the end that, being holy, harmless, undefiled, and full of grace and truth, he might be thoroughly furnished to execute the office of a mediator, and surety. Which office he took not unto himself, but was thereunto called by his Father, who put all power and judgment into his hand, and gave him commandment to execute the same.

IV. This office the Lord Jesus did most willingly undertake; which that he might discharge, he was made under the law, and did perfectly fulfill it; endured most grievous torments immediately in his soul, and most painful sufferings in his body; was crucified, and died, was buried, and remained under the power of death, yet saw no corruption. On the third day he arose from the dead, with the same body in which he suffered, with which also he ascended into heaven, and there sitteth at the right hand of his Father, making intercession, and shall return, to judge men and angels, at the end of the world.

V. The Lord Jesus, by his perfect obedience, and sacrifice of himself, which he through the eternal Spirit, once offered up unto God, hath fully satisfied the justice of his Father; and purchased, not only reconciliation, but an everlasting inheritance in the kingdom of heaven, for all those whom the Father hath given unto him.

VI. Although the work of redemption was not actually wrought by Christ till after his incarnation, yet the virtue, efficacy, and benefits thereof were communicated unto the elect, in all ages successively from the beginning of the world, in and by those promises, types, and sacrifices, wherein he was revealed, and signified to be the seed of the woman, which should bruise the serpent's head; and the Lamb slain from the beginning of the world; being yesterday and today the same, and forever.

VII. Christ, in the work of mediation, acts according to both natures, by each nature doing that which is proper to itself; yet, by reason of the unity of the person, that which is proper to one nature is sometimes in Scripture attributed to the person denominated by the other nature.

VIII. To all those for whom Christ hath purchased redemption, he doth certainly and effectually apply and communicate the same; making intercession for them, and revealing unto them, in and by the Word, the mysteries of salvation; effectually persuading them by his Spirit to believe and obey, and governing their hearts by his Word and Spirit; overcoming all their enemies by his almighty power and wisdom, in such manner, and ways, as are most consonant to his wonderful and unsearchable dispensation.

IX. Of Free Will

I. God hath endued the will of man with that natural liberty, that is neither forced, nor, by any absolute necessity of nature, determined to good, or evil.

II. Man, in his state of innocency, had freedom and power to will and to do that which was good and well pleasing to God; but yet, mutably, so that he might fall from it.

III. Man, by his fall into a state of sin, hath wholly lost all ability of will to any spiritual good accompanying salvation: so as, a natural man, being altogether averse from that good, and dead in sin, is not able, by his own strength, to convert himself, or to prepare himself thereunto.

IV. When God converts a sinner, and translates him into the state of grace, he freeth him from his natural bondage under sin; and, by his grace alone, enables him freely to will and to do that which is spiritually good; yet so, as that by reason of his remaining corruption, he doth not perfectly, nor only, will that which is good, but doth also will that which is evil.

V. The will of man is made perfectly and immutable free to good alone, in the state of glory only.

X. Of Effectual Calling

I. All those whom God hath predestinated unto life, and those only, he is pleased, in his appointed and accepted time, effectually to call, by his Word and Spirit, out of that state of sin and death, in which they are by nature, to grace and salvation, by Jesus Christ; enlightening their minds spiritually and savingly to understand the things of God, taking away their heart of stone, and giving unto them a heart of flesh; renewing their wills, and, by his almighty power, determining them to that which is good, and effectually drawing them to Jesus Christ: yet so, as they come most freely, being made willing by his grace.

II. This effectual call is of God's free and special grace alone, not from any thing at all foreseen in man, who is altogether passive therein, until, being quickened and renewed by the Holy Spirit, he is thereby enabled to answer this call, and to embrace the grace offered and conveyed in it.

III. Elect infants, dying in infancy, are regenerated, and saved by Christ, through the Spirit, who worketh when, and where, and how he pleaseth: so also are all other elect persons who are uncapable of being outwardly called by the ministry of the Word.

IV. Others, not elected, although they may be called by the ministry of the Word, and may have some common operations of the Spirit, yet they never truly come to Christ, and therefore cannot be saved: much less can men, not professing the Christian religion, be saved in any other way whatsoever, be they never so diligent to frame their lives according to the light of nature, and the laws of that religion they do profess. And, to assert and maintain that they may, is very pernicious, and to be detested.

XI. Of Justification

I. Those whom God effectually calleth, he also freely justifieth: not by infusing righteousness into them, but by pardoning their sins, and by accounting and accepting their persons as righteous; not for anything wrought in them, or done by them, but for Christ's sake alone; nor by imputing faith itself, the act of believing, or any other evangelical obedience to them, as their righteousness; but by imputing the obedience and satisfaction of Christ unto them, they receiving and resting on him and his righteousness, by faith; which faith they have not of themselves, it is the gift of God.

II. Faith, thus receiving and resting on Christ and his righteousness, is the alone instrument of justification: yet is it not alone in the person justified, but is ever accompanied with all other saving graces, and is no dead faith, but worketh by love.

III. Christ, by His obedience and death, did fully discharge the debt of all those that are thus justified, and did make a proper, real, and full satisfaction to his Father's justice in their behalf. Yet, inasmuch as he was given by the Father for them; and His obedience and satisfaction accepted in their stead; and both, freely, not for any thing in them; their justification is only of free grace; that both the exact justice and rich grace of God might be glorified in the justification of sinners.

IV. God did, from all eternity, decree to justify all the elect, and Christ did, in the fullness of time, die for their sins, and rise again for their justification: nevertheless, they are not justified, until the Holy Spirit doth, in due time, actually apply Christ unto them.

V. God doth continue to forgive the sins of those that are justified; and, although they can never fall from the state of justification, yet they may, by their sins, fall under God's fatherly displeasure, and not have the light of his countenance restored unto them, until they humble themselves, confess their sins, beg pardon, and renew their faith and repentance.

VI. The justification of believers under the old testament was, in all these respects, one and the same with the justification of believers under the new testament.

XII. Of Adoption

I. All those that are justified, God vouchsafeth, in and for his only Son

Jesus Christ, to make partakers of the grace of adoption, by which they are taken into the number, and enjoy the liberties and privileges of the children of God, have his name put upon them, receive the spirit of adoption, have access to the throne of grace with boldness, are enabled to cry, Abba, Father, are pitied, protected, provided for, and chastened by him, as by a Father: yet never cast off, but sealed to the day of redemption; and inherit the promises, as heirs of everlasting salvation.

XIII. Of Sanctification

I. They, who are once effectually called, and regenerated, having a new heart, and a new spirit created in them, are further sanctified, really and personally, through the virtue of Christ's death and resurrection, by his Word and Spirit dwelling in them: the dominion of the whole body of sin is destroyed, and the several lusts thereof are more and more weakened and mortified; and they more and more quickened and strengthened in all saving graces, to the practice of true holiness, without which no man shall see the Lord.

II. This sanctification is throughout, in the whole man; yet imperfect in this life, there abiding still some remnants of corruption in every part; whence ariseth a continual and irreconcilable war, the flesh lusting against the Spirit, and the Spirit against the flesh.

III. In which war, although the remaining corruption, for a time, may much prevail; yet, through the continual supply of strength from the sanctifying Spirit of Christ, the regenerate part doth overcome; and so, the saints grow in grace, perfecting holiness in the fear of God.

XIV. Of Saving Faith

I. The grace of faith, whereby the elect are enabled to believe to the saving of their souls, is the work of the Spirit of Christ in their hearts, and is ordinarily wrought by the ministry of the Word, by which also, and by the administration of the sacraments, and prayer, it is increased and strengthened.

II. By this faith, a Christian believeth to be true whatsoever is revealed in the Word, for the authority of God Himself speaking therein; and acteth differently upon that which each particular passage thereof containeth; yielding obedience to the commands, trembling at the threatenings, and embracing the promises of God for this life, and that which is to come. But the principal acts of saving faith are accepting, receiving, and resting upon Christ alone for justification, sanctification, and eternal life, by virtue of the covenant of grace.

III. This faith is different in degrees, weak or strong; may be often and many ways assailed, and weakened, but gets the victory: growing up in many to the attainment of a full assurance, through Christ, who is both the author and finisher of our faith.

XV. Of Repentance Unto Life

I. Repentance unto life is an evangelical grace, the doctrine whereof is to be preached by every minister of the Gospel, as well as that of faith in Christ.

II. By it, a sinner, out of the sight and sense not only of the danger, but also of the filthiness and odiousness of his sins, as contrary to the holy nature, and righteous law of God; and upon the apprehension of his mercy in Christ to such as are penitent, so grieves for, and hates his sins, as to turn from them all unto God, purposing and endeavouring to walk with him in all the ways of his commandments.

III. Although repentance be not to be rested in, as any satisfaction for sin, or any cause of the pardon thereof, which is the act of God's free grace in Christ; yet it is of such necessity to all sinners, that none may expect pardon without it.

IV. As there is no sin so small, but it deserves damnation; so there is no sin so great, that it can bring damnation upon those who truly repent.

V. Men ought not to content themselves with a general repentance, but it is every man's duty to endeavour to repent of his particular sins, particularly.

VI. As every man is bound to make private confession of his sins to God, praying for the pardon thereof; upon which, and the forsaking of them, he shall find mercy; so, he that scandalizeth his brother, or the church of Christ, ought to be willing, by a private or public confession, and sorrow for his sin, to declare his repentance to those that are offended, who are thereupon to be reconciled to him, and in love to receive him.

XVI. Of Good Works

I. Good works are only such as God hath commanded in his holy Word, and not such as, without the warrant thereof, are devised by men, out of blind zeal, or upon any pretense of good intention.

II. These good works, done in obedience to God's commandments, are the fruits and evidences of a true and lively faith: and by them believers manifest their thankfulness, strengthen their assurance, edify their brethren, adorn the profession of the gospel, stop the mouths of the adversaries, and glorify God, whose workmanship they are, created in Christ Jesus thereunto, that, having their fruit unto holiness, they may have the end, eternal life.

III. Their ability to do good works is not at all of themselves, but wholly from the Spirit of Christ. And that they may be enabled thereunto, beside the graces they have already received, there is required an actual influence of the same Holy Spirit, to work in them to will, and to do, of his good pleasure: yet are they not hereupon to grow negligent, as if they were not bound to perform any duty unless upon a special motion of the Spirit; but they ought to be diligent in stirring up the grace of God that is in them.

IV. They who, in their obedience, attain to the greatest height which is possible in this life, are so far from being able to supererogate, and to do more than God requires, as that they fall short of much which in duty they are bound to do.

V. We cannot by our best works merit pardon of sin, or eternal life at the hand of God, by reason of the great disproportion that is between them and the glory to come; and the infinite distance that is between us and God, whom, by them, we can neither profit, nor satisfy for the debt of our former sins, but when we have done all we can, we have done but our duty, and are unprofitable servants: and because, as they are good, they proceed from his Spirit; and as they are wrought by us, they are defiled, and mixed with so much weakness and imperfection, that they cannot endure the severity of God's judgment.

VI. Notwithstanding, the persons of believers being accepted through Christ, their good works also are accepted in him; not as though they were in this life wholly unblamable and unreproveable in God's sight; but that he, looking upon them in his Son, is pleased to accept and reward that which is sincere, although accompanied with many weaknesses and imperfections.

VII. Works done by unregenerate men, although for the matter of them they may be things which God commands; and of good use both to themselves and others: yet, because they proceed not from an heart purified by faith; nor are done in a right manner, according to the Word; nor to a right end, the glory of God, they are therefore sinful, and cannot please God, or make a man meet to receive grace from God: and yet, their neglect of them is more sinful and displeasing unto God.

XVII. Of The Perseverance of the Saints

I. They, whom God hath accepted in his Beloved, effectually called, and sanctified by His Spirit, can neither totally nor finally fall away from the state of grace, but shall certainly persevere therein to the end, and be eternally saved.

II. This perseverance of the saints depends not upon their own free will, but upon the immutability of the degree of election, flowing from the free and unchangeable love of God the Father; upon the efficacy of the merit and intercession of Jesus Christ, the abiding of the Spirit, and of the seed of God within them, and the nature of the covenant of grace: from all which ariseth also the certainty and infallibility thereof.

III. Nevertheless, they may, through the temptations of Satan and of the world, the prevalency of corruption remaining in them, and the neglect of the means of their preservation, fall into grievous sins; and, for a time, continue therein: whereby they incur God's displeasure, and grieve his Holy Spirit, come to be deprived of some measure of their graces and comforts, have their hearts hardened, and their consciences wounded; hurt and scandalize others, and bring temporal judgments upon themselves.

XVIII. Of the Assurance of Grace and Salvation

I. Although hypocrites and other unregenerate men may vainly deceive themselves with false hopes and carnal presumptions of being in the favor of God, and estate of salvation (which hope of theirs shall perish): yet such as truly believe in the Lord Jesus, and love him in sincerity, endeavouring to walk in all good conscience before him, may, in this life, be certainly assured that they are in the state of grace, and may rejoice in the hope of the glory of God, which hope shall never make them ashamed.

II. This certainty is not a bare conjectural and probable persuasion grounded upon a fallible hope; but an infallible assurance of faith founded upon the divine truth of the promises of salvation, the inward evidence of those graces unto which these promises are made, the testimony of the Spirit of adoption witnessing with our spirits that we are the children of God, which Spirit is the earnest of our inheritance, whereby we are sealed to the day of redemption.

III. This infallible assurance does not so belong to the essence of faith, but that a true believer may wait long, and conflict with many difficulties before he be partaker of it: yet, being enabled by the Spirit to know the things which are freely given him of God, he may, without extraordinary revelation, in the right use of ordinary means, attain thereunto. And therefore it is the duty of every one to give all diligence to make his calling and election sure, that thereby his heart may be enlarged in peace and joy in the Holy Ghost, in love and thankfulness to God, and in strength and cheerfulness in the duties of obedience, the proper fruits of this assurance; so far is it from inclining men to looseness.

IV. True believers may have the assurance of their salvation divers ways shaken, diminished, and intermitted; as, by negligence in preserving of it, by falling into some special sin which woundeth the conscience and grieveth the Spirit; by some sudden or vehement temptation, by God's withdrawing the light of his countenance, and suffering even such as fear him to walk in darkness and to have no light: yet are they never utterly destitute of that seed of God, and life of faith, that love of Christ and the brethren, that sincerity of heart, and conscience of duty, out of which, by the operation of the Spirit, this assurance may, in due time, be revived; and by the which, in the meantime, they are supported from utter despair.

Appendix 7
THE SECOND LONDON CONFESSION OF FAITH
III. Of Gods Decree

1. GOD hath *Decreed* in himself from all Eternity, by the most wise and holy Councel of his own will, freely and unchangeably, all things whatsoever comes to passe; yet so as thereby is God neither the author of sin, nor hath fellowship with any therin, nor is violence offered to the will of the Creature, nor yet is the liberty, or contingency of second causes taken away, but rather established, in which appears his wisdom in disposing all things, and power, and faithfulness in accomplishing his *Decree*.

2. Although God knoweth whatsoever may, or can come to passe upon all supposed conditions; yet hath he not *Decreed* anything, because he foresaw it as future, or as that which would come to pass upon such conditions.

3. By the *decree* of God, for the manifestation of his glory some men and Angels are predestinated, or fore-ordained to Eternal Life, through Jesus Christ, to the praise of his glorious grace; others being left to act in their sin to their just condemnation, to the praise of his glorious justice.

4. These Angels and Men thus predestinated, and fore-ordained, are particularly, and unchangeably designed, and their number so certain, and definite, that it cannot be either increased, or diminished.

5. Those of mankind that are predestinated to life, God, before the foundation of the world was laid, according to his eternal and immutable purpose, and the secret Councel and good pleasure of his will, hath chosen in Christ unto everlasting glory, out of his meer free grace and love; without any other thing in the creature as a condition or cause moving him thereunto.

6. As God hath appointed the Elect unto glory, so he hath by the eternal and most free purpose of his will, fore-ordained all the means thereunto, wherefore they who are elected, being faln in Adam, are redeemed by Christ, are effectually called unto faith in Christ, by his spirit working in due season, are justified, adopted, sanctified, and kept by his power through faith unto salvation; neither are any other redeemed by Christ, or effectually called, justified, adopted, sanctified, and saved, but the Elect only.

7. The Doctrine of this high mystery of predestination, is to be handled with special prudence, and care; that men attending to the will of God revealed in his word, and yielding obedience thereunto, may from the certainty of their effectual vocation, be assured of their eternal election; so shall this doctrine afford matter of praise, reverence, and admiration of God, and of humility, diligence, and abundant consolation, to all that sincerely obey the Gospel.

V. Of Divine Providence

1. GOD, the great *Creator* of all things, in *his* infinite power, and wisdom, doth uphold, direct, dispose, and govern all Creatures, and things, from the greatest even to the least, by *his* most wise and holy providence, to the end for the which they were *Created;* according unto his infallible foreknowledge, and the free and immutable Counsel of *his* own will; to the praise of the glory of *his* wisdom, power, justice, infinite goodness and mercy.

2. Although in relation to the foreknowledge and *Decree* of *God,* the first cause, all things come to pass immutably and infallibly; so that there is not any thing, befalls any by chance, or without *his Providence;* yet by the same *Providence* he ordereth them to fall out, according to the nature of second causes, either necessarily, freely, or contingently.

3. God in *his* ordinary *Providence* maketh use of means; yet is free to work, without, above, and against them, at *his* pleasure.

4. The Almighty power, unsearchable wisdom, and *infinite* goodness of *God,* so far manifest themselves in *his Providence,* that his determinate Councel extendeth it self even to the first fall, and all other sinful actions both of Angels, and Men; (and that not be a bare permission) which also he most wisely and powerfully boundeth, and otherwise ordereth, and governeth, in a manifold dispensation to *his* most holy ends: yet so, as the sinfulness of their acts proceedeth only from the Creatures, and not from *God;* who being most holy and righteous, neither is nor can be, the author or approver of sin.

5. The most wise, righteous, and gracious *God,* doth oftentimes, leave for a season *his* own children to manifold temptations, and the corruption of their own heart, to chastise them for their former sins, or to discover unto them the hidden strength of corruption, and deceitfulness of their hearts, that they may be humbled; and to raise them to a more close, and constant dependence for their support, upon himself; and to make them more watchful against all future occasions of sin, and for other just and holy ends.

So that whatsoever befalls any of his elect is by his appointment, for his glory, and their good.

6. As for those wicked and ungodly men, whom God as a righteous

judge, for former sin doth blind and harden; from them he not only withholdeth his Grace, whereby they might have been inlightened in their understanding, and wrought upon in their hearts; But sometimes also withdraweth the gifts which they had, and exposeth them to such objects as their *corruptions* makes occasion of sin; and withal gives them over to their own lusts, the temptations of the world, and the power of Satan; whereby it comes to pass, that they harden themselves, even under those means which God useth for the softening of others.

7. As the *Providence* of *God* doth, in general, reach to all *Creatures,* so after a most special manner it taketh care of his Church, and disposeth of all things to the good thereof.

VI. Of the fall of Man, of Sin, and of the Punishment thereof

1. Although *God created Man* upright, and perfect, and gave him a righteous law, which had been unto life had he kept it, and threatened death upon the breach thereof; yet he did not long abide in this honour; Satan using the subtilty of the serpent to seduce *Eve,* then by her seducing *Adam,* who without any compulsion, did wilfully transgress the Law of their *Creation,* and the command given unto them, in eating the forbidden fruit; which *God* was pleased according to *his* wise and holy *Councel* to permit, having purposed to order it, to *his* own glory.

2. Our first *Parents* by this *Sin,* fell from their original righteousness and communion with *God,* and we in them, whereby death came upon all; all becoming dead in *Sin,* and wholly defiled, in all the faculties, and parts, of soul, and body.

3. They being the root, and by *Gods* appointment, standing in the room, and stead of all mankind; the guilt of the *Sin* was imputed, and *corrupted* nature conveyed, to all their posterity descending from them by ordinary generation, being now conceived in *Sin,* and by nature children of wrath, the servants of *Sin,* the subjects of *death* and all other miseries, spiritual, temporal and eternal, unless the *Lord Jesus* set them free.

4. From this original *corruption,* whereby we are utterly indisposed, disabled, and made opposite to all good, and wholly inclined to all evil, do proceed all actual transgressions.

5. This *corruption* of nature, during this Life, doth remain in those that are regenerated: and although it be through *Christ* pardoned, and mortified, yet both it self, and the first motions thereof, are truly and properly *Sin.*

VII. Of Gods Covenant

1. THE distance between *God* and the *Creature* is so great, that

although reasonable *Creatures* do owe obedience unto him as their *Creator*, yet they could never have obtained any reward of Life, but by some voluntary condescension on *Gods part*, which he hath been pleased to express, by way of *Covenant*.

2. Moreover *Man* having brought himself under the *curse* of the Law by his fall, it pleased the *Lord* to make a *Covenant* of *Grace* wherein he freely offereth unto *Sinners*, Life and Salvation by *Jesus Christ*, requiring of them Faith in him, that they may be saved; and promising to give unto all those that are ordained unto eternal Life, his Holy *Spirit*, to make them willing, and able to believe.

3. This *Covenant* is revealed in the Gospel; first of all to *Adam* in the promise of Salvation by the seed of the woman, and afterwards by farther steps, until the full discovery thereof was compleated in the new Testament; and it is founded in that Eternal *Covenant* transaction, that was between the *Father* and the *Son*, about the Redemption of the *Elect;* and it is alone by the Grace of this *Covenant*, that all of the posterity of fallen *Adam*, that ever were saved, did obtain life and a blessed immortality; *Man* being now utterly uncapable of acceptance with *God* upon those terms, on which *Adam* stood in his state of innocency.

VIII. Of Christ the Mediator

1. IT pleased *God* in his eternal purpose, to chuse and ordain the *Lord Jesus* his only-begotten *Son*, according to the *Covenant* made between them both, to be the *Mediator* between *God* and *Man;* the Prophet, Priest and King; Head and Saviour of his Church, the heir or all things, and judge of the world: Unto whom he did from all Eternity, give a people to be his seed, and to be by him in time redeemed, called, justified, sanctified, and glorified.

2. The *Son* of *God*, the second Person in the *Holy Trinity*, being very and eternal *God*, the brightness of the Fathers glory, of one substance and equal with *him:* who made the World, who upholdeth and governeth all things he hath made: did when the fullness of time was come take upon him mans nature, with all the Essential properties, and common infirmities thereof, yet without sin: being conceived by the *Holy Spirit* in the *Womb* of the *Virgin Mary*, the *Holy Spirit* coming down upon her, and the power of the most *High* overshadowing her, and so was made of a *Woman*, of the Tribe of *Judah*, of the Seed of *Abraham*, and *David* according to the *Scriptures:* So that two whole, perfect, and distinct natures, were inseparably joined together in one *Person:* without *conversion, composition*, or *confusion:* which *Person* is very *God*, and very *Man;* yet one *Christ*, the only *Mediator* between *God* and *Man*.

3. The *Lord Jesus* in his human nature thus united to the divine, in the

Person of the *Son,* was sanctified, anointed with the *Holy Spirit,* above measure; having in him all the treasures of wisdom and knowledge; in whom it pleased the *Father* that all fullness should dwell: To the end that being holy, harmless, undefiled, and full of *Grace,* and *Truth,* he might be thoroughly furnished to execute the office of a *Mediator,* and *Surety;* which office he took not unto himself, but was thereunto called by his *Father;* who put all power and judgement in his hand, and gave him Commandment to execute the same.

4. This office the *Lord Jesus* did most willingly undertake, which that he might discharge he was made under the Law, and did perfectly fulfill it, and underwent the punishment due to us, which we should have born and suffered, being made *Sin* and a *Curse* for us: enduring most grievous sorrows in his Soul; and most painful sufferings in his body; was crucified, and died, and remained in the state of the dead; yet saw no *corruption:* on the third day he arose from the dead, with the same body in which he suffered; with which also he ascended into heaven: and there sitteth at the right hand of his *Father,* making intercession; and shall return to judge *Men* and *Angels,* at the end of the World.

5. The *Lord Jesus* by his perfect obedience and sacrifice of himself, which he through the Eternal *Spirit* once offered up unto *God,* hath fully satisfied the Justice of *God,* procured reconciliation, and purchased an Everlasting inheritance in the Kingdom of Heaven, for all those whom the *Father* hath given unto him.

6. Although the price of Redemption was not actually paid by *Christ,* till after his *Incarnation,* yet the vertue, efficacy, and benefit thereof were communicated to the Elect in all ages successively, from the beginning of the World, in and by those Promises, Types, and Sacrifices, wherein he was revealed, and signified to be the Seed of the *Woman,* which should bruise the Serpents head; and the Lamb slain from the foundation of the World: Being *the same yesterday, and to-day, and for ever.*

7. Christ in the work of *Mediation* acteth according to both natures, by each nature doing that which is proper to it self; yet by reason of the Unity of the Person, that which is proper to one nature, is sometimes in *Scripture* attributed to the Person denominated by the other nature.

8. To all those for whom Christ hath obtained eternal redemption, he doth certainly, and effectually apply, and communicate the same; making intercession for them, uniting them to himself by his spirit, revealing unto them, in and by the word, the mystery of salvation; perswading them to believe, and obey; governing their hearts by his word and spirit, and overcoming all their enemies by his Almighty power, and wisdom; in such manner, and wayes as are most consonant to his wonderful, and unsearchable dispensation; and all of free, and absolute Grace, without any condition foreseen in them, to procure it.

9. This office of Mediator between God and man, is proper onely to

Christ, who is the Prophet, Priest, and King of the Church of God; and may not be either in whole, or in part thereof transfer'ed from him to any other.

10. This number and order of Offices is necessary; for in respect of our ignorance, we stand in need of his prophetical Office; and in respect of our alienation from God, and imperfection of the best of our services, we need his Priestly office, to reconcile us, and present us acceptable unto God: and in respect of our averseness, and utter inability to return to God, and for our rescue, and security from our spiritual adversaries, we need his Kingly office, to convince, subdue, draw, uphold, deliver, and preserve us to his Heavenly Kingdome.

IX. Of Free Will

1. GOD hath endued the Will of Man, with that natural liberty, and power of acting upon choice; that is neither forced, nor by any necessity of nature determined to good or evil.

2. Man in his state of innocency, had freedom, and power, to will, and to do that which was good, and well-pleasing to God; but yet was mutable, so that he might fall from it.

3. Man by his fall into a state of sin hath wholly lost all ability of Will, to any spiritual good accompanying salvation; so as a natural man, being altogether averse from that good, and dead in *Sin*, is not able, by his own strength, to convert himself; or to prepare himself thereunto.

4 When God converts a sinner, and translates him into the state of Grace, he freeth him from his natural bondage under sin, and by his grace alone, enables him freely to will, and to do that which is spiritually good; yet so as that, by reason of his remaining corruption he doth not perfectly nor only will that which is good; but doth also will that which is evil.

5. The Will of Man is made perfectly, and immutable free to good alone, in the state of Glory only.

X. Of Effectual Calling

1. THose whom God hath predestinated unto Life, he is pleased, in his appointed, and accepted time, effectually to call by his word, and Spirit, out of that state of sin, and death, in which they are by nature, to grace and Salvation by Jesus Christ; inlightening their minds, spiritually, and savingly to understand the things of God; taking away their heart of stone, and giving unto them an heart of flesh; renewing their wills, and by his Almighty power determining them to that which is good, and effectually drawing them to Jesus Christ; yet so as they come most freely, being made willing by his Grace.

2. This Effectual Call is of God's free, and special grace alone not from any thing at all foreseen in man, nor from any power, or agency in the Creature, coworking with his special Grace, the Creature being wholly passive therein, being dead in sins and trespasses, until being quickened & renewed by the holy Spirit, he is thereby enabled to answer this call, and to embrace the Grace offered and conveyed in it; and that by no less power, then that which raised up Christ from the dead.

3. Elect Infants dying in infancy, are regenerated and saved by Christ through the Spirit; who worketh when, and where, and how he pleaseth: so also are all other elect persons, who are uncapable of being outwardly called by the Ministry of the Word.

4. Others not elected, although they may be called by the Ministry of the word, and may have some common operations of the Spirit, yet not being effectually drawn by the Father, they neither will nor can truly come to Christ; and therefore can not be saved: much less can men that receive not the Christian Religion be saved; be they never so diligent to frame their lives according to the light of nature, and the law of that Religion they do profess.

XI. Of Justification

1. THose whom God Effectually calleth, he also freely justifieth, not by infusing Righteousness into them, but by pardoning their sins, and by accounting, and accepting their Persons as Righteous; not for any thing wrought in them, or done by them, but for Christ's sake alone, not by imputing faith it self, the act of believing, or any other evangelical obedience to them, as their Righteousness; but by imputing Christs active obedience unto the whole Law, and passive obedience in his death, for their whole and sole Righteousness, they receiving, and resting on him, and his Righteousness, by Faith; which faith they have not of themselves, it is the gift of *God.*

2. Faith thus receiving and resting on Christ, and his Righteousness, is the alone instrument of Justification: yet is it not alone in the person justified, but is ever accompanied with all other saving Graces, and is no dead faith, but worketh by love.

3. Christ by his obedience, and death, did fully discharge the debt of all those that are thus justified; and did by the sacrifice of himself, in the blood of his cross, undergoing in their stead, the penalty due unto them: make a proper, real, and full satisfaction to *Gods* justice in their behalf: yet in asmuch as he was given by the Father for them, and his Obedience and Satisfaction accepted in their stead, and both freely, not for any thing in them; their Justification is only of Free Grace, that both the exact justice and rich Grace of *God,* might be glorified in the Justification of sinners.

4. God did from all eternity decree to justifie all the Elect, and Christ

did, in the fulness of time die for their sins, and rise again for their Justification; Nevertheless they are not justified, personally, untill the *Holy Spirit,* doth in due time actually apply *Christ* unto them.

5. God doth continue to Forgive the sins of those that are justified, and although they can never fall from the state of justification; yet they may by their sins fall under Gods Fatherly displeasure; and in that condition, they have not usually the light of his Countenance restored unto them, until they humble themselves, confess their sins, beg pardon, and renew their faith, and repentance.

6. The Justification of Believers under the Old Testament was in all these respects, one and the same with the justification of Believers under the New Testament.

XII. Of Adoption

ALL those that are justified, *God* vouchsafed, in, and for his only *Son Jesus Christ,* to make partakers of the Grace of *Adoption;* by which they are taken into the number, and enjoy the Liberties, and Privileges of the Children of *God;* have his name put upon them, receive the *Spirit of Adoption,* have access to the throne of Grace with boldness, are enabled to cry *Abba Father,* are pitied, protected, provided for, and chastned by him, as by a *Father;* yet never cast off; but sealed to the day of Redemption, and inherit the promises, as heirs, of everlasting Salvation.

XIII. Of Sanctification

1. THey who are united to *Christ,* Effectually called, and regenerated, having a new heart, and a new *Spirit created* in them, through the vertue of *Christ's* death, and Resurrection; are also farther sanctified, really, and personally, through the same vertue, by his word and *Spirit* dwelling in them; the dominion of the whole body of sin is destroyed, and the several lusts thereof, are more and more weakened, and mortified; and they more and more quickened, and strengthened in all saving graces, to the practice of all true holyness, without which no man shall see the Lord.

2. This Sanctification is throughout, in the whole man, yet imperfect in this life; there abideth still some remnants of *corruption* in every part, whence ariseth a continual, and irreconcilable war; the Flesh lusting against the Spirit, and the Spirit against the Flesh.

3. In which war, although the remaining *corruption* for a time may much prevail; yet through the continual supply of strength from the sanctifying *Spirit of Christ* the regenerate part doth overcome; and so the Saints grow in Grace, perfecting holiness in the fear of God, and pressing after an heavenly life, in Evangelical Obedience to all the commands

which *Christ* as *Head* and *King,* in his *Word* hath prescribed to them.

XIV. Of Saving Faith

1. THE Grace of *Faith,* whereby the Elect are enabled to believe to the saving of their souls, is the work of the *Spirit* of *Christ* in their hearts; and is ordinarily wrought by the Ministry of the Word; by which also, and by the administration of *Baptisme,* and the *Lords Supper, Prayer* and other *Means* appointed of *God,* it is increased, and strengthened.

2. By this *Faith* a Christian believeth to be true, whatsoever is revealed in the *Word,* for the Authority of *God* himself; and also apprehendeth an excellency therein, above all other *Writings;* and all things in the *world:* as it bears forth the glory of *God* in his *Attributes,* the excellency of *Christ* in his Nature and Offices; and the Power and Fullness of the *Holy Spirit* in his Workings, and Operations; and so is enabled to cast his Soul upon the truth thus believed; and also acteth differently, upon that which each particular, passage thereof containeth; yielding obedience to the commands, trembling at the threatenings, and embracing the promises of *God,* for this life, and that which is to come: But the principle acts of Saving Faith, have immediate relation to Christ, accepting, receiving, and resting upon him alone, for Justification, Sanctification, and Eternal Life, by vertue of the Covenant of Grace.

3. This *Faith* although it be different in degrees, and may be weak, or strong; yet it is in the least degree of it, different in the kind, or nature of it (as is all other saving Grace) from the Faith, and common grace of temporary believers; and therefore though it may be many times assailed, and weakened; yet it gets the victory; growing up in many, to the attainment of a full assurance through *Christ,* who is both the Author and finisher of our *Faith.*

XV. Of Repentance unto Life and Salvation

1. SUch of the Elect as are converted at riper years, having sometimes lived in the state of nature, and therein served divers lusts and pleasures, *God* in their *Effectual Calling* giveth them Repentance unto Life.

2. Whereas there is none that doth good, and sinneth not; and the best of men may, through the power, and deceitfulness of their corruption dwelling in them, with the prevalency of temptation, fall into great sins, and provocations; God hath in the Covenant of Grace, mercifully provided that Believers so sinning, and falling, be renewed through Repentance unto Salvation.

3. This saving Repentance is an evangelical Grace, whereby a person, being by the *Holy Spirit* made sensible of the manifold evils of his sin,

doth, by Faith in Christ, humble himself for it, with godly sorrow, detestation of it, and self-abhorrency; praying for pardon, and strength of grace, with a purpose and endeavour by supplies of the *Spirit,* to walk before God unto all well pleasing in all things.

4. As Repentance is to be continued through the whole course of our lives, upon the account of the body of death, and the motions thereof; so it is every mans duty, to repent of his particular known sins, particularly.

5. Such is the provision which God hath made through Christ in the Covenant of Grace, for the preservation of Believers unto Salvation, that although there is no sin so small, but it deserves damnation; yet there is no sin so great, that it shall bring damnation on them that repent; which makes the constant preaching of Repentance necessary.

XVI. Of Good Works

1. GOod works are only such as God hath commanded in his Holy word; and not such as without the warrant thereof, are devised by men, out of blind zeal, or upon any pretense of good intentions.

2. These good works, done in obedience to God's commandments, are the fruits, and evidences of a true, and lively faith; and by them Believers manifest their thankfullness, strengthen their assurance, edifie their brethren, adorn the profession of the Gospel, stop the mouths of the adversaries, and glorifie God, whose workmanship they are, created in Christ Jesus thereunto, that having their fruit unto holiness, they may have the end eternal life.

3. Their ability to do good works, is not at all of themselves; but wholly from the *Spirit* of Christ; and that they may be enabled thereunto, besides the graces they have already received, there is necessary an actual influence of the same *Holy Spirit,* to work in them to will, and to do, of his good pleasure; yet are they not hereupon to grow negligent, as if they were not bound to perform any duty, unless upon a special motion of the Spirit; but they ought to be diligent in stirring up the grace of God that is in them.

4. They who in their obedience, attain to the greatest height which is possible in this life, are so far from being able to superrogate, and to do more than God requires, that they fall short of much which in duty they are bound to do.

5. We cannot by our best works, merit pardon of Sin or Eternal Life at the hand of God, because of the great disproportion that is between them and the glory to come; and the infinite distance that is between us and God, whom by them we can neither profit, nor satisfie for the debt of our former sins; but when we have done all we can, we have done but our duty, and are unprofitable servants: and because as they are good they

proceed from his Spirit, and as they are wrought by us they are defiled and mixed with so much weakness and imperfection that they can not endure the severity of Gods judgment.

6. Yet notwithstanding the persons of Believers being accepted through Christ their good works also are accepted in him; not as though they were in this life wholly unblameable and unreprovable in Gods sight; but that he looking upon them in his Son is pleased to accept and reward that which is sincere although accomplished with many weaknesses and imperfections.

7. Works done by unregenerate men, although for the matter of them they may be things which God commands, and of good use, both to themselves and others; yet because they proceed not from a heart purified by faith, nor are done in a right manner according to the word, nor to a right end, the glory of God; they are therefore sinful and can not please God; nor make a man meet to receive grace from God; and yet their neglect of them is more sinful and displeasing unto God.

XVII. Of Perseverance of the Saints

1. THose whom God hath accepted in the beloved, effectually called and Sanctified by his *Spirit,* and given the precious faith of his Elect unto, can neither totally nor finally fall away from the state of grace; but shall certainly persevere therein to the end and be eternally saved, seeing the gifts and callings of God are without Repentance, (whence he still begets and nourisheth in them Faith, Repentance, Love, Joy, Hope, and all the graces of the Spirit unto immortality) and though many storms and floods arise and beat against them, yet they shall never be able to take them off that foundation and rock which by faith they are fastned upon: notwithstanding through unbelief and the temptations of Satan the sensible sight of the light and love of God, may for a time be clouded, and obscured from them, yet he is still the same, and they shall be sure to be kept by the power of God unto Salvation, where they shall enjoy their purchased possession, they being engraved upon the palms of his hands, and their names having been written in the book of life from all Eternity.

2. This perseverance of the Saints depends not upon their own free will; but upon the immutability of the decree of Election, flowing from the free and unchangeable love of God the Father; upon the efficacy of the merit and intercession of Jesus Christ and Union with him, the oath of God, the abiding of his Spirit & the seed of God with in them, and the nature of the Covenant of Grace from all which ariseth also the certainty and infallibility thereof.

3. And though they may, through the temptation of Satan and of the world, the prevalency of corruption remaining in them, and the neglect of the means of their preservation fall into grievous sins, and for a time

continue therein; whereby they incur Gods displeasure, and grieve his holy Spirit, come to have their graces and comforts impaired have their hearts hardened, and their Consciences wounded, hurt, and scandalize others, and bring temporal judgments upon themselves: yet they shall renew their repentance and be preserved through faith in Christ Jesus to the end.

XVIII. Of the Assurance of Grace and Salvation

1. ALthough temporary Believers, and other unregenerate men, may vainly deceive themselves with false hopes, and carnal presumptions, of being in the favour of God, and in a state of salvation, which hope of theirs shall perish; yet such as truly believe in the Lord Jesus, and love him in sincerity, endeavoring to walk in all good Conscience before him, may in this life be certainly assured that they are in the state of Grace; and may rejoice in the hope of the glory of God which hope shall never make them ashamed.

2. This certainty is not a bare conjectural and probable perswasion, grounded upon a fallible hope; but an infallible assurance of faith, founded on the Blood and Righteousness of Christ revealed in the Gospel; and also upon the inward evidence of those graces of the Spirit unto which promises are made, and on the testimony of the Spirit of adoption, witnessing with our Spirits that we are the children of God; and as a fruit thereof keeping the heart both humble and holy.

3. This infallible assurance doth not so belong to the essence of faith, but that a true Believer, may wait long and conflict with many difficulties before he be partaker of it; yet being enabled by the Spirit to know the things which are freely given him of God, he may without extraordinary revelation in the right use of means attain thereunto: and therefore it is the duty of every one, to give all diligence to make their Calling and Election sure, that thereby his heart may be enlarged in peace and joy in the holy Spirit, in love and thankfulness to God, and in strength and cheerfulness in the duties of obedience, the proper fruits of this Assurance; so far is it from inclining men to looseness.

4. True Believers may have the assurance of their Salvation divers ways shaken, diminished, and intermitted; as by negligence in preserving of it, by falling into some special Sin, which woundeth the conscience, and grieveth the *Spirit,* by some sudden or vehement temptation, by Gods withdrawing the light of his countenance and suffering even such as fear him to walk in darkness and to have no light; yet are they never destitute of that seed of God, and Life of Faith, that Love of Christ, and the brethren, that sincerity of Heart and Conscience of duty, out of which by the operation of the Spirit, this Assurance may in due time be revived: and by the which in the mean time they are preserved from utter despair.

NOTES

Preface

1. William Cunningham, *The Reformers and the Theology of the Reformation* (Edinburgh: The Banner of Truth Trust, 1967), p. 313.
2. Robert L. Sumner, *An Examination of Tulip* (Brownsburg: Biblical Evangelism, 1972); Peter S. Ruckman, *Hyper-Calvinism* (Pensacola: Bible Baptist Bookstore, 1984); John R. Rice, *Hyper-Calvinism: a False Doctrine* (Murfreesboro: Sword of the Lord Publishers, 1970); Curtis Hutson, *Why I Disagree With All Five Points of Calvinism* (Murfreesboro: Sword of the Lord Publishers, 1980); James Moffat, *Predestination* (Lancaster: Charles W. Duty & Sons, n.d.); Donald A. Waite, *Calvin's Error of Limited Atonement* (Collingswood: The Bible For Today, 1978); Alger Fitch, *Pick the Brighter Tulip* (Joplin: College Press Publishing Co., 1993); L. S. Ballard, *Election Made Plain,* 2nd ed. (n.p., n.d.).
3. J. R. Alexander, *The Tulip Doctrine* (Texarkana: Bogard Press, 1992); John R. Rice, *Predestinated for Hell? NO!* (Murfreesboro: Sword of the Lord Publishers, 1958); Peter S. Ruckman, *Why I Am Not a Calvinist* (Pensacola: Bible Baptist Bookstore, 1997); George L. Bryson, *The Five Points of Calvinism* (Costa Mesa: The Word for Today, 1996); O. Glenn McKinley, *Where Two Creeds Meet* (Kansas City: Beacon Hill Press, 1959); Max Younce, *Not Chosen to Salvation* (Madison: by the author, n.d.); James Wilkins, *Foreknowledge, Election, Predestination in the Light of Soul-Winning* (Mansfield: New Testament Ministries, 1985); Andrew Telford, *Subjects of Sovereignty* (Boca Raton: by the author, 1948); Robert P. Lightner, *The Death Christ Died* (Des Plains: Regular Baptist Press, 1967); Cornelius R. Stam, *Divine Election and Human Responsibility* (Chicago: Berean Bible Society, 1994).
4. Archer C. Wilcox, *Messianic Credentials of Jesus the Christ* (Burlington: Crown Publications, 1986); Samuel Fisk, *Divine Sovereignty and Human Freedom* (Neptune: Loizeaux Brothers, 1973); Samuel Fisk, *Calvinistic Paths Retraced* (Murfreesboro: Biblical Evangelism Press, 1985); Clark H. Pinnock, ed., *The Grace of God, The Will of Man* (Grand Rapids: Zondervan Publishing House, 1989); Clark H. Pinnock, ed., *Grace Unlimited* (Minneapolis: Bethany House Publishers, 1975); Kent Kelly, *Inside the Tulip Controversy* (Southern Pines: Calvary Press, 1986); Robert L. Shank, *Elect in the Son* (Springfield: Westcott Publishers, 1970); Robert L. Shank, *Life in the Son,* 2nd ed. (Springfield: Westcott Publishers, 1961); Roger T. Forster and V. Paul Marston, *God's Strategy in Human History* (Wheaton: Tyndale House Publishers, 1974); William W. Klein, *The New Chosen People* (Grand Rapids: Zondervan Publishing House, 1990).
5. Bob L. Ross, *The Killing Effects of Calvinism* (Pasadena: Pilgrim Publications, n.d.), p. 1.
6. Ohio Baptist College, *1992–1994 Catalog,* p. 8; Norris Bible Baptist

Institute, *1985–1986 Catalog,* p. 33.
7. Loraine Boettner, *The Reformed Doctrine of Predestination* (Phillipsburg: Presbyterian and Reformed Publishing Co., 1932), p. 1.
8. C. Samuel Storms, *Chosen for Life* (Grand Rapids: Baker Book House, 1987), p. 11.
9. David N. Steele and Curtis C. Thomas, *The Five Points of Calvinism* (Phillipsburg: Presbyterian and Reformed Publishing Co., 1963), p. 10.
10. W. J. Seaton, *The Five Points of Calvinism* (Edinburgh: The Banner of Truth Trust, 1970), p. 5.
11. Kenneth G. Talbot and W. Gary Crampton, *Calvinism, Hyper-Calvinism and Arminianism* (Edmonton: Still Waters Revival Books, 1990), p. 5.
12. John H. Gerstner, *Wrongly Dividing the Word of Truth* (Brentwood: Wolgemuth & Hyatt, Publishers, 1991), p. 107.
13. Bastian Kruithof, *The High Points of Calvinism* (Grand Rapids: Baker Book House, 1949), p. vii.
14. David J. Engelsma, *A Defense of Calvinism as the Gospel* (South Holland: The Evangelism Committee, Protestant Reformed Church, n.d.), p. 18.
15. Storms, Chosen for Life, p. 22.

Chapter 1
Introduction to Calvinism

1. Alister E. McGrath, *The Intellectual Origins of the European Reformation* (Grand Rapids: Baker, 1987), p. 6.
2. Boettner, Predestination, p. 7.
3. Benjamin B. Warfield, *Calvin and Augustine,* ed. Samuel G. Craig (Philadelphia: Presbyterian and Reformed Publishing Co., 1956), p. 287; Abraham Kuyper, *Lectures on Calvinism* (Grand Rapids: Wm. B. Eerdmans Publishing Co., 1931), pp. 13-15.
4. Robert L. Dabney, *The Five Points of Calvinism* (Harrisonburg: Sprinkle Publications, 1992), p. 6.
5. Engelsma, Defense of Calvinism, p. 3.
6. Ibid., p. 3.
7. Seaton, p. 5.
8. Boettner, Predestination, p. 340.
9. Engelsma, Defense of Calvinism, p. 3.
10. Seaton, p. 22; Engelsma, Defense of Calvinism, p. 3; D. James Kennedy, quoted in Talbot and Crampton, p. iv; Thomas R. Schreiner and Bruce A. Ware, Introduction to Thomas R. Schreiner and Bruce A. Ware, eds., *The Grace of God, the Bondage of the Will* (Grand Rapids: Baker Books, 1995), p. 14.
11. Warfield, Calvin, p. 497.
12. H. Henry Meeter, *The Basic Ideas of Calvinism,* 6th ed. (Grand Rapids: Baker, 1990), p. 17.
13. Boettner, Predestination, p. 335.
14. Warfield, Calvin, p. 507.
15. Samuel Taylor Coleridge, quoted in Eugene E. Brussell, ed., *Webster's New World Dictionary of Quotable Definitions,* 2nd ed. (Englewood Cliffs: Prentice Hall, 1988), p. 66.
16. Robert G. Ingersoll, quoted in Brussell, p. 66.

17. Kent Kelly, p. 8.

18. Aubrey Moore, quoted in Alan P. F. Sell, *The Great Debate* (Grand Rapids: Baker Book House, 1982), p. 21.

19. Samuel Miller, Introductory Essay to Thomas Scott, *The Articles of the Synod of Dort* (Harrisonburg: Sprinkle Publications, 1993), p. 63.

20. Seaton, pp. 17-18.

21. Leonard J. Coppes, *Are Five Points Enough? The Ten Points of Calvinism* (Denver: by the author, 1980), p. xi.

22. Edwin H. Palmer, *The Five Points of Calvinism,* enlar. ed. (Grand Rapids: Baker Book House, 1980), p. 5.

23. D. James Kennedy, quoted in Talbot and Crampton, p. iv.

24. Boettner, Predestination, p. 352.

25. Talbot and Crampton, p. 78.

26. Arthur C. Custance, *The Sovereignty of Grace* (Phillipsburg: Presbyterian and Reformed Publishing Co., 1979), p. 302.

27. Talbot and Crampton, p. 3.

28. Loraine Boettner, *The Reformed Faith* (Phillipsburg: Presbyterian and Reformed Publishing Co., 1983), p. 2.

29. Ibid.

30. Cunningham, Reformers, p. 338.

31. Warfield, Calvin, p. 506.

32. Ibid., p. 499.

33. Custance, p. 302.

34. Engelsma, Defense of Calvinism, p. 4.

35. Charles H. Spurgeon, *Spurgeon's Sovereign Grace Sermons* (Edmonton: Still Waters Revival Books, 1990), p. 129.

36. John Calvin, *Institutes of the Christian Religion,* ed. John T. McNeil, trans. Ford Lewis Battles (Philadelphia: The Westminster Press, 1960), p. 926 (III.xxi.5).

37. Engelsma, Defense of Calvinism, p. 18.

38. Boettner, Predestination, p. 333.

39. William G. T. Shedd, *Calvinism: Pure and Mixed* (Edinburgh: The Banner of Truth Trust, 1986), p. 149.

40. Robert C. Harbach, *Calvinism the Truth* (Grand Rapids: First Protestant Reformed Church, 1984), p. 3.

41. Gordon H. Clark, *Predestination* (Phillipsburg: Presbyterian and Reformed Publishing Co., 1987), p. 144.

42. Palmer, p. 26.

43. George L. Curtiss, *Arminianism in History* (Cincinnati: Cranston & Curts, 1894), p. 10.

44. David J. Engelsma, *Hyper-Calvinism and the Call of the Gospel* (Grand Rapids: Reformed Free Publishing Association, 1980), p. 7.

45. R. K. McGregor Wright, *No Place for Sovereignty* (Downers Grove: InterVarsity Press, 1996), p. 90.

46. Alexander Leighton, quoted in Christopher Ness, *An Antidote Against Arminianism* (Huntington: Paragon Printing Co., 1982), p. 2.

47. William MacLean, *Arminianism: Another Gospel* (Pensacola: Chapel Library, 1976), p. 5.

48. Ibid.

49. Herman Hanko, *God's Everlasting Covenant of Grace* (Grand Rapids:

Reformed Free Publishing Association, 1988), p. 16.

50. Harbach, p. 3.

51. N. S. McFetridge, *Calvinism in History* (Edmonton: Still Waters Revival Books, 1989), pp. 6-10.

52. Ibid., p. 5.

53. Clark, Predestination, p. 127.

54. George Whitefield, *Letter to John Wesley on Election* (Canton: Free Grace Publications, 1977), p. 15.

55. Duane Edward Spencer, *TULIP: The Five Points of Calvinism in the Light of Scripture* (Grand Rapids: Baker Book House, 1979), p. 65.

56. Grover E. Gunn, *The Doctrines of Grace* (Memphis: Footstool Publications, 1987), p. 3; Richard A. Muller, "Grace, Election, and Contingent Choice: Arminius's Gambit and the Reformed Response," in Schreiner and Ware, eds., *The Grace of God, the Bondage of the Will*, p. 277.

57. Gunn, p. 3.

58. Storms, Chosen for Life, p. 30.

59. Clark, Predestination, p. 95.

60. Palmer, p. 26.

61. J. I. Packer, *Introductory Essay to John Owen's The Death of Death in the Death of Christ* (Pensacola: Chapel Library, n.d.), pp. 6-7.

62. Boettner, Reformed Faith, p. 1.

63. Warfield, Calvin, p. 500.

64. Boettner, Predestination, p. 95.

65. MacLean, p. 5.

66. James Arminius, *The Works of James Arminius,* trans. James Nichols and William Nichols (Grand Rapids: Baker Book House, 1986), vol. 1, p. 1.

67. C. Gregg Singer, *JOHN CALVIN: His Roots and Fruits* (Atlanta: A Press, 1989), p. 29.

68. Ibid., p. 30.

69. Kuyper, p. 39.

70. Singer, pp. 46, 50.

71. Arthur Dakin, *Calvinism* (Philadelphia: The Westminster Press, 1946), p. 203.

72. W. Gary Crampton, *What Calvin Says* (Jefferson: The Trinity Foundation, 1992), p. 12.

73. Singer, p. 48.

74. For Weber's work in translation see Max Weber, *The Protestant Ethic and the Spirit of Capitalism,* trans. Talcott Parsons (New York: Charles Scribner's Sons, 1958). For an explanation see Michael H. Lessnoff, *The Spirit of Capitalism and the Protestant Ethic: An Enquiry into the Weber Thesis* (Hants: Edward Elgar Publishing, 1994). For a discussion of Calvinism and Capitalism by Calvinists see Alister E. McGrath, *A Life of John Calvin* (Oxford: Blackwell Publishers, 1990), pp. 219-245; Georgia Harkness, *John Calvin: The Man and His Ethics* (Nashville: Abingdon Press, 1958), pp. 178-220; Singer, pp. 48-51; Dakin, pp. 203-208.

75. John W. Robbins, "Our Comrades at Calvin College," *The Trinity Review,* November 1996, p. 1.

76. Henry Atherton, Introduction to Jerom Zanchius, *The Doctrine of Absolute Predestination,* trans. Augustus M. Toplady (Grand Rapids: Baker Book House, 1977), pp. 11-12.

77. Kuyper, p. 40.

78. Boettner, Predestination, p. 390.
79. Singer, pp. 42-43; McFetridge, p. 39.
80. Douglas F. Kelly, *The Emergence of Liberty in the Modern World* (Phillipsburg: Presbyterian and Reformed Publishing Co., 1992), p. 126; Samuel Miller, pp. 42, 52; Dakin, pp. 160-161.
81. Talbot and Crampton, pp. 80, 78.
82. Ibid., 78.
83. McFetridge, p. 14.
84. Talbot and Crampton, p. 79.
85. Ibid.
86. Ibid.
87. Boettner, Predestination, p. 2.
88. Ibid., pp. 2-3.
89. Ibid., p. 1.
90. R. Willis, quoted in Kuyper, p. 15.
91. Spencer, Tulip, p. 6.
92. Singer, p. 28.
93. R. C. Sproul, *Chosen by God* (Wheaton: Tyndale House, 1986), p. 15.
94. McFetridge, p. 81.
95. E.g., Seaton, p. 23; Spencer, Tulip, p. 7; Talbot and Crampton, pp. 79-80; Dabney, Calvinism, pp. 7-8.
96. Roy Mason, *What is to Be, Will Be* (n.p., n.d.), p. 1; Manford E. Kober, *Divine Election or Human Effort?* (n.p., n.d.), p. 52; Godwell Andrew Chan, "Spurgeon, the Forgotten Calvinist," *The Trinity Review*, August 1996, pp. 1-4; Kenneth H. Good, *Are Baptists Calvinists?* rev. ed. (Rochester: Backus Book Publishers, 1988), pp. 80, 147; Spencer, Tulip, p. 6; Steele and Thomas, p. 8; Seaton, pp. 8-9; Talbot and Crampton, pp. 2-3; Gerstner, Wrongly Dividing, p. 107.
97. J. Gresham Machen, *The Christian View of Man* (Edinburgh: The Banner of Truth Trust, 1965), p. 52; Mason, p. 9; Kober, p. 37; Kruithof, p. 40.
98. Boettner, Predestination, p. 382.
99. John H. Bratt, "The History and Development of Calvinism in America," in John H. Bratt, ed., *The Rise and Development of Calvinism*, 2nd ed. (Grand Rapids: Wm. B. Eerdmans Publishing Co., 1964), pp. 114-122; Boettner, Predestination, pp. 382-391; Dakin, pp. 158-165.
100. Boettner, Predestination, p. 397.
101. Bratt, Calvinism in America, pp. 124-127; Dakin, pp. 162-163; McFetridge, pp. 108-112; Thomas J. Nettles, "John Wesley's Contention with Calvinism: Interactions Then and Now," in Schreiner and Ware, eds., *The Grace of God, the Bondage of the Will*, pp. 302-303.
102. Bratt, Calvinism in America, p. 126.
103. Charles Hodge, *Systematic Theology* (Grand Rapids: Wm. B. Eerdmans Publishing Co., 1986), vol. 2, p. 333.
104. Sproul, Chosen by God, p. 15.
105. Curtis Pugh, "Six Reasons I Love the Doctrines of Grace," *The Berea Baptist Banner*, November 5, 1994, pp. 207-208; Thomas J. Nettles, *By His Grace and for His Glory* (Grand Rapids: Baker Book House, 1986), p. 13; Tom Ross, *Abandoned Truth: The Doctrines of Grace* (Xenia: Providence Baptist Church, 1991), pp. ix-x.
106. Joseph M. Wilson, "Sovereign Grace Versus Arminianism," *The Baptist*

Examiner, July 22, 1989, p. 1; Jack Warren, "For Sovereign Grace; Against Arminian Heresy," *Baptist Evangel,* January–March 1997, p. 2.

107. Ted Gower, "Am I a Calvinist?" *The Baptist Examiner,* November 21, 1992, p. 9; Jimmie B. Davis, in "The Berea Baptist Banner Forum," *The Berea Baptist Banner,* March 5, 1990, p. 51.

108. Forrest L. Keener, *Grace Not Calvinism* (Lawton: The Watchman Press, 1992).

109. Joseph M. Wilson, "From the Editor," *The Baptist Examiner,* June 22, 1991, p. 2.

110. Patrick H. Mell, *The Biblical Doctrine of Calvinism* (Cape Coral: Christian Gospel Foundation, 1988), p. 18.

111. Spurgeon, Sovereign Grace Sermons, p. 129.

112. Milburn Cockrell, Introduction to Tom Ross, *Abandoned Truth: The Doctrines of Grace,* p. v.

113. Milburn Cockrell, "Second Trip to the Philippines," *The Berea Baptist Banner,* January 5, 1995, p. 4.

114. Mason, pp. 5, 4-5.

115. Cockrell, Introduction to Tom Ross, p. vi.

116. Good, Calvinists, p. 85.

117. Ibid., p. 62.

118. Ibid., pp. 60-61, 96.

119. Keener, p. 21.

120. Cockrell, Introduction to Tom Ross, p. vi.

121. Wilson, Sovereign Grace, p.3.

122. Garner Smith, in "The Berea Baptist Banner Forum," *The Berea Baptist Banner,* September 5, 1992, p. 172.

123. Joseph M. Wilson, "Is There an Arminian Gospel?" *The Baptist Examiner,* December 7, 1991, p. 11.

124. Wilson, Sovereign Grace, p.3.

125. Ibid.

126. Keener, p. 18.

127. Joseph M. Wilson, "Sovereign Grace View and Arminian View of Salvation," *The Baptist Examiner,* July 18, 1992, p. 8.

128. Ibid.

129. Ibid.

130. Good, Calvinists, p. 63.

131. Ibid.

132. Charles H. Spurgeon, quoted in Good, Calvinists, p. 63.

133. Good, Calvinists, p. 2.

134. Ibid.

135. Ibid., p. 124.

136. Ibid.

137. Curtis Pugh, "The Biblicist Position," *The Berea Baptist Banner,* July 5, 1993, pp. 128-129.

138. Ibid., p. 121.

139. Good, Calvinists, pp. 124, 133, 140; Cockrell, Introduction to Tom Ross, p. v.

140. Thomas Crosby, *The History of the English Baptists* (Lafayette: Church History Research & Archives, 1979), vol. 1, p. 173.

141. John T. Christian, *A History of the Baptists* (Texarkana: Bogard Press,

1922), vol. 2, p. 407; Thomas Armitage, *The History of the Baptists* (Watertown: Maranatha Baptist Press, 1980), vol. 2, p. 731.

142. Good, Calvinists, p. 150.

143. Nettles, By His Grace, p. 73.

144. Good, Calvinists, p. 156.

145. Jack Warren, "More on Particular Baptists," *Baptist Evangel,* January 1994, p. 2.

146. David Benedict, *A General History of the Baptist Denomination in America, and Other Parts of the World* (Gallatin: Church History Research & Archives, 1985), vol. 1, p. 602.

147. Crosby, vol. 1, p. 174.

148. Robert G. Torbet, *A History of the Baptists,* 3rd ed. (Valley Forge: Judson Press, 1963), p. 70.

149. Mason, p. 5.

150. Cockrell, Introduction to Tom Ross, p. v.

151. Warren, For Sovereign Grace, p. 2.

152. Mason, p. 1.

153. Ibid., p. 2.

154. Fred Phelps, "The Five Points of Calvinism," *The Berea Baptist Banner,* February 5, 1990, p. 25

155. Mason, p. 3.

156. Garner Smith, in "The Berea Baptist Banner Forum," *The Berea Baptist Banner,* February 5, 1995, p. 30.

157. Kober, p. 46.

158. Warren, Particular Baptists, p. 2.

159. Wilson, Sovereign Grace, p. 1.

160. Charles H. Spurgeon, quoted in Iain H. Murray, *The Forgotten Spurgeon* (Edinburgh: The Banner of Truth Trust, 1978), p. 79.

161. Good, Calvinists, p. 156; Nettles, By His Grace, p. 42.

162. Mason, p. 24; Good, Calvinists, pp. 34-35, 66-67, 80; *The Biblical and Historical Faith of Baptists on God's Sovereignty* (Ashland: Calvary Baptist Church, n.d.), pp. 50-51.

163. Boettner, Predestination, p. 1.

164. McFetridge, p. 49.

165. Tom Ross, Abandoned Truth, pp. 21-28; Good, Calvinists, pp. 137-149.

166. Mason, chap. 3; Robert B. Selph, *Southern Baptists and the Doctrine of Election* (Harrisonburg: Sprinkle Publications, 1988), chap. 2.

167. Nettles, *By His Grace and for His Glory; The Biblical and Historical Faith of Baptists on God's Sovereignty.*

168. Nettles, By His Grace, p. 13.

169. Ibid., p. 73.

170. For a biography of Gill by his immediate successor, see John Rippon, *A Brief Memoir of the Life and Writings of the Late Rev. John Gill, D.D.* (Harrisonburg: Gano Books, 1992); for a more recent work, see George M. Ella, *John Gill and the Cause of God and Truth* (Durham: Go Publications, 1995).

171. The Baptist Standard Bearer, Number One Iron Oaks Dr., Paris, AR 72855.

172. Good, Calvinists, p. 147.

173. *Spurgeon's Sovereign Grace Sermons; Spurgeon's Sermons on Sovereignty* (Pasadena: Pilgrim Publications, 1990).

174. Pilgrim Publications, P.O. Box 66, Pasadena, TX 77501.

175. For the life of Pink, see Richard P. Belcher, *Arthur W. Pink: Born to Write* (Columbia: Richbarry Press, 1982), and Iain H. Murray, *The Life of Arthur W. Pink* (Edinburgh: The Banner of Truth Trust, 1981); for an examination and analysis of his Calvinism, see Richard P. Belcher, *Arthur W. Pink: Predestination* (Columbia: Richbarry Press, 1983).

176. Arthur W. Pink, *The Sovereignty of God,* 4th ed. (Grand Rapids: Baker Book House, 1949).

177. Arthur W. Pink, *The Sovereignty of God,* rev. ed. (Edinburgh: The Banner of Truth Trust, 1961).

178. Marc D. Carpenter, "The Banner of Truth Versus Calvinism," part 1, *The Trinity Review,* May 1997, pp. 1-4.

179. Most are published by Baker Book House, P.O. Box 6287, Grand Rapids, MI 49516.

180. Good, Calvinists, p. 79.

181. Ibid., p. 73.

182. See in the official journal of the Southern Baptist Convention, "A Study Tool for the Doctrine of Election," *SBC Life,* April 1995, pp. 8-9, and "Arminian/Calvinist Responses," *SBC Life,* August 1995, pp. 8-9.

183. Kenneth H. Good, *Are Baptists Reformed?* (Lorain: Regular Baptist Heritage Fellowship, 1986), p. 67.

184. R. B. Kuiper, *God-Centered Evangelism* (London: The Banner of Truth Trust, 1966), p. 9.

185. Boettner, Reformed Faith, p. 24.

186. Talbot and Crampton, p. 79.

187. Henry Zwaanstra, "Louis Berkhof," in David F. Wells, ed. *Dutch Reformed Theology* (Grand Rapids: Baker Book House, 1989), pp. 48, 53. His publisher, the Wm. B. Eerdmans Publishing Co., used to be known as "The Reformed Press."

188. For a brief assessment of Reformed theology, see George W. Zeller, *The Dangers of Reformed Theology* (Middletown: The Middletown Bible Church, n.d.); for a major critique, see Good, *Are Baptists Reformed?* for a comprehensive analysis of Covenant theology, see Renald E. Showers, *There Really is a Difference* (Bellmawr: The Friends of Israel Gospel Ministry, 1990).

189. R. C. Sproul, *Grace Unknown* (Grand Rapids: Baker Books, 1997), p. 99.

190. Coppes, p. x.

191. Boettner, Reformed Faith, p. 24.

192. John H. Leith, *Introduction to the Reformed Tradition,* rev. ed. (Atlanta: John Knox Press, 1981), p. 103.

193. D. James Kennedy, *Why I Am a Presbyterian* (Fort Lauderdale: Coral Ridge Ministries, n.d.), p. 1.

194. Kuyper, p. 41.

195. Talbot and Crampton, p. 78.

196. Herman Hanko, *We and Our Children* (Grand Rapids: Reformed Free Publishing Association, 1988), p. 11.

197. Hanko, Covenant of Grace, p. 2.

198. Hanko, We and Our Children, p. 12.

199. Arthur W. Pink, *The Doctrine of Sanctification* (Swengel: Reiner Publications, 1975), p. 9; Morton H. Smith, *Reformed Evangelism* (Clinton:

Multi-communication Ministries, 1975), p. 13; Palmer, p. 84; Good, Calvinists, p. 72; Talbot and Crampton, p. 76; Spurgeon, Sovereign Grace Sermons, p. 14.

200. E. D. Strickland, in "The Berea Baptist Banner Forum," *The Berea Baptist Banner,* March 5, 1990, p. 51; Talbot and Crampton, p. 76.

201. Belcher, Pink: Predestination, p. 8.

202. Iain Murray, Forgotten Spurgeon, p. 47.

203. Engelsma, Hyper-Calvinism, pp. 10-11.

204. Belcher, Pink: Predestination, p. 8.

205. Jimmie B. Davis, in "The Berea Baptist Banner Forum," *The Berea Baptist Banner,* March 5, 1990, p. 51.

206. Ruckman, Hyper-Calvinism, p. 3.

207. Iain H. Murray, *Spurgeon v. Hyper-Calvinism* (Edinburgh: The Banner of Truth Trust, 1995), pp. 40-46; A. J. Baxter, "C. H. Spurgeon: A Contempory View," in H. L. Williams and J. E. North, *Calvin versus Hyper-Spurgeonism* (E. Sussex: Berith Publications, 1997), pp. 5-12.

208. Marc D. Carpenter, "The Banner of Truth Versus Calvinism," part 2, *The Trinity Review,* June 1997, pp. 1-4; "Not So Sure With Mr. Spurgeon," in Williams and North, *Calvin versus Hyper-Spurgeonism,* pp. 23-33.

209. Charles H. Spurgeon, quoted in Iain Murray, Hyper-Calvinism, p. 38.

210. Engelsma, Hyper-Calvinism, p. 2.

211. Ibid.

212. Marc D. Carpenter, "A History of Hypo-Calvinism," part 1, *The Trinity Review,* March 1997, pp. 1-4, and "A History of Hypo-Calvinism," part 2, *The Trinity Review,* April 1997, pp. 1-4;

213. Keener, p. 21.

214. Iain Murray, Hyper-Calvinism, p. 40.

215. Engelsma, Hyper-Calvinism, p. 5; Iain Murray, Hyper-Calvinism, p. 49.

216. Charles H. Spurgeon, *The Two Wesleys* (Pasadena: Pilgrim Publications, 1975), pp. 4-5.

217. Peter Toon, *The Emergence of Hyper-Calvinism in English Nonconformity, 1689–1765* (London: The Olive Tree, 1967), pp. 28, 145; Sell, pp. 47-49; Ella, p. 157.

218. Toon, p. 74.

219. Sell, p. 51; Toon, pp. 93-96; Nettles, By His Grace, pp. 103-104, 390.

220. Sell, p. 78; Toon, p. 88.

221. Toon, p. 129.

222. Sell, pp. 78-79; Engelsma, Hyper-Calvinism, p. 11; Toon, p. 131.

223. Toon, p. 133.

224. Engelsma, Hyper-Calvinism, p. 11.

225. Henry C. Vedder, *A Short History of the Baptists* (Valley Forge: Judson Press, 1907), pp. 240-241; Torbet, p. 68; Toon, pp. 145, 151; Iain Murray, Hyper-Calvinism, p. 128.

226. Toon, pp. 98-101, 145.

227. Charles H. Spurgeon, *The Metropolitan Tabernacle: its History and Work* (Pasadena: Pilgrim Publications, 1990), p. 47.

228. Vedder, p. 249; Toon, p. 151.

229. David Benedict, *Fifty Years Among the Baptists* (Little Rock: Seminary Publications, 1977), p. 142.

230. Iain Murray, Hyper-Calvinism, p. 50.

231. Sell, pp. 86-87.

232. Andrew Fuller, quoted in Armitage, vol. 2, p. 584.
233. For the complete text of the second edition, see Andrew Fuller, *The Complete Works of the Rev. Andrew Fuller,* 3rd ed. rev. Joseph Belcher (Harrisonburg: Sprinkle Publications, 1988), vol. 2, pp. 328-416.
234. Andrew Fuller, quoted in Sell, p. 86.
235. Ibid., p. 87.
236. Toon, pp. 149-150; Engelsma, Hyper-Calvinism, p. 12.
237. For a critique of the Primitive Baptists by a Sovereign Grace Baptist, see Bob L. Ross, *The History and Heresies of Hardshellism* (Pasadena: Pilgrim Publications, n.d.).
238. Engelsma, Hyper-Calvinism, p. 1.
239. Kober, p. 44.
240. Palmer, p. 60.
241. Machen, Man, p. 58-59.
242. Benjamin B. Warfield, *The Plan of Salvation* (Boonton: Simpson Publishing Company, 1989), p. 27.
243. Wilson, Sovereign Grace View, p. 8.

Chapter Two
The Origin of Calvinism

1. Talbot and Crampton p. 78.
2. Dabney, Calvinism, p. 6.
3. Boettner, Predestination, pp. 3-4.
4. Palmer, p. 6.
5. Boettner, Predestination, p. 4.
6. Ibid.
7. Richard A. Muller, *Christ and the Decree* (Grand Rapids: Baker Book House, 1988), p. 22.
8. Alvin L. Baker, *Berkouwer's Doctrine of Election: Balance or Imbalance?* (Phillipsburg: Presbyterian and Reformed Publishing Co., 1981), p. 25.
9. Singer, p. vii.
10. Warfield, Calvin, p. 22.
11. Will Durant, *The Age of Faith* (New York: Simon and Schuster, 1950), p. 74.
12. Good, Calvinists, p. 49.
13. Charles H. Spurgeon, ed., *Exposition of the Doctrines of Grace* (Pasadena: Pilgrim Publications, n.d.), p. 298.
14. John Calvin, "A Treatise on the Eternal Predestination of God," trans. Henry Cole, in John Calvin, *Calvin's Calvinism* (Grand Rapids: Reformed Free Publishing Association, 1987), p. 38.
15. Kuyper, p. 13.
16. Warfield, Calvin, p. v.
17. Boettner, Predestination, p. 405.
18. Shedd, Calvinism, p. xi.
19. Mason, p. 2.
20. Warfield, Calvin, p. 323.
21. Good, Calvinism, p. 50.
22. Calvin Theological Seminary, *1996–1998 Catalog,* p. 110.

23. Palmer, p. 6; Custance, p. 50; George S. Bishop, *The Doctrines of Grace* (Grand Rapids: Baker Book House, 1977), p. 3.
24. Carl Bangs, *Arminius: A Study in the Dutch Reformation,* 2nd ed. (Grand Rapids: Zondervan Publishing House, 1985), pp. 192, 347.
25. *Christian History*, Vol. 5:4 (1986), p. 2.
26. Richard N. Ostling, "The Seconder Founder of the Faith," *Time*, September 29, 1986, p. 76.
27. Talbot and Crampton, p. 79.
28. Norman L. Geisler, *What Augustine Says* (Grand Rapids: Baker Book House, 1982), p. 9.
29. Alexander Souter, quoted in F. F. Bruce, *The Spreading Flame* (Grand Rapids: Wm. B. Eerdmans Publishing Co., 1958), p. 333.
30. Ibid.
31. S. L. Greenslade, quoted in Bruce, The Spreading Flame, p. 334.
32. *Christian History*, Vol. 6:3 (1987), p. 2.
33. N. L. Rice, *God Sovereign and Man Free* (Harrisonburg: Sprinkle Publications, 1985), p. 13.
34. Benjamin B. Warfield, "The Idea of Systematic Theology," in Mark A. Noll, ed., *The Princeton Theology* (Phillipsburg: Presbyterian and Reformed Publishing Co., 1983), p. 258.
35. Warfield, Calvin, p. 310.
36. Ibid., p. 318.
37. Ibid.
38. Ibid., p. 322.
39. Custance, p. 27.
40. *The Oxford Dictionary of the Christian Church,* 2nd ed. (London: Oxford University Press, 1974), s.v. "Augustine," p. 414.
41. *New Catholic Encyclopedia* (New York: McGraw-Hill Book Company, 1967), s.v. "Augustine, St.," vol. 1, p. 1041.
42. Ibid.
43. Pope John Paul II, quoted in Ostling, p. 76.
44. Joseph Cardinal Ratzinger, quoted in Ostling, p. 76.
45. *Christian History*, Vol. 6:3 (1987), pp. 34-35.
46. *The New Schaff-Herzog Encyclopedia of Religious Knowledge* (Grand Rapids: Baker Book House, 1949–1950), s.v. "Augustine," vol. 1, p. 368.
47. Warfield, Calvin, p. 313.
48. Philip Schaff, *History of the Christian Church* (Grand Rapids: Wm. B. Eerdmans Publishing Co., 1910), vol. 3, p. 1018.
49. Peter S. Ruckman, *The History of the New Testament Church* (Pensacola: Bible Baptist Bookstore, 1982–1984), vol. 1, p. 149.
50. Warfield, Calvin, pp. 321-322.
51. Tom Ross, Abandoned Truth, p. 11.
52. Ibid., p. 16.
53. See *The Catholic Encyclopedia* (New York: The Encyclopedia Press, 1913), s.v. "Augustine of Hippo," vol. 2, pp. 91-99.
54. Talbot and Crampton, p. 79.
55. Singer, pp. 1-6.
56. John Gill, *The Cause of God and Truth* (Paris: The Baptist Standard Bearer, 1992), pp. 220-328.
57. Paul K. Jewett, *Election and Predestination* (Grand Rapids: Wm. B.

Eerdmans Publishing Co., 1985), p. 5.

58. C. Norman Sellers, *Election and Perseverance* (Miami Springs: Schoettle Publishing Co., 1987), p. 3.

59. Boettner, Predestination, p. 365.

60. Ibid.

61. Warfield, Calvin, p. 321.

62. Custance, p. 18.

63. Ibid., p. 20.

64. Boettner, Predestination, p. 366.

65. Good, Calvinists, p. 49.

66. Edward Gibbon, *The History of the Decline and Fall of the Roman Empire* (New York: Modern Library, n.d.), vol. 2, p. 236.

67. Gill, God and Truth, p. 221.

68. Ibid., p. 220.

69. Tertullian *Apology* 50.

70. Eusebius *The Life of Constantine* 1.28.

71. Ibid., 1.29.

72. Eusebius *Church History* 10.5.

73. Schaff, History, vol. 3, p. 31; A. H. Newman, *A Manual of Church History* (Valley Forge: Judson Press, 1933), vol. 1, pp. 306-307.

74. Michael Grant, *Constantine the Great* (New York: Charles Scribner's Sons, 1993), p. 166.

75. Socrates Scholasticus *Ecclesiastical History* 1.9.

76. Eusebius *The Life of Constantine* 3.65.

77. Ibid., 3.62.

78. Will Durant, *Caesar and Christ* (New York: Simon and Schuster, 1972), p. 663.

79. Bruce, The Spreading Flame, p. 298.

80. Andrew Miller, *Miller's Church History* (Grand Rapids: Zondervan Publishing House, n.d.), p. 194.

81. Schaff, History, vol. 3, p. 38.

82. Ibid., p. 142.

83. Ibid.

84. Salaminius Sozomen *Ecclesiastical History* 7.9.

85. Schaff, History, vol. 3, pp. 63-64.

86. Salaminius Sozomen *Ecclesiastical History* 7.12.

87. Schaff, History, vol. 3, p. 142.

88. William Jones, *The History of the Christian Church,* 5th ed. (Gallatin: Church History Research and Archives, 1983), vol. 1, p. 306.

89. Gerald Bonner, *St Augustine of Hippo* (Philadelphia: The Westminster Press, 1963), p. 38.

90. Ibid., p. 53.

91. Augustine *Confessions* 2.3.6.

92. Ibid., 2.3.7.

93. Ibid., 3.1.1.

94. Peter Brown, *Augustine of Hippo* (Berkeley and Los Angeles: University of California Press, 1967), p. 39.

95. *New Dictionary of Theology* (Downers Grove: Inter-Varsity Press, 1988), s.v. "Augustine," p. 58.

96. Brown, p. 44.

97. Bonner, p. 161.
98. Ibid., p. 58.
99. Ibid.
100. Ibid., p. 59.
101. Ibid., p. 63.
102. *The New Schaff-Herzog Encyclopedia of Religious Knowledge,* s.v. "Augustine," Vol. 1, p. 366.
103. *A Dictionary of Christian Biography* (Peabody: Hendrickson Publishers, 1994), s.v. "Augustine," p. 72.
104. Bonner, p. 71.
105. Ibid., p. 80.
106. Ibid., p. 86; Brown, pp. 98-99.
107. Bonner, p. 72.
108. Schaff, History, vol. 3, p. 991; Bonner, p. 84.
109. Augustine *Confessions* 8.12.29.
110. Ibid.
111. Ibid.
112. Roy W. Battenhouse, ed., *A Companion to the Study of St. Augustine* (New York: Oxford University Press, 1955), p. 36.
113. Armitage, vol. 1, p. 218.
114. David Benedict, *History of the Donatists* (Gallatin: Church History Research & Archives, 1985), pp. 64-65.
115. Bonner, pp. 104-108.
116. Ibid., pp. 112-113.
117. Battenhouse, p. 41.
118. Ibid., p. 259.
119. Bonner, p. 105.
120. Ibid., p. 135.
121. John Laurence Mosheim, *An Ecclesiastical History, Ancient and Modern,* trans. Archibald MacLaine (Cincinnati: Applegate & Co., 1854), p. 101; Benedict, Donatists, pp. 19, 29, 113, 187; Battenhouse, p. 194.
122. Steele and Thomas, p. 19.
123. McFetridge, p. 4.
124. Boettner, Predestination, p. 47.
125. McFetridge, pp. 3-4.
126. John Ferguson, *Pelagius: A Historical and Theological Study* (Cambridge: W. Heffer & Sons, 1956), p. 79.
127. Louis Berkhof, *The History of Christian Doctrines* (Grand Rapids: Baker Book House, 1937), p. 132.
128. Ferguson, p. 100.
129. Bruce, The Spreading Flame, p. 335; Boettner, Predestination, p. 366; Schaff, History, vol. 3, p. 789; Berkhof, History, pp. 132, 133.
130. Bonner, p. 316.
131. Ferguson, p. 41.
132. Ibid., p. 47.
133. Bruce, The Spreading Flame, p. 335.
134. Berkhof, History, p. 132.
135. Schaff, History, vol. 3, p. 790.
136. Ferguson, p. 117.
137. Bonner, p. 317; Augustine *Confessions* 10.29.40.

138. *A Dictionary of Christian Biography,* s.v. "Pelagianism and Pelagius," p. 820.
139. Ferguson, p. 48.
140. Battenhouse, p. 204.
141. *New Catholic Encyclopedia,* s.v. "Augustine," p. 1046.
142. Bonner, p. 320.
143. Ferguson, p. 50.
144. Schaff, History, vol. 3, p. 793.
145. Ferguson, p. 52.
146. Brown, p. 368; Ferguson, p. 50.
147. Ferguson, p. 96.
148. Ibid., p. 97.
149. Ibid., p. 140.
150. Ibid., pp. 50, 135.
151. Ferguson, pp. 130-131, 164-165.
152. Brown, p. 357.
153. *The Westminster Dictionary of Christian Theology* (Philadelphia: The Westminster Press, 1983), s.v. "Pelagianism," p. 435.
154. *Evangelical Dictionary of Theology* (Grand Rapids: Baker Book House, 1984), s.v. "Augustine," p. 106.
155. Augustine *On Christian Doctrine* 2.8.
156. Augustine *City of God* 18.36.
157. Augustine *On Christian Doctrine* 2.8.
158. Augustine *City of God* 18.36.
159. Augustine *On the Correction of the Donatists* 5.19.
160. Augustine *On the Psalms* 3.4.
161. Augustine *City of God* 11.9.
162. Augustine *City of God* 18.42, 43.
163. Augustine *Letters* 71.4.6.
164. Bernard Ramm, *Protestant Biblical Interpretation,* 3rd rev. ed. (Grand Rapids: Baker Book House, 1970), pp. 34-35.
165. Ibid., p. 35.
166. Augustine *Confessions* 6.4.6; Ramm, p. 36.
167. Augustine *City of God* 11.6.
168. Ibid., 20.7.
169. Ibid.
170. Oswald T. Allis, *Prophecy and the Church* (Phillipsburg: Presbyterian and Reformed Publishing Co., 1947), p. 3; Schaff, History, vol. 3, p. 619.
171. John F. Walvoord, *The Millennial Kingdom* (Grand Rapids: Zondervan Publishing House, 1959), p. 49.
172. Augustine *City of God* 20.6-9.
173. Ibid., 20.8.
174. Ibid., 20.9.
175. Louis Berkhof, *Principles of Biblical Interpretation* (Grand Rapids: Baker Book House, 1950), p. 22.
176. *Baker's Dictionary of Theology* (Grand Rapids: Baker Book House, 1960), s.v. "Augustinianism," p. 80.
177. Warfield, Calvin, p. 319.
178. Schaff, History, vol. 3, p. 1010.
179. Augustine *Confessions* 11.3.5.

180. S. Angus, quoted in Bonner, p. 395.
181. Augustine *On the Merits and Forgiveness of Sins* 1.23, 26, 34.
182. Berkhof, History, p. 248, Schaff, History, vol. 3, p. 482.
183. Augustine *On the Merits and Forgiveness of Sins* 1.35.
184. Ibid., 1.33.
185. Ibid., 3.7.
186. Jewett, p. 127.
187. Augustine *On the Merits and Forgiveness of Sins* 1.21.
188. Augustine *City of God* 13.7.
189. Warfield, Calvin, p. 313.
190. Schaff, History, vol. 3, p. 1021.
191. Ibid., pp. 434, 435, 441.
192. Ibid., pp. 459-460.
193. Ibid., pp. 475, 1020.
194. Ibid., p. 478.
195. Ibid., pp. 498, 506, 1020.
196. Augustine *On the Correction of the Donatists* 11.50.
197. Schaff, History, p. 307.
198. F. F. Bruce, Foreword to Forster and Marston, *God's Strategy in Human History*, p. vii.
199. Bruce, The Spreading Flame, p. 339.
200. Loraine Boettner, *Immortality* (Phillipsburg: Presbyterian and Reformed Publishing Co., 1956), p. 135.
201. Schaff, History, vol. 3, pp. 202, 993, 994.
202. Christopher Dawson, *Religion and the Rise of Western Culture* (New York: Image Books, 1957), p. 47.
203. *The Westminster Dictionary of Christian Theology*, s.v. "Augustinianism," p. 58; Battenhouse, p. 385; Bonner, p.374.
204. Augustine *On Original Sin* 2.42.
205. Augustine *On the Morals of the Manichaeans* 18.65.
206. Augustine *On Christian Doctrine* 3.18.27.
207. Bonner, p. 129.
208. Augustine *On the Soul and its Origin* 4.16.
209. Augustine *On Rebuke and Grace* 39.
210. Ibid., 14.
211. Augustine *On the Gift of Perseverance* 47.
212. Augustine *On Rebuke and Grace* 40.
213. Augustine *On the Gift of Perseverance* 61.
214. Augustine *On the Spirit and the Letter* 61.
215. Ibid., 58.
216. Augustine *On the Predestination of the Saints* 7, 8, 16.
217. Augustine *Enchiridion* 95, 96, 100, 101.
218. Ibid., 103.
219. Berkhof, History, p. 136.
220. Augustine *On Rebuke and Grace* 22.
221. Ibid., 18.
222. Ibid., 36.
223. Berkhof, History, p. 208.
224. Schaff, History, vol. 3, p. 144.
225. Benedict, Donatists, p. 44.

226. Ibid., p. 60.
227. Ibid., pp. 64-65.
228. Gibbon, vol. 2, p. 233.
229. Schaff, History, vol. 3, p. 364.
230. Augustine *On the Correction of the Donatists* 4.17, 18; 5.19, 20; 6.21-24.
231. Ibid., 6.21.
232. J. A. Neander, quoted in Schaff, History, vol. 3, p. 145.
233. Boettner, Predestination, p. 367.
234. Custance, p. 37.
235. Berkhof, History, p. 137.
236. Schaff, History, vol. 3, p. 866; *New Dictionary of Theology,* s.v. "Semi-Pelagianism," p. 636; *Evangelical Dictionary of Theology,* s.v. "Semi-Pelagianism," p. 1000.
237. *New Dictionary of Theology,* s.v. "Semi-Pelagianism," p. 636.
238. Custance, pp. 37-38; Boettner, p. 367.
239. Schaff, History, vol. 4, p. 525.
240. Berkhof, History, p. 141.
241. Schaff, History, vol. 4, p. 527.
242. *New Dictionary of Theology,* s.v. "Gottschalk," p. 279.
243. *The Oxford Dictionary of the Christian Church,* s.v. "Bradwardine," p. 194.
244. Gordon Leff, *Bradwardine and the Pelagians* (Cambridge: Cambridge University Press, 1957), pp. 2-3.
245. Ibid., p. 206.
246. Ibid., pp. 17, 111.
247. George Park Fisher, *History of the Christian Church* (New York: Charles Scribner's Sons, 1900), p. 226.
248. *The Oxford Dictionary of the Christian Church,* s.v. "Gregory of Rimini," p. 600; *New Dictionary of Theology,* s.v. "Gregory of Rimini," p. 283.
249. Cunningham, Reformers, p. 1; Schaff, History, vol. 7, p. 1.
250. Roland H. Bainton, *The Reformation of the Sixteenth Century,* enlar. ed. (Boston: Beacon Press, 1985), p. 3.
251. William Cunningham, *Historical Theology* (Edmonton: Still Waters Revival Books, n.d.), vol. 2, p. 1.
252. Sproul, Grace Unknown, p. 60.
253. Ibid., p. 62.
254. Warfield, Calvin, p. 313.
255. Ibid., p. 322.
256. Ibid.
257. Custance, p. 27.
258. Bard Thompson, *Humanists and Reformers: A History of the Renaissance and Reformation* (Grand Rapids: Wm. B. Eerdmans Publishing Co., 1996), p. 388.
259. Boettner, Predestination, p. 367.
260. McFetridge, p. 14.
261. Martin Luther, quoted in Roland H. Bainton, *Here I Stand* (New York: Mentor Books, 1955), p. 34.
262. William R. Estep, *Renaissance and Reformation* (Grand Rapids: Wm. B. Eerdmans Publishing Co., 1986), pp. 114-115.

263. Timothy George, *Theology of the Reformers* (Nashville: Broadman Press, 1988), p. 55.
264. Martin Luther, quoted in Estep, p. 116.
265. Sproul, Grace Unknown, p. 66.
266. *Decrees of the Council of Trent,* canon 9, "Justification," in *Dogmatic Canons and Decrees* (Rockford: Tan Books and Publishers, 1977), p. 51.
267. Cunningham, Theology, vol. 2, p. 41.
268. Ibid.
269. Schaff, History, vol. 7, p. 123.
270. Berkhof, History, p. 207.
271. Ibid., p. 208.
272. Ibid., vol. 3, p. 812.
273. George, p. 8.
274. Ibid., p. 68.
275. Ibid., p. 65.
276. Ibid., p. 70.
277. Ibid., p. 64.
278. Martin Luther, quoted in George, p. 68.
279. Warfield, Calvin, p. 322.
280. Steele and Thomas, p. 21.
281. Charles Hodge, Theology, vol. 2, p. 333.
282. Boettner, Predestination, p. 367.
283. Sproul, Grace Unknown, p. 139.
284. Cunningham, Reformers, pp. 108-109.
285. George, p. 77; Schaff, History, vol. 8, p. 547.
286. Cunningham, Reformers, p. 109.
287. Sproul, Chosen by God, p. 15.
288. Augustus Toplady, Preface to Zanchius, *The Doctrine of Absolute Predestination,* p. 16.
289. J. I. Packer and O. R. Johnson, "Historical and Theological Introduction," in Martin Luther, *The Bondage of the Will,* trans. J. I. Packer and O. R. Johnson (Grand Rapids: Fleming H. Revell, 1957), pp. 37, 39.
290. Ibid., p. 40.
291. Luther, p. 109.
292. Schaff, History, vol. 8, pp. 91-93.
293. George, p. 119.
294. Ibid., p. 113.
295. Schaff, History, vol. 8, pp. 85-87.
296. George, p. 122.
297. Talbot and Crampton, p. 79; Boettner, Predestination, p. 1.
298. Schaff, History, vol. 8, pp. 210, 618.
299. George, p. 232; Talbot and Crampton, p. 79; Boettner, Predestination, p. 1.
300. Calvin, quoted in Hastings Eells, *Martin Bucer* (New Haven: Yale University Press, 1931), p. 233.
301. Ibid., p. 236.
302. Schaff, History, vol. 8, p. 873; Cunningham, Reformers, pp. 349, 358; Sell, p. 1.
303. Schaff, History, vol. 7, pp. 371-372.
304. Ibid., vol. 8, p. 392.

305. Cunningham, Reformers, p. 345.
306. Boettner, Predestination, pp. 3-4.

Chapter Three
John Calvin

1. Palmer, p. 6.
2. Boettner, Predestination, p. 4.
3. Custance, p. 3.
4. George, p. 167.
5. Otto Scott, *The Great Christian Revolution* (Windsor: The Reformer Library, 1994), p. 100.
6. William J. Bouwsma, *John Calvin: A Sixteenth Century Portrait* (New York: Oxford University Press, 1988), p. 235.
7. Earle E. Cairns, *Christianity Through the Centuries*, rev. and enlar. ed. (Grand Rapids: Zondervan Publishing House, 1981), p. 312.
8. Williston Walker, *John Calvin: The Organizer of Reformed Protestantism* (New York: Schocken Books, 1969), p. ix.
9. Westminster Theological Seminary, *1990–1992 Catalog*, p. 96; Calvin Theological Seminary, *1996–1998 Catalog*, p. 118; Reformed Bible College, *1990–1992 Catalog*, p. 43.
10. Harkness, p. 3.
11. Leith, p. 75.
12. Henry Cole, Translator's Preface to Calvin, *Calvin's Calvinism*, p. 6.
13. Daniel Gerdes, quoted in Schaff, History, vol. 8, p. 281.
14. Ernst Renan, quoted in Thomas M. Lindsay, *A History of the Reformation*, 2nd ed. (Edinburgh: T & T Clark, 1907), vol. 2, p. 159.
15. Francois Wendel, *Calvin: Origins and Development of His Religious Thought*, trans. Philip Mairet (Grand Rapids: Baker Books, 1997), p. 360.
16. Theodore Beza, quoted in Schaff, History, vol. 8, p. 272.
17. Boettner, Predestination, p. 5.
18. Ibid., p. 405.
19. McFetridge, p. 68.
20. John Calvin, "A Defence of the Secret Providence of God," trans. Henry Cole, in John Calvin, *Calvin's Calvinism*, p. 292.
21. Leopold von Ranke, quoted in Crampton, Calvin, p. vii.
22. Roland H. Bainton, quoted in *Christian History*, Vol. 5:4 (1986), p. 3.
23. Jimmy Swaggart, quoted in *Christian History*, Vol. 5:4 (1986), p. 3.
24. Oskar Pfister, quoted in *Christian History*, Vol. 5:4 (1986), p. 3.
25. Jones, vol. 2, p. 238.
26. Will Durant, *The Reformation* (New York: Simon and Schuster, 1957), p. 490.
27. Voltaire, quoted in Schaff, History, vol. 8, p. 287.
27. Schaff, History, vol. 8, p. 688.
29. Ibid., vol. 8, p. 283.
30. Ibid., vol. 8, p. 834.
31. Bouwsma, p. 2.
32. David Steinmetz, *Calvin in Context* (Oxford: Oxford University Press, 1995), p. 211.

33. John T. McNeil, *The History and Character of Calvinism,* paperback ed. (London: Oxford University Press, 1966), p. 239.
34. Ibid., p. 243.
35. Ibid., p. 245.
36. Ibid., p. 247.
37. Schaff, History, vol. 7, p. 319.
38. Ibid., pp. 320-321.
39. Ibid., p. 684.
40. Lindsay, vol. 1, p. 344.
41. Schaff, History, vol. 7, p. 686.
42. Alister E. McGrath, *Reformation Thought,* 2nd ed. (Grand Rapids: Baker, 1993), p. 6.
43. Hence, Augsburg Publishing House, now Augsburg Fortress Publishers.
44. Lindsay, vol. 1, p. 363.
45. Ibid., p. 373.
46. Ibid., pp. 374-375.
47. Ibid., pp. 390-391.
48. Leith, p. 34.
49. McGrath, Reformation Thought, pp. 8, 61.
50. Schaff, History, vol. 8, p. 6.
51. Ibid., p. 7.
52. McNeil, p. 22.
53. Ibid., p. 23.
54. Estep, p. 164.
55. Schaff, History, vol. 8, pp. 23-25.
56. Ibid., p. 24.
57. Ibid., p. 25.
58. Estep, pp. 165-166.
59. Huldreich Zwingli, quoted in Estep, p. 166.
60. George, p. 113.
61. Schaff, History, vol. 8, pp. 42-43, 47.
62. George, p. 114.
63. Huldreich Zwingli, quoted in George, p. 118.
64. Estep, p. 190.
65. Schaff, History, vol. 8, p. 108.
66. Ibid., p. 165.
67. Ibid., pp. 208, 219-221.
68. Schaff, History, vol. 8, p. 82.
69. Estep, p. 186.
70. Quoted in Estep, p. 186.
71. Schaff, vol. 8, p. 83.
72. Quoted in Armitage, vol. 1, p. 402.
73. Estep, pp. 130, 158, 184-185.
74. McGrath, Calvin, p. xi.
75. Bouwsma, p. 2.
76. McNeil, p. 94.
77. Schaff, vol. 8, pp. 298-299.
78. Ibid.
79. Quoted in T. H. L. Parker, *John Calvin* (Herts: Lion Publishing, 1975), p. 3.

80. George, p. 169.
81. Ibid.
82. Estep, p. 224.
83. Theodore Beza, *The Life of John Calvin,* new and expan. ed., ed. Gary Sanseri, trans. Henry Beveridge (Milwaukie: Back Home Industries, 1996), p. 15.
84. J. H. Merle d'Aubigne, *History of the Reformation of the Sixteenth Century* (Grand Rapids: Baker Book House, n.d.), p. 490.
85. Schaff, History, vol. 8, p. 302.
86. Wendel, p. 21.
87. Calvin, quoted in Bouwsma, p. 10.
88. John H. Bratt, *The Life and Teachings of John Calvin* (Grand Rapids: Baker Book House, 1958), p. 11.
89. Wendel, pp. 23-24.
90. Walker, p. 49.
91. John H. Bratt, "The Life and Work of John Calvin," in Bratt, ed., *The Rise and Development of Calvinism,* p. 11.
92. Walker, p. 55.
93. Ronald S. Wallace, *Calvin, Geneva, and the Reformation* (Grand Rapids: Baker Book House, 1990), p. 5.
94. Parker, p. 33.
95. Bouwsma, p. 10, McGrath, Calvin, p. 70.
96. Bratt, Teachings of Calvin, p. 13.
97. Walker, pp. 87-88.
98. Bratt, Teachings of Calvin, p. 13.
99. George, p. 172.
100. Bratt, Work of Calvin, p. 10; Walker, p. 86.
101. Bratt, Teachings of Calvin, p. 13.
102. Wallace, p. 9.
103. Parker, p. 27.
104. Wendel, p. 31.
105. Calvin, quoted in Walker, p. 76.
106. McNeil, p. 110.
107. Karl Barth, *The Theology of John Calvin,* trans. Geoffrey W. Bromiley (Grand Rapids: Wm. B. Eerdmans Publishing Co., 1995), p. 136.
108. George, p. 171.
109. Calvin, quoted in Walker, p. 72.
110. Ibid.
111. Parker, p. 195.
112. McGrath, Calvin, p. 73.
113. Walker, p. 61.
114. McNeil, p. 112.
115. Walker, pp. 62-63.
116. Wendel, p. 40.
117. Bratt, Work of Calvin, p. 13.
118. Barth, p. 142; Wendel, pp. 40-41.
119. Bratt, Work of Calvin, p. 13.
120. Bratt, Teachings of Calvin, pp. 16-17.
121. Walker, pp. 119-120.
122. Barth, p. 146; Walker, p. 119.
123. Barth, p. 146.

124. Ibid., p. 151.
125. Steinmetz, p. 9.
126. Schaff, History, vol. 8, pp. 320-321.
127. Ibid., p. 325.
128. Ibid., p. 326.
129. Parker, pp. 38-39.
130. McGrath, Calvin, pp. 77-78.
131. Ibid., p. 79.
132. Schaff, History, vol. 8, pp. 347-348.
133. Calvin, quoted in G. R. Potter and M. Greengrass, *John Calvin* (New York: St. Martin's Press, 1983), p. 46.
134. Parker, pp. 68-69.
135. Bratt, Work of Calvin, p. 17.
136. Schaff, History, vol. 8, p. 355.
137. Ibid., p. 356.
138. Ibid., p. 357.
139. Ibid., pp. 359-360.
140. Boettner, Predestination, p. 408.
141. McNeil, p. 144.
142. Calvin, quoted in Potter and Greengrass, p. 54.
143. Schaff, History, vol. 8, p. 369.
144. Walker, p. 221.
145. Bouwsma, p. 23.
146. Calvin, quoted in Schaff, History, vol. 8, p. 414.
147. Wulfert de Greef, *The Writings of John Calvin: An Introductory Guide*, trans. Lyle D. Bierman (Grand Rapids: Baker Books, 1993), p. 32.
148. Bouwsma, p. 23.
149. George, p. 182.
150. James Sadolet, quoted in Schaff, History, vol. 8, p. 401.
151. Schaff, History, vol. 8, p. 430.
152. Ibid., pp. 431, 433.
153. Calvin, quoted in Bratt, Teachings of Calvin, p. 31.
154. Walker, p. 259.
155. Bratt, Teachings of Calvin, p. 32.
156. de Greef, p. 41.
157. Calvin, quoted in Bratt, Teachings of Calvin, p. 71.
158. Walker, p. 439.
159. Schaff, History, vol. 8, p. 863.
160. Ibid., p. 232.
161. Walker, p. 162.
162. Ibid.
163. Schaff, History, vol. 8, p. 234.
164. Lindsay, vol. 2, pp. 71-73.
165. Schaff, History, vol. 8, p. 244.
166. Lindsay, vol. 2, p. 80.
167. Ibid., p. 89.
168. Minutes of the Council of 200, May 21, 1536, quoted in Potter and Greengrass, p. 48.
169. Harkness, p. 10.
170. McNeil, p. 135.

171. Walker, p. 178; McNeil, p. 135; Harkness, p. 10; George Park Fisher, *The Reformation* (New York: Scribner, Armstrong, and Co., 1873), p. 210.
172. Otto Scott, p. 44.
173. Barth, p. 258.
174. Lindsay, vol. 2, p. 110.
175. Fisher, Reformation, p. 212.
176. Schaff, vol. 8, pp. 350-351.
177. Bainton, Reformation, p. 119.
178. Schaff, vol. 8, p. 356.
179. Wendel, p. 53; Fisher, Reformation, p. 212.
180. Schaff, vol. 8, p. 348.
181. Bratt, Work of Calvin, p. 21.
182. McNeil, p. 185.
183. George, p. 185.
184. McNeil, pp. 163-164.
185. Wallace, p. 29.
186. Walker, p. 264.
187. Calvin, Institutes, p. 1487 (IV.xx.2).
188. Ibid., p. 1488 (IV.xx.3).
189. Boettner, Predestination, p. 370.
190. Ibid., p. 410.
191. Stefan Zweig, *The Right to Heresy* (London: Cassell and Company, 1936), p. 107.
192. Schaff, History, vol. 8, p. 490.
193. Ibid., pp. 490-491.
194. Durant, Reformation, p. 474.
195. *The Register of the Company of Pastors of Geneva in the Time of Calvin,* trans. and ed. Philip E. Hughes (Grand Rapids: Wm. B. Eerdmans Publishing Co., 1966), p. 58.
196. Ibid., p. 71.
197. Fisher, Reformation, p. 222.
198. McNeil, p. 172.
199. Harkness, p. 29-30.
200. Fisher, Reformation, p. 222.
201. McNeil, p. 189.
202. Ibid., 190.
203. Schaff, History, vol. 8, p. 464.
204. Dakin, p. 134-135.
205. McNeil, p. 189.
206. Register of Geneva, pp. 58-59.
207. McNeil, p. 189.
208. Schaff, History, vol. 8, p. 493.
209. Quoted in Schaff, History, vol. 8, p. 502.
210. Ibid., pp. 502-503.
211. Jacques Gruet, quoted in Parker, p. 128.
212. Quoted in Potter and Greengrass, p. 95.
213. McNeil, p. 171.
214. Schaff, History, vol. 8, p. 504.
215. Register of Geneva, pp. 137, 138.
216. Schaff, History, vol. 8, p. 618.

217. Potter and Greengrass, pp. 92-93.
218. Register of Geneva, p. 201.
219. Walker, p. 310.
220. Fisher, Reformation, p. 224.
221. Calvin, quoted in Schaff, History, vol. 8, p. 496.
222. McGrath, Calvin, p. 121.
223. John Knox, quoted in Thompson, p. 501.
224. McNeil, p. 179.
225. Estep, p. 246; McNeil, p. 181.
226. Bouwsma, p. 29.
227. Harkness, p. 15.
228. Schaff, History, vol. 8, pp. 805-806.
229. Bratt, Work of Calvin, p. 25.
230. Wallace, p. 48.
231. Otto Scott, p. 46.
232. Bratt, Work of Calvin, p. 23.
233. McNeil, p. 185; McGrath, Calvin, p. 109.
234. Charles Miller, "The Spread of Calvinism in Switzerland, Germany, and France," in Bratt, ed., *The Rise and Development of Calvinism,* p. 29.
235. Singer, p. 19.
236. Calvin, quoted in Fisher, Reformation, p. 224.
237. Newman, vol. 2, p. 219.
238. See Leonard Verduin, *The Reformers and Their Stepchildren* (Grand Rapids: Baker Book House, 1964).
239. Fisher, Reformation, pp. 223-224.
240. Paul Woolley, "Calvin and Toleration," in John H. Bratt, ed., *The Heritage of John Calvin* (Grand Rapids: Wm. B. Eerdmans Publishing Co., 1973), p. 156.
241. Schaff, History, vol. 8, p. 687.
242. Warfield, Calvin, p. 25.
243. Henry Cole, note to Dedicatory Preface of Calvin, Eternal Predestination, p. 20.
244. Kuyper, p. 100.
245. Philip E. Hughes, Introduction to *The Register of the Company of Pastors of Geneva in the Time of Calvin,* p. 243.
246. McGrath, Calvin, p. 116.
247. The date is sometimes given as 1509—Calvin's birthyear.
248. Schaff, History, vol. 8, p. 713.
249. Roland H. Bainton, *Hunted Heretic* (Boston: The Beacon Press, 1953), p. 16.
250. Schaff, History, vol. 8, pp. 714-715.
251. Parker, p. 138.
252. Schaff, History, vol. 8, p. 720.
253. Newman, vol. 2, p. 192.
254. Schaff, History, vol. 8, pp. 723-724.
255. Ibid., p. 724.
256. Bainton, Hunted Heretic, p. 118.
257. Ibid., p. 129.
258. Ibid.
259. Schaff, History, vol. 8, p. 787.

260. Bainton, Hunted Heretic, p. 130.
261. Schaff, History vol. 8, pp. 727-728.
262. Ibid., p. 728.
263. Calvin, quoted in Schaff, History, vol. 8, p. 728.
264. Schaff, History, vol. 8, p. 730.
265. Guillaume de Trie, quoted in Bainton, Hunted Heretic, p. 153.
266. Schaff, History, vol. 8, p. 762.
267. Quoted in Parker, p. 143.
268. Walker, p. 332.
269. Quoted in Schaff, History, vol. 8, p. 782.
270. Michael Servetus, quoted in Bainton, Hunted Heretic, p. 212.
271. Schaff, History, vol. 8, p. 737.
272. Ibid., pp. 769-770.
273. Michael Servetus, quoted in Bainton, Hunted Heretic, p. 20.
274. Schaff, History, vol. 8, p. 753.
275. Ibid., p. 733.
276. Michael Servetus, quoted in Schaff, History, vol. 8, p. 741.
277. Schaff, History, vol. 8, p. 742.
278. Ibid., p. 771.
279. Bainton, Hunted Heretic, p. 44-45; Schaff, History, vol. 8, p. 742.
280. Walker, p. 342.
281. Schaff, History, vol. 8, p. 770.
282. Ibid., p. 750.
283. Ibid., p. 725.
284. Ibid., pp. 754, 756.
285. Ibid., p. 749.
286. Steinmetz, p. 12.
287. de Greef, pp. 61, 62.
288. Letter from Calvin to Farel, February 13, 1546, in John Calvin, *Letters of John Calvin* (Edinburgh: The Banner of Truth Trust, 1980), p. 82.
289. Bainton, Hunted Heretic, p. 157; Schaff, History, vol. 8, pp. 758-759; Wallace, p. 76; Walker, pp. 331-332.
290. Schaff, History, vol. 8, 760.
291. Bainton, Hunted Heretic, p. 157.
292. Beza, p. 70.
293. Letter from Calvin to Farel, August 20, 1553, in Calvin, Letters, p. 158.
294. Calvin, quoted in Schaff, History, vol. 8, p. 765.
295. McGrath, Calvin, p. 116.
296. Wendel, p. 95.
297. Walker, p. 333.
298. Schaff, History, vol. 8, p. 769.
299. Letter from Calvin to Farel, August 20, 1553, in Calvin, Letters, p. 159.
300. McGrath, Calvin, p. 116.
301. Ibid.
302. Wallace, p. 77.
303. Boettner, Predestination, p. 418.
304. Calvin, quoted in Potter and Greengrass, p. 108.
305. Michael Servetus, quoted in Bainton, Hunted Heretic, p. 200.
306. Calvin, quoted in Schaff, History, vol. 8, p. 791.
307. Schaff, History, vol. 8, p. 792.

308. Calvin, quoted in Potter and Greengrass, p. 109.
309. Letter from Calvin to the marquis de Poet, quoted in Voltaire, *The Works of Voltaire* (New York: E. R. DuMont, 1901), vol. 4, p. 89. This is referred to by Robert Robinson, *Ecclesiastical Researches* (Gallatin: Church History Research & Archives, 1984), p. 348, and Benedict, History, vol. 1, p. 186.
310. Calvin, quoted in Schaff, History, vol. 8, pp. 690-691.
311. Hughes, p. 19; de Greef, p. 176; Wallace, pp. 73, 77; Cunningham, Reformers, p. 320; Parker, p. 145; George, p. 249; McNeil, p. 228; Otto Scott, p. 71.
312. Gordon H. Clark, *Thales to Dewey*, 2nd ed. (Jefferson: The Trinity Foundation, 1989), p. 111.
313. Letter from Calvin to Farel, August 20, 1553, in Calvin, Letters, p. 159.
314. Calvin, quoted in Schaff, History, vol. 8, p. 783.
315. Hughes, p. 18.
316. Verduin, Reformers, p. 52.
317. Leonard Verduin, *The Anatomy of a Hybrid* (Sarasota: The Christian Hymnary Publishers, 1976), p. 207.
318. Cunningham, Reformers, p. 316.
319. McGrath, Calvin, p. 116.
320. McNeil, p. 228.
321. Crampton, Calvin, p. 10.
322. Otto Scott, p. 72.
323. McGrath, Calvin, p. 116.
324. Bratt, Teachings of Calvin, p. 41.
325. McGrath, Calvin, p. 117.
326. Wendel, p. 97.
327. McNeil, p. 228.
328. Hughes, p. 17.
329. Ibid., p. 18.
330. Boettner, Predestination, p. 414.
331. Schaff, History, vol. 8, p. 709.
332. Register of Geneva, p. 290.
333. Heinrich Bullinger, quoted in Schaff, History, vol. 8, p. 709.
334. Philip Melanchthon, quoted in Schaff, History, vol. 8, p. 707.
335. Ibid., p. 707.
336. Martin Bucer, quoted in Schaff, History, vol. 8, p. 708.
337. Beza, p. 73.
338. Simon Kistemaker, *Calvinism: Its History, Principles and Perspectives* (Grand Rapids: Baker Book House, 1966), p. 23; Hughes, pp. 18, 20; Parker, pp. 144-145; McGrath, Calvin, p. 118.
339. Schaff, History, vol. 8, p. 691.
340. Wallace, pp. 81-82.
341. Hughes, p. 19.
342. Otto Scott, p. 71.
343. Bainton, Hunted Heretic, p. 210.
344. "The Life of John Calvin," in Calvin, *Letters of John Calvin*, p. 27.
345. Verduin, Reformers, p. 51.
346. Schaff, History, vol. 8, p. 684.
347. Gibbon, vol. 3, p. 314.
348. Jones, vol. 2, pp. 238, 239.

349. McNeil, p. 347.
350. Bratt, Teachings of Calvin, p. 41.
351. Cunningham, Reformers, pp. 316-317.
352. Quoted in Augustus H. Strong, *Systematic Theology* (Valley Forge: Judson Press, 1907), p. 778.
353. Singer, p. 7.
354. Parker, p. 39.
355. Introduction to Calvin, *Institutes of the Christian Religion,* p. xxxiii.
356. Walker, p. 132.
357. Schaff, History, vol. 8, p. 332.
358. John Calvin, "Prefatory Address to King Francis I of France," in Calvin, *Institutes of the Christian Religion,* p. 9.
359. Ibid.
360. Ibid.
361. Parker, p. 41.
362. Calvin, quoted in Estep, p. 228.
363. McGrath, Calvin, p. 137.
364. McNeil, p. 125.
365. Introduction to Calvin, Institutes, p. xxxiv.
366. Calvin, quoted in McGrath, Calvin, p. 137.
367. Parker, p. 88.
368. McNeil, p. 126.
369. McGrath, Calvin, p. 135.
370. Introduction to Calvin, Institutes, p. xxxviii.
371. Ibid., p. xxxvii.
372. Bratt, Teachings of Calvin, p. 20.
373. McGrath, Calvin, p. 141.
374. Warfield, Calvin, p. v.
375. Zweig, p. 35.
376. Schaff, History, vol. 8, p. 329.
377. Warfield, Calvin, p. 7.
378. McNeil, p. 127.
379. Cairns, p. 312.
380. Walker, p. 146.
381. Wendel, p. 131.
382. Warfield, Calvin, p. 22.
383. Wendel, p. 141.
384. Bouwsma, p. 22.
385. Wendel, p. 130.
386. Ibid., pp. 126-127.
387. Ibid., pp. 123-124.
388. Lindsay, vol. 2, p. 104.
389. Calvin, Institutes, p. 1303 (IV.xiv.26).
390. Talbot and Crampton, p. 79.
391. Introduction to Calvin, Institutes, p. lviii.
392. Ibid.
393. McGrath, Calvin, p. 151.
394. Introduction to Calvin, Institutes, p. lvii.
395. Ibid.
396. Wendel, p. 124.

397. Ibid.
398. Crampton, Calvin, p. 28.
399. Calvin, Eternal Predestination, pp. 39, 146, 148, 149.
400. Ibid., p. 38.
401. John Calvin, "John Calvin to the Reader," in Calvin, *Institutes of the Christian Religion,* p. 5.
402. McNeil, p. 153.
403. Parker, p. 127.
404. Calvin Theological Seminary, *1996–1998 Catalog,* p. 111.
405. McGrath, pp. 138, 147; Wendel, p. 111.
406. Philip Melanchthon, quoted in Schaff, History, vol. 8, p. 386.
407. Leith, p. 127.
408. John Mosheim, quoted in Schaff, History, vol. 8, p. 281.
409. Crampton, Calvin, p. 1.
410. Warfield, Calvin, p. 22.
411. Wendel, p. 359.
412. George, p. 179.
413. Martin Luther, quoted in George, p. 86.
414. George, p. 86.
415. John Mosheim, quoted in Schaff, History, vol. 8, p. 281.
416. Calvin, quoted in Potter and Greengrass, p. 117.
417. Calvin, Institutes, p. 1144 (IV.vii.25).
418. Schaff, History, vol. 8, p. 313.
419. Douglas Kelly, Liberty, p. 26.
420. Calvin, Institutes, p. 1021 (IV.i.7).
421. Ibid.
422. Ibid.
423. Verduin, Anatomy, p. 200.
424. Calvin, Institutes, p. 1024 (IV.i.10).
425. Ibid., p. 1016 (IV.1.4)
426. Ibid.
427. Wendel, p. 359.
428. Ford Lewis Battles, *An Analysis of the Institutes of the Christian Religion* (Grand Rapids: Baker Book House, 1980), p. 13.
429. Calvin, Institutes, pp. 1027, 1239 (IV.i.13, IV.xii.12).
430. Ibid., p. 1277 (IV.xiv.1).
431. Ibid., p. 1292 (IV.xiv.17).
432. Calvin, quoted in Wendel, p. 318.
433. Calvin, Institutes, p. 1290 (IV.xiv.15).
434. George, p. 239; Charles Miller, p. 28.
435. Wendel, p. 333.
436. Ibid., p. 330.
437. de Greef, pp. 134, 135, 191, 192.
438. Calvin, Institutes, p. 1430 (IV.xviii.2).
439. Ibid., p. 1413 (IV.xvii.36).
440. Ibid., p. 1426 (IV.xvii.48).
441. Ibid., p. 1421 (IV.xvii.43).
442. Barth, p. 266.
443. McNeil, p. 165.
444. Robert L. Dabney, *Systematic Theology,* 2nd ed. (Edinburgh: The Banner

of Truth Trust, 1985). p. 811.
445. Calvin, Institutes, p. 1360 (IV.xvii.1).
446. Ibid., p. 1370 (IV.xvii.10).
447. Ibid.
448. Ibid., p. 1403 (IV.xvii.32).
449. Louis Berkhof, *Systematic Theology,* 4th rev. and enlar. ed. (Grand Rapids: Wm. B. Eerdmans Publishing Co., 1941), p. 654.
450. Wendel, p. 354.
451. Calvin, Institutes, p. 1365 (IV.xvii.5).
452. Berkhof, Theology, p. 654.
453. Schaff, History, vol. 8, p. 592; Wendel, p. 332
454. Wendel, p. 332.
455. Calvin, Institutes, p. 1349 (IV.xvi.26).
456. Ibid., pp. 1303-1304 (IV.xv.1).
457. Ibid., p. 1304 (IV.xv.1).
458. Ibid., p. 1304 (IV.xv.2).
459. Ibid., p. 1305 (IV.xv.3).
460. Ibid., pp. 1304, 1307 (IV.xv.2, IV.xv.5).
461. Ibid., p. 1311 (IV.xv.10).
462. Ibid., p. 1327 (IV.xvi.4).
463. Ibid., p. 1331 (IV.xv.10).
464. Ibid., pp. 1324, 1332-1333 (IV.xvi.1, IV.xvi.10).
465. Ibid., p. 1332 (IV.xvi.9).
466. Wendel, p. 328.
467. Calvin, Institutes, p. 1343 (IV.xvi.20).
468. Ibid., p. 1328 (IV.xvi.6).
469. Ibid., p. 1329 (IV.xvi.7).
470. Ibid., p. 1137 (IV.xvi.15).
471. Wendel, p. 468.
472. Calvin, Institutes, p. 1320 (IV.xv.19).
473. Schaff, History, vol. 8, p. 587.
474. Crampton, Calvin, p. 102.
475. Calvin, Institutes, p. 995 (III.xxv.5).
476. Martin Luther, quoted in Berkhof, History, p. 263.
477. Crampton, Calvin, pp. 101-102.
478. Calvin, Institutes, p. 995 (III.xxv.5).
479. Boettner, Predestination, p. 406.
480. Bratt, Teachings of Calvin, p. 49.
481. McGrath, Reformation Thought, p. 124.
482. Charles Miller, p. 27.
483. McGrath, Calvin, pp. 166-167.
484. Meeter, p. 21.
485. Bratt, Teachings of Calvin, p. 49.
486. Willem Van't Spijker, quoted in de Greef, p. 200.
487. McGrath, Reformation Thought, p. 125.
488. Introduction to John Calvin, *The Bondage and Liberation of the Will: A Defence of the Orthodox Doctrine of Human Choice against Pighius,* ed. A. N. S. Lane, trans. G. I. Davies (Grand Rapids: Baker Books, 1996), p. xiv.
489. Ibid., pp. xiv-xv.
490. Ibid. p. xiv.

491. Ibid. p. xv.
492. Ibid.
493. Footnote in Calvin, Institutes, p. 920 (III.xxi.1); Wendel, p. 264; George, p. 232.
494. Calvin, Secret Providence, p. 209.
495. de Greef, p. 178.
496. Sebastian Castellio, quoted in Zweig, p. 24.
497. Register of Geneva, p. 302.
498. Ibid.
499. de Greef, p. 114.
500. Calvin, Institutes, p. 926 (III.xxi.4).
501. Heinrich Bullinger, quoted in Schaff, History, vol. 8, p. 618.
502. Jewett, p. 63.
503. Warfield, Calvin, p. 481.
504. Wendel, p. 359.

Chapter 4
James Arminius

1. Homer C. Hoeksema, *The Voice of Our Fathers* (Grand Rapids: Reformed Free Publishing Association, 1980), p. 5.
2. Samuel Miller, p. 6.
3. Cunningham, Theology, vol. 2, p. 375.
4. Sellers, p. 11.
5. James Nichols, quoted in Works of Arminius, vol. 1, p. 84.
6. Curtiss, p. 15.
7. Matthias Martinius, quoted in Works of Arminius, vol. 1, p. liii.
8. Philip Limborch, quoted in Works of Arminius, vol. 1, p. liii.
9. John Wilks, quoted in Works of Arminius, vol. 1, p. lxiii.
10. Homer Hoeksema, Voice of Our Fathers, p. 9.
11. Samuel Miller, p. 17.
12. Louis Praamsma, "The Background of the Arminian Controversy (1586–1618)," in Peter Y. De Jong, ed., *Crisis in the Reformed Churches* (Grand Rapids: Reformed Fellowship, 1968), p. 28.
13. Homer Hoeksema, Voice of Our Fathers, p. 9.
14. Custance, p. 195.
15. Samuel Miller, p. 17.
16. Homer Hoeksema, Voice of Our Fathers, p. 9.
17. Custance, p. 195.
18. Lindsay, vol. 2, pp. 229-237.
19. Quoted in McNeil, p. 260.
20. McNeil, p. 242.
21. Lindsay, vol. 2, pp. 252-253.
22. Jonathan Israel, *The Dutch Republic* (New York: Oxford University Press, 1995), p. 155.
23. Gerard Brandt, quoted in Lindsay, vol. 2, p. 257.
24. Israel, pp. 185-186.
25. Lindsay, vol. 2, p. 267.
26. Ibid.

27. Lindsay, vol. 2, pp. 552-555.
28. Israel, p. 417.
29. Lindsay, vol. 2, p. 565.
30. Estep, p. 279.
31. Lindsay, vol. 2, pp. 572-573.
32. Estep, p. 280.
33. Lindsay, vol. 2, p. 604.
34. Estep, p. 284.
35. Lindsay, vol. 2, pp. 228-229, 270.
36. McNeil, p. 255.
37. W. B. Lockwood, "Vernacular Scriptures in Germany and the Low Countries Before 1500," in *The Cambridge History of the Bible,* Vol. 2: *The West from the Fathers to the Reformation,* ed. G. W. H. Lampe (Cambridge: Cambridge University Press, 1969), pp. 431-434.
38. Israel, pp. 44-47.
39. Ibid., p. 46.
40. Peter Y. De Jong, "The Rise of the Reformed Churches in the Netherlands," in De Jong, ed., *Crisis in the Reformed Churches,* pp. 7, 9.
41. Walter Lagerwey, "The History of Calvinism in the Netherlands," in Bratt, ed., *The Rise and Development of Calvinism,* p. 65.
42. Armitage, vol. 1, pp. 411-416.
43. Bangs, Arminius: A Study, pp. 21-22.
44. Carl Bangs, "Arminius as a Reformed Theologian," in Bratt, ed., *The Heritage of John Calvin,* pp. 211-214.
45. De Jong, Reformed Churches, p. 9; Israel, p. 101.
46. Lagerwey, p. 67.
47. Ibid.
48. McNeil, p. 261.
49. Lagerwey, p. 71.
50. *Evangelical Dictionary of Theology,* s.v. "Heidelberg Catechism," p. 514.
50. Lagerwey, p. 72.
52. *Evangelical Dictionary of Theology,* s.v. "Belgic Confession," p. 132.
53. Charles Miller, p. 61.
54. McNeil, p. 260.
55. Lagerwey, p. 72.
56. De Jong, Reformed Churches, p. 14.
57. Ibid.
58. Lagerwey, p. 72.
59. Homer Hoeksema, Voice of Our Fathers, p. 4.
60. The traditional date for the birth of Arminius is 1560, but Carl Bangs *(Arminius: A Study in the Dutch Reformation)* makes a good case for 1559 as being the correct date.
60. Arminius' name can be found as: Hermann, Harmensen, Van Herman, Hermanss, Van Harmin, Harmenszoon, Harmensen, Harmenson, Hermanszoon, Hermandszoon, Hermans, Harmens, Harmsen, Hermannson, van Hermanns, Haemensz, and Harmanzoon.
62. Bangs, Arminius: A Study, p. 25.
63. Works of Arminius, vol. 1, p. ix.
64. Ibid.
65. Ibid., pp. ix-x.

66. Bangs, Arminius: A Study, p. 37.
67. Ibid., p. 38.
68. Ibid., p. 37.
69. Works of Arminius, vol. 1, p. 21.
70. Ibid.
71. Ibid., p. 22.
72. Bangs, Arminius: A Study, p. 65.
73. Quoted in Bangs, Arminius: A Study, p. 65
74. Bangs, Arminius: A Study, p. 65.
75. Curtiss, p. 18.
76. Bangs, Arminius: A Study, p. 71.
77. Ibid.
78. Ibid., pp. 72-73.
79. Ibid., p. 78.
80. Works of Arminius, vol. 1, p. 26.
81. Ibid., p. xii.
82. Ibid.
83. Ibid., p. 28.
84. Ibid., p. 29.
85. Bangs, Arminius: A Study, p. 155.
86. Works of Arminius, vol. 1, pp. xiv-xv.
87. Bangs, Arminius: A Study, p. 253.
88. Ibid., p. 186.
89. Works of Arminius, p. xv.
90. See Works of Arminius, vol. 1, pp. xx-xxix, for the history of the publication of Arminius' writings.
91. Works of Arminius, p. xvi.
92. Bangs, Arminius: A Study, p. 329.
93. Richard A. Muller, *God, Creation, and Providence in the Thought of Jacob Arminius* (Grand Rapids: Baker Book House, 1991), p. 269.
94. Works of Arminius, vol. 2, p. 324.
95. Ibid., p. 323.
96. Ibid., pp. 323-324.
97. Ibid., vol. 1, p. 247.
98. Ibid., p. 295.
99. Ibid., vol. 2, p. 81.
100. Ibid., vol. 1, p. 103.
101. Ibid., vol. 2, pp. 264-265.
102. Ibid., vol. 1, p. 49.
103. Ibid., vol. 2, p. 306.
104. Ibid., vol. 1, p. 299.
105. Ibid., p. 298.
106. Ibid.
107. Ibid., vol. 2, p. 444.
108. Ibid., p. 243.
109. Ibid., vol. 1, p. 644.
110. Ibid., vol. 2, p. 138.
111. Ibid., p. 355.
112. Ibid., p. 353.
113. Ibid., pp. 115-118

114. Ibid., p. 143.
115. Ibid., p. 379.
116. Ibid., p. 141.
117. Ibid., p. 379.
118. Ibid., p. 387.
119. Ibid., pp. 387-388.
120. Ibid., p. 443.
121. Ibid., p. 145.
122. Ibid., p. 151.
123. Ibid., pp. 156-157.
124. Ibid., p. 157.
125. Ibid., vol. 1, pp. 659-660.
126. Ibid., p. 700.
127. Ibid., vol. 2, p. 256.
128. Ibid., vol. 1, p. 700.
129. Ibid., vol. 2, p. 408.
130. Ibid., vol. 1, p. 741.
131. Ibid., p. 667.
132. Ibid., vol. 2, pp. 440-441.
133. Bangs, Arminius: A Study, p. 167.
134. Ibid.
135. Ibid., p. 168.
136. Works of Arminius, vol. 1, p. 103.
137. Ibid., vol. 2, p. 703.
138. Ibid., vol. 1, p. 45.
139. Bangs, Arminius as a Theologian, pp. 214-221.
140. Peter Bertius, quoted in Bangs, Arminius: A Study, p. 331.
141. Hugo Grotius, quoted in Curtiss, p. 50.
142. Bangs, Arminius: A Study, pp. 19, 171.
143. Theodore Beza, quoted in Bangs, Arminius: A Study, p. 74.
144. Works of Arminius, vol. 1, p. 296.
145. Ibid., p. 700.
146. Ibid., p. 295.
147. Bangs, Arminius: A Study, pp. 19, 171.
148. Ibid., p. 139.
149. de Greef, pp. 139-140.
150. Dirck Coornhert, quoted in Curtiss, p. 23.
151. Curtiss, p. 23.
152. Bangs, Arminius: A Study, p. 138.
153. Ibid., p. 139.
154. Works of Arminius, vol. 1, p. 30.
155. Bangs, p. 139; Thomas Scott, p. 8; R. C. Sproul, *Willing to Believe* (Grand Rapids: Baker Books, 1997), p. 134.
156. Curtiss, p. 24; Schaff, History, vol. 8, p. 510; Custance, p. 76; Sellers, p. 8; Homer Hoeksema, Voice of Our Fathers, p. 7; *Encyclopedia of Religion and Ethics* (New York: Charles Scribner's Sons, n.d.), s.v. "Arminianism," vol. 1, p. 808; *Dictionary of Christianity in America* (Downers Grove: InterVarsity Press, 1990), s.v. "Arminianism," p. 78; Praasma, p. 24; J. L. Neve, *A History of Christian Thought* (Philadelphia: The Muhlenberg Press, 1946), vol. 2, p. 16.
157. *The Oxford Dictionary of the Christian Church,* s.v. "Arminianism," p.

90; *The Westminster Dictionary of Christian Theology,* s.v. "Arminianism," p. 43; *New Catholic Encyclopedia,* s.v. "Arminius, Jacobus," vol. 1, p. 840; *Baker's Dictionary of Theology,* s.v. "Arminianism," p. 64; Frederick D. Kershner, *Pioneers of Christian Thought* (Freeport: Books for Libraries Press, 1958), p. 305; *The New Schaff-Herzog Encyclopedia of Religious Knowledge,* s.v. "Arminius, Jacobus," vol. 1, p. 296.

158. Arminius, quoted in Bangs, Arminius: A Study, p. 139.
159. Ibid., p. 296.
160. Bangs, Arminius: A Study, p. 178.
161. Ibid., p. 119.
162. Ibid.
163. Ibid., pp. 147, 272.
164. Works of Arminius, vol. 3, p. 1.
165. Ibid., p. 266.
166. Bangs, Arminius: A Study, p. 209.
167. Ibid., pp. 283, 327-328.
168. Curtiss, p. 65.
169. Israel, p. 393.
170. Bangs, Arminius: A Study, pp. 264, 307.
171. Ibid., p. 273.
172. Works of Arminius, vol. 2, p. 686; Bangs, Arminius: A Study, p. 282.
173. Berkhof, History, pp. 96, 185.
174. Steele and Thomas, pp. 20-21; Spencer, Tulip, p. 65; Boettner, Predestination, p. 47; Mason, p. 5.
175. Curtiss, p. 39; Bangs, Arminius: A Study, pp. 114, 216, 272; Works of Arminius, vol. 1, pp. 102, 113, 289.
176. Bangs, Arminius: A Study, pp. 144, 192; Works of Arminius, vol. 1, p. 102.
177. Works of Arminius, vol. 1, p. 617.
178. de Greef, pp. 162-163.
179. Bangs, Arminius: A Study, p. 144; Works of Arminius, vol. 1, p. 101.
180. Works of Arminius, vol. 1, pp. 106, 110, 113, 600.
181. Ibid., vol. 2, p. 690.
182. Ibid., vol. 1, p. 702.
183. Ibid., p. 724.
184. Ibid.
185. *The Three Forms of Unity* (Grand Rapids: Protestant Reformed Churches in America, 1991), p. 10.
186. *The Three Forms of Unity,* p. 28.
187. Bangs, Arminius: A Study, p. 149.
188. Ibid., pp. 101, 225, 314.
189. Ibid., p. 314.
190. *The Three Forms of Unity,* p. 5.
191. Works of Arminius, vol. 1, p. 623.
192. Ibid., vol. 2, p. 698.
193. Ibid.
194. Ibid., vol. 1, p. 643.
195. Berkhof, History, p. 155.
196. Cunningham, Reformers, p. 451.
197. Good, Calvinists, p. 63; Wright, p. 29; Sellers, p. 8; Cunningham,

Reformers, p. 451.

198. Bangs, Arminius: A Study, p. 147; Works of Arminius, p. xxii.

199. Curtiss, p. 137; *The Oxford Dictionary of the Christian Church*, s.v. "Arminianism," p. 90; *Dictionary of Christianity in America*, s.v. "Arminianism," pp. 77, 78; Nicholas Tyacke, *Anti-Calvinists: the Rise of English Arminianism c. 1590–1640* (Oxford: Clarendon Press, 1987), pp. 4, 245.

200. Neve, vol. 2, p. 31.

201. Gordon H. Clark, *What Do Presbyterians Believe?* (Phillipsburg: Presbyterian and Reformed Publishing Co., 1965), p. iii.

202. For the history of Princeton Seminary see David B. Calhoun, *Princeton Seminary*, Vol. 1: *Faith and Learning (1812-1868)* (Edinburgh: The Banner of Truth Trust, 1994), and *Princeton Seminary*, Vol. 2: *The Majestic Testimony (1868-1929)* (Edinburgh: The Banner of Truth Trust, 1996).

203. Charles Miller, p. 61.

204. *Dictionary of Christianity in America*, s.v. "Arminianism," p. 79.

205. Spurgeon, Sermons on Sovereignty, p. 14.

206. James Haskins, *The Methodists* (New York: Hippocrene Books, 1992), pp. 39-40, 57.

207. *Evangelical Dictionary of Theology*, s.v. "Wesley, John," p. 1164.

208. Ibid., s.v. "Methodism," p. 713.

209. Gerald O. McCulloh, "The Influence of Arminius on American Theology," in Gerald O. McCulloh, ed., *Man's Faith and Freedom* (Nashville: Abingdon Press, 1962), p. 74.

210. Haskins, p. 70.

211. *Evangelical Dictionary of Theology*, s.v. "Asbury, Francis," p. 85.

212. Ibid., s.v. "Methodism," p. 713.

213. Spurgeon, Two Wesleys, p. 4.

214. Nettles, Wesley, pp. 302-313.

215. John Wesley, quoted in Nettles, Wesley, p. 301.

216. Susanna Wesley, quoted in A. W. Harrison, *Arminianism* (London: Duckworth, 1937), p. 189.

217. Howard A. Slaatte, *The Arminian Arm of Theology* (Washington D.C.: University Press of America, 1979), p. 118; Harrison, Arminianism, p. 210.

218. John Wesley, quoted in Nettles, Wesley, p. 309.

219. Spurgeon, Two Wesleys, p. 9.

220. Frank S. Mead, *Handbook of Denominations in the United States*, 8th ed., rev. Samuel S. Hill (Nashville: Abingdon Press, 1985), p. 260.

221. Ibid., p. 92.

222. William Cathcart, *The Baptist Encyclopedia* (Philadelphia: Louis H. Everts, 1881), s.v. "Free-Will Baptists," pp. 416-417.

223. Quoted in Works of Arminius, vol. 1, p. 306.

Chapter Five
The Five Points of Calvinism

1. Boettner, Predestination, p. 59.

2. Engelsma, Defense of Calvinism, p. 6.

3. Roger Nicole, Preface to Steele and Thomas, *The Five Points of Calvinism*, p. 7.

4. Tom Ross, Abandoned Truth, p. 16.
5. Engelsma, Defense of Calvinism, p. 7.
6. Spencer, Tulip, p. 9.
7. Custance, pp. 223-224.
8. Ibid., p. 71.
9. Mason, p. 4.
10. Coppes, p. xi.
11. Palmer, p. 5.
12. Ibid.
13. Ibid.
14. George W. Knight, Foreword to Coppes, *Are Five Points Enough? The Ten Points of Calvinism,* p. iv.
15. Dabney, Calvinism, p. 3.
16. Kenneth H. Good, *God's Gracious Purpose* (Rochester: Backus Book Publishers, 1979), p. 11.
17. Seaton, p. 8.
18. Gunn, p. 4.
19. Boettner, Predestination, p. 59.
20. Clyde T. Everman, in "The Baptist Examiner Pulpit Forum," *The Baptist Examiner,* December 1, 1995, p. 4.
21. Mark Duncan, *The Five Points of Christian Reconstruction from the Lips of Our Lord* (Edmonton: Still Waters Revival Books, 1990), p. 10.
22. Jimmie B. Davis, in "The Berea Baptist Banner Forum," *The Berea Baptist Banner,* February 5, 1995, p. 30.
23. David O'Neil, in "The Berea Baptist Banner Forum," *The Berea Baptist Banner,* February 5, 1995, p. 30.
24. Jack C. Whitt, in "The Baptist Examiner Pulpit Forum," *The Baptist Examiner,* December 1, 1995, p. 4.
25. Joseph M. Wilson, "The World's Three Great Errors About the Church," *The Baptist Examiner,* November 23, 1991, p. 2.
26. Sproul, Grace Unknown, p. 115.
27. Ben Lacy Rose, *T.U.L.I.P.: The Five Disputed Points of Calvinism,* 2nd ed. (Franklin: Providence House Publishers, 1996), p. vii.
28. Duncan, p. 3.
29. Ibid., p. 2.
30. Steve Lally, "Overcoming the #1 Prostate Problem," *Prevention,* January 1992, p. 126.
31. Coppes, p. xi.
32. Steele and Thomas, p. 9.
33. Coppes, p. 55.
34. Phelps, p. 26.
35. Ibid., p. 21.
36. Ibid., p. 26.
37. Charles H. Spurgeon, "The Sum and Substance of All Theology," in Charles H. Spurgeon, *Election* (Pasadena: Pilgrim Publications, 1978), p. 579.
38. Brian G. Armstrong, *Calvinism and the Amyraut Heresy* (Madison: The University of Wisconsin Press, 1969), pp. xviii, 1.
39. Paul Helm, *Calvin and the Calvinists* (Edinburgh: The Banner of Truth Trust, 1982), pp. 36-37.
40. Lewis Sperry Chafer, *Systematic Theology* (Dallas: Dallas Seminary Press,

1948), vol. 3, p. 184.
  41. See Lightner, pp. 45-49; Kober, pp. 14-15.
  42. For a discussion of Calvinism in the GARBC see the section entitled "The Retreat of the General Association of Regular Baptists" in Good, *Are Baptists Calvinists?* pp. 217-239.
  43. Charles W. Bronson, *The Extent of the Atonement* (Pasadena: Pilgrim Publications, 1992), p. 19.
  44. Palmer, p. 27.
  45. Gunn, p. 4.
  46. Joseph M. Wilson, "How is the Atonement Limited?" *The Baptist Examiner,* December 9, 1989, p. 1.
  47. Boettner, Predestination, p. 59.
  48. Custance, p. 71.
  49. Wilson, Atonement, p. 1.
  50. De Jong, Reformed Churches, p. 13.
  51. Homer Hoeksema, Voice of Our Fathers, p. 17.
  52. Bangs, Arminius: A Study, pp. 224-225.
  53. De Jong, Reformed Churches, p. 17.
  54. Lagerwey, p. 82.
  55. Bangs, Arminius: A Study, p. 21.
  56. Simon Kistemaker, "Leading Figures at the Synod of Dort," in De Jong, ed., *Crisis in the Reformed Churches,* p. 47.
  57. Ibid., p. 48.
  58. Ibid., p. 42.
  59. Israel, p. 459.
  60. *Evangelical Dictionary of Theology,* s.v. "Grotius, Hugo," p. 489.
  61. *The Oxford Encyclopedia of the Reformation* (New York: Oxford University Press, 1996), s.v. "Grotius, Hugo," vol. 2, pp. 197-198.
  62. A. W. Harrison, *The Beginnings of Arminianism to the Synod of Dort* (London: University of London Press, 1926), pp. 148-149. This number is also given as forty-five (Curtiss, p. 64); forty-four (Israel, p. 425; Bangs, Arminius: A Study, p. 356); and forty-three (*The New Schaff-Herzog Encyclopedia of Religious Knowledge,* s.v. "Remonstrants," vol. 9, p. 481).
  63. Harrison, Beginnings of Arminianism, pp. 148-149.
  64. Quoted in Curtiss, p. 69.
  65. Philip Schaff, *The Creeds of Christendom,* 6th ed. (Grand Rapids: Baker Book House, 1990), vol. 3, pp. 545-549.
  66. Bangs, Arminius: A Study, p. 318.
  67. Israel, p. 426.
  68. Harrison, Beginnings of Arminianism, p. 152.
  69. Bangs, Arminius: A Study, p. 318.
  70. Quoted in Harrison, Beginnings of Arminianism, p. 152.
  71. Also known as the Contra-Remonstrance.
  72. De Jong, ed., *Crisis in the Reformed Churches,* pp. 211-213.
  73. Harrison, Beginnings of Arminianism, p. 154.
  74. Israel, p. 425.
  75. Harrison, Beginnings of Arminianism, pp. 157-159.
  76. Ibid., pp. 194-196.
  77. *The New Schaff-Herzog Encyclopedia of Religious Knowledge,* s.v. "Remonstrants," vol. 9, p. 481.

NOTES 689

78. Harrison, Beginnings of Arminianism, pp. 224-225.
79. Israel, pp. 425, 440.
80. Harrison, Beginnings of Arminianism, p. 207.
81. Ibid., pp. 226-228.
82. Bangs, Arminius: A Study, p. 356; Israel, pp. 450-456.
83. Praamsma, p. 33.
84. Homer Hoeksema, Voice of Our Fathers, p. 101.
85. Israel p. 460.
86. De Jong, ed., p. 220.
87. *The New Schaff-Herzog Encyclopedia of Religious Knowledge,* s.v. "Dort, Synod of," vol. 3, p. 494.
88. See De Jong, ed., pp. 215-219, for a list of delegates; however, sources vary on these numbers.
89. Cunningham, Theology, vol. 2, p. 380.
90. Ibid., p. 381.
91. The synod ended on May 9, but the Dutch delegates met again from May 13 to 29; hence, sources vary on the closing date.
92. Homer Hoeksema, Voice of Our Fathers, p. 25.
93. Quoted in Samuel Miller, p. 37.
94. Schaff, Creeds, vol. 1, 513.
95. John Bogerman, quoted in Harrison, Beginnings of Arminianism, p. 87.
96. Arminius, quoted in Harrison, Beginnings of Arminianism, p. 88.
97. Homer Hoeksema, Voice of Our Fathers, p. 25.
98. *The Oxford Encyclopedia of the Reformation,* s.v. "Dordrecht, Synod of," vol. 2, p. 2.
99. John Breitinger, quoted in Schaff, Creeds, vol. 1, p. 514.
100. Joseph Hall, quoted in Samuel Miller, p. 33.
101. Harrison, Beginnings of Arminianism, p. 336.
102. Quoted in Harrison, Beginnings of Arminianism, p. 336.
103. Schaff, Creeds, vol. 1, p. 513.
104. John Wesley, quoted in Works of Arminius, vol. 1, p. lxiii.
105. Matthias Martinius, quoted in Homer Hoeksema, Voice of Our Fathers, p. 23.
106. De Jong, ed., p. 213.
107. Schaff, Creeds, vol. 1, p. 512; De Jong, ed., p. 214.
108. Schaff, Creeds, vol. 1, p. 512.
109. Harrison, Beginnings of Arminianism, p. 309.
110. Kistemaker, Dort, p. 41; see De Jong, ed., pp. 220-221, for a list of the Remonstrants.
111. Homer Hoeksema, Voice of Our Fathers, p. 103.
112. Ibid., pp. 103-109.
113. John Bogerman, quoted in Homer Hoeksema, Voice of Our Fathers, p. 27.
114. Simon Episcopius, quoted in Harrison, Beginnings of Arminianism, p. 329.
115. Harrison, Beginnings of Arminianism, p. 329.
116. Ibid., p. 385.
117. Israel, pp. 462-463.
118. Harrison, Beginnings of Arminianism, pp. 386-387; Lagerwey, p. 82.
119. Schaff, Creeds, vol. 1, p. 515.

120. Bangs, Arminius: A Study, p. 357.
121. Quoted in Thomas Scott, p. 241.
122. Cunningham, Theology, vol. 2, p. 379.
123. Berkhof, History, p. 152.
124. Homer Hoeksema, Voice of Our Fathers, p. 114.
125. Peter Y. De Jong, "Preaching and the Synod of Dort," in De Jong, ed., *Crisis in the Reformed Churches,* p. 115.
126. *The Three Forms of Unity,* pp. 37-55.
127. Schaff, Creeds, vol. 1, p. 514.
128. Lagerwey, p. 84.
129. Ibid.
130. Ibid., p. 96.
131. Ibid., p. 97.
132. Reformed Bible College, *1990–1992 Catalog,* p. 43
133. Ibid., p. 5.
134. Calvin Theological Seminary, *1996–1998 Catalog,* p. 114.
135. Ibid., p. 115.
136. Quoted in Fred H. Klooster, "Doctrinal Deliverances of Dort," in De Jong, ed., *Crisis in the Reformed Churches,* p. 93.
137. Homer Hoeksema, Voice of Our Fathers, p. 42.
138. Good, Calvinists, p. 80.
139. Ibid.
140. Ibid., p. 66.
141. Herman Hanko, "Total Depravity," in Herman Hanko, Homer C. Hoeksema, and Gise J. Van Baren, *The Five Points of Calvinism* (Grand Rapids: Reformed Free Publishing Association, 1976), p. 10.
142. Custance, p. 71.
143. Marten H. Woudstra, "The Synod and Bible Translation," in De Jong, ed., *Crisis in the Reformed Churches,* p. 95.
144. Ibid., p. 101.
145. Ibid., pp. 101, 103.
146. Bangs, Arminius: A Study, p. 101.
147. Schaff, Creeds, vol. 1, p. 505.
148. M. Howard Rienstra, "The History and Development of Calvinism in Scotland and England," in Bratt, ed., *The Rise and Development of Calvinism,* p. 110.
149. For a more detailed look at the development of the English Bible see the author's *A Brief History of English Bible Translations.*
150. A. R. Myers, ed. *English Historical Documents (1327–1515),* vol. 4 of *English Historical Documents,* ed. David C. Douglas (New York: Oxford University Press, 1969), p. 696.
151. John Wycliffe, quoted in J. H. Merle d'Aubigne, *The Reformation in England,* ed. S. M. Houghton, trans. H. White (Edinburgh: Banner of Truth Trust, 1962), vol. 1, p. 92.
152. Henry Gee and William John Hardy, eds. *Documents Illustrative of English Church History* (London: Macmillan and Co., 1910), p. 108.
153. Paul L. Hughes and James F. Larkin, eds., *Tudor Royal Proclamations,* Vol. I: *The Early Tudors (1485–1553)* (New Haven and London: Yale University Press, 1964), p. 6.
154. Alfred W. Pollard, ed., *Records of the English Bible* (London: Oxford

University Press, 1911), p. 1.
   155. Andreas Ammonius, quoted in H. Maynard Smith, *Pre-Reformation England* (New York: Russell & Russell, 1963), p. 289.
   156. d'Aubigne, Reformation in England, vol. 1, pp. 157-158.
   157. Ibid., p. 177.
   158. G. R. Elton, *Reform and Reformation, England 1509–1598* (Cambridge: Harvard University Press, 1977), p. 75.
   159. Newman, vol. 2, p. 66.
   160. Hughes and Larkin, vol. 1, p. 183.
   161. Ibid., p. 185.
   162. Ibid., p. 196.
   163. Ibid.
   164. William Tyndale, quoted in David Daniell, *William Tyndale: A Biography* (New Haven & London: Yale University Press, 1994), p. 383.
   165. G. R. Elton, ed., *The Tudor Constitution: Documents and Commentary* (Cambridge: Cambridge University Press, 1960), p. 335.
   166. Henry Bettenson, ed., *Documents of the Christian Church*, 2nd ed. (London: Oxford University Press, 1963), p. 229.
   167. Gee and Hardy, p. 257.
   168. Lindsay, vol. 2, pp. 333-334.
   169. Gee and Hardy, p. 307.
   170. C. H. Williams, ed., *English Historical Documents (1485–1558)*, vol. 5 of *English Historical Documents,* ed. David C. Douglas (New York: Oxford University Press, 1971), p. 824.
   171. Thomas Cranmer, quoted in C. H. Williams, p. 825.
   172. Gee and Hardy, p. 275.
   173. Hughes and Larkin, vol. 1, p. 297.
   174. Ibid., p. 374.
   175. Ibid., p. 393.
   176. Thompson, p. 594.
   177. Gee and Hardy, p. 366.
   178. Hughes and Larkin, vol. 1, p. 395.
   179. Gee and Hardy, pp. 358, 369.
   180. Quoted in E. N. Williams, *A Documentary History of England,* Vol. 2: *(1559–1931)* (Baltimore: Penguin Books, 1965), p. 20.
   181. Schaff, Creeds, vol. 1, p. 614.
   182. Edward VI, quoted in Thompson, p. 609.
   183. Paul L. Hughes and James F. Larkin, eds., *Tudor Royal Proclamations,* Vol. II: *The Later Tudors (1553–1587)* (New Haven and London: Yale University Press, 1969), p. 6.
   184. C. H. Williams, pp. 860, 862.
   185. Hughes and Larkin, vol. 2, p. 59.
   186. Ibid., p. 91.
   187. Gee and Hardy, p. 384.
   188. Thompson, p.617.
   189. Hugh Latimer, quoted in Thompson, p. 617.
   190. John Knox, *The First Blast of the Trumpet Against the Monstrous Regiment of Women* (Dallas: Presbyterian Heritage Publications, 1993), p. 87.
   191. Charles D. Cremeans, *The Reception of Calvinistic Thought in England* (Urbana: University of Illinois Press, 1949), p. 35.

192. Gee and Hardy, p. 442.
193. Ibid., p. 458.
194. Elton, The Tudor Constitution, p. 424.
195. Hughes and Larkin, vol. 2, p. 119.
196. Ibid.
197. Ibid., p. 126.
198. Quoted in Brooke F. Westcott, *A General View of the History of the English Bible,* 3rd ed. rev. William A. Wright (London: Macmillan and Co., 1905), p. 101.
199. Pollard, p. 303.
200. Schaff, Creeds, vol. 1, p. 616.
201. Gee and Hardy, p. 477.
202. Everett H. Emerson, *English Puritanism from John Hooper to John Milton* (Durham: Duke University Press, 1968), p. 15.
203. Ibid., p. 17.
204. William Haller, *Elizabeth I and the Puritans* (Charlottesville: The University Press of Virginia, 1972), p. 31.
205. Douglas Kelly, Liberty, p. 57.
206. Ibid., p. 63.
207. James H. Smylie, *A Brief History of the Presbyterians* (Louisville: Geneva Press, 1996), p. 31.
208. Quoted in William M. Hetherington, *History of the Westminster Assembly of Divines,* 3rd ed. (Edmonton: Still Waters Revival Books, 1993), p. 61.
209. Emerson, p. 31.
210. John Reynolds, quoted in Schaff, Creeds, vol. 1, p. 709.
211. Schaff, Creeds, vol. 1, pp. 710-712.
212. Benjamin B. Warfield, *The Westminster Assembly and its Work* (Edmonton: Still Waters Revival Books, 1991), pp. 4-5.
213. Quoted in Schaff, Creeds, vol. 1, pp. 687-688.
214. Douglas Kelly, Liberty, p. 67.
215. Schaff, Creeds, vol. 1, pp. 689, 718-719.
216. McNeil, p. 309.
217. Calvin, Letters, pp. 87, 113, 119, 125, 130, 138, 140, 145, 147.
218. Cremeans, p. 28.
219. Schaff, Creeds, vol. 1, p. 602.
220. McNeil, p. 311.
221. Ibid., p. 314.
222. Schaff, Creeds, vol. 1, p. 603.
223. R. T. Kendall, *Calvin and English Calvinism* (Oxford: Oxford University Press, 1979), p. 52.
224. McNeil, p. 313.
225. Horton Davies, *Worship and Theology in England,* Vol. I: *From Cranmer to Hooker* (Grand Rapids: Wm. B. Eerdmans Publishing Co., 1996), p. 424.
226. Kendall, pp. 52-53.
227. Curtiss, p. 132.
228. Cunningham, Reformers, p. 426.
229. Schaff, Creeds, vol. 3, pp. 523-524.
230. Ibid., vol. 1, p. 661.
231. Patrick Collinson, "England and International Calvinism, 1558–1640," in

Menna Prestwich, *International Calvinism* (Oxford: Oxford University Press, 1985), pp. 213, 220.

232. John Reynolds, quoted in Schaff, Creeds, vol. 1, p. 661.

233. Quoted in Harrison, Beginnings of Arminianism, p. 181.

234. Emerson, p. 31.

235. Kenneth Fincham and Peter Lake, "The Ecclesiastical Policies of James I and Charles I," in Kenneth Fincham, ed., *The Early Stuart Church, 1603–1642* (Stanford: Stanford University Press, 1993), p. 32.

236. Peter White, "The *via media* in the early Stuart Church," in Fincham, ed., *The Early Stuart Church, 1603–1642*, pp. 218, 225; Fincham and Lake, p. 31-32.

237. Fincham and Lake, p. 32.

238. Quoted in Schaff, Creeds, vol. 1, p. 513.

239. Tyacke, Anti-Calvinists, p. 102.

240. Neve, vol. 2, p. 29.

241. Quoted Harrison, Arminianism, p. 133.

242. Harrison, Arminianism, p. 128; Collinson, pp. 218, 220; Tyacke, Anti-Calvinists, p. 127.

243. Harrison, Arminianism, p. 133.

244. Robert Montagu, quoted in Harrison, Arminianism, p. 131.

245. Emerson, p. 37.

246. Neve, vol. 2, p. 30.

247. Quoted in Nicholas Tyacke, "Archbishop Laud," in Fincham, ed., *The Early Stuart Church, 1603–1642*, p. 65.

248. Tyacke, Anti-Calvinists, pp. 47, 49, 57, 126, 137, 138, 167, 186.

249. Ibid., pp. 127-139.

250. John Owen, *The Death of Christ,* volume 10 of *The Works of John Owen,* ed. William H. Goold (Edinburgh: The Banner of Truth Trust, 1967), pp. 1, 4.

251. McNeil, p. 322.

252. Quoted in Hetherington, p. 97.

253. John R. de Witt, "The Form of Church Government," in John L. Carson and David W. Hall, eds., *To Glorify and Enjoy God: A Commemoration of the 350th Anniversary of the Westminster Assembly* (Edinburgh: The Banner of Truth Trust, 1994), p. 150.

254. Clark, Presbyterians, p. xi.

255. Schaff, Creeds, vol. 1, p. 730.

256. William S. Barker, "The Men and Parties of the Assembly," in Carson and Hall, eds., *To Glorify and Enjoy God: A Commemoration of the 350th Anniversary of the Westminster Assembly,* p. 52.

257. Richard Baxter, quoted in Schaff, Creeds, vol. 1, p. 729.

258. Samuel T. Logan, "The Context and Work of the Assembly," in Carson and Hall, eds., *To Glorify and Enjoy God: A Commemoration of the 350th Anniversary of the Westminster Assembly,* p. 34.

259. Quoted in Hetherington, p. 117.

260. Barker, p. 52.

261. Schaff, Creeds, vol. 1, p. 733.

262. Warfield, Westminster Assembly, p. 17.

263. Works of Arminius, vol. 1, p. 649.

264. Sell, p. 63.

265. Schaff, Creeds, vol. 1, p. 733.
266. Hetherington, p. 136.
267. Schaff, Creeds, vol. 1, pp. 737-738.
268. Ibid., p. 739.
269. Ibid., p. 736.
270. Quoted in Hetherington, p. 129.
271. Schaff, Creeds, vol. 1, pp. 745-747.
272. Quoted in Hetherington, p. 97.
273. Ibid.
274. Hetherington, p. 98.
275. McNeil, p. 324.
276. Logan, p. 36.
277. de Witt, Church Government, p. 148.
278. Quoted in de Witt, Church Government, p. 147.
279. Logan, p. 35.
280. Schaff, Creeds, vol. 1, p. 730.
281. Warfield, Westminster Assembly, pp. 3, 17.
282. Ibid., p. 3.
283. Logan, p. 37.
284. Schaff, Creeds, vol. 1, p. 754.
285. Quoted in Hetherington, p. 130.
286. Warfield, Westminster Assembly, p. 36.
287. Quoted in Hetherington, p. 158.
288. Warfield, Westminster Assembly, pp. 82-86.
289. Quoted in Warfield, Westminster Assembly, p. 63.
290. Hetherington, p. 310.
291. Henry O. Wakeman, *An Introduction to the History of the Church of England,* 7th ed. (London: Rivingtons, 1912), p. 377.
292. William L. Lumpkin, *Baptist Confessions of Faith,* rev. ed. (Valley Forge: Judson Press, 1969), p. 150.
293. For the particulars see the preface and introduction to Carson and Hall, eds., *To Glorify and Enjoy God: A Commemoration of the 350th Anniversary of the Westminster Assembly.*
294. James E. Bordwine, *A Guide to the Westminster Standards* (Jefferson: The Trinity Foundation, 1991), p. v.
295. Hetherington, pp. 342-343.
296. Warfield, Westminster Assembly, pp. 43, 45.
297. Hetherington, pp. 342-343.
298. Warfield, Westminster Assembly, pp. 339-340.
299. Ibid., p. 340.
300. Schaff, Creeds, vol. 1, p. 758.
301. Warfield, Westminster Assembly, p. 341.
302. Ibid., p. 63.
303. Ibid., pp. 63-64.
304. Benjamin B. Warfield, quoted in Jay E. Adams, "Afterword: The Influence of Westminster," in Carson and Hall, eds., *To Glorify and Enjoy God: A Commemoration of the 350th Anniversary of the Westminster Assembly,* p. 250.
305. Dr. Currey, quoted in Schaff, Creeds, vol. 1, p. 789.
306. Dean Stanley, quoted in Schaff, Creeds, vol. 1, p. 789.
307. Boettner, Predestination, p. 13.

308. McNeil, p. 325.
309. Benjamin B. Warfield, quoted in Kendall, p. 2.
310. Kendall, p. 212.
311. Shedd, Calvinism, p. 146.
312. John Richardson, Introduction to Clark, *What Do Presbyterians Believe?* p. xii.
313. Westminster Theological Seminary, *1990–1992 Catalog,* p. 96.
314. Warfield, Westminster Assembly, pp. 361-367.
315. *The Westminster Confession of Faith* (Philadelphia: Great Commission Publications, n.d.).
316. Schaff, Creeds, vol. 1, pp. 665, 761.
317. Warfield, Westminster Assembly, p. 106.
318. For the sections that have been changed, see Bordwine, p. v.
319. Warfield, Westminster Assembly, p. 64.
320. W. Robert Godfrey, "The Westminster Larger Catechism," in Carson and Hall, eds., *To Glorify and Enjoy God: A Commemoration of the 350th Anniversary of the Westminster Assembly,* p. 130.
321. McNeil, p. 326.
322. Richard Baxter, quoted in Douglas F. Kelly, "The Westminster Shorter Catechism," in Carson and Hall, eds., *To Glorify and Enjoy God: A Commemoration of the 350th Anniversary of the Westminster Assembly,* p. 102.
323. Warfield, Westminster Assembly, p. 64.
324. McNeil, p. 325.
325. Richard Baxter, quoted in Douglas Kelly, Catechism, p. 102.
326. Schaff, Creeds, vol. 1, p. 787.
327. Reformed Theological Seminary, *1990–1991 Catalog,* p. 39.
328. Schaff, Creeds, vol. 1, p. 783.
329. Warfield, Westminster Assembly, p. 389.
330. Ibid., p. 788.
331. Shedd, Calvinism, p. 116.
332. Schaff, Creeds, vol. 1, p. 815.
333. Kendall, p. 212.
334. Lumpkin, p. 144.
335. Ibid., p. 147.
336. Ibid.
337. Ibid.
338. Quoted in W. J. McGlothlin, *Baptist Confessions of Faith* (Philadelphia: American Baptist Publications Society, 1911), p. 190.
339. Richard P. Belcher and Tony Mattia, *A Discussion of Seventeenth Century Baptist Confessions of Faith* (Columbia: Richbarry Press, 1983), p. 18.
340. Lumpkin, p. 150.
341. *The First London Confession of Faith With an Appendix by Benjamin Cox* (New York: Backus Book Publishers, 1981).
342. Lumpkin, pp. 150-152.
343. Schaff, Creeds, vol. 1, p. 832.
344. Lumpkin, p. 236.
345. Quoted in Lumpkin, pp. 238-239.
346. Lumpkin, p. 239; Kiffin and Keach had also signed the 1644 confession.
347. Lumpkin, pp. 241-295.
348. Good, Calvinists, p. 67.

349. Ibid., p. 66.
350. Gary Long, Contemporary Preface to *The First London Confession of Faith With an Appendix by Benjamin Cox,* p. iii.
351. Belcher and Mattia, p. 29.
352. Introduction to Erroll Hulse, et al., *Our Baptist Heritage* (Leeds: Reformation Today Trust, 1993), p. ix.
353. Lumpkin, p. 349.
354. Ibid.
355. Ibid.
356. Steele and Thomas, p. 23.

Chapter Six
Total Depravity

1. Palmer, p. 13.
2. Frank B. Beck, *The Five Points of Calvinism* (Ashland: Calvary Baptist Church, n.d.), p. 4.
3. Steele and Thomas, p. 25.
4. Storms, Chosen for Life, p. 34.
5. Jewett, p. 15; Coppes, p. 56.
6. Storms, Chosen for Life, p. 34.
7. Sproul, Chosen by God, p. 104.
8. Harold Harvey, in "The Berea Baptist Banner Forum," *The Berea Baptist Banner*, October 5, 1989, p. 190.
9. Good, God's Purpose, p. 16.
10. Rose, p. 2.
11. Talbot and Crampton, p. 20.
12. Pink, Sovereignty, p. 149.
13. Ibid., p. 136.
14. Canons of Dort, III,IV:3.
15. Boettner, Predestination, p. 60; Seaton, p. 8; Good, God's Purpose, p. 16.
16. Kober, p. 7; Kruithof, p. 33; Steele and Thomas, p. 24; Talbot and Crampton, p. 17.
17. Hanko, Total Depravity, p. 18.
18. Palmer, p. 14.
19. E. D. Strickland, in "The Berea Baptist Banner Forum," *The Berea Baptist Banner*, October 5, 1989, p. 190.
20. Palmer, p. 9; Spencer, Tulip, p. 24.
21. Sproul, Chosen by God, p. 104.
22. John H. Gerstner, *A Predestination Primer* (Grand Rapids: Baker Book House, 1960), p. 10.
23. Spencer, Tulip, p. 24.
24. Talbot and Crampton, p. 18.
25. Hanko, Total Depravity, p. 17.
26. Ibid., p. 16.
27. David J. Engelsma, "The Death of Confessional Calvinism in Scottish Presbyterianism," *Standard Bearer,* December 1, 1992, p. 102.
28. Hanko, Total Depravity, p. 23.
29. Engelsma, Confessional Calvinism, p. 103.

NOTES

30. Hanko, Total Depravity, p. 23.
31. Gerstner, Predestination, p. 11.
32. Ibid., p. 12.
33. Seaton, p. 9.
34. Arthur W. Pink, *Gleanings from the Scriptures* (Chicago: Moody Press, 1969), p. 12.
35. Hanko, Total Depravity, p. 14.
36. Boettner, Predestination, p. 28.
37. Rose, p. 3.
38. Custance, p. 9.
39. Arthur W. Pink, *Gleanings in Genesis* (Chicago: Moody Press, 1950), p. 35.
40. Ibid., p. 47.
41. Arthur W. Pink, *The Divine Covenants* (Grand Rapids: Baker Book House, 1973), p. 30.
42. Timothy Dwight, quoted in Chafer, Theology, vol. 2, p. 221.
43. Jonathan Edwards, *Original Sin,* ed. Clyde A. Holbrook (New Haven and London: Yale University Press, 1970), p. 136.
44. Ibid., p. 137.
45. Ruckman, Church History, vol. 1, p. 72.
46. Works of Arminius, vol. 2, p. 151.
47. Ibid., pp. 156-157.
48. Ibid., vol. 1, pp. 659-660.
49. Sproul, Willing to Believe, p. 126.
50. Cunningham, Theology, vol. 2, p. 389.
51. John Wesley, quoted in Arthur S. Wood, "The Contribution of John Wesley to the Theology of Grace," in Pinnock, ed., *Grace Unlimited,* p. 214.
52. Ibid., p. 213.
53. John Wesley, *A Compend of Wesley's Theology,* ed. Robert W. Burtner and Robert E. Chiles (Nashville: Abingdon Press, 1954), p. 127.
54. Jewett, p. 17.
55. Pink, Sovereignty, p. 136.
56. Ibid.
57. Spencer, Tulip, p. 27.
58. Steele and Thomas, p. 25.
59. Talbot and Crampton, p. 19.
60. Custance, p. 40.
61. Jonathan Edwards, *Freedom of the Will,* ed. Paul Ramsey (New Haven and London: Yale University Press, 1957), p. 137.
62. Pink, Sovereignty, p. 130.
63. Tom Ross, Abandoned Truth, p. 46.
64. Walter J. Chantry, *Man's Will—Free Yet Bound* (Canton: Free Grace Publications, 1988), p. 2; Tom Wells, *Faith: The Gift of God* (Edinburgh: The Banner of Truth Trust, 1983), p. 47; Bishop, p. 145.
65. Pink, Sovereignty, p. 139.
66. Talbot and Crampton, p. 21.
67. Chantry, p. 4.
68. Charles H. Spurgeon, *Free Will—A Slave* (Canton: Free Grace Publications, 1977), p. 3.
69. David O. Wilmoth, in "The Baptist Examiner Forum II," *The Baptist*

Examiner, September 16, 1989, p. 5.

70. Tom Ross, Abandoned Truth, p. 56.

71. W. E. Best, *Free Grace Versus Free Will* (Houston: W. E. Best Book Missionary Trust, 1977), p. 35.

72. Boettner, Predestination, p. 221.

73. John H. Gerstner, *A Primer on Free Will* (Phillipsburg: Presbyterian and Reformed Publishing Co., 1982), p. 10.

74. Clark, Predestination, p. 114.

75. Steven R. Houck, *The Bondage of the Will* (Lansing: Peace Protestant Reformed Church, n.d.), p. 1.

76. Tom Ross, Abandoned Truth, p. 48.

77. Boettner, Predestination, p. 221.

78. Tom Wells, p. 52.

79. Dewey J. Hoitenga, *John Calvin and the Will: A Critique and Corrective* (Grand Rapids: Baker Books, 1997), p. 70.

80. Gill, God and Truth, p. 197; Bishop, p. 149.

81. Gill, God and Truth, p. 198.

82. Pink, Sovereignty, p. 134.

83. Gill, God and Truth, p. 197; Pink, Sovereignty, p. 135; Bishop, p. 148.

84. Pink, Sovereignty, pp. 134-135.

85. E.g., Matt. 7—Gunn, p. 7; Steele and Thomas, p. 29. Matt. 12—Pink, Gleanings from the Scriptures, p. 217; Chantry, p. 1.

86. Pink, Sovereignty, pp. 151, 152.

87. Boettner, Predestination, p. 65.

88. Ibid.

89. Ibid.

90. Ibid.

91. J. B. Heard, *The Tripartite Nature of Man: Spirit, Soul, and Body,* 5th ed. (Edinburgh: T & T Clark, 1882), p. 100.

92. Ibid., pp. 96, 209.

93. Arthur W. Pink, *The Doctrine of Salvation* (Grand Rapids: Baker Book House, 1975), p. 23.

94. Calvinistic trichotomists include Pink (Salvation, p. 23) and Chafer, Theology (vol. 2, p. 181); Calvinistic dichotomists include Berkhof (Theology, p. 194) and Charles Hodge (Theology, vol. 2, p. 249).

95. Boettner, Immortality, p. 123.

96. Pink, Genesis, pp. 37-38.

97. Homer Hoeksema, Voice of Our Fathers, pp. 453-464.

98. Canons of Dort, III, IV:4.

99. Pink, Genesis, p. 38.

100. Hoitenga, p. 70.

101. Ibid., p. 111.

102. Ibid.

103. Ibid.

104. Arthur W. Pink, *Exposition of the Gospel of John* (Grand Rapids: Zondervan Publishing House, 1975), p. 385.

105. Boettner, Predestination, p. 63.

106. Edwards, Original Sin, p. 139.

107. Donald Grey Barnhouse, "God's Wrath," in *Expositions of Bible Doctrines Taking the Epistle to the Romans as a Point of Departure* (Grand

Rapids: Wm. B. Eerdmans Publishing Co., 1953), vol. 1, p. 216.
　108. Palmer, p. 12.
　109. Storms, Chosen for Life, p. 35.
　110. Hanko, Total Depravity, p. 17.
　111. Houck, Bondage of the Will, p. 9.
　112. Chantry, p. 8.
　113. Desiderius Erasmus, in *Erasmus—Luther Discourse on Free Will,* trans. and ed. by Ernst F. Winter (New York: Frederick Ungar Publishing Co., 1961), p. 20.
　114. Ibid., p. 29.
　115. Ibid., p. 31.
　116. Works of Arminius, vol. 2, p. 192.
　117. Wesley, p. 132.
　118. Pink, Sovereignty, p. 151.
　119. Ibid., p. 152.
　120. Luther, p. 107.
　121. Tom Ross, Abandoned Truth, p. 45.
　122. Best, Free Grace, p. 43.
　123. Bishop, p. 146.
　124. Spurgeon, Free Will, p. 3.
　125. Gerstner, Free Will, p. 10; Storms, Chosen for Life, pp. 36-37; Kober, p. 33; N. L. Rice, p. 75; Best, Free Grace, p. 20.
　126. Palmer, p. 36.
　127. Charles Hodge, Theology, vol. 2, p. 260.
　128. Eddie K. Garrett, "Freedom of the Will?" *The Hardshell Baptist,* July 1989, p. 1.
　129. Pink, Sovereignty, p. 143.
　130. Talbot and Crampton, p. 18.
　131. Pink, Sovereignty, p. 138.
　132. Beck, p. 9.
　133. Gerstner, Free Will, p. 10.
　134. Pink, Sovereignty, p. 128.
　135. Pink, Gleanings from the Scriptures, p. 216.
　136. Steven R. Houck, *God's Sovereignty in Salvation* (Lansing: Peace Protestant Reformed Church, n.d.), p. 17.
　137. Bishop, p. 146.
　138. Kober, p. 31.
　139. Custance, p. 188.
　140. Pink, John, p. 30.
　141. Houck, Bondage of the Will, p. 14.
　142. Pink, Gleanings from the Scriptures, p. 226.
　143. Steele and Thomas, p. 55.
　144. Edwards, Freedom of the Will, p. v.
　145. Boettner, Predestination, p. 63.
　146. Sproul, Chosen by God, p. 113.
　147. Palmer, p. 18; Boettner, Predestination, p. 165; Sproul, Chosen by God, p. 121; Seaton, p. 11; Storms, Chosen for Life, p. 49; Spencer, Tulip, p. 28.
　148. Gordon H. Clark, *The Biblical Doctrine of Man* (Jefferson: The Trinity Foundation, 1984), p. 102.
　149. Pink, Sovereignty, p. 141.

150. Gerstner, Predestination, p. 18.
151. Dabney, Calvinism, p. 35.
152. Custance, p. 18.
153. Sproul, Chosen by God, p. 120.
154. Pink, Gleanings from the Scriptures, p. 276.
155. Dabney, Calvinism, p. 35.
156. Palmer, p. 17.
157. Ness, p. 88.
158. Pink, Sovereignty, p. 72.
159. Pink, Salvation, p. 26.
160. Gunn, p. 23.
161. Palmer, p. 17.
162. Pink, Salvation, pp. 26-27.
163. Rose, p. 5.
164. W. E. Best, *Regeneration and Conversion* (Houston: W. E. Best Book Missionary Trust, n.d.), p. 11; Boettner, Predestination, p. 81; Tom Ross, Abandoned Truth, p. 43; Spencer, Tulip, p. 26.
165. Coppes, p. 46.
166. Keener, p. 51.
167. Robert A. Morey, *Studies in the Atonement* (Southbridge: Crowne Publications, 1989), p. 82. The word *one* in this quote appears in the book misspelled as "on."
168. Boettner, Predestination, p. 65; Spencer, Tulip, p. 28; Coppes, p. 45; Gunn, p. 6; Tom Ross, Abandoned Truth, p. 44.
169. John Calvin, *Calvin's New Testament Commentaries* (Grand Rapids: Wm. B. Eerdmans Publishing Co., 1994), p. 227.
170. D. A. Carson, *Divine Sovereignty and Human Responsibility* (Atlanta: John Knox Press, 1981), p. 166.
171. Robert W. Yarbrough, "Divine Election in the Gospel of John," in Schreiner and Ware, eds., *The Grace of God, the Bondage of the Will,* p. 51; Best, Regeneration, p. 11.
172. Jay E. Adams, *The Grand Demonstration* (Santa Barbara: EastGate Publishers, 1991), p. 69; Thomas R. Schreiner, "Does Scripture Teach Prevenient Grace in the Wesleyan Sense?" in Schreiner and Ware, eds., *The Grace of God, the Bondage of the Will,* p. 368; Boettner, Predestination, p. 71; Gunn, p. 6; Storms, Chosen for Life, p. 42; Palmer, p. 15; Tom Ross, Abandoned Truth, p. 42.
173. Douglas Moo, *The Epistle to the Romans* (Grand Rapids: Wm. B. Eerdmans Publishing Co., 1996), p. 488.
174. John Murray, *The Epistle to the Romans* (Grand Rapids: Wm. B. Eerdmans Publishing Co., 1959, 1965), vol. 1, p. 287.
175. Gerstner, Predestination, p. 16.
176. Keith A. Mathison, *Dispensationalism: Rightly Dividing the People of God?* (Phillipsburg: Presbyterian and Reformed Publishing Co., 1995), p. 50; Clark, Predestination, p. 111; Gunn, p. 6; Boettner, Reformed Faith, p. 7; Gerstner, Predestination, p. 19; Tom Ross, Abandoned Truth, p. 53; Beck, p. 9; Spencer, Tulip, p. 25; Sproul, Grace Unknown, p. 124.
177. Sproul, Chosen by God, p. 110.
178. Sproul, Grace Unknown, p. 125.
179. Barnhouse, "God's Wrath," vol. 1, pp. 216-217.
180. Gunn, p. 6; Kruithof, p. 35; Storms, Chosen for Life, p. 42; Spencer,

Tulip, p. 26; Beck, p. 7; Steele and Thomas, p. 30; Talbot and Crampton, p. 20.
    181. Boettner, Predestination, p. 63.
    182. Wright, p. 111.
    183. Custance, p. 123.
    184. Calvin, Commentaries, vol. 9, p. 62.
    185. Eddie K. Garrett, "The Purpose of the Gospel," *The Hardshell Baptist*, December 1990, p. 1.
    186. Gordon H. Clark, *First Corinthians,* 2nd ed. (Jefferson: The Trinity Foundation, 1991), p. 42.
    187. Charles Hodge, *A Commentary on 1 & 2 Corinthians* (Edinburgh: The Banner of Truth Trust, 1974), p. 43.
    188. Wright, p. 111.
    189. Ibid.
    190. Tom Ross, Abandoned Truth, p. 45.
    191. Hanko, Total Depravity, p. 23.
    192. Custance, pp. 117-118.
    193. Ibid., p. 117.
    194. Tom Ross, Abandoned Truth, p. 51.
    195. Ibid., p. 50.
    196. Pink, Gleanings from the Scriptures, p. 337.
    197. Pink, Sovereignty, p. 159.
    198. Houck, Bondage of the Will, p. 14.
    199. Edwards, Freedom of the Will, pp. 156-162.
    200. Pink, Sovereignty, p. 153.
    201. Ibid., p. 154.
    202. Ibid.
    203. Ibid., p. 152.
    204. Ibid.
    205. Ibid., p. 151.
    206. Ibid., p. 154.
    207. Boettner, Predestination, p. 64.
    208. John Wesley, quoted in Wood, p. 211.
    209. Desiderius Erasmus, quoted in Luther, p. 171.
    210. Ronald VanOverloop, "Calvinism and Missions: 1. Total Depravity," *Standard Bearer,* September 15, 1992, p. 493.
    211. Ibid.

Chapter Seven
Unconditional Election

    1. Seaton, p. 11.
    2. Ibid.
    3. Boettner, Predestination, p. 95.
    4. Seaton, p. 12.
    5. Gerstner, Predestination, p. 12.
    6. Spencer, Tulip, p. 28.
    7. Arthur W. Pink, *The Doctrines of Election and Justification* (Grand Rapids: Baker Book House, 1974), p. 12.
    8. Storms, Chosen for Life, p. 18.

9. Sproul, Chosen by God, p. 155.
10. Coppes, p. 56; Sproul, Chosen by God, p. 155; Morton Smith, p. 7.
11. See any issue of *The Berea Baptist Banner* or *The Baptist Examiner*.
12. John L. Dagg, *Manual of Theology and Church Order* (Harrisonburg: Sprinkle Publications, 1982), p. 309.
13. Herman Hanko, "Unconditional Election," in Hanko, et al., *The Five Points of Calvinism*, p. 33.
14. Beck, p. 12.
15. J. Oliver Buswell, *A Systematic Theology of the Christian Religion* (Grand Rapids: Zondervan Publishing House, 1962), vol. 2, pp. 149-150; Herman Hoeksema, *Reformed Dogmatics* (Grand Rapids: Reformed Free Publishing Association, 1966), p. 161; Millard J. Erickson, *Christian Theology* (Grand Rapids: Baker Book House, 1985), p. 346; A. A. Hodge, *Evangelical Theology* (Edinburgh: The Banner of Truth Trust, 1976), pp. 126-127; James P. Boyce, *Abstract of Systematic Theology* (North Pompano Beach: den Dulk Christian Foundation, n.d.), p. 347; Wayne A. Grudem, *Systematic Theology* (Grand Rapids: Zondervan Publishing House, 1994), p. 670; William G. T. Shedd, *Dogmatic Theology*, 2nd ed. (Nashville: Thomas Nelson Publishers, 1980), vol. 1, p. 426; Thomas P. Simmons, *A Systematic Study of Bible Doctrine*, 6th ed. (Clarksville: Bible Baptist Books & Supply, 1979), p. 194; *The Zondervan Pictorial Bible Dictionary* (Grand Rapids: Zondervan Publishing House, 1967), s.v. "Election," p. 242; Floyd H. Barackman, *Practical Christian Theology* (Old Tappan: Fleming H. Revell, 1984), p. 247; James M. Pendleton, *Christian Doctrines* (Valley Forge: Judson Press, 1906), p. 107; Emery H. Bancroft, Christian Theology, 2nd rev. ed. (Grand Rapids: Zondervan Publishing House, 1976), p. 237; *Baker's Dictionary of Theology*, s.v. "Elect, Election," p. 179; *Evangelical Dictionary of Theology*, s.v. "Elect, Election," p. 348; Berkhof, Theology, p. 114; Strong, p. 779; Dagg, p. 309; Charles Hodge, Theology, vol. 2, p. 333; Chafer, Theology, vol. 7, pp. 134-135.
16. Westminster Confession of Faith, III:3.
17. Canons of Dort, I:7.
18. Nettles, By His Grace, p. 267.
19. Hanko, Unconditional Election, p. 28.
20. Warfield, Calvin, p. 291.
21. Gunn, p. 15.
22. Robert Haldane, *Commentary on Romans* (Grand Rapids: Kregel Publications, 1988), p. 487.
23. Nettles, By His Grace, p. 267.
24. Mathison, p. 57.
25. Hanko, Unconditional Election, p. 28.
26. Reformed Theology Seminary, *1990-1991 Catalog*, p. 72.
27. Custance, p. 3.
28. Rose, p. 19.
29. Storms, Chosen for Life, p. 55.
30. Gerstner, Predestination, p. 12.
31. Carl Morton, "Does the Bible Teach Election?" *The Berea Baptist Banner*, January 5, 1995, p. 19.
32. Boettner, Predestination, p. 95.
33. Rose, p. 20.
34. Mason, p. 34.
35. Ibid., pp. 39-40.

36. Bishop, p. 167.
37. Chafer, Theology, vol. 1, p. 246.
38. Seaton, p. 12.
39. Charles Halff, "God's Predestination," messages 4 through 6, *The Baptist Examiner*, December 23, 1989, p. 6.
40. Clark, Predestination, p. 181.
41. Custance, p. 7.
42. Num. 16:5; 1 Kgs. 19:18; Psa. 65:4; Psa. 80:18-19; Psa. 110:3; Pro. 16:1; Isa. 26:12; Jer. 10:23; Jer. 31:18-19; Jer. 50:20; Lam. 5:21.
43. Boettner, Predestination, p. 346.
44. "Five Common Questions on the Doctrine of Election Simply and Clearly Answered," *The Baptist Examiner*, November 20, 1993, p. 5.
45. Mason, p. 1.
46. Jewett, pp. 3-4.
47. Mason, p. 32.
48. Boettner, Predestination, p. 2.
49. Gary North, *Dominion and Common Grace* (Tyler: Institute for Christian Economics, 1987), p. 231; Talbot and Crampton, p. 4; Coppes, p. 23.
50. Seaton, p. 13.
51. Machen, Man, p. 65.
52. Engelsma, Hyper-Calvinism, p. 53.
53. Boettner, Predestination, p. 260.
54. Coppes, p. 43.
55. W. E. Best, *God's Eternal Decree* (Houston: W. E. Best Book Missionary Trust, n.d.), p. 1.
56. Buswell, vol. 1, p. 164.
57. Charles Hodge, Theology, vol. 1, p. 537.
58. Herman Hoeksema, Dogmatics, p. 157.
59. Berkhof, Theology, p. 104.
60. Gunn, p. 14.
61. Boettner, Predestination, p. 6.
62. Boettner, Reformed Faith, p. 2.
63. Singer, p. 32.
64. Engelsma, Hyper-Calvinism, p. 133.
65. Talbot and Crampton, p. 14.
66. Ibid.
67. Coppes, p. 15.
68. Pink, Election, p. 9.
69. John Gill, *A Body of Doctrinal and Practical Divinity* (Paris: Baptist Standard Bearer, 1987), p. 173.
70. Boettner, Predestination, p. 15.
71. David S. West, in "The Baptist Examiner Forum II," *The Baptist Examiner*, March 18, 1989, p. 5.
72. Philip Melanchthon, quoted in Boettner, Predestination, p. 15.
73. Arthur W. Pink, *Gleanings in Joshua* (Chicago: Moody Press, 1964), p. 338.
74. Gill, Divinity, p. 174.
75. Boettner, Predestination, p. 234.
76. Zanchius, p. 88.
77. Pink, Sovereignty, p. 147.

78. Ibid., p. 249.
79. Gill, Divinity, p. 319.
80. Muller, Christ and the Decree, p. 81.
81. Palmer, p. 82.
82. Shedd, Calvinism, p. 37.
83. Machen, Man, p. 46.
84. Shedd, Calvinism, p. 31.
85. Franciscus Gomarus, quoted in Newman, vol. 2, p. 339.
86. John Piscator, quoted in Newman, vol. 2, p. 338.
87. Gunn, p. 13.
88. David S. West, in "The Baptist Examiner Forum II," *The Baptist Examiner,* March 18, 1989, p. 5.
89. Pink, Sovereignty, p. 110.
90. Ness, p. 7.
91. Boettner, Predestination, p. 124.
92. Palmer, p. 87.
93. Ibid., p. 86.
94. Strong, p. 361.
95. Pink, Sovereignty, p. 19; Sproul, Chosen by God, p. 26.
96. Pink, Sovereignty, p. 21.
97. Ibid., p. 17.
98. Arthur W. Pink, *The Satisfaction of Christ* (Grand Rapids: Zondervan Publishing House, 1955), p. 20.
99. Pink, Covenants, p. 176.
100. Arthur W. Pink, *An Exposition of Hebrews* (Grand Rapids: Baker Book House, 1954), p. 737.
101. Herman Hoeksema, *Whosoever Will* (Grand Rapids: Reformed Free Publishing Association, 1945), p. 144.
102. Arthur W. Pink, *Gleanings in Exodus* (Chicago: Moody Press, 1981), p. 78.
103. Arthur W. Pink, *Gleanings from Paul* (Chicago: Moody Press, 1967), p. 153.
104. Boettner, Predestination, p. 9.
105. Clark, Predestination, p. 9.
106. Pink, Sovereignty, p. 42.
107. Clark, Predestination, p. 125.
108. Custance, pp. 6, 7; Talbot and Crampton, pp. 12, 13.
109. David S. West, in "The Baptist Examiner Forum II," *The Baptist Examiner,* March 18, 1989, p. 5.
110. Pink, Joshua, p. 317.
111. Clark, Predestination, p. 170.
112. Milburn Cockrell, "Dying on Time," *The Berea Baptist Banner,* November 5, 1997, p. 202.
113. Ibid., p. 203.
114. Clark, Predestination, p. 63.
115. Ibid., p. 64.
116. Pink, Sovereignty, p. 57.
117. Ibid.
118. Pink, Election, p. 172.
119. Calvin, Commentaries, vol. 6, p. 65.

120. Ibid., vol. 12, p. 249.
121. Shedd, Calvinism, p. 37.
122. Alvin C. Plantinga, *God, Freedom, and Evil* (Grand Rapids: Wm. B. Eerdmans Publishing Co., 1977), p. 10.
123. See Marilyn McCord Adams, "Horrendous Evils and the Goodness of God," in Marilyn McCord Adams and Robert Merrihew Adams, eds., *The Problem of Evil* (New York: Oxford University Press, 1990), p. 209; Plantinga, p. 17.
124. Plantinga, pp. 29-34.
125. Clark, Predestination, p. 185.
126. Custance, pp. 263, 264, 265, 268, 269.
127. Pink, Sovereignty, pp. 15, 55, 109, 168, 225, 240.
128. Baker, p. 174.
129. John S. Feinberg, "God Ordains All Things," in David Basinger and Randall Basinger, eds., *Predestination and Free Will* (Downers Grove: InterVarsity Press, 1986), p. 29.
130. Clark, Predestination, pp. 74-75.
131. Theodore Beza, quoted in Muller, Christ and the Decree, p. 84.
132. Charles Hodge, *A Commentary on Romans* (Edinburgh: The Banner of Truth Trust, 1972), p. 316.
133. Jay Adams, Grand Demonstration, p. 67.
134. Gunn, p. 14.
135. Jay Adams, Grand Demonstration, p. 61.
136. Westminster Confession of Faith, III:1.
137. Palmer, p. 87.
138. Gunn, p. 14.
139. Palmer, p. 87.
140. J. I. Packer, *Evangelism and the Sovereignty of God* (Downers Grove: Inter-Varsity Press, 1961), p. 21.
141. Gordon H. Clark, *Today's Evangelism: Counterfeit or Genuine?* (Jefferson: The Trinity Foundation, 1990), pp. 57-58; W. Gary Crampton, "Does the Bible Contain Paradox?" *The Trinity Review,* November/December 1990, pp. 1-4; Sproul, Chosen by God, p. 40.
142. Ibid., pp. 45-46.
143. Clark, Evangelism, p. 58.
144. Gerstner, Free Will, p. 1.
145. Ibid.
146. Ibid., p.6.
147. Boettner, Predestination, p. 208.
148. Clark, Presbyterians, p. 111.
149. Ibid., p. 112.
150. James O. Wilmoth, David S. West, and Dan Phillips, in "The Baptist Examiner Forum II," *The Baptist Examiner,* February 18, 1989, p. 5.
151. Joseph M. Wilson, "Does Prayer Change Things?" *The Baptist Examiner,* June 8, 1991, p. 8.
152. Selph, p. 144.
153. N. L. Rice, p. 9.
154. Palmer, p. 85.
155. Dabney, Calvinism, p. 49; 112. Talbot and Crampton, pp. 70-71; N. L. Rice, pp. 48-49; Chafer, Theology, vol. 1, p. 236.
156. Talbot and Crampton, pp. 70, 71.

157. G. C. Berkouwer, quoted in Baker, p. 8.
158. Jimmie B. Davis and Garner Smith, in "The Berea Baptist Banner Forum," *The Berea Baptist Banner*, August 5, 1992, p. 150.
159. S. T. Tolley, "Who's Who Among Primitive Baptists?" *The Christian Baptist*, August/September 1989, pp. 1, 5.
160. Coppes, p. 23; Keener, p. 83; Sproul, Chosen by God, p. 191; Kruithof, p. 47; Jay Adams, Grand Demonstration, p. 67; Best, Free Grace, p. 49; Garner Smith, in "The Berea Baptist Banner Forum," *The Berea Baptist Banner*, June 5, 1997, p. 110.
161. Desiderius Erasmus, in Erasmus—Luther Discourse on Free Will, pp. 11-12.
162. N. L. Rice, p. 10.
163. Best, God's Decree, p. 6.
164. Westminster Confession of Faith, III:3.
165. Charles Hodge, Theology, vol. 2, p. 320.
166. Machen, Man, p. 50.
167. Berkhof, Theology, p. 113.
168. John L. Girardeau, *Calvinism and Evangelical Arminianism* (Harrisonburg: Sprinkle Publications, 1984), pp. 9-10.
169. Sproul, Grace Unknown, p. 141.
170. Pink, Election, p. 15.
171. Best, God's Decree, p. 9.
172. Berkhof, Theology, p. 104.
173. G. C. Berkouwer, *Divine Election*, trans. Hugo Bekker (Grand Rapids: Eerdmans Publishing Co., 1960), p. 257.
174. Ibid., 258.
175. Works of Arminius, vol. 1, pp. 623, 624, 625, 626, 628, 629, 630, 631, 633.
176. Ibid., p. 630.
177. Ibid., p. 639.
178. James Orr, quoted in Sell, p. 7.
179. James I, quoted in Works of Arminius, vol. 1, p. 213.
180. Boettner, Predestination, p. 129.
181. Cunningham, Reformers, pp. 349, 358; Sell, p. 1.
182. Custance, pp. 159-160.
183. Ibid., p. 160.
184. Best, God's Decree, p. 10.
185. Schaff, Creeds, vol. 1, p. 453.
186. Kent Kelly, p. 12; Gill, Divinity, p. 185; Shedd, Theology, vol. 1, p. 409.
187. Custance, p. 75; Leith, p. 114.
188. A. A. Hodge, *The Atonement* (Memphis: Footstool Publishers, 1987), p. 389; George Park Fisher, *History of Christian Doctrine* (New York: Charles Scribner's Sons, 1899), p. 300; Shank, Life in the Son, p. 345; Berkhof, Theology, p. 110; Works of Arminius, vol. 1, p. 92; Introduction to Calvin, Institutes, p. lviii; Cairns, p. 310; Jewett, p. 89; Neve, vol. 2, p. 16.
189. Klass Dijk, quoted in Berkouwer, pp. 260-261.
190. Fred H. Klooster, *Calvin's Doctrine of Predestination*, 2nd ed. (Grand Rapids: Baker Book House, 1977), pp. 13-14.
191. Ibid., p. 14.
192. George, p. 233.

193. Calvin, Institutes, p. 926 (III.xxi.5).
194. Ibid., p. 931 (III.xxi.7).
195. Klooster, Calvin, p. 26.
196. Ibid., p. 88.
197. Ibid., p. 25.
198. Calvin, Institutes, p. 955 (III.xxiii.7)
199. Quoted in Schaff, History, vol. 8, p. 567.
200. Quoted in Sell, p. 72.
201. Clark, Presbyterians, p. 40.
202. Calvin, Secret Providence, p. 267.
203. Calvin, Eternal Predestination, p. 93.
204. Calvin, Secret Providence, p. 266.
205. Ibid.
206. Calvin, Institutes, p. 955 (III.xxiii.7).
207. Ibid., p. 956 (III.xxiii.8).
208. Ibid., p. 201 (I.xvi.3).
209. Calvin, Eternal Predestination, p. 185.
210. Theodore Beza, quoted in Muller, Christ and the Decree, p. 86.
211. Ibid.
212. Bangs, Arminius: A Study, pp. 208, 263-264.
213. Engelsma, Hyper-Calvinism, p. 10; Works of Arminius, vol. 1, p. 75.
214. Schaff, Creeds, vol. 1, p. 553; Works of Arminius, vol. 1, pp. 648-649.
215. Louis Berkhof, *Introduction to Systematic Theology* (Grand Rapids: Baker Book House, 1979), p. 81.
216. Gill, Divinity, p. 185.
217. Pink, Election, p. 66.
218. Letter from Arthur W. Pink to John C. Blackburn, November 11, 1935, in Arthur W. Pink, *Letters of Arthur W. Pink* (Edinburgh: The Banner of Truth Trust, n.d.), pp. 74-75.
219. Belcher, Pink: Born to Write, p. 10.
220. Iain Murray, Life of Pink, p. 19.
221. Arno Gaebelein, quoted in Fisk, Divine Sovereignty, p. 24.
222. Belcher, Pink: Predestination, p. 61.
223. Pink, Sovereignty, p. 100.
224. Ibid., p. 82.
225. Ibid.
226. Ibid., p. 84.
227. Iain Murray, Life of Pink, p. 196.
228. Zwaanstra, p. 51; Berkouwer, p. 177.
229. Berkhof, Theology, p. 124; Berkouwer, p. 261.
230. Berkouwer, p. 255.
231. Herman Hoeksema, Dogmatics, p. 164.
232. Berkouwer, p. 263.
233. Gerstner, Predestination, p. 7; Sproul, Grace Unknown, p. 158; Best, God's Decree, p. 25; Chafer, Theology, vol. 1, p. 236.
234. Gill, Divinity, p. 192.
235. Ibid., p. 197.
236. Calvin, Institutes, p. 978 (III.xxiv.12).
237. Ibid.
238. Engelsma, Hyper-Calvinism, p. 45.

239. Ibid.
240. Boettner, Predestination, p. 123.
241. John Wesley, quoted in Sell, p. 72.
242. Hanko, Unconditional Election, p. 36.
243. Boettner, Predestination, p. 105.
244. Sproul, Grace Unknown, p. 158.
245. Ibid.
246. Ibid.
247. Best, God's Decree, p. 23.
248. Warfield, Salvation, p. 21.
249. Boettner, Predestination, p. 127.
250. Shedd, Calvinism, p. 35.
251. Spurgeon, Two Wesleys, p. 54.
252. Sproul, Chosen, p. 96.
253. Girardeau, pp. 175-176.
254. Cunningham, Theology, vol. 2, pp. 429-430.
255. Canons of Dort, I:15.
256. Charles Hodge, Theology, vol. 2, p. 321; Dabney, Theology, p. 235.
257. Palmer, p. 110.
258. Berkhof, Theology, p. 105.
259. Berkouwer, p. 261.
260. Chafer, Theology, vol. 1, p. 228.
261. Berkouwer, p. 261.
262. Boettner, Predestination, p. 125.
263. Chafer, Theology, vol. 1, p. 237.
264. Dabney, Theology, p. 239.
265. Ibid.
266. Berkouwer, p. 267.
267. Pink, Sovereignty, p. 239.
268. Benjamin Warfield, quoted in Storms, Chosen for Life, p. 122.
269. Baker, p. 66.
270. Palmer, p. 87.
271. Quoted in George, p. 333.
272. John W. Robbins, ed., *Gordon H. Clark: Personal Recollections* (Jefferson: The Trinity Foundation, 1989), p. 77.
273. Baker, p. 24.
274. Cornelius Van Til, quoted in Iain H. Murray, *The Life of John Murray* (Edinburgh: The Banner of Truth Trust, 1982), p. 40.
275. Boettner, Predestination, p. 23.
276. Ibid., inside front dust cover.
277. Ned B. Stonehouse, *J. Gresham Machen: A Biographical Memoir*, 3rd ed. (Edinburgh: The Banner of Truth Trust, 1987), p. 7.
278. Ibid., p. 67.
279. Gordon H. Clark, *The Trinity* (Jefferson: The Trinity Foundation, 1985), p. 68.
280. Stonehouse, p. 67.
281. Douglas F. Kelly, "Robert Lewis Dabney," in David F. Wells, ed., *Southern Reformed Theology* (Grand Rapids: Baker Book House, 1989), p. 37.
282. Baker, pp. 31-32.
283. Iain Murray, Life of Murray, p. 35.

284. Boettner, Predestination, p. 143.
285. Benjamin B. Warfield, *Biblical and Theological Studies*, ed. Samuel G. Craig (Philadelphia: Presbyterian and Reformed Publishing Co., 1968), p. 258.
286. Machen, Man, p. 81.
287. Boettner, Predestination, p. 136.
288. Gertrude Hoeksema, *Therefore Have I Spoken* (Grand Rapids: Reformed Free Publishing Association, 1969), p. 240.
289. Stonehouse, p. 85.
290. Iain Murray, Life of Murray, p. 113.
291. Calvin, Institutes, p. 947 (III.xxxiii.1)
292. Engelsma, Hyper-Calvinism, p. 44.
293. Gill, Divinity, p. 192.
294. Engelsma, Hyper-Calvinism, p. 46.
295. Ibid.
296. Baker, p. 156.
297. Ibid., p. 179.
298. John Murray, Romans, vol. 2, p. 49.
299. Gordon H. Clark, *The Pastoral Epistles* (Jefferson: The Trinity Foundation, 1983), p. 173.
300. Charles Hodge, Corinthians, p. 682.
301. Ibid.
302. John Murray, "Calvin, Dort, and Westminster on Predestination—A Comparative Study," in De Jong, ed., *Crisis in the Reformed Churches,* p. 155.
303. Dabney, Theology, p. 238.
304. Ibid., pp. 238-239.
305. Pink, Sovereignty, p. 85.
306. Ibid., p. 124.
307. Pink, Joshua, p. 319.
308. Clark, Predestination, p. 178.
309. Pink, Sovereignty, p. 85.
310. Ibid., 98.
311. Joseph M. Wilson, "Not Appointed to Wrath, But to Salvation," *The Baptist Examiner,* February 2, 1991, p. 1.
312. Arthur W. Pink, *Studies in Saving Faith* (Petersburg: Pilgrim Brethren Press, 1992), p. 4.
313. Tom Ross, *Elementary Eschatology: A Study of Premillennial Prophecy* (n.p., n.d.), p. 69.
314. Ibid.
315. Chafer, Theology, vol. 5, p. 223.
316. Pink, Sovereignty, pp. 98-99.
317. Warfield, Studies, p. 305.
318. Pink, Sovereignty, p. 99.
319. Ibid., p. 124.
320. Ibid., p. 99.
321. Ibid.
322. John Bunyan, *Reprobation Asserted* (Swengel: Reiner Publications, 1969), pp. 80, 81.
323. Pink, Sovereignty, p. 99.
324. Thomas Manton, *A Commentary on Jude* (Edinburgh: The Banner of Truth Trust, 1958), p. 128.

325. Baker, p. 160.
326. Herman Hoeksema, Dogmatics, p. 161; Clark, Predestination, p. 98; Schreiner, Prevenient Grace, p. 376.
327. Pink, Sovereignty, pp. 91-92.
328. Ibid., p. 91.
329. Ibid., p. 92.
330. Ibid., p. 124.
331. Pink, John, pp. 689-690.
332. Gill, God and Truth, p. 73.
333. Carson, p. 196.
334. Pink, Sovereignty, p. 98.
335. W. E. Best, *The Most Neglected Chapter in the Bible (Romans 9)* (Houston: W. E. Best Book Missionary Trust, n.d.).
336. Benjamin B. Warfield, quoted in Boettner, Predestination, p. 86.
337. Pink, Sovereignty, p. 98.
338. Kenneth D. Johns, *Election: Love Before Time* (Phillipsburg: Presbyterian and Reformed Publishing Co., 1976), p. 6.
339. Herman Hoeksema, *God's Eternal Good Pleasure*, ed. and rev. Homer C. Hoeksema (Grand Rapids: Reformed Free Publishing Association, 1979); Charles H. Cosgrove, *Elusive Israel: The Puzzle of Election in Romans* (Louisville: Westminster John Knox Press, 1997); Stephen Motyer, *Israel in the Plan of God* (Leicester: Inter-Varsity Press, 1989); H. L. Ellison, *The Mystery of Israel*, rev. and enlar. ed. (Devon: The Paternoster Press, 1968); John Piper, *The Justification of God*, 2nd ed. (Grand Rapids: Baker Books, 1993); Best, Romans 9.
340. Helen Thomas, "Jacob and Esau—'rigidly Calvinistic'?" *Studies in English Literature 1500–1900* 9 (Spring 1969), p. 200.
341. Johns, p. 7.
342. Herman Hoeksema, Good Pleasure, p. 24.
343. Haldane, p. 462.
344. Piper, Justification, pp. 203-204.
345. Cosgrove, p. 28.
346. Herman Hoeksema, Good Pleasure, p. 19.
347. Ballard, p. 15.
348. Calvin, Institutes, p. 930 (III.xxi.7).
349. Baker, p. 153; Berkouwer, p. 71.
350. John Murray, Romans, vol. 2, pp. 20-21.
351. Haldane, p. 465.
352. Owen, p. 227.
353. Pink, Sovereignty, p. 200.
354. Ibid., p. 201.
355. Buswell, vol. 2, p. 149.
356. Storms, Chosen for Life, p. 87.
357. Herman Hoeksema, Good Pleasure, p. 46.
358. Pink, Sovereignty, p. 90.
359. Berkouwer, pp. 212-213.
360. Herman Hoeksema, Good Pleasure, p. 46.
361. Storms, Chosen for Life, p. 88.
362. John Murray, Romans, vol. 2, p. 29.
363. Herman Hoeksema, Good Pleasure, p. 60.
364. Ibid., p. 63.

365. Charles Hodge, Romans, p. 319; Pink, Sovereignty, p. 97.
366. Patrick H. Mell, *A Southern Baptist Looks at Predestination* (Cape Coral: Christian Gospel Foundation, n.d.), p. 31; Best, Romans 9, pp. 193-198.
367. Pink, Sovereignty, p. 96.
368. Cosgrove, p. 27.
369. Piper, Justification, p. 204.
370. Ibid., p. 212.
371. John Murray, Romans, vol. 2, p. 37.
372. Ibid., pp. 32-33.
373. Charles Hodge, Romans, p. 319.
374. Berkouwer, p. 214.
375. John Murray, Romans, vol. 2, p. 36.
376. Charles Hodge, Romans, p. 321.
377. Haldane, p. 493.
378. John Murray, Romans, vol. 2, p. 35.
379. Berkouwer, p. 214.
380. Calvin, Eternal Predestination, p. 149.
381. Bunyan, pp. 46-47.
382. Baker, p. 161.
383. Herman Bavinck and Klaas Dijk, quoted in Berkouwer, p. 202.
384. Jewett, p. 97.
385. Palmer, p. 110.
386. Spencer, Tulip, p. 66.
387. Herman Hoeksema, *The Wonder of Grace*, 2nd ed. (Grand Rapids: Reformed Free Publishing Association, 1982), p. 13.
388. Herman Hoeksema, Whosoever Will, p. 119.
389. Ibid., p. 14.
390. Ibid., p. 24.
391. Ibid., p. 144.
392. Boettner, Reformed Faith, p. 11.
393. Chafer, Theology, vol. 6, p. 252.
394. Englesma, Hyper-Calvinism, p. 57.
395. David Nettleton, *Chosen to Salvation* (Schaumburg: Regular Baptist Press, 1983), p. 161.
396. Pink, Sovereignty, p. 100.
397. Custance, p. 245.
398. Clark, Predestination, p. 190.
399. Talbot and Crampton, p. 27.
400. Ballard, pp. 25-26.
401. Pink, Satisfaction, pp. 251-252.
402. Dan Phillips, "The Atonement," *The Baptist Examiner,* September 15, 1990, p. 3.
403. Pink, John, p. 536.
404. Custance, p. 300.
405. Ibid., p. 183.
406. Pink, John, p. 460.
407. Custance, p. 151.
408. Parker, p. 132; Calvin, Commentaries, vol. 4, p. 229-230.
409. Custance, p. 145.
410. Palmer, p. 27.

411. Machen, Man, p. 64.
412. Custance, p. 201.
413. Carson, p. 187.
414. Custance, p. 201.
415. Nettleton, p. 16.
416. Shank, Elect in the Son, p. 183; Fisk, Calvinistic Paths, p. 76; Younce, p. 23; Ballard, p. 20; Kent Kelly, p. 159; William G. MacDonald, "The Biblical Doctrine of Election," in Pinnock, ed., *The Grace of God, the Will of Man,* p. 227.
417. Milburn Cockrell, "KJV Vindicated on Acts 13:48," *The Berea Baptist Banner,* March 5, 1992, p. 57, and April 5, 1992, pp. 77-78.
418. Palmer, p. 29.
419. Pink, Sovereignty, p. 52.
420. Luther, pp. 246-247.
421. Buswell, vol. 2, p. 152.
422. Clark, Predestination, p. 69.
423. Wright, p. 122; Storms, Chosen for Life, p. 17; Pink, Sovereignty, p. 54; Steele and Thomas, p. 32.
424. Clark, Predestination, p. 98.
425. Boettner, Predestination, p. 87.
426. Nettleton, p. 22.
427. Clyde T. Everman, "Studies in Acts," *The Baptist Examiner,* August 5, 1989, pp. 3-4.
428. Custance, p. 283.
429. Buswell, vol. 2, p. 148.
430. Storms, Chosen for Life, p. 28.
431. Custance, p. 150; Steele and Thomas, p. 33; Boettner, Predestination, p. 94.
432. Storms, Chosen for Life, p. 28.
433. Custance, p. 7; Clark, Predestination, p. 99; Steele and Thomas, p. 32.
434. Berkouwer, p. 27.
435. Beck, p. 40.
436. Nettles, By His Grace, p. 269.
437. Milburn Cockrell, "What God Does for the Poor," *The Berea Baptist Banner,* August 5, 1992, p. 158.
438. Clark, Predestination, p. 100.
439. Pink, Sovereignty, p. 56.
440. Palmer, p. 29.
441. Fisk, Divine Sovereignty, pp. 139-140.
442. Storms, Chosen for Life, p. 97.
443. Leon Morris, *The First and Second Epistles to the Thessalonians,* rev. ed. (Grand Rapids: Wm. B. Eerdmans Publishing Co., 1991), p. 238.
444. Phillips, p. 3.
445. Gill, God and Truth, p. 84.
446. Storms, Chosen for Life, p. 91.
447. Milburn Cockrell, "Chosen in Christ," *The Berea Baptist Banner,* February 5, 1994, p. 21.
448. Storms, Chosen for Life, p. 335.
449. Ibid., p. 96.
450. Charles Hodge, *A Commentary on Ephesians* (Edinburgh: The Banner of Truth Trust, 1964), p. 9.

451. Thomas R. Schreiner, "Does Romans 9 Teach Individual Election to Salvation," in Schreiner and Ware, eds., *The Grace of God, The Bondage of the Will,* p. 103.
452. Pink, Election, p. 77.
453. Ibid.
454. Storms, Chosen for Life, p. 94.
455. Custance, p. 245; Spencer, Tulip, p. 31; Steele and Thomas, p. 33.
456. Calvin, Commentaries, vol. 10, p. 297.
457. Baker, p. 102.
458. W. E. Best, *Life Brought to Light* (Houston: W. E. Best Book Missionary Trust, n.d.), p. 129.
459. Arthur W. Pink, *Spiritual Union and Communion* (Grand Rapids: Baker Book House, 1971), p. 45.
460. Cockrell, Chosen in Christ, p. 23.
461. Pink, Spiritual Union, p. 50.
462. John Gill, *The Doctrines of God's Everlasting Love to His Elect, and Their Eternal Union with Christ* (Paris: The Baptist Standard Bearer, 1987), p. 24.
463. Ibid., pp. 25, 27.
464. Pink, Spiritual Union, pp. 54, 56; Gill, Everlasting Love, pp. 30-31.
465. Phillips, p. 3.
466. Steve Cornett, in "The Berea Baptist Banner Forum," *The Berea Baptist Banner,* August 5, 1990, p. 151.
467. John Lenegar, in "The Baptist Examiner Forum I," *The Baptist Examiner,* June 23, 1990, p. 4.
468. Sam Wilson, in "The Baptist Examiner Forum I," *The Baptist Examiner,* June 23, 1990, p. 4.
469. Steve Cornett, in "The Berea Baptist Banner Forum," *The Berea Baptist Banner,* May 5, 1990, p. 91.
470. Homer C. Hoeksema, "Limited Atonement," in Hanko, et al., *The Five Points of Calvinism,* pp. 56, 57.
471. Pink, Election, p. 66.
472. Ibid., pp. 45-46.
473. Ibid., pp. 64-65.
474. Pink, Spiritual Union, pp. 55-56.
475. Pink, Exodus, p. 19.
476. Morey, p. 95.
477. Joseph M. Wilson, "I'm Going to Heaven Someday," *The Baptist Examiner,* June 24, 1989, p. 2.
478. John Brine, *A Defence of the Doctrine of Eternal Justification* (Chicago: Leory Rhodes, n.d.), p. 16.
479. Herman Hoeksema, Grace, p. 73.
480. Talbot and Crampton, p. 26.
481. Nettles, By His Grace, p. 267.
482. Engelsma, Defense of Calvinism, p. 15.
483. Kober, p. 42.
484. Sellers, p. 12.
485. Keener, p. 89; Boettner, pp. 88-91.
486. H. H. Rowley, *The Biblical Doctrine of Election* (London: Lutterworth Press, 1950), p. 15.
487. Keener, p. 90.

488. Pink, Election, p. 37.
489. Ibid.
490. Westminster Confession of Faith, III:3.
491. Boettner, Predestination, p. 92.
492. Gill, Divinity, p. 193.
493. Ibid., p. 192.
494. Chafer, Theology, vol. 4, p. 319.
495. Pink, Election, p. 129.
496. Ibid., p. 36.
497. Calvin, Commentaries, vol. 8, p. 257; John Murray, Romans, vol. 2, p. 101; Haldane, p. 553.
498. John Murray, Romans, vol. 2, p. 72.
499. Charles Hodge, Romans, p. 355.
500. John Murray, Romans, vol. 2, p. 71.
501. Ibid.
502. Berkouwer, p. 74.
503. Doug Bookman, "God's Sovereign Pleasure," *Masterpiece,* July/August 1990, p. 25.
504. Pink, Election, p. 137.
505. Ibid., p. 138.
506. Ibid., pp. 137-138, 162.
507. Calvin, Commentaries, vol. 12, p. 333.
508. Custance, p. 249.
509. E. g., Clark, Predestination; Custance, and Palmer.
510. Buswell, vol. 2, pp. 140-141, 141.
511. Gill, Divinity, p. 182.
512. Henry C. Thiessen, *Introductory Lectures in Systematic Theology* (Grand Rapids: Wm. B. Eerdmans Publishing Co., 1949), p. 344.
513. Buswell, vol. 2, p. 140.
514. Pink, Sovereignty, pp. 57, 58.
515. Calvin, Commentaries, vol. 12, p. 229.
516. Warfield, Studies, p. 305.
517. Buswell, vol. 2, p. 141.
518. Pink, Sovereignty, p. 75.
519. Best, Light to Life, p. 128.
520. Forster and Marston, p. 137.
521. Klein, p. 265.
522. Herman Hanko, review of *The New Chosen People: A Corporate View of Election,* by William W. Klein, in *Standard Bearer,* June 1, 1992, p. 406.
523. Herman Hoeksema, Grace, p. 68.
524. Ness, p. 46.
525. Benjamin B. Warfield, quoted in Samuel G. Craig, "Benjamin B. Warfield," in Warfield, *Biblical and Theological Studies,* p. xxxv.
526. Calvin, Eternal Predestination, p. 145.
527. John Alber, "God's Predestination," *The Berea Baptist Banner,* August 5, 1990, p. 147.
528. Buswell, vol. 2, p. 148.
529. Calvin, Institutes, p. 923 (III.xxi.2).
530. Ness, p. 5.
531. Kruithof, p. 44.

532. Westminster Confession of Faith, III:3.

533. Jewett, p. 33; Palmer, p. 30; Steele and Thomas, p. 37; Girardeau, p. 44; Custance, p. 140.

534. Berkhof, Theology, p. 516.

535. Pink, Election, p. 69.

536. William Cooper, *The Doctrine of Predestination Unto Life*, 2nd ed. (New Ipswich: Pietan Publications, n.d.); Milburn Cockrell, "God's Golden Chain of Grace," *The Berea Baptist Banner*, January 5, 1998, p. 241; Joseph M. Wilson, "God's Plan of Salvation," *The Baptist Examiner*, August 4, 1990, p. 2; Palmer, p. 32; Sproul, Grace Unknown, p. 143; Warfield, Studies, p. 311.

537. Cockrell, Golden Chain, p. 241.

538. Johns, p. 17.

539. Jonathan Dickinson, *The True Scripture Doctrine Concerning Some Important Points of Christian Faith* (Harrisonburg: Sprinkle Publications, 1992), pp. 32-33, 33.

540. Storms, Chosen for Life, p. 73.

541. Sproul, Grace Unknown, p. 144; Berkhof, Theology, p. 416.

542. Herman Hoeksema, Dogmatics, p. 446.

543. Pink, Exodus, p. 18.

544. Brine, p. 35.

545. Ibid.

546. Ibid., p. 38.

547. Clark, Predestination, p. 69; Palmer, p. 32; Cockrell, Golden Chain, p. 243.

548. Cockrell, Golden Chain, p. 243.

549. Nettles, By His Grace, p. 272.

550. John Miley, *Systematic Theology* (Peabody: Hendrickson Publishers, 1989), vol. 2, p. 261.

551. Ibid., p. 270.

552. Storms, Chosen for Life, p. 74.

553. Thiessen, pp. 344-345.

554. Nettles, By His Grace, p. 275.

555. Pink, Election, p. 172.

556. Boettner, Predestination, p. 99.

557. Pink, Election, p. 172.

558. Pink, Sovereignty, p. 57.

559. J. A. Crabtree, "Does Middle Knowledge Solve the Problem of Divine Sovereignty?" in Schreiner and Ware, eds., *The Grace of God, The Bondage of the Will*, p. 429.

560. For a explanation of the different types of God's knowledge, see David Basinger, *The Case for Freewill Theism: A Philosophical Assessment* (Downers Grove: InterVarsity Press, 1996).

561. Robert Merrihew Adams, "Middle Knowledge and the Problem of Evil," in Adams and Adams eds., *The Problem of Evil*, p. 111; Clark H. Pinnock, "God Limits His Knowledge," in Basinger and Basinger, eds., *Predestination and Free Will*, pp. 143-162; Richard Rice, *God's Foreknowledge and Man's Free Will* (Minneapolis: Bethany House Publishers, 1985), pp. 53-59; John Martin Fischer, ed., *God, Foreknowledge, and Freedom* (Stanford: Stanford University Press, 1989).

562. Richard Rice, p. 56.

563. Zanchius, pp. 44-45.
564. Works of Arminius, vol. 2, p. 120.
565. Ibid.
566. See Fischer, ed., *God, Foreknowledge, and Freedom.*
567. John Martin Fischer, "Freedom and Foreknowledge," in Fischer, ed., *God, Foreknowledge, and Freedom,* p. 86.
568. Pinnock, p. 157.
569. William Lane Craig, *The Only Wise God* (Grand Rapids: Baker Book House, 1987), p. 74.
570. Boettner, Reformed Faith, p. 17.
571. Warfield, Studies, p. 312.
572. Talbot and Crampton, p. 23.
573. Storms, Chosen for Life, pp. 75-76.
574. Palmer, p. 32.
575. Kober, p. 20.
576. Keener, p. 93.
577. Houck, Sovereignty, p. 9.
578. John F. MacArthur, *Saved Without a Doubt* (Wheaton: Victor Books, 1992), p. 59.
579. Talbot and Crampton, p. 24.
580. Calvin, Commentaries, vol. 6, p. 65.
581. Ibid., vol. 8, p. 180.
582. Wilson, Salvation, p. 2.
583. Talbot and Crampton, p. 24.
584. John Murray, Romans, vol. 1, p. 317.
585. Sproul, Chosen by God, p. 131.
586. Talbot and Crampton, p. 24.
587. Alber, p. 147.
588. Haldane, p. 532; Charles Hodge, Romans, p. 354.
589. John Murray, Romans, vol. 2, pp. 67-68.
590. Ibid., vol. 1, pp. 318-319.
591. Westminster Confession of Faith, X:3.
592. R. A. Webb, *The Theology of Infant Salvation* (Harrisonburg: Sprinkle Publications, 1981), pp. 305-308; Boettner, Predestination, pp. 146-147; Shedd, Calvinism, pp. 62-66; Schaff, Creeds, vol. 1, p. 795.
593. Webb, p. 306.
594. Spurgeon, Doctrines of Grace, p. 300.
595. Webb, pp. 312-313; Schaff, History, vol. 8, p. 556.
596. Schaff, History, vol. 8, p. 559-560.
597. George, p. 95.
598. Boettner, Predestination, p. 147.
599. Schaff, History, vol. 8, pp. 558-559.
600. Jewett, p. 82.
601. Girardeau, p. 272.
602. Gill, God and Truth, p. 188.
603. Boettner, Predestination, p. 143.
604. Harold Harvey, E. D. Strickland, Jimmie B. Davis, and James Green, in "The Berea Baptist Banner Forum," *The Berea Baptist Banner,* March 5, 1989, p. 51.
605. Quoted in Sell, p. 72.

606. R. B. Kuiper, *To Be or Not to Be Reformed* (Grand Rapids: Zondervan Publishing House, 1959), p. 69.
607. Shedd, Calvinism, p. 66.
608. W. E. Best, *Justification Before God (Not by Faith)* (W. E. Best Book Missionary Trust, n.d.), p. 10.
609. Boettner, Predestination, p. 143.
610. Canons of Dort, I:17.
611. Hanko, Covenant of Grace, pp. 99-100, 109-110.
612. Ibid., p. 100.
613. Herman Hoeksema, Dogmatics, p. 680.
614. Ibid., p. 694.
615. Charles H. Spurgeon, *Infant Salvation* (Pasadena: Pilgrim Publications, n.d.), p. 3.
616. Ibid., p. 35.
617. Johns, p. 83.
618. Pink, Election, pp. 69-70.
619. Hanko, Unconditional Election, p. 41.
620. Clark, Presbyterians, p. 39.
621. Ibid.
622. Martyn Lloyd-Jones, *Saved in Eternity*, ed. Christopher Catherwood (Westchester: Crossway Books, 1988), p. 16.
623. Boettner, Predestination, p. 126.
624. Coppes, p. 25.
625. Ronald VanOverloop, "Calvinism and Missions: 2. Unconditional Election," *Standard Bearer,* January 15, 1993, p. 185.
626. Ibid.
627. Shedd, Calvinism, p. 81; Warfield, Studies, p. 349.
628. Zanchius, p. 92.
629. Storms, Chosen for Life, p. 105.
630. John Wesley, quoted in Sell, p. 73.

Chapter Eight
Limited Atonement

1. Good, Reformed, p. 51.
2. Boettner, Predestination, p. 151.
3. Homer Hoeksema, Limited Atonement, p. 46.
4. Spencer, Tulip, p. 35.
5. Gunn, p. 16.
6. Talbot and Crampton, p. 37.
7. John R. de Witt, *What is the Reformed Faith?* (Edinburgh: The Banner of Truth Trust, 1981), p.11.
8. John Murray, *Redemption Accomplished and Applied* (Grand Rapids: Wm. B. Eerdmans Publishing Co., 1955), p. 59; A. A. Hodge, Atonement, pp. 348-349.
9. Wilson, Atonement, p. 2.
10. Ibid.
11. A. A. Hodge, Atonement, p. 348.
12. Ibid.
13. Mathison, pp. 58, 58-59.

14. Good, Calvinists, p. 68.
15. Palmer, p. 42.
16. Rose, p. 28.
17. Gary D. Long, *Definite Atonement* (Rochester: Backus Book Publishers, 1977), p. 3; Gerstner, Wrongly Dividing, 116; de Witt, Reformed Faith, p. 11; Morton Smith, p. 8; Coppes, p. 56; Palmer, p. 42.
18. Jewett, p. 15; Palmer, p. 42; Talbot and Crampton, p. 30.
19. Rose, p. 28; Gerstner, Wrongly Dividing, p. 116.
20. Homer Hoeksema, Limited Atonement, p. 55.
21. Rose, p. 30.
22. Homer Hoeksema, Limited Atonement, p. 59.
23. Dabney, Theology, p. 528.
24. Seaton, p. 8; de Witt, Reformed Faith, p. 11; Morey, p. 58; Long, Atonement, p. 3; Steele and Thomas, p. 38; Dabney, Calvinism, p. 60.
25. Coppes, p. 49.
26. Boettner, Predestination, p. 150.
27. John Murray, Redemption, p. 64.
28. Seaton, p. 15.
29. Gunn, p. 17.
30. Westminster Confession, VIII:5.
31. James Daane, *The Freedom of God* (Grand Rapids: Wm. B. Eerdmans Publishing Co., 1973), p. 138.
32. Canons of Dort, II:8
33. Gunn, p. 17.
34. Zanchius, p. 53.
35. Seaton, p. 15.
36. Spencer, Tulip, p. 42.
37. Homer Hoeksema, Limited Atonement, p. 49.
38. Gordon H. Clark, *The Atonement* (Jefferson: The Trinity Foundation, 1987), p. 140.
39. A. A. Hodge, Atonement, pp. 372-373.
40. Boettner, Predestination, p. 218.
41. Rose, p. 30.
42. Ibid., p. 31.
43. Boettner, Predestination, p. 155.
44. Palmer, p. 41.
45. Hanko, Covenant of Grace, p. 15.
46. Dabney, Calvinism, p. 61.
47. Boettner, Predestination, p. 151.
48. Talbot and Crampton, p. 37.
49. Ibid., p. 29.
50. Phillips, p. 3.
51. A. A. Hodge, Atonement, p. 402.
52. Homer Hoeksema, Limited Atonement, p. 65.
53. Herman Hoeksema, Whosoever Will, p. 24.
54. Coppes, p. 49.
55. Morey, p. 64.
56. Good, Calvinists, p. 67.
57. Custance, p. 149.
58. Good, Calvinists, p. 69.

59. Tom Ross, Abandoned Truth, p. 103.
60. Pink, Sovereignty, p. 261.
61. Chafer, Theology, vol. 3, p. 186.
62. Sproul, Chosen by God, p. 204.
63. Palmer, p. 50.
64. Gerstner, Wrongly Dividing, p. 105.
65. Ibid., pp. 118-121.
66. Shank, Life in the Son, p. 354.
67. A. A. Hodge, Atonement, p. 13.
68. Berkhof, Theology, pp. 384-385.
69. Ibid., p. 385.
70. Ibid.
71. Ibid., p. 386.
72. Ibid., p. 387.
73. Paul P. Enns, *The Moody Handbook of Theology* (Chicago: Moody Press, 1989), p. 320.
74. Berkhof, Theology, pp. 388.
75. Ibid., p. 389.
76. Arthur W. Pink, *Gleanings in the Godhead* (Chicago: Moody Press, 1975), p. 40.
77. John Murray, Atonement, p. 9; A. A. Hodge, Atonement, pp. 33-34.
78. Homer Hoeksema, Limited Atonement, p. 48.
79. Talbot and Crampton, p. 30; Boettner, Predestination, p. 152; Kruithof, p. 60.
80. Custance, p. 153.
81. Dabney, Theology, p. 527.
82. A. A. Hodge, *Outlines of Theology,* rev. and enlar. ed. (Edinburgh: The Banner of Truth Trust, 1972), p. 416; Shedd, Theology, vol. 2, p. 468.
83. Sproul, Grace Unknown, p. 165.
84. Nettles, By His Grace, p. 305.
85. Ibid., p. 319.
86. Dabney, Calvinism, p. 62, 63.
87. Boettner, Predestination, p. 160.
88. Kruithof, p. 60; Talbot and Crampton, p. 30; Gunn, p. 17; Palmer, p. 54.
89. Cunningham, Theology, vol. 2, p. 333.
90. Boettner, Predestination, p. 161.
91. North, p. 43.
92. Homer Hoeksema, Limited Atonement, p. 61.
93. Sproul, Grace Unknown, p. 165.
94. Seaton, p. 15.
95. Mathison, pp. 59-60.
96. Whitefield, p. 568.
97. Long, Atonement, p. 33.
98. Custance, p. 156.
99. Boettner, Reformed Faith, p. 14.
100. Seaton, p. 17; Boettner, Predestination, p. 155.
101. Steele and Thomas, p. 39.
102. Gerstner, Wrongly Dividing, p. 121.
103. Owen, p. 235.
104. Dabney, Calvinism, p. 66.

105. Hodge, Theology, vol. 2, pp. 551-552.

106. Best, Justification, p. 23; Lawrence Reti, "15 Rotten Fruits of the Universal Atonement Theory," *The Berea Baptist Banner,* July 5, 1997, pp. 136-137; Dennis Fry, *Questions on the Atonement* (Pensacola: Chapel Library, n.d.), p. 4; Phillips, p. 3; Seaton, p. 15; Beck, pp. 24-25; Talbot and Crampton, pp. 38-39; Wright, pp. 172-173; Sproul, Chosen by God, p. 206; Long, Atonement, p. 112;

107. Owen, pp. 173-174.
108. Ibid., p. 209.
109. John Murray, Redemption, p. 63.
110. Pink, Satisfaction, pp. 264-265.
111. Homer Hoeksema, Limited Atonement, pp. 50-51.
112. Rose, p. 31.
113. Owen, p. 97.
114. Best, Justification, p. 26.
115. Ibid.
116. Pink, Exodus, p. 88.
117. Ibid., p. 84.
118. Gerstner, Wrongly Dividing, p. 123.
119. Boettner, Predestination, p. 155.
120. Chafer, Theology, vol. 3, p. 193.

121. John Murray, Romans, vol. 1, pp. 192-193, 203; Charles Hodge, Romans, pp. 164, 171-172.

122. George Smeaton, *Christ's Doctrine of the Atonement,* 2nd ed. (Edinburgh: The Banner of Truth Trust, 1991), pp. 157-158; John Murray, Romans, vol. 1, pp. 199, 203.

123. Owen, p. 238.
124. Gerstner, Wrongly Dividing, p. 123.
125. Sproul, Chosen by God, p. 206.
126. Steele and Thomas, p. 46.
127. Sproul, Chosen by God, p. 207.
128. Custance, p. 149.
129. Pink, Sovereignty, p. 61.
130. Gunn, p. 18.
131. Owen, p. 338.
132. Pink, Sovereignty, p. 204.
133. Owen, p. 342.

134. Homer C. Hoeksema, *God So Loved The World* (South Holland: The Evangelism Committee, Protestant Reformed Church, n.d.), p. 11.

135. Ness, p. 75.
136. Talbot and Crampton, p. 36.
137. Kuiper, Evangelism, p. 30.
138. Pink, Sovereignty, p. 204.
139. Dabney, Theology, p. 525.
140. Kuiper, Evangelism, p. 23.
141. Spencer, Tulip, p. 35.

142. Custance, pp. 168-169; Spencer, Tulip, pp. 35-36; Sproul, Grace Unknown, p. 177; Owen, p. 304; Homer Hoeksema, God So Loved, p. 11; Pink, Sovereignty, pp. 253-255.

143. R. B. Kuiper, *For Whom Did Christ Die?* (Grand Rapids: Wm. B.

Eerdmans Publishing Co., 1959), p. 28; Sproul, Grace Unknown, p. 177; Spencer, Tulip, p. 36.

144. Sproul, Chosen by God, p. 206.
145. Herman Hoeksema, Whosoever Will, p. 86.
146. Kuiper, Evangelism, p. 23.
147. Sproul, Grace Unknown, p. 177.
148. Long, Atonement, p. 107.
149. Pink, Sovereignty, p. 204.
150. George Smeaton, *The Doctrine of the Atonement According to the Apostles* (Peabody: Hendrickson Publishers, 1988), p. 220.
151. Owen, p. 339.
152. Long, Atonement, p. 103.
153. Ibid., p. 102.
154. Sproul, Grace Unknown, p. 176.
155. John Murray, Redemption, p. 72.
156. Pink, Sovereignty, p. 257.
157. Ibid., p. 259.
158. Ibid.
159. Ibid.
160. Ibid., p. 260.
161. Ibid., p. 258.
162. Arthur W. Pink, *The Application of the Scriptures* (Canton: Free Grace Publications, 1977), p. 5.
163. Jimmie B. Davis, in "The Berea Baptist Banner Forum," *The Berea Baptist Banner,* August 5, 1989, p. 151; Keener, p. 190; Long, Atonement, p. 95; Ness, p. 77; Owen, p. 338; John Murray Redemption, p. 73.
164. Long, Atonement, p. 92.
165. Ibid., p. 93.
166. Smeaton, Apostles, p. 460.
167. Ibid.
168. Dabney, Theology, p. 525.
169. Pink, Satisfaction, p. 263.
170. Pink, Sovereignty, p. 259.
171. Ibid., p. 66.
172. Ibid.
173. Smeaton, Christ, p. 370.
174. Mathison, p. 66; Pink, Satisfaction, p. 262; Custance, p. 162; Owen, p. 309.
175. Pink, Satisfaction, p. 262; A. A. Hodge, Atonement, p. 424; Kuiper, For Whom Did Christ Die, p. 28.
176. Owen, p. 245.
177. Pink, Satisfaction, p. 263.
178. Palmer, p. 49.
179. John Murray, Redemption, p. 72.
180. Pink, Sovereignty, p. 67.
181. Ibid., p. 68.
182. Palmer, p. 49; Pink, Sovereignty, p. 67; John Murray, Redemption, p. 71.
183. Dabney, Theology, p. 525.
184. Custance, p. 171.
185. Ibid., p. 172.

186. Ibid., pp. 172-173.
187. Smeaton, Apostles, p. 325.
188. Custance, p. 162.
189. Pink, Sovereignty, p. 68.
190. Sproul, Chosen by God, p. 207.
191. Pink, Satisfaction, p. 264; Beck, p. 26; Custance, pp. 166-167; Simmons, p. 270.
192. North, p. 44.
193. Bronson, p. 41; Pink, Sovereignty, p. 70; Beck, p. 36.
194. John Murray, Redemption, p. 61.
195. Boettner, Predestination, p. 288.
196. Henry Alford, *The New Testament for English Readers* (Grand Rapids: Baker Book House, 1983), vol. 4, p. 1459.
197. Kenneth S. Wuest, *Hebrews in the Greek New Testament* (Grand Rapids: Wm. B. Eerdmans Publishing Co., 1947), p. 59.
198. Archibald Thomas Robertson, *Word Pictures in the New Testament* (Nashville: Broadman Press, 1930), vol. 5, p. 346.
199. Pink, Hebrews, p. 106.
200. Ferrell Griswold, *Particular Redemption* (Birmingham: First Baptist Church, n.d.), p. 26; Owen, p. 350; Beck, p. 36; Smeaton, Apostles, p. 351; John Murray, Redemption, p. 61.
201. Alford, vol. 4, p. 1459.
202. Beck, p. 127.
203. John Murray, Redemption, p. 59.
204. W. E. Best, *The Saviour's Definite Redemption* (Houston: W. E. Best Book Missionary Trust, 1982), p. 30.
205. Loraine Boettner, *Studies in Theology* (Phillipsburg: Presbyterian and Reformed Publishing Co., 1947), p. 317; Steele and Thomas, pp. 46-47; Talbot and Crampton, p. 34; Sproul, Chosen by God, p. 205; Custance, p. 150; Seaton, p. 16; Owen, p. 214; Shedd, Theology, vol. 2, p. 476.
206. Charles Hodge, Theology, vol. 2, p. 549.
207. Pink, Satisfaction, p. 251.
208. Spencer, Tulip, p. 41.
209. Boettner, Predestination, p. 155.
210. Pink, Satisfaction, pp. 251-252.
211. Smeaton, Christ, p. 369.
212. Tom Ross, Abandoned Truth, p. 134.
213. Charles Hodge, Romans, p. 163.
214. John Murray, Romans, vol. 1, pp. 193-194.
215. Pink, Sovereignty, p. 65.
216. Owen, p. 214.
217. Pink, Satisfaction, p. 277.
218. Bronson, p. 45.
219. Dabney, Theology, p. 525.
220. Beck, p. 52.
221. Gill, God and Truth, p. 58.
222. Owen, p. 365.
223. Pink does not comment on this verse in his books *The Sovereignty of God, Sanctification,* or his Hebrews commentary.
224. Smeaton, Apostles, p. 446.

225. Ibid., p. 447.
226. Shedd, Theology, vol. 2, p. 481.
227. A. A. Hodge, Atonement, p. 428.
228. Gill, God and Truth, p. 61.
229. Owen, p. 362; Tom Ross, Abandoned Truth, p. 153; Beck, p. 34; Simmons, p. 270; Ness, p. 82.
230. Ness, p. 82.
231. Tom Ross, Abandoned Truth, p. 153; Simmons, p. 270; Beck, p. 34; Owen, p. 363; Long, Atonement, pp. 76-77.
232. Owen, p. 363.
233. Smeaton, Apostles, p. 447; Long, Atonement, pp. 70-71.
234. Long, Atonement, p. 71.
235. Ibid., p. 76.
236. Smeaton, Apostles, p. 447.
237. Jimmie B. Davis, in "The Berea Baptist Banner Forum," *The Berea Baptist Banner,* June 5, 1998, p. 351.
238. Ibid.
239. Kendall, p. 149; Cunningham, Reformers, p. 395; Stam, p. 33; Waite, p. 16; Kent Kelly, p. 115; Sumner, p. 8; Kober, pp. 15-16; Lightner, pp. 13-14; John Rice, Predestinated to Hell, pp. 11-12; Thiessen, p. 343.
240. James Richards, *Lectures on Mental Philosophy and Theology* (New York: M. W. Dodd, 1846), p. 308; Lightner, pp. 13-14, Strong, p. 777.
241. Cunningham, Reformers, pp. 395-396; Kendall, p. 210.
242. Cunningham, Reformers, p. 398; Helm, pp. 30-31; Morey, p. 295; A. A. Hodge, Atonement, p. 389; Smeaton, Apostles, p. 222; Custance, p. 153; Cairns, p. 310.
243. Schaff, History, vol. 8, p. 873.
244. Cunningham, Reformers, p. 395.
245. Schaff, Creeds, vol. 3, p. 507.
246. Ibid., p. 189.
247. Lumpkin, p. 162.
248. Lightner, p. 13.
249. Robert A. Peterson, *Calvin's Doctrine of the Atonement* (Phillipsburg: Presbyterian and Reformed Publishing Co., 1983), p. 90.
250. A. A. Hodge, Atonement, p. 388.
251. Calvin, Commentaries, vol. 2, p. 273.
252. Ibid., vol. 3, p. 139.
253. Ibid., vol. 8, p. 115.
254. Ibid., vol. 12, p. 131.
255. Ibid., pp. 148-149.
256. Ibid., p. 346.
257. Ibid., vol. 5, p. 43.
258. Ibid., vol. 8, p. 118.
259. Ibid., vol. 10, p. 74.
260. Ibid., vol. 11, p. 312.
261. Ibid., vol. 10, p. 210.
262. Ibid., p. 245.
263. Ibid., vol. 12, p. 24.
264. Ibid., vol. 4, p. 32.
265. Ibid., pp. 74-75.

266. Ibid., p. 110.
267. Ibid., vol. 10, p. 78.
268. John Rice, Predestinated to Hell, p. 12; Sumner, p. 8; Kent Kelly, p. 115; Waite, p. 16; Thiessen, p. 343.
269. Strong, p. 777.
270. Morey, p. 295.
271. Strong, p. 778.
272. Calvin, Commentaries, vol. 5, p. 244.
273. John Calvin, *Commentary on the Catholic Epistles*, ed. and trans. John Owen (Grand Rapids: Wm. B. Eerdmans Publishing Co., 1948), p. 173.
274. A. A. Hodge, Atonement, p. 390.
275. Peterson, p. 90.
276. Calvin, Eternal Predestination, p. 94.
277. Ibid., pp. 165-166.
278. Calvin, quoted in Helm, p. 21.
279. "Last Will and Testament of Calvin," quoted in Schaff, History, vol. 8, p. 829.
280. "Last Will and Testament of Calvin," quoted in Calvin, Letters, p. 250.
281. "Last Will and Testament of Calvin," quoted in "Life of Calvin," in Calvin, Letters, p. 29.
282. Calvin, Commentaries, vol. 10, p. 245.
283. Morey, p. 296.
284. A. A. Hodge, Atonement, p. 389.
285. Steele and Thomas, p. 38.
286. Custance, p. 286.
287. John Murray, Redemption, p. 65.
288. R. B. Kuiper, quoted in Morton Smith, p. 21.
289. Talbot and Crampton, p. 33.
290. Bronson, p. 31.
291. Arthur W. Pink, *Interpretation of the Scriptures* (Grand Rapids: Baker Book House, 1972), p. 54.
292. Gunn, p. 19.
293. Bronson, p. 47.
294. Palmer, p. 54.
295. Steele and Thomas, p. 38.
296. Custance, p. 294.
297. Ibid., p. 169.
298. Talbot and Crampton, p. 35.

Chapter Nine
Irresistible Grace

1. Gerstner, Wrongly Dividing, p. 131.
2. Gise J. Van Baren, "Irresistible Grace," in Hanko, et al., *The Five Points of Calvinism*, p. 75.
3. Ibid.
4. Pink, Sovereignty, p. 136.
5. Seaton, p. 17.
6. Tom Ross, Abandoned Truth, p. 156.

7. Gunn, p. 20.
8. Tom Ross, Abandoned Truth, p. 156.
9. Bruce A. Ware, "The Place of Effectual Calling and Grace in a Calvinist Soteriology," in Schreiner and Ware, eds., *The Grace of God, The Bondage of the Will,* p. 345.
10. Van Baren, Irresistible Grace, p. 73.
11. Gerstner, Wrongly Dividing, p. 131.
12. Palmer, pp. 57-58.
13. Spencer, Tulip, p. 73.
14. Canons of Dort, III, IV:10.
15. Benjamin B. Warfield, quoted in Samuel Craig, "Benjamin B. Warfield," in Warfield, Studies, p. xxxv.
16. Palmer, p. 57.
17. Sproul, Chosen by God, pp. 120, 121, 123.
18. Gunn, p. 20.
19. Steele and Thomas, p. 48; Coppes, p. 56; Boettner, Predestination, p. 178; Jewett, p. 15.
20. Dabney, Theology, p. 585; Rose, p. 38; Leith, p. 39.
21. Keener, p. 199; Good, Calvinists, p. 98; Tom Ross, Abandoned Truth, p. 156; Nettles, By His Grace, p. 285; Bob Ross, Calvinism, p. 8.
22. Sproul, Grace Unknown, p. 191.
23. Houck, Bondage of the Will, p. 2.
24. Mell, Predestination, p. 53.
25. Best, Free Grace, p. 6.
26. John Piper, "Are There Two Wills in God? Divine Election and God's Desire for All to be Saved," in Schreiner and Ware, eds., *The Grace of God, the Bondage of the Will,* p. 109.
27. Pink, Sovereignty, p. 244.
28. Ibid.
29. Ibid.
30. Best, Free Grace, p. 6; Pink, Sovereignty, p. 243.
31. Houck, Bondage of the Will, p. 2.
32. Pink, Sovereignty, p. 244.
33. Ibid., p. 246.
34. Theodore Beza, quoted in Muller, Christ and the Decree, p. 86.
35. Sproul, Chosen by God, p. 26.
36. Pink, Sovereignty, p. 243.
37. Houck, Bondage of the Will, p. 3.
38. Boettner, Reformed Faith, p. 19.
39. Gill, God and Truth, p. 28.
40. Ibid.
41. Fitch, p. 53.
42. Boettner, Reformed Faith, p. 19.
43. Piper, Two Wills, p. 107.
44. Wright, p. 168.
45. Pink, Sovereignty, p. 104.
46. Calvin, Commentaries, vol. 10, p. 208.
47. Ibid., pp. 208-209.
48. Boettner, Reformed Faith, p. 20; Jewett, p. 104.
49. Wright, p. 171.

50. Gill, God and Truth, p. 51.
51. Piper, Two Wills, p. 108.
52. Ibid., p. 130.
53. Ibid.
54. Iain Murray, Hyper-Calvinism, pp. 149-150.
55. "Not So Sure With Mr. Spurgeon," in Williams and North, p. 25.
56. Sproul, Chosen by God, p. 206.
57. W. E. Best, *God's Longsuffering is Salvation* (Houston: W. E. Best Book Missionary Trust, n.d.), p. 27.
58. Boettner, Reformed Faith, p. 19.
59. Gordon H. Clark, *New Heavens, New Earth,* 2nd ed. (Jefferson: The Trinity Foundation, 1993), p. 231.
60. Pink, Sovereignty, p. 207.
61. Garner Smith and Jimmie B. Davis, in "The Berea Baptist Banner Forum," *The Berea Baptist Banner,* October 5, 1997, pp. 190, 193; Best, God's Longsuffering, p. 29.
62. Berkouwer, p. 238.
63. Piper, Two Wills, p. 108; Custance, pp. 152, 166; Gill, God and Truth, p. 62; John Murray and Ned B. Stonehouse, *The Free Offer of the Gospel* (n.p., n.d.), pp. 21-22.
64. Calvin, Commentaries, vol. 12, p. 364.
65. Ibid.
66. Tom Ross, Abandoned Truth, p. 184.
67. Clark, Predestination, p. 139.
68. Van Baren, Irresistible Grace, p. 76.
69. Beck, p. 42.
70. Ibid., p. 39.
71. Spencer, Tulip, p. 48.
72. Tom Ross, Abandoned Truth, p. 56.
73. Works of Arminius, vol. 1, p. 525.
74. Ness, p. 98.
75. Tom Ross, Abandoned Truth, p. 184.
76. Good, God's Purpose, p. 99; Seaton, p. 18; Tom Ross, Abandoned Truth, p. 158; Best, Life to Light, p. 42; Ware, p. 346.
77. Kruithof, p. 64; Rose, p. 38; Storms, Chosen for Life, p. 104; Custance, p. 364; Selph, p. 98.
78. Gerstner, Free Will, p. 21.
79. Mathison, p. 73; Seaton, p. 18.
80. Calvin, Institutes, p. 974 (III.xxiv.8); Charles H. Spurgeon, "Particular Election," in Spurgeon, *Election,* p. 130.
81. Steele and Thomas, p. 18; Talbot and Crampton, p. 43; Gunn, pp. 21, 22.
82. Sumner, p. 9.
83. Ware, p. 346.
84. Talbot and Crampton, p. 43.
85. Seaton, p. 18.
86. Gunn, p. 22.
87. Storms, Chosen for Life, p. 104.
88. Steele and Thomas, p. 18.
89. Tom Ross, Abandoned Truth, p. 163.
90. Seaton, p. 18.

91. Louis Berkhof, *Manual of Christian Doctrine* (Grand Rapids: Wm. B. Eerdmans Publishing Co., 1933), p. 231.
92. Tom Ross, Abandoned Truth, p. 162.
93. Tom Ross, Abandoned Truth, p. 161; Talbot and Crampton, pp. 43-44.
94. Sproul, Grace Unknown, p. 189.
95. Ware, p. 347.
96. Palmer, p. 36.
97. Rose, p. 37.
98. Tom Ross, Abandoned Truth, p. 161.
99. Steele and Thomas, p. 49; Good, God's Purpose, p. 99.
100. Gerstner, Wrongly Dividing, p. 120.
101. Arthur W. Pink, *Comfort for Christians* (Grand Rapids: Baker Book House, 1976), p. 15.
102. Rose, p. 39.
103. Storms, Chosen for Life, p. 103; Engelsma, Hyper-Calvinism, p. 65; Dagg, p. 332.
104. Best, Life to Light, p. 42.
105. Ware, p. 361.
106. Eddie K. Garrett, "The Tulip Series: Irresistible Grace," *The Hardshell Baptist,* December 1987, p. 1.
107. Johns, p. 17.
108. Ware, p. 361; Sproul, Grace Unknown, p. 143.
109. Ware, p. 362.
110. Haldane, p. 411.
111. Ware, p. 356.
112. Clark, First Corinthians, p. 23.
113. Ware, p. 359.
114. Sproul, Grace Unknown, p. 184; Shedd, Calvinism, p. 92; Rose, pp. 37, 39; Boettner, Predestination, p. 180; Schreiner, Prevenient Grace, p. 371.
115. Boettner, Predestination, p. 179.
116. Rose, p. 37.
117. Shedd, Calvinism, p. 92.
118. Ibid.
119. Ibid., p. 94.
120. Ibid.
121. Ibid., pp. 94-95.
122. Rose, p. 37.
123. Boettner, Predestination, p. 179.
124. Quoted in Kuiper, Reformed, pp. 105-106.
125. See Barry L. Gritters, *Grace Uncommon* (Bryon Center: The Evangelism Society, Byron Center Protestant Reformed Church, n.d.); Kuiper, Reformed, pp. 105-113; Engelsma, Hyper-Calvinism, pp. 109-125; North, pp. 6-7.
126. North, p. 3.
127. Shedd, Calvinism, p. 92.
128. Clark, Predestination, p. 98.
129. Ibid., pp. 98-100.
130. Wright, p. 133.
131. Clark, Predestination, p. 198.
132. Ibid., p. 199.
133. Ibid, p. 210.

134. Ibid., p. 200.
135. Pink, Gleanings from the Scriptures, p. 90; Tom Ross, Abandoned Truth, p. 157.
136. Beck, p. 40; Tom Ross, Abandoned Truth, pp. 56, 156; Shedd, Calvinism, p. 93; Talbot and Crampton, p. 41; Best, Free Grace, p. 25; Pink, Gleanings from the Scriptures, p. 174; Chantry, p. 8.
137. Joseph M. Wilson, "From the Editor," *The Baptist Examiner,* September 14, 1991, p. 2.
138. Clark, Predestination, p. 174.
139. Ibid.
140. Wilson, Salvation, p. 3.
141. Ibid.
142. Ibid.
143. Beck, p. 41; Steele and Thomas, pp. 51, 56; Spencer, Tulip, p. 46; Houck, Bondage of the Will, p. 12; Custance, p. 188; Gunn, p. 22; Keener, p. 212.
144. Clark, Predestination, p. 97.
145. Ibid., p. 100.
146. Custance, p. 188.
147. Ibid.
148. Gunn, p. 21; Spencer, Tulip, p. 49; Steele and Thomas, p. 53; Ware, p. 347.
149. Van Baren, Irresistible Grace, p. 78.
150. Palmer, p. 66.
151. Seaton, p. 19.
152. Eddie K. Garrett, "Lydia," *The Hardshell Baptist,* July 1990, p. 1.
153. Mason, p. 44; Best, Free Grace, p. 5; Gill, God and Truth, p. 29; Boettner, Reformed Faith, p. 19.
154. Gordon H. Clark, *Philippians* (Jefferson: The Trinity Foundation, 1996), p. 71.
155. Clark, Predestination, p. 120.
156. Kober, p. 36; Tom Ross, Abandoned Truth, p. 160; Steele and Thomas, p. 56; Wright, p. 135; Pink, Sovereignty, p. 138; Keener, pp. 210-211; Shedd, Calvinism, p. 93.
157. Herman Hoeksema, Grace, p. 82.
158. Clark, Philippians, p. 71.
159. Carson, p. 174.
160. Rose, p. 36; Houck, Bondage of the Will, p. 12; Boettner, Reformed Faith, p. 11; Seaton, p. 18; Kober, p. 35; Talbot and Crampton, p. 40; Tom Ross, Abandoned Truth, p. 156; Wright, p. 133; Palmer, p. 61; Custance, p. 188; Van Baren, Irresistible Grace, p. 77.
161. Pink, John, pp. 337-338.
162. Herman Hoeksema, Whosoever Will, p. 122.
163. Pink, Salvation, p. 88.
164. Pink, John, p. 338.
165. John Gill, *Exposition of the Old and New Testaments* (Paris: The Baptist Standard Bearer, 1989), vol. 4, p. 634.
166. Storms, Chosen for Life, pp. 66-67.
167. Ibid., p. 65.
168. Pink, John, p. 338.
169. Pink, Sovereignty, p. 64.

170. Herman Hoeksema, Whosoever Will, p. 14.
171. Spencer, Tulip, p. 45.
172. Palmer, pp. 20, 58.
173. Boettner, Predestination, p. 178.
174. Boettner, Reformed Faith, p. 11.
175. Yarbrough, p. 50; Pink, John, p. 338; Palmer, pp. 61-62; Storms, Chosen for Life, p. 66.
176. Sproul, Chosen, p. 69.
177. Pink, John, p. 338.
178. W. E. Best, *Simple Faith (A Misnomer)* (Houston: W. E. Best Book Missionary Trust, 1993), p. 39.
179. Pink, John, p. 339.
180. Herman Hoeksema, Whosoever Will, p. 123.
181. Calvin, Commentaries, vol. 5, p. 43.
182. Pink, John, p. 682.
183. Schreiner, Prevenient Grace, p. 378.
184. Pink, John, p. 682.
185. Calvin, Commentaries, vol. 4, p. 15.
186. Duane Edward Spencer, *Word Keys Which Unlock Scripture: Draw* (San Antonio: Word of Grace, 1974), p. 4.
187. Storms, Chosen for Life, p. 46.
188. Herman Hoeksema, Grace, p. 73.
189. Steele and Thomas, p. 49.
190. Houck, Sovereignty, p. 25; Gunn, p. 21; Steele and Thomas, p. 53; Boettner, Predestination, pp. 101-102; Wright, p. 134.
191. Pink, Salvation, p. 51.
192. Rose, p. 45.
193. Mathison, p. 99.
194. C. Samuel Storms, "Prayer and Evangelism under God's Sovereignty," in Schreiner and Ware, eds., *The Grace of God, the Bondage of the Will,* p. 221.
195. Clark, Predestination, p. 102.
196. Coppes, p. 47.
197. W. Robertson Nicoll, ed., *The Expositor's Greek Testament* (Grand Rapids: Wm. B. Eerdmans Publishing Co., n.d.), vol. 3, p. 289; Kenneth S. Wuest, *Ephesians and Colossians in the Greek New Testament* (Grand Rapids: Wm. B. Eerdmans Publishing Co., 1953), p. 69; Robertson, vol. 4, p. 525; Alford, vol. 3, p. 1216; Marvin R. Vincent, *Word Studies in the Greek New Testament* (McLean: MacDonald Publishing Co., n.d.), vol. 3, p. 376.
198. Eddie K. Garrett, "Faith: The Gift of God," *The Hardshell Baptist*, June 1987, p. 1; Clark, Predestination, pp. 102-103; Best, Justification, pp. 54-55; Storms, Chosen for Life, pp. 47-48.
199. Homer Hoeksema, Voice of Our Fathers, p. 145.
200. F. F. Bruce, Foreword to Forster and Marston, *God's Strategy in Human History,* p. vii.
201. F. F. Bruce, *The Epistles to the Colossians, to Philemon, and to the Ephesians* (Grand Rapids: Wm. B. Eerdmans Publishing Co., 1984), p. 290.
202. Calvin, Commentaries, vol. 11, p. 145.
203. Augustine *On the Predestination of the Saints* 7, 8, 16.
204. Houck, Sovereignty, p. 23.
205. Rose, p. 45; Houck, Bondage of the Will, p. 13; Spencer, Tulip, p. 45.

206. Hoeksema, Grace, p. 62.
207. Hodge, Ephesians, p. 78.
208. Hodge, Theology, vol. 2, p. 365.
209. J. Gresham Machen, *What is Faith?* (Edinburgh: The Banner of Truth Trust, 1991), p. 195.
210. Calvin, Commentaries, vol. 11, p. 144.
211. Ibid.
212. Pink, Sovereignty, pp. 50, 103.
213. Pink, Salvation, pp. 116-117.
214. Houck, Sovereignty, p. 16.
215. Ibid., p. 22.
216. Keener, p. 205.
217. Gene D. Abbott, "Consistent Grace," *The Baptist Examiner,* September 14, 1991, p. 1.
218. Sproul, Chosen by God, p. 72.
219. Ibid.
220. Best, Simple Faith, p. 34.
221. Boettner, Predestination, p. 101.
222. Arthur W. Pink, *The Holy Spirit* (Grand Rapids: Baker Book House, 1978), p. 55.
223. Gunn, p. 8.
224. Sproul, Chosen by God, p. 73.
225. Pink, Sovereignty, p. 73.
226. Bryson, p. 80.
227. Storms, Chosen for Life, p. 108.
228. A. W. Martin, *The Practical Implications of Calvinism* (Edinburgh: The Banner of Truth Trust, 1979), p. 13.
229. Custance, pp. 359-364.
230. Sproul, Grace Unknown, p. 184.
231. Ibid., p. 183.
232. Ibid., p. 189.
233. Ibid., p. 184.
234. Custance, pp. 359-360.
235. Ibid., p. 364.
236. Sproul, Willing to Believe, p. 196.
237. Ibid.
238. Custance, p. 364.
239. Gerstner, Wrongly Dividing, pp. 149-169; Sproul, Grace Unknown, pp. 192-195; Mathison, pp. 45-106.
240. Custance, p. 364.
241. Sproul, Grace Unknown, p. 186.
242. Homer Hoeksema, God So Loved, p. 4.
243. Herman Hoeksema, Grace, pp. 49-50.
244. Ibid., p. 41.
245. Berkhof, Theology, p. 472.
246. Garrett, Purpose of the Gospel, 1990, p. 1.
247. Garrett, Faith, p. 1.
248. Eddie K. Garrett, "Two Salvations," *The Hardshell Baptist,* February 1992, p. 1.
249. Ibid., p. 2.

250. Ibid.
251. Ibid., p. 3.
252. Garrett, Purpose of the Gospel, 1990, p. 4.
253. Garrett, Lydia, p. 1.
254. Best, Regeneration, p. 105.
255. Keener, p. 205.
256. Sproul, Willing to Believe, pp. 194, 193.
257. Ibid.
258. Strong, p. 793.
259. Ibid.
260. Warren, Particular Baptists, p. 2.
261. Gerstner, Predestination, p. 9.
262. See Bob Ross, *The History and Heresies of Hardshellism,* and Eddie K. Garrett, "A Review of A. H. Strong on Regeneration," *The Hardshell Baptist,* September 1992, pp. 1, 3-4, "Contending for the Faith, A Reply to Bob Ross," *The Hardshell Baptist,* January 1993, pp. 1, 3-4.
263. Eddie K. Garrett, "The Purpose of the Gospel," *The Hardshell Baptist,* May 1988, p. 1.
264. Garrett, Purpose of the Gospel, 1990, p. 1.
265. Kevin Fralick, "The Idea of Acceptance," *The Christian Baptist,* June/July 1998, p. 9.
266. Garrett, Two Salvations, p. 3.
267. S. T. Tolley, "Is Gospel Faith Necessary in Order to Be Saved in Heaven?" *The Christian Baptist,* April 1996, p. 4.
268. Joseph M. Wilson, "Soul Winning and the Doctrines of Grace," *The Baptist Examiner,* February 29, 1992, p. 3.
269. Eddie K. Garrett, "The Design of the Gospel," *The Hardshell Baptist,* October 1991, p. 4.
270. S. T. Tolley, "Is Gospel Faith Necessary in Order to Be Saved in Heaven?" *The Christian Baptist,* August 1996, p. 3.
271. Garrett, Purpose of the Gospel, 1990, p. 4.
272. Garrett, Review of Strong, p. 1.
273. Garrett, Reply to Ross, p. 1.
274. Eddie K. Garrett, "Who Are 'Born Again'?" *The Hardshell Baptist,* June 1988, p. 4.
275. Webb, p. v.
276. Boettner, Predestination, p. 121.
277. Talbot and Crampton, p. 45.
278. Shedd, Theology, vol. 2, p. 512.
279. Westminster Confession of Faith, X:3.
280. Philadelphia Confession of Faith, X:3.
281. Shedd, Calvinism, p. 60.
282. Ibid., p. 128.
283. Ibid., pp. 128-129.
284. Ibid., p. 128.
285. Ibid., pp. 60, 61.
286. Ibid.
287. George, p. 124.
288. Zanchius, p. 104.
289. Boettner, Predestination, pp. 119-120.

290. James E. Hobbs, in "The Baptist Examiner Pulpit Forum," *The Baptist Examiner,* August 1, 1996, p. 4.
291. George R. Sledd, in "The Baptist Examiner Pulpit Forum," *The Baptist Examiner,* August 1, 1996, p. 4.
292. Boettner, Predestination, pp. 144-145.
293. Shedd, Calvinism, p. 64.
294. Webb, p. 280.
295. Samuel Craig, "Benjamin B. Warfield," in Warfield, Studies, p. xxxviii.
296. Garner Smith, in "The Berea Baptist Banner Forum," *The Berea Baptist Banner,* November 5, 1992, p. 211.
297. Jimmie B. Davis, in "The Berea Baptist Banner Forum," *The Berea Baptist Banner,* November 5, 1992, p. 211.
298. Tom Ross, in "The Berea Baptist Banner Forum," *The Berea Baptist Banner,* July 5, 1998, p. 370.
299. Webb, pp. 280-281.
300. Strong, p. 663.
301. Garrett, Review of Strong, p. 4.
302. Gerstner, Wrongly Dividing, pp. 152-153.
303. Hanko, Covenant of Grace, p. 101.
304. McFetridge, p. 107.
305. Engelsma, Hyper-Calvinism, p. 70.
306. David J. Engelsma, *Evangelism and the Reformed Faith* (South Holland: The Evangelism Committee, Protestant Reformed Church, n.d.), p. 8.
307. Kruithof, p. 61.
308. Kenneth H. Good, *Christ's Teaching on the Theology of Evangelism* (Rochester: Backus Book Publishers, 1988), p. vii.
309. Kober, p. 43.
310. Packer, pp. 94-95.
311. Custance, p. 277.
312. Pink, Interpretation, p. 54.
313. Johns, p. 46.
314. Packer, p. 196.
315. Custance, p. 24.
316. Zanchius, p. 99.
317. Pink, Sovereignty, p. 207.
318. Pink, Election, p. 156.
319. Tom Ross, Abandoned Truth, p. 165.
320. Arthur W. Pink, *Present-Day Evangelism* (Mifflinburg: Bible Truth Depot, n.d.), p. 3.
321. Iain H. Murray, *The Invitation System* (Edinburgh: The Banner of Truth Trust, 1967), p. 25.
322. Coppes, p. 162; Iain Murray, Invitation System, pp. 4-6.
323. Engelsma, Evangelism, p. 4.
324. Morton Smith, p. 5.
325. Packer, p. 100.
326. Morton Smith, p. 12.
327. Murray and Stonehouse, p. 4.
328. Morton Smith, p. 12.
329. Engelsma, Evangelism, p. 11.
330. Custance, p. 157.

331. Ibid., pp. 157-158.
332. Ibid., p. 158.
333. Engelsma, Hyper-Calvinism, pp. 17-18.
334. Daane, pp. 27, 28.
335. Engelsma, Hyper-Calvinism, p. 37.
336. Herman Hoeksema, Good Pleasure, p. 204.
337. Herman Hoeksema, Grace, p. 62.
338. Engelsma, Hyper-Calvinism, p. 67.
339. Ibid., p. 13.
340. Garrett P. Johnson, "The Myth of Common Grace," *The Trinity Review,* March/April 1987, pp. 1-8.
341. Murray and Stonehouse, p. 3.
342. Ibid.
343. Charles H. Spurgeon, *The Soul Winner* (Grand Rapids: Wm. B. Eerdmans Publishing Co., 1963), p. 15.
344. Wilson, Soul Winning, p. 1.
345. Ibid., p. 3.
346. Packer, p. 99.
347. Engelsma, Hyper-Calvinism, p. 67.
348. Jay E. Adams, *Decisional Regeneration* (Canton: Free Grace Publications, 1972), p. 12.
349. Ibid.
350. Westminster Confession of Faith, VII:3.
351. Wilson, Soul Winning, p. 1.
352. Ibid.
353. Ibid., p. 3.
354. Joseph M. Wilson, "Soul Winning," *The Baptist Examiner,* February 15, 1992, pp. 1-2.
355. Jay Adams, Regeneration, p. 8; Engelsma, Evangelism, p. 3; Iain Murray, Invitation System, p. 10.
356. Talbot and Crampton, p. 41.
357. Engelsma, Hyper-Calvinism, p. 140.
358. E. R. Roberts, "The Public Invitation," *The Berea Baptist Banner,* April 5, 1988, pp. 1, 8.
359. Pink, Election, p. 179.
360. Boettner, Predestination, p. 285.
361. Pink, Election, p. 129.
362. Jay Adams, Regeneration, pp. 3-4.
363. Clark, Evangelism, p. 59.
364. Engelsma, Evangelism, p. 14.
365. Pink, Saving Faith, p. 3.
366. John W. Robbins, "What is the Gospel?" *The Trinity Review,* March/April 1988, pp. 1-2.
367. Good, Evangelism, p. 14.
368. Ibid., p. 15.
369. Custance, p. 302.
370. Engelsma, Defense of Calvinism, p. 4.
371. Although Daane (p. 24) is here arguing against Herman Hoeksema, his conclusion actually applies to any form of Calvinism.
372. Custance, p. 288.

373. Jay Adams, Grand Demonstration, p. 89.
374. Keith Ellis, "Does God Perform His Will?" *The Christian Baptist,* April 1993, p. 11.
375. Ibid., p. 3.
376. Shedd, Theology, vol. 2, pp. 524-528.
377. Best, Life to Light, pp. 155-156.
378. Best, Regeneration, p. 109.
379. Garrett, Irresistible Grace, p. 1.
380. T. L. Webb, quoted in Garrett, Purpose of the Gospel, 1988, p. 1.
381. Ibid.
382. Garrett, Purpose of the Gospel, 1988, p. 4.
383. Eddie K. Garrett, "An Examination of Roman Catholicism," *The Hardshell Baptist,* July 1987, p. 3.
384. Garrett, Purpose of the Gospel, 1990, p. 1.
385. Kober, p. 27.
386. Zanchius, p. 52.
387. Engelsma, Hyper-Calvinism, p. 68.
388. Kober, p. 43.
389. Engelsma, Hyper-Calvinism, p. 51.
390. Custance, p. 289.
391. Kuiper, Reformed, p. 77.
392. Ibid., p. 79.
393. Custance, p. 280.
394. Pink, Sovereignty, p. 141.
395. Engelsma, Evangelism, p. 12.
396. Charles H. Spurgeon, *For Whom Did Christ Die?* (Pasadena: Pilgrim Publications, n.d.), p. 503.
397. Spurgeon, Sermons on Sovereignty, p. 93.
398. W. E. Best, *The Born Again Phenomenon (A Cover-up for Heresy)* (Houston: W. E. Best Book Missionary Trust, n.d.), p. 29.
399. Palmer, p. 66.
400. Sproul, Chosen by God, p. 125.
401. Boettner, Predestination, p. 140.
402. Van Baren, Irresistible Grace, p. 77.
403. Boettner, Predestination, p. 170.
404. Herman Hoeksema, Whosoever Will, p. 24.
405. Boettner, Reformed Faith, p. 11.
406. Custance, p. 281.
407. Ibid.
408. Good, God's Purpose, pp. 27-30.
409. Palmer, p. 60.
410. Sproul, Chosen by God, p. 125; VanOverloop, Election, p. 183.
411. John Wesley, quoted in Schaff, History, vol., 8, p. 566.
412. Works of Arminius, vol. 1, pp. 301-302.
413. Leith, p. 38.

Chapter Ten
Perseverance of the Saints

1. Boettner, Predestination, p. 182.
2. Kruithof, p. 73.
3. Spencer, Tulip, p. 54.
4. Gunn, p. 24.
5. Berkhof, Theology, pp. 545-546.
6. Arthur W. Pink, *Eternal Security* (Grand Rapids: Baker Books, 1974), p. 16; L. R. Shelton, *Eternal Security: God's Preservation—Man's Perseverance* (Pensacola: Mt. Zion Publications, n.d.), vol. 1, p. 3; Ness, p. 102; Boettner, Predestination, p. 2; A. A. Hodge, Outlines, p. 542; Nettles, By His Grace, p. 323; Tom Ross, Abandoned Truth, p. 215.
7. Beck, p. 46.
8. Palmer, p. 68; Coppes, p. 56; Kruithof, p. 75.
9. Palmer, p. 68.
10. Rose, p. 50.
11. Custance, p. 84; Palmer, p. 69; Sproul, Grace Unknown, p. 197.
12. Pink, Eternal Security, pp. 14, 15.
13. Berkhof, Theology, p. 546.
14. Rose, p. 49.
15. Gunn, p. 24;
16. Gerstner, Wrongly Dividing, p. 142.
17. Milburn Cockrell, "The Perseverance of the Saints," *The Berea Baptist Banner,* February 5, 1989, p. 39.
18. John Murray, Redemption, p. 155.
19. Gise J. Van Baren, "The Perseverance of the Saints," in Hanko, et al., *The Five Points of Calvinism,* p. 90.
20. Sproul, Chosen by God, p. 175.
21. Houck, Sovereignty, p. 30.
22. Mathison, p. 76.
23. Pink, Interpretation, p. 54.
24. Westminster Confession of Faith, XVII:1.
25. Canons of Dort, V:3.
26. Gunn, p. 24.
27. Van Baren, Perseverance, p. 89.
28. Palmer, p. 68.
29. Mathison, p. 79.
30. John Murray, Redemption, p. 155.
31. Houck, Sovereignty, p. 32.
32. Curtis Pugh, "Perseverance and Preservation of the Saints," *The Berea Baptist Banner,* May 5, 1993, p. 81.
33. Cockrell, Perseverance, p. 39.
34. Calvin, Eternal Predestination, p. 41.
35. John F. MacArthur, *The Gospel According to Jesus* (Grand Rapids: Zondervan Publishing House, 1988), p. 98.
36. Cockrell, Perseverance, p. 39.
37. Pink, Eternal Security, p. 28.
38. Boettner, Predestination, p. 182.

39. Talbot and Crampton, p. 50.
40. Sproul, Chosen by God, p. 177.
41. Houck, Sovereignty, p. 32.
42. Sproul, Grace Unknown, p. 209.
43. Steele and Thomas, p. 56.
44. Gunn, p. 25.
45. John M. Otis, *Who is the Genuine Christian?* (n.p., n.d.), p. 40.
46. Shelton, vol. 1, p. 1; Rose, p. 49; Sproul, Chosen by God, p. 175; Palmer, p. 69; Custance, p. 197.
47. MacArthur, p. 98; John Murray, Redemption, p. 154.
48. Mathison, p. 75.
49. Talbot and Crampton, p. 52.
50. Gerstner, Wrongly Dividing, p. 131.
51. Palmer, p. 79.
52. Pink, Eternal Security, p. 11.
53. Rose, p. 50.
54. Talbot and Crampton, p. 52.
55. Pink, Eternal Security, p. 21.
56. Anthony A. Hoekema, *Saved by Grace* (Grand Rapids: Wm. B. Eerdmans Publishing Co., 1989), pp. 253, 254.
57. Fitch, p. 71; McKinley, p. 45; Guy Duty, *If Ye Continue* (Minneapolis: Bethany House Publishers, 1966), p. 17.
58. Gerstner, Wrongly Dividing, p. 146.
59. Mason, p. 32.
60. Palmer, p. 69.
61. Van Baren, Perseverance, p. 91.
62. Palmer, p. 71.
63. Tom Ross, Abandoned Truth, p. 227.
64. Sproul, Chosen by God, p. 174.
65. Guy Duty, *If Ye Continue* (Minneapolis: Bethany House Publishers, 1966).
66. Ibid., p. 17.
67. Ibid., pp. 105, 106, 108, 110.
68. Ibid., p. 111.
69. Ibid., p. 65.
70. Ibid., p. 169.
71. Ibid., p. 141.
72. Robert L. Shank, *Life in the Son,* 2nd ed. (Springfield: Westcott Publishers, 1961).
73. Ibid., pp. 289-300.
74. Ibid., pp. 64, 93, 107, 170, 171, 300.
75. Ibid., pp. 37, 56, 77, 79, 107, 117, 179.
76. Ibid., pp. 60, 62, 76.
77. Ibid., p. 219.
78. Ibid.
79. Ibid., p. 293.
80. Ibid., pp. 301-303.
81. Ibid., p. 301.
82. Arthur W. Pink, quoted in Iain Murray, Life of Pink, pp. 248-249.
83. Otis, pp. 22-23.

84. Ibid., p. 24.
85. Ibid.
86. Arthur W. Pink, *Practical Christianity* (Grand Rapids: Guardian Press, 1974), p. 16.
87. Pink, Sanctification, p. 28.
88. Hodge, Corinthians, p. 181.
89. Sproul, Grace Unknown, p. 198.
90. Pink, Sanctification, p. 28.
91. Joseph C. Dillow, *The Reign of the Servant Kings* (Miami Springs: Schoettle Publishing Co., 1992), p. 232.
92. Lewis Sperry Chafer, *Salvation* (Grand Rapids: Zondervan Publishing House, 1945), p. 33.
93. Dillow, p. 11.
94. Calvin, Commentaries, vol. 9, p. 197.
95. Hodge, Corinthians, p. 169.
96. Duty, pp. 105, 107.
97. Shank, Life in the Son, p. 37.
98. R. C. H. Lenski, *The Interpretation of St. Paul's First & Second Epistles to the Corinthians* (Minneapolis: Augsburg Publishing House, 1963), p. 388.
99. Calvin, Commentaries, vol. 10, p. 248.
100. Duty, p. 116.
101. Calvin, Commentaries, vol. 3, p. 82.
102. Pink, Hebrews, p. 597.
103. Tom Ross, Abandoned Truth, pp. 189, 228; Sproul, Grace Unknown, p. 198.
104. R. C. H. Lenski, *The Interpretation of St. Matthew's Gospel* (Minneapolis: Augsburg Publishing House, 1961), p. 935.
105. Shank, Life in the Son, p. 159.
106. McKinley, p. 64.
107. Hutson, p. 16.
108. Cockrell, Perseverance, p. 39.
109. Eddie K. Garrett, "Can a Child of God Fall?" *The Hardshell Baptist*, February 1990, p. 2.
110. Van Baren, Perseverance, p. 85.
111. Dillow, p. 10.
112. Kenneth L. Gentry, *Lord of the Saved: Getting to the Heart of the Lordship Debate* (Phillipsburg: Presbyterian and Reformed Publishing Co., 1992); Curtis I. Crenshaw, *Lordship Salvation: The Only Kind There Is* (Memphis: Footstool Publications, 1994); Richard P. Belcher, *A Layman's Guide to the Lordship Controversy* (Southbridge: Crowne Publications, 1990); Robert H. Lescelius, *Lordship Salvation: Some Crucial Questions and Answers* (Asheville: Revival Literature, 1992); Michael S. Horton, ed., *Christ the Lord: The Reformation and Lordship Salvation* (Grand Rapids: Baker Book House, 1992); John F. MacArthur, *The Gospel According to Jesus,* rev. and expand. ed. (Grand Rapids: Zondervan Publishing House, 1994); John F. MacArthur, *Faith Works: The Gospel According to the Apostles* (Dallas: Word Publishing, 1993).
113. Zane C. Hodges, *Absolutely Free!* (Dallas: Redencion Viva, 1989); Charles C. Ryrie, *So Great Salvation* (Wheaton: Victor Books, 1989).
114. Pink, Sanctification, p. 177.
115. Otis, p. 7.

116. Gentry, p. 87.
117. Pink, Evangelism, p. 20.
118. Gentry, p. 8.
119. MacArthur, Gospel According to Jesus, pp. 28-29.
120. Ibid., p. 28.
121. Ibid., p. 209.
122. Ibid., p. 217.
123. Ibid., p. 30.
124. Ibid., p. xii.
125. Ibid., p. xiv.
126. Ibid., pp. 221-237.
127. Mathison, pp. 95-106; Crenshaw, p. 4.
128. Belcher, Lordship, p. 99.
129. Gentry, p. 8.
130. Michael S. Horton, "Don't Judge a Book by Its Cover," in Horton, ed. *Christ the Lord: The Reformation and Lordship Salvation,* pp. 16, 17; Crenshaw, pp. 6, 7.
131. Gentry, pp. xi, 9.
132. MacArthur, Gospel According to Jesus, xiii.
133. Ibid., pp. 110, 146.
134. Ibid., p. 98.
135. Shank, Life in the Son, p. 15.
136. Ibid., p. 16.
137. Ibid., p. 198.
138. Ibid., p. 189.
139. Crenshaw, pp. 3-4; Lescelius, p. 117; Mathison, pp. 95-96.
140. Mathison; Gerstner, Wrongly Dividing; Crenshaw, pp. 151-164; Belcher, Lordship, pp. 101-102.
141. MacArthur, Gospel According to Jesus, p. 25.
142. Ibid., pp. 26, 27, 89.
143. Crenshaw, pp. 2-3, 151-164; Robert B. Strimple, "Repentance in Romans," in Horton, ed. *Christ the Lord: The Reformation and Lordship Salvation,* p. 65; Lescelius, p. 117; MacArthur, Faith Works, pp. 94-96.
144. Ernest C. Reisinger, *The Carnal Christian?* (Edinburgh: The Banner of Truth Trust, n.d.); MacArthur, Gospel According to Jesus, pp. 97-98; Gentry, p. 7; Gerstner, Wrongly Dividing, p. 213; Crenshaw, p. 2.
145. Morey, pp. 130-131; Gerstner, Wrongly Dividing, pp. 144-145; Crenshaw, p. 2.
146. Gerstner, Wrongly Dividing, pp. 144, 213; MacArthur, Faith Works, p. 57.
147. Tom Ross, Abandoned Truth, p. 3; MacArthur, Faith Works, pp. 55-56; MacArthur, Gospel According to Jesus, p. 21; Crenshaw, p. 46.
148. Gentry, pp. 67-82; Lescelius, pp. 105-108; MacArthur, Gospel According to Jesus, pp. 29-30.
149. Crenshaw, pp. 88-89; MacArthur, Faith Works, pp. 96-97.
150. Gentry, pp. 15-31, 33-49; Crenshaw, pp. 45-86.
151. MacArthur, Gospel According to Jesus, pp. 207, 209; Gentry, pp. 60, 62, 64; Crenshaw, p. 75.
152. Garrett, Child of God, p. 2.
153. Pink, Salvation, p. 27.

154. Shank, Life in the Son, p. 212.

155. Eddie K. Garrett, "Sinless Perfection," *The Hardshell Baptist,* February 1990, p. 1.

156. John W. Robbins, "The Gospel According to John MacArthur," part 1, *The Trinity Review,* April 1993, p. 3.

157. Shank, Life in the Son, pp. 131-132.

158. Gentry, pp. 20-21; MacArthur, Gospel According to Jesus, p. 31.

159. W. Stanford Reid, "J. Gresham Machen," in David F. Wells, ed., *The Princeton Theology* (Grand Rapids: Baker Book House, 1989), p. 102; see also Machen's *What is Faith?* pp. 192-195.

160. Kim Riddlebarger, "What is Faith?" in Horton, ed. *Christ the Lord: The Reformation and Lordship Salvation,* pp. 93-95, 104-105.

161. Dillow, p. 29.

162. Clark, Predestination, p. 107.

163. MacArthur, Gospel According to Jesus, p. 162; Gentry, p. 39.

164. Otis, p. 21.

165. Ibid., p. 24.

166. Hodges, p. 221.

167. James O. Combs, "The Gospel According to John MacArthur," *Baptist Bible Tribune,* April 26, 1989, pp. 14-15, 27; Robbins, MacArthur, part 1, part 2.

168. Robbins, MacArthur, part 1, p. 1.

169. Ibid.

170. Ibid., p. 3.

171. Ibid., p. 4.

172. John W. Robbins, "The Gospel According to John MacArthur," part 2, *The Trinity Review,* May 1993, p. 2.

173. Ibid., p. 4.

174. Pink, Exodus, p. 18.

175. Ibid., p. 19.

176. Murray, Redemption, p. 161.

177. MacArthur, Gospel According to Jesus, p. 172; Shank, Life in the Son, pp. 56, 60.

178. MacArthur, Gospel According to Jesus, p. 172; Shank, Life in the Son, pp. 96, 171, 212, 278.

179. Good, Calvinists, p. 63; Wright, p. 29; Sellers, p. 8; Cunningham, Reformers, p. 451.

180. Works of Arminius, vol. 2, p. 725.

181. Ibid., p. 67.

182. Ibid., vol. 1, p. 667.

183. Ibid., pp. 664-667.

184. Pink, Saving Faith, p. 8.

185. Shank, Life in the Son, p. 93.

186. Pink, Evangelism, p. 16; Shank, Life in the Son, p. 135.

187. John H. Gerstner, *A Primer on Dispensationalism* (Phillipsburg: Presbyterian and Reformed Publishing Co., 1992), pp. 14-15.

188. Best, Simple Faith, p. 20.

189. Shank, Life in the Son, p. 170.

190. Pink, Eternal Security, p. 15.

191. Cockrell, Perseverance, p. 39.

192. Coppes, p. 55.

193. Martin, p. 18.
194. Garrett, Child of God, p. 2.
195. Talbot and Crampton, p. 53.
196. Boettner, Predestination, p. 191.
197. Letter from Arthur W. Pink to Robert C. Harbach, January 18, 1947, in Arthur W. Pink, *Letters to a Young Pastor* (Grandville: The Grandville Protestant Reformed Evangelism Committee, 1993), p. 27.
198. Otis, p. 39.
199. Coppes, p. 27.
200. Charles Hodge, Romans, p. 292.
201. Boettner, Predestination, p. 309.
202. Shank, Life in the Son, p. 293.
203. Ibid.

BIBLIOGRAPHY

"A Study Tool for the Doctrine of Election." *SBC Life,* April 1995.
A Dictionary of Christian Biography. Peabody: Hendrickson Publishers, 1994.
Abbott, Gene D. "Consistent Grace." *The Baptist Examiner,* September 14, 1991.
Adams, Jay E. *Decisional Regeneration.* Canton: Free Grace Publications, 1972.
_____. *The Grand Demonstration.* Santa Barbara: EastGate Publishers, 1991.
Adams, Marilyn McCord, and Robert Merrihew Adams, eds. *The Problem of Evil.* New York: Oxford University Press, 1990.
Alber, John. "God's Predestination." *The Berea Baptist Banner,* August 5, 1990.
Alexander, J. R. *The Tulip Doctrine.* Texarkana: Bogard Press, 1992.
Alford, Henry. *The New Testament for English Readers.* Grand Rapids: Baker Book House, 1983.
Allis, Oswald T. *Prophecy and the Church.* Phillipsburg: Presbyterian and Reformed Publishing Co., 1947.
"Arminian/Calvinist Responses." *SBC Life,* August 1995.
Arminius, James. *The Works of James Arminius.* Trans. by James Nichols and William Nichols. Grand Rapids: Baker Book House, 1986.
Armitage, Thomas. *The History of the Baptists.* Watertown: Maranatha Baptist Press, 1980.
Armstrong, Brian G. *Calvinism and the Amyraut Heresy.* Madison: The University of Wisconsin Press, 1969.
Augustine. *City of God.*
_____. *Confessions.*
_____. *Enchiridion.*
_____. *Letters.*
_____. *On Christian Doctrine.*
_____. *On Original Sin.*
_____. *On Rebuke and Grace.*
_____. *On the Correction of the Donatists.*
_____. *On the Gift of Perseverance.*
_____. *On the Merits and Forgiveness of Sins.*
_____. *On the Morals of the Manichaeans.*
_____. *On the Predestination of the Saints.*
_____. *On the Psalms.*
_____. *On the Spirit and the Letter.*
_____. *On the Soul and its Origin.*
Bainton, Roland H. *Here I Stand.* New York: Mentor Books, 1955.
_____. *Hunted Heretic.* Boston: The Beacon Press, 1953.
_____. *The Reformation of the Sixteenth Century,* enlar. ed. Boston: Beacon Press, 1985.

Baker, Alvin L. *Berkouwer's Doctrine of Election: Balance or Imbalance?* Phillipsburg: Presbyterian and Reformed Publishing Co., 1981.
Baker's Dictionary of Theology. Grand Rapids: Baker Book House, 1960.
Ballard, L. S. *Election Made Plain,* 2nd ed. n.p., n.d.
Bancroft, Emery H. *Christian Theology,* 2nd rev. ed. Grand Rapids: Zondervan Publishing House, 1976.
Bangs, Carl. *Arminius: A Study in the Dutch Reformation,* 2nd ed. Grand Rapids: Zondervan Publishing House, 1985.
Barackman, Floyd H. *Practical Christian Theology.* Old Tappan: Fleming H. Revell, 1984.
Barnhouse, Donald Grey. "God's Wrath," in *Expositions of Bible Doctrines Taking the Epistle to the Romans as a Point of Departure.* Grand Rapids: Wm. B. Eerdmans Publishing Co., 1953.
Barth, Karl. *The Theology of John Calvin.* Trans. Geoffrey W. Bromiley. Grand Rapids: Wm. B. Eerdmans Publishing Co., 1995.
Basinger, David. *The Case for Freewill Theism: A Philosophical Assessment.* Downers Grove: InterVarsity Press, 1996.
Basinger, David, and Randall Basinger, eds. *Predestination and Free Will.* Downers Grove: InterVarsity Press, 1986.
Battenhouse, Roy W., ed. *A Companion to the Study of St. Augustine.* New York: Oxford University Press, 1955.
Battles, Ford Lewis. *An Analysis of the Institutes of the Christian Religion.* Grand Rapids: Baker Book House, 1980.
Beck, Frank B. *The Five Points of Calvinism.* Ashland: Calvary Baptist Church, n.d.
Belcher, Richard P. *A Layman's Guide to the Lordship Controversy.* Southbridge: Crowne Publications, 1990.
_____. *Arthur W. Pink: Born to Write.* Columbia: Richbarry Press, 1982.
_____. *Arthur W. Pink: Predestination.* Columbia: Richbarry Press, 1983.
Belcher, Richard P., and Tony Mattia. *A Discussion of Seventeenth Century Baptist Confessions of Faith.* Columbia: Richbarry Press, 1983.
Benedict, David. *A General History of the Baptist Denomination in America, and Other Parts of the World.* Gallatin: Church History Research & Archives, 1985.
_____. *Fifty Years Among the Baptists.* Little Rock: Seminary Publications, 1977.
_____. *History of the Donatists.* Gallatin: Church History Research & Archives, 1985.
Berkhof, Louis. *Introduction to Systematic Theology.* Grand Rapids: Baker Book House, 1979.
_____. *Manual of Christian Doctrine.* Grand Rapids: Wm. B. Eerdmans Publishing Co., 1933.
_____. *Principles of Biblical Interpretation.* Grand Rapids: Baker Book House, 1950.
_____. *Systematic Theology,* 4th rev. and enlar. ed. Grand Rapids: Wm. B. Eerdmans Publishing Co., 1941.
_____. *The History of Christian Doctrines.* Grand Rapids: Baker Book House, 1937.
Berkouwer, G. C. *Divine Election.* Trans. by Hugo Bekker. Grand Rapids: Eerdmans Publishing Co., 1960.

Best, W. E. *Free Grace Versus Free Will.* Houston: W. E. Best Book Missionary Trust, 1977.
_____. *God's Eternal Decree.* Houston: W. E. Best Book Missionary Trust, n.d.
_____. *God's Longsuffering is Salvation.* Houston: W. E. Best Book Missionary Trust, n.d.
_____. *Justification Before God (Not by Faith).* W. E. Best Book Missionary Trust, n.d.
_____. *Life Brought to Light.* Houston: W. E. Best Book Missionary Trust, n.d.
_____. *Regeneration and Conversion.* Houston: W. E. Best Book Missionary Trust, n.d.
_____. *Simple Faith (A Misnomer).* Houston: W. E. Best Book Missionary Trust, 1993.
_____. *The Born Again Phenomenon (A Cover-up for Heresy).* Houston: W. E. Best Book Missionary Trust, n.d.
_____. *The Most Neglected Chapter in the Bible (Romans 9).* Houston: W. E. Best Book Missionary Trust, n.d.
_____. *The Saviour's Definite Redemption.* Houston: W. E. Best Book Missionary Trust, 1982.
Bettenson, Henry, ed. *Documents of the Christian Church,* 2nd ed. London: Oxford University Press, 1963.
Beza, Theodore. *The Life of John Calvin,* new and expand. ed. Ed. by Gary Sanseri. Trans. by Henry Beveridge. Milwaukie: Back Home Industries, 1996.
Bishop, George S. *The Doctrines of Grace.* Grand Rapids: Baker Book House, 1977.
Boettner, Loraine. *Immortality.* Phillipsburg: Presbyterian and Reformed Publishing Co., 1956.
_____. *Studies in Theology.* Phillipsburg: Presbyterian and Reformed Publishing Co., 1947.
_____. *The Reformed Doctrine of Predestination.* Phillipsburg: Presbyterian and Reformed Publishing Co., 1932.
_____. *The Reformed Faith.* Phillipsburg: Presbyterian and Reformed Publishing Co., 1983.
Bonner, Gerald. *St Augustine of Hippo.* Philadelphia: The Westminster Press, 1963.
Bookman, Doug. "God's Sovereign Pleasure." *Masterpiece,* July/August 1990.
Bordwine, James E. *A Guide to the Westminster Standards.* Jefferson: The Trinity Foundation, 1991.
Bouwsma, William J. *John Calvin: A Sixteenth Century Portrait.* New York: Oxford University Press, 1988.
Boyce, James P. *Abstract of Systematic Theology.* North Pompano Beach: den Dulk Christian Foundation, n.d.
Bratt, John H. *The Life and Teachings of John Calvin.* Grand Rapids: Baker Book House, 1958.
_____., ed. *The Heritage of John Calvin.* Grand Rapids: Wm. B. Eerdmans Publishing Co., 1973.
_____., ed. *The Rise and Development of Calvinism,* 2nd ed. Grand Rapids: Wm. B. Eerdmans Publishing Co., 1964.
Brine, John. *A Defence of the Doctrine of Eternal Justification.* Chicago: Leory Rhodes, n.d.

Bronson, Charles W. *The Extent of the Atonement.* Pasadena: Pilgrim Publications, 1992.

Brown, Peter. *Augustine of Hippo.* Berkeley and Los Angeles: University of California Press, 1967.

Bruce, F. F. *The Epistles to the Colossians, to Philemon, and to the Ephesians.* Grand Rapids: Wm. B. Eerdmans Publishing Co., 1984.

_____. *The Spreading Flame.* Grand Rapids: Wm. B. Eerdmans Publishing Co., 1958.

Brussell, Eugene E., ed., *Webster's New World Dictionary of Quotable Definitions,* 2nd ed. Englewood Cliffs: Prentice Hall, 1988.

Bryson, George L. *The Five Points of Calvinism.* Costa Mesa: The Word for Today, 1996.

Bunyan, John. *Reprobation Asserted.* Swengel: Reiner Publications, 1969.

Buswell, J. Oliver. *A Systematic Theology of the Christian Religion.* Grand Rapids: Zondervan Publishing House, 1962.

Cairns, Earle E. *Christianity Through the Centuries,* rev. and enlar. ed. Grand Rapids: Zondervan Publishing House, 1981.

Calhoun, David B. *Princeton Seminary,* Vol. 1: *Faith and Learning (1812–1868).* Edinburgh: The Banner of Truth Trust, 1994.

_____. *Princeton Seminary,* Vol. 2: *The Majestic Testimony (1868–1929).* Edinburgh: The Banner of Truth Trust, 1996.

Calvin, John. *Calvin's Calvinism.* Grand Rapids: Reformed Free Publishing Association, 1987.

_____. *Calvin's New Testament Commentaries.* Grand Rapids: Wm. B. Eerdmans Publishing Co., 1994.

_____. *Commentary on the Catholic Epistles.* Ed. and trans. by John Owen. Grand Rapids: Wm. B. Eerdmans Publishing Co., 1948.

_____. *Institutes of the Christian Religion.* Ed. by John T. McNeil. Trans. by Ford Lewis Battles. Philadelphia: The Westminster Press, 1960.

_____. *Letters of John Calvin.* Edinburgh: The Banner of Truth Trust, 1980.

_____. *The Bondage and Liberation of the Will: A Defence of the Orthodox Doctrine of Human Choice against Pighius.* Ed. by A. N. S. Lane. Trans. by G. I. Davies. Grand Rapids: Baker Books, 1996.

Calvin Theological Seminary. *1996–1998 Catalog.*

Carpenter, Marc D. "A History of Hypo-Calvinism," part 1. *The Trinity Review,* March 1997.

_____. "A History of Hypo-Calvinism," part 2. *The Trinity Review,* April 1997.

_____. "The Banner of Truth Versus Calvinism," part 1. *The Trinity Review,* May 1997.

_____. "The Banner of Truth Versus Calvinism," part 2. *The Trinity Review,* June 1997.

Carson, D. A. *Divine Sovereignty and Human Responsibility.* Atlanta: John Knox Press, 1981.

Carson, John L., and David W. Hall, eds. *To Glorify and Enjoy God: A Commemoration of the 350th Anniversary of the Westminster Assembly.* Edinburgh: The Banner of Truth Trust, 1994.

Cathcart, William. *The Baptist Encyclopedia.* Philadelphia: Louis H. Everts, 1881.

Chafer, Lewis Sperry. *Salvation.* Grand Rapids: Zondervan Publishing House, 1945.

_____. *Systematic Theology*. Dallas: Dallas Seminary Press, 1948.
Chan, Godwell Andrew. "Spurgeon, the Forgotten Calvinist," *The Trinity Review*, August 1996.
Chantry, Walter J. *Man's Will—Free Yet Bound*. Canton: Free Grace Publications, 1988.
Christian History, Vol. 6:3 (1987).
Christian History, Vol. 5:4 (1986).
Christian, John T. *A History of the Baptists*. Texarkana: Bogard Press, 1922.
Clark, Gordon H. *First Corinthians*, 2nd ed. Jefferson: The Trinity Foundation, 1991.
_____. *New Heavens, New Earth*, 2nd ed. Jefferson: The Trinity Foundation, 1993.
_____. *Philippians*. Jefferson: The Trinity Foundation, 1996.
_____. *Predestination*. Phillipsburg: Presbyterian and Reformed Publishing Co., 1987.
_____. *Thales to Dewey*, 2nd ed. Jefferson: The Trinity Foundation, 1989.
_____. *The Atonement*. Jefferson: The Trinity Foundation, 1987.
_____. *The Biblical Doctrine of Man*. Jefferson: The Trinity Foundation, 1984.
_____. *The Pastoral Epistles*. Jefferson: The Trinity Foundation, 1983.
_____. *The Trinity*. Jefferson: The Trinity Foundation, 1985.
_____. *Today's Evangelism: Counterfeit or Genuine?* Jefferson: The Trinity Foundation, 1990.
_____. *What Do Presbyterians Believe?* Phillipsburg: Presbyterian and Reformed Publishing Co., 1965.
Cockrell, Milburn. "Chosen in Christ." *The Berea Baptist Banner*, February 5, 1994.
_____. "Dying on Time." *The Berea Baptist Banner*, November 5, 1997.
_____. "God's Golden Chain of Grace." *The Berea Baptist Banner*, January 5, 1998.
_____. "KJV Vindicated on Acts 13:48." *The Berea Baptist Banner*, March 5, 1992, and April 5, 1992.
_____. "Second Trip to the Philippines." *The Berea Baptist Banner*, January 5, 1995.
_____. "The Perseverance of the Saints." *The Berea Baptist Banner*, February 5, 1989.
_____. "What God Does for the Poor." *The Berea Baptist Banner*, August 5, 1992.
Combs, James O. "The Gospel According to John MacArthur." *Baptist Bible Tribune*, April 26, 1989.
Cooper, William. *The Doctrine of Predestination Unto Life*, 2nd ed. New Ipswich: Pietan Publications, n.d.
Coppes, Leonard J. *Are Five Points Enough? The Ten Points of Calvinism*. Denver: by the author, 1980.
Cosgrove, Charles H. *Elusive Israel: The Puzzle of Election in Romans*. Louisville: Westminster John Knox Press, 1997.
Craig, William Lane. *The Only Wise God*. Grand Rapids: Baker Book House, 1987.
Crampton, W. Gary. "Does the Bible Contain Paradox?" *The Trinity Review*, November/December 1990.
_____. *What Calvin Says*. Jefferson: The Trinity Foundation, 1992.
Cremeans, Charles D. *The Reception of Calvinistic Thought in England*. Urbana:

University of Illinois Press, 1949.
Crenshaw, Curtis I. *Lordship Salvation: The Only Kind There Is.* Memphis: Footstool Publications, 1994.
Crosby, Thomas. *The History of the English Baptists.* Lafayette: Church History Research & Archives, 1979.
Cunningham, William. *Historical Theology.* Edmonton: Still Waters Revival Books, n.d.
_____. *The Reformers and the Theology of the Reformation.* Edinburgh: The Banner of Truth Trust, 1967.
Curtiss, George L. *Arminianism in History.* Cincinnati: Cranston & Curts, 1894.
Custance, Arthur C. *The Sovereignty of Grace.* Phillipsburg: Presbyterian and Reformed Publishing Co., 1979.
d'Aubigne, J. H. Merle. *History of the Reformation of the Sixteenth Century.* Grand Rapids: Baker Book House, n.d.
_____. *The Reformation in England.* Ed. by S. M. Houghton. Trans. by H. White (Edinburgh: Banner of Truth Trust, 1962.
Daane, James. *The Freedom of God.* Grand Rapids: Wm. B. Eerdmans Publishing Co., 1973.
Dabney, Robert L. *Systematic Theology,* 2nd ed. Edinburgh: The Banner of Truth Trust, 1985.
_____. *The Five Points of Calvinism.* Harrisonburg: Sprinkle Publications, 1992.
Dagg, John L. *Manual of Theology and Church Order.* Harrisonburg: Sprinkle Publications, 1982.
Dakin, Arthur. *Calvinism.* Philadelphia: The Westminster Press, 1946.
Daniell, David. *William Tyndale: A Biography.* New Haven & London: Yale University Press, 1994.
Davies, Horton. *Worship and Theology in England,* Vol. I: *From Cranmer to Hooker.* Grand Rapids: Wm. B. Eerdmans Publishing Co., 1996.
Dawson, Christopher. *Religion and the Rise of Western Culture.* New York: Image Books, 1957.
de Greef, Wulfert. *The Writings of John Calvin: An Introductory Guide.* Trans. by Lyle D. Bierman. Grand Rapids: Baker Books, 1993.
De Jong, Peter Y., ed. *Crisis in the Reformed Churches.* Grand Rapids: Reformed Fellowship, 1968.
de Witt, John R. *What is the Reformed Faith?* Edinburgh: The Banner of Truth Trust, 1981.
Dickinson, Jonathan. *The True Scripture Doctrine Concerning Some Important Points of Christian Faith.* Harrisonburg: Sprinkle Publications, 1992.
Dictionary of Christianity in America. Downers Grove: InterVarsity Press, 1990.
Dillow, Joseph C. *The Reign of the Servant Kings.* Miami Springs: Schoettle Publishing Co., 1992.
Dogmatic Canons and Decrees. Rockford: Tan Books and Publishers, 1977.
Duncan, Mark. *The Five Points of Christian Reconstruction from the Lips of Our Lord.* Edmonton: Still Waters Revival Books, 1990.
Durant, Will. *Caesar and Christ.* New York: Simon and Schuster, 1972.
_____. *The Age of Faith.* New York: Simon and Schuster, 1950.
_____. *The Reformation.* New York: Simon and Schuster, 1957.
Duty, Guy. *If Ye Continue.* Minneapolis: Bethany House Publishers, 1966.
Edwards, Jonathan. *Freedom of the Will,* ed. Paul Ramsey. New Haven and

London: Yale University Press, 1957.
_____. *Original Sin,* ed. Clyde A. Holbrook. New Haven and London: Yale University Press, 1970.
Eells, Hastings. *Martin Bucer.* New Haven: Yale University Press, 1931.
Ella, George M. *John Gill and the Cause of God and Truth.* Durham: Go Publications, 1995.
Ellis, Keith. "Does God Perform His Will?" *The Christian Baptist,* April 1993.
Ellison, H. L. *The Mystery of Israel,* rev. and enlar. ed. Devon: The Paternoster Press, 1968.
Elton, G. R. *Reform and Reformation, England 1509–1598.* Cambridge: Harvard University Press, 1977.
_____., ed. *The Tudor Constitution: Documents and Commentary.* Cambridge: Cambridge University Press, 1960.
Emerson, Everett H. *English Puritanism from John Hooper to John Milton.* Durham: Duke University Press, 1968.
Encyclopedia of Religion and Ethics. New York: Charles Scribner's Sons, n.d.
Engelsma, David J. *A Defense of Calvinism as the Gospel.* South Holland: The Evangelism Committee, Protestant Reformed Church, n.d.
_____. *Evangelism and the Reformed Faith.* South Holland: The Evangelism Committee, Protestant Reformed Church, n.d.
_____. *Hyper-Calvinism and the Call of the Gospel.* Grand Rapids: Reformed Free Publishing Association, 1980.
_____. "The Death of Confessional Calvinism in Scottish Presbyterianism." *Standard Bearer,* December 1, 1992.
Enns, Paul P. *The Moody Handbook of Theology.* Chicago: Moody Press, 1989.
Erasmus—Luther Discourse on Free Will. Trans. and ed. by Ernst F. Winter. New York: Frederick Ungar Publishing Co., 1961.
Erickson, Millard J. *Christian Theology.* Grand Rapids: Baker Book House, 1985.
Estep, William R. *Renaissance and Reformation.* Grand Rapids: Wm. B. Eerdmans Publishing Co., 1986.
Eusebius. *Church History.*
_____. *The Life of Constantine.*
Evangelical Dictionary of Theology. Grand Rapids: Baker Book House, 1984.
Everman, Clyde T. "Studies in Acts." *The Baptist Examiner,* August 5, 1989.
Ferguson, John. *Pelagius: A Historical and Theological Study.* Cambridge: W. Heffer & Sons, 1956.
Fincham, Kenneth, ed. *The Early Stuart Church, 1603–1642.* Stanford: Stanford University Press, 1993.
Fischer, John Martin, ed. *God, Foreknowledge, and Freedom.* Stanford: Stanford University Press, 1989.
Fisher, George Park. *History of Christian Doctrine.* New York: Charles Scribner's Sons, 1899.
_____. *History of the Christian Church.* New York: Charles Scribner's Sons, 1900.
_____. *The Reformation.* New York: Scribner, Armstrong, and Co., 1873.
Fisk, Samuel. *Calvinistic Paths Retraced.* Murfreesboro: Biblical Evangelism Press, 1985.
_____. *Divine Sovereignty and Human Freedom.* Neptune: Loizeaux Brothers, 1973.
Fitch, Alger. *Pick the Brighter Tulip.* Joplin: College Press Publishing Co., 1993.

"Five Common Questions on the Doctrine of Election Simply and Clearly Answered." *The Baptist Examiner,* November 20, 1993.
Forster, Roger T., and Paul V. Marston. *God's Strategy in Human History.* Wheaton: Tyndale House Publishers, 1974.
Fralick, Kevin. "The Idea of Acceptance." *The Christian Baptist,* June/July 1998.
Fry, Dennis. *Questions on the Atonement.* Pensacola: Chapel Library, n.d.
Fuller, Andrew. *The Complete Works of the Rev. Andrew Fuller,* 3rd ed. Rev. by Joseph Belcher. Harrisonburg: Sprinkle Publications, 1988.
Garrett, Eddie K. "A Review of A. H. Strong on Regeneration." *The Hardshell Baptist,* September 1992.
_____. "Can a Child of God Fall?" *The Hardshell Baptist,* February 1990.
_____. "Sinless Perfection." *The Hardshell Baptist,* February 1990.
_____. "An Examination of Roman Catholicism." *The Hardshell Baptist,* July 1987.
_____. "Contending for the Faith, A Reply to Bob Ross." *The Hardshell Baptist,* January 1993.
_____. "Faith: The Gift of God." *The Hardshell Baptist,* June 1987.
_____. "Freedom of the Will?" *The Hardshell Baptist,* July 1989.
_____. "Lydia." *The Hardshell Baptist,* July 1990.
_____. "The Design of the Gospel." *The Hardshell Baptist,* October 1991.
_____. "The Purpose of the Gospel." *The Hardshell Baptist,* May 1988.
_____. "The Purpose of the Gospel." *The Hardshell Baptist,* December 1990.
_____. "The Tulip Series: Irresistible Grace." *The Hardshell Baptist,* December 1987.
_____. "Two Salvations." *The Hardshell Baptist,* February 1992.
_____. "Who Are 'Born Again'?" *The Hardshell Baptist,* June 1988.
Gee, Henry, and William John Hardy, eds. *Documents Illustrative of English Church History.* London: Macmillan and Co., 1910.
Geisler, Norman L. *What Augustine Says.* Grand Rapids: Baker Book House, 1982.
Gentry, Kenneth L. *Lord of the Saved: Getting to the Heart of the Lordship Debate.* Phillipsburg: Presbyterian and Reformed Publishing Co., 1992.
George, Timothy. *Theology of the Reformers.* Nashville: Broadman Press, 1988.
Gerstner, John H. *A Predestination Primer.* Grand Rapids: Baker Book House, 1960.
_____. *A Primer on Dispensationalism* Phillipsburg: Presbyterian and Reformed Publishing Co., 1992.
_____. *A Primer on Free Will.* Phillipsburg: Presbyterian and Reformed Publishing Co., 1982.
_____. *Wrongly Dividing the Word of Truth.* Brentwood: Wolgemuth & Hyatt, Publishers, 1991.
Gibbon, Edward. *The History of the Decline and Fall of the Roman Empire.* New York: Modern Library, n.d.
Gill, John. *A Body of Doctrinal and Practical Divinity.* Paris: Baptist Standard Bearer, 1987.
_____. *Exposition of the Old and New Testaments.* Paris: The Baptist Standard Bearer, 1989.
_____. *The Cause of God and Truth.* Paris: The Baptist Standard Bearer, 1992.
_____. *The Doctrines of God's Everlasting Love to His Elect, and Their Eternal Union with Christ.* Paris: The Baptist Standard Bearer, 1987.

Girardeau, John L. *Calvinism and Evangelical Arminianism.* Harrisonburg: Sprinkle Publications, 1984.
Good, Kenneth H. *Are Baptists Calvinists?* rev. ed. Rochester: Backus Book Publishers, 1988.
_____. *Are Baptists Reformed?* Lorain: Regular Baptist Heritage Fellowship, 1986.
_____. *Christ's Teaching on the Theology of Evangelism.* Rochester: Backus Book Publishers, 1988.
_____. *God's Gracious Purpose.* Rochester: Backus Book Publishers, 1979.
Gower, Ted. "Am I a Calvinist?" *The Baptist Examiner,* November 21, 1992.
Grant, Michael. *Constantine the Great.* New York: Charles Scribner's Sons, 1993.
Griswold, Ferrell. *Particular Redemption.* Birmingham: First Baptist Church, n.d.
Gritters, Barry L. *Grace Uncommon.* Bryon Center: The Evangelism Society, Byron Center Protestant Reformed Church, n.d.
Grudem, Wayne A. *Systematic Theology.* Grand Rapids: Zondervan Publishing House, 1994.
Gunn, Grover E. *The Doctrines of Grace.* Memphis: Footstool Publications, 1987.
Haldane, Robert. *Commentary on Romans.* Grand Rapids: Kregel Publications, 1988.
Halff, Charles. "God's Predestination," messages 4 through 6. *The Baptist Examiner,* December 23, 1989.
Haller, William. *Elizabeth I and the Puritans.* Charlottesville: The University Press of Virginia, 1972.
Hanko, Herman. *God's Everlasting Covenant of Grace.* Grand Rapids: Reformed Free Publishing Association, 1988.
_____. Review of *The New Chosen People: A Corporate View of Election,* by William W. Klein. In *Standard Bearer,* June 1, 1992.
_____. *We and Our Children.* Grand Rapids: Reformed Free Publishing Association, 1988.
Hanko, Herman, Homer C. Hoeksema, and Gise J. Van Baren. *The Five Points of Calvinism.* Grand Rapids: Reformed Free Publishing Association, 1976.
Harbach, Robert C. *Calvinism the Truth.* Grand Rapids: First Protestant Reformed Church, 1984.
Harkness, Georgia. *John Calvin: The Man and His Ethics.* Nashville: Abingdon Press, 1958.
Harrison, A. W. *Arminianism.* London: Duckworth, 1937.
_____. *The Beginnings of Arminianism to the Synod of Dort.* London: University of London Press, 1926.
Haskins, James. *The Methodists.* New York: Hippocrene Books, 1992.
Heard, J. B. *The Tripartite Nature of Man: Spirit, Soul, and Body,* 5th ed. Edinburgh: T & T Clark, 1882.
Helm, Paul. *Calvin and the Calvinists.* Edinburgh: The Banner of Truth Trust, 1982.
Hetherington, William M. *History of the Westminster Assembly of Divines,* 3rd ed. Edmonton: Still Waters Revival Books, 1993.
Hodge, A. A. *Evangelical Theology.* Edinburgh: The Banner of Truth Trust, 1976.
_____. *Outlines of Theology,* rev. and enlar. ed. Edinburgh: The Banner of Truth Trust, 1972.
_____. *The Atonement.* Memphis: Footstool Publications, 1987.
Hodge, Charles. *A Commentary on 1 & 2 Corinthians.* Edinburgh: The Banner of

Truth Trust, 1974.
_____. *A Commentary on Ephesians.* Edinburgh: The Banner of Truth Trust, 1964.
_____. *A Commentary on Romans.* Edinburgh: The Banner of Truth Trust, 1972.
_____. *Systematic Theology.* Grand Rapids: Wm. B. Eerdmans Publishing Co., 1986.
Hodges, Zane C. *Absolutely Free!* Dallas: Redencion Viva, 1989.
Hoekema, Anthony A. *Saved by Grace.* Grand Rapids: Wm. B. Eerdmans Publishing Co., 1989.
Hoeksema, Gertrude. *Therefore Have I Spoken.* Grand Rapids: Reformed Free Publishing Association, 1969.
Hoeksema, Herman. *God's Eternal Good Pleasure.* Ed. and rev. by Homer C. Hoeksema. Grand Rapids: Reformed Free Publishing Association, 1979.
_____. *Reformed Dogmatics.* Grand Rapids: Reformed Free Publishing Association, 1966.
_____. *The Wonder of Grace,* 2nd ed. Grand Rapids: Reformed Free Publishing Association, 1982.
_____. *Whosoever Will.* Grand Rapids: Reformed Free Publishing Association, 1945.
Hoeksema, Homer C. *God So Loved The World.* South Holland: The Evangelism Committee, Protestant Reformed Church, n.d.
_____. *The Voice of Our Fathers.* Grand Rapids: Reformed Free Publishing Association, 1980.
Hoitenga, Dewey J. *John Calvin and the Will: A Critique and Corrective.* Grand Rapids: Baker Books, 1997.
Horton, Michael S., ed. *Christ the Lord: The Reformation and Lordship Salvation.* Grand Rapids: Baker Book House, 1992.
Houck, Steven R. *God's Sovereignty in Salvation.* Lansing: Peace Protestant Reformed Church, n.d.
_____. *The Bondage of the Will.* Lansing: Peace Protestant Reformed Church, n.d.
Hughes, Paul L., and James F. Larkin, eds., *Tudor Royal Proclamations,* Vol. I: *The Early Tudors (1485–1553).* New Haven and London: Yale University Press, 1964.
_____., eds. *Tudor Royal Proclamations,* Vol. II: *The Later Tudors (1553–1587).* New Haven and London: Yale University Press, 1969.
Hulse, Erroll, et al. *Our Baptist Heritage.* Leeds: Reformation Today Trust, 1993.
Hutson, Curtis. *Why I Disagree With All Five Points of Calvinism.* Murfreesboro: Sword of the Lord Publishers, 1980.
Israel, Jonathan. *The Dutch Republic.* New York: Oxford University Press, 1995.
Jewett, Paul K. *Election and Predestination.* Grand Rapids: Wm. B. Eerdmans Publishing Co., 1985.
Johns, Kenneth D. *Election: Love Before Time.* Phillipsburg: Presbyterian and Reformed Publishing Co., 1976.
Johnson, Garrett P. "The Myth of Common Grace." *The Trinity Review,* March/April 1987.
Jones, William. *The History of the Christian Church,* 5th ed. Gallatin: Church History Research and Archives, 1983.
Keener, Forrest L. *Grace Not Calvinism.* Lawton: The Watchman Press, 1992.
Kelly, Douglas F. *The Emergence of Liberty in the Modern World.* Phillipsburg: Presbyterian and Reformed Publishing Co., 1992.

Kelly, Kent. *Inside the Tulip Controversy.* Southern Pines: Calvary Press, 1986.
Kendall, R. T. *Calvin and English Calvinism.* Oxford: Oxford University Press, 1979.
Kennedy, D. James. *Why I Am a Presbyterian.* Fort Lauderdale: Coral Ridge Ministries, n.d.
Kershner, Frederick D. *Pioneers of Christian Thought.* Freeport: Books for Libraries Press, 1958.
Kistemaker, Simon. *Calvinism: Its History, Principles and Perspectives.* Grand Rapids: Baker Book House, 1966.
Klein, William W. *The New Chosen People.* Grand Rapids: Zondervan Publishing House, 1990.
Klooster, Fred H. *Calvin's Doctrine of Predestination,* 2nd ed. Grand Rapids: Baker Book House, 1977.
Knox, John. *The First Blast of the Trumpet Against the Monstrous Regiment of Women.* Dallas: Presbyterian Heritage Publications, 1993.
Kober, Manford E. *Divine Election or Human Effort?* n.p., n.d.
Kruithof, Bastian. *The High Points of Calvinism.* Grand Rapids: Baker Book House, 1949.
Kuiper, R. B. *For Whom Did Christ Die?* Grand Rapids: Wm. B. Eerdmans Publishing Co., 1959.
_____. *God-Centered Evangelism.* London: The Banner of Truth Trust, 1966.
_____. *To Be or Not to Be Reformed.* Grand Rapids: Zondervan Publishing House, 1959.
Kuyper, Abraham. *Lectures on Calvinism.* Grand Rapids: Wm. B. Eerdmans Publishing Co., 1931.
Lally, Steve. "Overcoming the #1 Prostate Problem." *Prevention,* January 1992.
Leff, Gordon. *Bradwardine and the Pelagians.* Cambridge: Cambridge University Press, 1957.
Leith, John H. *Introduction to the Reformed Tradition,* rev. ed. Atlanta: John Knox Press, 1981.
Lenski, R. C. H. *The Interpretation of St. Matthew's Gospel.* Minneapolis: Augsburg Publishing House, 1961.
_____. *The Interpretation of St. Paul's First & Second Epistles to the Corinthians.* Minneapolis: Augsburg Publishing House, 1963.
Lescelius, Robert H. *Lordship Salvation: Some Crucial Questions and Answers.* Asheville: Revival Literature, 1992.
Lessnoff, Michael H. *The Spirit of Capitalism and the Protestant Ethic: An Enquiry into the Weber Thesis.* Hants: Edward Elgar Publishing, 1994.
Lightner, Robert P. *The Death Christ Died.* Des Plaines: Regular Baptist Press, 1967.
Lindsay, Thomas M. *A History of the Reformation,* 2nd ed. Edinburgh: T & T Clark, 1907.
Lloyd-Jones, Martyn. *Saved in Eternity*, ed. Christopher Catherwood. Westchester: Crossway Books, 1988.
Long, Gary D. *Definite Atonement.* Rochester: Backus Book Publishers, 1977.
Lumpkin, William L. *Baptist Confessions of Faith,* rev. ed. Valley Forge: Judson Press, 1969.
Luther, Martin. *The Bondage of the Will.* Trans. by J. I. Packer and O. R. Johnson. Grand Rapids: Fleming H. Revell, 1957.

MacArthur, John F. *Faith Works: The Gospel According to the Apostles.* Dallas: Word Publishing, 1993.
_____. *Saved Without a Doubt.* Wheaton: Victor Books, 1992.
_____. *The Gospel According to Jesus.* Grand Rapids: Zondervan Publishing House, 1988.
_____. *The Gospel According to Jesus,* rev. and expand. ed. Grand Rapids: Zondervan Publishing House, 1994.
MacLean, William. *Arminianism: Another Gospel.* Pensacola: Chapel Library, 1976.
Machen, J. Gresham. *The Christian View of Man.* Edinburgh: The Banner of Truth Trust, 1965.
_____. *What is Faith?* Edinburgh: The Banner of Truth Trust, 1991.
Manton, Thomas. *A Commentary on Jude.* Edinburgh: The Banner of Truth Trust, 1958.
Martin, A. W. *The Practical Implications of Calvinism.* Edinburgh: The Banner of Truth Trust, 1979.
Mason, Roy. *What is to Be, Will Be.* n.p., n.d.
Mathison, Keith A. *Dispensationalism: Rightly Dividing the People of God?* Phillipsburg: Presbyterian and Reformed Publishing Co., 1995.
McCulloh, Gerald O., ed. *Man's Faith and Freedom.* Nashville: Abingdon Press, 1962.
McFetridge, N. S. *Calvinism in History.* Edmonton: Still Waters Revival Books, 1989.
McGlothlin, W. J. *Baptist Confessions of Faith.* Philadelphia: American Baptist Publications Society, 1911.
McGrath, Alister E. *A Life of John Calvin.* Oxford: Blackwell Publishers, 1990.
_____. *Reformation Thought,* 2nd ed. Grand Rapids: Baker, 1993.
_____. *The Intellectual Origins of the European Reformation.* Grand Rapids: Baker, 1987.
McKinley, O. Glenn. *Where Two Creeds Meet.* Kansas City: Beacon Hill Press, 1959.
McNeil, John T. *The History and Character of Calvinism,* paperback ed. London: Oxford University Press, 1966.
Mead, Frank S. *Handbook of Denominations in the United States,* 8th ed. Rev. by Samuel S. Hill. Nashville: Abingdon Press, 1985.
Meeter, H. Henry. *The Basic Ideas of Calvinism,* 6th ed. Grand Rapids: Baker, 1990.
Mell, Patrick H. *A Southern Baptist Looks at Predestination.* Cape Coral: Christian Gospel Foundation, n.d.
_____. *The Biblical Doctrine of Calvinism.* Cape Coral: Christian Gospel Foundation, 1988.
Miley, John. *Systematic Theology.* Peabody: Hendrickson Publishers, 1989.
Miller, Andrew. *Miller's Church History.* Grand Rapids: Zondervan Publishing House, n.d.
Moffat, James. *Predestination.* Lancaster: Charles W. Duty & Sons, n.d.
Moo, Douglas. *The Epistle to the Romans.* Grand Rapids: Wm. B. Eerdmans Publishing Co., 1996.
Morey, Robert A. *Studies in the Atonement.* Southbridge: Crowne Publications, 1989.

BIBLIOGRAPHY

Morris, Leon. *The First and Second Epistles to the Thessalonians,* rev. ed. Grand Rapids: Wm. B. Eerdmans Publishing Co., 1991.

Morton, Carl. "Does the Bible Teach Election?" *The Berea Baptist Banner,* January 5, 1995.

Mosheim, John Laurence. *An Ecclesiastical History, Ancient and Modern.* Trans. by Archibald MacLaine. Cincinnati: Applegate & Co., 1854.

Motyer, Stephen. *Israel in the Plan of God.* Leicester: Inter-Varsity Press, 1989.

Muller, Richard A. *Christ and the Decree.* Grand Rapids: Baker Book House, 1988.

_____. *God, Creation, and Providence in the Thought of Jacob Arminius.* Grand Rapids: Baker Book House, 1991.

Murray, Iain H. *Spurgeon v. Hyper-Calvinism.* Edinburgh: The Banner of Truth Trust, 1995.

_____. *The Forgotten Spurgeon.* Edinburgh: The Banner of Truth Trust, 1978.

_____. *The Invitation System.* Edinburgh: The Banner of Truth Trust, 1967.

_____. *The Life of Arthur W. Pink.* Edinburgh: The Banner of Truth Trust, 1981.

_____. *The Life of John Murray.* Edinburgh: The Banner of Truth Trust, 1982.

Murray, John. *Redemption Accomplished and Applied.* Grand Rapids: Wm. B. Eerdmans Publishing Co., 1955.

_____. *The Epistle to the Romans.* Grand Rapids: Wm. B. Eerdmans Publishing Co., 1959, 1965.

Murray John, and Ned B. Stonehouse. *The Free Offer of the Gospel.* n.p., n.d.

Myers, A. R., ed. *English Historical Documents (1327–1515),* vol. 4 of *English Historical Documents.* Ed. by David C. Douglas. New York: Oxford University Press, 1969.

Ness, Christopher. *An Antidote Against Arminianism.* Huntington: Paragon Printing Co., 1982.

Nettles, Thomas J. *By His Grace and for His Glory.* Grand Rapids: Baker Book House, 1986.

Nettleton, David. *Chosen to Salvation.* Schaumburg: Regular Baptist Press, 1983.

Neve, J. L. *A History of Christian Thought.* Philadelphia: The Muhlenberg Press, 1946.

New Catholic Encyclopedia. New York: McGraw-Hill Book Company, 1967.

New Dictionary of Theology. Downers Grove: Inter-Varsity Press, 1988.

Newman, A. H. *A Manual of Church History.* Valley Forge: Judson Press, 1933.

Nicoll, W. Robertson, ed. *The Expositor's Greek Testament.* Grand Rapids: Wm. B. Eerdmans Publishing Co., n.d.

Noll, Mark A., ed. *The Princeton Theology.* Phillipsburg: Presbyterian and Reformed Publishing Co., 1983.

Norris Bible Baptist Institute, *1985–1986 Catalog.*

North, Gary. *Dominion and Common Grace.* Tyler: Institute for Christian Economics, 1987.

Ohio Baptist College, *1992–1994 Catalog.*

Ostling, Richard N. "The Seconder Founder of the Faith." *Time,* September 29, 1986.

Otis, John M. *Who is the Genuine Christian?* n.p., n.d.

Owen, John. *The Death of Christ,* volume 10 of *The Works of John Owen.* Ed. by William H. Goold. Edinburgh: The Banner of Truth Trust, 1967.

Packer, J. I. *Evangelism and the Sovereignty of God.* Downers Grove: Inter-Varsity

Press, 1961.

_____. *Introductory Essay to John Owen's The Death of Death in the Death of Christ.* Pensacola: Chapel Library, n.d.

Palmer, Edwin H. *The Five Points of Calvinism,* enlar. ed. Grand Rapids: Baker Book House, 1980.

Parker, T. H. L. *John Calvin.* Herts: Lion Publishing, 1975.

Pendleton, James M. *Christian Doctrines.* Valley Forge: Judson Press, 1906.

Peterson, Robert A. *Calvin's Doctrine of the Atonement.* Phillipsburg: Presbyterian and Reformed Publishing Co., 1983.

Phelps, Fred. "The Five Points of Calvinism." *The Berea Baptist Banner,* February 5, 1990.

Phillips, Dan. "The Atonement." *The Baptist Examiner,* September 15, 1990.

Pink, Arthur W. *An Exposition of Hebrews.* Grand Rapids: Baker Book House, 1954.

_____. *Comfort for Christians.* Grand Rapids: Baker Book House, 1976.

_____. *Eternal Security.* Grand Rapids: Baker Books, 1974.

_____. *Exposition of the Gospel of John.* Grand Rapids: Zondervan Publishing House, 1975.

_____. *Gleanings from Paul.* Chicago: Moody Press, 1967.

_____. *Gleanings from the Scriptures.* Chicago: Moody Press, 1969.

_____. *Gleanings in Exodus.* Chicago: Moody Press, 1981.

_____. *Gleanings in Genesis.* Chicago: Moody Press, 1950.

_____. *Gleanings in Joshua.* Chicago: Moody Press, 1964.

_____. *Gleanings in the Godhead.* Chicago: Moody Press, 1975.

_____. *Interpretation of the Scriptures.* Grand Rapids: Baker Book House, 1972.

_____. *Letters of Arthur W. Pink.* Edinburgh: The Banner of Truth Trust, n.d.

_____. *Letters to a Young Pastor.* Grandville: The Grandville Protestant Reformed Evangelism Committee, 1993.

_____. *Practical Christianity.* Grand Rapids: Guardian Press, 1974.

_____. *Present-Day Evangelism.* Mifflinburg: Bible Truth Depot, n.d.

_____. *Spiritual Union and Communion.* Grand Rapids: Baker Book House, 1971.

_____. *Studies in Saving Faith.* Petersburg: Pilgrim Brethren Press, 1992.

_____. *The Application of the Scriptures.* Canton: Free Grace Publications, 1977.

_____. *The Divine Covenants.* Grand Rapids: Baker Book House, 1973.

_____. *The Doctrine of Salvation.* Grand Rapids: Baker Book House, 1975.

_____. *The Doctrine of Sanctification.* Swengel: Reiner Publications, 1975.

_____. *The Doctrines of Election and Justification.* Grand Rapids: Baker Book House, 1974.

_____. *The Holy Spirit.* Grand Rapids: Baker Book House, 1978.

_____. *The Satisfaction of Christ.* Grand Rapids: Zondervan Publishing House, 1955.

_____. *The Sovereignty of God,* rev. ed. Edinburgh: The Banner of Truth Trust, 1961.

_____. *The Sovereignty of God,* 4th ed. Grand Rapids: Baker Book House, 1949.

Pinnock, Clark H., ed. *Grace Unlimited.* Minneapolis: Bethany House Publishers, 1975.

_____., ed. *The Grace of God, The Will of Man.* Grand Rapids: Zondervan Publishing House, 1989.

Piper, John. *The Justification of God,* 2nd ed. Grand Rapids: Baker Books, 1993.

Plantinga, Alvin C. *God, Freedom, and Evil.* Grand Rapids: Wm. B. Eerdmans Publishing Co., 1977.

Pollard, Alfred W., ed. *Records of the English Bible.* London: Oxford University Press, 1911.

Potter, G. R., and M. Greengrass. *John Calvin.* New York: St. Martin's Press, 1983.

Prestwich, Menna. *International Calvinism.* Oxford: Oxford University Press, 1985.

Pugh, Curtis. "Perseverance and Preservation of the Saints." *The Berea Baptist Banner,* May 5, 1993.

_____. "Six Reasons I Love the Doctrines of Grace." *The Berea Baptist Banner,* November 5, 1994.

_____. "The Biblicist Position." *The Berea Baptist Banner,* July 5, 1993.

Ramm, Bernard. *Protestant Biblical Interpretation,* 3rd rev. ed. Grand Rapids: Baker Book House, 1970.

Reformed Bible College, *1990–1992 Catalog.*

Reformed Theological Seminary, *1990–1991 Catalog.*

Reisinger, Ernest C. *The Carnal Christian?* Edinburgh: The Banner of Truth Trust, n.d.

Reti, Lawrence. "15 Rotten Fruits of the Universal Atonement Theory." *The Berea Baptist Banner,* July 5, 1997.

Rice, John R. *Hyper-Calvinism: a False Doctrine.* Murfreesboro: Sword of the Lord Publishers, 1970.

_____. *Predestinated for Hell? NO!* Murfreesboro: Sword of the Lord Publishers, 1958.

Rice, N. L. *God Sovereign and Man Free.* Harrisonburg: Sprinkle Publications, 1985.

Rice, Richard. *God's Foreknowledge and Man's Free Will.* Minneapolis: Bethany House Publishers, 1985.

Richards, James. *Lectures on Mental Philosophy and Theology.* New York: M. W. Dodd, 1846.

Rippon, John. *A Brief Memoir of the Life and Writings of the Late Rev. John Gill, D.D.* Harrisonburg: Gano Books, 1992.

Robbins, John W. "Our Comrades at Calvin College." *The Trinity Review,* November 1996.

_____. "The Gospel According to John MacArthur," part 1. *The Trinity Review,* April 1993.

_____. "The Gospel According to John MacArthur," part 2. *The Trinity Review,* May 1993.

_____. "What is the Gospel?" *The Trinity Review,* March/April 1988.

_____., ed. *Gordon H. Clark: Personal Recollections.* Jefferson: The Trinity Foundation, 1989.

Roberts, E. R. "The Public Invitation." *The Berea Baptist Banner,* April 5, 1988.

Robertson, Archibald Thomas. *Word Pictures in the New Testament.* Nashville: Broadman Press, 1930.

Robinson, Robert. *Ecclesiastical Researches.* Gallatin: Church History Research & Archives, 1984.

Rose, Ben Lacy. *T.U.L.I.P.: The Five Disputed Points of Calvinism,* 2nd ed. Franklin: Providence House Publishers, 1996.

Ross, Tom. *Abandoned Truth: The Doctrines of Grace.* Xenia: Providence Baptist Church, 1991.

_____. *Elementary Eschatology: A Study of Premillennial Prophecy.* n.p., n.d.

Ross, Bob L. *The History and Heresies of Hardshellism.* Pasadena: Pilgrim Publications, n.d.

_____. *The Killing Effects of Calvinism.* Pasadena: Pilgrim Publications, n.d.

Rowley, H. H. *The Biblical Doctrine of Election.* London: Lutterworth Press, 1950.

Ruckman, Peter S. *Hyper-Calvinism.* Pensacola: Bible Baptist Bookstore, 1984.

_____. *The History of the New Testament Church.* Pensacola: Bible Baptist Bookstore, 1982–1984.

_____. *Why I Am Not a Calvinist.* Pensacola: Bible Baptist Bookstore, 1997.

Ryrie, Charles C. *So Great Salvation.* Wheaton: Victor Books, 1989.

Schaff, Philip. *History of the Christian Church.* Grand Rapids: Wm. B. Eerdmans Publishing Co., 1910.

_____. *The Creeds of Christendom,* 6th ed. Grand Rapids: Baker Book House, 1990.

Scholasticus, Socrates. *Ecclesiastical History.*

Schreiner, Thomas R., and Bruce A. Ware, eds. *The Grace of God, the Bondage of the Will.* Grand Rapids: Baker Books, 1995.

Scott, Otto. *The Great Christian Revolution.* Windsor: The Reformer Library, 1994.

Scott, Thomas. *The Articles of the Synod of Dort.* Harrisonburg: Sprinkle Publications, 1993.

Seaton, W. J. *The Five Points of Calvinism.* Edinburgh: The Banner of Truth Trust, 1970.

Sell, Alan P. F. *The Great Debate.* Grand Rapids: Baker Book House, 1982.

Sellers, C. Norman. *Election and Perseverance.* Miami Springs: Schoettle Publishing Co., 1987.

Selph, Robert B. *Southern Baptists and the Doctrine of Election.* Harrisonburg: Sprinkle Publications, 1988.

Shank, Robert L. *Elect in the Son.* Springfield: Westcott Publishers, 1970.

_____. *Life in the Son,* 2nd ed. Springfield: Westcott Publishers, 1961.

Shedd, William G. T. *Calvinism: Pure and Mixed.* Edinburgh: The Banner of Truth Trust, 1986.

_____. *Dogmatic Theology,* 2nd ed. Nashville: Thomas Nelson Publishers, 1980.

Shelton, L. R. *Eternal Security: God's Preservation—Man's Perseverance.* Pensacola: Mt. Zion Publications, n.d.

Showers, Renald E. *There Really is a Difference.* Bellmawr: The Friends of Israel Gospel Ministry, 1990.

Simmons, Thomas P. *A Systematic Study of Bible Doctrine,* 6th ed. Clarksville: Bible Baptist Books & Supply, 1979.

Singer, C. Gregg. *JOHN CALVIN: His Roots and Fruits.* Atlanta: A Press, 1989.

Slaatte, Howard A. *The Arminian Arm of Theology.* Washington D.C.: University Press of America, 1979.

Smeaton, George. *Christ's Doctrine of the Atonement,* 2nd ed. Edinburgh: The Banner of Truth Trust, 1991.

_____. *The Doctrine of the Atonement According to the Apostles.* Peabody: Hendrickson Publishers, 1988.

Smith, H. Maynard. *Pre-Reformation England.* New York: Russell & Russell, 1963.
Smith, Morton H. *Reformed Evangelism.* Clinton: Multi-communication Ministries, 1975.
Smylie, James H. *A Brief History of the Presbyterians.* Louisville: Geneva Press, 1996.
Sozomen, Salaminius. *Ecclesiastical History.*
Spencer, Duane Edward. *TULIP: The Five Points of Calvinism in the Light of Scripture.* Grand Rapids: Baker Book House, 1979.
_____. *Word Keys Which Unlock Scripture: Draw.* San Antonio: Word of Grace, 1974.
Sproul, R. C. *Chosen by God.* Wheaton: Tyndale House, 1986.
_____. *Grace Unknown.* Grand Rapids: Baker Books, 1997.
_____. *Willing to Believe.* Grand Rapids: Baker Books, 1997.
Spurgeon, Charles H. *Election.* Pasadena: Pilgrim Publications, 1978.
_____. *For Whom Did Christ Die?* Pasadena: Pilgrim Publications, n.d.
_____. *Free Will—A Slave.* Canton: Free Grace Publications, 1977.
_____. *Infant Salvation.* Pasadena: Pilgrim Publications, n.d.
_____. *Spurgeon's Sermons on Sovereignty.* Pasadena: Pilgrim Publications, 1990.
_____. *Spurgeon's Sovereign Grace Sermons.* Edmonton: Still Waters Revival Books, 1990.
_____. *The Metropolitan Tabernacle: its History and Work.* Pasadena: Pilgrim Publications, 1990.
_____. *The Soul Winner.* Grand Rapids: Wm. B. Eerdmans Publishing Co., 1963.
_____. *The Two Wesleys.* Pasadena: Pilgrim Publications, 1975.
_____., ed. *Exposition of the Doctrines of Grace.* Pasadena: Pilgrim Publications, n.d.
Stam, Cornelius R. *Divine Election and Human Responsibility.* Chicago: Berean Bible Society, 1994.
Steele, David N., and Curtis C. Thomas, *The Five Points of Calvinism.* Phillipsburg: Presbyterian and Reformed Publishing Co., 1963.
Steinmetz, David. *Calvin in Context.* Oxford: Oxford University Press, 1995.
Stonehouse, Ned B. *J. Gresham Machen: A Biographical Memoir*, 3rd ed. Edinburgh: The Banner of Truth Trust, 1987.
Storms, C. Samuel. *Chosen for Life.* Grand Rapids: Baker Book House, 1987.
Strong, Augustus H. *Systematic Theology.* Valley Forge: Judson Press, 1907.
Sumner, Robert L. *An Examination of Tulip.* Brownsburg: Biblical Evangelism, 1972.
Talbot, Kenneth G., and W. Gary Crampton. *Calvinism, Hyper-Calvinism and Arminianism.* Edmonton: Still Waters Revival Books, 1990.
Telford, Andrew. *Subjects of Sovereignty.* Boca Raton: by the author, 1948.
Tertullian. *Apology.*
"The Baptist Examiner Forum I." *The Baptist Examiner,* June 23, 1990.
"The Baptist Examiner Forum II." *The Baptist Examiner,* February 18, 1989; March 18, 1989; September 16, 1989.
"The Baptist Examiner Pulpit Forum." *The Baptist Examiner,* December 1, 1995; August 1, 1996.
"The Berea Baptist Banner Forum." *The Berea Baptist Banner,* March 5, 1989; August 5, 1989; October 5, 1989; March 5, 1990; May 5, 1990; August 5,

1990; August 5, 1992; September 5, 1992; November 5, 1992; February 5, 1995; June 5, 1997; October 5, 1997; June 5, 1998; July 5, 1998.

The Biblical and Historical Faith of Baptists on God's Sovereignty. Ashland: Calvary Baptist Church, n.d.

The Cambridge History of the Bible, Vol. 2: *The West from the Fathers to the Reformation.* Ed. by G. W. H. Lampe. Cambridge: Cambridge University Press, 1969.

The Catholic Encyclopedia. New York: The Encyclopedia Press, 1913.

The First London Confession of Faith With an Appendix by Benjamin Cox. New York: Backus Book Publishers, 1981.

The New Schaff-Herzog Encyclopedia of Religious Knowledge. Grand Rapids: Baker Book House, 1949–1950.

The Oxford Dictionary of the Christian Church, 2nd ed. London: Oxford University Press, 1974.

The Oxford Encyclopedia of the Reformation. New York: Oxford University Press, 1996.

The Register of the Company of Pastors of Geneva in the Time of Calvin. Trans. and ed. by Philip E. Hughes. Grand Rapids: Wm. B. Eerdmans Publishing Co., 1966.

The Three Forms of Unity. Grand Rapids: Protestant Reformed Churches in America, 1991.

The Westminster Dictionary of Christian Theology. Philadelphia: The Westminster Press, 1983.

The Westminster Confession of Faith. Philadelphia: Great Commission Publications, n.d.

The Zondervan Pictorial Bible Dictionary. Grand Rapids: Zondervan Publishing House, 1967.

Thiessen, Henry C. *Introductory Lectures in Systematic Theology.* Grand Rapids: Wm. B. Eerdmans Publishing Co., 1949.

Thomas, Helen. "Jacob and Esau—'rigidly Calvinistic'?" *Studies in English Literature 1500–1900* 9 (Spring 1969).

Thompson, Bard. *Humanists and Reformers: A History of the Renaissance and Reformation.* Grand Rapids: Wm. B. Eerdmans Publishing Co., 1996.

Tolley, S. T. "Is Gospel Faith Necessary in Order to Be Saved in Heaven?" *The Christian Baptist,* April 1996.

_____. "Is Gospel Faith Necessary in Order to Be Saved in Heaven?" *The Christian Baptist,* August 1996.

_____. "Who's Who Among Primitive Baptists?" *The Christian Baptist,* August/September 1989.

Toon, Peter. *The Emergence of Hyper-Calvinism in English Nonconformity, 1689–1765.* London: The Olive Tree, 1967.

Torbet, Robert G. *A History of the Baptists,* 3rd ed. Valley Forge: Judson Press, 1963.

Tyacke, Nicholas. *Anti-Calvinists: the Rise of English Arminianism c. 1590–1640.* Oxford: Clarendon Press, 1987.

VanOverloop, Ronald. "Calvinism and Missions: 1. Total Depravity." *Standard Bearer,* September 15, 1992.

_____. "Calvinism and Missions: 2. Unconditional Election." *Standard Bearer,* January 15, 1993.

Vedder, Henry C. *A Short History of the Baptists*. Valley Forge: Judson Press, 1907.
Verduin, Leonard. *The Anatomy of a Hybrid*. Sarasota: The Christian Hymnary Publishers, 1976.
_____. *The Reformers and Their Stepchildren*. Grand Rapids: Baker Book House, 1964.
Vincent, Marvin R. *Word Studies in the Greek New Testament*. McLean: MacDonald Publishing Co., n.d.
Voltaire. *The Works of Voltaire*. New York: E. R. DuMont, 1901.
Waite, Donald A. *Calvin's Error of Limited Atonement*. Collingswood: The Bible For Today, 1978.
Wakeman, Henry O. *An Introduction to the History of the Church of England*, 7th ed. London: Rivingtons, 1912.
Walker, Williston. *John Calvin: The Organizer of Reformed Protestantism*. New York: Schocken Books, 1969.
Wallace, Ronald S. *Calvin, Geneva, and the Reformation*. Grand Rapids: Baker Book House, 1990.
Walvoord, John F. *The Millennial Kingdom*. Grand Rapids: Zondervan Publishing House, 1959.
Warfield, Benjamin B. *Biblical and Theological Studies*. Ed. by Samuel G. Craig. Philadelphia: Presbyterian and Reformed Publishing Co., 1968.
_____. *Calvin and Augustine*. Ed. by Samuel G. Craig. Philadelphia: Presbyterian and Reformed Publishing Co., 1956.
_____. *The Plan of Salvation*. Boonton: Simpson Publishing Company, 1989.
_____. *The Westminster Assembly and its Work*. Edmonton: Still Waters Revival Books, 1991.
Warren, Jack. "For Sovereign Grace; Against Arminian Heresy." *Baptist Evangel*, January–March 1997.
_____. "More on Particular Baptists." *Baptist Evangel*, January 1994.
Webb, R. A. *The Theology of Infant Salvation*. Harrisonburg: Sprinkle Publications, 1981.
Weber, Max. *The Protestant Ethic and the Spirit of Capitalism*. Trans. by Talcott Parsons. New York: Charles Scribner's Sons, 1958.
Wells, David F., ed. *Dutch Reformed Theology*. Grand Rapids: Baker Book House, 1989.
_____., ed. *Southern Reformed Theology*. Grand Rapids: Baker Book House, 1989.
_____., ed. *The Princeton Theology*. Grand Rapids: Baker Book House, 1989.
Wells, Tom. *Faith: The Gift of God*. Edinburgh: The Banner of Truth Trust, 1983.
Wendel, Francois. *Calvin: Origins and Development of His Religious Thought*. Trans. by Philip Mairet. Grand Rapids: Baker Books, 1997.
Wesley, John. *A Compend of Wesley's Theology*. Ed. by Robert W. Burtner and Robert E. Chiles. Nashville: Abingdon Press, 1954.
Westcott, Brooke F. *A General View of the History of the English Bible*, 3rd ed. Rev. by William A. Wright. London: Macmillan and Co., 1905.
Westminster Theological Seminary, *1990–1992 Catalog*.
Whitefield, George. *Letter to John Wesley on Election*. Canton: Free Grace Publications, 1977.
Wilcox, Archer C. *Messianic Credentials of Jesus the Christ*. Burlington: Crown Publications, 1986.

Wilkins, James. *Foreknowledge, Election, Predestination in the Light of Soul-Winning.* Mansfield: New Testament Ministries, 1985.
Williams, C. H., ed. *English Historical Documents (1485–1558),* vol. 5 of *English Historical Documents.* Ed. by David C. Douglas. New York: Oxford University Press, 1971.
Williams, E. N. *A Documentary History of England,* Vol. 2: *(1559–1931).* Baltimore: Penguin Books, 1965.
Williams, H. L., and J. E. North. *Calvin versus Hyper-Spurgeonism.* E. Sussex: Berith Publications, 1997.
Wilson, Joseph M. "Does Prayer Change Things?" *The Baptist Examiner,* June 8, 1991.
_____. "From the Editor." *The Baptist Examiner,* June 22, 1991.
_____. "From the Editor." *The Baptist Examiner,* September 14, 1991.
_____. "God's Plan of Salvation." *The Baptist Examiner,* August 4, 1990.
_____. "How is the Atonement Limited?" *The Baptist Examiner,* December 9, 1989.
_____. "I'm Going to Heaven Someday." *The Baptist Examiner,* June 24, 1989.
_____. "Is There an Arminian Gospel?" *The Baptist Examiner,* December 7, 1991.
_____. "Not Appointed to Wrath, But to Salvation." *The Baptist Examiner,* February 2, 1991.
_____. "Soul Winning." *The Baptist Examiner,* February 15, 1992.
_____. "Soul Winning and the Doctrines of Grace." *The Baptist Examiner,* February 29, 1992.
_____. "Sovereign Grace Versus Arminianism." *The Baptist Examiner,* July 22, 1989.
_____. "Sovereign Grace View and Arminian View of Salvation." *The Baptist Examiner,* July 18, 1992.
_____. "The World's Three Great Errors About the Church." *The Baptist Examiner,* November 23, 1991.
Wright, R. K. McGregor. *No Place for Sovereignty.* Downers Grove: InterVarsity Press, 1996.
Wuest, Kenneth S. *Ephesians and Colossians in the Greek New Testament.* Grand Rapids: Wm. B. Eerdmans Publishing Co., 1953.
_____. *Hebrews in the Greek New Testament.* Grand Rapids: Wm. B. Eerdmans Publishing Co., 1947.
Younce, Max. *Not Chosen to Salvation.* Madison: by the author, n.d.
Zanchius, Jerom. *The Doctrine of Absolute Predestination.* Trans. by Augustus M. Toplady. Grand Rapids: Baker Book House, 1977.
Zeller, George W. *The Dangers of Reformed Theology.* Middletown: The Middletown Bible Church, n.d.
Zweig, Stefan. *The Right to Heresy.* London: Cassell and Company, 1936.

SUBJECT INDEX

Absolute depravity–189
Academy of Saumur–147
Act of Abjuration–118
Act of Supremacy–162, 165
Act of Toleration–180
Act of Uniformity–165
Adoption–383
Allegorical method–48, 53, 54
Amillennialism–15, 33, 35, 53, 112, 368, 379, 501
Amsterdam–125, 131, 133, 134, 135
Anabaptists–76, 80, 81, 88, 101, 107, 118, 121, 130
Angels–366, 367, 381, 382, 423, 472
Anglicanism–159, 174
Antinomianism–30, 258, 562, 580, 590
Apocrypha–53, 119
Arianism–8, 45, 92, 410
Arminianism–5, 10, 12, 14, 17, 18, 19, 20, 28, 30, 34, 49, 50, 115, 116, 133, 138, 139, 141, 142, 148, 149, 150, 152, 153, 154, 156, 168, 169, 170, 202, 214, 215, 269, 285, 325, 376, 378, 385, 388, 390, 391, 393, 402, 403, 406, 410, 411, 412, 422, 423, 424, 456, 460, 483, 484, 485, 502, 516, 524, 529, 530, 540, 541, 543, 549, 552, 562, 563, 564-569, 570, 571, 572, 573, 574, 579, 580, 581, 585, 588, 589, 590, 593, 594, 596
Assurance of salvation–130, 403, 586, 591, 595, 596
Athanasian Creed–92
Atheism–4, 11
Atonement of Christ–52, 128, 135, 154, 252, 297, 374, 398, 405, 406, 407, 409, 411, 413, 414-422, 423, 424, 425, 426, 427, 428, 429, 430, 431, 433, 435, 442, 443, 451, 456, 457, 459, 460, 461, 466, 468, 469, 470, 471, 475, 539
Atonement theories–414-415
Auburn Affirmation–139
Augsburg Confession–67, 73
Augsburg Diet–73
Augsburg Interim–73
Augustinianism–38, 39, 40, 49, 52, 54, 60, 62, 103, 143, 410
Back loading the Gospel–569, 577
Baptism–15, 23, 28, 46, 49, 51, 52, 54, 55, 60, 76, 87, 98, 110, 111, 121, 130, 144, 181, 398, 400, 401, 411, 430, 549
Baptismal regeneration–54, 55, 92, 162
Baptist Confessions–178-182
Baptists–5, 12, 13, 14, 15-28, 29, 31, 32, 33, 34, 35, 38, 41, 42, 43, 64, 76, 88, 91, 92, 99, 140, 141, 143, 144, 145, 146, 147, 158, 174, 178, 179, 180, 181, 182, 244, 248, 262, 276, 277, 289, 290, 301, 302, 350, 353, 357, 360, 361, 377, 393, 395, 398, 399, 400, 401, 405, 421, 502, 520, 526, 528, 529, 530, 531, 534, 536, 537, 542, 543, 549, 574, 580
Belgic Confession of Faith–122, 136, 137, 148, 149, 154, 157
Biblicists–19
Bishops Bible–166
Book of Common Prayer–164, 165, 175
Brethren of the Common Life–120
Buddhism–48
Calling–266, 329, 349, 374, 375, 385, 386, 387, 389, 492, 493, 495, 496, 497, 518, 524
Calminians–19
Calvin Theological Seminary–39, 104, 158, 286, 562
Calviphobia–19

Cambridge University–166, 168
Canons of Dort–148, 156-159, 182, 188, 207, 244, 296, 400, 408, 460, 478, 558, 562
Capitalism–11
Carnal Christians–580, 581
Chance–279
Charismatics–17
Chiliasts–53, 112
Chosen to salvation–348-364
Christian Reconstructionism–145
Christian Reformed Church–291, 399, 498, 499
Christian History magazine–39
Church and State–12, 44, 45, 46, 47, 73, 83, 84, 87, 89, 100, 105, 122, 130, 149, 158, 159, 166, 173
Church Fathers–15, 41, 42, 43, 78, 100, 248
Church of England–140, 162, 168, 170, 172
Closet-Calvinists–25, 147
Common grace–35, 471, 497, 498, 499
Communism–11
Congregationalism–24, 180
Conscience–207, 208
Convocation of Canterbury–160, 165
Corporate election–368, 379
Council of Carthage–52, 58
Council of Milevis–52
Council of Nicaea–45
Council of Trent–63, 64, 106, 119, 154
Counter-Reformation–117, 119
Counter-Remonstrance–151
Counter-Remonstrants–152, 153
Covenant theology–26, 35, 144, 145, 400, 401
Coverdale Bible–162, 163, 164
Crucifixion of Christ–52, 265, 266, 267
Cumberland Presbyterians–178, 397
Decrees of God–35, 42, 60, 86, 138, 146, 245, 250-281, 282, 290, 291, 297, 299, 300, 301, 302, 307, 308, 310, 313, 314, 315, 326, 332, 334, 344, 345, 347, 348, 351, 356, 366, 367, 369, 370, 373, 378, 382, 397, 401, 403, 414, 472, 479, 481, 482, 487, 488, 551, 589
Deism–8

Depravity of man–35, 42, 128, 185, 187, 188, 190, 191-200, 205, 206, 209, 211, 212, 213, 219, 223, 228, 229, 231, 232, 239, 241, 307, 421, 475, 476, 550, 553, 586
Dichotomy–206
Diet of Nuremberg–73
Diet of Speyer–72, 73
Diet of Worms–72
Dispensationalism–23, 34, 35, 147, 440, 451, 524, 580
Doctrines of Grace–2, 15, 16, 21, 22, 413, 537, 541, 544
Donatists–45, 49, 51, 55, 58, 59, 107
Douay-Rheims Bible–165, 166
Drawing–508, 509, 510, 511, 512
Dutch Reformed–12, 28, 117, 122, 138, 149, 157, 207, 422, 475, 506, 517, 590
Easy believism–580, 581
Economics–11
Edict of Milan–44, 45
Edict of Nantes–72
Edict of Worms–73
Effectual calling–476, 478, 478, 490-500, 502, 524, 531, 536, 550, 551, 563, 595
Elected to salvation–364-380, 405, 551
Election–21, 31, 69, 84, 114, 137, 241, 242, 243, 244, 245, 246, 247, 248, 251, 254, 256, 266, 281, 282, 291, 294, 297, 298, 300, 302, 303, 319, 320, 321, 322, 325, 333, 348, 350, 353, 357, 358, 364-380, 383, 385, 386, 387, 392, 393, 397, 401, 402, 404, 406, 413, 475, 494, 495, 499, 510, 518, 537, 538, 543, 563, 595, 596
Episcopacy–166, 167, 169, 174, 175
Episcopalians–169, 171, 179
Erastians–171
Eternal justification–299, 301, 364, 387
Eternal security–10, 28, 130, 386, 555, 561, 562-563, 565, 566, 574, 579, 586, 590, 594
Evangelism–239, 403, 471, 528, 536-550
Evolution–302
Faith–31, 62, 67, 249, 373, 379, 427, 478, 513-521, 522, 524, 525, 526, 528,

SUBJECT INDEX

531, 534, 535, 539, 542, 546, 580, 582, 585
Fall of Adam–51, 52, 128, 186, 191, 192, 199, 205, 206, 208, 215, 232, 239, 242, 253, 254, 267, 282, 283, 292, 294, 298, 299, 300, 362, 363, 364, 425, 430, 469
Fatalism–278, 402
Finneyites–202
First Council of Constantinople–46
First Great Awakening–14
First Helvetic Confession–75
First London Confession–179
Five Points of Calvinism–143, 144, 145, 147, 154, 156, 157, 159, 182, 241, 245, 250, 281
Foreknowledge–56, 265, 266, 268, 298, 327, 349, 376, 377, 378, 379, 385, 388, 389, 391, 392, 393, 394, 395, 396, 494
Foreordination–251, 252, 254, 259, 260, 261, 262, 263, 264, 265, 266, 268, 271, 272, 274, 277, 278, 279, 280, 281, 288, 298, 312, 329, 346, 349, 367, 375, 377, 378, 382, 390, 391, 392, 393, 395, 396, 397, 481, 500, 538
Forty-two Articles–164
Four-point Calvinism–147-148, 297, 298, 412, 424, 428, 466
Free agency–35, 214, 215
Free will–7, 35, 43, 51, 52, 57, 61, 66, 67, 121, 134, 136, 188, 200, 201, 202, 203, 211, 212, 214, 215, 216, 217, 219, 234, 238, 269, 274, 275, 276, 280, 334, 368, 391, 476, 500, 503, 506, 519, 551, 552, 594
Free Will Baptists–142
Front loading the Gospel–577
GARBC–147, 336
General calling–35, 491, 492, 493, 494, 496
Geneva–70, 71, 80, 81, 82-89, 91, 92, 93, 96, 97, 98, 100, 107, 114, 124, 125, 132, 133, 149, 159, 165, 168
Geneva Bible–165, 168
Gentiles–196, 229, 230, 339, 346, 347, 371, 380, 432, 440, 441, 442, 485, 496, 505, 512, 514
Georgetown University–119

Given to Salvation–341-344
Glorification–385, 387, 494, 595
Gnostics–50
God's People–335-341, 369, 453, 454, 546
Gospel–4, 5, 9, 18, 31, 85, 94, 98, 146, 147, 181, 200, 208, 220, 224, 226, 227, 230, 231, 233, 235, 245, 246, 346, 356, 361, 364, 365, 369, 370, 374, 383, 421, 431, 471, 492, 496, 505, 506, 524, 525, 530, 533, 535, 539, 540, 541, 544, 545, 546, 547, 548, 555, 568, 569, 577, 578, 580, 582, 584, 585
Governmental view of Atonement–150
Grand Rapids, MI–157, 158
Great Bible–163, 165
Greek Language–161, 166, 449, 517, 565, 571
Hampton Court Conference–167, 168
Hardening–306, 307, 308, 309, 326, 327, 373
Hardshellism–28, 32, 524, 542
Harvard University–14
Heidelberg Catechism–121, 122, 136, 137, 138, 148, 149, 150, 154, 157
Holiness–17, 140, 141, 142
Horrible decree–287, 288, 292, 332, 354
Huguenots–21
Humanism–4
Hyper-Calvinism–28-33, 189, 285, 413, 539, 540
Hypothetical redemption–297
Inability–35, 187, 188, 189, 190, 191, 200, 205, 206, 208, 211, 213, 215, 219, 220, 223, 224, 225, 226, 227, 229, 230, 231, 232, 233, 234, 235, 236, 239, 241, 316, 403, 475, 477, 535
Incarnation–410, 415
Independents–171, 174, 180
Index of Prohibited Books–120
Infant salvation–55, 60, 61, 110, 236, 397, 398, 399, 400, 530-536, 543
Infralapsarianism–35, 282, 283, 286, 289, 290, 291, 292, 294, 296, 297, 309, 332, 367
Inquisition–120
Institutes of the Christian Religion–80, 86, 90, 92, 100-104, 108, 111, 113,

114, 121, 122, 129, 132, 168, 287, 467, 468
Interregnum–174
Irish Articles–177
Islam–248, 249
Jesuits–119
Jews–43, 94, 196, 197, 225, 226, 229, 230, 278, 306, 308, 311, 312, 315, 317, 318, 319, 320, 322, 323, 327, 328, 330, 331, 339, 340, 344, 346, 347, 367, 368, 369, 371, 372, 373, 374, 379, 380, 395, 396, 400, 432, 434, 435, 439, 440, 441, 442, 451, 453, 454, 483, 496, 501, 510, 511, 512, 514
Judgment of God–332, 382
Justification–46, 61, 62, 63, 65, 119, 129, 141, 385, 386, 387, 426, 427, 494, 495, 518, 526, 539, 585, 588, 595
King James Bible–33, 167, 169
Lambeth Articles–168, 169
Latin Vulgate–119, 120, 160
London Confession of Faith–179, 180, 181, 460
Long Parliament–170, 174
Lordship salvation–577-586
Lord's Supper–55, 66, 75, 80, 107, 108, 109
Loyola University–119
Lutheranism–66, 72, 73, 76, 78, 118, 169, 456
Manichaeism–48, 49, 50, 51
Marburg Colloquy–75
Matthew Bible–162, 163
Mennonites–121, 140
Methodism–139, 140, 141
Middle Ages–13, 14, 40, 61, 87
Middle knowledge–389
Millenary Petition–166
Missions–238, 239, 403, 471
Modern Question–31
Monasticism–56
Monergism–35, 522, 523
National Covenant–167
Nature of man–206, 208
Nazarenes–140, 141
Neoplatonism–48, 54
New Testament salvation–521-530
Nicene creed–46
Nonconformists–140, 380

Omnipotence of God–269, 395, 488, 551
Omnipresence of God–332, 551
Omniscience of God–259, 260, 265, 332, 389, 390, 391, 392, 395, 551
Opinions of the Remonstrants–155, 157, 593
Ordained to Salvation–344-348
Ordo salutis–385, 386, 387, 397, 494
Original sin–51, 134, 241
Oxford University–168
Pacification of Ghent–118
Papists–77, 98, 127, 165
Peace of Augsburg–73
Pedobaptists–13, 14, 23
Pelagianism–8, 18, 31, 49, 50-52, 60, 61, 136, 141, 152, 202, 410, 436, 540, 579
Pentecostals–17, 140
Perfectionism–141, 582, 584, 585
Perseverance–35, 57, 141, 376, 377, 386, 472, 555, 556, 557, 558, 559, 560, 561, 563, 564, 565, 566, 567, 569, 570, 573-577, 580, 586, 587, 590, 591, 593, 594, 595, 596
Philadelphia Baptist Association–21, 182
Philadelphia Confession of Faith–182, 277, 531
Philosophy–48, 54, 65, 390, 391
Pilgrims–14
Politics–11, 12, 83, 88
Popery–7, 17, 81, 164
Postmillennialism–15, 53, 112, 145, 368, 379
Prayer–276, 277, 370, 574
Predestinated to salvation–380-397
Predestination–1, 15, 21, 28, 35, 37, 42, 52, 56, 57, 59, 60, 61, 65, 66, 67, 69, 86, 92, 103, 107, 112, 113, 114, 121, 133, 134, 137, 138, 141, 149, 151, 169, 170, 177, 201, 218, 220, 242, 243, 244, 245, 247, 248, 249, 256, 264, 276, 278, 281, 282, 283, 284, 286, 287, 288, 289, 291, 294, 297, 299, 306, 319, 321, 326, 327, 329, 333, 348, 350, 356, 366, 367, 375, 376, 380-397, 402, 403, 404, 406, 412, 470, 494, 500, 503, 507, 521, 543, 563, 588, 589, 595

SUBJECT INDEX

Prelacy–166
Premillennialism–15, 23, 33, 35, 53, 92, 369, 520
Presbyterianism–1, 3, 6, 14, 15, 17, 21, 26, 27, 33, 35, 70, 92, 139, 144, 145, 164, 166, 167, 171, 174, 175, 178, 180, 301, 411, 497, 520, 528, 534, 570, 579
Present knowledge–389
Preservation–35, 386, 495, 556, 558, 563, 566, 573, 576, 577, 586-590, 593, 595
Presumptive regeneration–301
Preterition–35, 295, 297, 299, 300, 317, 367, 403, 450, 499
Pride's Purge–174
Primitive Baptists–277, 524, 525, 529, 530, 545
Princeton Seminary–14, 139
Propitiation–428, 431, 442, 443, 446, 460
Protestant Reformed Church–33, 189, 291, 293, 335, 336, 401, 499, 540
Protestantism–12, 27, 40, 63, 69, 71, 72, 73, 75, 76, 80, 82, 83, 87, 88, 91, 94, 99, 101, 102, 118, 119, 120, 122, 123, 125, 132, 140, 164, 165, 167, 174, 177
Public invitation–543
Purgatory–56
Puritanism–12, 14, 21, 166, 167, 168, 169, 170, 171, 174
Quakers–12
Reconciliation–437, 438, 439, 588
Redemption–458, 588
Reformation–7, 13, 26, 40, 45, 59, 60, 61, 72, 73, 74, 75, 78, 80, 83, 87, 96, 98, 106, 117, 119, 120, 159, 160, 161, 163, 164, 167, 286, 594
Reformed–13, 14, 15, 17, 21, 26, 27, 28, 33, 35, 64, 70, 76, 84, 102, 109, 120, 121, 124, 125, 127, 130, 131, 134, 137, 144, 147, 152, 158, 168, 172, 192, 244, 254, 282, 297, 301, 302, 400, 401, 405, 440, 472, 492, 520, 521, 524, 525, 528, 534, 536, 549, 552, 563, 579
Reformed Baptists–181
Reformed Bible College–157
Reformed Faith–26, 27, 102, 143, 159, 176, 245, 251, 536, 543, 544
Reformed Theological Seminary–177, 246
Reformers–14, 15, 64, 65-68, 73, 77, 84, 97, 98, 103, 105, 106, 119, 120, 238, 398
Regeneration–31, 383, 385, 478, 494, 506, 520, 521, 522, 523, 524, 525, 526, 526, 528, 529, 531, 535, 539, 541, 542, 543, 546, 550, 551, 588
Religious liberty–12, 44, 73, 114
Remonstrance–150, 151, 155, 157, 376, 592
Remonstrant Brotherhood–156
Remonstrants–152, 153, 155, 156, 157
Renaissance–7, 74, 87
Repentance–31, 513-521, 525, 526, 528, 531, 534, 535, 542, 580, 582, 583
Reprobation–35, 114, 228, 248, 254, 282, 284, 290, 291, 292, 293, 294, 295, 297, 298, 299, 302-333, 338, 363, 366, 367, 371, 376, 380, 382, 399, 402, 403, 405, 406, 469
Responsibility of man–234, 235, 236, 471
Roman Catholicism–8, 37, 40, 41, 49, 55, 60, 63, 64, 67, 72, 73, 74, 75, 76, 77, 78, 79, 80, 81, 83, 88, 89, 90, 91, 94, 98, 101, 102, 105, 106, 107, 108, 112, 118, 119, 120, 121, 124, 125, 127, 135, 160, 161, 162, 163, 164, 165, 166, 197, 202, 410, 555, 585
Roman Empire–40, 44, 72, 89, 98, 117
Rump Parliament–174
Sabellianism–91
Sacramentarians–121
Sacraments–55, 107, 181
Salvation by grace–8, 9, 10, 28, 34, 42, 62, 64, 67, 214, 233, 239, 247, 410, 414, 470, 505, 536, 550, 553, 555, 564, 568, 569
Salvation by works–8, 9, 35, 62, 67, 246, 247, 564, 568
Sanctification–52, 64, 129, 266, 378, 383, 385, 386, 455, 457, 494, 495, 580, 582, 588
Savoy Declaration–180
Saxon Visitation Articles–460
Schmalkald League–73
Scotch Confession–166

Second Council of Orange—60
Second Diet of Speyer—73, 76
Second Helvetic Confession—76
Second London Confession—181
Second Royal Injunctions—163
Septuagint—53
Shelf-Calvinists—25
Sin of unbelief—425, 431
Six Articles—162, 163
Socialism—11, 135
Socinianism—8, 152, 410, 415
Solemn League and Covenant—167, 172, 173
Soul winning—471, 541, 542
Southern Baptist Convention—25
Sovereign grace—15, 16, 17, 18, 21, 50, 189, 243, 276, 299, 363, 513, 536, 537, 579
Sovereignty of God—24, 42, 248, 251, 256, 257, 258, 259, 260, 269, 271, 274, 276, 290, 291, 375, 391, 392, 406, 440, 594
Special calling—35, 491
Special grace—35, 497, 498, 499
Spiritual death—193, 194, 206, 220
Sublapsarianism—282, 296, 297, 332
Supralapsarianism—35, 282, 283, 284, 285, 286, 289, 290, 291, 292, 293, 294, 296, 309, 330, 332, 335, 363, 367, 405, 506, 540
Supremacy of God—257
Synergism—35, 522, 523
Synod of Dort—148-156, 157, 159, 169, 170, 171, 172, 173, 241, 284, 289, 412, 593
Synod of Emden—121
Synod of Mainz—60
Synod of Utrecht—291
Ten Articles—162
Thirty Years' War—173
Thirty-nine Articles—166, 168, 460
Three Forms of Unity—157, 158
Time magazine—39
Tower of Babel—196
Trichotomy—206
Trinity—91, 410
TULIP—145, 146, 189, 190, 200, 214, 229, 233, 238, 321, 324, 359, 374, 376, 387, 388, 389, 397, 401, 405, 413, 432, 442, 448, 452, 454, 459, 475, 487, 490, 500, 501, 503, 505, 520, 528, 541, 547, 555, 556, 563, 570, 596
Tyndale's New Testament—161, 163, 164
Union of Utrecht—150
Unitarianism—8, 91, 135, 139
University of Basel—74, 124
University of Bourges—78
University of Leiden—123, 125, 134, 148, 149, 150, 169
University of Marburg—123, 124
University of Orleans—77
University of Paris—77
University of Saragossa—89
University of Toulouse—89
University of Vienna—74
Wesleyans—140, 141
Westminster Abbey—173, 175
Westminster Assembly—14, 159-175, 177, 179, 289
Westminster Confession of Faith—159, 175, 178, 180, 181, 182, 186, 188, 244, 250, 273, 281, 289, 296, 366, 367, 381, 397, 402, 408, 460, 477, 478, 490, 522, 531, 532, 542, 558
Westminster Larger Catechism—176, 177, 178
Westminster Shorter Catechism—176, 178, 252
Westminster Standards—175-178
Westminster Theological Seminary—176
Whosoever believeth—279, 309, 311, 334, 335, 380, 459, 540, 551
Will of God—217, 280, 292, 298, 309, 342, 367, 479-490, 503, 504, 507, 546
Will of man—35, 201-219, 223, 236
Yale—14
Zoroastrianism—48

NAME INDEX

Abelard–415
Adams, Jay–273, 542, 543, 545
Aemilius, Theodorus–123
Alaric the Goth–49
Alber, John–395
Alciati, Andrea–78
Alexander, Archibald–301
Alford, Henry–449, 450
Ambrose–41, 48
Ammonius, Andreas–161
Amyraut, Moyse–147, 297, 412
Anselm–103, 415
Aquinas, Thomas–15, 103
Aristotle–40, 124
Arminius, James–5, 10, 17, 19, 39, 50, 51, 87, 114, 115-142, 148, 149, 150, 154, 156, 168, 169, 171, 198, 199, 212, 254, 284, 390, 553, 590, 591, 592
Asbury, Francis–140
Augustine, Aurelius–15, 37-68, 69, 70, 78, 103, 104, 107, 109, 110, 113, 158, 159, 199, 301, 331, 332, 398, 485
Backus, Isaac–22
Baillie, Robert–172
Bainton, Roland–98
Baker, Alvin–271, 300, 314, 332
Ballard, L. S.–322
Bangs, Carl–149
Baro, Peter–168
Barth, Karl–78, 79
Bavinck, Herman–33, 291, 301, 332
Baxter, Richard–177
Beck, Frank–450, 455, 489, 556
Benedict, David–20
Berkhof, Louis–26, 33, 54, 57, 58, 60, 64, 109, 138, 249, 250, 255, 282, 286, 289, 291, 297, 301, 302, 383, 491, 524, 556
Berkouwer, G. C.–33, 277, 283, 298, 299, 301, 323, 326, 353, 487, 594
Bernard–103

Bertius, Peter–123, 125
Best, W. E.–281, 282, 286, 294, 400, 426, 450, 479, 487, 493, 525, 545, 593
Beza, Theodore–67, 70, 75, 77, 82, 87, 93, 97, 124, 132, 133, 134, 149, 254, 272, 286, 289, 460, 481
Bloody Mary–87, 164, 165, 168
Boettner, Loraine–1, 4, 6, 12, 13, 14, 21, 27, 37, 42, 50, 56, 59, 81, 84, 97, 112, 176, 191, 203, 205, 206, 219, 236, 241, 248, 256, 275, 285, 293, 294, 298, 301, 302, 335, 350, 367, 392, 400, 402, 411, 421, 423, 428, 449, 484, 487, 497, 509, 533, 534, 543, 551, 555
Bogerman, John–154, 155
Boleyn, Anne–162
Bolsec, Jerome–86, 113
Booth, Abraham–22
Bouwsma, William–72
Boyce, James–22
Bradwardine, Thomas–60
Bratt, John–87, 113
Brine, John–22, 31, 364, 387
Broadus, John–22
Bronson, Charles–455, 471
Bruce, F. F.–46, 55, 517
Bucer, Martin–67, 75, 81, 97, 103, 118, 168
Buddha–414
Bullinger, Heinrich–67, 75, 80, 94, 97, 114, 286
Bunyan, John–22, 331
Buswell, J. Oliver–33, 325, 348, 351, 370, 377, 378, 381
Caelestius–51
Calvin, Charles–77
Calvin, Gerald–77
Calvin, John–1, 5, 10, 11, 13, 15, 16, 17, 21, 25, 28, 32, 37, 38, 39, 42, 49, 50, 51, 59, 65, 66, 67, 68, 69-114,

115, 116, 118, 120, 121, 122, 127, 129, 130, 131, 132, 133, 136, 137, 138, 141, 143, 144, 159, 160, 164, 167, 168, 176, 199, 203, 208, 225, 231, 249, 266, 285, 286, 287, 288, 289, 292, 295, 301, 302, 323, 326, 330, 331, 332, 370, 374, 380, 381, 393, 398, 459, 461, 466, 467, 469, 470, 485, 486, 512, 517, 519, 570, 572, 596
Calvin, Marie–77
Carey, William–22, 24
Carroll, B. H.–22
Carson, D. A.–225, 317
Carson, Alexander–22
Cartwright, Thomas–166
Castellio, Sebastian–113, 114
Castro, Fidel–257
Catherine of Aragon–162
Chafer, Louis–147, 298, 311, 335, 369, 424, 429, 580
Chantry, Walter–211
Charles I–167, 170
Charles II–174
Charles V–72, 89, 117, 118
Cicero–47
Clark, Gordon–8, 95, 203, 232, 248, 264, 265, 266, 269, 271, 274, 275, 305, 337, 348, 350, 354, 402, 488, 496, 500, 501, 502, 503, 506, 515, 543, 582
Clarke, John–22, 33
Cockrell, Milburn–16, 17, 18, 21, 357, 360, 384
Cole, Henry–89
Constantine–43, 44, 45, 46
Coornhert, Dirck–133, 134
Cop, Nicholas–79, 80
Coppes, Leonard–114, 145, 224, 249, 403, 516, 595
Cordier, Mathurin–78
Corneliszoon, Arent–133, 134
Cosgrove, Charles–321, 328
Coverdale, Myles–162, 163, 164
Cox, Benjamin–180
Craig, William–391
Crampton, W. Gary–4, 27, 96, 103, 187, 189, 215, 251, 277, 285, 337, 406, 491, 531, 543
Cranmer, Thomas–162, 163, 164, 168
Crenshaw, Curtis–579

Crisp, Tobias–31
Cromwell, Oliver–174
Cromwell, Richard–174
Cromwell, Thomas–162, 163
Crosby, Thomas–20
Cunningham, William–33, 61, 64, 66, 67, 96, 138, 153, 295, 421
Curtiss, George–6,
Custance, Arthur–40, 59, 69, 117, 143, 159, 191, 217, 220, 248, 269, 286, 337, 341, 375, 423, 433, 445, 446, 471, 472, 504, 523, 540, 544, 548, 549, 551
Dabney, Robert–1, 33, 37, 108, 109, 144, 255, 291, 296, 297, 298, 299, 301, 306, 407, 411, 421, 424, 434, 440, 445, 455
Dagg, John–22
Dargan, Edwin–22
Darwin, Charles–192
Davenant, John–147, 154, 412
Davis, Jimmie–399, 458
Davis, Richard–31
Day, Doris–253
de Bres, Guido–122
de Bure, Idelette–81
de la Fountaine–93
de Trie, Guillaume–90
deWitt, John–406
Dick, John–33
Dijk, Klaas–286, 332
Dillow, Joseph–568
Donteklok, Reynier–133, 134
Duke of Alva–118
Duncan, Mark–145
Durant, Will–38
Duty, Guy–565, 567, 570, 572
Eaton, John–30
Edward III–60
Edward IV–160
Edward VI–163, 164, 166, 168,
Edwards, Jonathan–14, 15, 33, 195, 202, 218, 235
Elizabeth I–112, 165, 166, 168
Engelsma, David–1, 5, 30, 31, 189, 190, 293, 302, 303, 336, 536, 540, 541, 543, 544, 549
English, E. Schuyler–580
Episcopius, Simon–149, 152, 155
Erasmus, Desiderius–66, 74, 78, 79, 103, 120, 121, 161, 211, 212, 238, 280

NAME INDEX

Erastus, Thomas–171
Eusebius–44, 46
Everman, Clyde–145, 350
Farel, Guillaume–80, 81, 82, 83, 87, 92, 93
Featley, Daniel–179
Feinberg, John–271
Finney, Charles–14, 543, 549
Fisher, George–88
Fletcher, John–141
Forster, Roger–379
Francis I–72, 100
Franklin, Benjamin–182
Frederick Henry–156
Friedrich III–122
Fuller, Andrew–22, 24, 32
Furman, Richard–22
Gaebelein, Arno–290
Gambrell, J. B.–22
Gano, John–22
Garrett, Eddie–215, 494, 524, 525, 529, 530, 535, 545, 546, 574, 580, 581, 594
Gaudentius–58
Gentry, Kenneth–578, 579
George, Timothy–64, 65, 66, 69, 105, 398
Gerstner, John–189, 203, 242, 274, 413, 424, 428, 432, 492, 527, 562, 563, 578, 593
Gibbon, Edward–58, 99
Gill, John–22, 23, 31, 32, 42, 43, 141, 252, 253, 289, 292, 296, 301, 302, 317, 357, 360, 367, 377, 400, 455, 456, 483, 485, 508
Girardeau, John–282, 295, 296
Gomarus, Franciscus–135, 149, 153, 154, 289
Good, Kenneth–17, 19, 20, 23, 27, 38, 144, 158, 413, 537
Goodwin, John–10
Gottschalk–60
Graham, Billy–539, 549
Graves, J. R.–22
Green, James–399
Gregory of Rimini–60
Gregory the Great–40
Groot, Gerard–120
Grotius, Hugo–131, 150, 152, 415
Gruet, Jacques–85, 86
Gunn, Grover–245, 274, 434, 478, 491, 556
Haldane, Robert–245, 324, 495
Hall, Joseph–154
Hall, Robert–22
Hanko, Herman–28, 158, 189, 190, 191, 223, 379, 400, 401
Harvey, Harold–399
Harvey, William–90
Heard, J. B.–206
Helmichius–133
Henry II–72
Henry VII–160
Henry VIII–160, 162, 163, 164
Heshusius, Tileman–468
Hitler, Adoph–258
Hodge, A. A.–33, 286, 301, 406, 407, 414, 456, 461, 467
Hodge, Caspar–301
Hodge, Charles–14, 33, 50, 214, 232, 255, 273, 281, 291, 301, 305, 306, 329, 401, 425, 452, 453, 518, 519, 570, 596
Hodges, Zane–584
Hoekema, Anthony–562
Hoeksema, Herman–33, 250, 258, 291, 302, 321, 326, 327, 328, 335, 364, 379, 385, 400, 401, 435, 499, 506, 508, 509, 518, 524, 540
Hoeksema, Homer C.–117, 158, 207, 294, 417, 422, 434, 517, 524
Holbein, Hans–163
Hommius, Festus–152, 153
Houck, Steven–479, 520
Hovey, Alva–22
Howell, R. B. C.–22
Hughes, Philip–89, 95, 97, 98
Hume, David–268
Hussein, Saddam–257
Hussey, Joseph–31
Hutson, Curtis–574
Irenaeus–414
James I–153, 166, 169, 284
Jerome–41, 50, 53
Jessey, Henry–22
Jewett, Paul–114, 248, 332
Johns, Kenneth–401, 494
Johnson, W. B.–22
Jones, William–47, 99
Judson, Adoniram–22, 24
Junius, Franciscus–125, 134, 137
Kampschulte, Wilhem–102

Keach, Benjamin–22, 181
Keach, Elias–182
Keener, Forrest–18, 224
Kennedy, D. James–3, 27
Kiffin, William–22, 181
Klein, William–379
Klooster, Fred–286, 287
Knollys, Hanserd–22, 181
Knox, John–87, 165, 166, 168
Kober, Manford–216, 365, 537
Kruithof, Bastian–536, 556
Kuiper, R. B.–434, 435, 471, 549
Kuyper, Abraham–12, 27, 33, 89, 157, 291, 301
Lagerwey, Walter–122
Larkin, Clarence–580
Latimer, Hugh–164
Laud, William–167, 170
Leith, John–553
Leland, John–22
Lenski, Richard–570, 573
Licinius–44
Lightfoot, John–171
Lightner, Robert–428
Lloyd-Jones, Martyn–402
Lombard–103
Long, Gary–437, 439, 457
Loyola, Ignatius–77, 119
Luther, Martin–15, 40, 62, 64, 65, 66, 67, 72, 73, 74, 75, 76, 78, 79, 103, 105, 108, 112, 118, 119, 120, 121, 129, 160, 161, 164, 199, 211, 213, 286, 398
Lydius, Martinus–133
MacArthur, John–578, 579, 580, 582, 585
Machen, J. Gresham–33, 281, 301, 302, 519, 582
Mani–48
Manly, Basil, Jr.–22
Manly, Basil, Sr.–22
Manton, Thomas–314
Manz, Felix–76
Mao Tse-tung–258
Margaret–118
Marston, Paul–379
Martinius, Matthias–154
Mason, Roy–17, 21, 144, 247, 248, 563
Mathison, Keith–246, 407, 515, 562, 579

Maxentius–44
McFetridge, N. S.–8, 13, 21, 50, 62, 536
McGrath, Alister–89, 93, 94, 96, 112, 113
McNeil, John–85, 96, 97, 170, 176
Meeter, H. Henry–69, 113
Melanchthon, Philip–67, 73, 75, 97, 103, 105, 123, 160, 286
Mell, Patrick–22
Melville, Andrew–166
Mercer, Jesse–22
Miley, John–388
Miller, Charles–88, 139
Milton, John–367
Mohammed–414
Montagu, Richard–169, 170
Moody, D. L.–14
Morey, Robert–224, 363,
Morris, Leon–355
Mosheim, John–99, 106
Muller, Richard–254
Murray, John–33, 301, 302, 304, 306, 323, 327, 329, 371, 372, 373, 393, 449, 450, 452, 453, 471, 539, 541, 588
Neander–59
Ness, Christopher–256, 380, 434, 456, 490
Nettles, Tom–245, 246, 387, 421
Nettleton, David–336, 345, 350
Newman, A. H.–88
Nichols, James–115, 125
Nichols, William–125
North, Gary–448, 499
Oecolampadius, John–75, 89, 118
Olevianus, Caspar–122
Olivetan–78, 80
Origen–53, 414
Orr, James–284
Otis, John–567, 584
Owen, John–170, 424, 425, 431, 434, 438, 444, 455, 456, 457, 469
Packer, J. I.–274, 539, 540, 541, 578
Palmer, Edwin–37, 144, 188, 214, 256, 274, 277, 300, 332, 341, 345, 407, 471, 477, 478, 509, 552, 562, 563
Parker, Matthew–165
Paton, John–307
Patton, Francis–301
Paul, the Apostle–5, 13, 21, 37, 38, 40, 41, 42, 56, 64, 65, 70, 71, 197, 205,

NAME INDEX

226, 228, 249, 263, 280, 304, 305, 320, 322, 325, 326, 328, 330, 336, 346, 351, 352, 355, 356, 365, 371, 372, 373, 380, 385, 387, 392, 438, 447, 448, 453, 454, 455, 457, 463, 482, 504, 505, 507, 513, 514, 516, 517, 518, 526, 547, 548, 571, 572, 584, 586
Pelagius–49, 50, 51, 52, 64, 67
Pendleton, J. M.–22
Perkins, William–135, 168, 171
Peterson, Robert–461, 467
Phelps, Fred–146
Philip II–117, 118, 164
Phillips, Dan–277
Philpot, J. C.–22
Pighius, Albert–113, 468
Pink, Arthur–22, 23, 24, 33, 187, 191, 192, 193, 200, 202, 204, 206, 207, 209, 213, 215, 217, 220, 221, 222, 234, 235, 243, 249, 251, 257, 258, 259, 263, 266, 271, 282, 290, 291, 299, 307, 308, 309, 310, 311, 312, 313, 314, 316, 317, 324, 328, 337, 338, 341, 345, 354, 358, 360, 363, 366, 367, 369, 374, 377, 383, 386, 389, 401, 413, 416, 427, 434, 437, 439, 440, 442, 444, 445, 446, 447, 449, 452, 453, 454, 476, 479, 480, 481, 484, 492, 508, 509, 510, 514, 520, 522, 538, 543, 544, 549, 556, 558, 562, 566, 567, 570, 572, 578, 580, 583, 587, 593, 594
Piper, John–321, 329, 484, 485
Piscator, John–254
Plancius, Petrus–130, 134, 152
Plotinus–48
Pope Innocent VIII–160
Pope John Paul II–40
Pope Leo X–161
Pope Paul III–119, 120, 162
Pope Paul IV–120
Pope Pius IV–120
Porphyry–48
Pride, Thomas–174
Prince Maurice–149, 152, 156
Pugh, Curtis–19
Quintana, Juan–89
Ramus, Peter–124
Randall, Benjamin–142
Reynolds, John–167, 168

Rice, Luther–22, 24
Rice, N. L.–40, 277
Richards, James–460, 466
Ridderbos, Herman–323
Ridley, Nicholas–164
Rippon, John–22
Ritschl, Otto–292
Robbins, John–585
Robertson, A. T.–449
Rogers, John–162, 164
Rose, Ben–145, 191, 223, 407, 492, 493, 514, 556
Ross, Tom–41, 143, 203, 234, 311, 413, 476, 488, 490, 491, 492, 530, 535, 538, 563
Rowley, H. H.–365
Ryland, John–22, 24
Ryrie, Charles–580
Sadoleto, Joseph–81, 82, 106
Saltmarsh, John–30
Schaff, Philip–41, 54, 64, 71, 80, 84, 85, 94, 98, 100, 106, 154, 172, 286, 398
Schweitzer, Albert–415
Scott, Otto–69, 87, 96, 98
Seaton, W. J.–1, 191, 242, 249, 409, 476
Sellers, C. Norman–42
Selph, Robert–277
Servetus, Michael–69, 72, 79, 89, 90, 91, 92, 93, 94, 95, 96, 97, 98, 99, 100, 107, 114
Seymour, Edward–163
Shank, Robert–414, 565, 567, 570, 573, 579, 581, 593, 594, 596
Shedd, William–6, 33, 178, 268, 291, 294, 301, 403, 456, 531, 532, 534
Shields, Dr.–398
Siculus, Georgius–468
Simons, Menno–121
Singer, Gregg–100
Skepp, John–22, 31
Smeaton, George–437, 440, 446, 456, 457
Smith, Adam–11
Smith, Garner–21
Smith, Henry–33
Smith, Morton–539
Snellias, Rudolphus–123
Socinus, Faustus–135
Socinus, Laelius–135

Somerset, Protector–168
Spencer, Duane–8, 13, 200, 242, 334, 406, 435, 477, 509, 512, 556
Spilsbery, John–22
Sproul, R. C.–13, 26, 61, 63, 66, 145, 187, 189, 220, 243, 274, 282, 294, 421, 432, 436, 447, 478, 486, 509, 521, 522, 523, 526, 550, 552, 578
Spurgeon, Charles–5, 13, 14, 19, 21, 22, 23, 28, 29, 30, 31, 32, 38, 140, 141, 147, 249, 294, 301, 397, 401, 541, 542, 549
Steele, David–49, 182, 432, 472
Steinmetz, David–72
Stephanus–104
Stonehouse, Ned–539, 541
Storms, C. Samuel–187, 243, 325, 327, 353, 357, 358, 385, 403, 491, 509, 515
Strickland, E. D.–399
Strong, A. H.–22, 256, 302, 466, 467, 535
Sunday, Billy–14
Talbot, Kenneth–4, 27, 103, 187, 189, 215, 251, 277, 285, 337, 406, 491, 531, 543
Taylor, H. Boyce–22
Tertullian–43
Theodosius–46, 58
Thiessen, Henry–377
Thomas, Curtis–49, 182, 432, 472
Thornwell, James–33
Tidwell, J. B.–22
Toplady, Augustus–66, 141
Torquemada, Tomas–98, 120
Trolliet, Jean–86, 113
Turretin, Francis–33
Twisse, William–171, 289
Tyndale, William–161, 162, 163, 164
Ursinus, Zacharias–122
Ussher, James–171, 177
Uytenbogaert, John–149, 150, 151, 152, 154
Van Baren, Gise–475, 477, 488, 551, 563, 574
Van Oldenbarnevelt, John–150, 151, 152, 152
Van Til, Cornelius–33, 291, 301
VanOverloop, Ronald–403
Veluanus, Anastasius–121
Verduin, Leonard–95, 98

Viret, Peter–82
Voltaire–71
Vorstius, Conrad–169, 254
Vos, Geerhardus–33, 291
Walker, Williston–91, 103
Wallace, Ronald–98
Walvoord, John–563
Ward, Samuel–154
Ware, Bruce–476, 494, 496
Warfield, Benjamin–33, 34, 40, 41, 42, 54, 61, 89, 103, 114, 176, 177, 245, 294, 299, 301, 302, 311, 335, 377, 380, 403, 440, 478, 534
Warren, Jack–20, 21, 527
Watson, Richard–141, 567
Wayland, Francis–22
Wayman, Lewis–31
Webb, R. A.–534, 535
Weber, Max–11
Wells, Tom–203
Wendel, Francois–93, 96, 103, 105, 109, 110, 111
Wesley, Charles–140, 141, 287, 399
Wesley, John–14, 139, 140, 141, 142, 154, 156, 171, 198, 199, 212, 236, 293, 403, 553, 567
Wesley, Samuel–140
Wesley, Susanna–140, 141
West, David–262, 276
White, John–171
Whitefield, George–8, 14, 140, 142
Whitgift, John–166
Whittingham, William–87, 165
William of Orange–118, 122, 123, 149, 150
Wilmoth, James–276
Wilson, Joseph–15, 18, 21, 34, 277, 310, 406, 502, 541, 542
Wolmar, Melchior–78
Wright, R. K.–484, 485
Wuest, Kenneth–449
Wycliffe, John–160
Zanchius, Jerom–390, 403, 532
Zwingli, Huldreich–65, 66, 67, 73, 74, 75, 76, 103, 108, 118, 120, 160, 286, 398, 532

SCRIPTURE INDEX

Genesis

1:1–309, 352
1:16–309
1:26–192
1:28–192
1:31–192
2:16–275
2:25–207
3:7–207
4:1–393
6:2–367
6:3–488
6:5–196
6:11-12–196
8:21–194
11:4-8–262
11:7-6–196
12:1-3–196
17:7-8–322
17:19–196
19:33-36–575
20:6–259
22:2–210
25:22-23–322
25:23–322, 322
26:3-4–322, 196
26:27–210
26:29–210
33:3–322
33:5–322
33:8–322
33:11–322
35:11-12–322
37:4–213
47:29–264
49:24–311

Exodus

1:7–197

2:24-25–197
3:19–327
4:21–327
4:22-197
5:1-2–37
6:6-7–326
7:3–327
7:3-4–327
7:5–326
7:13–327
7:22–327
8:15–327
8:32–327
9:12–327
9:14–326
9:16–326
9:34–327
9:35–327
10:1–327
10:1-2–326
10:20–327
10:27–327
11:5–390
12:6–427
12:7–427
12:21–427
12:22-427
13:14-16–326
14:4–326
14:8–327
14:17–259, 331
14:17-18–326
14:18–326
14:31–326
15:11–259
16:23–197
17:25–326
19:6–379
32:9–197
32:10–197

33:18-19–218
33:19–332
33:22–218
34:12–197
34:13–308
34:15–308

Leviticus

5:17–236
10:1-2–324
16:8-10–262
18:6–307
18:20–307
18:21–308
18:21-24–279
18:22–308
18:23–308
18:24–197
18:24-25–307
24:16–94

Numbers

11:1–197
11:33–197
16:31-33–324
21:6-9–436
21:8–436, 512
21:25–308
23:7-8–45
24:1–227
25:5–45
28:6–345
31:16–45

Deuteronomy

1:39–535
2:30–308
5:29–483
5:33–278
6:1-3–278
7:2–197, 308
7:7–320
7:16–197
7:23–308
8:20–308
9:7–197
9:8–197

9:18-20–276
11:16-17–278
14:2–367
14:22–197
22:6–279
25:1–63
29:29–256, 480
31:14–264
32:39–503
33:9–393

Joshua

2:10-11–326
7:20-21–213
11:19-20–307

Judges

5:2–275
16:17–352
19:29–279

Ruth

1:16–368

1 Samuel

2:3–390
2:6–503
4:7-8–326
12:22–227
16:7–595

2 Samuel

17:14–270
24:1–273

1 Kings

3:8–320
3:10–227
8:46–211
12:32–345
14:10–270
21:1-13–263
21:21–270
22:17–339

SCRIPTURE INDEX

2 Kings

5:7–503
17:8–197
20:1-6–276
23:5–345

1 Chronicles

9:22–345
16:11–230
17:9–345
21:1–273
21:15–583
28:9–276, 390
29:11-12–257

2 Chronicles

11:15–345
12:14–230
15:13–230
23:18–345
29:27–345
33:9–197, 263, 576

Ezra

1:1-2–263
5:13–255
6:1–255
7:13–275

Nehemiah

9:16–483
11:2–276
13:18–270

Esther

9:32–255

Job

1:11–273
1:12–273
1:21–273
2:5–273
2:7–273, 194
11:12–194

14:4–193
14:5–263
15:15–194
20:11–194
21:30–313
25:4–199
25:6–194
28:26–255
33:13–280
34:10–270
37:16–390
38:10–255
42:11–273

Psalms

2:5–332
2:7–255
5:4–270
7:11–324
7:13–345
8:3–345, 346
8:5–192
9:17–332
10:4–230
11:6–332
33:10–310
33:13-15–310, 334, 495
33:15–499
33:21–259
34:22–458
37:20–332
39:5–195
39:6–194
44:11–339
44:21–390
44:22–339
47:2–257
47:8–259
51:5–193
55:23–264
58:3–194
65:4–353, 502
73:24–259
74:1–339
76:10–259, 310
78:41–483
78:52–339
79:13–339
81:11–483

86:5–528
90:10–264
92:15–332
94:11–194
95:7–339
100:3–339
103:14–194
110:3–502
115:3–257
118:22–311
119:2–230
119:18–505
119:36–259
119:176–339
135:4–320
139:4–390
139:24–259
145:17–258
148:6–255
149:9–314

Proverbs

1:24–483
1:25–272, 483
1:26–332
1:28–230
1:30–272
3:6–259
8:29–255
13:22–209
15:3–332
16:1–260, 262
16:4–309
16:7–227
16:9–260, 262
16:33–260, 262
17:15–63
17:22–209
18:21–528
19:21–260, 262
20:24–260, 262
21:1–260, 262
21:4–195
21:27–195, 324
29:1–308
29:26–261
29:60–262
31:8–312

Ecclesiastes

3:2–263
6:12–194
7:17–264
7:20–194, 210
7:29–192, 309
8:11–195
9:5–220

Song of Solomon

1:1–508
1:2–508
1:4–508

Isaiah

1:6–552
1:9–372
6:3–258
6:9-10–315
8:14–311
10:1–256, 297
10:22–255, 372
14:24–480
26:12–345
28:16–311, 311, 366
29:16–328
30:33–345
38:5–264
40:6-7–194
42:1–354
42:9–259, 390
42:21–227
45:4–320, 367
45:7–269
45:9–328
45:19–230, 238, 273
45:22–237, 581
46:10–259, 309, 390
53–451
53:6–194, 339, 428, 443, 450, 451
53:8–451
53:10–227, 267, 417
53:11-12–450
54:13–510
55:6–229, 318
55:8–280
55:8-9–256

56:4–227
57:20–194
59:1-2–528
63:17–308, 327
64:6–195
64:8–328
65:9–367
65:12–483
65:22–367

Jeremiah

1:5–345, 352
5:3–483
5:22–256
6:13–303
6:16–303
6:17–303
6:19–271, 304
6:30–303
7:13–483
11:10-11–271
13:10–483
16:10-11–271
17:9–195, 210
18:1-6–328
18:6–328
19:3-5–271
19:5–271, 272
23:1–339
25:9–263
29:13-14–230
30:7–368
31:1-2–501
31:3–361, 501
31:4–501
31:7–501
32:30–197
36:3–271
50:6–339, 339
50:17–339

Lamentations

3:26–42, 200, 331, 402, 476, 551
3:38–269

Ezekiel

2:7–549
14:22–270

18:24–575
28:15-17–309
33:11–309
34:6–339, 339
34:11–339
34:11-16–340
34:12–339
37:1-6–500
37:11-12–501

Daniel

1:1-2–197
2:24–345
3:10–255
4:24–256
4:35–257, 480
9:14–270

Hosea

7:2–332

Amos

3:6–269
5:4–229

Jonah

4:11–535

Habakkuk

1:13–270

Zephaniah

2:3–230
3:8–263

Malachi

1:1-3–323

Matthew

1:1–508
1:21–451, 453, 454, 461
2:6–454
2:7–492
2:16–263
3:17–227

4:21–493
5:45–499
7:6–339
7:11–210
7:15–205
7:16–205
7:17–205
7:17-18–204
7:21–205
7:21-23–586
7:23–394
8:10–519
8:11–532
8:20–430
8:25–582
9:2–519
9:13–497
9:22–519
9:27–219
10:1–447, 486
10:6–339, 340
10:22–443, 570
11:21–278
11:23–278
11:25-27–303
11:27–510
11:28–237, 581
12:18–354
12:34-35–204
12:36–332
12:50–482
13:14-15–315, 316
13:33–247
13:42–221
15:22–219
15:24–339, 340, 454
15:26-27–339
15:28–519
16:17–510
16:28–451
17:5–227
17:15–219
19:8–355
19:14–111
19:25–200
20:1–349, 349, 493
20:16–348, 385, 493, 494
20:28–418, 451, 461
20:30–219
21:28-29–583

21:44–311
22:2–349, 493
22:3–349, 493
22:9–49, 349, 493
22:10–349, 493
22:11–349
22:14–266, 348, 349, 385, 494
22:41–493
23:37–483
24–369
24:13–369, 572, 573
24:14–580
24:21–368, 573
24:22–368
24:24–368
24:29–368, 573
24:31–368
25:31–367
26:28–462, 510
26:41–575
26:50–458
26:56–582
26:60–262
27:25–197, 267, 331
28:20–573

Mark

1:15–187, 237, 513
3:13-14–351
3:14–345, 346
4:7–205
4:9–510
4:12–315
6:52–308
7:5–377
7:20-23–195
8:17–308
9:12–430
10:18–211
10:22–324
10:52–519
13:19–355
13:28–394
14:21–268

Luke

1:1-2–355
1:5-6–340

1:15–352
1:68–454
1:71–572
2:1–255
2:8-20–340
2:25–340, 510
2:36-38–340
6:33-209
6:35–499
7:14–503
7:30–272, 483
7:34–458
7:50–519
8:10–315
8:12–238, 278, 318
8:54–503
10:30–300
10:31–279
10:34–300
10:37–300
10:31-32–300
10:33-34–300
11:50–337
14:23–59
15:24–221
16:23-28–220
16:26–199, 208
18:1–370
18:7–369, 376
19:10–430, 457
22:19-20–454
22:22–267
23:34–331
24:45–505

John

1:1–431
1:3–309
1:9–512
1:10–435
1:10-11–453
1:10-13–217
1:11–344, 510
1:12–232, 383, 526, 581
1:13–216, 503
1:17–546
1:24–492
1:29–418, 428, 433, 434, 465
1:31–344, 510

1:40-49–340
2:11–581
2:23-24–395
3:2–589
3:3–219, 223, 224, 225
3:4–595
3:5–54, 225
3:6–194
3:7–194
3:8–224
3:13–430
3:14–512
3:14-15–436, 512
3:15–436, 551
3:16–229, 279, 380, 422, 433, 434, 435, 436, 447, 465, 505, 508, 527, 551, 568
3:18–199, 380, 431, 528, 533, 569, 571
3:19–436, 447
3:36–199, 310, 380, 499, 528, 569
4:22–454
4:42–433, 458, 466
5:3–552
5:6–552
5:20–503
5:21–503
5:24–220, 299, 380, 571, 588, 588
5:24-25–503
5:25–386, 524
5:40–219, 238, 278, 486, 553
6:27–344
6:27-29–436
6:33–434
6:36–225, 344
6:37–341, 342, 343, 510, 537
6:39–341, 342
6:40–342, 586
6:44–223, 227, 344, 507, 508, 509, 511
6:44-45–515
6:45–510, 510
6:47–527, 568
6:51–433, 436, 581
6:64–355
6:65–224, 227, 344, 510
6:66–342, 582
6:70–342, 346, 351
7:7–435
7:16–209

7:17–482
7:37–237, 334, 581
7:39–510
8:21–225
8:23–225, 435
8:24–225, 230, 528, 533, 569
8:25–355
8:34–226
8:43–223, 225
8:44–225, 226, 355
8:45–225
8:46–225
8:47–225, 341
10–303
10:14–340, 344, 510, 588
10:14-16–338
10:15–451, 461
10:17-18–416
10:18–267
10:26–338, 339, 341
10:27–340, 344, 431, 510
10:28–339, 340, 587, 589, 592
11:43–503
11:43-44–220
11:49-52–442, 443
11:50–442
11:51–442
11:52–442, 443
12:4–581
12:19–435
12:31–435, 512
12:31-33–511
12:32–463, 511, 512
12:37-40–316, 317
12:39-40–224, 227, 315
12:46–309, 436
13:1–435
14:6–230, 533
14:17–223, 226, 435, 588
14:19–435, 590
14:22–435
14:30–435
15:5–588
15:7–276
15:13–458
15:16–350, 345
15:18–435
15:19–435
15:27–355
16:7-11–513
16:8–431, 499, 533
16:8-11–553
16:9–431, 533
16:11–435
16:33–435
17–342
17:2–342
17:6–342, 343, 343, 435, 504
17:8–343
17:9–342, 435
17:11–342
17:12–342, 342, 343, 343
17:14–435
17:16–435
17:17–209, 582
17:18–435
17:20–343
17:24–314, 343
17:25–435
17:26–344
18:10–509
18:36–435
19:11–484
19:30–416
19:38-39–581
20:29–225
20:31–526
21:6–509

Acts

1:22–345
1:24-26–262
2:23–265, 266, 297, 304, 312, 349, 375, 378, 385, 386, 388, 389, 392, 393, 394, 494
2:36–267
2:39–111, 400
3:13–268
3:13-15–267
4:1-3–43
4:10–267
4:12–533
4:17-18–43
4:27-28–265
4:34–346
5:2-5–262
5:30–267
5:31–514, 514, 515
5:36–346

5:37–509
7:51–488, 490
7:52–267
7:54–346
7:58-59–43
8:30-35–451
9:15–351, 351
10:1–347
10:2–229, 347
10:4–347
10:22–229
10:31–347
10:34–499
10:35–347
10:38–211
10:39–267
10:42–345
10:43–309, 334, 347, 459, 551
11:1–347
11:4–355
11:14–229
11:17–347
11:18–347, 514, 514, 515
12:1-2–43
13:2–352
13:13–575
13:42–347
13:46–346
13:48–345, 346, 346, 347, 347, 348, 376, 515
13:49–348
14:1–315, 318
14:16–196
14:23–345
14:27–347, 505
15:7–347
15:14–346
15:18–355
16:4–255, 345
16:9-10–356
16:10–356, 505
16:11–356
16:12–356, 356
16:14–356, 504, 505, 515
16:30-31–200
16:30-34–356
16:31–527, 545, 567, 568, 585
17:1–356
17:7–255
17:10–356
17:11–228
17:14–356
17:15–356
17:25–263
17:30–187, 196, 237, 540
17:31–345
18:1–305
18:2–336
18:4–305
18:5–336, 356
18:6–346
18:7–336
18:8–305, 336, 336
18:9-10–335
18:27–515
20:21–513, 582
20:24–349, 493, 580
20:27–331
20:28–451, 457, 461
20:29-30–197
20:30–42, 509
21:20–315, 318
22:14–351, 351
26:4-5–394
26:5–355
26:16–351
26:18–225, 351, 505
26:20–583
27:31–572
28:24–553
28:25-27–316
28:28–346

Romans

1-8–319
1:1–492
1:10–482
1:16–346, 459, 526, 546, 584
1:23–304
1:24–304
1:25–304
1:26–304
1:28–304, 304
2:2–377
2:10–209
2:14-15–208
2:16–332, 547
3–506
3:1–229, 506

3:6–506
3:8–506
3:9–229, 441
3:10-18–228
3:10-20–228
3:11–224, 228
3:12–210
3:14–354
3:19–199
3:20–518
3:22–449, 588
3:23–193, 194
3:25–419, 427
3:26–416, 419, 528
4:4-5–518
4:5–372, 373, 506, 568, 581
4:5-6–63
4:16–373, 518
4:22-24–526
5:1–519, 581, 588
5:6–194, 457
5:8–229, 428, 454, 505, 508
5:10-199, 420
5:11–416
5:12–193, 364, 453
5:12-19–193
5:15–429, 452, 461, 462, 581
5:15-18–516
5:16–430
5:17–373, 430, 588
5:18–430, 453, 463
5:19–193, 430, 453
6:1–506
6:2–220
6:4–587
6:15–506
6:16–212
6:17–219
6:20–194, 205
6:23–349, 493, 516
7:7–506
7:13–506
7:15-20–206
7:18–575
8–329, 384, 385, 387, 494
8:4–226
8:7-8–223, 226
8:8–199, 226
8:15–383, 384
8:17–384

8:18–387
8:19–387
8:23–383, 383, 384, 384
8:28–389, 392, 395
8:28-29–389
8:28-30–329, 384, 494
8:29–266, 349, 376, 377, 378, 382, 384, 385, 388, 389, 392, 393, 394, 396, 494, 589
8:30–376, 382, 386, 387, 494, 495
8:33–375, 376
8:33-34–595
8:38-39–571
9–137, 217, 303, 314, 319, 323, 325, 328, 329, 331, 357, 506
9-11–514, 319, 320, 329, 371, 376
9:1-3–320, 369
9:1-5–320
9:4–383
9:6–13, 322, 370
9:6-9–321
9:6-13–329
9:10-13–320
9:11–322, 322, 370, 518
9:12–322
9:13–320, 323
9:14–263, 332, 506
9:15-16–218
9:15-18–331, 325
9:16–216, 503
9:17–309
9:19–505, 506
9:20-24–328
9:21–320, 329, 329
9:22–329
9:26–493
9:27–371
9:29–371
9:30-31–320
9:31–372
9:31-32–311
9:32–311, 331, 518
9:32-33–372
9:33–309, 311, 334, 380
10:1-3–320, 320, 369
10:3–320, 372
10:4–373
10:8–520
10:9–527, 569, 583
10:11–459, 551

10:12–320
10:13–459
10:14–547
10:16–311, 582
10:17–520, 530, 547
10:21–320
11:1–320
11:1-2–396
11:1-4–371
11:1-10–320
11:2–394
11:5–370, 371, 373
11:5-7–372
11:6–373, 518
11:7–370, 373
11:7-8–319
11:11–346
11:11-12–320
11:12–441
11:12-14–320, 369
11:14–548
11:15–441
11:25–311, 318, 319, 346, 373
11:25-27–368
11:28–331, 370
11:30-31–331
11:30-32–219
11:33–390
11:33-35–280
12-16–319
12:1–585
12:2–482
12:3–520
13:1–345
13:14–49
14:10–571
14:23–213
15:8–454
15:20–369, 547
15:32–482
16:7–354
16:18–210
16:26–582

1 Corinthians

1:2–493
1:7–547
1:7-8–573
1:8–588
1:9–493
1:18–146, 496
1:21–227, 437, 496, 527
1:22–496
1:22-24–496
1:23–496
1:24–496
1:26–496, 497
2:4-5–515
2:6–437
2:7–348
2:8–267, 268, 437
2:9-15–231
2:12–231, 437, 438
2:13–453
2:14–224, 231, 585
2:18–496
3:1–580
3:6–548
3:13-15–571, 576
3:14–571
3:19–437
3:23–587
4:15–530, 548
4:19–482
5:5–575
5:7–417
5:14–446
5:17–438
6:2–437
6:3–367
6:6–517
6:8–517
6:9-10–304
6:11–304, 386, 495, 582, 588
6:17–359, 587, 588
6:20–457
7:2–56
7:14–111
7:15–493
7:17–345
8:6–587
8:11–454
8:12–208
9:14–345, 346
9:16–547
9:17–276
9:22–548
9:24-27–570
9:25–571, 571

9:27–571, 572
10:12–595
10:20–196
10:31–576
10:32–196, 441, 454
12:2–196
12:3–583
12:9–516
12:12–588
14:33–297
15:1-4-5, 544
15:3-4–431
15:8–352
15:21–193
15:22–193, 299, 354, 362, 430, 587, 588
15:45–204, 430
15:47–204, 430
15:49–193, 387, 396, 589
15:58–575
16:7–482

2 Corinthians

1:6–572
1:21–588
2:6-8–575
2:15-16–496
2:17–448
3:6–53
4:4–194, 318, 437, 552
4:5–583
4:6–515
5:9–581
5:10–571, 577
5:14–443, 444
5:14-15–444
5:15–445, 464
5:17–220, 222, 588
5:18–428, 588
5:18-19–420
5:18-21–438
5:19–428, 433, 436, 437, 466
5:20–438
5:21–267, 416, 418, 428, 454
6:1–490
7:8–583
10:16–548
11:9–356
11:23-27–369

12:9–596
13:3–305
13:5–305
13:5-7–305
13:7–305

Galatians

1:4–437, 438, 454
1:6–493, 495, 528, 568, 569
1:8–9
1:9–528
1:15-16–352
1:16–227
2:7–547
2:20–454, 587
2:21–490
3:2–518
3:13–416
3:22–198
3:26–443, 519, 527
3:28–441
4:3–437
4:4-5–457
4:5–383, 383, 588
4:6–231, 384
4:7–384
4:8-9–395
5:4–490
5:13–493
5:17–206
6:10–448

Ephesians

1:1–587
1:3–362, 363, 388, 588
1:3-4–359, 361
1:4–314, 354, 354, 357, 360, 360, 383, 387, 388, 431
1:5–376, 382, 384, 384,
1:6–384, 581, 588
1:11–271, 284, 297, 304, 309, 367, 382, 383, 383, 588
1:12–384
1:13–232, 383, 384, 546, 581
1:14–384, 384
1:15–548
1:17-18–505, 515
1:19–488

1:20–359
1:22-23–379
2:1–193, 201, 205, 219, 220, 221, 339, 383, 427, 535
2:1-3–362
2:2–225, 336, 377
2:2-3–220
2:3–128, 193, 194, 198, 205, 331, 336, 362, 427, 443
2:5–587, 593
2:6–359, 388, 588
2:8–199, 349, 493, 515, 516, 517, 571
2:8-9–515, 568
2:9–199, 506, 518
2:10–345, 346, 576
2:12–339, 362, 362, 395, 552
2:15-16–420
2:16–420
2:20–507
2:20-22–588
3:7–547
3:9–355
3:20–507
4:1–493
4:17–196
4:18–199
4:30–588
4:32–588
5:2–417
5:17–482
5:23–588
5:25–451, 452, 461, 508
5:27–588
5:30–359, 587, 589
5:30-32–588
6:6–482
6:18–574

Philippians

1:1–589
1:6–588
1:29–344, 515
2:7–204
2:9-11–309
2:12–575, 594
2:12-13–506
2:15–437
2:16–547
3:9–519

3:10-11–584
3:15–511
3:21–204, 582, 589
4:3–369
4:6–276
4:7–581
4:8–577
4:15–356
4:15-16–355
4:16–356
4:18–356

Colossians

1:4–548
1:9–482
1:10–576
1:13–588
1:14–418, 428, 588
1:16–309
1:18–379
1:19–227
1:20–439, 464
1:20-21–420, 439
1:21–439
1:23–574
1:27–587
1:29–507
2:6–583
2:11–588
2:20–437, 587
3:1–587
3:3–220
3:3-4–587
3:4–589
3:6–194, 443
3:12–375, 376
3:17–576
4:3–548
4:12–482

1 Thessalonians

1:4–374
1:5–356
1:10–311
2:1-2–356
2:9–356
2:12–356, 387, 495
2:13–375, 500, 507, 552

2:16–197, 238, 278, 310, 320, 547
2:19–571
4:3–480, 582
4:5–196
4:7–493
4:9–510, 310, 311
5:17–276
5:18–480
5:22–577
5:23–587

2 Thessalonians

2:11-12–312
2:12–312
2:13–354, 356, 374, 376, 385, 494
2:14–356, 388, 493, 495, 546
3:1–547
3:8–356

1 Timothy

1:1–448
1:6–574
1:12–572
1:13–331
1:15–352, 416, 457
1:16–331
1:19–574
1:20–575
2:1-5–484
2:1-6–446, 448
2:2–448, 486
2:3–448
2:4–57, 276, 448, 484, 486, 487
2:5–416, 447, 486
2:6–418, 443, 446, 447, 448, 455, 464
2:7–345
2:14–192
2:15–572
3:16–416
4:1–198, 574,
4:2–208
4:3–56
4:8–546
4:10–428, 444, 448, 455, 465, 469
4:16–572
5:8–574
5:12–574
5:21–366

6:10–574
6:20–574

2 Timothy

1:1–482
1:9–266, 349, 359, 360, 361, 374, 386, 428, 495, 518, 546
1:10–360, 545, 546
2:9–xi, 588
2:10–369, 386, 386
2:12–369, 574, 589
2:13–250, 297, 589
2:15–305
2:19–595
2:20–328
2:25–514
2:24-26–515
3:7–305
3:8–304
4:3-4–198
4:8–571, 572
4:10–575
4:11–575
4:18–587

Titus

1:1–375, 376
1:3–448
1:5–345
1:15–208
1:16–304
2:10–448
2:11–499
2:11-12–450
2:14–418, 454
3:3–194
3:4–499
3:5–54, 218, 385, 494, 568, 588
3:8–346, 576
3:14–346, 448

Philemon

10–548

Hebrews

1:3–419

2:6–450
2:6-9–450
2:9–428, 444, 447, 449, 450, 465
2:10–449
2:11–449
2:12–449
2:13–449
2:17–420
3:10–394
3:13–308
3:15–308
4:16–204, 210
5:1–345, 346
5:4–493
7:26–416
7:27–417
9:6–345
9:12–418
9:14–419
9:15–429
9:17–510
9:26–419
9:28–451, 462
10:5–416
10:10–416, 417, 428, 582, 588
10:10-14–346
10:12–343, 417
10:14–416
10:22–208
10:24–455, 576
10:26–456
10:29–428, 455, 463, 490
10:30–456
11:5–227
11:6–230
12:8–442
12:15–490
13:4–56
13:16–227
13:21–507

James

1:12–571
1:13–504
1:14–504
1:14-15–213
1:15–504
1:17–504
1:18–503, 504
1:21–504, 530
2:5–353
3:7–447, 486
4:8–508
4:15–482
4:17–214

1 Peter

1:1–378
1:2–266, 356, 375, 376, 376, 377, 378, 378, 385, 385, 386, 388, 392, 394, 494
1:4–384, 588
1:5–588
1:16–584
1:18-19–418
1:20–265, 314
1:22–588
1:23–221, 383, 530, 588
2:1–457
2:6–311, 334, 366
2:7–311
2:8–303, 311
2:9–194, 352, 379, 493, 495, 588
2:10–331, 588
2:18-209
2:21–456
2:24-25–451
3:18–419, 458
3:20–488
3:21–54
4:14–387
5:1–387, 587
5:4–571
5:10–387
5:13–373

2 Peter

1:1–515, 571
1:3–387
1:4–587
1:8–574
1:9–588
1:10–266, 349, 374, 386, 495
1:20–311
2:1–312, 313, 339, 374, 428, 455, 456, 463
2:4–313, 366, 367
2:7–575

2:8–575
2:9–313
2:12–312, 313
2:13–313
2:14–213
2:17–313
2:22–339
3:4–355
3:7–313
3:9–386, 484, 487
3:15–488
3:17–394, 574

1 John

1:1–355
1:2–431
1:3–441
1:7–434
2:1–441
2:2–419, 428, 433, 439, 440, 441, 442, 443, 446, 461, 466, 467, 468
2:7–355
2:13–355
2:14–355
2:15–441
2:16–441
2:17–441
2:28–574
3:1–441, 493
3:2–367, 383, 387, 396, 582
3:4–213
3:5–428
3:8–355
3:9–221
3:16–454
3:23–237
4:3–441
4:10–419, 428
4:14–433, 439, 458
4:19–229, 505, 508
5:1–309, 334, 459
5:4–441
5:11–571
5:13–192, 380, 441, 588
5:17–213
5:19–441

2 John

1–375
5–355
6–355
13–375

Jude

1–349, 374, 385, 386, 494, 495, 587
4–303, 313, 314, 490
5–313
5-7–314
6–313, 367
10–312, 313
11–314
12-13–314
13–313
14–590
14-15–314
21–575
24–588

Revelation

2:14–45
3:5–338
4:11–192, 309
5:9–448, 486
6:8–317
6:9-10–370
6:17–311
9:11–165
11:8–493
11:18–311
12:4–366, 367
13:8–265, 336
15:1–311
16:1–311
17:8–337
17:17–263
20–54
20:7-9–262
20:14–221
20:14-15–193
22:17–237, 279, 334, 459, 551, 581
22:19–338